Pro ASP.NET 3.5 Server Controls and AJAX Components

Rob Cameron and
Dale Michalk

Apress®

Pro ASP.NET 3.5 Server Controls and AJAX Components

ISBN-13 (pbk): 978-1-59059-865-8

ISBN-10 (pbk): 1-59059-865-2

ISBN-13 (electronic): 978-1-4302-0462-6

ISBN-10 (electronic): 1-4302-0462-1

Printed and bound in the United States of America 9 8 7 6 5 4 3 2 1

Lead Editor: Ewan Buckingham
Technical Reviewer: Fabio Claudio Ferracchiati
Editorial Board: Clay Andres, Steve Anglin, Ewan Buckingham, Tony Campbell, Gary Cornell, Jonathan Gennick, Matthew Moodie, Joseph Ottinger, Jeffrey Pepper, Frank Pohlmann, Ben Renow-Clarke, Dominic Shakeshaft, Matt Wade, Tom Welsh
Project Manager: Kylie Johnston
Copy Editor: Heather Lang
Associate Production Director: Kari Brooks-Copony
Production Editor: Ellie Fountain
Compositor: Susan Glinert
Proofreader: Liz Welch
Indexer: Brenda Miller
Artist: Kinetic Publishing Services, LLC
Cover Designer: Kurt Krames
Manufacturing Director: Tom Debolski

Distributed to the book trade worldwide by Springer-Verlag New York, Inc., 233 Spring Street, 6th Floor, New York, NY 10013. Phone 1-800-SPRINGER, fax 201-348-4505, e-mail orders-ny@springer-sbm.com, or visit http://www.springeronline.com.

For information on translations, please contact Apress directly at 2855 Telegraph Avenue, Suite 600, Berkeley, CA 94705. Phone 510-549-5930, fax 510-549-5939, e-mail info@apress.com, or visit http://www.apress.com.

Apress and friends of ED books may be purchased in bulk for academic, corporate, or promotional use. eBook versions and licenses are also available for most titles. For more information, reference our Special Bulk Sales–eBook Licensing web page at http://www.apress.com/info/bulksales.

The source code for this book is available to readers at http://www.apress.com.

To my beautiful wife, Ally, and daughters Amanda and Anna,
who bring so much happiness to my life
—Rob Cameron

Contents at a Glance

Contents

About the Authors

ROB CAMERON is employed with Microsoft Corporation in Atlanta, GA. He has been with Microsoft since 2001 assisting communications sector and media and entertainment companies build solutions on the Microsoft platform. Prior to employment at Microsoft, he worked as an independent consultant developing software on the Microsoft platform for over five years. He has a master's degree in information technology management and a bachelor's degree in computer science. A former naval officer and United States Naval Academy graduate, he enjoys spending his free time with his wife and two daughters.

DALE MICHALK is employed with Microsoft Corporation in Dallas, Texas. He has been with Microsoft since 2001, where he helps promote .NET as a development platform and assists companies interested in migrating to new technologies such as ASP.NET. He is a former U.S. Army officer and West Point graduate.

About the Technical Reviewer

FABIO CLAUDIO FERRACCHIATI is a senior consultant and a senior analyst/developer using Microsoft technologies. He works for Brain Force (`www.brainforce.com`) in its Italian branch (`www.brainforce.it`). He is a Microsoft Certified Solution Developer for .NET, a Microsoft Certified Application Developer for .NET, a Microsoft Certified Professional, and a prolific author and technical reviewer. Over the past ten years, he's written articles for Italian and international magazines and coauthored more than ten books on a variety of computer topics. You can read his LINQ blog at `www.ferracchiati.com`.

Acknowledgments

Writing a book is a long and incredible journey that requires the support and care of a lot of people. The first and foremost of those I would like to recognize are my family members. Without their support and patience with all those long hours on the computer, this book would never have come to pass. I would like to thank Dale Michalk for inviting me on this journey, starting with our first book *Building ASP.NET Server Controls*. Dale's contributions to the first book are no doubt a significant part of this effort as well, and that is why Dale's name appears on the front cover of this book.

Apress is a fantastic company to work for as an author, as evidenced by their care and feeding in getting this book into production. This is a publishing house run by those who actually write for a living; they understand the balance in ensuring high quality versus meeting deadlines. Thanks especially to Matthew and Kylie for all the patience in the slipped schedules and author changes. Thanks to the editing folks from Apress—Kylie, Heather, and Ellie—as well as to those who I don't know by name but whose efforts helped to make this book possible. I would also like to thank Fabio Claudio Ferracchiati, who reviewed the book and provided technical assistance and support.

A final thanks is owed to the ASP.NET product team who provided the Microsoft web development community with an awesome product and are busy at work on future versions that will reach new heights.

Rob Cameron

Introduction

With the explosion of the Internet, web development tools evolved as a combination of HTML and a scripting language, such as ASP or Perl, to generate dynamic output. With the advent of Microsoft's .NET Framework, ASP.NET turned web development on its head by combining a design-time interface similar to Visual Basic with an HTML and JavaScript output that requires nothing more than a web browser for rending. With ASP.NET 3.5, HTML and JavaScript are combined in powerful ways via ASP.NET AJAX technology that helps connect client-side and server-side connection without losing point-and-click design-time support. We wrote this book to document the major improvements since ASP.NET 1.1, while also covering the fundamentals for those new to custom server control development.

At the core of ASP.NET is server control technology. From the `Page` class to the `Label` control to web parts, all objects in ASP.NET are server controls. Server controls combine server-side execution in a well defined life cycle with browser-friendly rendering that includes down-level browsers as well as a plethora of mobile clients. Regardless of the target output, all server controls behave in a similar manner. Understanding this technology and how to leverage it in your own development efforts are the subjects of this book.

Who This Book Is For

The target audience for this book consists of developers with an intermediate to advanced experience level looking to deepen their understanding of ASP.NET and its underlying server control architecture. The example code in this book is written in C#. However, if you are a VB. NET developer, the examples translate pretty easily, as ASP.NET development is language agnostic. The .NET Framework and the ASP.NET object model are what's important, not the language.

If you are a developer in need of learning a particular technique, each major facet of control development is presented with simple example code to highlight that particular topic. For example, if you are looking for information on how to add events to your server controls, or how to understand how events work in ASP.NET, you can drill into that chapter to get the details.

If you are a developer looking for full-featured example code, you'll find that here too. One example shows how to implement data binding and templates that can connect to a database backend. The rich example in the last part of the book pulls techniques described throughout this book into a holistic demonstration of how to build a rich, complex server control that is fully localized and includes licensing support.

How This Book Is Structured

This book is about server control technology as the underlying foundation of ASP.NET. It will provide you with a deep understanding of how server control technology works, as well as explaining how to build your own custom server controls as part of a web development project or for resale in the component marketplace.

The first section of the book provides an introduction to server control technology. We also discuss the different ways to build a server control including inheritance from a base control (such as `Control` or `WebControl`) encapsulation, or composite controls, as well as inheritance from an existing or rich control, like the `TextBox` server control.

The second section of the book dives into deep a discussion on critical topics such as state management, server-side event handling, templates, data binding, and integrating client-side script, as well as considering advanced base classes such as `CompositeControl` and `DataBoundControl`. A common theme for all of these discussions is how the topic relates to the control life cycle. Understanding the control life cycle is critical to server control development as well as to ASP.NET development in general. Of course, there are copious amounts of code to support our discussions as well.

The third section of the book covers advanced development techniques such as building ASP.NET AJAX controls and extenders. We also cover web part development for ASP.NET or SharePoint. We round out the section with a discussion of control adapters for modifying an existing server control's HTML output and device adapters for mobile control development.

The last section of the book covers design-time support in detail. Many of the controls built in earlier chapters include design-time support; however, we centralize discussion of the design-time support capabilities in ASP.NET and server controls to facilitate understanding without cluttering up the earlier chapters. We finish up this last section of the book by walking through how to create a professional-quality server control with a discussion on licensing, globalization, and localization.

Prerequisites

The following applications would be helpful in working through the examples in this book, but access to them isn't required:

- Visual Studio 2008, Express edition
- SQL Server 2005 Express (for a couple of the database samples)
- Internet Information Services (for the mobile web project)

Downloading the Code

The source code for this book is available to readers at `www.apress.com` in the Source Code section of this book's home page. Please feel free to visit the Apress web site and download all the code there. You can also check for errata and find related titles from Apress.

Contacting the Authors

You can contact Rob Cameron via `http://blogs.msdn.com/robcamer`; there is a contact link to send Rob an e-mail there.

CHAPTER 1

Server Control Basics

To create server controls, you need to understand how they work. This chapter provides a very high-level run-through of the various server control namespaces to set the scene for the rest of this book. To begin our journey, we'll start by reviewing what a server control provides to clients and taking a look at some of the prebuilt controls supplied by ASP.NET. We'll study the controls' inheritance bloodlines for the HTML and web controls, examining how the namespaces are organized, so that you become familiar with what is available for immediate use in ASP.NET. Because inheritance and composition of existing server controls are important timesaving control-building techniques available in ASP.NET, this rapid journey through the object model is well worth the effort.

To begin this chapter, we start out with a "Hello, World" form to demonstrate master pages. The `MasterPage` class can trace its inheritance back to the user control functionality introduced in ASP.NET 1.0. We next discuss the basic server control construction, as well as how server controls are organized in an ASP.NET web form. Finally, we cover the root server control namespaces with an example of the types of server controls found in the different namespaces.

Source Code

The source code for this book is available for download from the Apress web site for those who want to follow along by running the code in Visual Studio 2008. The web site project is file based, so having IIS installed and configured isn't required. There is a main solution file titled `ControlsBook2Solution.sln` that, when opened, will load all of the projects. Please refer to the read-me file included with the source code download for detailed instructions on how to get the code running. The full source code is also printed in this book, so those who want to read while not in front of a computer can still enjoy reading the source code.

The Heart and Soul of ASP.NET

Each piece of HTML delivered by an ASP.NET page, whether a `<span>` tag without server-side interactivity, a complex list control such as the `DataGrid` that supports templates, or the web form itself that hosts the HTML tags, is generated by an object that inherits from the `System.Web.UI.Control` base class. These objects, or server controls, are the engine that drives the ASP.NET page-rendering process. The fact that every snippet of rendered HTML exists as a server control allows for a consistent page parsing process that permits easy control configuration and manipulation to create dynamic and powerful content. The clean, consistent object model provided by ASP.NET also facilitates extension through custom server controls that share a common object model.

A .NET Framework "Hello, World" Web Form

The first stop on our journey through the ASP.NET server controls is construction of a "Hello, World" web form. Before actually creating the "Hello, World" web form, we need to create a master page to provide a consistent UI for the book web site. A master page, one of the many new features in ASP.NET 2.0 and later versions, has a `@Master` directive at the top of the code instead of the `@Page` directive on a standard web form.

■ **Note** ASP.NET 3.5 includes additional master page item templates to support AJAX functionality and nested master pages called AJAX Master Page and Nested Master Page respectively.

The `@Master` directive takes most of the same options as the `@Control` directive. If you have not migrated to ASP.NET 2.0 or later, master pages are a welcome addition in ASP.NET and should often be used for page layout and template purposes in situations where ASP.NET user controls were in ASP.NET 1.1 but came up short. Figure 1-1 shows the master page used in this book's sample web site.

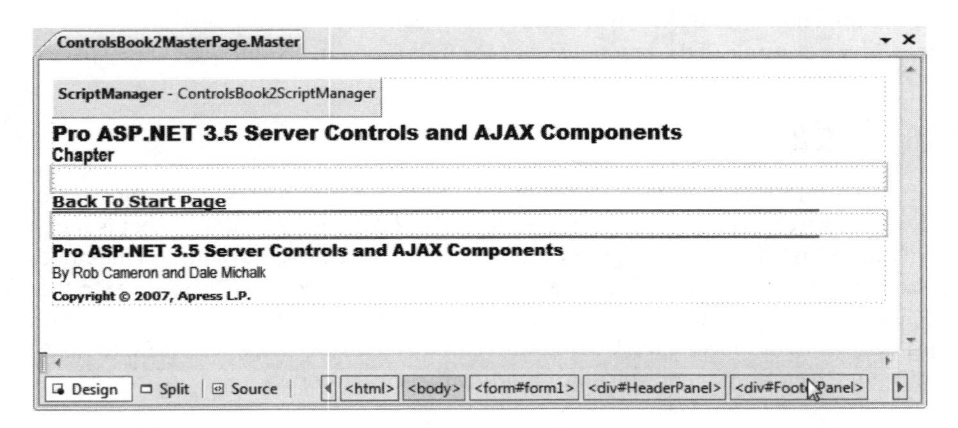

Figure 1-1. *The Controls Book 2 web site's master page*

Web forms added to the project can be configured to use the master page rendering at design time, like Figure 1-2.

Notice in Figure 1-2 that the master page area is grayed out (and cannot be edited) at design time in a web content form. The design-time view displays the master page HTML and the web content form HTML, providing a more accurate view of the rendered web form. Listings 1-1 and 1-2 show the master page source page and code-behind file.

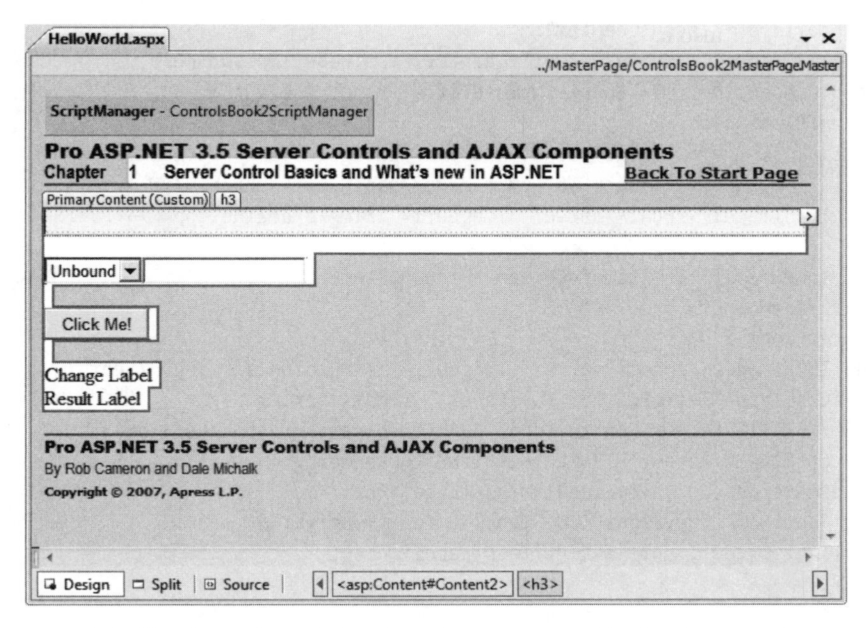

Figure 1-2. *The Controls Book 2 web site's master page displayed in a web content form*

Listing 1-1. *The ControlsBook2 Master Page File*

```
<%@ Master Language="C#" AutoEventWireup="true"
CodeBehind="ControlsBook2MasterPage.master.cs"
  Inherits="ControlsBook2Web.MasterPage.ControlsBook2MasterPage" %>

<!DOCTYPE html PUBLIC "-//W3C//DTD XHTML 1.0 Transitional//EN"
"http://www.w3.org/TR/xhtml1/DTD/xhtml1-transitional.dtd">
<html xmlns="http://www.w3.org/1999/xhtml">
<head runat="server">
  <title>Master Page</title>
  <link href="../css/ControlsBook2Master.css" rel="stylesheet" type="text/css" />
  <link href="../css/SkinnedControl.css" rel="stylesheet" type="text/css" />
  <asp:ContentPlaceHolder ID="HeadSection" runat="server">
  </asp:ContentPlaceHolder>
</head>
<body>
  <form id="form1" runat="server">
  <div id="HeaderPanel">
    <asp:ScriptManager ID="ControlsBook2ScriptManager" runat="server">
      <Scripts>
        <asp:ScriptReference Path="../ch09/hoverbutton.js" />
      </Scripts>
    </asp:ScriptManager>
    <asp:Label ID="Label2" CssClass="TitleHeader" runat="server" Height="18px"
Width="604px">Pro ASP.NET 3.5 Server Controls and AJAX Components</asp:Label>
<br />
```

```
    <div id="ChapterInfo" class="Chapter">
      <asp:Label ID="label1" runat="server">Chapter</asp:Label>  
      <asp:ContentPlaceHolder ID="ChapterNumAndTitle" runat="server">
      </asp:ContentPlaceHolder>
      <asp:HyperLink ID="DefaultPage" runat="server" NavigateUrl="~/Default.aspx">
                                   Back To Start Page</asp:HyperLink><br />
      <asp:Image ID="Image1" runat="server" ImageUrl="~/img/blueline.jpg" /><br />
    </div>
    <asp:ContentPlaceHolder ID="PrimaryContent" runat="server">
    </asp:ContentPlaceHolder>
    <div id="FooterPanel">
      <asp:Image ID="Image2" runat="server" ImageUrl="~/img/blueline.jpg" /><br />
      <asp:Label CssClass="TitleFooter" ID="Label5" runat="server">
          Pro ASP.NET 3.5 Server Controls and AJAX Components</asp:Label><br />
      <asp:Label CssClass="Author" ID="Label6" runat="server">
           By Rob Cameron and Dale Michalk</asp:Label><br />
      <asp:Label CssClass="Copyright" ID="Label7" runat="server">
            Copyright © 2007, Apress L.P.</asp:Label> 
    </div>
  </div>
  </form>
</body>
</html>
```

Listing 1-2. *The ControlsBook2MasterPage Master Page Code-Behind Class File*

```
using System;

namespace ControlsBook2Web.MasterPage
{
    public partial class ControlsBook2MasterPage : System.Web.UI.MasterPage
    {
        protected void Page_Load(object sender, EventArgs e)
        {

        }
    }
}
```

In the master page for the Controls Book 2 web site, the chapter number and chapter title have `ContentPlaceHolder` placeholder tags to allow content pages to update the chapter number and title.

Each web form sets values for the chapter title and number by simply placing the value in the corresponding `Content` tag in the content page. This is a simple example of providing a consistent user interface in a web site, but still allowing customization.

Tip ASP.NET User Controls are still present in ASP.NET 3.5. In fact the `MasterPage` class inherits from the `UserControl` class.

The resulting arrangement is shown in Figure 1-3 with a `DropDownList` control, a `TextBox` control, two `Label` controls, and a `Button` control. The resulting source code generated by Visual Studio 2008 is shown in Listings 1-3 and 1-4.

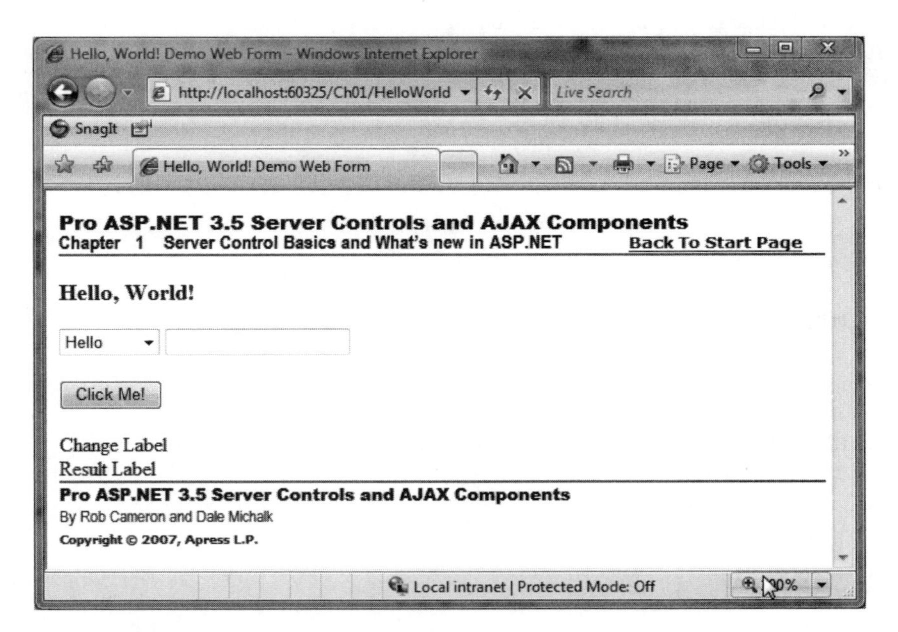

Figure 1-3. *The HelloWorld server control web form*

Listing 1-3. *The HelloWorld Demo Web Form .aspx File*

```
<%@ Page Language="C#"
MasterPageFile="~/MasterPage/ControlsBook2MasterPage.Master"
  AutoEventWireup="true" CodeBehind="HelloWorld.aspx.cs"
Inherits="ControlsBook2Web.Ch01.HelloWorld"
  Title="Hello, World! Demo Web Form" %>

<asp:Content ID="Content1" ContentPlaceHolderID="ChapterNumAndTitle" runat="server">
  <asp:Label ID="ChapterNumberLabel" runat="server"
Width="14px">1</asp:Label>  <asp:Label
    ID="ChapterTitleLabel" runat="server" Width="360px">
Server Control Basics and What's new in ASP.NET</asp:Label>
</asp:Content>
<asp:Content ID="Content2" ContentPlaceHolderID="PrimaryContent" runat="server">
  <h3><asp:Label ID="Label1" runat="server" Text=
```

```
"Hello, World!"></asp:Label></h3>
  <asp:DropDownList ID="Greeting" runat="server" ToolTip="Select a greeting">
  </asp:DropDownList>
  <asp:TextBox ID="Name" runat="server" Font-Italic="True" ToolTip="Enter your name"
    OnTextChanged="Name_TextChanged"></asp:TextBox><br />
  <br />
  <asp:Button ID="ClickMe" runat="server" Text="Click Me!"
OnClick="ClickMe_Click"></asp:Button><br />
  <br />
  <asp:Label ID="ChangeLabel" runat="server">Change Label</asp:Label><br />
  <asp:Label ID="Resultlabel" runat="server">Result Label</asp:Label>
  <br />
</asp:Content>
```

Listing 1-4. *The HelloWorld Server Control Demo Code-Behind Class File*

```
using System;
using System.Collections;

namespace ControlsBook2Web.Ch01
{
  public partial class HelloWorld : System.Web.UI.Page
  {
    protected void Page_Load(object sender, EventArgs e)
    {
      ArrayList list = new ArrayList();
      list.Add("Hello");
      list.Add("Goodbye");

      Greeting.DataSource = list;
      Greeting.DataBind();
    }

    protected void ClickMe_Click(object sender, EventArgs e)
    {
      Resultlabel.Text = "Your new message: " + Greeting.SelectedItem.Value +
     " " + Name.Text + "!";
    }

    protected void Name_TextChanged(object sender, EventArgs e)
    {
      ChangeLabel.Text = "Textbox changed to " + Name.Text;
    }
  }
}
```

The server controls on our "Hello, World" web form (specifically, the `Label`, `TextBox`, and `DropDownList` objects) render as HTML and, for the `TextBox` control, remember what is typed in the control between postback cycles. The HTML rendered to the browser is backed by powerful objects that can be wired up to programming logic to perform useful work on the web server. During server-side processing, the object-oriented nature of server controls provides us with three main constructs to interact with controls as objects: properties, methods, and events. We discuss these constructs in the sections that follow.

Control Properties

The most common means of working with a server control is through the properties it exposes. Properties allow the control to take information from the web form to configure its output or modify its behavior in the HTML-generation process.

■ **Note** Properties are different and more powerful than public data members. Properties provide an additional layer of abstraction through the use of `get` and `set` methods; `get` and `set` methods or function calls provide a convenient location for programming logic, such as displaying an error if a value is out of range or otherwise invalid, enforcing read-only access (implementing a `get` method only), and so on. Properties can be declared as public, protected, or private.

Properties are easily viewable in the Properties window available when you select a control in the Visual Studio Design view of the `.aspx` page. Figure 1-4 shows the Properties window when the `Name` `TextBox` is selected. Notice that the `Font` property has been configured to show the `TextBox`'s `Text` property text in italics.

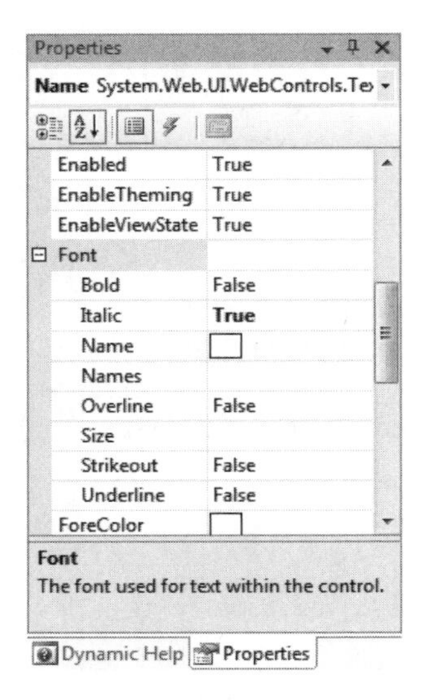

Figure 1-4. *The Properties window for the TextBox control*

The Visual Studio Designer translates the entries in the Properties window into attribute values on the HTML view of the .aspx page. To see this, set a property for a control in the Properties tool window and then switch to HTML view. Likewise, if you modify attribute values in the HTML view of the .aspx page, these changes will be reflected in the Designer, assuming you typed in the values correctly. This behavior can be very handy for quickly duplicating attributes between controls. Simply copy the HTML version of the attributes and then paste the HTML into the target control that you want to match the original. You can think of the Designer as a code generator that allows you to declaratively work with the look and feel of the ASP.NET application without having to write the code. As an example, the Font settings set in the Properties window for the TextBox control described previously map directly to Font attributes:

```
<asp:TextBox id="Name" runat="server" Font-Italic="True"
             ToolTip="Enter your name" OnTextChanged="Name_TextChanged">
</asp:TextBox>
```

The Label and TextBox controls work a little differently than most, in that the content between the opening and closing tags is controlled by the Text property:

```
<asp:Label id="Resultlabel" runat="server">Result Label</asp:Label>
```

You can also set a control's properties programmatically in the code-behind class file. The "Hello, World" demonstration sets the Text property for Label1 to a blank string each time the web form is loaded, to overwrite the Label value that is declaratively set in the .aspx page. The activity happens in a method named Page_Load that is mapped to the Page object's Load event:

```
protected void Page_Load(object sender, EventArgs e)
{
  Resultlabel.Text = "";
  ChangeLabel.Text = "";

  if (!Page.IsPostBack)
  {
    UpdateMaster();
    LoadDropDownList();
  }
  DataBind();
}
```

You can also use the properties exposed by the control to read input from the client browser during postback on the server side. The Button click event handling routine in the "Hello, World" web form reads the Text property of the TextBox control and the Value property of the SelectedItem property on the DropDownList control to display the greeting to the client of the web browser:

```
 protected void ClickMe_Click(object sender, EventArgs e)
{
  Resultlabel.Text =
    "Your new message: " + Greeting.SelectedItem.Value + " " + Name.Text + "!";
}
```

Control Methods

The second feature exposed by a server control is a collection of object methods. Functionality implemented using methods typically goes beyond the features of a property's set or get method; they usually perform a more complex action against the control. One of the best examples in ASP.NET of using methods for a server control is the data-binding process that links a control with a data source.

In the "Hello, World" web form example, the Page_Load event checks to see if the page is requested via a form postback or if it was called for the first time using HTTP GET so that the page can generate the initial HTML for the browser, creating the option list. In the postback scenario, the code to create the option list is not necessary for the DropDownList control via the LoadDropDownList() method, because the server control DropDownList1 maintains its internal option list via the web form ViewState mechanism for subsequent postback operations to the server. We cover ViewState extensively in Chapter 3.

The page's LoadDropDownList() method's first task is to create an ArrayList collection and load it with the string values "Hello" and "Goodbye". It also links the ArrayList to the DropDownList by setting the DataSource property to the ArrayList:

```
private void LoadDropDownList()
{
  ArrayList list = new ArrayList();
  list.Add("Hello");
  list.Add("Goodbye");

  Greeting.DataSource = list;
}
```

Note that we do not call the DataBind() method directly for DropDownList. Instead, we call the DataBind() method on the Page_Load handler itself. The DataBind() method of the Page class recursively calls the DataBind() methods for all its child controls that have references to a data source. In this case, when the Page class's DataBind() method is invoked, the DropDownList control data binds to the ArrayList object as shown previously.

Control Events

Events are the final constructs used for interacting with controls that we discuss in this chapter. Events provide a mechanism to notify clients of state changes inside the control. In ASP.NET, events always coincide with an HTTP POST submission back to the web server. Through the automatic postback mechanism, events in ASP.NET appear to behave very much like their counterparts in a Windows Forms application.

■ **Note** Events provide an object-oriented mechanism for a control to communicate with other controls that care to know about state changes within that control. If events did not exist, objects would have to resort to polling to know about state changes in other objects. The asynchronous nature of events provides an elegant means for communicating between objects. Event handler methods are generally protected to the control class (the event subscriber), as it would not make sense to call event handlers outside the consuming class.

The Page class in the "Hello, World" example consumes the Click event raised by the Button to read values and sets the first Label control. The Button Click event is easy to map in the Designer by simply double-clicking the button. Double-clicking a control in Visual Studio automatically generates the default event handler for the control. In the case of the Button, it is the Click event. In addition, Visual Studio performs other housekeeping tasks, such as wiring up the event delegate exposed by the Button control to the generated method (in this case, Button1_Click) in the Page class.

Note In the .NET Framework 2.0 and later, the concept of a partial class exists where a class can be split across multiple files. This allows Visual Studio or similar non-Microsoft tools to provide better design-time support.

Events in ASP.NET take advantage of delegates as the infrastructure for this communication among objects. In Chapter 5, we discuss how to work with events in detail.

The Properties window in the Design view of the Visual Studio Designer can help map the events from a control that don't result from double-clicking the control.

Note Click the yellow lightning bolt icon at the top of the Properties window to filter the view to show only events exposed by a particular control.

Each available event for a control is listed on a separate line, and creating a wired up event handler is as simple as either double-clicking the blank area next to the event name to generate an event with the default naming scheme (ControlName_EventName) or typing a name and pressing the Enter key. Figure 1-5 illustrates creating the event handler for the TextBox control.

The end result of using the Properties window to add the protected event handler to the Page class is a method named TextBox_TextChanged that is wired to the TextChanged event of the TextBox control. You can add code to this handling routine to announce the state change of the TextBox control by setting the Text property of the Label2 control on the web form:

```
protected void Name_TextChanged(object sender, EventArgs e)
{
  ChangeLabel.Text = "Textbox changed to " + Name.Text;
}
```

Visual Studio 2008 provides much cleaner code generation when compared to Visual Studio .NET 2003. There is no longer a code region named "Web Form Designer generated code" present in the code file. Much of the boilerplate code that existed in ASP.NET 1.1 is no longer present, which makes developers' lives a bit simpler.

The result of all the not-so-hard work to this point is the browser view in Figure 1-6, which shows what happens when Rob enters his name and selects a polite greeting.

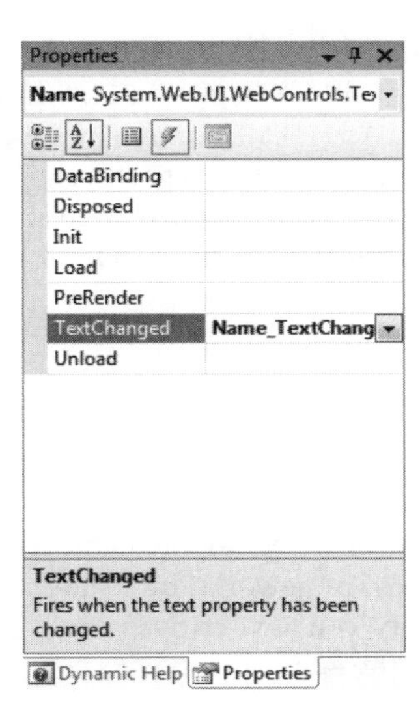

Figure 1-5. *Adding an event handler to the TextChanged event of the TextBox control*

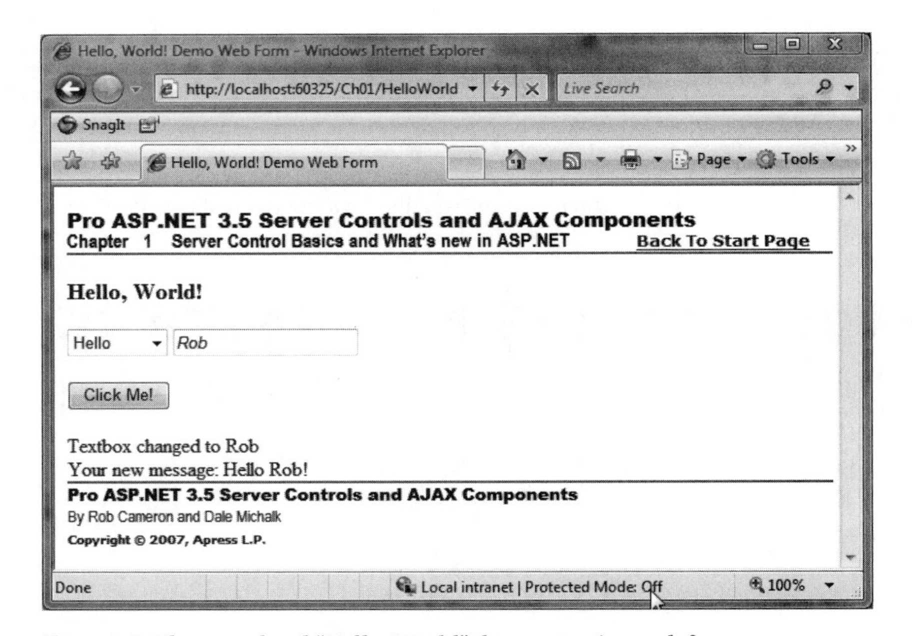

Figure 1-6. *The completed "Hello, World" demonstration web form*

The Web Page As a Control Tree

ASP.NET provides full programmatic access to the tags on an HTML page in an object-oriented way. The architecture in ASP.NET that provides this capability is the `.aspx` page control tree. In this section, we discuss the control tree as it relates to the "Hello, World" example.

At first glance, the "Hello, World" web form would seem to contain only a few visible server controls that were explicitly placed on the form. The reality is that the entire display surface of the `.aspx` page becomes a cornucopia of controls during processing. Any HTML content in the web form that is not part of the server controls laid out in the Visual Studio Designer is packaged into a server control that renders the HTML. The control structure of the web form can be seen by turning on the trace features of ASP.NET through setting the `Trace=True` attribute on the `Page` directive:

```
<%@ Page Language="C#" Trace="true"
        MasterPageFile="../Master Page/ControlsBook2MasterPage.master"
        AutoEventWireup="true" CodeFile="HelloWorld.aspx.cs"
        Inherits="Ch01_HelloWorld" Title="Ch01 Hello World!"  %>
```

You no longer need to make sure that tracing is enabled in the `<trace>` XML element inside of the `web.config` configuration file for the web application with .NET Framework 2.0 and later. However, if you wish to enable and customize the trace functionality, you have to paste the element within the `<system.web>` element of the `web.config` file for the application:

```
<trace
enabled="true"
requestLimit="10"
pageOutput="false"
traceMode="SortByTime"
localOnly="true"
/>
```

Figure 1-7 shows the portion of the trace output that displays the control tree for the web form.

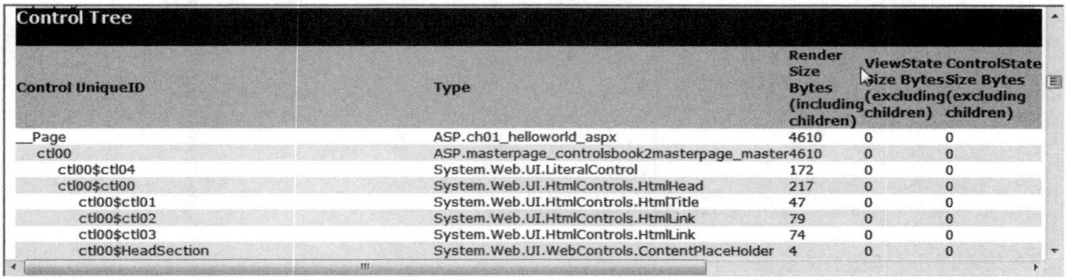

Control Tree

Control UniqueID	Type	Render Size Bytes (including children)	ViewState Size Bytes (excluding children)	ControlState Size Bytes (excluding children)
__Page	ASP.ch01_helloworld_aspx	4610	0	0
ctl00	ASP.masterpage_controlsbook2masterpage_master	4610	0	0
ctl00$ctl04	System.Web.UI.LiteralControl	172	0	0
ctl00$ctl00	System.Web.UI.HtmlControls.HtmlHead	217	0	0
ctl00$ctl01	System.Web.UI.HtmlControls.HtmlTitle	47	0	0
ctl00$ctl02	System.Web.UI.HtmlControls.HtmlLink	79	0	0
ctl00$ctl03	System.Web.UI.HtmlControls.HtmlLink	74	0	0
ctl00$HeadSection	System.Web.UI.WebControls.ContentPlaceHolder	4	0	0

Figure 1-7. *Tracing the control tree of the "Hello, World" web form*

The X-ray vision into ASP.NET provided by the trace feature dissects the web form in gory detail. At the top is the `Page` control that represents the web form of type `ASP.ch01_helloworld_aspx`. Below it are the server controls that you would expect to be there: `DropDownList`, `TextBox`, `Button`, and `Label`. What you might not expect to see are the `HtmlForm`, `DataBoundLiteralControl`, and `LiteralControl` objects in the control tree trace.

HtmlForm is responsible for representing the <form> tag on the .aspx page and providing the missing method and action properties to ensure the page is always sent back to the original URL via an HTTP POST. The form server control looks like the following in the ControlsBook2MasterPage.master master page at design time:

```
<form id="form1" runat="server">
```

There isn't a form server control in HelloWorld.aspx, because it is a content page that renders within a master page, which is where the HTML form exists. At runtime in the browser, the generated HTML has this <form> tag:

```
<form name="aspnetForm" method="post" action="HelloWorld.aspx" id="aspnetForm">
```

The HtmlForm server control renders HTML with all the necessary information to post the page back to itself, as shown in the preceding line of code. This allows each control on the page to remember its previous state via the ViewState mechanism and raise the appropriate server control event.

The literal controls have the responsibility for rendering the generic text and HTML tags in the web form without much of a server-side presence. These are the flyweight classes of the ASP.NET server control framework. The literal controls pick up text or tags in the master page or .aspx page that do not have the runat="server" attribute identifying them as a server control.

The LiteralControl class is the simplest of the two shown in the control dump, because it is a pure text-in and text-out operation. Notice how the control tree picks up the <br/> tags between the other server controls as well as the closing <body> and <html> tags as LiteralControl objects. The ResourceBasedLiteralControl that was present in ASP.NET 1.1 was removed in ASP.NET 2.0. That is not a backward compatibility concern, because the class is an internally implemented class in the ASP.NET 1.1 framework that is not creatable or accessible by the programmer.

The DataBoundLiteralControl is the most complex of the literal controls, because it represents a data-binding expression like the one in the document that binds to the GetTitle() method of the Page object. It has a DataBind() method that must be called by the Page class to resolve its value, just like the DropDownList control had to read from the ArrayList data source in its DataBind() operations.

The Root Controls

The previous demonstration highlighted the server-control-centric nature of the ASP.NET web form page execution process. We now shift gears to briefly discuss where the various controls exist inside the .NET Framework and what features they provide in rendering HTML. The controls are factored into three primary namespaces in the .NET Framework: System.Web.UI, System.eb.UI.HtmlControls, and System.Web.UI.WebControls (see Figure 1-8).

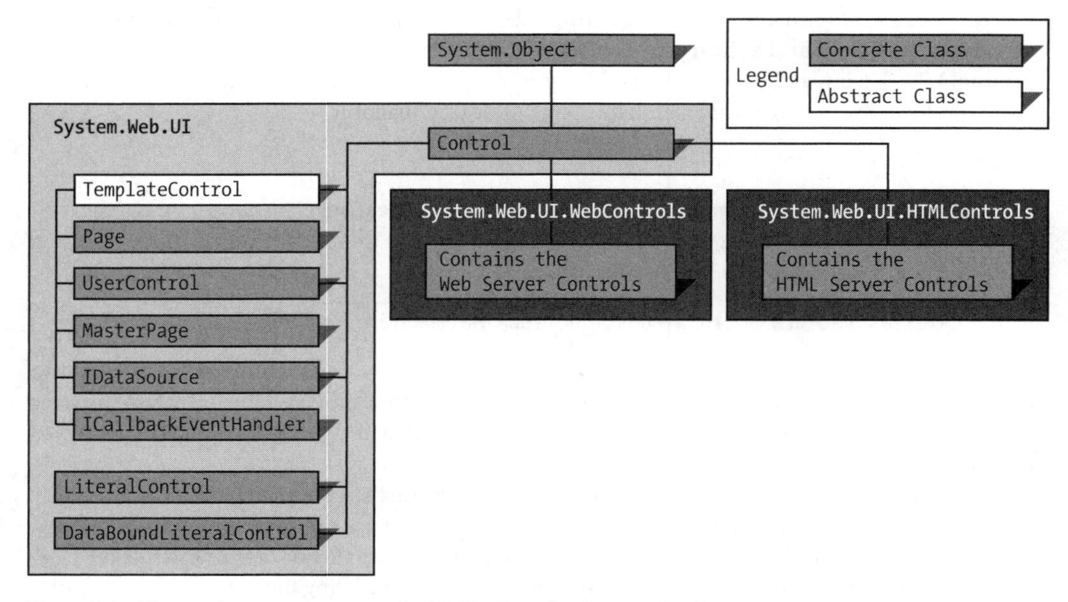

Figure 1-8. *The major namespaces of ASP.NET under System.Web.UI*

The System.Web.UI Namespace

At the top of the hierarchy is our first destination—the `System.Web.UI` namespace and its root controls. It contains the `Control` class, which is the mandatory parent class for all objects that want to call themselves controls. Directly inheriting from the `Control` class in this namespace is a set of specialized classes that implement the web form through the `Page` class, the user control through the `UserControl` class, and the literal controls. The `Page` class and the literal controls are discussed in detail in the previous "Hello, World" web form demonstration. We focus in more detail on the `UserControl` class in the next chapter when we cover control creation.

System.Web.UI.HtmlControls Namespace

The controls under `System.Web.UI.HtmlControls` have the capability to take existing HTML content and make it available as a server control with the addition of a `runat="server"` attribute. The canonical example of this type of control is turning an HTML text box into a server control:

```
<input type="text" id="name" runat="server"/>
```

The ASP.NET parsing engine is responsible for mapping the HTML tag to the correct control type in `System.Web.UI.HtmlControls` when it sees this marker attribute. The preceding example adds an instance of the `HtmlInputText` control to the web form's control collection.

■ **Note** If you want to modify or interact with any of the literal controls on the server side, you have two options. One option is to walk the page's control tree collection to find the desired control. The other option is declare the control in the code-behind class file. In the previous input example, the declaration would look like this: `protected System.Web.UI.HtmlControls.HtmlInputText name;`.

Although they may look like their HTML cousins, these controls set themselves apart by remembering state, raising events, allowing themselves to be programmatically manipulated in server-side code, and providing other value-add services such as file upload when the form post has reached the Web. The full list of HTML controls available in the `System.Web.UI.HtmlControls` namespace is depicted in Figure 1-9.

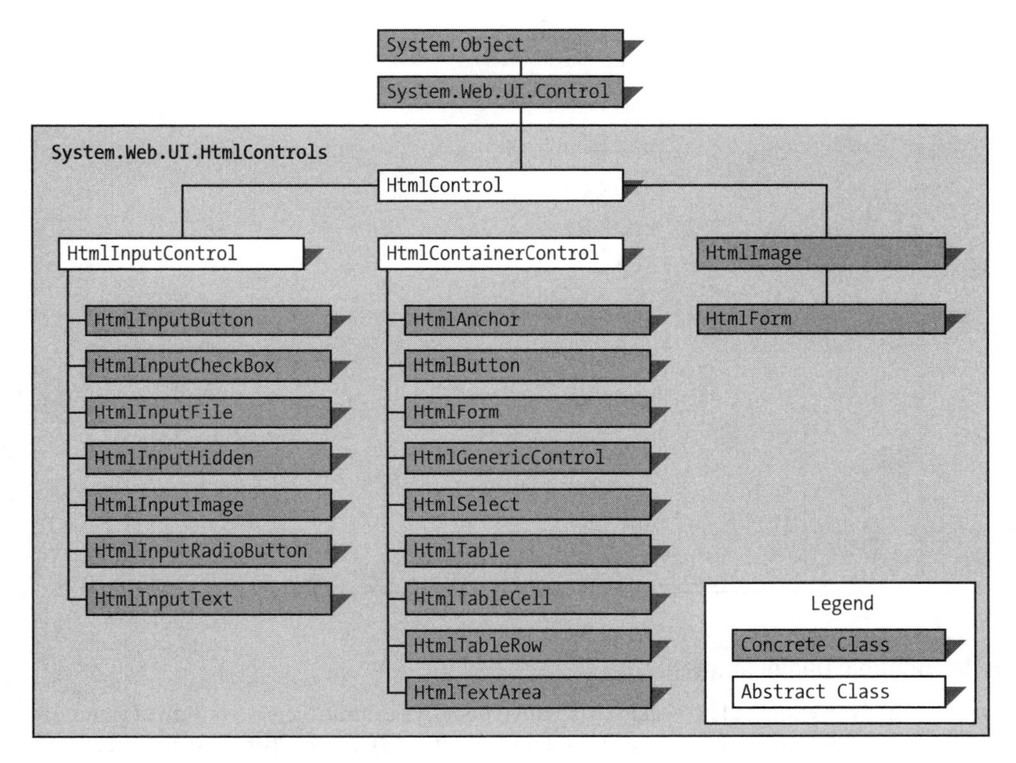

Figure 1-9. *Controls in the System.Web.UI.HtmlControls namespace*

Table 1-1 is useful for figuring out which of the HTML tags maps to a specific HTML control. Note that some of controls (such as the `HtmlInputText` control) map to multiple HTML tags on an `.aspx` page. For tags that do not have a specific control mapping, the `HtmlGeneric` control is used to represent them as a server-side control object when they have a `runat="server"` attribute.

Table 1-1. *HTML Tags and Their HTML Server Control Counterparts*

HTML Tag	HTML Server Control
`<form>`	`HtmlForm`
`<input type="text">`	`HtmlInputText`
`<input type="password">`	`HtmlInputText`
`<input type="radio">`	`HtmlInputRadioButton`

Table 1-1. *HTML Tags and Their HTML Server Control Counterparts (Continued)*

HTML Tag	HTML Server Control
`<input type="checkbox">`	HtmlInputCheckBox
`<input type="submit">`	HtmlInputButton
`<input type="hidden">`	HtmlInputHidden
`<input type="button">`	HtmlInputButton
`<input type="reset">`	HtmlInputButton
`<input type="image">`	HtmlInputImage
`<input type="file">`	HtmlInputFile
`<button>`	HtmlButton
`<select>`	HtmlSelect
`<textarea>`	HtmlTextArea
`<img>`	HtmlImage
`<a>`	HtmlAnchor
`<table>`	HtmlTable
`<tr>`	HtmlTableRow
`<td>`	HtmlTableCell
All other tags	HtmlGenericControl

An HTML Controls Demonstration

To examine the `System.Web.UI.HtmlControls` namespace, we examine the execution of a demonstration showing the controls in action. This demonstration dynamically constructs an HTML table from X and Y coordinates that are present on the web form using the code shown in Listings 1-5 and 1-6. We discuss this code after the listings.

Listing 1-5. *The HTMLControls Web Form .aspx File*

```
<%@ Page Language="C#"
MasterPageFile="~/MasterPage/ControlsBook2MasterPage.Master"
  AutoEventWireup="true" CodeBehind="HtmlControls.aspx.cs"
Inherits="ControlsBook2Web.Ch01.HtmlControls"
  Title="HTML Controls Demo" %>

<asp:Content ID="Content1" ContentPlaceHolderID="ChapterNumAndTitle" runat="server">
  <asp:Label ID="ChapterNumberLabel" runat="server"
Width="14px">1</asp:Label>  <asp:Label
    ID="ChapterTitleLabel" runat="server" Width="360px">
Server Control Basics and What's new in ASP.NET</asp:Label>
```

```
</asp:Content>
<asp:Content ID="Content2" ContentPlaceHolderID="PrimaryContent" runat="server">
  <h3>
    HTML Controls</h3>
  X
  <input type="text" id="XTextBox" runat="server" /><br />
  <br />
  Y
  <input type="text" id="YTextBox" runat="server" /><br />
  <br />
  <input type="submit" id="BuildTableButton" runat="server"
value="Build Table" onserverclick="BuildTableButton_ServerClick" /><br />
  <br />
  <span id="Span1" runat="server"></span>
</asp:Content>
```

Listing 1-6. *The HTMLControls Code-Behind Class File*

```
using System;
using System.Web;
using System.Web.UI;
using System.Web.UI.WebControls;
using System.Web.UI.HtmlControls;

namespace ControlsBook2Web.Ch01
{
  public partial class HtmlControls : System.Web.UI.Page
  {
    protected void Page_Load(object sender, EventArgs e)
    {

    }

    protected void BuildTableButton_ServerClick(object sender, EventArgs e)
    {
      int xDim = Convert.ToInt32(XTextBox.Value);
      int yDim = Convert.ToInt32(YTextBox.Value);
      BuildTable(xDim, yDim);
    }

    private void BuildTable(int xDim, int yDim)
    {
      HtmlTable table;
      HtmlTableRow row;
      HtmlTableCell cell;
      HtmlGenericControl content;
```

```
      table = new HtmlTable();
      table.Border = 1;
      for (int y = 0; y < yDim; y++)
      {
        row = new HtmlTableRow();
        for (int x = 0; x < xDim; x++)
        {
          cell = new HtmlTableCell();
          cell.Style.Add("font", "16pt verdana bold italic");
          cell.Style.Add("background-color", "red");
          cell.Style.Add("color", "yellow");

          content = new HtmlGenericControl("SPAN");
          content.InnerHtml = "X:" + x.ToString() +
             "Y:" + y.ToString();
          cell.Controls.Add(content);
          row.Cells.Add(cell);
        }
        table.Rows.Add(row);
      }
      Span1.Controls.Add(table);
    }
  }
}
```

Dynamically adding controls to an existing control structure is a common way to implement web forms that vary their content and structure according to the user's input. The BuildTable() method encapsulates this dynamic functionality in this HTML controls demonstration by rendering the table when passed X and Y parameters. The variables passed in to BuildTable() are retrieved using the Value property of the HtmlInputText controls:

```
int xDim = Convert.ToInt32(XTextBox.Value);
int yDim = Convert.ToInt32(YTextBox.Value);
BuildTable(xDim,yDim);
```

The bulk of the work in this HTML controls demonstration is located in the BuildTable() method. This method starts by creating an HtmlTable control representing the outer <table> tag and then jumps into nested For loops to add HtmlTableRow controls representing the <tr> tags along with HtmlTableCell controls rendering <td> tags.

One of the more interesting sections of this routine is the cell creation and CSS styling configuration code. Once the HtmlTableCell control is created, the CSS styles are set as strings and then added to the Style property representing the cell's CSS attributes. This is a manual, string-based process that is not helped by any type or enumeration from the System.Web.UI.HtmlControls namespace:

```
cell = new HtmlTableCell();
cell.Style.Add("font","16pt verdana bold italic");
cell.Style.Add("background-color","red");
cell.Style.Add("color","yellow");
```

After the styling is set, the cell adds an `HtmlGenericControl` representing a `<span>` tag to its control collection. The `HtmlGenericControl`'s `InnerHtml`, or content, is then set to the X and Y values for the cell. The result is that the `<span>` tag is nested in the table cell's `<td>` tag. The final step in the process is to add the cell to its parent row:

```
content = new HtmlGenericControl("SPAN");
content.InnerHtml = "X:" + x.ToString() +
   "Y:" + y.ToString();
cell.Controls.Add(content);
row.Cells.Add(cell);
```

The HTML rendered in the browser client shows the direct insertion of the CSS attributes into the `<td>` tag and the `HtmlGenericControl` production of the `<span>` content:

```
<td style="font:16pt verdana bold italic;
background-color:red;color:yellow;">
<span>X:0Y:0</span>
</td>
```

Figure 1-10 shows the output of all this work. When the page initially loads, the red and yellow table is not present. Once values are entered for X and Y, in this case **3** and **3**, clicking the Build Table button results in the page shown in Figure 1-10.

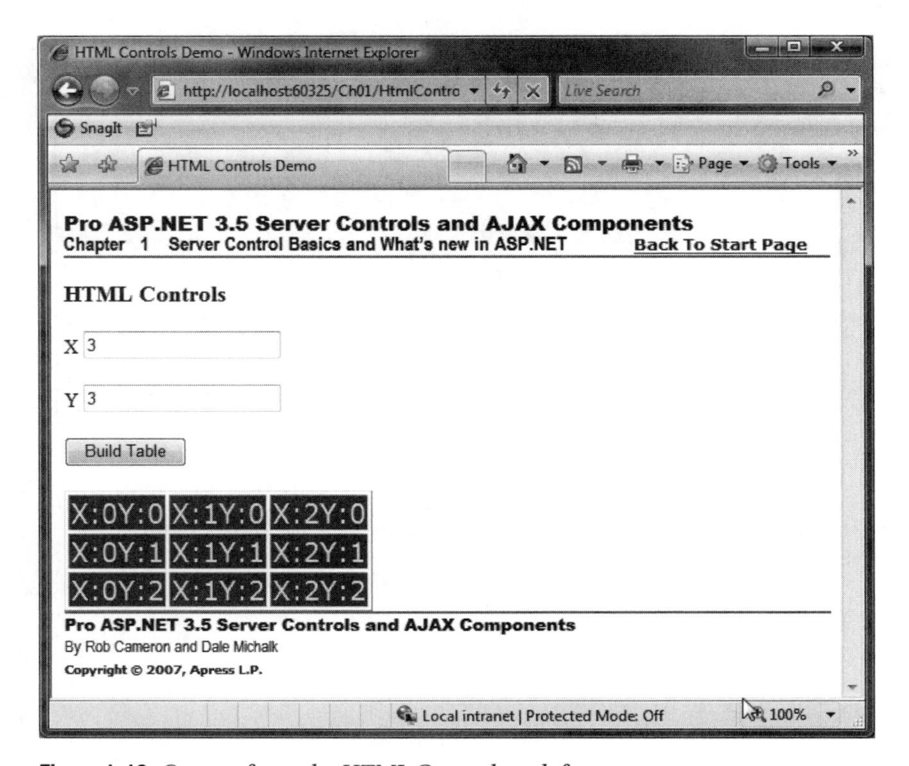

Figure 1-10. *Output from the HTML Controls web form*

The System.Web.UI.WebControls Namespace

Like the HTML controls in the previous section, the web controls occupy a separate namespace in the .NET Framework—namely, `System.Web.UI.WebControls`. Figure 1-11 shows the graphical breakdown of the namespace and the myriad server control objects available.

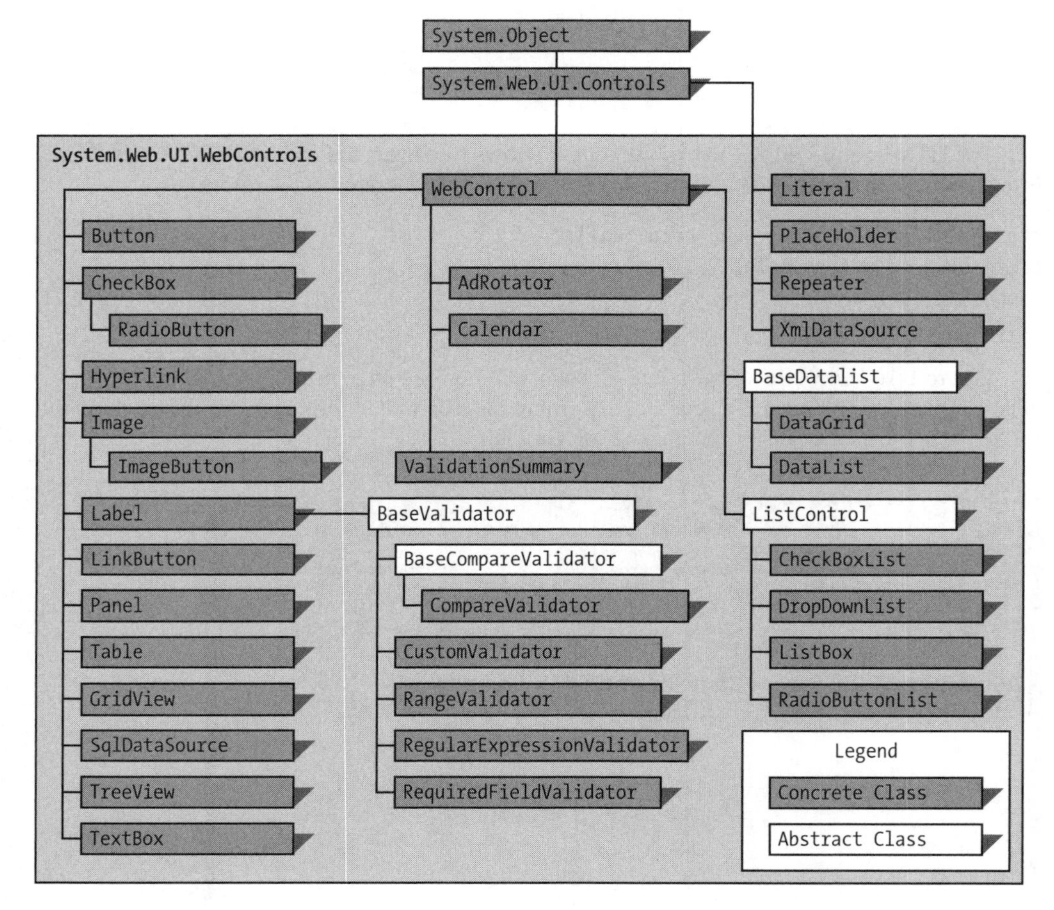

Figure 1-11. *Controls in the System.Web.UI.WebControls namespace*

The controls under the `System.Web.UI.WebControls` namespace are grouped into a few primary categories:

- Simple
- List
- Rich
- Validation

The following sections cover each category.

Simple Controls

The simple controls are the web control cousins to the HTML controls in that they generally map one-to-one to an HTML tag. Some good examples of this are the mappings of the `Label` control to the `<span>` tag and the `TextBox` control to the `<input type="text">` tag.

Because simple controls map closely to a single HTML tag, we bring back the ever-popular tag-to-control mapping table in a manner similar to our discussion in the last section on HTML controls. Like the previous table, some controls in Table 1-2 handle more than one tag by property settings. The `LiteralControl` from the `System.Web.UI` namespace is used for tags that are not represented in `System.Web.UI.WebControls` as a control.

Table 1-2. *HTML Tags and Their Web Control Counterparts*

HTML Tag	Simple Web Control
`<input type="text">`	`TextBox` with `TextMode=Single`
`<input type="password">`	`TextBox` with `TextMode=Password`
`<textarea>`	`TextBox` with `TextMode=MultiLine`
`<input type="checkbox">`	`CheckBox`
`<input type="radio">`	`RadioButton`
`<input type="submit">`	`Button`
`<input type="image">`	`ImageButton`
`<button>`	`Button`
`<select>`	`DropDownList`
`<select size=3>`	`SelectList` with `Rows=3`
`<textarea>`	`HtmlTextArea`
`<img>`	`Image`
`<a>`	`HyperLink`, `LinkButton`
`<table>`	`Table`
`<tr>`	`TableRow`
`<td>`	`TableCell`
`<table>`	`Panel`
`<span>`	`Label`

A Simple Controls Demonstration

The following simple controls demonstration is a port of the original HTML controls demonstration to show the same output using dynamically built controls from the `System.Web.UI.WebControls` namespace. Listings 1-7 and 1-8 contain the code.

Listing 1-7. *The SimpleControls Web Form .aspx File*

```
<%@ Page Language="C#" MasterPageFile="~/MasterPage/ControlsBook2MasterPage.Master"
  AutoEventWireup="true" CodeBehind="SimpleControls.aspx.cs"
Inherits="ControlsBook2Web.Ch01.SimpleControls"
  Title="Simple Controls Demo" %>

<asp:Content ID="Content1" ContentPlaceHolderID="ChapterNumAndTitle" runat="server">
  <asp:Label ID="ChapterNumberLabel" runat="server"
Width="14px">1</asp:Label>  <asp:Label\
    ID="ChapterTitleLabel" runat="server" Width="360px">
Server Control Basics and What's new in ASP.NET</asp:Label>
</asp:Content>
<asp:Content ID="Content2" ContentPlaceHolderID="PrimaryContent" runat="server">
  <h3>
    Simple Controls</h3>
  X
  <asp:TextBox ID="XTextBox" runat="server"></asp:TextBox><br />
  <br />
  Y
  <asp:TextBox ID="YTextBox" runat="server"></asp:TextBox><br />
  <br />
  <asp:Button ID="BuildTableButton" runat="server"
Text="Build Table" OnClick="BuildTableButton_Click">
  </asp:Button><br />
  <asp:PlaceHolder ID="TablePlaceHolder" runat="server"></asp:PlaceHolder>
</asp:Content>
```

Listing 1-8. *The SimpleControls Code-Behind Class File*

```
using System;
using System.Web;
using System.Web.UI;
using System.Web.UI.WebControls;
using System.Drawing;

namespace ControlsBook2Web.Ch01
{
  public partial class SimpleControls : System.Web.UI.Page
  {
    protected void Page_Load(object sender, EventArgs e)
    {

    }
```

```
    protected void BuildTableButton_Click(object sender, EventArgs e)
    {
      int xDim = Convert.ToInt32(XTextBox.Text);
      int yDim = Convert.ToInt32(YTextBox.Text);
      BuildTable(xDim, yDim);
    }

    private void BuildTable(int xDim, int yDim)
    {
      Table table;
      TableRow row;
      TableCell cell;
      Literal content;

      table = new Table();
      table.BorderWidth = 1;
      table.BorderStyle = BorderStyle.Ridge;
      for (int y = 0; y < yDim; y++)
      {
        row = new TableRow();
        for (int x = 0; x < xDim; x++)
        {
          cell = new TableCell();
          cell.BackColor = Color.Blue;
          cell.BorderWidth = 1;
          cell.ForeColor = Color.Yellow;
          cell.Font.Name = "Verdana";
          cell.Font.Size = 16;
          cell.Font.Bold = true;
          cell.Font.Italic = true;

          content = new Literal();
          content.Text = "<SPAN>X:" + x.ToString() +
             "Y:" + y.ToString() + "</SPAN>";
          cell.Controls.Add(content);
          row.Cells.Add(cell);
        }
        table.Rows.Add(row);
      }
      TablePlaceHolder.Controls.Add(table);
    }
  }
}
```

Comparing this simple controls demonstration to the HTML controls demonstration shows little difference beyond changes to control names and namespaces. One minor difference is the fact that in the simple controls demonstration, a `PlaceHolder` control (yes, there really is a `PlaceHolder` class) acts as the container for holding the cell content. The `PlaceHolder` control does not have a UI; instead, it renders only the UI of its child controls. This is in contrast to the HTML controls demonstration, which used `HtmlGenericControl` representing a `<span>` tag for holding the cell content.

The bigger difference between the two examples is the Cascading Style Sheet (CSS) style configuration. In the HTML controls demonstration, we had to use a more explicit syntax without the benefit of help from the control object model or IntelliSense in Visual Studio. However, in this simple controls demonstration, we have full access to the assistance provided by the Framework and Visual Studio. The following code snippet shows how easy it is to set color and other font styling in with simple controls:

```
cell = new TableCell();
cell.BackColor = Color.Blue;
cell.BorderWidth = 1;
cell.ForeColor = Color.Yellow;
cell.Font.Name = "Verdana";
cell.Font.Size = 16;
cell.Font.Bold = true;
cell.Font.Italic = true;
```

The content rendered in the browser demonstrates the nice abstraction of CSS styling made available to controls by the `System.Web.UI.WebControls` namespace:

```
<td style="color:Yellow;background-color:Blue;border-width:1px;border-style:solid;
font-family:Verdana;font-size:16pt;font-weight:bold;font-style:italic;">
<span>X:0Y:0</span>
</td>
```

Figure 1-12 shows the output from this simple controls demonstration.

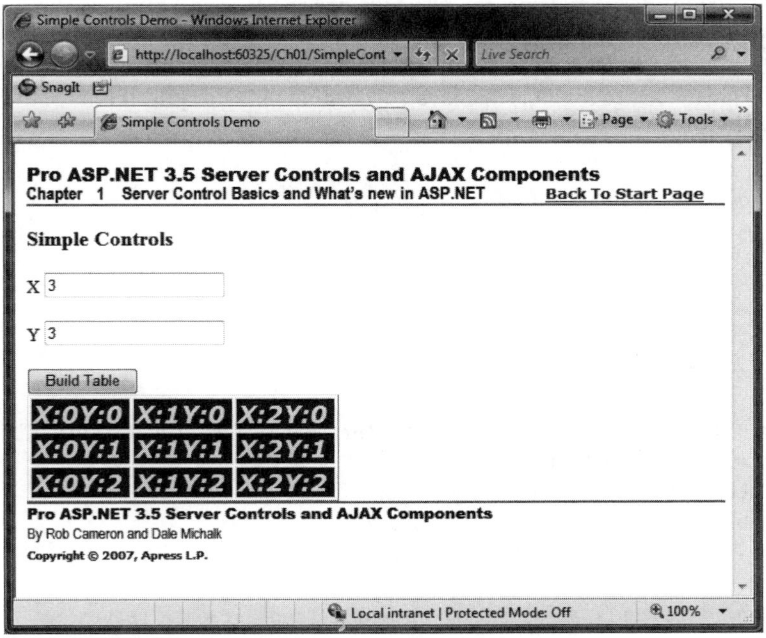

Figure 1-12. *Output from the simple controls web form*

List Controls

List controls provide enhanced capabilities beyond those of the simple controls by generating their content using an external data source. They range from the simple `CheckBoxList` and `RadioButtonList` controls, which build a group of simple HTML tags, to the more complex `DataGrid`, `DataList`, and `Repeater` controls, which support a highly customizable UI. In ASP.NET 2.0, the `GridView` was added to the arsenal, providing a very powerful list-based control, and in Chapter 2, the simple user control demonstration includes a `GridView` control. List controls are a key instrument in the toolkit of the ASP.NET developer, because they provide broad functionality when tasked with quickly getting a data-oriented web site up and running.

A List Controls Demonstration

The following list controls demonstration uses a `Repeater` control to build an HTML table representing data from a simple Access database containing a `Books` table with information from the Apress web site; the source code is provided in Listings 1-9 and 1-10. The previous edition of this book used the SQL `Northwind` database `Customer` table, but in this edition, we've made things a bit simpler by using an Access database. However, generally, you would want to use an enterprise-quality database such as SQL Server for a real application. The demonstration illustrates two key features of ASP.NET UI development: templates and data binding, which we cover in Chapter 7.

With templates and data binding available, the programmer can focus on building the data access class library in the n-tier model and hooking up the control to a data source via data binding in the code-behind page, while the UI designer can tweak the HTML content and templates on the .aspx page to ensure that it is displayed according to the requirements of the web development project.

Listing 1-9. *The ListControls Web Form .aspx File*

```
<%@ Page Language="C#"
MasterPageFile="~/MasterPage/ControlsBook2MasterPage.Master"
  AutoEventWireup="true" CodeBehind="ListControls.aspx.cs"
Inherits="ControlsBook2Web.Ch01.ListControls"
  Title="List Controls Demo" %>

<asp:Content ID="Content1" ContentPlaceHolderID="ChapterNumAndTitle" runat="server">
  <asp:Label ID="ChapterNumberLabel" runat="server"
Width="14px">1</asp:Label>  <asp:Label
    ID="ChapterTitleLabel" runat="server" Width="360px">
Server Control Basics and What's new in ASP.NET</asp:Label>
</asp:Content>
<asp:Content ID="Content2" ContentPlaceHolderID="PrimaryContent" runat="server">
  <h3>
    List Controls</h3>
  <asp:Repeater ID="Repeater1" runat="server" DataSourceID="ApressBooksds">
    <HeaderTemplate>
      <table>
        <th>
          Title</th>
        <th>
          Author</th>
        <th>
          ISBN</th>
        <th>
          Date Published</th>
    </HeaderTemplate>
    <ItemTemplate>
      <tr style="background-color: Silver">
        <td>
          <%# DataBinder.Eval(Container.DataItem,"Title") %></td>
        <td>
          <%# DataBinder.Eval(Container.DataItem,"Author") %></td>
        <td>
          <%# DataBinder.Eval(Container.DataItem,"ISBN") %></td>
        <td>
          <%# DataBinder.Eval(Container.DataItem,"DatePublished") %></td>
      </tr>
    </ItemTemplate>
```

```
    <AlternatingItemTemplate>
      <tr style="background-color: White">
        <td>
          <%# DataBinder.Eval(Container.DataItem,"Title") %></td>
        <td>
          <%# DataBinder.Eval(Container.DataItem,"Author") %></td>
        <td>
          <%# DataBinder.Eval(Container.DataItem,"ISBN") %></td>
        <td>
          <%# DataBinder.Eval(Container.DataItem,"DatePublished") %></td>
      </tr>
    </AlternatingItemTemplate>
    <FooterTemplate>
      </table>
    </FooterTemplate>
  </asp:Repeater>
  <asp:AccessDataSource ID="ApressBooksds" runat="server"
DataFile="~/App_Data/ApressBooks.mdb"
    SelectCommand="SELECT [Title], [Author], [ISBN], [DatePublished]
FROM [Books]"></asp:AccessDataSource>
  <br />
</asp:Content>
```

Listing 1-10. *The ListControls Web Form Code-Behind Class File*

```
using System;
using System.Web.UI.WebControls;

namespace ControlsBook2Web.Ch01
{
  public partial class ListControls : System.Web.UI.Page
  {
    protected void Page_Load(object sender, EventArgs e)
    {

    }
  }
}
```

The data source in the list controls example is an AccessDataSource named ApressBooksds that contains rows from a sample database of Apress books. The Repeater control is bound directly to the ApressBooksds control.

The Repeater control is templated to produce an HTML table with HTML rows representing each data row in the ApressBooksds data-source control. The HeaderTemplate and FooterTemplate give us the table opening and closing tags, and the ItemTemplate and AlternatingItemTemplate give us the structure for each row in the table.

The data in each row of the `DataSet` is available via the `Container.DataItem` reference available for use inside the template content. A string index name something like "Title" is used to grab a particular column for display. Although using code-behind over inline script as much as possible is preferable, `DataBinder.Eval()` is a late-bound formatting method that we use to keep from having to do ugly casts to satisfy the strongly typed nature of C# and ASP.NET. Interestingly, the `Repeater` control is the only list-based control that allows HTML formatting to span across the templates. Figure 1-13 shows the output from this list controls demonstration.

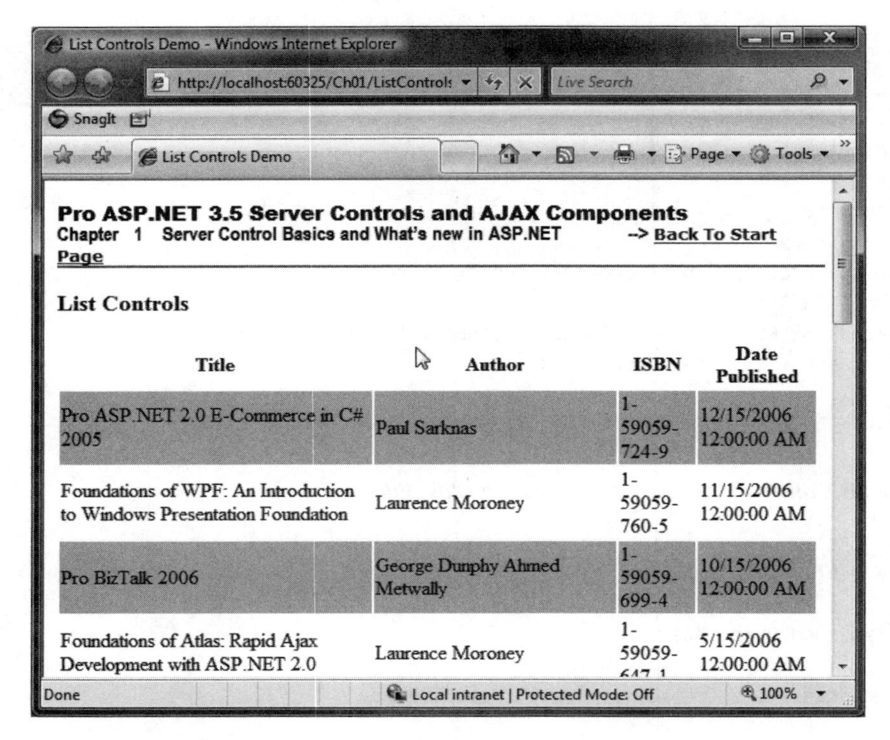

Figure 1-13. *Output from the list controls web form*

Rich Controls

The list controls are nice for working with data sources and building templated user interfaces, but sometimes, a web project needs more help from a control when building dauntingly complex pieces of HTML content. This is the domain of rich controls, such as the `Calendar` and `AdRotator`, in `System.Web.UI.WebControls`. They make hard-to-generate HTML appear easy, as they require little in the way of development to generate significant HTML output.

A Rich Controls Demonstration

This rich controls web form demonstration shows the `Calendar` control in action. The source code is provided in Listings 1-11 and 1-12.

Listing 1-11. *The RichControls Web Form .aspx File*

```
<%@ Page Language="C#"
MasterPageFile="~/MasterPage/ControlsBook2MasterPage.Master"
  AutoEventWireup="true" CodeBehind="RichControls.aspx.cs"
Inherits="ControlsBook2Web.Ch01.RichControls"
  Title="Rich Controls Demo" %>

<asp:Content ID="Content1" ContentPlaceHolderID="ChapterNumAndTitle" runat="server">
  <asp:Label ID="ChapterNumberLabel" runat="server"
Width="14px">1</asp:Label>  <asp:Label
    ID="ChapterTitleLabel" runat="server" Width="360px">
Server Control Basics and What's new in ASP.NET</asp:Label>
</asp:Content>
<asp:Content ID="Content2" ContentPlaceHolderID="PrimaryContent" runat="server">
  <h3>
    Rich Controls</h3>
  <p>
    <asp:Calendar ID="Calendar1" runat="server" BackColor="White" Width="220px"
ForeColor="#003399"
      Height="200px" Font-Size="8pt" Font-Names="Verdana"
BorderColor="#3366CC" BorderWidth="1px"
      DayNameFormat="FirstLetter" CellPadding="1"
       OnSelectionChanged="Date_Selected">
      <TodayDayStyle ForeColor="White" BackColor="#99CCCC"></TodayDayStyle>
      <SelectorStyle ForeColor="#336666" BackColor="#99CCCC"></SelectorStyle>
      <NextPrevStyle Font-Size="8pt" ForeColor="#CCCCFF"></NextPrevStyle>
      <DayHeaderStyle Height="1px" ForeColor="#336666"
BackColor="#99CCCC"></DayHeaderStyle>
      <SelectedDayStyle Font-Bold="True" ForeColor="#CCFF99"
BackColor="#009999"></SelectedDayStyle>
      <TitleStyle Font-Size="10pt" Font-Bold="True" Height="25px"
BorderWidth="1px" ForeColor="#CCCCFF"
        BorderStyle="Solid" BorderColor="#3366CC" BackColor="#003399"></TitleStyle>
      <WeekendDayStyle BackColor="#CCCCFF"></WeekendDayStyle>
      <OtherMonthDayStyle ForeColor="#999999"></OtherMonthDayStyle>
    </asp:Calendar>
  </p>
  <p>
    <asp:Label ID="Label1" runat="server"></asp:Label></p>
</asp:Content>
```

Listing 1-12. *The RichControls Web Form Code-Behind Class File*

```
using System;
using System.Web;
using System.Web.UI;
using System.Web.UI.WebControls;

namespace ControlsBook2Web.Ch01
{
  public partial class RichControls : System.Web.UI.Page
  {
    protected void Page_Load(object sender, EventArgs e)
    {

    }

    protected void Date_Selected(object sender, EventArgs e)
    {
      Label1.Text = "Selected: " + Calendar1.SelectedDate.ToLongDateString();
    }
  }
}
```

The rich controls demonstration has the least amount of code surface area of all the demonstrations we've shown in this chapter. The .aspx page contains the Calendar control and all the declarative settings to have the Calendar render in a manner pleasing to the eye, along with a Label control to display the selected date. The code-behind has a Date_Selected() method mapped to the SelectionChanged event of the Calendar control to set the value of the Label control to the date we select (by clicking it). Figure 1-14 shows the output from this rich controls demonstration.

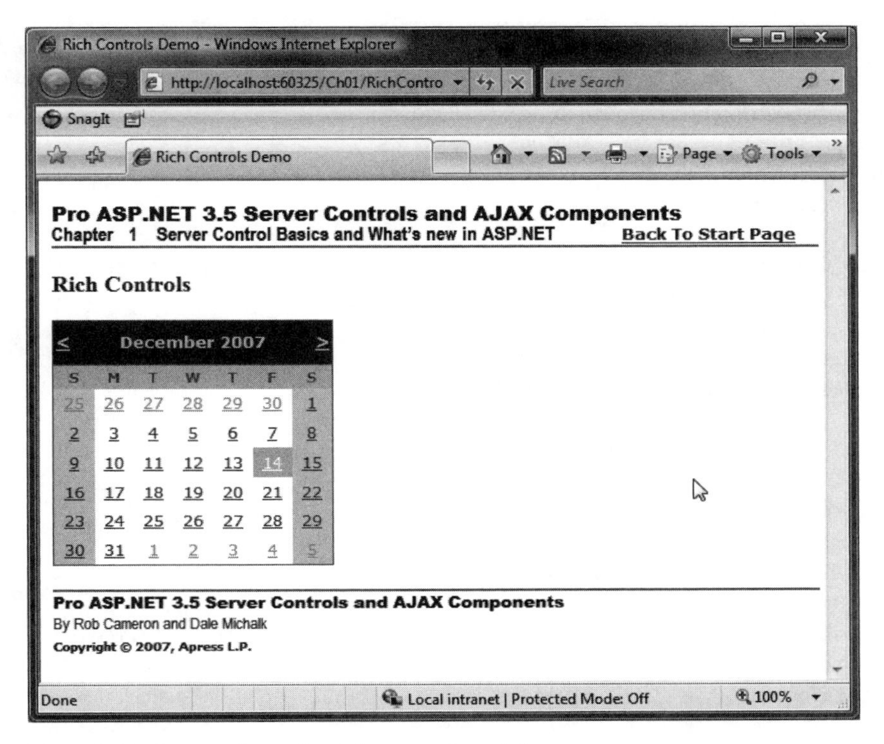

Figure 1-14. *Output from the rich controls web form*

Rich Controls and XSLT

Another interesting control from the rich controls portion of the `System.Web.UI.WebControls` namespace is the XML control. This control takes both an XML data source and an XML Style Sheet Language Transformations (XSLT) style sheet to generate the final HTML output. An XSLT style sheet can be brought to bear as an alternate UI generation paradigm that separates the display of data from its source in a similar fashion to what we accomplished with templates and data binding in the previous list controls demonstration.

An XML Control and XSLT Demonstration

The XML control web form generates an HTML table similar to the list controls demonstration, using the same data source and the native XML support available in ADO.NET. Listings 1-13 and 1-14 provide the source code for our demonstration. Listing 1-13 presents the XML control web form's `ApressBooks.xslt` file, and Listing 1-14 shows the code-behind file.

Listing 1-13. *The XMLControl Web Form .aspx File*

```
<%@ Page Language="C#"
MasterPageFile="~/MasterPage/ControlsBook2MasterPage.Master"
  AutoEventWireup="true" CodeBehind="XMLControl.aspx.cs"
Inherits="ControlsBook2Web.Ch01.XMLControls"
  Title="XML Control Demo" %>

<asp:Content ID="Content1" ContentPlaceHolderID="ChapterNumAndTitle" runat="server">
  <asp:Label ID="ChapterNumberLabel" runat="server"
Width="14px">1</asp:Label>  <asp:Label
    ID="ChapterTitleLabel" runat="server" Width="360px">
Server Control Basics and What's new in ASP.NET</asp:Label>
</asp:Content>
<asp:Content ID="Content2" ContentPlaceHolderID="PrimaryContent" runat="server">
  <h3>
    XML Control</h3>
  <asp:Xml ID="Xml1" runat="server"></asp:Xml><br />
  <asp:AccessDataSource ID="ApressBooksds" runat="server"
DataFile="~/App_Data/ApressBooks.mdb"
    SelectCommand="SELECT [ISBN], [Author], [DatePublished], [NumPages], [Price]
FROM [Books]">
  </asp:AccessDataSource>
</asp:Content>
```

Listing 1-14. *The XMLControl Web Form Code-Behind Class File*

```
using System;
using System.Data;
using System.Web.UI;
using System.Web.UI.WebControls;

namespace ControlsBook2Web.Ch01
{
  public partial class XMLControls : System.Web.UI.Page
  {
    protected void Page_Load(object sender, EventArgs e)
    {
      if (!Page.IsPostBack)
      {
        LoadXMLControl();
      }
    }
```

```
    private void LoadXMLControl()
    {
      //Create a DataView from the AccessDataSource control
      DataView dv = (DataView)ApressBooksds.Select(new DataSourceSelectArguments());
      try
      {
        dv.Table.TableName = "Books";
        DataSet ds = dv.Table.DataSet;
        ds.DataSetName = "ApressBooks";

        // give the XML control the XML and xslt
        Xml1.DocumentContent = ds.GetXml();
        Xml1.TransformSource = "ApressBooks.xslt";
      }
      finally
      {
        dv.Dispose();
      }
    }
  }
}
```

The code has a copy of the AccessDataSource ApressBooksds used in the list controls demonstration to generate a DataSet from the AccessDataSource:

```
DataView dv = new DataView();
dv = (DataView)ApressBooksds.Select(new DataSourceSelectArguments());
 dv.Table.TableName = "Books";
 DataSet ds = dv.Table.DataSet;
 ds.DataSetName = "ApressBooks";
```

The code from the first version of this book uses now obsolete methods for ASP.NET 2.0. This code no longer uses the XslTransform class or obsolete properties on the XML control. Instead, the DocumentContent and TransformSource properties are set in the code-behind class:

```
Xml1.DocumentSource = ds.GetXml();
Xml1.TransformSource = "ApressBooks.xslt";
```

These changes in the ASP.NET 2.0 object model simplify the code required. Figure 1-15 shows the output from this XML and XSLT demonstration.

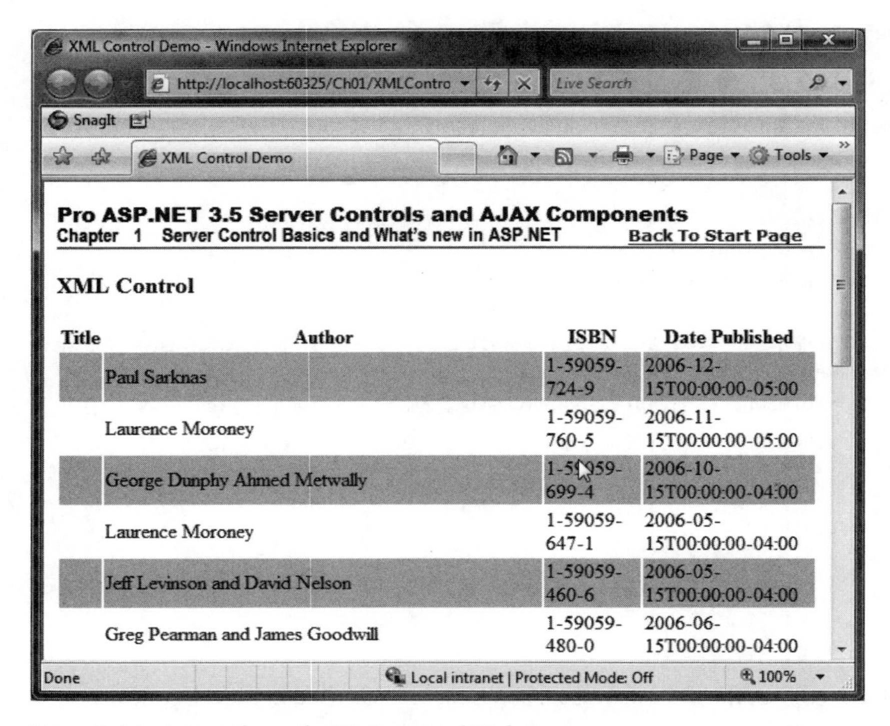

Figure 1-15. *Output from the XML control Web Form*

Although the XML control seems to be a great way to build UIs, we do not recommend the XSLT technique as a way to take advantage of ASP.NET and its server control mechanism for several reasons:

- All UI layout information must be specified declaratively inside the XSLT document, which requires the programmer to take over the task of rendering the entire HTML document.
- It is not possible to leverage server controls, which have the capability to render conditional UI based on browser capabilities in this model, nor is it possible to capture events during postback on the server side that are connected to the HTML tags rendered by the XSLT.
- Extra steps are required to debug the XSLT style sheet outside of Visual Studio. The programmer must either manually look at the HTML output or buy a third-party XSLT debugger, such as XML Spy, to be able to step through the XSLT code. Contrast this with the ability to completely step through the page generation process with templates and data binding.

Validation Controls

Checking user input on a web page is one of the least favorite tasks on a web developer's to-do list. It falls somewhere between maintenance of old code and sitting in another project planning meeting. Fortunately, ASP.NET comes to the rescue with a set of controls that not only take care of validation of input when it reaches the web server but also handle the task of generating

JavaScript validation routines to check the validity of input on the client side, minimizing additional round-trips to the server. This is accomplished by setting the `EnableClientScript` property to `true`.

Table 1-3 shows the various validation controls that are available in the `System.Web.UI.WebControls` namespaces and the input-checking features they provide.

Table 1-3. *Validation Controls Available in ASP.NET*

Validation Control	Description
`RequiredFieldValidator`	Checks for a null or empty value in a server control
`CompareValidator`	Compares two server controls by various operators
`RangeValidator`	Ensures the values of a server control fall in a specific range
`RegularExpressionValidator`	Uses a regular expression to validate the input of a server control
`CustomValidator`	Allows the programmer to specify client-side and server-side validation routines to constrain a server control's input
`ValidationSummary`	Shows a summary of all the error messages generated by validator controls on a web form

A Validation Controls Demonstration

The following validation controls web form demonstrates all of the validation controls in action. Full source code is provided in Listings 1-15 and 1-16. The web form has `TextBox` controls to test input and a `Label` to display the success or failure of the web form postback according to the validation process.

Listing 1-15. *The ValidationControls Web Form .aspx File*

```
<%@ Page Language="C#"
MasterPageFile="~/MasterPage/ControlsBook2MasterPage.Master"
  AutoEventWireup="true" CodeBehind="ValidationControls.aspx.cs"
Inherits="ControlsBook2Web.Ch01.ValidationControls"
  Title="Validation Controls Demo" %>

<asp:Content ID="Content1" ContentPlaceHolderID="ChapterNumAndTitle" runat="server">
  <asp:Label ID="ChapterNumberLabel" runat="server"
Width="14px">1</asp:Label>  <asp:Label
    ID="ChapterTitleLabel" runat="server" Width="360px">
Server Control Basics and What's new in ASP.NET</asp:Label>
</asp:Content>
<asp:Content ID="Content2" ContentPlaceHolderID="PrimaryContent" runat="server">

  <script type="text/javascript">
    function ValidateEvent(oSrc, args){
      args.IsValid = ((args.Value % 2) == 0);
    }
  </script>
```

```
  <asp:Label ID="Label1" runat="server"> RequiredField</asp:Label><br />
  <asp:TextBox ID="RequiredField" runat="server"></asp:TextBox>
  <asp:RequiredFieldValidator ID="RequiredFieldValidator1" runat="server"
ErrorMessage="RequiredField needs an input value!"
    ControlToValidate="RequiredField"></asp:RequiredFieldValidator><br />
  <asp:Label ID="Label2" runat="server"> ComparedField</asp:Label><br />
  <asp:TextBox ID="ComparedField" runat="server"></asp:TextBox>
  <asp:CompareValidator ID="CompareValidator1" runat="server"
ErrorMessage="RequiredField and ComparedField are not equal!"
    ControlToValidate="ComparedField"
ControlToCompare="RequiredField"></asp:CompareValidator><br />
  <asp:Label ID="Label3" runat="server"> RangeField</asp:Label><br />
  <asp:TextBox ID="RangeField" runat="server"></asp:TextBox>
  <asp:RangeValidator ID="RangeValidator1" runat="server" ErrorMessage="RangeField
value must be between 1-10!"
    ControlToValidate="RangeField" MaximumValue="10" MinimumValue="1"
Type="Integer"></asp:RangeValidator><br />
  <asp:Label ID="Label4" runat="server"> RegexField (Phone)</asp:Label><br />
  <asp:TextBox ID="RegexField" runat="server"></asp:TextBox>
  <asp:RegularExpressionValidator ID="RegularExpressionValidator1" runat="server"
ErrorMessage="RegexField must be a valid US phone number!"
    ControlToValidate="RegexField" ValidationExpression=
"((\(\d{3}\) ?)|(\d{3}-))?\d{3}-\d{4}"></asp:RegularExpressionValidator><br />
  <asp:Label ID="Label5" runat="server">CustomField (Even Number)</asp:Label><br />
  <asp:TextBox ID="CustomField" runat="server"></asp:TextBox>
  <asp:CustomValidator ID="CustomValidator1" runat="server" ErrorMessage=
"CustomField must be an even number!"
    ControlToValidate="CustomField" ClientValidationFunction="ValidateEvent"
OnServerValidate="ValidateEvent"></asp:CustomValidator><br />
  <br />
  <asp:Button ID="ValidateButton" runat="server" Text="Submit"
OnClick="ValidateButton_Click">
  </asp:Button><br />
  <asp:Label ID="ResultsLabel" runat="server"></asp:Label><br />
  <br />
  <asp:ValidationSummary ID="ValidationSummary1"
runat="server"></asp:ValidationSummary>
</asp:Content>
```

Listing 1-16. *The ValidationControls Web Form Code-Behind Class File*

```
using System;
using System.Web;
using System.Web.UI;
using System.Web.UI.WebControls;

namespace ControlsBook2Web.Ch01
{
  public partial class ValidationControls : System.Web.UI.Page
  {
    protected void Page_Load(object sender, EventArgs e)
    {

    }

    protected void ValidateButton_Click(object sender, EventArgs e)
    {
      ResultsLabel.Text = "Page submitted at " + DateTime.Now + "
        IsValid: " + Page.IsValid;
    }

    protected void ValidateEvent(object source, ServerValidateEventArgs args)
    {
      if ((Convert.ToInt32(args.Value) % 2) == 0)
        args.IsValid = true;
      else
        args.IsValid = false;
    }
  }
}
```

The web form button that submits the `.aspx` page uses the `IsValid` property of the `Page` class to determine if the form post was successful. It also displays the time.

Of course, this `Label` output won't be displayed on the browser window, like in Figure 1-17, unless the form post has successfully passed through the client-side validation that occurs when the demonstration is executed using a JavaScript-capable browser, such as Internet Explorer 6.0. Figure 1-16 shows the result of erroneous client-side input with the JavaScript features enabled. You should also notice the display of the error messages by the input elements and the summary at the bottom generated by the `ValidationSummary` control.

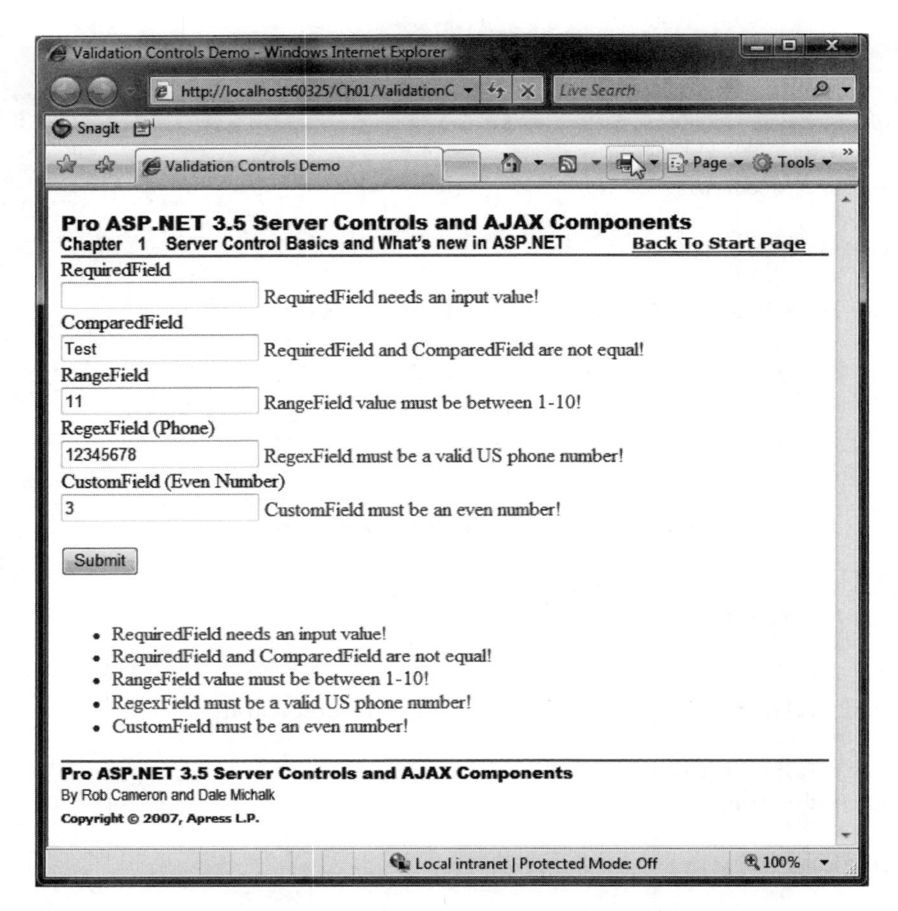

Figure 1-16. *Output from the validation controls web form with validation errors*

If the posted data makes its way past the guard of client-side validation, it has a second hurdle to overcome: validation on the server side. Each validation control is checked once again for correctness of values. This prevents spoofing or tampering with the HTTP postback to the web server in an attempt to get around the validation process.

The validation system in ASP.NET also provides the ability to customize the client-side and server-side routines that verify input. The preceding example demonstrates this with the `CustomValidator` control that is linked to the `CustomField` `TextBox` control. The first step is to wire up custom client-side validation through the `ClientValidationFunction` property. We set the value of this property to `ValidateEvent` and include a like-named JavaScript function in our `.aspx` page in the `<head>` section of the HTML content:

```
<script type="text/javascript">
   function ValidateEvent(oSrc, args){
      args.IsValid = ((args.Value % 2) == 0);
   }
</script>
```

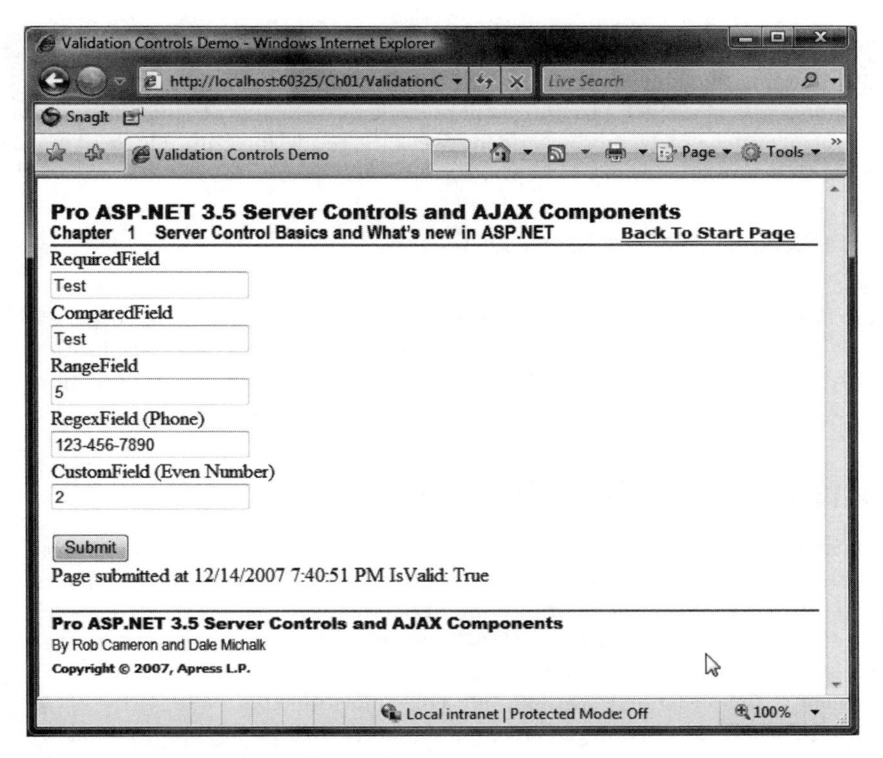

Figure 1-17. *Successful output from the validation controls web form*

The arguments passed to our routine provide us with the means to check the state of the validated HTML element and communicate the results of our validation work. The second argument is a structure with an `IsValid` property that is set to `true` or `false` to signal the results as well as a `Value` property representing the input value. The `ValidateEvent` routine uses modulo arithmetic to detect if a number is even or odd.

Configuring the server-side validation for the same control is done by wiring up the `ValidateEvent` method in the code-behind file with the `ServerValidate` event of the `CustomValidator` control. The parameters work in a similar fashion to their JavaScript counterparts with a `Value` and `IsValid` property.

```
private void ValidateEvent(object source,
  System.Web.UI.WebControls.ServerValidateEventArgs args)
{
   if ((Convert.ToInt32(args.Value) % 2) == 0)
      args.IsValid = true;
   else
      args.IsValid = false;
}
```

The next two sections provide a high-level overview of namespaces introduced in ASP.NET 2.0 or later.

System.Web.UI.WebControls.Adapters Namespace

`System.Web.UI.WebControls.Adapters` was introduced in ASP.NET 2.0. It allows developers to build control adapters. An ASP.NET 2.0 control adapter allows developers to plug into any ASP.NET server control and override, modify, and/or tweak the rendering output logic of that control. We provide an example adapter in Chapter 10.

System.Web.UI.WebControls.WebParts Namespace

`System.Web.UI.WebControls.WebParts` was introduced in ASP.NET 2.0 and allows developers to build `WebPart` functionality into ASP.NET 2.0 or later applications. The `WebParts` namespace was previously only available via the SharePoint SDK for use in a SharePoint portal application but was mainstreamed in ASP.NET 2.0. In Chapter 10, we cover `WebPart`-based controls in more detail.

Web Controls vs. HTML Controls

The controls discussed in this chapter span both the `System.Web.UI.WebControls` and `System.Web.UI.HtmlControls` namespaces. On the surface, the functionality in these two namespaces appears to overlap, particularly when generating content that maps to a single HTML tag such as `<input type="text">` or `<textarea>`. Both the HTML control `HtmlInputText` and web control `TextBox` handle this with equal functionality when added to a web form as a server control. Deciding which to use in this situation is a commonly asked question about ASP.NET.

The HTML controls have the advantage of looking similar to their HTML brethren, taking on attributes that are familiar to web developers. This eases the porting process and helps keep people comfortable with the changes to ASP.NET. This is both a blessing and a curse. It is easy to overlook the `runat="server"` attribute and assume that the control is raw HTML. This is especially a problem late at night, when things on the monitor don't look as they should to tired eyes.

The web controls provide a more consistent attribute model for specifying properties on controls. The best example is the use of the more intuitive `Text` property on a `Label` and `TextBox` control, contrasted with the `Value` or `Name` property that is used in the `HtmlControls` namespace. The CSS styling support is also much better with web controls, as the web controls example demonstrated in the CSS-related types added to the `System.Web.UI.WebControls` namespace.

Also, notice that web controls have an `asp:` tag prefix added to the HTML tag on the `.aspx` page to identify the tag as a server control within a particular namespace. The classes in the `HtmlControls` namespace do not have a tag prefix and cannot be used as a base class for a custom server control.

We would have been remiss not to include a detailed discussion of what is available in the `HtmlControls` namespace, as these controls can provide a potential interim step to help ease the migration challenges to ASP.NET from ASP. However, it is our opinion that, outside the necessary `HtmlForm` control for web form construction and the file upload functionality of the `HtmlInputFile` control, programmers should stay away from using the HTML controls in ASP.NET applications. We recommend that developers strive to fully migrate toward the web control classes in application development to gain the benefits from the level of abstraction web controls provide as well as the rich programming model available. This is especially true if custom control development is planned or desired.

Summary

This chapter was devoted to the topic of server controls. Server controls are objects, and as such, they provide the time-honored constructs of properties, methods, and events. The HTML content rendered to the browser client is generated in its entirety by a tree of server controls representing each item on the page.

Controls in ASP.NET are separated into three hierarchies: `System.Web.UI`, `System.Web.UI.HtmlControls`, and `System.Web.UI.WebControls`. `System.Web.UI` contains the `Page` class, which represents the web form, and the `Control` class, which is the root base class of all the other server controls in ASP.NET.

`System.Web.UI.HtmlControls` contains controls that directly map to HTML tags and make porting from HTML pages easier. `HtmlInputText`, `HtmlForm`, and `HtmlInputHidden` are examples of HTML controls.

`System.Web.UI.WebControls` contains a full-featured set of controls, including simple, list, rich, and validation controls. Simple controls are web controls that provide server-side mapping to HTML tags. `TextBox`, `Button`, and `DropDownList` are examples of simple controls. List controls support building HTML content through data binding and templates. The `DataList`, `DataGrid`, and `Repeater` controls are some examples of list controls. Rich controls generate complex UI from a minimal amount of input. The `Calendar` control is an example of a rich control.

Validation controls simplify the tedious nature of web form input validation. Validation can occur on the client side for JavaScript-capable browsers. It is also possible to write custom validation scripts using the `CustomValidator` control.

There is overlapping functionality between `WebControls` and `HtmlControls`. We recommend using the `System.Web.UI.WebControls` namespace over `System.Web.UI.HtmlControls` due to its rich control set, enhanced styling features, and powerful abstraction layer around HTML rendering. Also, it is not possible to create a custom server control that derives from an `HtmlControl` class.

CHAPTER 2

Encapsulating Functionality in ASP.NET

The previous chapter provided a high-level overview of the large number of prebuilt controls available in ASP.NET, highlighting some of the powerful new controls available in ASP.NET 3.5. These battle-tested components serve admirably in a variety of scenarios that web application designers can dream up. The ASP.NET development team had a goal of reducing the amount of code that developers must write and have done an admirable job in ASP.NET 2.0 through ASP.NET 3.5. Of course, developers can always dream up new functionality for applications, giving an opportunity for control builders to extend and enhance the capabilities of the components delivered out of the box through inheritance and encapsulation as well as build brand-new server controls.

In this chapter, we discuss the various methods available in ASP.NET to encapsulate functionality such as master pages, user controls, or of course, server controls that have the same amount of modularity and reuse potential as the built-in controls. We provide a high-level overview of ASP.NET AJAX 1.0, which was released after .NET Framework 2.0 and is enhanced in .NET Framework 3.5, as an introduction to the new technology. Once we cover the basics, we dive right in and encapsulate the same functionality using the different techniques available to help drive the concepts.

Packaging Content in ASP.NET

The rich, object-oriented framework of ASP.NET 2.0 and later provides two control-building options (which generally fall into four categories):

- User controls
- Custom server controls

User controls are a great option when you are packaging common UI layout for reuse across a project or group of projects. In ASP.NET 1.1, user controls were often the method of abstracting the areas, such as top and side banners, that are common to every page in a web site, but this method met with varying success. In ASP.NET 2.0 and later, the `MasterPage` class, which inherits from the `UserControl` class, along with the `Content` class provide a much more powerful and flexible means to create a page template for a web site, as discussed in Chapter 1. Custom server controls are more akin to what is traditionally considered a control or widget.

Web parts are custom server controls that were originally available as part of the SharePoint Server 2003 software development kit (SDK) and worked only within the Windows SharePoint Services 2.0 in ASP.NET 1.1. In ASP.NET 2.0 and later, support for web parts is baked directly into ASP.NET and no longer requires Windows SharePoint Services to run. Before we discuss these two methods of creating controls in ASP.NET, we first cover a couple of key concepts: inheritance and encapsulation.

Inheritance

One way to package new functionality and take advantage of the rich, object-oriented framework in ASP.NET is to use inheritance. This elegant, tried-and-true technique is the central theme of this book and the topic on which we spend the most time.

Inheritance works because of the polymorphic behavior of objects. This capability permits you to override methods defined as `virtual` in the base object class so that you can add or customize the objects' behavior, with the option of still leveraging the functionality available in the original base class method. To put it another way, you don't have to reinvent the wheel to add new functionality. In terms of code, this will generally look something like the following:

```
//overide virtual method "Render"
protected override void Render(HtmlTextWriter output)
{
    //add some new style to output
    output.AddStyleAttribute("somestylename","somevalue");
    base.Render(output);  //render the output using the base class Render method
}
```

In this code snippet, we override the virtual method `Render()`, which is defined in the base class `System.Web.UI.Control`. This syntax may look a little strange at first. For example, where is `base` defined? Like the `this` reference, the object that `base` actually references is context defined and made available by the framework. As its name suggests, `base` is a convenient way to reference the base class that the custom server control inherits from in its class definition. In our version of the `Render()` method, we tack on some styling to the output class (of type `HtmlTextWriter`) and then call the base class's `Render()` method to display the control's new styled output on the ASP.NET page.

In the preceding example, if `Render()` were not defined as virtual in the base class, the ease with which we perform this task would not have been possible. Without the `virtual` modifier, the base class's `Render()` method would have been hidden or redefined when we declared a method named `Render()` in the derived server control class. We would not have been able to make use of the base object's `Render()` method in our new `Render()` method, and we would have been forced to re-create all of the base class's `Render()` functionality.

■ **Note** Keep in mind the role that modifiers such as `virtual` play when you add new methods to your custom server controls and would like to support polymorphic behavior.

All custom server controls inherit from an ASP.NET server control class to ensure that the new control falls in line with the .NET Framework. There are several choices for a base class, including System.Web.UI.Control, System.Web.UI.WebControl, or one of the full-featured server controls such as TextBox. We discuss what factors affect this decision and provide several introductory examples of custom server controls later in this chapter.

Encapsulation

Another construct available to package functionality within an object-oriented framework, such as .NET, is encapsulation. Encapsulation is also referred to as composition or building composite controls. Composite controls can inherit from any ASP.NET server control, but generally, they are inherited from System.Web.UI.Control or System.Web.UI.WebControls.CompositeControl. This inheritance is necessary to gain access to the necessary ASP.NET plumbing (rendering, state management, postback, and so on); however, composition does not rely on inheritance or polymorphism to achieve reuse.

Composite controls package functionality by combining server controls as children controls, but they are still treated as a single entity. This promotes information hiding and eases development by allowing the composite control developer/user to focus on the combined functionality of the parent control without worrying about setting individual properties or calling methods on the children controls.

ASP.NET provides two different methods for building composite controls: composition through custom server controls and composition through user controls. We discuss what factors can go into choosing one method over the other and provide several introductory examples later on in this chapter.

Comparing the Control-Building Techniques

As described earlier in this chapter, there are primarily two methods of packing content in ASP.NET: user controls and custom server controls. We provide a high-level overview of these methods in the following sections. To assist with this discussion, we'll create user controls and custom server controls that implement the same functionality to help us compare and contrast the two construction methodologies.

User Controls

User controls are a form of composite control that you can use to package functionality such as HTML and server controls like the TextBox within ASP.NET. Generally, the focus of user control development is to encapsulate application-specific business logic that can be shared within a single application or within a family of related applications.

Of the two primary means of building controls in ASP.NET, user controls are the simpler control type to create. Constructing user controls is similar to building ASP.NET web forms, as they support a declarative style of development through dragging and dropping controls from the toolbox in Visual Studio onto the user control design surface.

A user control page has intermixed HTML tags and server controls like an .aspx page, except they are stored in an .ascx file. Like web forms, user controls also support separation of the HTML tags and UI from the page logic through the code-behind mechanism. The Design view of a user control is almost identical to that of a web form, as shown in Figure 2-1.

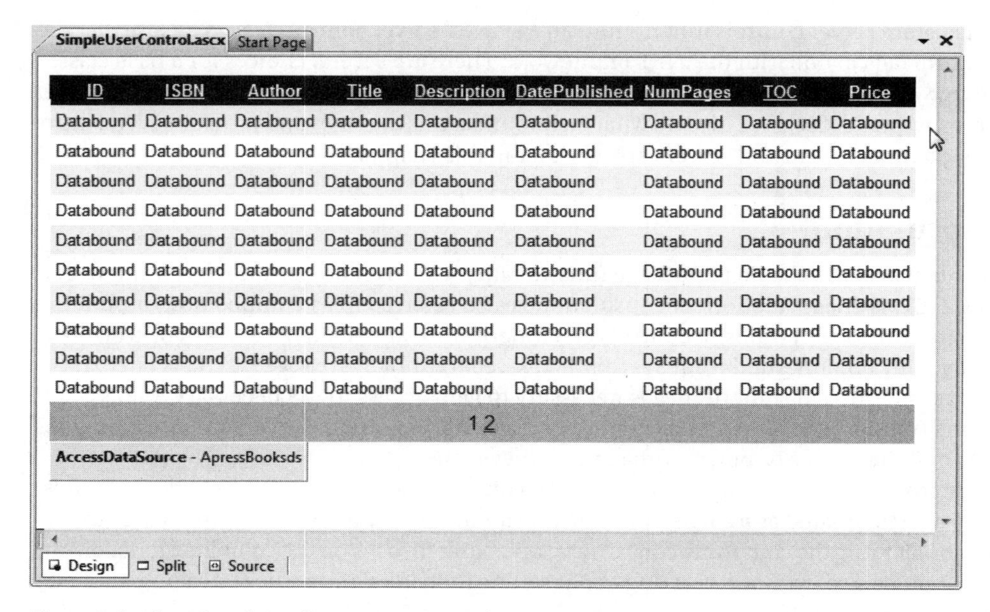

Figure 2-1. *The Visual Studio Design view of a user control*

You will typically implement a user control when you want to build a control that requires a fair number of declarative HTML tags with the least amount of effort. This option makes it easier for the UI designer to go back in and modify the output of the control using the Visual Studio 2008 web page designer WYSIWYG interface than the option to use custom server controls, which are programmatically designed in code. In ASP.NET 1.1 or earlier, user controls were often used to templatize web sites with varying success. In ASP.NET 2.0 and later, master pages replace one of the most common reasons why developers implement user controls, but there are still many places where user controls can be beneficial. Here is a list of other important characteristics of user controls:

- User controls are a great way to package HTML and modularize web development for application-specific logic. They are also a great way to replace the use of `HTML` include files.
- User controls support properties and methods that can be set either in the HTML as attributes or in the code-behind page of the hosting `.ascx` page.
- User controls can be cached in the ASP.NET cache based on a number of different parameters to speed web application performance (details on this are available in the ASP.NET documentation).
- Certain tags are not permitted in a user control, because user controls are hosted in web forms that will already have these tags—specifically, the `<html>`, `<head>`, `<body>`, and `<form>` tags. Using these tags would interfere with the functioning of the hosting `.aspx` page.
- User control tag declarations should appear between the hosting `.aspx` page's beginning and ending `<form>` tags to ensure proper operation.

In the previous version of this book, the header and footer displayed in the example web forms were user controls. With master pages in, the header and footer information has been moved to a master page template, as discussed in Chapter 1. Instead of the header and footer, we have the simple user control shown in Figure 2-1. Listing 2-1 shows the code for the `SimpleUserControl` user control.

Listing 2-1. *The SimpleUserControl User Control .ascx File*

```
<%@ Control Language="C#" AutoEventWireup="true"
CodeBehind="SimpleUserControl.ascx.cs"
  Inherits="ControlsBook2Web.Ch02.SimpleUserControl" %>
<asp:GridView ID="GridView1" runat="server" AllowPaging="True" AllowSorting="True"
  AutoGenerateColumns="False" CellPadding="4" DataKeyNames="ID"
DataSourceID="ApressBooksds"
  EmptyDataText="There are no data records to display." Font-Names="Arial"
  Font-Size="X-Small"
  ForeColor="#333333" GridLines="None">
  <Columns>
    <asp:BoundField DataField="ID" HeaderText="ID" ReadOnly="True"
    SortExpression="ID"
      InsertVisible="False" />
    <asp:BoundField DataField="ISBN" HeaderText="ISBN" SortExpression="ISBN" />
    <asp:BoundField DataField="Author" HeaderText="Author" SortExpression=
   "Author" />
    <asp:BoundField DataField="Title" HeaderText="Title" SortExpression="Title" />
    <asp:BoundField DataField="Description" HeaderText="Description"
SortExpression="
    Description" />
    <asp:BoundField DataField="DatePublished" HeaderText="DatePublished"
SortExpression="DatePublished" />
    <asp:BoundField DataField="NumPages" HeaderText="NumPages"
     SortExpression="NumPages" />
    <asp:BoundField DataField="TOC" HeaderText="TOC" SortExpression="TOC" />
    <asp:BoundField DataField="Price" HeaderText="Price" SortExpression="Price" />
  </Columns>
  <FooterStyle BackColor="#990000" Font-Bold="True" ForeColor="White" />
  <RowStyle BackColor="#FFFBD6" ForeColor="#333333" />
  <SelectedRowStyle BackColor="#FFCC66" Font-Bold="True" ForeColor="Navy" />
  <PagerStyle BackColor="#FFCC66" ForeColor="#333333" HorizontalAlign="Center" />
  <HeaderStyle BackColor="#990000" Font-Bold="True" ForeColor="White" />
  <AlternatingRowStyle BackColor="White" />
</asp:GridView>
<asp:AccessDataSource ID="ApressBooksds" runat="server"
DataFile="~/App_Data/ApressBooks.mdb"
  SelectCommand="SELECT * FROM [Books]"></asp:AccessDataSource>
```

Listing 2-2 has the code-behind file for SimpleUserControl.

Listing 2-2. *The SimpleUserControl User Control Code-Behind Class File*

```
using System;
using System.Drawing;

namespace ControlsBook2Web.Ch02
{
  public partial class SimpleUserControl : System.Web.UI.UserControl
  {
    protected void Page_Load(object sender, EventArgs e)
    {

    }

    public Color HeaderColor
    {
      get { return GridView1.HeaderStyle.BackColor; }
      set { GridView1.HeaderStyle.BackColor = value; }
    }

    public int RecordsPerPage
    {
      get { return GridView1.PageSize; }
      set { GridView1.PageSize = value; }
    }
  }
}
```

SimpleUserControl.aspx provides a test container for our newly created user control as well as exercises the two custom public properties HeaderColor and RecordsPerPage on SimpleUserControl.ascx. Listing 2-3 has the source code for the SimpleUserControl demonstration web form.

Listing 2-3. *The SimpleUserControlDemo Web Form .aspx File*

```
<%@ Page Language="C#" MasterPageFile="~/MasterPage/ControlsBook2MasterPage.Master"
  AutoEventWireup="true" CodeBehind="SimpleUserControlDemo.aspx.cs"
  Inherits="ControlsBook2Web.Ch02.SimpleUserControlDemo"
  Title="Simple User Control Demo" %>

<%@ Register Src="SimpleUserControl.ascx" TagName="SimpleUserControl" ]
  TagPrefix="apressuc" %>
<asp:Content ID="Content1" ContentPlaceHolderID="ChapterNumAndTitle" runat="server">
  <asp:Label ID="ChapterNumberLabel" runat="server"
```

```
  Width="14px">2</asp:Label>  <asp:Label
    ID="ChapterTitleLabel" runat="server" Width="360px">
  Encapsulating Functionality in ASP.NET</asp:Label>
</asp:Content>
<asp:Content ID="Content2" ContentPlaceHolderID="PrimaryContent" runat="server">
  <apressuc:SimpleUserControl ID="SimpleUserControl1" runat="server" />
</asp:Content>
```

Listing 2-4 contains the code-behind file for the SimpleUserControl demonstration web form.

Listing 2-4. *The SimpleUserControlDemo Web Form Code-Behind Class File*

```
using System;

namespace ControlsBook2Web.Ch02
{
  public partial class SimpleUserControlDemo : System.Web.UI.Page
  {
    protected void Page_Load(object sender, EventArgs e)
    {

    }
  }

}
```

For the SimpleUserControl user control, properties such as HeaderColor and RecordsPerPage can be set in the HTML through attributes or in the code-behind page, such as with SimpleUserControl.aspx. In ASP.NET 1.1, to access the Header user control in the code-behind page, we had to first add a declaration for the user control to the code-behind class as well as add a runat="server" attribute to the declaration in the .aspx file. In ASP.NET 2.0 and later, we can simply access the user control by name in the code-behind file:

```
SimpleUserControl1.RecordsPerPage = 5;
SimpleUserControl1.HeaderColor = Color.CadetBlue;
```

When compared to building custom server controls, user controls are easier on the development staff in terms of the learning curve; any developer capable of building web forms can build user controls.

Custom Server Controls

Custom server controls, the other option for control development in ASP.NET, package functionality through inheritance, composition, or both. Server controls do not support declarative, drag-and-drop–style UI development as with a user control. Everything that is rendered by the control is programmatically specified within a code class. In Chapter 6, we examine templates, which allow UI designers to specify the UI of a custom control in a declarative fashion. These compensate to some degree for the lack of a tag page that is edited in the Designer during server control development. The requirement to put everything (UI layout, functionality, and so on) in code does provide server controls a superior packaging and deployment mechanism over user controls, because they compile into an assembly. The resulting assembly can be copied between web development projects and stored in the global assembly cache (GAC).

Custom controls are a fully programmatic way of packaging reusable content in ASP.NET. They allow developers to tap into the underlying ASP.NET plumbing, replacing or adding core functionality, such as how a control renders, in order to achieve the desired behavior. They tend to implement richer functionality and exhibit greater reuse from project to project, as shown by advanced controls such as the `TextBox`, `DataGrid`, and `Calendar` controls that exist in the ASP.NET `WebControls` namespace.

■ **Note** Building server controls in ASP.NET 2.0 or later is very similar to building server controls in ASP.NET 1.1. However, there are many new features, such as improved design-time support, the ability to create web parts outside of SharePoint, easier client-side script integration, and so on, which can be fully leveraged in ASP.NET 2.0 or later custom-built server controls.

In ASP.NET 1.1, a custom control had better support than user controls in the Design view of the control when placed on a web form `.aspx` page by the developer/user. In the Design view, a custom control renders the HTML output that it normally would when generating for HTML browser consumption, while user controls are rendered as a gray box. In ASP.NET 2.0, user controls also render the design-time HTML output just like custom server controls. Compare Figure 2-1 and 2-2 to see the similarities between a user control as displayed at design time and how the user control renders when hosted with an ASP.NET web form at design time.

Another major difference between user controls and custom controls that existed in ASP.NET 1.1 is in their deployment model. Reusing a user control requires copying its `.ascx` files along with code-behind assemblies, if necessary, in order to reuse it in different web applications in ASP.NET 1.1. In contrast to user controls in ASP.NET 1.1, user controls in ASP.NET 2.0 and later can compile down to an assembly. In ASP.NET 2.0 and later, we can take advantage of precompilation features to compile a user control into an assembly that can be deployed to other applications without source code.

■ **Note** The user control should be as self-contained as possible, in much the same way as a custom-built server control, meaning the user control should not have dependencies on images being located at a particular URL or be dependent on objects declared in `Global.asax` in order to render properly.

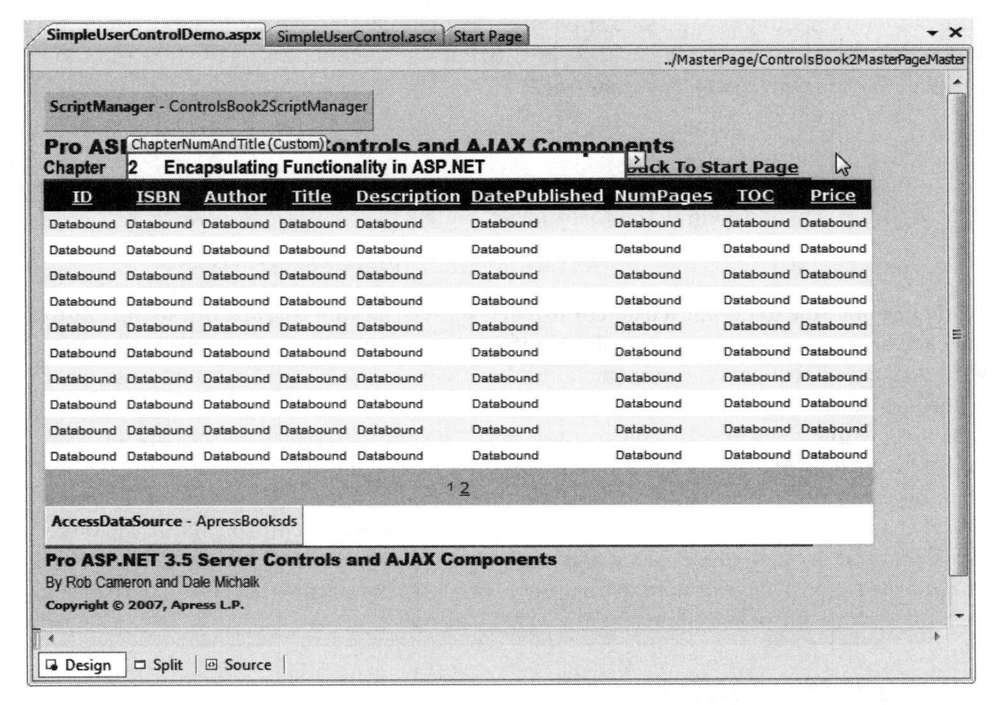

Figure 2-2. *The Visual Studio Design view of the same user control hosted on a web form*

It is possible in ASP.NET 2.0 and later to precompile a web site in its current location or precompile a web site for deployment to another server. For our purposes with packaging a user control in an assembly, we need to follow the steps to precompile a site for deployment. The first step is to create the user control and test it. One item of note is to add a `ClassName` attribute with the namespace to the `@Control` directive for the user control like this:

```
<%@ Control Language="C#" AutoEventWireup="true"
CodeBehind="SimpleUserControl.ascx.cs"
Inherits="ControlsBook2Web.Ch02.SimpleUserControl" %>
```

Once the user control has been created and tested, use the publish functionality available under the Visual Studio menu item Build ➤ Publish Web Site.

The Publish dialog requires a target location for the precompiled site. Also, it is recommended that you check the "Use fixed naming and single page assemblies" box to allow the user control to be published in a single assembly. Otherwise, the user control will be compiled with other application code in a combined assembly with a randomly generated file name. Another potentially useful option is to enable strong naming on precompiled assemblies.

After publishing is completed, go to the target location specified in the Publish dialog, and look in the bin directory for an assembly named something like `App_Web_simpleusercontrol.ascx.5b4d926a.dll`. This is the `SimpleUserControl.ascx` compiled to an assembly and is ready to be used as a server control.

Next, add the assembly to a test web application by right-clicking the application, selecting Add Reference, and browsing to the user control assembly. The next step is to make the server control available on a web form by registering it:

```
<%@ Register TagPrefix="apressuc" Namespace="ControlsBook2"
          Assembly="App_Web_simpleusercontrol.ascx.5b4d926a.dll" %>
```

The final step is to add a tag to the `.aspx` page:

```
<apressUC:SimpleUserControl ID="SimpleUserControl1" runat="server" />
```

While it is possible to deploy a user control in a similar manner to a custom server control as shown in the preceding example, deployment of a user control as an `.ascx` file is a bit more straightforward and probably more applicable where user controls are of most interest, which is for sharing code internal to an organization.

The design-time rendering of user controls and the ability to deploy a user control as an assembly are welcome ASP.NET improvements; custom server controls provide superior design-time capabilities, simpler deployment, and finer control over functionality. Naturally, all the benefits of custom controls do not come for free. Generally, custom controls require a longer development cycle and a higher skill level from the development staff. The focus of this book is on custom server control development with the goal of easing the learning curve and developing some useful server control samples to help you get started.

Building a User Control

So far, we've discussed user controls and custom server controls, and their benefits and differences. User controls and server controls have differing strengths and trade-offs that we highlight in this section by building two families of controls:

- A static hyperlink menu control
- A dynamically generated HTML table control

The example controls we present may seem simple and somewhat removed from real-world web projects, but we do this for a reason. We believe that you must start simple and build toward more complexity to achieve a deep understanding of the process. In upcoming chapters, we explore controls that leverage the complete functionality available to controls in ASP.NET as well as provide interesting capabilities.

ASP.NET developers typically look to the user control as the first option for creating controls due to its ease of construction and simplicity. Building a user control closely mirrors the construction techniques and technical details of a web form. User controls support drag-and-drop development with the Visual Studio control toolbox, a fully editable design surface in the IDE, and a code-behind class file structure to support a separation of UI and logic programming. User controls are built in two ways:

- From scratch
- By taking out reusable content from an existing web form

The first method is used when enough planning and design work is done ahead of time to figure out which portions of the UI are going to be reused on the web site. The second technique results from refactoring the content of a site after it has been built to make it modular and easier to maintain.

The MenuUserControl User Control

Our first example takes advantage of the declarative nature of the user control to encapsulate a simple hyperlink menu as a control that we build from scratch. The control is pure, static HTML without a single embedded server control. It consists of nothing more than a list of fixed hyperlinks to a variety of web sites.

The simplicity is shown in the tags present in the `.ascx` file in Listing 2-5. The code-behind class in Listing 2-6 is left unchanged from the blank template Visual Studio produces when you add a user control to a web application.

Listing 2-5. *The MenuUserControl User Control .ascx File*

```
<%@ Control Language="C#" AutoEventWireup="true"
 CodeBehind="MenuUserControl.ascx.cs"
  Inherits="ControlsBook2Web.Ch02.MenuUserControl" %>
<div>
  <span><a href="http://www.apress.com">Apress</a></span> | <span>
  <a href="http://www.microsoft.com">
    Microsoft</a></span> | <span><a href="http://msdn.microsoft.com">MSDN</a></span>
  | <span><a href="http://asp.net">ASP.NET</a></span>
</div>
```

Listing 2-6. *The MenuUserControl User Control Code-Behind Class File*

```
using System;

namespace ControlsBook2Web.Ch02
{
  public partial class MenuUserControl : System.Web.UI.UserControl
  {
    protected void Page_Load(object sender, EventArgs e)
    {

    }
  }
}
```

The `Control` directive at the top of the user control `.ascx` file shown in Listing 2-5 identifies it as a user control to the ASP.NET parsing engine. The format is similar to that of the `Page` directive in an `.aspx` page file.

The `Control` directive helps set up the code-behind system through its `CodeFile` and `Inherits` properties. In ASP.NET 1.1, the attribute name was `CodeBehind`, but in ASP.NET 2.0 and later, the attribute is `CodeFile`. The `CodeFile` attribute points to the location of the class file, and the `Inherits` attribute specifies the class name the `.ascx` tag page inherits from. The `CodeFile` attribute for the `@Control` (and the `@Page`) directive in conjunction with the `partial class` declaration in the code-behind file is part of the new code-behind model in ASP.NET 2.0 and later. The model also removes the requirement to have protected declarations of all server controls used on a web form or user control page in the code behind file, removing what was a fragile relationship in ASP.NET 1.1 between the `.aspx`/`.ascx` page and the code-behind file, as well as generally making the code-behind files cleaner and shorter.

■ **Note** The partial class model applies only if the `CodeFile` attribute exists in the `@Page` or `@Control` directive. If the `Inherits` or `src` attribute is used without the `CodeFile` attribute, ASP.NET 2.0 and later resorts to ASP.NET 1.1 code-behind style and places the class as the sole base class for the `.aspx` or `.ascx` file. If there isn't a code-behind file, class generation is also similar to ASP.NET 1.1. Features like strongly typed master page access and previous page access are dependent on the new partial class/code-behind model in ASP.NET 2.0 and later.

Notice that the inheritance tree in an `.ascx` file uses the `System.Web.UI.UserControl` class instead of the `System.Web.UI.Page` base class (as in an `.aspx` file).

Using the MenuUserControl User Control

To actually see the content of the user control, we must host the user control on a web form. Doing so requires a registration step to give the web form enough information to find the user control content and bring it into the scope of the page via a tag associated with the user control. The menu user control demonstration web form accomplishes this task. Figure 2-3 shows the final output of the web form in the browser.

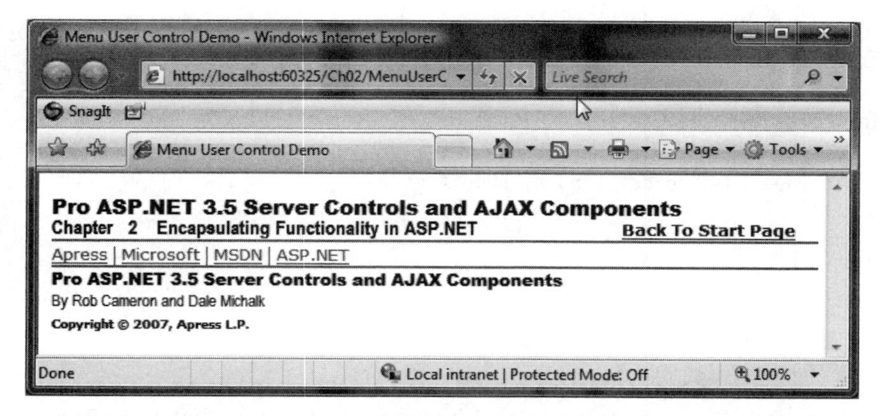

Figure 2-3. *The browser view of the HTML output from the menu user control demonstration web form*

Listing 2-7 shows the source code for the `MenuUserControlDemo .aspx` file.

Listing 2-7. *The MenuUserControlDemo Web Form .aspx File*

```
<%@ Page Language="C#" MasterPageFile="~/MasterPage/ControlsBook2MasterPage.Master"
  AutoEventWireup="true" CodeBehind="MenuUserControlDemo.aspx.cs"
Inherits="ControlsBook2Web.Ch02.MenuUserControlDemo"
  Title="Menu User Control Demo" %>

<%@ Register Src="MenuUserControl.ascx" TagName="MenuUserControl"
TagPrefix="apressuc" %>
<asp:Content ID="Content1" ContentPlaceHolderID="ChapterNumAndTitle" runat="server">
  <asp:Label ID="ChapterNumberLabel" runat="server"
Width="14px">2</asp:Label>  <asp:Label
    ID="ChapterTitleLabel" runat="server" Width="360px">
   Encapsulating Functionality in ASP.NET</asp:Label>
</asp:Content>
<asp:Content ID="Content2" ContentPlaceHolderID="PrimaryContent" runat="server">
  <apressuc:MenuUserControl ID="MenuUserControl1" runat="server" />
</asp:Content>
```

The `Register` directive does its part by locating the `.ascx` file representing the user control with its `src` attribute and determining its look on the page with the `TagName` and `TagPrefix` attributes:

```
<%@ Register Src="MenuUserControl.ascx"
TagName="MenuUserControl" TagPrefix="apressuc" %>
```

As a common convention in this book, we use `apressuc` as the tag prefix for our user controls and `apress` for custom controls. You are free to choose a prefix to suit your organizational or company standards. In the example, we use `MenuUserControl` as the name of the tag and identify our single instance with the `id` attribute `menu1`. The `runat="server"` attribute is also present to signify that it is a server control and must be handled appropriately by the ASP.NET parsing system:

```
<apressuc:MenuUserControl id="menu1" runat="server" />
```

An interesting thing to note about this example is how the user control displays on the web form when you view the hosting web form in Design view. It is shown as a gray box that provides little feedback as to what the final output in the browser will be.

The TableUserControl User Control

Our second user control example raises the degree of difficulty by demonstrating how to use the dynamic control-building features of ASP.NET inside a user control. Because the `UserControl` class itself has an inheritance chain back to the root `System.Web.UI.Control` class and is a full-blown control in its own right, we can add controls to its `Controls` collection at runtime to build up its content structure. We can also manipulate the child controls on its surface programmatically.

This example has similar functionality to the examples in Chapter 1. Here, the action is orchestrated according to the properties that the control exposes to the web form at runtime in its declaration, specifically the `X` and `Y` properties. Listing 2-8 shows the source code for the `TableUserControlascx` file. Listing 2-9 shows the source code for the `TableUserControl` code-behind class file.

Listing 2-8. *The TableUserControl User Control .ascx File*

```
<%@ Control Language="C#" AutoEventWireup="true" CodeBehind=
  "TableUserControl.ascx.cs"
  Inherits="ControlsBook2Web.Ch02.TableUserControl" %>
<h3>
  TableUserControl<br />
  X:<asp:Label ID="XLabel" runat="server"></asp:Label>
  Y:<asp:Label ID="YLabel" runat="server"></asp:Label>
</h3>
<table id="Table1" border="1" runat="server">
</table>
```

Listing 2-9. *The TableUserControl User Control Code-Behind Class File*

```
using System;
using System.Web.UI.HtmlControls;

namespace ControlsBook2Web.Ch02
{
  public partial class TableUserControl : System.Web.UI.UserControl
  {
    protected void Page_Load(object sender, EventArgs e)
    {
      XLabel.Text = X.ToString();
      YLabel.Text = Y.ToString();

      BuildTable(X, Y);
    }

    // properties to access dimensions of HTML table
    public int X {get; set;}

    public int Y {get; set;}

    // HTML table building routine
    private void BuildTable(int xDim, int yDim)
    {
      HtmlTableRow row;
      HtmlTableCell cell;
      HtmlGenericControl content;

      for (int y = 0; y < yDim; y++)
      {
        // create <TR>
        row = new HtmlTableRow();
```

```
        for (int x = 0; x < xDim; x++)
        {
          // create <TD cellspacing=1>
          cell = new HtmlTableCell();
          cell.Attributes.Add("border", "1");

          // create a <SPAN>
          content = new HtmlGenericControl("SPAN");
          content.InnerHtml = "X:" + x.ToString() +
             "Y:" + y.ToString();
          cell.Controls.Add(content);

          row.Cells.Add(cell);
        }
        Table1.Rows.Add(row);
      }
    }
  }
}
```

In this example, the .ascx page is a mix of HTML content and server controls. The two Label controls come from the System.Web.UI.WebControls namespace. The labels display the X and Y properties' configuration of the user control:

```
X:<asp:label id="XLabel" Runat="server"></asp:label>;
Y:<asp:label id="YLabel" Runat="server"></asp:label>
```

The HtmlTable control comes from the System.Web.UI.HtmlControls namespace and is declared as a table with a border size of 1 on the .ascx page.

The table control in the HtmlControl namespace was chosen over the table in the WebControl namespace, because it does not automatically add styling information to the final output. This is desirable at this point in the book; we defer the control styling discussion until Chapter 4.

The code-behind class file of the user control is much more interesting in this example, because it contains the content-building code. The X and Y properties exposed by the user control map to private variables in a demonstration of data encapsulation. These properties are exposed to the containing web forms in their .aspx page file via attributes on the user control tag or programmatically in the code-behind class file via a variable reference to an instance of the user control. We could have exposed public methods, fields, and events from the user control as well.

The Page_Load() method that is mapped to the web form's Page.Load event is responsible for transferring the data from the dimension properties to build the table hierarchy via the BuildTable() routine. It also configures the display of the Label controls on the user control to indicate what data was passed in to build the table. We pass on examining the BuildTable() routine in more detail here, because it is very similar to the HTML table building routine from Chapter 1.

Using the TableUserControl User Control

Like the menu demonstration, the table user control demonstration web form hosts the user control in order for us to realize its output. The table user control demonstration web form sets the X and Y properties of the TableUserControl control in both the .aspx tag page and the code-behind class file. This demonstrates how you can work with the user control in a declarative and a programmatic fashion on a web form. Figure 2-4 shows the table user control demonstration web form at design time, and Figure 2-5 shows our web form at runtime.

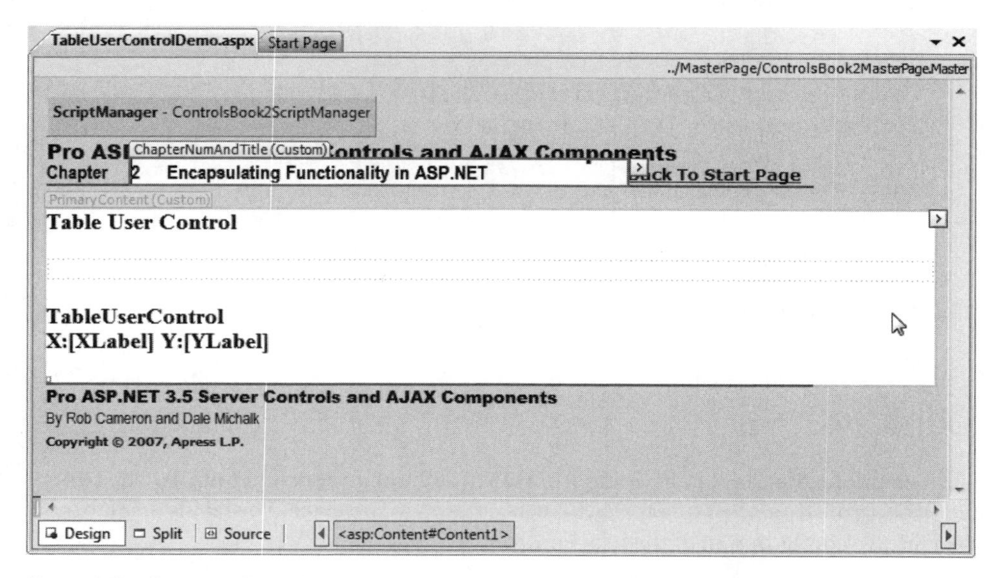

Figure 2-4. *The Visual Studio Design view of the table user control demonstration web form*

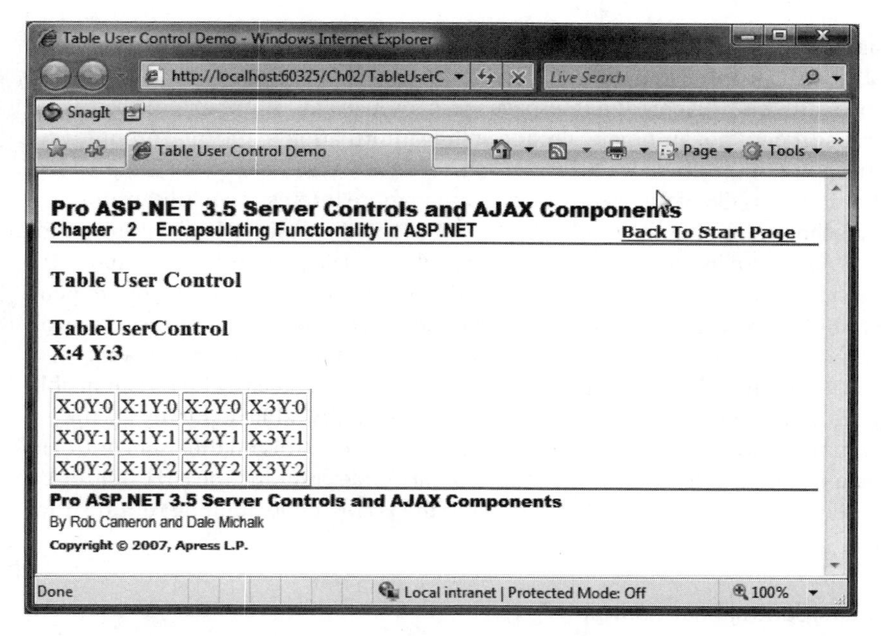

Figure 2-5. *The browser view of the HTML output from the table user control demonstration web form*

Listings 2-10 and 2-11 show TableUserControlDemo's .aspx page file and its code-behind class file, respectively.

Listing 2-10. *The TableUserControlDemo Web Form .aspx File*

```
<%@ Page Language="C#" MasterPageFile="~/MasterPage/ControlsBook2MasterPage.Master"
  AutoEventWireup="true" CodeBehind="TableUserControlDemo.aspx.cs"
Inherits="ControlsBook2Web.Ch02.TableUserControlDemo"
  Title="Table User Control Demo" %>

<%@ Register Src="TableUserControl.ascx" TagName="TableUserControl"
TagPrefix="apressuc" %>
<asp:Content ID="Content1" ContentPlaceHolderID="ChapterNumAndTitle" runat="server">
  <asp:Label ID="ChapterNumberLabel" runat="server"
Width="14px">2</asp:Label>  <asp:Label
    ID="ChapterTitleLabel" runat="server" Width="360px">
    Encapsulating Functionality in ASP.NET</asp:Label>
</asp:Content>
<asp:Content ID="Content2" ContentPlaceHolderID="PrimaryContent" runat="server">
  <h3>
    Table User Control</h3>
  <p>
    <apressuc:TableUserControl ID="TableUserControl1" runat="server" X="1" Y="1" />
</asp:Content>
```

Listing 2-11. *The TableUserControlDemo Code-Behind Class File*

```
using System;

namespace ControlsBook2Web.Ch02
{
  public partial class TableUserControlDemo : System.Web.UI.Page
  {
    protected void Page_Load(object sender, EventArgs e)
    {
      TableUserControl1.X = 4;
      TableUserControl1.Y = 3;
    }
  }
}
```

The user control is registered at the top of the .aspx page and declared via an apressuc tag prefix as before. Although we declare the HTML table structure to be a 1 × 1 grid declaratively in the .aspx page file, the code-behind class file programmatically changes it to 4 × 3. The Page_Load() method is executed after the ASP.NET system has set the value of the control declaratively, so it wins the contest over the value of the X and Y parameters.

Unlike in ASP.NET 1.1, we did not need to declare a member variable with the name and type of our user control to gain access to the user control in the code-behind class file and programmatically set the parameters. In ASP.NET 1.1, we would have had to add a protected member in the code behind page, like in the following code, but this additional typing is no longer required in the ASP.NET 2.0 and later code-behind model:

```
protected ControlsBook2Web.Ch02.TableUserControl TableUserControl1;
```

After this chapter, we do not touch on building user controls, as this book focuses on building custom server controls. For more information on building ASP.NET user controls, please refer to the ASP.NET documentation.

Building a Custom Control

We now turn our attention to creating custom server controls. The first decision that we must make when building a custom server control is what base class to inherit from. In the next section, we cover the generic base classes that are available to inherit from in addition to some decision-making guidelines on which base class to use.

Which Base Class?

The discussion of the control hierarchy in Chapter 1covered the various families of controls in the three main namespaces: `System.Web.UI`, `System.Web.UI.WebControls`, and `System.Web.UI.HtmlControls`. You have the option to inherit from any of the controls in these namespaces.

For those who prefer to start with a blank slate, which is the approach we take in this section, three control classes stand out as a potential starting point:

- `System.Web.UI.Control` is the base class that all controls directly or indirectly inherit from. It provides the bare minimum features required to call a class a server control.
- `System.Web.UI.WebControls.WebControl` adds CSS styling management to the rendering process, which makes it easier to build a styled custom control.
- `System.Web.UI.WebControls.WebParts` adds web part functionality to ASP.NET 2.0 and later, whereas with ASP.NET 1.1 web part functionality was only available within the SharePoint runtime environment. It is still possible to create SharePoint-specific web parts to take advantage of the features and capabilities available within the SharePoint runtime environment, but it is no longer a requirement with ASP.NET 2.0 and later.

Still a blank state but a bit more specific are the following potential base classes that became available in .NET Framework 2.0 and later:

- `System.Web.UI.WebControls.CompositeControl` can serve as a great starting point when building composite controls. It also removes the need to create a custom designer for composite controls to render correctly at design-time as was required in .NET Framework 1.1.
- `System.Web.UI.WebControls.DataBoundControl` can serve as a great starting point when building custom server controls that include data binding, since it takes care of much of the data binding plumbing code. `DataBoundControl` also includes a custom designer that can serve most needs when building a data-bound control.

- System.Web.UI.WebControls.CompositeDataBoundControl can serve as a great starting point when building a custom composite server control that includes data binding, since it also helps to manage the data binding and includes a designer.

Except for the composite control TableCompCustomControl, the examples in this chapter inherit from System.Web.UI.Control to keep things as simple as possible and provide you with a foundation in the features of the root control class. In later chapters, we examine the extra features that make System.Web.UI.WebControls.WebControl the best starting point for most projects as well as what is available when inheriting from the System.Web.UI.WebControls.WebParts base class.

Another option for building controls is inheriting from existing controls that are available in the framework. An example would be to inherit from the TextBox control and add validation capabilities to ensure that only a phone number is entered into it. You could also take a more complex control, such as the DataGrid, and customize it to your needs. Though we do provide a simple example of inheriting from an existing control, this chapter concentrates on building custom controls from scratch or, more accurately, from the base System.Web.UI.Control class.

Rendered or Composite Control?

The second major decision in building a custom control concerns the construction technique. The two main options available relate to how a control generates its HTML:

- A server control that renders its own HTML
- A composite control that relies on its children controls to perform the HTML rendering

Figure 2-6 shows these two control options.

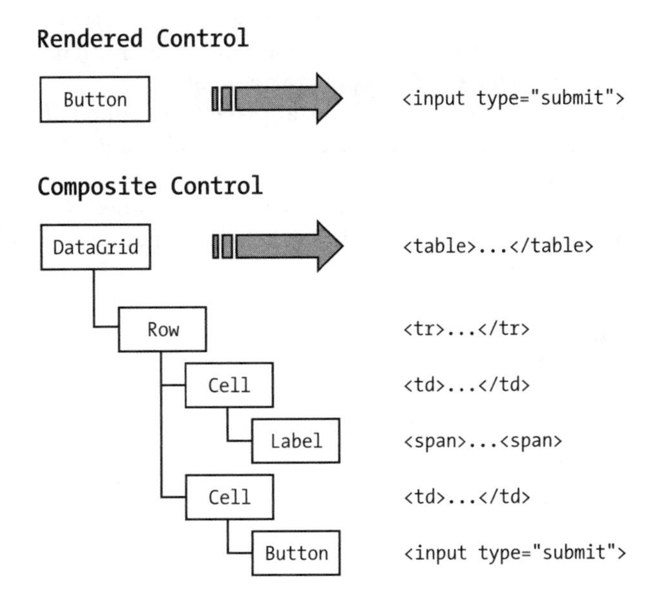

Figure 2-6. *Rendered versus composite custom controls*

Rendered controls tend to be simpler in nature and have a close relationship with individual HTML tags. Examples of this type of control in the ASP.NET Framework are the `TextBox` and `Button` controls that emit the `<input>` tag into the HTML stream. Nothing prevents a developer from putting more complex HTML rendering into these custom controls, but at some point, maintaining large amounts of rendered HTML can present a code maintenance problem.

Composite controls are able to take on more complex UI rendering tasks, because they follow good object-oriented principles of abstraction and encapsulation. Instead of trying to generate all the output through direct HTML emission, they break down the content generation process into a hierarchy of child controls that are responsible for rendering the portion of HTML that is their responsibility. A great example of this is the `GridView` control, which builds a fairly complex hierarchy of controls to generate its HTML table output. In .NET Framework 2.0 and later, there is a new base class `System.Web.UI.CompositeControl` that includes a custom designer to ensure proper rendering at design time. We inherit from `CompositeControl` when building the `TableCompCustomControl` example.

Separating the Web Application and Control Library

The examples demonstrated so far in the book have all been built under the assumption that they are part of the same ASP.NET web application. Custom ASP.NET server control development should deviate from this method and be constructed in a separate library project to generate an assembly independent of any web application code. The sample source code for the book follows this advice, as it has a web application project and a control library project holding the source code for all the custom controls.

The MenuCustomControl Server Control

The `MenuCustomControl` class is a clone of its user control cousin, rendering a simple HTML hyperlink menu. Because custom controls do not have the luxury of declaratively specifying the HTML output using drag and drop with the Visual Studio Toolbox and the Designer surface, we must use the facilities of the `HtmlTextWriter` class to generate the HTML output programmatically.

`HtmlTextWriter` is passed as the only parameter to the all-important `Render()` method of the `System.Web.UI.Control` base class. `Render()` is overridden by a custom control to inject the appropriate HTML content into the output stream.

The `Render()` method in Listing 2-12 calls on the services of a helper method named `RenderMenuItem()` that does the work for each item in the menu. Using helper methods is a good habit, as it keeps the rendering code more manageable.

Listing 2-12. *The MenuCustomControl Class File*

```
using System;
using System.Web;
using System.Web.UI;

namespace ControlsBook2Lib.Ch02
{
```

```
  [ToolboxData("<{0}:menucustomcontrol runat=server></{0}:menucustomcontrol>")]
  public class MenuCustomControl : Control
  {
    protected override void Render(HtmlTextWriter writer)
    {
      base.Render(writer);

      writer.WriteLine("<div>");
      RenderMenuItem(writer, "Apress", "http://www.apress.com");
      writer.Write(" | ");
      RenderMenuItem(writer, "Microsoft", "http://www.microsoft.com");
      writer.Write(" | ");
      RenderMenuItem(writer, "MSDN", "http://msdn.microsoft.com");
      writer.Write(" | ");
      RenderMenuItem(writer, "ASP.NET", "http://asp.net");
      writer.WriteLine("</div>");
    }

    private void RenderMenuItem(HtmlTextWriter writer, string title, string url)
    {
      writer.Write("<span><a href=\"");
      writer.Write(url);
      writer.Write("\">");
      writer.Write(title);
      writer.WriteLine("</a><span>");
    }
  }
}
```

HtmlTextWriter in this example is used in its basic mode by sticking to its Write() and WriteLine() methods. These methods should be familiar to the ASP developer, as they are analogous to the Response.Write() and Response.WriteLine() methods that take string input and pass it directly to the output stream.

Using the MenuCustomControl Server Control

Like user controls, custom controls cannot stand alone without the hosting support of a web form .aspx page. The registration process with custom controls is similar to that of user controls except for describing the location of the control content. Instead of providing a path to an .ascx file, we are looking for an assembly and namespace that contains the code of the custom control:

```
<%@ Register TagPrefix="apress" Namespace="ControlsBookLib.Ch02"
             Assembly="ControlsBookLib" %>
```

You have to remember to make the control assembly, like ControlsBookLib in this example, available to the web application either through the GAC or the web application's bin directory. If things are set up properly, the MenuCustomControl provides an accurate representation in the Design view of its HTML output, as shown in Figure 2-7.

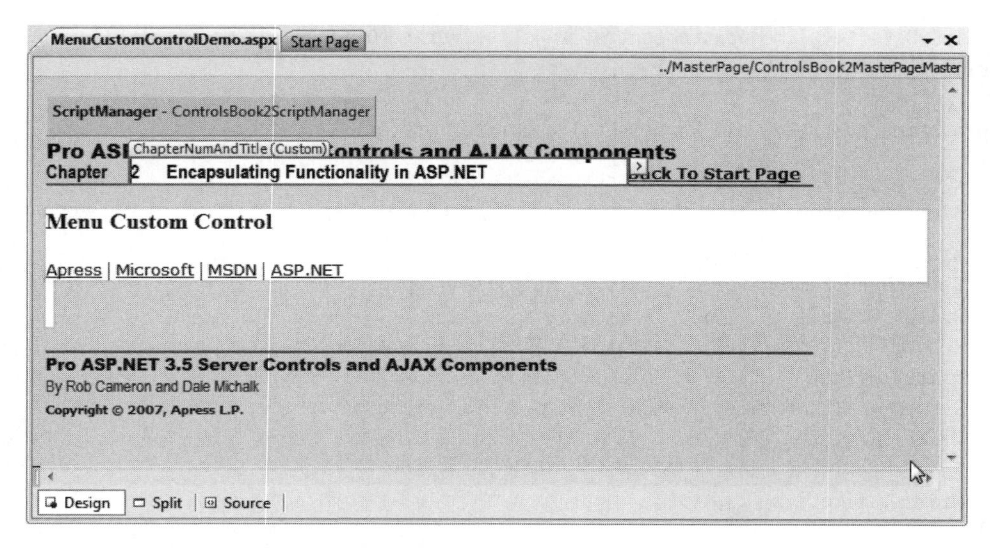

Figure 2-7. *The Visual Studio Design view of the MenuCustomControl on a web form*

Figure 2-8 confirms that the HTML output from our `MenuCustomControl` custom server control is the same as that of the user control in a browser. Listing 2-13 presents `MenuCustomControlDemo`'s `.aspx` file.

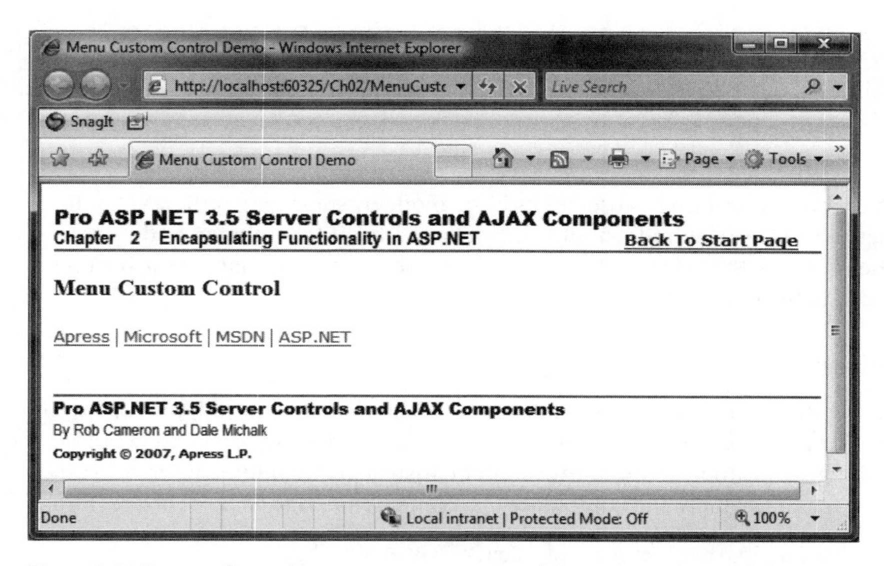

Figure 2-8. *Output from the menu custom control demonstration web form*

Listing 2-13. *The MenuCustomControlDemo Web Form .aspx File*

```
<%@ Page Language="C#" MasterPageFile="~/MasterPage/ControlsBook2MasterPage.Master"
  AutoEventWireup="true" CodeBehind="MenuCustomControlDemo.aspx.cs"
Inherits="ControlsBook2Web.Ch02.MenuCustomControlDemo"
  Title="Menu Custom Control Demo" %>

<%@ Register TagPrefix="apress" Namespace="ControlsBook2Lib.Ch02"
Assembly="ControlsBook2Lib" %>
<asp:Content ID="Content1" ContentPlaceHolderID="ChapterNumAndTitle" runat="server">
  <asp:Label ID="ChapterNumberLabel" runat="server"
Width="14px">2</asp:Label>  <asp:Label
    ID="ChapterTitleLabel" runat="server" Width="360px">
   Encapsulating Functionality in ASP.NET</asp:Label>
</asp:Content>
<asp:Content ID="Content2" ContentPlaceHolderID="PrimaryContent" runat="server">
  <h3>
    Menu Custom Control</h3>
  <apress:MenuCustomControl ID="menu1" runat="server" />
  <br />
  <br />
</asp:Content>
```

The TableCustomControl Server Control via Rendering

We continue our task of duplicating the user control examples via custom controls by implementing the dynamic HTML table. To make things more interesting, we demonstrate some of the more advanced techniques of the `HtmlTextWriter` class, and we use control composition to build the HTML table content. The rendering version is on deck first. Listing 2-14 shows the `TableCustomControl` class file.

Listing 2-14. *The TableCustomControl Class File*

```
using System;
using System.Web;
using System.Web.UI;

namespace ControlsBook2Lib.Ch02
{
  [ToolboxData("<{0}:tablecustomcontrol runat=server></{0}:tablecustomcontrol>")]
  public class TableCustomControl : Control
  {
    // Properties to access dimensions of HTML table
    // New property declaration syntax in C# 3.0
    public int X { get; set; }
    public int Y { get; set; }
```

```
protected override void Render(HtmlTextWriter writer)
{
  base.Render(writer);

  RenderHeader(writer);
  RenderTable(writer, X, Y);
}

private void RenderHeader(HtmlTextWriter writer)
{
  // write just <H3
  writer.WriteBeginTag("h3");
  // write >
  writer.Write(HtmlTextWriter.TagRightChar);
  writer.Write("TableCustomControl");
  // write <br/>
  writer.WriteFullBeginTag("br");
  writer.Write("X:" + X.ToString() + " ");
  writer.WriteLine("Y:" + Y.ToString() + " ");
  // write </h3>
  writer.WriteEndTag("h3");
}

private void RenderTable(HtmlTextWriter writer, int xDim, int yDim)
{
  // write <TABLE border="1">
  writer.AddAttribute(HtmlTextWriterAttribute.Border, "1");
  writer.RenderBeginTag(HtmlTextWriterTag.Table);

  for (int y = 0; y < yDim; y++)
  {
    // write <TR>
    writer.RenderBeginTag(HtmlTextWriterTag.Tr);

    for (int x = 0; x < xDim; x++)
    {
      // write <TD cellspacing="1">
      writer.AddAttribute(HtmlTextWriterAttribute.Cellspacing, "1");
      writer.RenderBeginTag(HtmlTextWriterTag.Td);

      // write <SPAN>
      writer.RenderBeginTag(HtmlTextWriterTag.Span);
      writer.Write("X:" + x.ToString());
      writer.Write("Y:" + y.ToString());
      // write </SPAN>
      writer.RenderEndTag();
```

```
          // write </TD>
          writer.RenderEndTag();
        }
        // write </TR>
        writer.RenderEndTag();
      }
      // write </TABLE>
      writer.RenderEndTag();
    }
  }
}
```

The property declarations for the X and Y dimensions of the HTML table demonstrate the new C# 3.0 syntax available to declare simple properties in a compact manner. Instead of declaring a private member variable and essentially empty getter and setter methods, this syntax will create a private member variable automatically:

```
public int X { get; set; }
public int Y { get; set; }
```

More interestingly, the `Render()` method drives the process of rendering the control output.

Rendering the Table Header

The `RenderHeader()` method is responsible for displaying information about the `X` and `Y` properties inside of an `<h3>` section. The code to build the `<h3>` tag demonstrates the ability to use the special `Write()` methods of the `HtmlTextWriter` class.

`WriteBeginTag()` writes the starting portion of a tag, including the opening bracket and the name of the tag, without closing it:

```
// write just <h3
writer.WriteBeginTag("h3");
```

At this point, you can manually add HTML attributes, such as borders and styles, using the `Write()` method of `HtmlTextWriter` if necessary. You also have the responsibility of explicitly closing the tag.

A handy way to write out special characters is to use the helper fields exposed by `HtmlTextWriter` to produce the correct strings, which sure beats the escaping that has to occur inside the C# string for special characters if you do all the work on your own. Table 2-1 shows the fields that are available.

Table 2-1. *String Fields Exposed by HtmlTextWriter*

HtmlTextWriter Field	String Output
`DefaultTabString`	Single tab character
`DoubleQuoteChar`	" "
`EndTagLeftChars`	</
`EqualsChar`	=

Table 2-1. *String Fields Exposed by HtmlTextWriter (Continued)*

HtmlTextWriter Field	String Output
EqualsDoubleQuoteString	=""
SelfClosingChars	/
SelfClosingTagEnd	/>
SemicolonChar	;
SingleQuoteChar	'
SlashChar	/
SpaceChar	Space
StyleEqualsChar	:
TagLeftChar	<
TagRightChar	>

The RenderHeader() code uses TagRightChar to generate the closing bracket for the <h3> tag:

```
// write >
writer.Write(HtmlTextWriter.TagRightChar);
```

An easier method to write a fully formed tag is to use the WriteFullBegin() tag method. This is useful for HTML tags such as <br/> that are commonly used without attributes:

```
// write <br/>
writer.WriteFullBeginTag("br");
```

Closing the <h3> tag requires a tag that contains a closing slash before the name (e.g., </h3>). WriteEndTag() can be used to generate this content in one atomic action:

```
// write </h3>
writer.WriteEndTag("h3");
```

Rendering the Table

Once the control header content is rendered, we move on to building the HTML table in the RenderTable() method. This portion of the control demonstrates a nifty feature of the HtmlTextWriter in working with HTML attributes. The AddAttribute() method takes a key/value string pair for each attribute you wish to render on an HTML tag. You can call this method multiple times to build up as many attributes to the follow-on tag as necessary. Once you've finished adding attributes, the next step is to use the RenderBeginTag() method. This method is smart enough to look at the attributes that were added previously and render them into the final output stream along with the tag name and brackets. The RenderTable() method uses this functionality to build the <table> tag and add a Border attribute to it:

```
// write <table border="1">
writer.AddAttribute(HtmlTextWriterAttribute.Border,"1");
writer.RenderBeginTag(HtmlTextWriterTag.Table);
```

The HtmlTextWriterTag enumeration is used for the <table> tag and the Border attribute strings as a simplified means of specifying the correct HTML name. Many of the HtmlTextWriter methods are overloaded to accept this enumeration and return the appropriate string value. See the ASP.NET documentation for full details on what names are supported.

If you use the RenderBeginTag() to build your opening tag, you must remember to pair it with a RenderEndTag() call to generate the closing tag. Fortunately, the HtmlTextWriter class is smart enough to remember the nesting and the order of the two routines to match them up and generate the correct closing tags. Closing our table is a direct call to RenderEndTag() with no parameters:

```
// write </table>
writer.RenderEndTag();
```

The rest of the RenderTable() routine uses RenderBeginTag() and RenderEndTag() in a two-loop scenario to build the <tr> and <td> tags along with their content according to the size specified in the X and Y dimension fields of the control.

The TableCustomControl Server Control via Control Composition

The second table custom control example accomplishes the same task as the first but does not bother with getting its hands dirty with HTML rendering. It follows the lead of the table user control and builds up its control content programmatically by adding child controls such as the table and its cells.

■ **Note** Because we are building a composite control, we inherit from System.UI.Web.CompositeControl, which implements the INamingContainer interface, to ensure that unique names are generated for each server control instance on the same page to prevent name conflicts. We discuss why this is necessary in Chapter 5. CompositeControl also brings in a custom designer automatically via the base class to ensure proper design-time rendering.

Listing 2-15 shows TableCompCustomControl's class file.

Listing 2-15. *The TableCompCustomControl Class File*

```
using System;
using System.ComponentModel;
using System.Web.UI;
using System.Web.UI.HtmlControls;
using System.Web.UI.WebControls;
using System.Text;

namespace ControlsBook2Lib.Ch02
{
  [ToolboxData("<{0}:tablecompcustomcontrol runat=server></{0}:
   tablecompcustomcontrol>")]
```

```
public class TableCompCustomControl : CompositeControl
{
  private HtmlTable table;

  // properties to access dimensions of HTML table
  int xDim;
  public int X
  {
    get
    {
      return xDim;
    }
    set
    {
      xDim = value;
    }
  }

  int yDim;
  public int Y
  {
    get
    {
      return yDim;
    }
    set
    {
      yDim = value;
    }
  }

  public override ControlCollection Controls
  {
    get
    {
      EnsureChildControls();
      return base.Controls;
    }
  }

  protected override void CreateChildControls()
  {
    Controls.Clear();
    BuildHeader();
    BuildTable(X, Y);
  }

  private void BuildHeader()
  {
```

```
      StringBuilder sb = new StringBuilder();
      sb.Append("TableCompCustomControl<br/>");
      sb.Append("X:");
      sb.Append(X.ToString());
      sb.Append(" ");
      sb.Append("Y:");
      sb.Append(Y.ToString());
      sb.Append(" ");

      HtmlGenericControl header = new HtmlGenericControl("h3");
      header.InnerHtml = sb.ToString();
      Controls.Add(header);
    }

    private void BuildTable(int xDim, int yDim)
    {
      HtmlTableRow row;
      HtmlTableCell cell;
      HtmlGenericControl content;

      // create <table border=1>
      table = new HtmlTable();
      table.Border = 1;

      for (int y = 0; y < Y; y++)
      {
        // create <tr>
        row = new HtmlTableRow();

        for (int x = 0; x < X; x++)
        {
          // create <td cellspacing=1>
          cell = new HtmlTableCell();
          cell.Attributes.Add("border", "1");

          // create a <span>
          content = new HtmlGenericControl("span");
          content.InnerHtml = "X:" + x.ToString() +
             "Y:" + y.ToString();
          cell.Controls.Add(content);

          row.Cells.Add(cell);
        }
        table.Rows.Add(row);
      }
      Controls.Add(table);
    }
  }
}
```

Composite custom controls typically do not override the Render() method. They rely on the base class implementation of Render() provided by the System.Web.UI.Control class that locates the Controls collection and calls Render() for each child control. This recursive call, in turn, causes the child controls to either render or do the same with their children, recursively walking through the render tree. In the end, we have a nice HTML output.

Although the composite control doesn't override the Render() method, it needs to override the CreateChildControls() method that is called by the ASP.NET Framework. This method is called to give the custom server control the opportunity to create its Controls collection, populating it with the appropriate child controls for rendering the desired output.

One extra task we need to perform is to override the Controls property exposed by the base Control class. This ensures that when an outside client attempts to access our composite control, the child control content will always be created and ready for access.

The EnsureChildControls() method does the work for us. Calling it will call CreateChildControls() if the child controls have not been initialized. Overriding Controls is always recommended in composite controls.

It is also recommended to call EnsureChildControls() for properties in a composite control right at the beginning of the Get and Set methods. This prevents any chance of accessing a child control before it is created. We deviate from this practice for the TableCompCustomControl control, because the X and Y properties must be set and available before we can create the control hierarchy. Otherwise, we wouldn't know what dimensions to use for the table.

Our implementation of CreateChildControls() calls into routines responsible for adding the child controls representing the header and the HTML table of the control, which are named BuildHeader() and BuildTable(), respectively. It is also the linkage point for evaluating the X and Y dimensions of the table.

BuildHeader() demonstrates the use of an HtmlGenericControl control from the System.Web.UI.HtmlControls namespace to render the <h3> content. This control was chosen due to its lack of built-in styling capabilities to keep the example simple. We build up the string content of the control by using the StringBuilder class. This class is a more efficient way of building up strings in .NET than concatenating literals as Strings, because StringBuilder uses a buffer. Variables of type String are immutable, and a concatenation operation actually builds a third string from the two strings brought together, literal or otherwise. For those who were worried about the HtmlTextWriter class and its efficiencies, the Render() and Write() methods write to a buffer, so there aren't any performance concerns about calling these methods multiple times.

Once we have built up the string content, we next use the InnerHtml property to easily load the HTML information inside the <h3> control. The final step is to add the HtmlGenericControl to the Controls collection of our new custom server control.

Building the HTML table in the BuildTable() method follows the well worn process of programmatically building up the HtmlTable control's child content. The result is almost an exact image of the user control version of the table. This is a good indication of the strength of custom controls when it comes to dynamic generation. The declarative advantages of the user control are not as powerful when content is built on the fly.

Using the Custom Table Controls

To verify that both custom controls provide identical HTML output, we use a web form that hosts them side by side in an HTML table. Figure 2-9 shows that they have the same Designer capability, though TableCompCustomControl requires the additional Designer attribute on its class to render correctly at design time, as discussed previously. Figure 2-10 shows that the final output is identical in the browser.

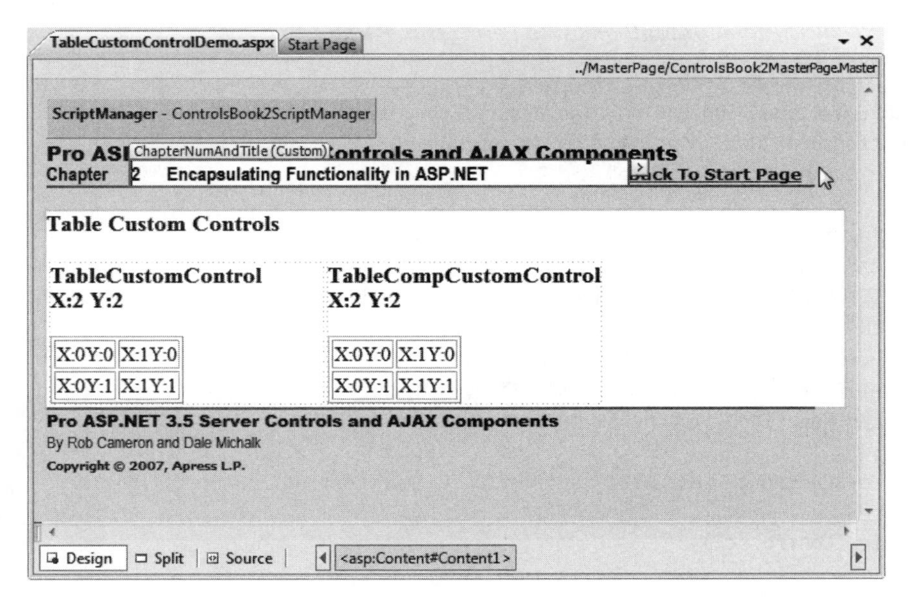

Figure 2-9. *The Visual Studio Design view of custom table controls on a web form*

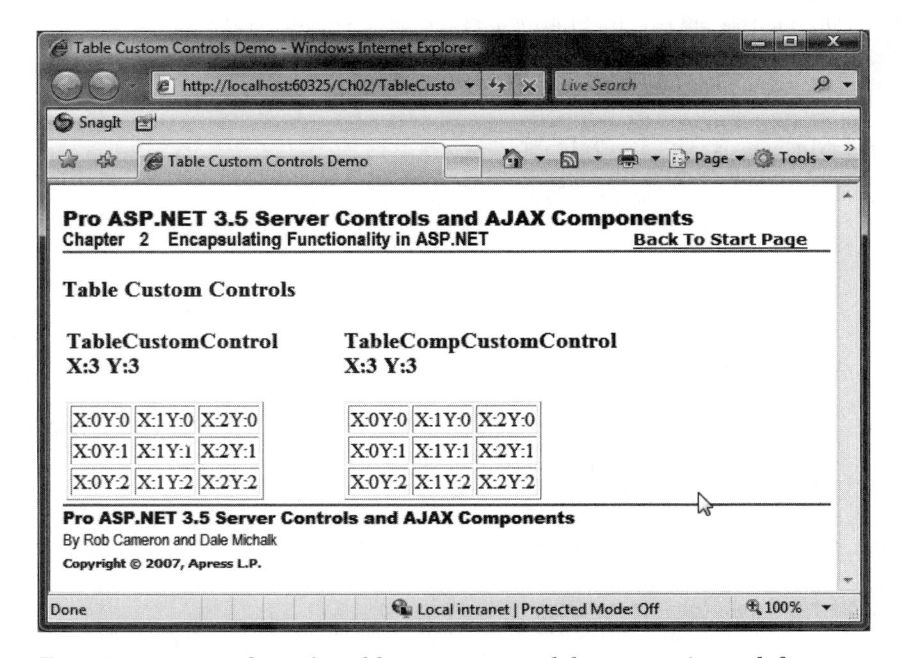

Figure 2-10. *Output from the table custom control demonstration web form*

Listings 2-16 and 2-17 show `TableCustomControlDemo`'s `.aspx` and class files.

Listing 2-16. *The TableCustomControlDemo Web Form .aspx File*

```
<%@ Page Language="C#" MasterPageFile="~/MasterPage/ControlsBook2MasterPage.Master"
  AutoEventWireup="true" CodeBehind="TableCustomControlDemo.aspx.cs"
Inherits="ControlsBook2Web.Ch02.TableCustomControlDemo"
  Title="Table Custom Controls Demo" %>

<%@ Register TagPrefix="apress" Namespace="ControlsBook2Lib.Ch02"
Assembly="ControlsBook2Lib" %>
<asp:Content ID="Content1" ContentPlaceHolderID="ChapterNumAndTitle" runat="server">
  <asp:Label ID="ChapterNumberLabel" runat="server"
Width="14px">2</asp:Label>  <asp:Label
    ID="ChapterTitleLabel" runat="server" Width="360px">
   Encapsulating Functionality in ASP.NET</asp:Label>
</asp:Content>
<asp:Content ID="Content2" ContentPlaceHolderID="PrimaryContent" runat="server">
  <h3>
    Table Custom Controls</h3>
  <table>
    <tr>
      <td style="width: 50%">
        <apress:TableCustomControl ID="TableCust1" runat="server" Y="2" X="2">
        </apress:TableCustomControl>
      </td>
      <td>
        <apress:TableCompCustomControl ID="TableCompCust1"
         runat="server" X="2" Y="2"></apress:TableCompCustomControl>
      </td>
    </tr>
  </table>
</asp:Content>
```

Listing 2-17. *The TableCustomControlDemo Code-Behind Class File*

```
using System;

namespace ControlsBook2Web.Ch02
{
  public partial class TableCustomControlDemo : System.Web.UI.Page
  {
    protected void Page_Load(object sender, EventArgs e)
    {
      if (!Page.IsPostBack)
      {
        TableCust1.X = 3;
        TableCust1.Y = 3;
        TableCompCust1.X = 3;
        TableCompCust1.Y = 3;
      }
```

```
    }
  }
}
```

Inheriting from an Existing Server Control

The previous examples are very simple controls in concept. This was by design; we focused on the details required to build the simplest of controls in order to give you a taste of the control-building process. In this section, we demonstrate how, with just a little bit of code, it is possible to add pleasing functionality through inheritance to one of the existing ASP.NET controls.

In this simple inheritance example, we'll add a 3-D look to the `WebControl` `TextBox` class. To add this UI behavior, we take advantage of the DHTML features of Internet Explorer when rendering our new server control. Listing 2-18 contains `TextBox3d`'s class file.

Listing 2-18. *The TextBox3d Class File*

```
using System;
using System.Web.UI;
using System.Web.UI.WebControls;
using System.ComponentModel;
using System.Drawing;

namespace ControlsBook2Lib.Ch02
{
  [ToolboxData("<{0}:textbox3d runat=server></{0}:textbox3d>"),
  ToolboxBitmap(typeof(ControlsBook2Lib.Ch02.TextBox3d),
  "ControlsBook2Lib.Ch03.TextBox3d.bmp")]
  public class TextBox3d : TextBox// Inherit from rich control
  {
    public TextBox3d()
    {
      Enable3D = true;
    }

    // Custom property to set 3D appearance
    [DescriptionAttribute("Set to true for 3d appearance"), DefaultValue("True")]
    public bool Enable3D
    {
      get
      {
        object enable3D = ViewState["Enable3D"];
        if (enable3D == null)
          return false;
        else
          return (bool)enable3D;
      }
      set
      {
```

```
        ViewState["Enable3D"] = value;
      }
    }

    protected override void Render(HtmlTextWriter output)
    {
      // Add DHTML style attribute
      if (Enable3D)
        output.AddStyleAttribute("FILTER",  "progid:DXImageTransform.Microsoft.
        dropshadow(OffX=2, OffY=2, Color='gray', Positive='true'");

      base.Render(output);
    }
  }
}
```

In our inheritance example, we have two main features: a property called `Enable3D` and an overridden `Render()` method. The property is used to determine whether or not to render with a 3-D look. Providing a Boolean property that allows the developer to revert to the default behavior of the base class server control is a good design guideline to follow when inheriting from rich server controls in ASP.NET.

We make this property available so that it is possible to revert to the `TextBox` base class's look and feel without having to swap out the control. The property uses `ViewState`, which we cover in Chapter 3, to store the value, with a default value of `true` set in the control's constructor.

The only other interesting code in this simple control is the `Render()` method. Here, we add a `style` attribute to the output variable to provide the 3-D look to the base `TextBox` control. We round out this method with a call to the base class's `Render()` method to finish off all the work.

As in previous examples, we need an `.aspx` page to host our custom control and show off our new 3-D look. Figure 2-11 shows the 3-D `TextBox` at runtime.

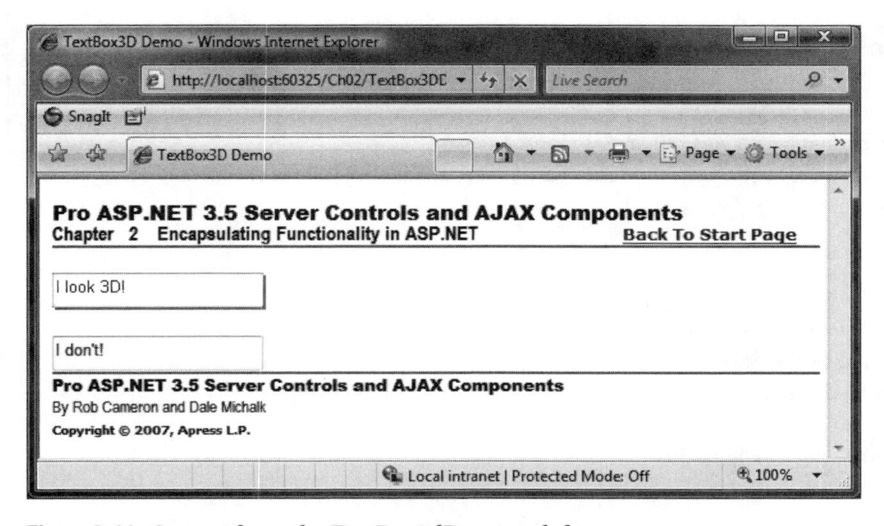

Figure 2-11. *Output from the TextBox3dDemo web form*

Listings 2-19 and 2-20 contain TextBox3dDemo's .aspx and class files, respectively.

Listing 2-19. *The TextBox3dDemo Web Form .aspx File*

```
<%@ Page Language="C#" MasterPageFile="~/MasterPage/ControlsBook2MasterPage.Master"
  AutoEventWireup="true" CodeBehind="TextBox3DDemo.aspx.cs"
Inherits="ControlsBook2Web.Ch02.TextBox3DDemo"
  Title="TextBox3D Demo" %>

<%@ Register TagPrefix="apress" Namespace=
  "ControlsBook2Lib.Ch02" Assembly="ControlsBook2Lib" %>
<asp:Content ID="Content1" ContentPlaceHolderID="ChapterNumAndTitle" runat="server">
  <asp:Label ID="ChapterNumberLabel" runat="server"
Width="14px">2</asp:Label>  <asp:Label
    ID="ChapterTitleLabel" runat="server" Width="360px">
   Encapsulating Functionality in ASP.NET</asp:Label>
</asp:Content>
<asp:Content ID="Content2" ContentPlaceHolderID="PrimaryContent" runat="server">
  <br />
  <apress:TextBox3d ID="TextBox3d1" runat="server" Width="159px" Height="22px"
  Enable3D="True">I look 3D!</apress:TextBox3d>
  <br />
  <br />
  <apress:TextBox3d ID="Textbox3d2" runat="server" Width="159px" Height="22px"
   Enable3D="false">I don't!</apress:TextBox3d>
  <br />
</asp:Content>
```

Listing 2-20. *The TextBox3dDemo Code-Behind Class File*

```
using System;

namespace ControlsBook2Web.Ch02
{
  public partial class TextBox3DDemo : System.Web.UI.Page
  {
    protected void Page_Load(object sender, EventArgs e)
    {

    }
  }
}
```

Having a rich server control as the base class is a powerful means of packaging functionality that takes advantage of browser DHTML capabilities to generate pleasing output, as this example demonstrates.

In the preceding examples, we did not provide persistent state for control properties to keep the example code simple. The lack of a persistent state requires that the control's value be set in the page's Load event if the desired value is different than what is set declaratively in the page. In the next chapter, we discuss how to take advantage of state management in server controls, but first, we provide a quick introduction to the new AJAX functionality first available in ASP.NET 3.0 and enhanced in ASP.NET 3.5.

ASP.NET AJAX

ASP.NET AJAX 1.0 released after .NET Framework 2.0 as an officially supported product that installs on top of .NET Framework 2.0. ASP.NET AJAX 1.0 provides a set of technologies to add AJAX (Asynchronous JavaScript and XML) support to ASP.NET 2.0. It consists of a client-side script framework and server controls, as well as the underlying plumbing for the AJAX functionality with ASP.NET.

In addition to the ASP.NET AJAX 1.0 release, the ASP.NET AJAX Control Toolkit released as a shared-source implementation built on top of the ASP.NET AJAX Extensions 1.0 core functionality.

■ **Note** The ASP.NET AJAX Control Toolkit is not supported by Microsoft directly as a stand-alone product; it is shipped as source code. This means that customers using the Control Toolkit can modify the source code directly as well as seek help from the community and user forum resources.

The Control Toolkit has lots of useful and powerful AJAX controls and extenders with source code that can be used as-is in applications or server as example code for building your own AJAX-enabled server controls or an extender control that can apply AJAX functionality to an existing server control.

The .NET Framework 3.5 provides additional enhancements to ASP.NET, building on the currently available ASP.NET AJAX functionality, which we cover in Chapter 9. In this chapter, we provide a quick demonstration of writing AJAX-enabled web pages—ASP.NET style—through the use of the `UpdatePanel` control.

ASP.NET AJAX UpdatePanel Server Control

In Visual Studio 2008 with .NET Framework 3.5, a new node is available in the Toolbox window, shown in Figure 2-12.

For a quick example, we've copied the `HtmlControls` sample from Chapter 1 into the `Ch02` folder in the web project and renamed it `HtmlControlsAJAX.aspx`. As a quick review, in Chapter 1, this example took X and Y values to dynamically build a table that had X columns and Y rows. To quickly make this page more responsive with less page flickering (i.e., to add AJAX functionality), the `<input>` tag that renders as the button and the `<span>` tag that serves as a container for the resulting table are moved into an `UpdatePanel` server control available on the AJAX Extensions Toolbox node. An additional change is required: an ASP.NET AJAX `ScriptManager` server control must appear somewhere on the page before the AJAX server controls appear in terms. In our scenario, a `ScriptManager` server control was added to the `MasterPage` `ControlsBook2MasterPage.master` so that it is always present.

Figure 2-12. *The AJAX Extensions Toolbox node*

This worked great in terms of only updating the <span> tag and not reloading the whole page, but if you enter fairly large values for X and Y, such as 200 × 200, several seconds will pass before the table renders without providing any visual queue as to what is going on. This could cause the user to click the button multiple times, thinking that the first click didn't work.

ASP.NET AJAX UpdateProgress Server Control

In building this sample, we immediately saw the value that the ASP.NET AJAX extensions provide in terms of quickly adding AJAX-style functionality to an existing web page. To take the AJAX example to the next level, we added an `UpdateProgress` server control to provide a visual cue to the end user that work is occurring. This is a very important design requirement in building effective AJAX-enabled web applications. Listings 2-21 and 2-22 contain the `HtmlControlsAJAX` demonstration `.aspx` and code-behind class files, respectively.

Listing 2-21. *The HtmlControlsAJAX Web Form .aspx File*

```
<%@ Page Language="C#" MasterPageFile="~/MasterPage/ControlsBook2MasterPage.Master"
  AutoEventWireup="true" CodeBehind="HtmlControlsAJAX.aspx.cs"
Inherits="ControlsBook2Web.Ch02.HtmlControlsAJAX"
  Title="HTML Controls Demo" %>

<asp:Content ID="Content1" ContentPlaceHolderID="ChapterNumAndTitle" runat="server">
  <asp:Label ID="ChapterNumberLabel" runat="server"
Width="14px">2</asp:Label>  <asp:Label
    ID="ChapterTitleLabel" runat="server" Width="360px">
   Encapsulating Functionality in ASP.NET</asp:Label>
</asp:Content>
```

```
<asp:Content ID="Content2" ContentPlaceHolderID="PrimaryContent" runat="server">
  <h3>
    HTML Controls</h3>
  X
  <input type="text" id="XTextBox" runat="server" /><br />
  <br />
  Y
  <input type="text" id="YTextBox" runat="server" /><br />
  <asp:UpdatePanel ID="UpdatePanel1" runat="server">
    <ContentTemplate>
      <input type="submit" id="BuildTableButton" runat="server" value=
       "Build Table" onserverclick="BuildTableButton_ServerClick" />
      <asp:UpdateProgress ID="UpdateProgress1" runat="server"
      AssociatedUpdatePanelID="UpdatePanel1">
        <ProgressTemplate>
          Updating...</ProgressTemplate>
      </asp:UpdateProgress>
      <span id="Span1" runat="server"></span>
    </ContentTemplate>
  </asp:UpdatePanel>
</asp:Content>
```

Listing 2-22. *The TextBox3dDemo Code-Behind Class File*

```
using System;
using System.Web;
using System.Web.UI;
using System.Web.UI.WebControls;
using System.Web.UI.HtmlControls;

namespace ControlsBook2Web.Ch02
{
  public partial class HtmlControlsAJAX : System.Web.UI.Page
  {
    protected void Page_Load(object sender, EventArgs e)
    {

    }

    protected void BuildTableButton_ServerClick(object sender, EventArgs e)
    {
      int xDim = Convert.ToInt32(XTextBox.Value);
      int yDim = Convert.ToInt32(YTextBox.Value);
      BuildTable(xDim, yDim);
    }
```

```
    private void BuildTable(int xDim, int yDim)
    {
      HtmlTable table;
      HtmlTableRow row;
      HtmlTableCell cell;
      HtmlGenericControl content;

      table = new HtmlTable();
      table.Border = 1;
      for (int y = 0; y < yDim; y++)
      {
        row = new HtmlTableRow();
        for (int x = 0; x < xDim; x++)
        {
          cell = new HtmlTableCell();
          cell.Style.Add("font", "16pt verdana bold italic");
          cell.Style.Add("background-color", "red");
          cell.Style.Add("color", "yellow");

          content = new HtmlGenericControl("SPAN");
          content.InnerHtml = "X:" + x.ToString() +
             "Y:" + y.ToString();
          cell.Controls.Add(content);
          row.Cells.Add(cell);
        }
        table.Rows.Add(row);
      }
      Span1.Controls.Add(table);
    }
  }
}
```

When reviewing the source code, you will find that no changes were needed in the code-behind class file. All of the hard AJAX programming is automatically handled by the ASP.NET AJAX extensions server controls and associated JavaScript file that ships with ASP.NET AJAX. Figure 2-13 shows the page loading with the phrase "Updating . . ." displayed under the Build Table button while waiting for the update HTML to return from the AJAX call.

ASP.NET AJAX provides a rapid ability to add AJAX-like functionality to existing web sites. In Chapter 9, we cover building server controls that are AJAX aware as well as considerations to make sure that any custom server controls you develop work properly within the ASP.NET AJAX popular `UpdatePanel` server control.

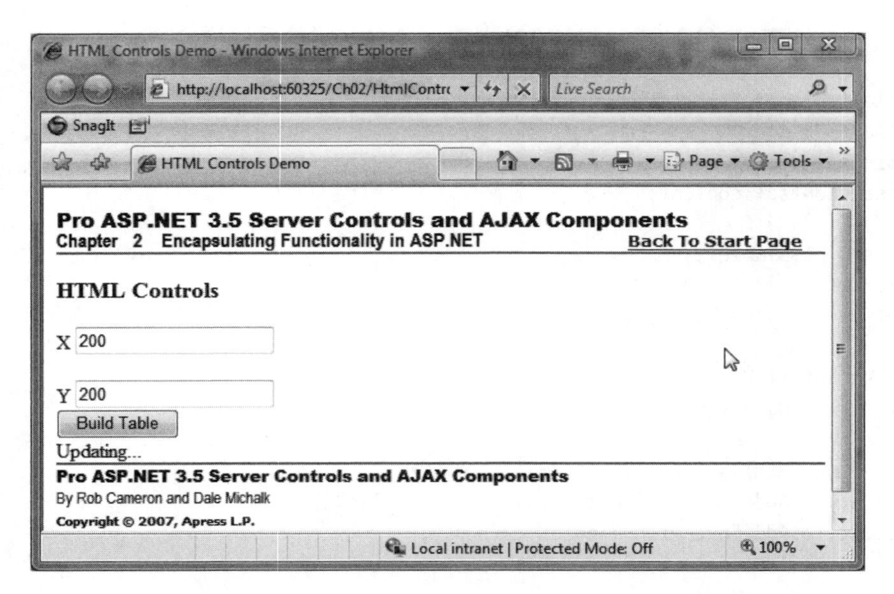

Figure 2-13. *The Web form demonstrating ASP.NET AJAX partial updates with progress status*

Using Design-Time Attributes

Visual Studio provides a rich, powerful development environment with automatic completion and default properties, as well as custom property editors to speed developers' coding efforts. There are a few different technologies available to integrate and extend the Visual Studio environment. Attributes provide one means to extend Visual Studio and are used to integrate custom server controls into the environment. Before we present a quick overview of the most important design-time attributes, we provide a short background on attributes.

What's an Attribute?

An attribute is essentially a class that contains properties and methods used to modify other classes, class methods, or class properties. Attribute information is stored with the metadata of the element and can be retrieved at runtime through reflection.

Attributes can be applied to an entire class or to a specific class method or property. Attribute classes are defined as public classes. All attributes derive directly or indirectly from the `System.Attribute` class, and attribute classes generally end in the word `Attribute` to enhance readability. Here is a sample attribute declaration:

```
public class SampleAttribute : Attribute
{
}
```

An attribute is declared within brackets just before the element to which it is applied. The syntax consists of calling a constructor on the attribute. Here is how an attribute is applied to a class method:

```
public class SampleClass
{
   [SampleAttribute]
   public virtual void SampleMethod()
   {
      //...
   }
}
```

Attributes provide an object-oriented way to extend the declarative syntax of the .NET Framework without having to resort to macros or some other outside mechanism to store configuration information such as the registry.

Common Design-Time Attributes

Now that you have a bit of background on attributes, let's move on to design-time attributes for server controls. Design-time attributes exist in the `System.ComponentModel` namespace. Table 2-2 provides a brief description of the most common design-time attributes.

Table 2-2. *Common Design-Time Attributes*

Attribute	Description
`BindableAttribute`	Indicates whether or not a property supports two-way data binding
`BrowsableAttribute`	Indicates whether or not a property or event should be listed in a property browser
`CategoryAttribute`	Specifies in which category a property or event should be listed in the property browser
`DefaultEvent`	Specifies the name of the default event for a class
`DefaultProperty`	Specifies the name of the default property for a class
`DefaultValue`	Sets the default value for a property
`DescriptionAttribute`	Allows the property browser to display a brief description of a property
`DesignOnlyAttribute`	Specifies that a property can be set only at design time
`EditorAttribute`	Associates a UI type editor with a property
`TagPrefix`	Assembly-level attribute that indicates the tag prefix for a control or set of controls within an assembly
`ToolboxData`	Specifies default values for control attributes and customizes the initial HTML content
`TypeConverterAttribute`	Defines a custom type converter for a property

You can apply multiple attributes to a particular class, method, or property. There are two ways to do this. One syntax is to separate attributes by a comma within a set of brackets:

```
[DefaultProperty("Text"), toolboxdata("<{0}:mylabel runat=server></{0}:mylabel>")]
  public class SuperLabel : Label
  {...}
```

The other syntax is to put each attribute in its own set of brackets:

```
[DefaultProperty("Text")]
[ToolboxData("<{0}:mylabel runat=server></{0}:mylabel>")]
  public class SuperLabel : Label
  {...}
```

This completes our whirlwind tour of attributes and of the most common design-time attributes available for use on custom controls. In this section we provided a short overview of basic Designer attributes that we use in the code samples in this book. We cover design-time support in more detail in Chapter 11.

Summary

The ASP.NET object model fully supports inheritance as a method of providing additional functionality to existing controls. Given the object-oriented nature of the Framework, it is quite easy to add powerful functionality with just a few lines of code.

ASP.NET provides two primary means of building controls: user controls and custom controls. Encapsulation or composition is another method available in ASP.NET to package functionality. Server control encapsulation is more applicable when focused on generic logic. User control encapsulation is more applicable when packaging application-specific logic.

User controls have the benefit of declarative UI development and require less skill from the development staff. Custom controls provide bare-bones access to the ASP.NET plumbing, myriad design options, a superior deployment mechanism as an assembly, and better Designer support for the developer/user.

Custom controls typically inherit from `System.Web.UI.Control`, `System.Web.UI.WebControls.WebControl`, or `System.Web.UI.WebControls.WebPart` and are built using one of two primary techniques: direct rendering or control composition. The `HtmlTextWriter` class provides a significant amount of assistance with rendering HTML content from a custom control through its `Write()` and `Render()` methods. Custom controls that use control composition speed development time by letting child controls handle their own HTML generation through the application of good object-oriented design principles.

CHAPTER 3

ASP.NET State Management

The need to maintain state in a web application has driven vendors and those who participate in the evolution of web protocols to provide additional tools and standards to make life easier for web developers. Through these clever techniques, you can make it appear to the user as if the browser is intimately linked to the web application and maintains an ongoing, connected relationship, as experienced when using a thick-client application running locally on the user's desktop. AJAX functionality takes these state management techniques to the next level by reducing the number of full-page postback cycles giving the application an appearance even more like a Windows application. In this chapter, we cover the various techniques available in ASP.NET 3.5 to maintain state and demonstrate how these techniques relate to building server controls, such as using ASP.NET `ViewState` and `ControlState` to leverage the ASP.NET infrastructure.

Web developers can choose to maintain application state in a web application in two locations: on the client side or on the web server. Client-side state management techniques include cookies and hidden form fields. Server-side state management techniques include `Session` and `Application` variables, as well as additional options that we discuss later in this chapter.

ASP.NET Request-Processing Architecture

When you develop web-based applications, managing user state and implementing a secure robust application are high on the list of requirements. On the Internet, ensuring state and application integrity (i.e., authorization, authentication, and auditing) is even more important because of the wild nature of the Web. In this section, we provide a quick overview of the ASP.NET request processing architecture. While not strictly required for server control development, understanding the basics of the ASP.NET processing architecture, as well as `HttpModules` and `HttpHandlers`, can help a developer understand where to plug in custom server controls or where an `HttpModule` or `HttpHandler` may be more appropriate.

When a browser client makes a request to Internet Information Services (IIS) for a resource such as an `.aspx` file, by default, ASP.NET initiates and then maintains user state for the duration of the user's site interaction, which can include multiple request/response HTTP sessions. Figure 3-1 shows the logical data flow for a typical ASP.NET request. The request is made to IIS, which checks the file extension mappings to determine how to handle the request. If it is an ASP.NET request, IIS hands off the request to the ASP.NET Internet Server Application Programming Interface (ISAPI) library, `aspnet_isapi.dll`. That library next funnels the request into the ASP.NET pluggable architecture, handing off the request to the ASP.NET worker process, `aspnet_wp.exe`.

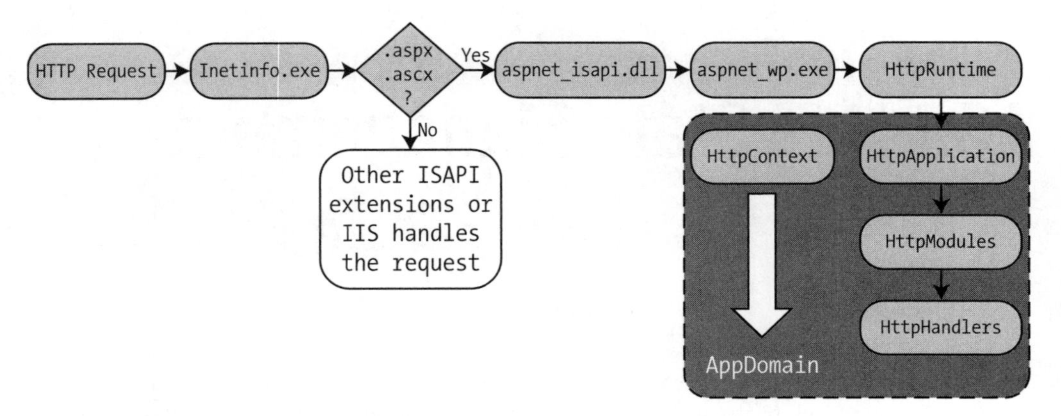

Figure 3-1. *ASP.NET request data flow*

The worker process implements the HttpRuntime object, which handles ASP.NET requests within the same process space and achieves isolation using separate AppDomains. The HttpRuntime object uses an HttpApplicationFactory object to locate the correct AppDomain and create an HttpApplication object to process the request. The global.asax file can be used to subscribe to events available via the HttpApplication object. User state information for the current user session within the application is made available through the Context property of the HttpApplication-derived object. We cover Context in more detail in the "ASP.NET and Server-Side State Management" section. At this point in the processing pipeline, any objects that implement the HttpModule class and are registered in the application will have their events fired. For example, Session_Start and Session_End are implemented in an HTTP module named SessionStateModule. HttpModule objects can be used to implement a variety of sitewide functionality, such as a custom authentication architecture that verifies requests based on custom HTTP header information.

After all registered HttpModule objects have a chance to process events, the request is shepherded to the appropriate HTTP handler by calling its ProcessRequest() method. The ProcessRequest() method takes one parameter of type HttpContext containing the user state of the current request. Next, HttpHandler is responsible for generating a response to the request using the Context.Response.Write() method. This entire process is illustrated in Figure 3-1.

As you can see, request processing flows through a series of ASP.NET objects that have full access to the ASP.NET state. The ASP.NET classes in Figure 3-2 can examine the state of a user request to implement authentication, authorization, and auditing in a web application. These objects also implement numerous useful events that can be extended. The ASP.NET classes that manage user state flow and request processing are shown in the figure. Note that the familiar Request, Response, Application, and Session objects are implemented via classes in this section of the ASP.NET class hierarchy as part of the HttpContext class.

The ASP.NET request processing architecture permits developers to plug into the architecture by authoring custom objects that implement the HttpHandler or HttpModule class. As a point of reference, the HttpHandler class has similar behavior to ISAPI extensions. Likewise, the HttpModule class provides similar functionality to ISAPI filters. These two .NET classes greatly expand the ISAPI library concept, as the classes are fully integrated into the ASP.NET architecture.

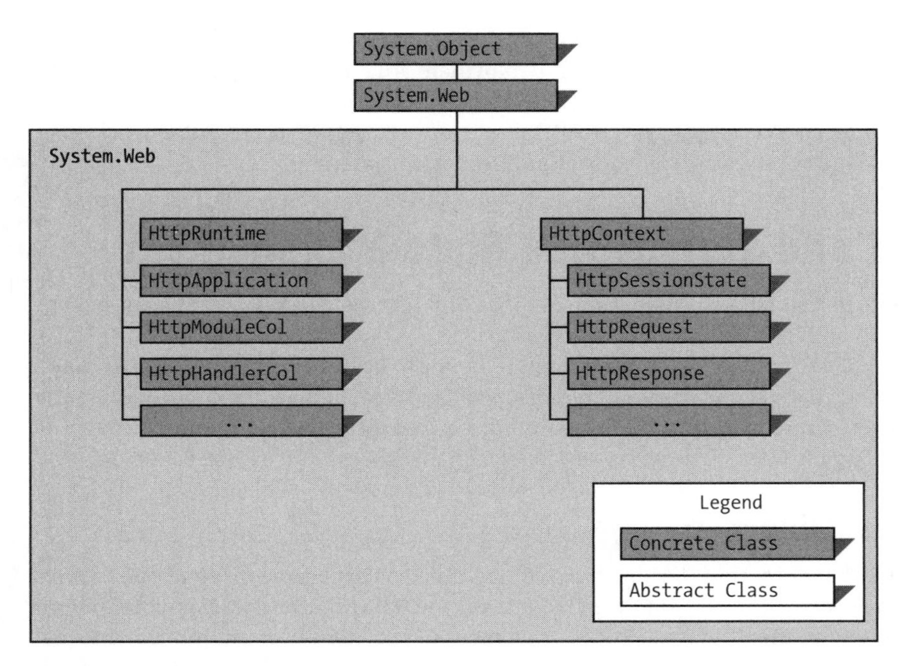

Figure 3-2. *ASP.NET request processing classes*

HttpHandler

HttpHandler objects deserve special attention, because ASP.NET uses this same architecture to process requests for .aspx and .asmx pages. HttpHandlers enable processing of individual HTTP URLs or groups of URL extensions within an application. Table 3-1 shows examples of the HttpHandlers provided in ASP.NET by default.

Table 3-1. *Built-in ASP.NET Handlers*

Handler	Description
ASP.NET service handler	Default HttpHandler for all ASP.NET service (.asmx) pages
ASP.NET page handler	Default HttpHandler for all ASP.NET (.aspx) pages

The ASP.NET page handler PageHandlerFactory performs the important task of receiving the user request and creating the Page object for manipulation by the developer. The Page object makes user state easily accessible; this state information includes application and session state, data stored in ViewState, and data stored in control state, which is new in ASP.NET 2.0 and later.

In general, an HttpHandler can be either synchronous or asynchronous. As you would guess, a synchronous handler does not return data until it finishes processing the HTTP request for which it is called. An asynchronous handler returns data immediately and is usually tasked with launching a process that can be lengthy. As mentioned previously, HttpHandlers have a simple implementation compared to writing an ISAPI extension library. After writing and compiling code to implement an HttpHandler, deployment is a matter of registering the handler in the application's web.config file.

The single drawback when you compare HttpHandlers to ISAPI extensions is that you cannot use HttpModules and HttpHandlers outside of ASP.NET in this manner.

ASP.NET and Server-Side State Management

Server-side state in ASP.NET consists of the familiar Application and Session objects, which store application and user state data in a collection.

In general, data stored in Application variables tends to be like constants, shared by application users and unchanging. Application variables are usually set in the global.asax file. Session variables are user-connection specific and quite convenient for maintaining state throughout an application. To gain access to these server-side state mechanisms, you use the Context object.

The Context Object

We mentioned previously that the HttpApplication class makes user state available to the developer in the Context property of the HttpContext type. The HttpContext class implements HttpSessionState and HttpApplicationState instances to provide server-side state management. In this section, we cover these classes in detail, because they are important features of the ASP.NET request-processing engine, as they provide server-side state mechanisms to web applications.

Table 3-2 contains a partial description of some of the important properties attached to the HttpContext class and what capabilities they provide. Refer to the .NET Framework documentation for more detailed information on the HttpContext class.

Table 3-2. *Properties of the HttpContext Class*

Property	Description
Application	Provides server-side state management for all clients of the web application
ApplicationInstance	Reference controls the execution process of the ASP.NET web request
Cache	Provides access to the server-side cache in ASP.NET
Error	Provides access to the error exceptions that occur during ASP.NET execution
Items	Key/value pair collection used to pass information between the components in a request
Request	Contains information from the client request, including browser type, cookies, and values encoded in form and URL query string collections
Response	Key/value pair collection used to pass information between the requesting components
Server	Provides utilities including Server.Transfer, Server.HtmlEncode, and Server.MapPath

Table 3-2. *Properties of the HttpContext Class*

Property	Description
`Session`	State collection maintained on behalf of a web application user
`Trace`	Debugging utility for writing to the trace output of the web form
`User`	Makes security information available when a user is authenticated

Web forms and controls have different methods to obtain a reference to the `HttpContext` instance. A static property, `HttpContext.Current`, returns an instance of the current `HttpContext` to any class that is interested, even if it is not inside an ASP.NET page. For example, the `Current` static property can be referenced in helper classes used within the web form page's server-side code to gain access to any of the properties in Table 3-2, such as `Cache`. This ease of access allows for more modular code that's easier to read.

Controls inherit a `Context` property from `System.Web.UI.Control` that is mapped to the current instance of `HttpContext` as a convenient reference for use in server control development. The `Page` class has a `Context` property as well, but it goes one step further by providing properties that are mapped to their `Context` counterparts, such as `Request` and `Response`.

Server-Side State Considerations

In general, we do not recommend using server-side state management techniques in server control development, especially when most, if not all, state storage requirements can be met using client-side state management, which we discuss in the next section.

In situations where server-side state is feasible and the limitations, such as requiring browser cookies, are acceptable, server-side state can be a convenient method to store state for custom controls. However, in this book, we do not use server-side state management techniques in any of the samples, because doing so would require developer users of the server controls to enable server-side state in order for the controls to work. Forcing server-side state on users is not a good practice and would limit the desirability of the server controls.

ASP.NET and Client-Side State Management

ASP.NET provides access to a variety of client-side state management techniques to give you a helping hand in building useful, interactive web sites. Control developers can leverage these state management features to provide extra value in their controls by making it look as if the controls can remember their previous values or obviate the need to go back to a data source to display information for tabular controls. What makes this capability wonderful is that these options do not require any special-purpose mechanism on the web server; instead, they use the everyday features of a web browser to make this magic happen. In this section, we provide an overview of the client-side state options that are available:

- URL strings
- Cookies
- Hidden HTML variables
- View state

URL Strings

Encoding information in the URL string passed to the web server is one of the simplest and most widely used techniques for storing client state. A great example is your favorite e-commerce store that puts the category and product-identifying information in a list of hyperlinks for the rows of products that fit a category. The embedded information in the URL allows the web site to remember what category the user came from when choosing to follow a link for a particular product. Developers can also add nonnavigational information at the end of the URL string by just appending another variable, to track such information as the customer's buying history with the web site to provide a discount, for example:

```
http://acme.com/product.aspx?categoryid=1&productid=1&custtype=preferred
```

ASP.NET parses the URL string that it receives as part of the page request and provides easy access to the key/value pairs through two properties of the `HttpRequest` class: `QueryString` and `Params`. `HttpRequest` itself is available through the `Request` property of the `Context` object. The following code snippet shows how either the `QueryString` or `Params` collection can read the incoming `product.aspx` URL string for category and custom information:

```
string categoryID = Request.QueryString["categoryid"];
string productID = Request.Params["productid"];
string custType = Request.Querystring["custtype"];
```

Adding extra variables or removing variables from the URL string in maintaining an application is something that the programmer must do manually. Forgetting to add variables or neglecting to modify all hyperlinks on a web form is a common mistake. Finally, URL strings have size limitations that vary among browser devices, so developers must take a one-size-fits-all approach when attempting to store state in the URL string.

Cookies

The second client-side state feature of ASP.NET we discuss here is the client-side cookie, a mechanism familiar to most web developers that is added to the HTTP protocol to allow the web server and web browser to collaborate in storing information on the user's machine. A cookie can store site-specific data for a defined period of time, after which the cookie expires. The cookie time limit is put to use by server-side state mechanisms in ASP.NET, such as session state, and security mechanisms, such as ASP.NET forms authentication. Both emit cookies to identify the user and track information related to storing data on the web server or authenticating the user browsing the web site.

The cookie information passed between browser and server is delivered via HTTP headers. The web server will send down to the browser client an HTTP header named `Set-Cookie` with the information it wants the browser to persist on the user's local machine. The next time the user visits that site (and only that site), the browser responds with a `Cookie` HTTP header containing the locally stored site-specific data, as long as the cookie hasn't expired.

ASP.NET provides access to outgoing cookies via the `Cookies` property of the `HttpResponse` class. `HttpResponse` represents the output of the web form and is reached through the `Response` property of the `Context` object, which is available to server controls via the `System.Web.UI.Control` class. The `Cookies` collection is serialized to a set of string values attached to HTTP headers.

The following code adds two differently named cookies representing the first and last name of one of the authors to the Cookies collection:

```
Response.Cookies["firstname"] = "Dale";
Response.Cookies["lastname"] = "Michalk";
```

The Cookies collection serialization process generates two Set-Cookie headers, one for each cookie being sent down to the browser:

```
Set-Cookie: firstname=Dale; path=/
Set-Cookie: lastname=Michalk; path=/
```

The HttpRequest class has a Cookies collection that allows the developer to read incoming cookies in a manner identical to the outgoing collection. In our example, when the browser comes back to the same web form, it will send the cookie information for both cookies in a single HTTP header named Cookie:

```
Cookie: firstname=Dale; lastname=Michalk
```

The following code shows you how to read the two cookies via the Cookies collection on a web form:

```
string firstname = Request.Cookies["firstname"];
string lastname = Request.Cookies["lastname"];
```

Common sense dictates that you should not store a large value, because the information stored in a cookie is transmitted as part of the web page automatically, unlike a URL string parameter, which must be continuously refreshed by the programmer, or an HTML hidden variable, which must be sent via an HTTP POST request for a specific page. The cookie technique also presents challenges when the user either disables cookies or has problems with maintaining or deleting them from the local cookie store. Some browsing devices don't support cookies at all, so you may have to avoid them entirely as an option for storing state in your controls.

HTML Hidden Variables

Hidden input variables inside an HTML form are the third method of client-side state management available in ASP.NET that we discuss in this section. This technique is familiar to many developers who created web applications with technologies such as Common Gateway Interface (CGI) and ASP. Unlike the URL string and cookie options, size limitations and device support issues are not pressing concerns, so hidden input variables as part of an HTML form are a heavily used technique for client-side state management.

For data stored in an HTML form to be available, the use of the HTTP POST mechanism is required to transmit the state information back to the web server. ASP.NET helps ensure this through the System.Web.UI.HtmlControls.HtmlInputForm server control. HtmlInputForm is smart enough to render a method="post" attribute, along with an action attribute that directs the page back to the original URL. The following tag on a hypothetical web form named first.aspx is rendered as a server control because of the runat="server" attribute:

```
<form id="first" method="post" runat="server">
```

The server control representing the form tag emits the following HTML output:

```
<form id="first" method="post" action="first.aspx">
```

Notice that the tag is tied to the HTTP POST protocol and has an action attribute to submit the page back to the original URL of the web page. Ensuring that all emitted form variables, hidden or not, can be read upon form submission is a key requirement. Here's the complete form output for our simple example:

```
<form id="first" method="post" action="first.aspx">
   <input id="names" type="text" value="Dale Michalk Rob Cameron">
   <input id="task" type="text" value="write book">
</form>
```

Once the web form is submitted via a button click or a JavaScript submission of the form, ASP.NET parses the input values to allow web form and control code to extract the values and drive the logic of the web application. The variables in an HTTP POST are encoded using HTML encoding rules and are separated in the body of the request via ampersand characters:

```
names=dale+michalk+rob+cameron&task=writebook
```

ASP.NET provides the Form or Params collections attached to the HttpRequest class in the current HttpContext to read the values:

```
string names = Request.Form["names"];
string task = Request.Params["task"];
```

As you can see, form data is made available on the server through the construct of the ASP.NET postback mechanism and the HttpContext object. Figure 3-3 shows the ASP.NET postback mechanism.

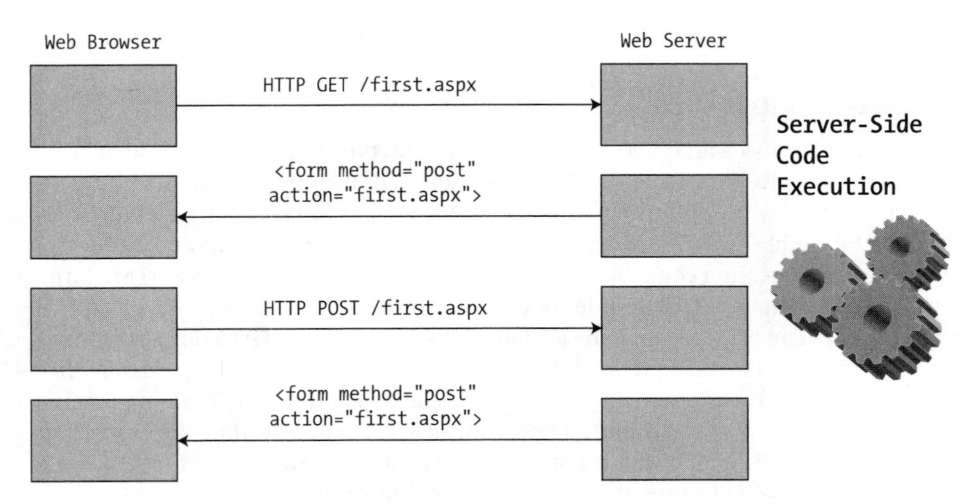

Figure 3-3. *The ASP.NET postback mechanism*

Most of the time, when building web applications, developers need to store state information that shouldn't be exposed to the user, such as application-specific logic to aid in processing a request. Hidden input fields give developers the ability to store additional information as part of the web form without making the data directly visible to the user. The <input type="hidden"> tag can carry the additional state information as part of the <form> tag inside an HTML document:

```
<form id="writing" method="post" action="writing.aspx">
   <input id="names" value="Dale Michalk Rob Cameron">
   <input id="task" value="write book">
   <input id="SessionNumber" type="hidden" value="234234222">
   <input id="progress" type="hidden" value="50%">
</form>
```

Naturally, the hidden form fields can be accessed in server-side code in the same way as the text form fields were previously, by using either the Request.Form or Request.Params collection. Hidden form variables do have some potential drawbacks:

- As with URL query string variables, programmers must manually track changes to hidden variables and emit values each time a page is rendered in order to maintain the user's state within the application.
- Although hidden fields are not immediately visible to the user, selecting View ➤ Source in the browser enables the user to see what information is available in hidden fields. In most cases, this may not be an issue, but it is important to be cognizant of this and either refrain from storing sensitive data or manually add an additional processing layer of encryption to prevent exposure.
- Storing a large amount of data in hidden variables can become a performance issue, depending on the amount of network bandwidth and processing available. Like the previous drawback, developers can manually add an additional processing layer that implements compression to minimize data size.

Despite these limitations, hidden form fields remain a popular method for developers to maintain application state. ASP.NET takes its cue from this and adds a layer of abstraction called view state on top of the HTML form hidden variable mechanism to make life easier on web developers wishing to take advantage of client-side state with a minimal amount of fuss and effort.

ViewState

As mentioned in the previous section, the ViewState server control state management technique builds on the hidden form field client-side method, taking advantage of its well documented benefits while minimizing its potential drawbacks. ViewState addresses hidden form variable limitations by providing built-in data management, compression, encoding, and tamper resistance, so web developers and control builders can focus on the application requirements and business logic.

In ASP.NET 2.0 and later, `ViewState` is greatly improved compared to .NET Framework 1.1 or earlier by a reduction in encoding size, which reduces the size of pages with `ViewState` enabled. Also, `ViewState` in ASP.NET 2.0 and later does a much better job of integrating with data controls like `GridView` by intelligently using `ViewState` when data controls are bound to declarative data source controls—meaning, if `ViewState` is enabled, ASP.NET 2.0 and later will not go back to the database to get data. However, if `ViewState` is disabled, ASP.NET 2.0 and later will automatically go back and bind to the data source. This functionality is building into the `DataBoundControl` base class.

Another improvement in ASP.NET 2.0 and later is control state, which allows a control to store important control-related data items required for proper function even if `ViewState` is disabled. We cover control state in more detail later in this chapter.

The StateBag Class and the IStateManager Interface

The client-side state management technique `ViewState` exists in the .NET Framework class hierarchy as a member property of the `System.Web.UI.Control` class called `ViewState`, of type `StateBag`, which implements a dictionary data structure to store name/value pairs. The `StateBag` class implements the interfaces in Table 3-3.

Table 3-3. *Interfaces Implemented by the StateBag Class*

Interface	Description
`ICollection`	Defines enumerators, synchronization methods, and size for collections
`IDictionary`	Specialized collection interface that implements a collection of name/value pairs
`IEnumerable`	Provides the enumerator for iteration over a collection
`IStateManager`	Defines the properties and methods required to support ViewState management in server controls

The interfaces `ICollection` and `IEnumerable` are standard interfaces used to give collection functionality to a class. `IDictionary` provides the name/value storage mechanism required when working with `ViewState`. `IStateManager` is the interface that handles all the tedious state maintenance functions during server-side processing and greatly contributes to the Visual Basic–like ease of programming model for ASP.NET web developers.

As you can see, the `IStateManager` interface is the most interesting interface implemented by the `StateBag` class, as it includes methods to load and save a control's data or state. Because all server controls descend from `System.Web.UI.Control`, the .NET Framework uses the methods and properties implemented by `IStateManager` to dehydrate controls before serialization into a hidden form field named `__VIEWSTATE`. Likewise, ASP.NET calls on `IStateManager` during postback to rehydrate server control objects for server-side processing.

State Data Management

Because both custom controls and the Page class inherit from Control, ViewState is easily accessible to the ASP.NET developer from either the web form or from within a custom control class. As described in the previous section, the type of the ViewState collection that is serialized into the __VIEWSTATE hidden form field is System.Web.UI.StateBag, a strongly typed dictionary data structure that stores name/value pairs with the value having a type that is either serializable or has a TypeConverter defined.

Native data types such as int, string, and so forth have default TypeConverters that provide string-to-value conversions, so no additional work is required on the part of the developer. In situations where a developer creates a custom type for use in a server control, we recommend that the developer create a TypeConverter class for the custom type in place of implementing ISerializable. The reason is that types that are only defined as serializable are slower and generate much larger ViewState than types that have a TypeConverter implemented. We discuss how to create a TypeConverter in Chapter 11.

An alternative to implementing a TypeConverter is to customize how property data is stored in ViewState. The System.Web.UI.Control class provides two methods for this purpose: SaveViewState and LoadViewState. As you would guess, these methods must be implemented in tandem.

Compression and Integrity

State information placed inside of the ViewState collection is kept separate for each control as well as from the web form itself. During page processing, ViewState data is converted into a hashed, compressed, and encoded blob that is streamed to the client as a hidden form field named __VIEWSTATE.

■ **Tip** To see what ViewState looks like on the client side, simply load one of the book's sample web forms (you can find them on the book's page on the Apress web site at http://www.apress.com) and select View ➤ Source in your web browser. You will find a hidden form field named __VIEWSTATE and its value.

The output that is sent to the browser by ViewState overcomes one of the big weaknesses of other client-side state systems whose values can be mimicked in an attempt to spoof the server. Any attempts to manipulate ViewState outside of the page's life cycle process will be detected by the ASP.NET, minimizing the possibility of tampering.

Ease of Use

Having a tamper-resistant, efficient state management technology is one thing, but what truly makes ViewState successful is how easy it is to put to work. Using ViewState is like using any of the collection types available in .NET. The following code snippet adds the value writebook with a key value of task:

```
ViewState["task"] = "writebook";
```

Accessing ViewState in this way results in a hidden form variable, like the following one, that contains not only the values loaded by all controls with ViewState enabled but also the data loaded in our example:

```
<input type="hidden" name="__VIEWSTATE" value="dDw2MDQ5NjY2NDk7dDxw... " />
```

Reading back the value is a simple process of accessing the ViewState collection when the form is posted back to the web server. ASP.NET checks the ViewState data for its hash value and ensures no unscheduled modifications have taken place prior to populating the collection:

```
string name = ViewState["task"];
```

As described previously, ViewState uses the well-known <input type="hidden" name="__VIEWSTATE"> HTML tag to hold the page's state data. No special browser techniques or proprietary mechanisms are required to work with ViewState.

The primary consideration with ViewState is the serialization process used to dehydrate and rehydrate state for each server control in the page's control tree. On a web form with either numerous server controls or controls with large amounts of data, the size of the __VIEWSTATE hidden variable can be large. Because ViewState data is transported over the wire for each round-trip, it's recommended that developers turn off ViewState for controls that don't need to retain state. This can greatly decrease the size of the generated ViewState transported with the HTML document. ViewState emissions are handled through the EnableViewState property that all controls inherit from System.Web.UI.Control. Developers need to be cognizant of this ability to disable ViewState when building server controls.

A Client State Workshop

Before jumping into server control development using client-side state, let's quickly review the different client-side state management techniques, as well as highlight how performing an HTTP GET or HTTP POST affects state. The ClientState.aspx web form demonstrates the process of working with the client side in general. It is a rather contrived but sufficient example with a single TextBox that provides the input device for storing a name on the client using a cookie, URL query string, hidden fields, and ViewState.

The web form has two buttons that can submit the page back to the web server using the HTTP POST mechanism. One button, Set State, causes the page to post back to the web server and change the name that is persisted to the client. The other button, Submit Page, posts the page back to the server without changing any state information. This button simply causes a round-trip to test the holding power of each of the state mechanisms. There is also a hyperlink on the page to test the use of the URL query string as a state-persistence device.

Figure 3-4 shows the web page generated from ClientState.aspx after an initial HTTP GET request from the browser. Listings 3-1 and 3-2 contain the .aspx file and code-behind class, respectively. One of this book's author's names is entered into the TextBox control in order to set the page up for saving that name via client-side state. The bottom portion of the web form has readouts for all the client-state mechanisms: URL strings, cookies, hidden variables, and ViewState. It shows the result of an attempt to read the state mechanism, which is initially blank because no state has been set just yet.

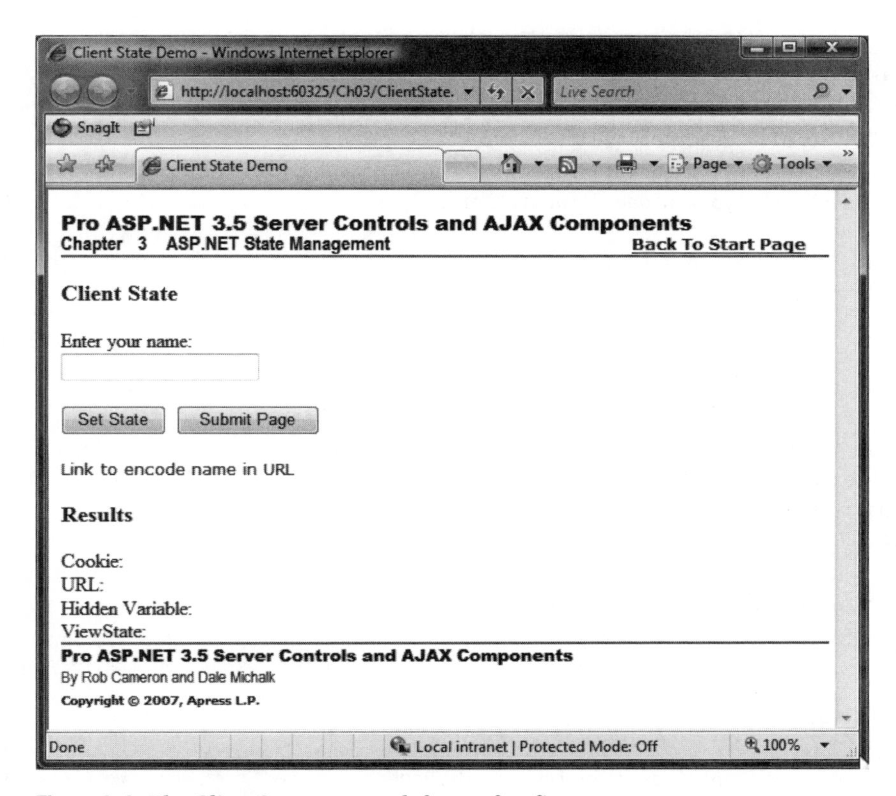

Figure 3-4. *The ClientState.aspx web form after first request*

Listing 3-1. *The ClientState Web Form .aspx File*

```
<%@ Page Language="C#"
MasterPageFile="~/MasterPage/ControlsBook2MasterPage.Master"
  AutoEventWireup="true" CodeBehind="ClientState.aspx.cs"
 Inherits="ControlsBook2Web.Ch03.ClientState"
  Title="Client State Demo" %>

<asp:Content ID="Content1" ContentPlaceHolderID="ChapterNumAndTitle" runat="server">
  <asp:Label ID="ChapterNumberLabel" runat="server"
  Width="14px">3</asp:Label>  <asp:Label
    ID="ChapterTitleLabel" runat="server" Width="360px">
    ASP.NET State Management</asp:Label>
</asp:Content>
<asp:Content ID="Content2" ContentPlaceHolderID="PrimaryContent" runat="server">
  <h3>
    Client State</h3>
  Enter your name:<br />
  <asp:TextBox ID="NameTextBox" runat="server"></asp:TextBox><br />
  <br />
```

```
  <asp:Button ID="SetStateButton" runat="server" Text="Set State"
  OnClick="SetStateButton_Click">
  </asp:Button> 
  <asp:Button ID="SubmitPageButton" runat="server"
  Text="Submit Page"></asp:Button><br />
  <input id="HiddenName" type="hidden" runat="server" />
  <br />
  <asp:HyperLink ID="URLEncodeLink" runat="server">
  Link to encode name in URL</asp:HyperLink><br />
  <br />
  <h3>
    Results</h3>
  Cookie:<asp:Label ID="CookieLabel" runat="server"></asp:Label><br />
  URL:<asp:Label ID="URLLabel" runat="server"></asp:Label><br />
  Hidden Variable:<asp:Label ID="HiddenLabel" runat="server"></asp:Label><br />
  ViewState:<asp:Label ID="ViewStateLabel" runat="server"></asp:Label><br />
</asp:Content>
```

Listing 3-2. *The ClientState Web Form Code-Behind Class File*

```
using System;

namespace ControlsBook2Web.Ch03
{
  public partial class ClientState : System.Web.UI.Page
  {
    protected void Page_Load(object sender, EventArgs e)
    {
      GetClientState();
    }

    protected void SetStateButton_Click(object sender, EventArgs e)
    {
      SetClientState();
    }

    private void SetClientState()
    {
      string name = NameTextBox.Text;

      // set the name Cookie value
      Response.Cookies["cookiename"].Value = name;

      // encode the name in the redirect URL
      URLEncodeLink.NavigateUrl = "ClientState.aspx?urlname=" + name;
```

```
      // put the name in the hidden variable
      HiddenName.Value = name;

      // put the name in ViewState
      ViewState["viewstatename"] = name;
    }

    private void GetClientState()
    {
      // check the cookiename Cookie
      CookieLabel.Text = "";
      if (Request.Cookies["cookiename"] != null)
        CookieLabel.Text = Request.Cookies["cookiename"].Value;

      // check the URL for urlname variable
      URLLabel.Text = "";
      if (Request.QueryString["urlname"] != null)
        URLLabel.Text = Request.Params["urlname"];

      // check the form data for hiddenname variable
      // Must use UniqueID to get correct HTML Form name
      HiddenLabel.Text = "";
      if (Context.Request.Form[HiddenName.UniqueID] != null)
        HiddenLabel.Text = Request.Form[HiddenName.UniqueID];

      // check the Viewstate for the viewstatename variable
      ViewStateLabel.Text = "";
      if (ViewState["viewstatename"] != null)
        ViewStateLabel.Text = ViewState["viewstatename"].ToString();
    }
  }
}
```

Clicking the Set State button submits the page via postback to ASP.NET, which retrieves the name gathered from the NameTextBox control on the ClientState.aspx web form and pushes it out to the client-state mechanisms we are interested in testing.

The page that renders after the server-side execution of Set State is complete contains the client state for the name entered into the NameTextBox control. The URL has the name embedded as part of the query string. If you click the link, it will force a read of the query string state, which allows the URL field at the bottom of the page a chance to show the value through this state mechanism. The web form has two hidden variables; one is populated with ViewState and used to hold the name entered by the user in the web form, as a developer would code using just hidden input tags. To see this, select View ➤ Source in the browser. Finally, the Cookie value is included in the HTTP response.

Interestingly, the URL fields at the bottom of the page are blank. Not until the next round-trip to the server does ASP.NET have a chance to access the current state and populate the fields at the bottom of the page. The reason for this is that when you click Set State, the Page_Load event fires first, which executes the GetClientState() helper method. GetClientState() loads the current values from the various state storage mechanisms into the labels on the bottom portion of the web form. Because the server-side click event `SetStateButton_Click` has not had a chance to fire just yet, the state loaded into the fields at the bottom of the web form by `GetClientState()` in `Page_Load` is the previous state, as shown in Figure 3-4. After the `Page_Load` event completes, `SetStateButton_Click` executes next, calling `SetClientState()`, which loads the value from the `TextBox` control into all the client-state mechanisms. The resulting page shows that all the state mechanisms are storing the value.

Now that the state has been set, clicking the Submit button one more time forces a round-trip to the server, executing the `Page_Load` event. This time around, the fields at the bottom of the page have a chance to pick up the current state in `GetClientState()` and display the expected values. The only difference between Figure 3-4 and Figure 3-5 is that the browser notices our hyperlink has a nonblank URL and displays the link text in blue underlined font.

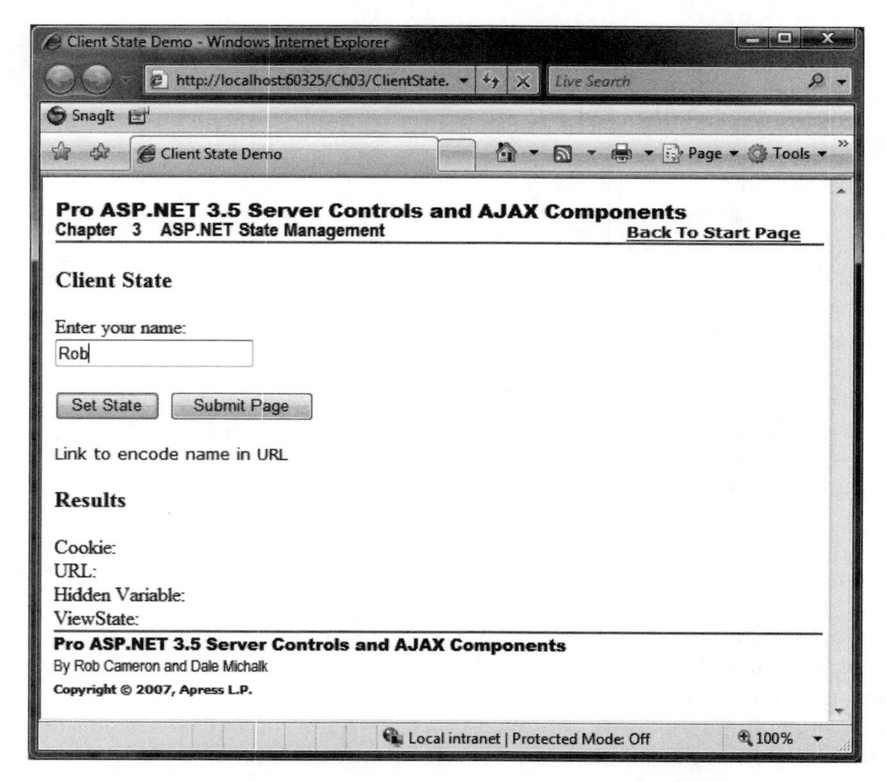

Figure 3-5. *The ClientState.aspx web form during the Set State button postback*

Reading the Client State

Click the Submit Page button to submit the web form back to the server one more time. There is no button-handling routine for this button on the server, so the only logic that executes is the `Page_Load` event handler. All this simple routine does is call `GetClientState()`. The `GetClientState()` routine pulls back values for all systems except the URL-encoding scheme, as shown in Figure 3-6.

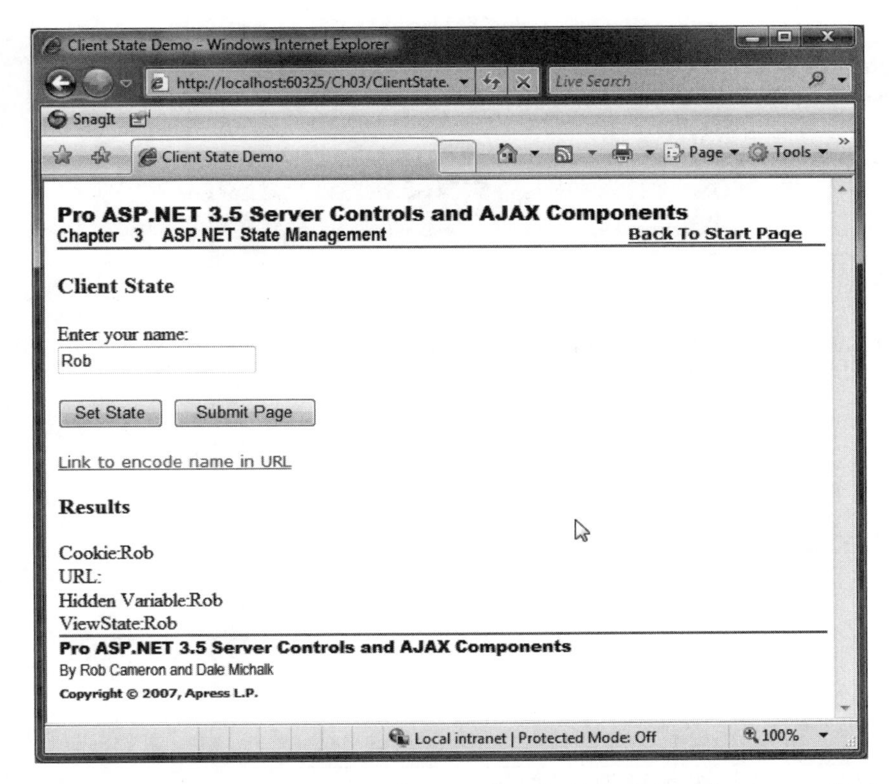

Figure 3-6. *The ClientState.aspx web form after the Submit Page button postback*

GetClientState() is careful when accessing the state collections; it checks for null values and sets the name to a blank string where appropriate. This provides more reliable code that is capable of operating under failure conditions. The following excerpt of the code from Listing 3-2 reads values from ViewState. See Listing 3-2 for the details on the code for the other state mechanisms.

```
// check the Viewstate for the viewstatename variable
ViewStateLabel.Text = "";
if (ViewState["viewstatename"] != null)
ViewStateLabel.Text = ViewState["viewstatename"].ToString();
```

Getting the URL State

The URL string did not display in the previous attempts, because we navigated to the same page through the postback mechanism enforced by the HtmlInputForm control and its <form> tag generation, which uses an HTTP POST. The URL string state mechanism is activated in our demonstration only through clicking the hyperlink on the web form.

Figure 3-7 displays the values from the URL string but loses the information that was available for our HTML hidden variable and ViewState. The reason for the change in behavior is a switch from an HTTP POST request using the postback mechanism to an HTTP GET request by clicking the hyperlink. Because we bypassed the form postback with an HTTP GET, all values based on HTML form information, such as hidden variables and ViewState, are lost. ViewState must go through the postback cycle to the original page it was produced from for it to work and give our controls the capability to remember state.

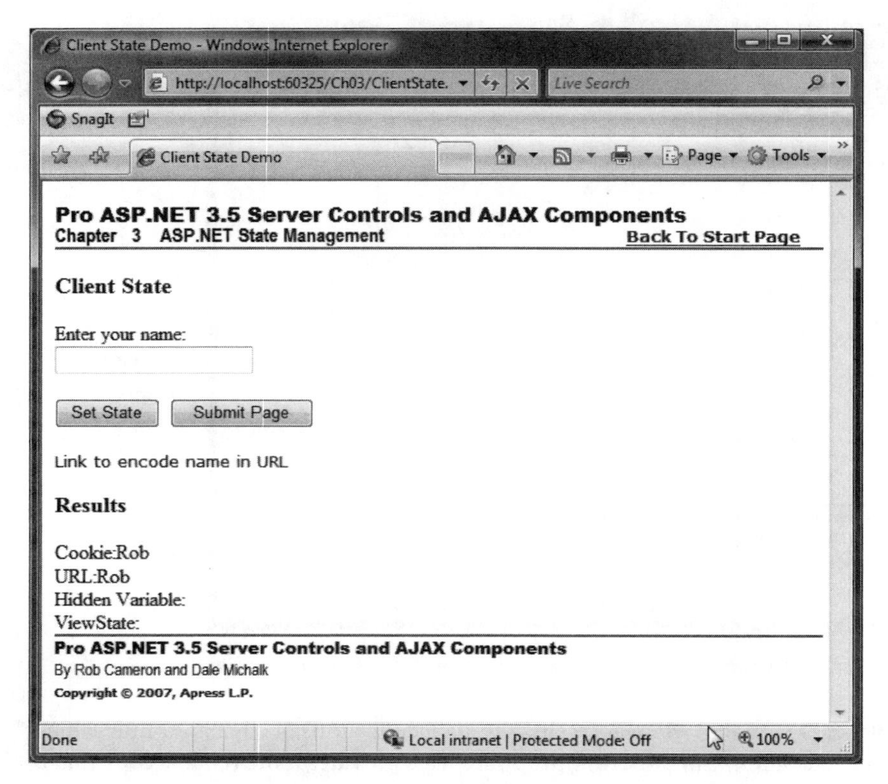

Figure 3-7. *The ClientState.aspx web form after hyperlink navigation*

ASP.NET Server Controls and State

Now that we have demonstrated a web form taking advantage of the various client-side state management techniques, we transition to using it inside server controls. Taking into account all the client-side state facilities available, we strongly recommended that you follow the lead of the prebuilt controls in ASP.NET and use ViewState and control state within your server controls. With extensive support in the ASP.NET framework, using ViewState in custom control development will greatly reduce development time and ensure consistent behavior. Likewise, using the new control state functionality in ASP.NET 2.0 and later helps ensure consistent server control behavior whether or not ViewState is enabled; we cover control state later in this chapter.

The StatelessLabel Server Control

The first label control we build here does not take advantage of any of the state mechanisms in ASP.NET as an example of working without state. StatelessLabel inherits from System.Web.UI.Control and provides a string Text property that it uses to render its content inside a <span>.

The Text property is mapped to a private field named text that is not persisted and is available only when the control is in memory on the web server. Listing 3-3 shows the code for the StatelessLabel server control.

Listing 3-3. *The StatelessLabel Class File*

```
using System;
using System.Web.UI;
using System.ComponentModel;

namespace ControlsBook2Lib.Ch03
{
  [ToolboxData("<{0}:statelesslabel runat=server></{0}:statelesslabel>"),
  DefaultProperty("Text")]
  public class StatelessLabel : Control
  {
    public string Text { get; set; }

    override protected void Render(HtmlTextWriter writer)
    {
      base.Render(writer);

      writer.RenderBeginTag(HtmlTextWriterTag.Span);
      writer.Write(Text);
      writer.RenderEndTag();
    }
  }
}
```

The StatefulLabel Server Control

To spiff up things and take advantage of ViewState, the second label control, StatefulLabel, has a different mechanism for storing the information passed to the Text property. It uses the ViewState collection to read/write the property information in its get and set methods. Listing 3-4 contains the source code for the StatefulLabel class file.

Listing 3-4. *The StatefulLabel Class File*

```
using System;
using System.Web.UI;
using System.ComponentModel;

namespace ControlsBook2Lib.Ch03
{
  [ToolboxData("<{0}:statefullabel runat=server></{0}:statefullabel>"),
  DefaultProperty("Text")]
```

```
  public class StatefulLabel : Control
  {
    public virtual string Text
    {
      get
      {
        object text = ViewState["Text"];
        if (text == null)
          return string.Empty;
        else
          return (string)text;
      }
      set
      {
        ViewState["Text"] = value;
      }
    }

    override protected void Render(HtmlTextWriter writer)
    {
      base.Render(writer);

      writer.RenderBeginTag(HtmlTextWriterTag.Span);
      writer.Write(Text);
      writer.RenderEndTag();
    }
  }
}
```

The get method for the Text property uses some guard code to correctly deal with the ViewState collection if the key we are looking for is not available. If the return value is null, it returns an empty string.

Returning an empty string is a good habit to get into, especially for control properties that are more complex than a primitive, such as a string or integer.

Comparing the Labels

Label Controls is a web form example that directly compares both the stateless and stateful controls in their use, or lack, of client-side state. The GUI layout setup is similar to the one we used for ClientState.aspx in the previous demonstration but changes the bottom portion of the web form layout to display the two label controls. Navigating to the web form URL directly renders the output shown in Figure 3-8. Listings 3-5 and 3-6 contain the .aspx page and code-behind class file for the Label Controls demonstration.

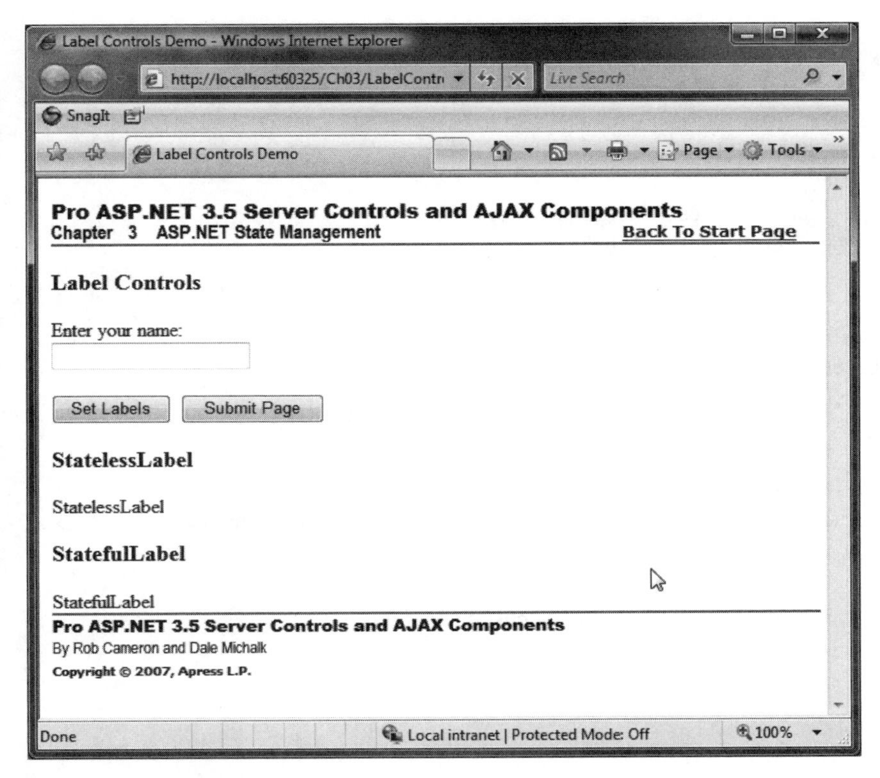

Figure 3-8. *LabelControls.aspx after the first request*

Listing 3-5. *The LabelControls Web Form .aspx Page File*

```
<%@ Page Language="C#" MasterPageFile="~/MasterPage/ControlsBook2MasterPage.Master"
  AutoEventWireup="true" CodeBehind="LabelControls.aspx.cs"
 Inherits="ControlsBook2Web.Ch03.LabelControls"
  Title="Label Controls Demo" %>

<%@ Register TagPrefix="apress" Namespace="ControlsBook2Lib.Ch03"
 Assembly="ControlsBook2Lib" %>
<asp:Content ID="Content1" ContentPlaceHolderID="ChapterNumAndTitle" runat="server">
  <asp:Label ID="ChapterNumberLabel" runat="server"
Width="14px">3</asp:Label>  <asp:Label
ID="ChapterTitleLabel" runat="server" Width="360px">
ASP.NET State Management</asp:Label>
</asp:Content>
<asp:Content ID="Content2" ContentPlaceHolderID="PrimaryContent" runat="server">
  <h3>
    Label Controls</h3>
  Enter your name:
```

```
  <br />
  <asp:TextBox ID="NameTextBox" runat="server"></asp:TextBox><br />
  <br />
  <asp:Button ID="SetLabelButton" runat="server" Text="Set Labels"
 OnClick="SetLabelButton_Click">
  </asp:Button> 
  <asp:Button ID="SubmitPageButton" runat="server"
  Text="Submit Page"></asp:Button><br />
  <br />
  <h3>
    StatelessLabel</h3>
  <apress:StatelessLabel ID="StatelessLabel1"
  Text="StatelessLabel" runat="server" />
  <br />
  <h3>
    StatefulLabel</h3>
  <apress:StatefulLabel ID="StatefulLabel1" Text="StatefulLabel" runat="server" />
</asp:Content>
```

Listing 3-6. *The LabelControls Web Form Code-Behind Class File*

```
using System;

namespace ControlsBook2Web.Ch03
{
  public partial class LabelControls : System.Web.UI.Page
  {
    protected void Page_Load(object sender, EventArgs e)
    {

    }

    protected void SetLabelButton_Click(object sender, EventArgs e)
    {
      StatelessLabel1.Text = "Set by " + NameTextBox.Text;
      StatefulLabel1.Text = "Set by " + NameTextBox.Text;
    }
  }
}
```

Setting the Label Control State

Click the Set Labels button to post the web page back to the server. The `SetLabelButton_Click` routine is executed by ASP.NET when the `SetLabelButton` button is notified that the HTML button it represents caused the postback.

`SetLabelButton_Click` has the simple job of setting the `Text` property of the `StatelessLabel` and `StatefulLabel` controls:

```
protected void SetLabelButton_Click(object sender, EventArgs e)
{
  StatelessLabel1.Text = "Set by " + NameTextBox.Text;
  StatefulLabel1.Text = "Set by " + NameTextBox.Text;
}
```

The output of the web form for these controls is identical, because they both render their contents into HTML based on the recently set Text property, as shown in Figure 3-9.

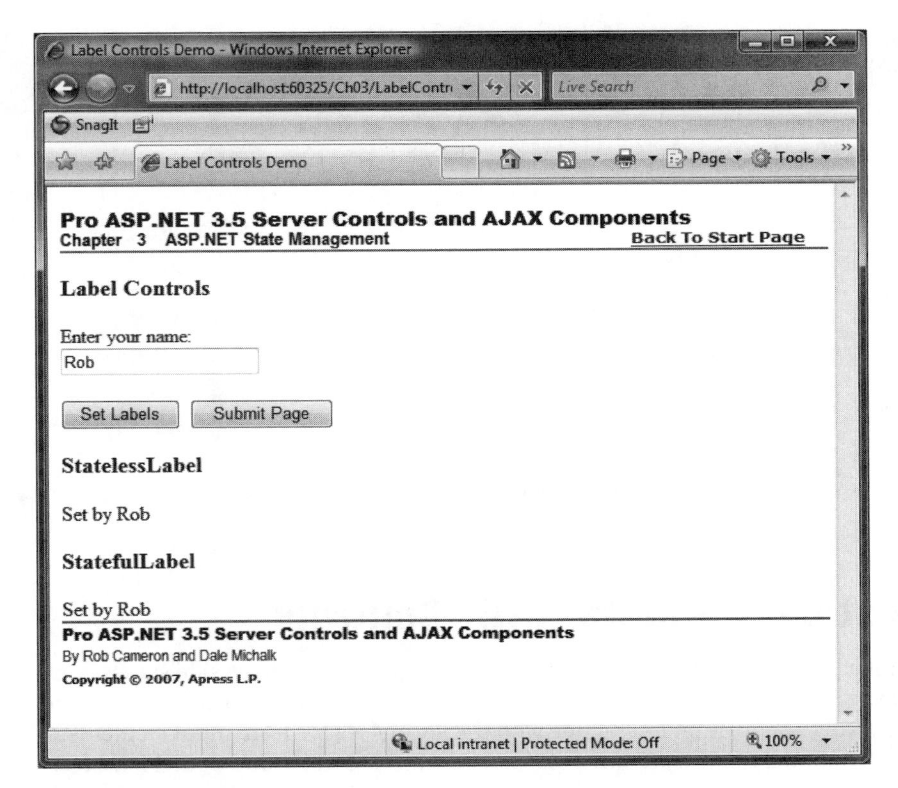

Figure 3-9. *LabelControls.aspx after the Set Labels button postback*

Testing Control ViewState

To test the state-saving features of ViewState and its impact on controls, click the Submit Page button. The SubmitPageButton control has no event-handling routines defined, and our Page_Load event handler is blank, so the net result of clicking the button is a recycling of the web form without any explicit web form code.

In this sample page, the only action in the controls is getting and setting properties during the page life cycle through postback. The controls are involved in regenerating their HTML content and the possibility of taking advantage of the ViewState that was posted back from the client. In Figure 3-10, you can see that the StatefulLabel control was able to remember its previous Text property value, while the StatelessLabel control reverted to the initial value set in its Text attribute as part of the .aspx page markup.

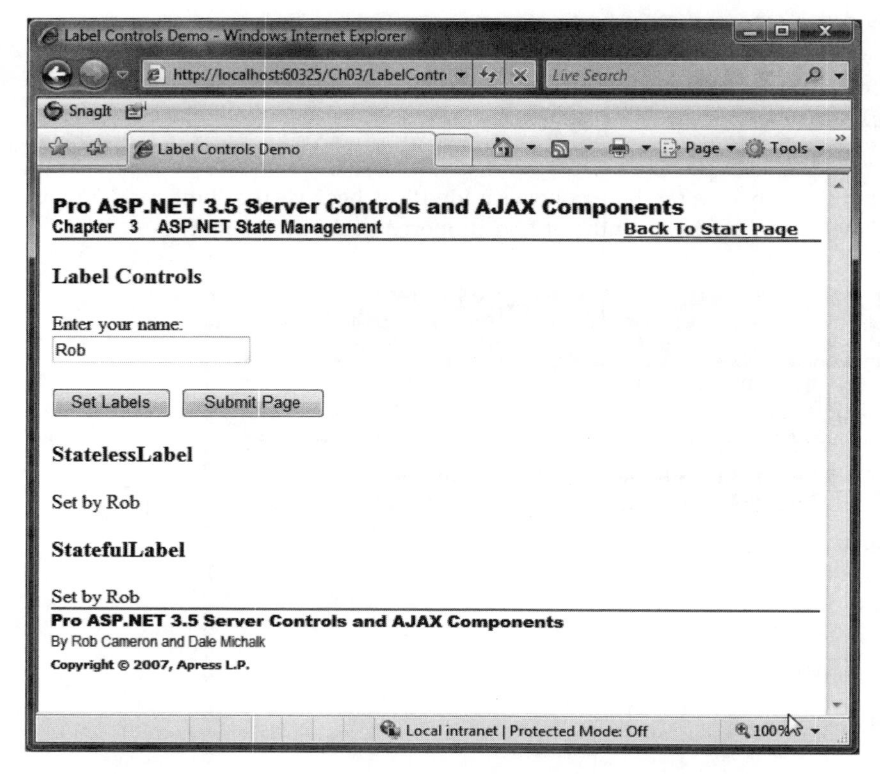

Figure 3-10. *LabelControls.aspx after the Submit Page button postback*

Form Post Data and ASP.NET Controls

The postback mechanism in ASP.NET provides a means of generating client-side state as well as the opportunity to receive input from the user. The first part of this chapter concentrated on client-side state. Now, we focus on interacting with the normal HTML form input elements.

Many controls model themselves after `<input>` tags and provide value-added features, such as remembering state and raising events to their clients when internal state changes occur. To work with the HTTP `POST` mechanism to retrieve data, one implementation would be for the client to simply read all of the form variables directly. Fortunately, ASP.NET provides a more organized mechanism to server controls that implement the `IPostBackDataHandler` interface.

The IPostBackDataHandler Interface

The `IPostBackDataHandler` interface is the recommended method to read form post data from a control in ASP.NET without having to use the `Page` class and its `Request` object.

Note In general, we do not recommend that you directly access the Request or Response object provided by the Page class (HttpContext), as this would interfere with normal page processing. If you need to write to the output stream, use the HtmlTextWriter class for this purpose.

IPostBackDataHandler also provides a framework to allow the control to raise change events at a later point in time if the state of the control has changed sufficiently to warrant such an action. Listing 3-7 shows the interface definition for IPostBackDataHandler. LoadPostData is the interface method we concentrate on in this section, as it provides the means to retrieve data posted to the web server.

Listing 3-7. *The IPostBackDataHandler Interface Definition*

```
public interface IPostBackDataHandler{
   public bool LoadPostData(string postDataKey,
                            NameValueCollection postCollection);
   public void RaisePostDataChangedEvent();
}
```

On a postback of a web form to the web server, the ASP.NET framework searches the posted form values for matches between the corresponding id of the form element and the UniqueID property of the matching control. It then calls the LoadPostData() method for each control where there is a match to give the control a chance to retrieve its posted data. The UniqueID property of a control is the same as the ID value. The ID value is determined by its value in the .aspx page for a control. As an example, the following StatefulLabel control tag would have an ID and UniqueID property value equal to StatefulLabel1:

```
<apress:StatefulLabel id="StatefulLabel1" Text="StatelessLabel" runat="server" />
```

The two id properties need to differ only when working with composite controls that may contain multiple versions of the same control definition via templates. However, they are still required to have a way to uniquely identify themselves to ASP.NET. We examine how the INamingContainer interface solves this problem in Chapter 5.

The return value from LoadPostData() provides a means for a control to raise a state change event at a later point in time. If you return true in your implementation of LoadPostData in your server control, the ASP.NET framework will call your RaisePostDataChangedEvent() method further down in the page processing life cycle. If you return false, ASP.NET will skip the callback notification for your control.

The Textbox Control

A commonly used HTML form input element is the <input type="text"> tag. The ASP.NET framework provides controls that render this type of tag, including System.Web.UI.HtmlControls.HtmlInputText and System.Web.UI.WebControls.TextBox. We reinvent the wheel here (see Listing 3-8) to show you how these controls use ViewState and work with the postback data submitted from a web form.

Listing 3-8. *The Textbox Class File*

```
using System;
using System.Web;
using System.Web.UI;
using System.Collections.Specialized;
using System.ComponentModel;

namespace ControlsBook2Lib.Ch03
{
   [ToolboxData("<{0}:textbox runat=server></{0}:textbox>"),
   DefaultProperty("Text")]
   public class Textbox : Control, IPostBackDataHandler
   {
       public virtual string Text
      {
         get
         {
            object text = ViewState["Text"];
            if (text == null)
               return string.Empty;
            else
               return (string) text;
         }
         set
         {
            ViewState["Text"] = value;
         }
      }

      public bool LoadPostData(string postDataKey,
         NameValueCollection postCollection)
      {
         string postedValue = postCollection[postDataKey];
         Text = postedValue;
         return false;
      }

      public virtual void RaisePostDataChangedEvent()
      {

      }

      override protected void Render(HtmlTextWriter writer)
      {
         Page.VerifyRenderingInServerForm(this);

         base.Render(writer);
```

```
            // write out the <INPUT type="text"> tag
            writer.Write("<INPUT type=\"text\" name=\"");
            writer.Write(this.UniqueID);
            writer.Write("\" value=\"" + this.Text + "\" />");
        }
    }
}
```

The Textbox control in Listing 3-8 inherits from System.Web.UI.Control and reuses the same Text property ViewState handling from our previous StatefulLabel control class. This provides the control all the memory it needs to rehydrate itself completely.

The Render() method override has to do a little more work by inserting the UniqueID and Text properties of our control into the output, along with some quote-character escapes in the string. The UniqueID property is used by ASP.NET to identify our control and retrieve its data from the postback.

Notice the call to VerifyRenderingInServerForm() in the Render() method. Developers should call this method when building a server control that requires rendering inside a <form runat="server"> tag. ASP.NET will throw an exception if a developer or user attempts to put such a control outside an HTML <form> tag.

The IPostBackDataHandler interface is implemented by our LoadPostData() and RaisePostDataChangedEvent() methods. RaisePostDataChangedEvent() is blank, because we are not emitting events from our control based on state changes, but it still must be present to satisfy the terms of the interface. In the next chapter, we go further into raising our own events and examine what kind of code you would normally put into the RaisePostDataChangedEvent().

LoadPostData() has the necessary logic to read the information posted by our <input type="text"> tag rendered in the HTML document. LoadPostData() uses the passed-in key to read from the postCollection collection passed into the routine. The type of the collection is NameValueCollection, so you can expect a string value to be passed back when you access the data with your key.

Once we pull out the data, we store it immediately in ViewState via the Text property so the control can remember what was sent to it as well as render the correct HTML for the <input> tag with the value filled in upon return to the browser. The LoadPostData() routine closes by returning false, because it does not need to have RaisePostDataChangedEvent() called, as no events are implemented.

Using the Textbox Control

The Postback Data web form is identical to the previous Label Controls demonstration except for removal of the ASP.NET TextBox control and substitution of the one we just created. It has the button setup you have become familiar with: one button sets the value of the labels, and the other button recycles the form to exercise ViewState. Because the Textbox control receives its own postback data, we do not need to set its value in the code-behind class explicitly or worry about maintaining its state.

The initial page in Figure 3-11 looks identical to the previous web form that demonstrated our labels. Our Textbox control performs admirably well as a substitute for the ASP.NET built-in version of the control. Listings 3-9 and 3-10 contain the source code for this demonstration.

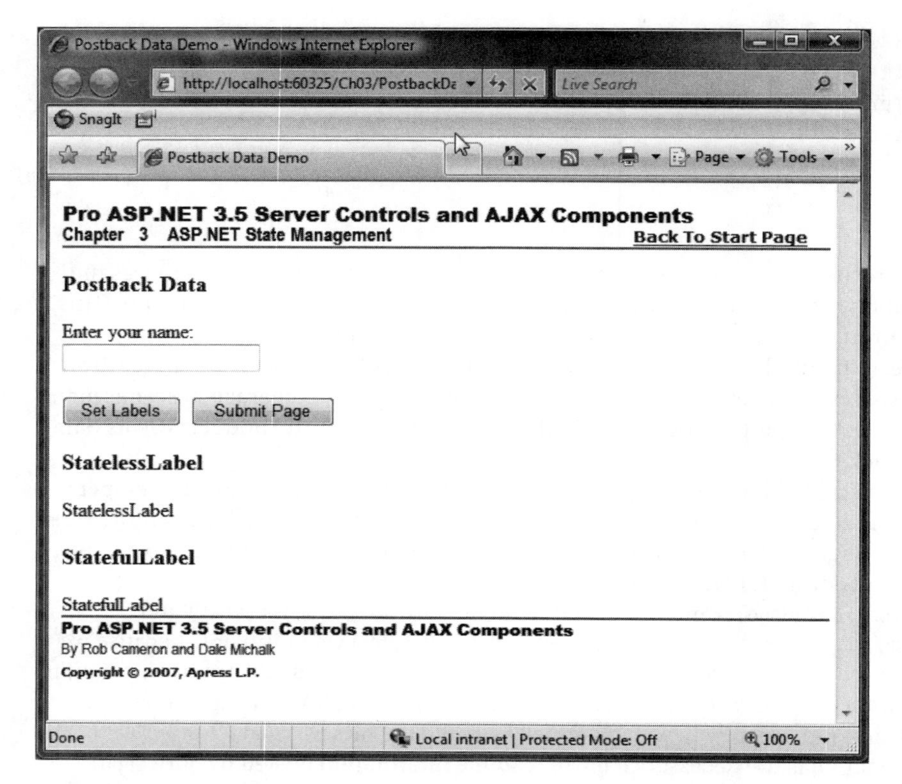

Figure 3-11. *PostbackData.aspx after the first request*

Listing 3-9. *The Postback Data Web Form .aspx File*

```
<%@ Page Language="C#" MasterPageFile="~/MasterPage/ControlsBook2MasterPage.Master"
  AutoEventWireup="true" CodeBehind="PostbackData.aspx.cs"
  Inherits="ControlsBook2Web.Ch03.PostbackData"
  Title="Postback Data Demo" %>

<%@ Register TagPrefix="apress" Namespace="ControlsBook2Lib.Ch03"
Assembly="ControlsBook2Lib" %>
<asp:Content ID="Content1" ContentPlaceHolderID="ChapterNumAndTitle" runat="server">
  <asp:Label ID="ChapterNumberLabel" runat="server"
  Width="14px">3</asp:Label>  <asp:Label
  ID="ChapterTitleLabel" runat="server" Width="360px">
   ASP.NET State Management</asp:Label>
</asp:Content>
```

```
<asp:Content ID="Content2" ContentPlaceHolderID="PrimaryContent" runat="server">
  <h3>
    Postback Data</h3>
  Enter your name:<br />
  <apress:Textbox ID="NameTextBox" runat="server">
  </apress:Textbox>
  <br />
  <br />
  <asp:Button ID="SetLabelButton" runat="server" Text=
"Set Labels" OnClick="SetLabelButton_Click">
  </asp:Button> 
  <asp:Button ID="SubmitPageButton" runat="server"
  Text="Submit Page"></asp:Button><br />
  <br />
  <h3>
    StatelessLabel</h3>
  <apress:StatelessLabel ID="StatelessLabel1" runat="server" Text="StatelessLabel">
  </apress:StatelessLabel>
  <br />
  <h3>
    StatefulLabel</h3>
  <apress:StatefulLabel ID="StatefulLabel1" runat="server" Text="StatefulLabel">
  </apress:StatefulLabel>
</asp:Content>
```

Listing 3-10. *The Postback Data Web Form Code-Behind Class File*

```
using System;

namespace ControlsBook2Web.Ch03
{
  public partial class PostbackData : System.Web.UI.Page
  {
    protected void Page_Load(object sender, EventArgs e)
    {

    }

    protected void SetLabelButton_Click(object sender, EventArgs e)
    {
      StatelessLabel1.Text = "Set by " + NameTextBox.Text;
      StatefulLabel1.Text = "Set by " + NameTextBox.Text;
    }
  }
}
```

To test the page, click the Set Labels button on the web form to generate a postback to the web server. The button-click code in the code-behind class file sets the two label controls' `Text` properties. The postback itself gives our `Textbox` control the opportunity to receive data from the HTML form and set its `Text` property in its `LoadPostData()` implementation without any additional work needed in the test `.aspx` page. The emitted HTML control from the `Textbox` `Render()` method also sets the value of the `<input type="text">` tag, as shown in Figure 3-12.

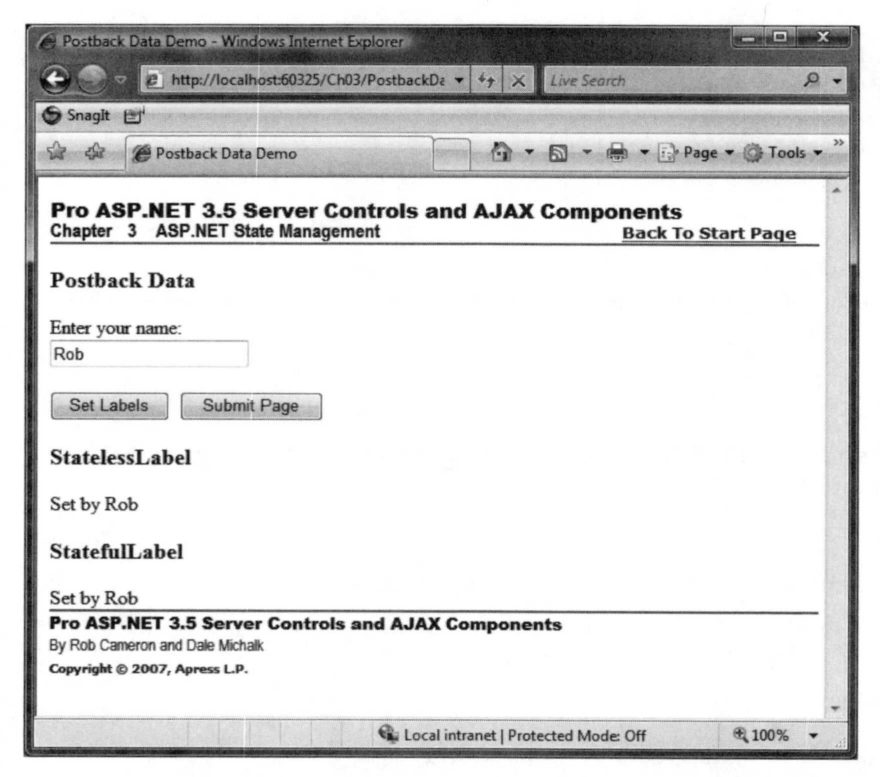

Figure 3-12. *PostbackData.aspx after the first postback via the SetLabelButton control*

Next, click the Submit Page button to test the `ViewState` capabilities of the label controls and submit the `Textbox` data to the `Textbox` control yet again via another postback. The net result is that one label control can read from `ViewState`, and the other control reverts to its initial value, as shown in Figure 3-13.

The use of `ViewState` for our `Textbox` control was not really necessary. A control based on an `<input>` tag has built-in state management within the ASP.NET framework. The posted data of the tag is always returned to the control via `LoadPostData()`. However, we put the extra work here with `ViewState` to good use in the next chapter, which covers server control events. The control will be extended to take the value persisted in `ViewState` and check it against the post-back data in order to raise a state change event.

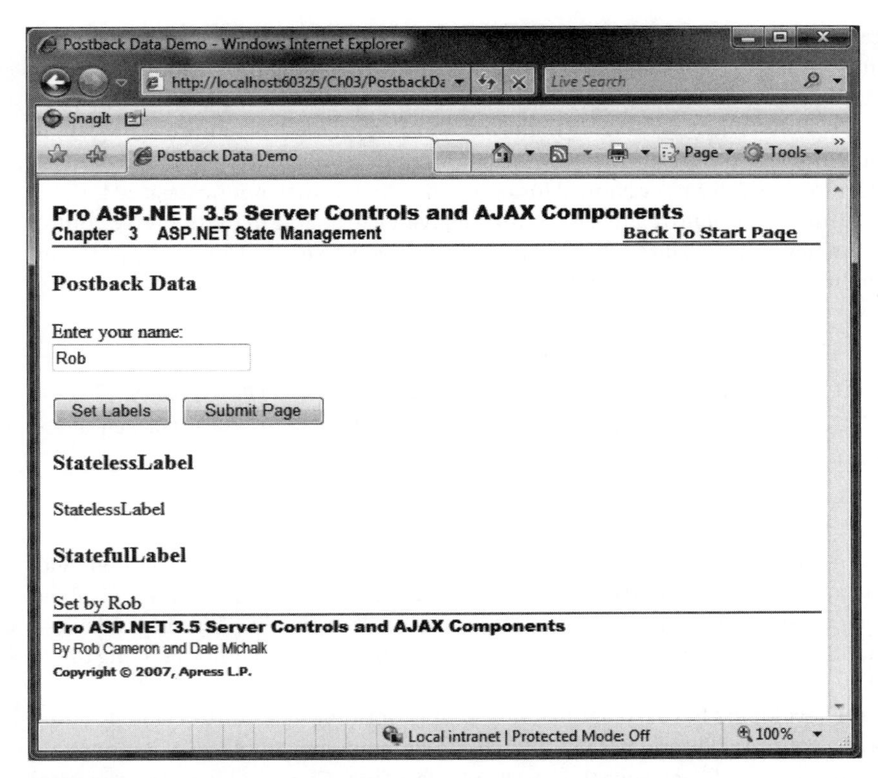

Figure 3-13. *PostbackData.aspx after the second postback via the SubmitPageButton control*

In the next section, we cover the new ASP.NET 2.0 and later control state functionality.

ASP.NET Control State

Control state was briefly discussed in the preceding `ViewState` section primarily because control state was added to ASP.NET 2.0 and later to provide more flexibility to server control developers. Control state allows a server control developer to maintain non-user-related state data between page post back cycles to still have correct control behavior even when the developer user disables `ViewState`.

ViewState Is Now Application User State

`ViewState` provides a very convenient way to maintain state in an application. The one drawback to `ViewState` is that it transports the page state down to the user's browser on every round-trip. This can lead to performance issues on busy web sites with complex web forms. ASP.NET developers know to disable `ViewState` when not required or when redundant. For example, enabling `ViewState` on a `DataGrid` control that retrieves fresh data on each request is redundant, because the data is retrieved and rendered as well as persisted in ViewState, essentially, it's transmitted twice. In ASP.NET 1.1, ViewState is an all or nothing proposition, meaning, if you disable ViewState for an entire page, it reduces functionality for some built-in server controls like DataGrid. Behaviors like paging in the DataGrid server control require ViewState to be enabled to function correctly. This had an effect of forcing web page developers to enable ViewState in order to have full server control functionality when it may not be desired.

In ASP.NET 2.0 and later, state related to control behavior like paging in the GridView control can be stored in the new control state functionality. This allows server controls to support core control functionality without requiring that ViewState be enabled.

■ **Caution** The DataGrid control has not been redesigned to use control state. Luckily, ASP.NET 2.0 and later has the new GridView control, which does take advantage of control state as well as other enhancements that DataGrid does not.

Control state operations, similar to ViewState, store control state in the same hidden field; with control state appended to the end of the ViewState data. However, if ViewState is disabled for the individual control or the whole page, control state is still persisted. This allows developers to store state related to basic control functionality in control state without having to enable ViewState.

Server control developers have a responsibility to appropriately use control state for the behavioral state of a control only, and not use it for all states including content. To demonstrate a good use of control state, we'll enhance the TextBox3d class from Chapter 2 to support control state for its Enable3D property, so ViewState is not required but the control still functions as expected without ViewState enabled.

New TextBox3d Demonstration Web Form

Let's copy the TextBox3d class into the ControlsBook2Lib.Ch03 namespace as our starting point for updating the server control to support control state for the Enable3D property. We'll also copy the demonstration page for the original TextBox3d control and update it to include an instance of our new version of TextBox3d that supports control state. Figure 3-14 shows the TextBox3DControlStateDemo web form at design time.

When this web form is run with the EnableViewState property on the page or on both controls set to true, the Toggle3d button dutifully toggles the Enable3D property on both controls, and pressing the Submit button results in the expected postback with state maintained for both controls.

If the EnableViewState property on the page or on the controls is set to false, clicking the Toggle3d button will enable the Enable3D property on both controls for that postback. However, the setting of true does not persist between the Submit button clicks; instead, the value reverts to the default value of false. Listings 3-11 and 3-12 have the code for the TextBox3DControlStateDemo web form.

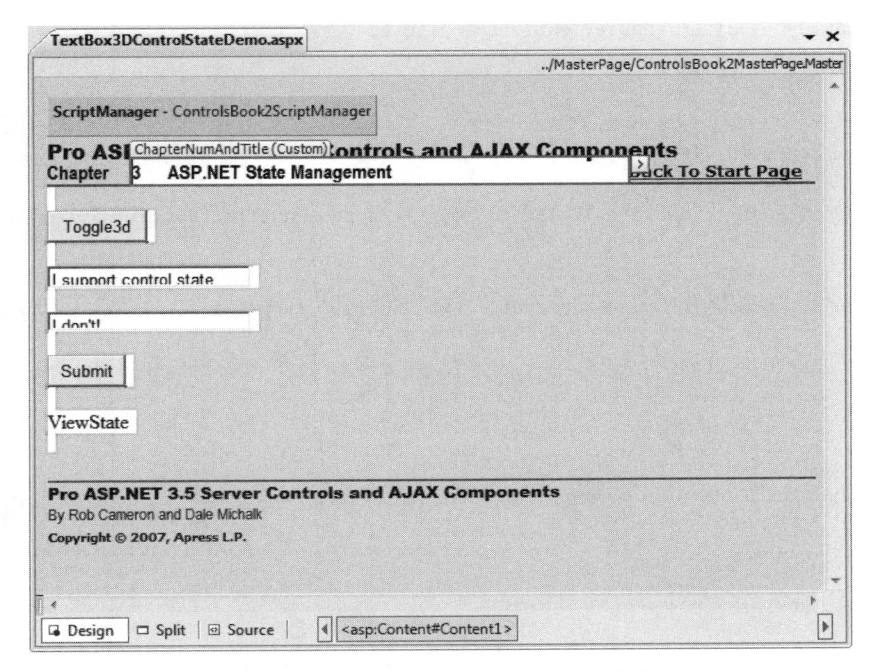

Figure 3-14. *TextBox3DControlStateDemo web form at design time*

Listing 3-11. *The TextBox3DControlStateDemo Web Form .aspx File*

```
<%@ Page Language="C#" MasterPageFile="~/MasterPage/ControlsBook2MasterPage.Master"
  AutoEventWireup="true" CodeBehind="TextBox3DControlStateDemo.aspx.cs"
  Inherits="ControlsBook2Web.Ch03.TextBox3DControlStateDemo"
  Title="Control State Demo" %>

<%@ Register TagPrefix="apressCh02" Namespace="ControlsBook2Lib.Ch02"
Assembly="ControlsBook2Lib" %>
<%@ Register TagPrefix="apressCh03" Namespace="ControlsBook2Lib.Ch03"
Assembly="ControlsBook2Lib" %>
<asp:Content ID="Content1" ContentPlaceHolderID="ChapterNumAndTitle" runat="server">
  <asp:Label ID="ChapterNumberLabel" runat="server"
Width="14px">3</asp:Label>  <asp:Label
    ID="ChapterTitleLabel" runat="server" Width="360px">
ASP.NET State Management</asp:Label>
</asp:Content>
<asp:Content ID="Content2" ContentPlaceHolderID="PrimaryContent" runat="server">
  <br />
  <asp:Button ID="buttonToggle3d" runat="server" Text="Toggle3d"
  OnClick="buttonToggle3d_Click" /><br />
  <br />
  <apressCh03:TextBox3d ID="Textbox3CtrlState" runat="server" Width="159px"
```

```
Height="18px" Enable3D="False" EnableViewState="False">I
  support control state</apressCh03:TextBox3d>
  <br />
  <br />
  <apressCh02:TextBox3d ID="TextBox3dBasic" runat="server"
  Width="159px" Height="16px"
    Enable3D="False" EnableViewState="False">I don't!</apressCh02:TextBox3d>
  <br />
  <br />
  <asp:Button ID="ButtonSubmit" runat="server" Text="Submit" /><br />
  <br />
  <asp:Label ID="LabelViewState" runat="server" Text="ViewState"></asp:Label><br />
  <br />
</asp:Content>
```

Listing 3-12. *The TextBox3DControlStateDemo Web Form .aspx File*

```
using System;

namespace ControlsBook2Web.Ch03
{
  public partial class TextBox3DControlStateDemo : System.Web.UI.Page
  {
    protected void Page_Load(object sender, EventArgs e)
    {
      LabelViewState.Text = "ViewState Enabled = " +
Textbox3CtrlState.EnableViewState.ToString();
    }

    protected void buttonToggle3d_Click(object sender, EventArgs e)
    {
      Textbox3CtrlState.Enable3D = !Textbox3CtrlState.Enable3D;
      TextBox3dBasic.Enable3D = !TextBox3dBasic.Enable3D;
    }
  }
}
```

In the next section, we cover how we added support for control state to the `TextBox3D` custom server control.

Adding Control State to TextBox3D

The first step is to override the control's `OnInit()` member to notify the page that control state is required for our new and improved `TextBox3D` control:

```
protected override void OnInit(EventArgs e)
{
  base.OnInit(e);
  Page.RegisterRequiresControlState(this);
}
```

Next, the Enable3D property is updated to no longer use ViewState and instead store the Enable3D property using the new C# 3.0 property declaration syntax:

```
[DescriptionAttribute("Set to true for 3d appearance"), DefaultValue("True")]
public bool Enable3D {get; set; }
```

The Enable3D property is saved and loaded by overriding the control's SaveControlState() and LoadControlState() (described later) to save the value and load the value for the _enable3D private member variable. This enables the new and improved TextBox3D class to maintain the value of the Enable3D property when ViewState disabled. The source code for the control state-aware version of TextBox3D is shown in Listing 3-13.

Listing 3-13. *The TextBox3D with a Control State Class File*

```
using System;
using System.Web.UI;
using System.Web.UI.WebControls;
using System.ComponentModel;
using System.Drawing;

namespace ControlsBook2Lib.Ch03
{
  [ToolboxData("<{0}:textbox3d runat=server></{0}:textbox3d>"),
  ToolboxBitmap(typeof(ControlsBook2Lib.Ch03.TextBox3d),
  "ControlsBook2Lib.Ch02.TextBox3d.bmp")]
  public class TextBox3d : TextBox// Inherit from rich control
  {
    public TextBox3d()
    {
      Enable3D = true;
    }

    // Custom property to set 3D appearance
    [DescriptionAttribute("Set to true for 3d appearance"), DefaultValue("True")]
    public bool Enable3D {get; set; }

    protected override void Render(HtmlTextWriter output)
    {
      // Add DHTML style attribute
      if (Enable3D)
        output.AddStyleAttribute("FILTER", "progid:DXImageTransform.Microsoft.
       dropshadow(OffX=2, OffY=2, Color='gray', Positive='true'");
```

```
        base.Render(output);
    }

    //Notify the page that control state is required
    protected override void OnInit(EventArgs e)
    {
        base.OnInit(e);
        Page.RegisterRequiresControlState(this);
    }

    protected override object SaveControlState()
    {
        object obj = base.SaveControlState();
        if (_enable3D != false)
        {
            if (obj != null)
            {
                return new Pair(obj, _enable3D);
            }
            else
            {
                return (_enable3D);
            }
        }
        else
        {
            return obj;
        }
    }

    protected override void LoadControlState(object state)
    {
        if (state != null)
        {
            Pair p = state as Pair;
            if (p != null)
            {
                base.LoadControlState(p.First);
                _enable3D = (bool)p.Second;
            }
            else
            {
                if (state is bool)
                {
                    _enable3D = (bool)state;
                }
```

```
        else
        {
          base.LoadControlState(state);
        }
      }
    }
  }
 }
}
```

An instance of the new control's state-aware version maintains state and looks 3-D when ViewState is disabled, while the old version that relied on ViewState for all state information does not look 3-D, as shown in Figure 3-15.

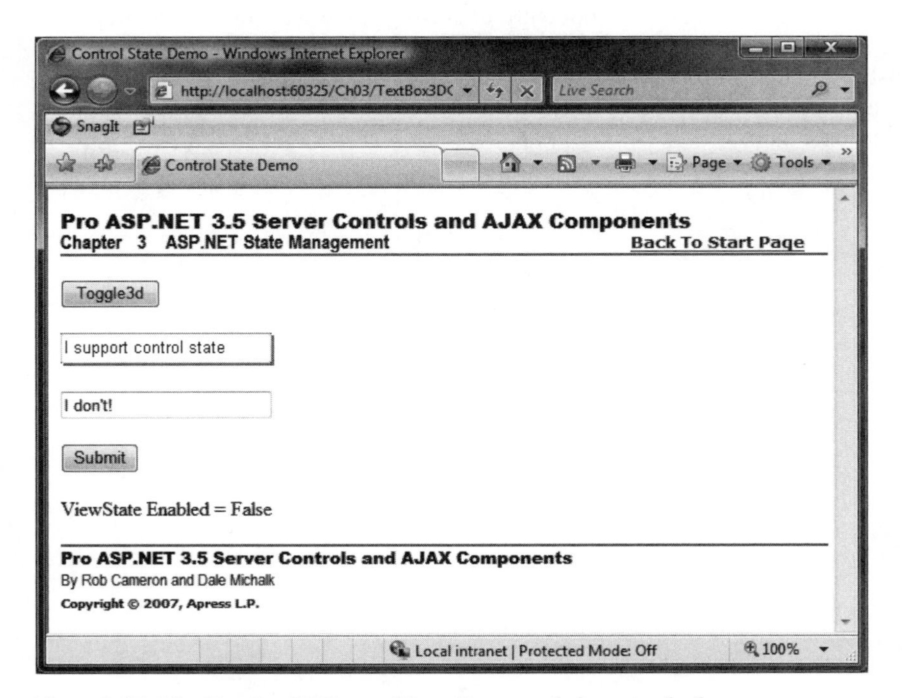

Figure 3-15. *The TextBox3DControlStateDemo web form in the browser*

Summary

Client-side state takes on four forms in ASP.NET: URL strings, cookies, HTML hidden form variables, and ViewState. HttpContext bundles together the important classes in ASP.NET for working with the request/response cycle of a web form in ASP.NET, including Session and Application server-side state mechanisms. Controls access the HttpContext class through the Context property they inherit from System.Web.UI.Control.

Variables in URL strings can be accessed through the QueryString or Params collection properties attached to the HttpRequest class. Cookies can be manipulated via the Request.Cookies or Response.Cookies collections attached to the Page class. HTML form hidden variables are accessible through the Form and QueryString properties attached to the HttpRequest class.

ViewState is a client-side state management technology built on top of the hidden HTML form variable state management technique. It abstracts the details of managing state for web form and server control programmers. ViewState is manipulated through the ViewState property available to all controls through inheritance from System.Web.UI.Control. ViewState requires the postback system, where a web form always executes an HTTP POST back to the same page. This allows all controls to read their previous states and provide memory in the application for server-side page processing.

Control state is a new feature in ASP.NET 2.0 and later that allows server controls to maintain critical control-related state when ViewState is disabled. This allows web form developers to decide whether to enable ViewState or not without loosing any server control functionality.

IPostBackDataHandler is the interface a control implements to receive HTML form's post data from a postback. The control must emit an <input> tag with its UniqueID property to be called by the framework. LoadPostData() is the method in IPostBackDataHandler that allows a control to read its post data.

CHAPTER 4

The WebControl Base Class and Control Styles

The ability to configure how a web page renders its HTML elements is an essential requirement of any web development model. As you would expect, the .NET Framework and ASP.NET 3.5 provide a rich architecture to support styling of web page elements through server controls on the web form.

In this chapter, we introduce a new server control construction model and build several custom server controls that inherit from `WebControl` (instead of `Control`) as a means to examine how to customize control styling using the `System.Web.UI.WebControls.Style` class, as well as a means to introduce the more powerful rendering model provided by the `WebControl` class.

In the final portion of the chapter, we discuss how to customize ViewState storage to preserve any applied styling and we show how to override the `Style` property to support your own customized style class for further customization of appearance. This section also highlights the benefits the strongly typed styling mechanism provided by ASP.NET.

Customizing the Appearance of Controls

Controls have a tough crowd to please. Programmers want them to be powerful, easy to use, robust, high performing, and fully customizable in their look and feel. Not a short list by any means. The last item, look and feel, garners most of the attention. After all, who cares what the control does on the inside if the HTML it produces is a pain to configure or is rigidly fixed to a certain output? Because many controls will be distributed to their consumer as an assembly, without source code, a customizable look and feel is a requirement.

Controls based on `System.Web.UI.WebControls.WebControl` benefit from a wonderful amount of prebuilt functionality to customize themselves with Cascading Style Sheet (CSS) styling. Controls of type `WebControl` are also smart enough to appropriately render HTML tags for browsers that support HTML 3.2 so that many of the style features are not lost in down-level browsers.

HTML: Content and Appearance

The HTML document that renders in your favorite browser has two core aspects to its makeup. The first is the textual content placed in the document—the information that users seek. The second is the appearance and layout of the content on the page. The style of the document determines whether the text is a certain font, is italicized, or has a particular color. Style also involves how information is laid out on the page, which determines the position and flow of text and other content such as images.

Styling Using Tags

HTML was invented to provide access to textual information that can be easily navigated and cross-referenced via hyperlinks. Commercialization of the Internet drove the need for rich HTML content, and the ensuing browser competition generated strong demand for styling capability. The initial wave of style support came in the form of tags that would modify the output of text or attributes such as color. The `<font>`, `<b>`, and `<i>` tags are a perfect example of the style tags added to HTML.

The following piece of HTML displays text using an Arial font with bold and italic styling:

```
<font face="Arial" color="blue">
  <b><i>This text is Bold, Italic Blue Text</i></b>
</font>
```

Layout tags such as `<center>` and `<table>` can also be considered part of the style of the document. Originally designed to display data in a tabular format, these tags have been co-opted for layout purposes by web designers. Most of the HMTL sites you see on the Web use the `<table>` tag to lay out content. Unfortunately, tables render differently in different browsers and much tweaking is required to get them "just right." Having a more precise layout mechanism would go a long way toward reducing the amount of work needed.

Another unfortunate side effect of using style tags to manage the appearance of an HTML document is tag maintenance. Modifying `<font>` tags scattered throughout a complex HTML document, let alone an entire site, is an error-prone and time-consuming undertaking. Luckily, as the Internet has evolved, so have the technologies used to present content to web surfers. One such technological advancement is the topic of the next section: CSS, which permits separation of content from styling and layout.

Styling Using Cascading Style Sheets

CSS technology permits web developers to separate the concerns of HTML content from its appearance by defining a system for applying styling rules to informational content. The heart of CSS is a set of style properties that are defined separately from the content. CSS can be defined inline on an HTML tag or defined in a separate file with an extension of `.css`. Here is an example CSS class that would apply to the `<title>` tag for a web form:

```
.title {
  padding: 0;
  border-bottom: 0;
  margin: 0;
  font-size: 22px;
}
```

If the CSS class is stored in a separate file, the file would need to be referenced in the web form <head> tag using a <link> tag like this:

```
<link href="ListsStyleSheet.css" rel="stylesheet" type="text/css" />
```

The syntax for a CSS style property is simple. It consists of a property name followed by a colon (:) and then the value of that property. Multiple properties are separated by semicolons (;). The following style properties specify that the textual content be displayed in blue Arial font with bold and italic effects:

```
<span style="font-family: Arial; color: Blue;  font-weight:bold;
font-style:italic;">This text is Bold, Italic Blue Text</span>
```

Contrast this with the use of the <font>, <b>, and <i> tags in the previous section to describe the same textual styling. If the style properties are not defined inline with the HTML element, they take on a slightly different appearance. A mechanism called a *selector* is needed to join style rules to HTML elements. The following style sheet snippet defines a rule for <span> elements where the textual content should be displayed in blue Arial font with bold and italic effects:

```
span
{ font-family: Arial; color: Blue;  font-weight:bold;  font-style:italic; }
```

The span keyword is an HTML element selector in CSS, because it uses HTML element names to modify the selection process. HTML element selectors are good for setting up default styles for specific tags that a web site uses for its content.

Sometimes, you want to target a specific group of HTML elements with CSS styles instead of all instances of an element type. Putting a period in front of the CSS style class name defines a class selector, as you can see in the following code snippet. The class selector applies to all HTML tags with a class attribute equal to the selector name. The period in front of the class name makes it a class selector.

```
 .second
{ font-family: Arial; color: Blue;  font-weight:bold;  font-style:italic; }
```

The second class style rule would apply to the following <span> because of its class attribute:

```
<span id="class_style" class="second">Bold, Italic Blue Text</span>
```

A selector with a hash (#) character in front of it signals the use of an id selector. It applies to HTML elements that have the same id attribute value as the selector name. Because id attributes for HTML elements on a page need to be unique, this specifies a style setting for a specific tag. If we changed the selector from the previous style definition to

```
#third
{ font-family: Arial; color: Blue;  font-weight:bold;  font-style:italic; }
```

then to use it we need a <span> with an id attribute equal to third:

```
<span id="third">Bold, Italic Blue Text</span>
```

You can combine the id or class technique along with the tag selector to separate the CSS classes from the tags they mark up. The following CSS definition shows the <span> and <div> HTML element selector names combined with the same class selector:

```
span.first
{ font-family: Arial; color: Blue;  font-weight:bold; font-style:italic; }
div.first
{ font-family: Arial; color: Red;  font-weight:bold;  font-style:italic; }
```

This produces different text layout depending on whether the class attribute `first` is used with a `<span>` or `<div>` tag:

```
<span class="first">Bold, Italic Blue Text</span>
<div class="first">Bold,  Italic Red Text</span>
```

There are additional selectors that do more specialized selection of HTML elements, such as the ability to group several selectors via commas. Please refer to a good text on CSS styling, such as *CSS Mastery: Advanced Web Standards Solutions* (Andy Budd, Simon Collison, Cameron Moll. friends of ED, 2006.), for more information on CSS selectors.

CSS provides several ways to formulate the style rules. You can place styles in their own separate CSS file and bring them in via a `<link>` tag as described previously, or you can place CSS styles in a `<style>` block in the `<head>` section of the document:

```
<style type="text/css">
   .bluetext
   {
      color: blue;
      background-color: yellow;
   }
</style>
```

You can also place CSS styles inline with the `style` attribute:

```
<span class="bluetext" style="color: red;">Yellow background, red text</span>
```

This begs the question, what happens when style properties that are defined in several different locations come together on the same document? CSS is built to handle this situation and this is where the "cascading" part of the CSS acronym comes in to play. The process can be summarized this way: if the styles do not conflict, the attributes are combined in an additive process. Also, style settings in the parent container apply to the parent's child elements.

When conflicts do arise because of the flow of style properties, there is a pecking order to determine which style takes precedence. The rule is simple: definitions closer to the tag take precedence over the more remote definitions, in terms of location on the page. The following order is taken into consideration, with the last bullet taking precedence over the first bullet:

- Browser defaults
- External style sheet
- Internal style sheet (inside the `<head>` tag)
- Inline style (`style` attribute on HTML element)

The previous <span> example displays with a yellow background that it inherits from the class selector, and its inline style color displays the text in red.

Style Properties and Visual Studio

Trying to remember what the various CSS properties are and how to use them can be a daunting task. You either need to have a thick reference close at hand or use the CSS editing features bundled with Visual Studio. Figure 4-1 shows a CSS style sheet in the main window and the Explorer view of its rules on the left side.

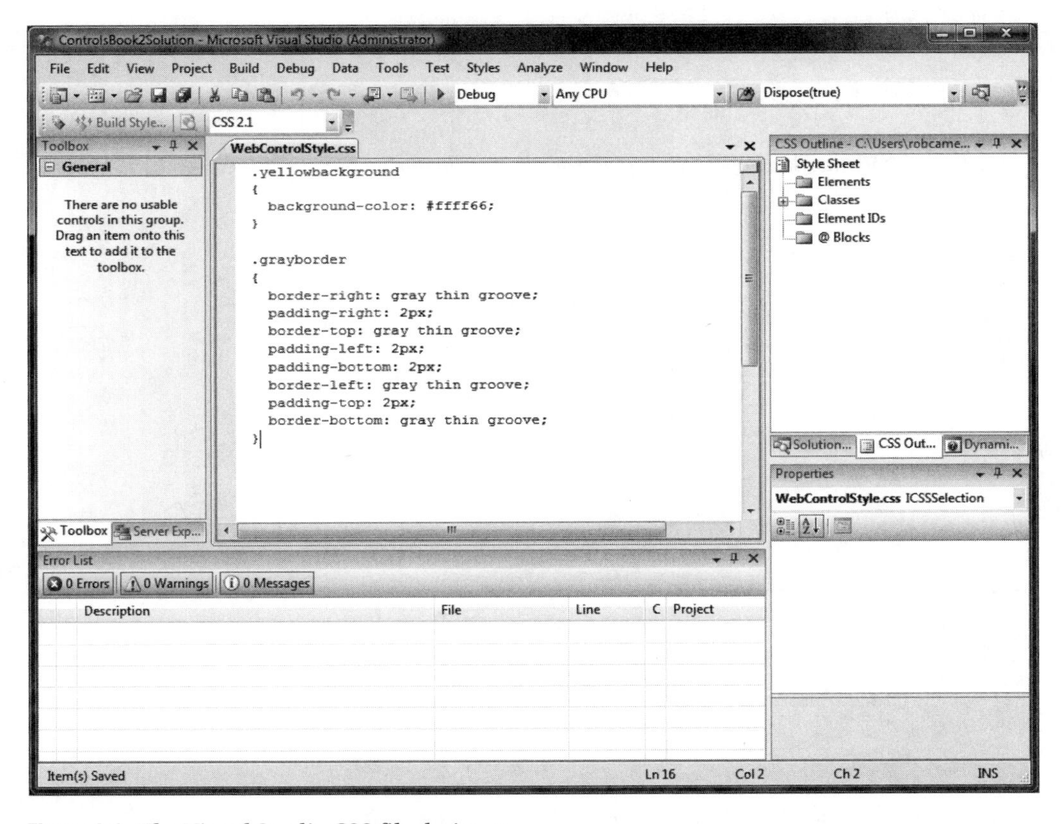

Figure 4-1. *The Visual Studio CSS file designer*

Right-click the design surface to add new styles or build on existing styles. The Add Style Rule dialog box shown in Figure 4-2 helps build the selector and outlines how the cascading style rules are applied.

Once you've added a new style selector to a CSS file, you can right-click the selector in the outline view to get the Style Builder dialog box, as shown in Figure 4-3. This is an excellent way to configure CSS classes, as it previews the style in the dialog box as it is created.

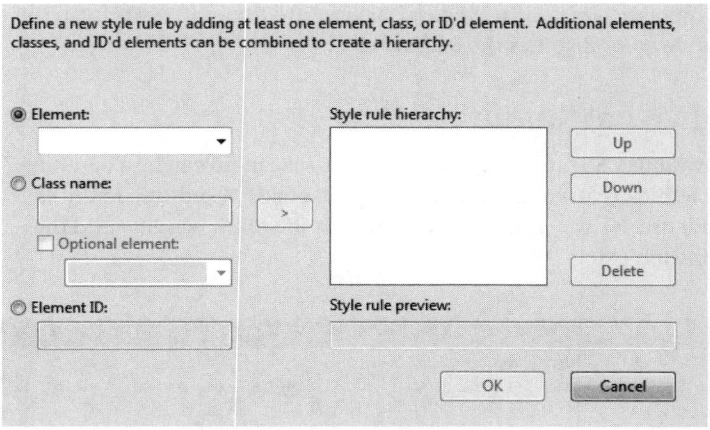

Figure 4-2. *The Visual Studio CSS designer Add Style Rule dialog box*

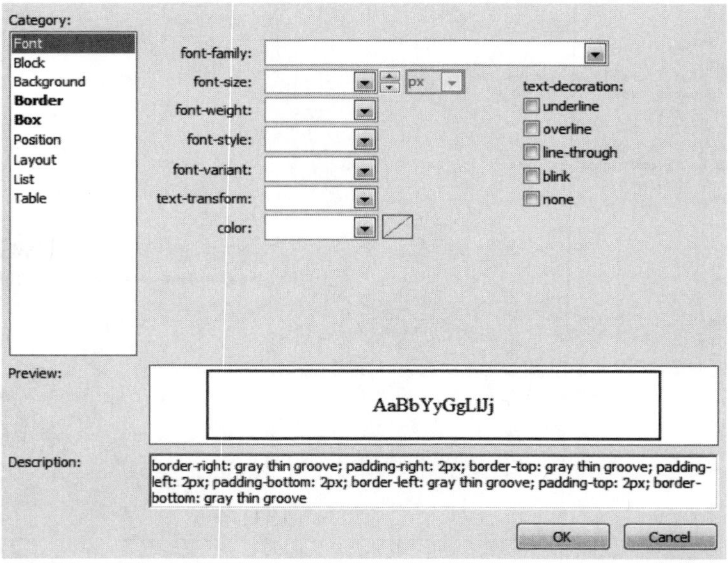

Figure 4-3. *The Visual Studio CSS designer Style Builder dialog box*

Visual Studio .NET 2003 included a page property called `pageLayout`, which enabled precise positioning of server controls when the `pageLayout` property is set to `GridLayout`. Visual Studio and ASP.NET 2.0 and later do not have a `pageLayout` property on web form documents, but there is a similar capability in the HTML designer. Go to Tools ➤ Options, and expand the HTML Designer node. Select the CSS Positioning node, check the option "Change positioning to the following for controls", and select "Absolutely positioned" in the combo box. Note that this is a global setting that will affect all subsequent web forms. Figure 4-4 shows the Options dialog box.

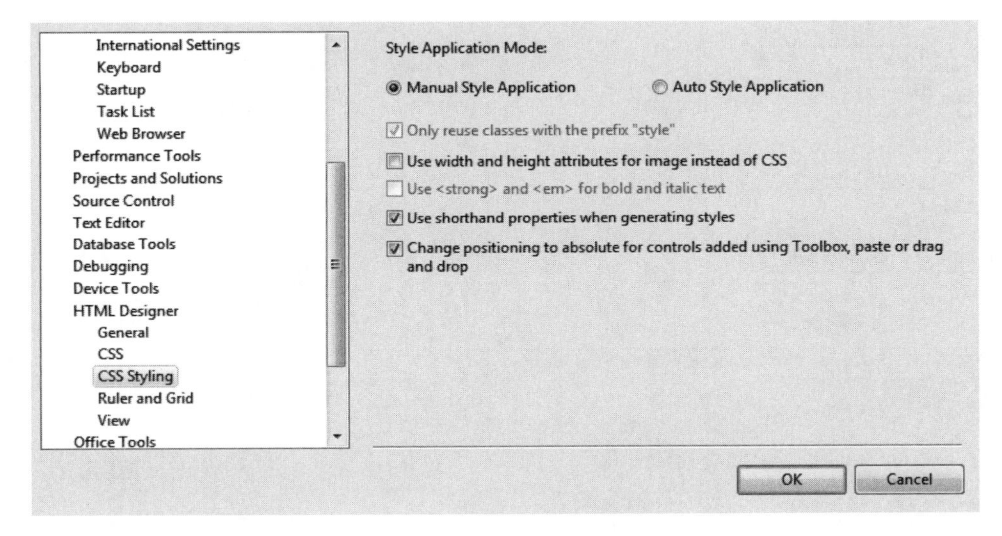

Figure 4-4. *The Visual Studio HTML Designer Options dialog box for setting the web form layout to "Absolutely positioned"*

The "Absolutely positioned" option uses the features of CSS absolute positioning, specifying pixel locations for server control objects, as shown in Figure 4-5. Visual Studio translates the developer's drag-and-drop movements of controls on the Designer surface into CSS style properties.

The following server control style properties position a button 133 pixels from the top of the document and 252 pixels from the left edge.

```
<asp:Button id="Button1" style="Z-INDEX: 101; LEFT: 252px; POSITION: absolute;
TOP: 133px" runat="server" Text="Button"></asp:Button>
```

CSS absolute positioning is enabled with the position property having an absolute value. The z-index provides a way to position the HTML elements in a third dimension: depth. This allows for overlapping content and some interesting visual effects.

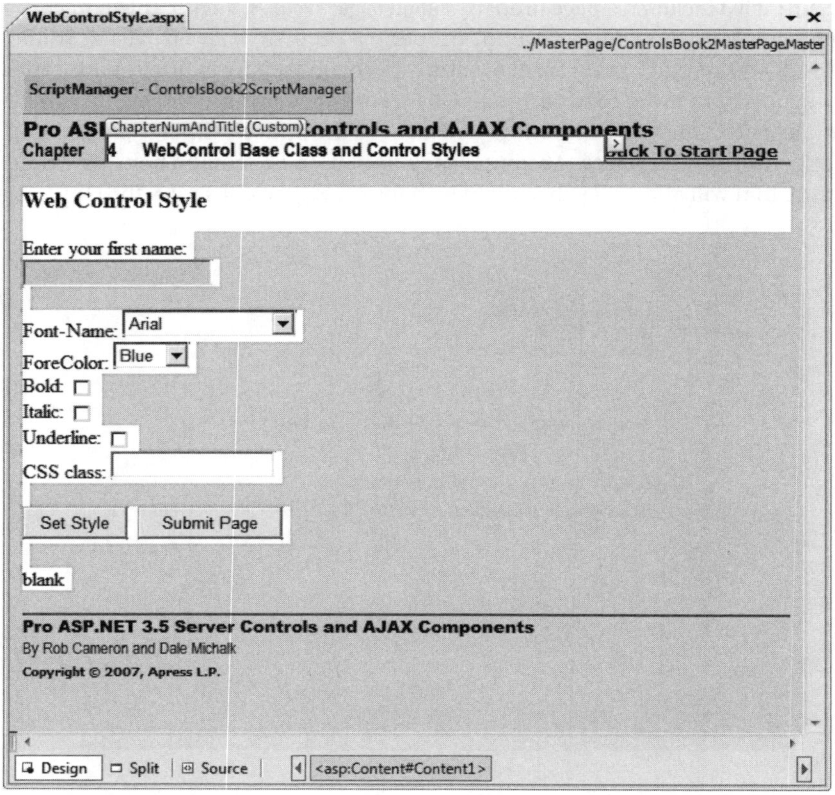

Figure 4-5. *A Visual Studio Designer web form using "Absolutely positioned"*

WebControl and Control Styling

Up to this point in this book, we built our server controls by inheriting from `System.Web.UI.Control` as the base class. We did this to keep things simple, concentrating on the basics of control development. However, `Control` as a base class starts to show its inherent limitations when we start working with styling and cross-browser support. When inheriting from `Control`, developers are responsible for manually building up the HTML tags, providing a style property and manually emitting the style property into the HTML output stream. To avoid this work, a better choice is inheriting from the `WebControl` class, as you will see in the ensuing discussion.

■ **Note** There will be times when inheriting from `Control` is desired in order to have full control over the rendering process and the capabilities built into `WebControl` are not required. When this is not the case, we recommend inheriting from `WebControl` or `WebPart` discussed later in this book whenever possible.

In this section, we discuss how to add styling capabilities to server controls. We also introduce a new method of building server controls that inherit from the `WebControl` class. The `WebControl` class provides an abstraction layer over the rendering process to support strong styling capabilities and rendering in down-level browsers.

The `WebControl` class from the `System.Web.UI.WebControls` namespace provides a wealth of style support in the form of style properties and automatic style rendering. Not only does it take care of rendering CSS style properties, but it also goes the extra mile to support HTML 3.2 with explicit style tags for down-level browsers.

Control styling and rendering are closely coupled, because at the end of the day, raw HTML is the output from a server control. In the next section, we dive into the styling capabilities available in `WebControl`. Along the way, we discuss the new rendering model in `WebControl` that provides the necessary support for styling and down-level browsers without requiring too much effort on the developer's part to make it happen.

WebControl's ControlStyle Property

`ControlStyle` is the property of interest in the `WebControl` class for manipulating styling. It is a read-only property that provides access to an instance of the `System.Web.UI.WebControls.Style` class. The `Style` class captures most of the commonly used style properties that a web developer needs to use with a control, focusing on text, font, color, and borders. Table 4-1 shows the properties that hang from the `Style` class and the CSS property that is rendered in conjunction with the property.

Table 4-1. *Properties of the System.Web.UI.WebControls.Style Class*

Style Property	CSS Property
`BackColor`	`background-color`
`BorderColor`	`border-color`
`BorderStyle`	`border-style`
`BorderWidth`	`border-width`
`CssClass`	CSS class name
`Font`	Font weight, style, family, and so on
`ForeColor`	`color`
`Height`	`height`
`Width`	`width`

`CssClass` is a string property that translates directly to rendering a class attribute on the control tag. Setting the `CssClass` property in the `.aspx` page for the ASP.NET `Label` `WebControl`

```
<asp:label id="myspan" runat="server" CssClass="mycssclass" Text="blank" />
```

translates into the following HTML:

```
<span id="myspan" class="mycssclass">blank</span>
```

The Font property exposes a set of subproperties, so we continue our property examination with Table 4-2 for the System.Web.UI.FontInfo class.

Table 4-2. *Properties of the System.Web.UI.WebControls.FontInfo Class*

Font Property	CSS Property
Bold	font-weight: bold
Italic	font-style: italic
Name	font-family
Names	font-family
Overline	text-decoration: overline
Size	font-size
Strikeout	text-decoration: line-through
Underline	text-decoration: underline

WebControl Top-Level Style Properties

Going through the ControlStyle property to access these attributes would require a lot of extra typing when setting style properties in either the .aspx control tag or the code-behind class file. The WebControl class makes life easier by exposing all of the properties listed in Tables 4-1 and 4-2 directly as properties (see Figure 4-6), which saves a lot of typing.

The top-level property exposure as shown in Figure 4-6 shortens the syntax from this

```
Mycontrol.ControlStyle.ForeColor = red;
```

to the more pleasant

```
MyControl.ForeColor = red;
```

The style properties are also available for configuration of the control tag via attributes in the .aspx page as well:

```
<apress:textbox id="MyControl" runat="server" forecolor="red" font-bold="true"  />
```

These top-level properties are convenient to use, but there are other styling attributes available too numerous to hang off of the WebControl class. Instead, you can access these styling capabilities through the Style property.

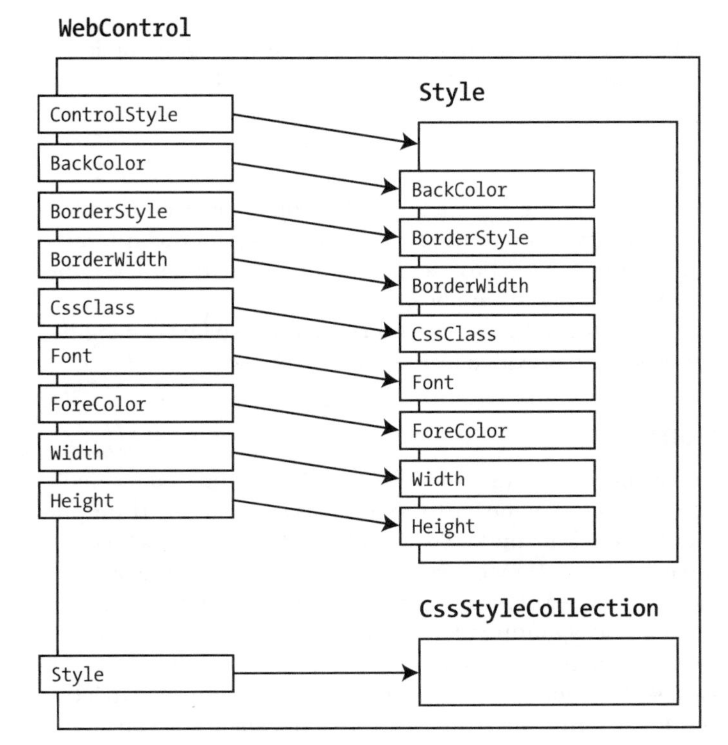

Figure 4-6. *WebControl and top-level style properties*

The Style Property

The ControlStyle property and top-level properties of WebControl do not expose the complete spectrum of CSS styling capabilities. The most notable omissions are the placement attributes that allow you to do CSS absolute positioning.

To handle these "other" style properties, WebControl exposes a collection via the Style property. The Style property is an instance of type CssStyleCollection. CssStyleCollection is a string-based collection that uses string names as indexers into the values. This is similar to the Hashtable class, except it mandates strings for both keys and values.

You can set the Style property programmatically, but it is more commonly set by adding style properties to the .aspx page. The WYSIWYG designers, such as the ASP.NET Designer in Visual Studio in "Absolutely positioned" mode, are the best examples of this. The ASP.NET Designer uses the Style property on the .aspx page to control the layout of the controls when it is set to be absolutely positioned:

```
<asp:button id="Button2" runat="server" style="Z-INDEX: 101; LEFT: 252px;
POSITION: absolute;"></asp:button>
```

Parsing an .aspx page creates start-up code that initializes a control's Style property collection with declarative style properties. You can modify the Style property programmatically as well. The following line of code changes the button's text color from its declarative red value to a programmatically set blue value:

```
Button1.Style[color] = blue;
```

The primary drawback to adding style properties via the Style property collection is that it isn't browser-aware. Although ControlStyle properties render HTML tags for down-level browsers, the Style properties are streamed to the browser verbatim as CSS properties. If the browser doesn't understand the CSS properties, it simply ignores them.

We next move on to discuss how to provide cross-browser compatible styling capabilities by taking advantage of the rendering system provided by the WebControl class.

A New Rendering System

As we stated earlier, the custom controls we have developed so far inherit from Control and require that we override the Render() method of the base Control class to emit HTML output. Going forward in this chapter, we will inherit from the WebControl class, which overrides Render() by default to save us from having to emit raw HTML tags and style content into the output stream. Instead, we override RenderContents(), which is a method in the WebControl class.

RenderContents() provides a method signature identical to that of Render() with an HtmlTextWriter reference as its sole parameter. The difference is that you have the task of emitting what is inside the outermost HTML tag for the control. For this reason, you need to let WebControl know what kind of HTML tag formulates your control's outer shell. You can do this in one of two ways: by passing the tag via the HtmlTextWriterTag enumeration to the base WebControl constructor or by setting either the TagKey or TagName property of WebControl. The more common way is to use the base constructor:

```
public Label() : base(HtmlTextWriterTag.Span)
{
}
```

In the next section, we dive into WebControl-based control building and create a simple Label control.

A Styled Label Control

Label controls are probably the simplest controls in the ASP.NET server control arsenal. They have a single mission: to render a piece of content within a <span> tag. To demonstrate the styling powers of the WebControl class, we will build our own version of the Label control. Listing 4-1 shows how easy this truly is.

Listing 4-1. *The Label Control*

```
using System;
using System.Web.UI;
using System.Web.UI.WebControls;
using System.ComponentModel;
```

```
namespace ControlsBook2Lib.Ch04
{
  [ToolboxData("<{0}:label runat=server></{0}:label>"),
  DefaultProperty("Text")]
  public class Label : WebControl
  {
    public Label()
      : base(HtmlTextWriterTag.Span)
    {
    }

    public virtual string Text
    {
      get
      {
        object text = ViewState["Text"];
        if (text == null)
          return string.Empty;
        else
          return (string)text;
      }
      set
      {
        ViewState["Text"] = value;
      }
    }

    override protected void RenderContents(HtmlTextWriter writer)
    {
      writer.Write(Text);
    }
  }
}
```

The constructor of the Label control calls the base constructor of WebControl to have it emit the content inside of <span> tags via the HtmlTextWriterTag.Span enumeration value. This sets up the control to call our overridden RenderContents() method. Note that we do not emit a single HTML tag directly. The RenderContents() method simply has to write out the Text property to complete the control functionality. We next create a TextBox control to demonstrate further how to work with WebControl, laying the groundwork for building stylized server controls that take full advantage of the capabilities built into ASP.NET and the WebControl class.

The AddAttributesToRender() Method

The Label was an easy enough control to build, but its limited functionality did not require the use of attributes on the <span> tag. What happens when you have an <input> tag like our various TextBox controls from previous chapters? It needs to output type and value attributes inside the <input> tag.

For those who need to render attributes on the outer tag, the AddAttributesToRender() method is a method override available when inheriting from WebControl that fits the bill. It is part of the customized Render() process that WebControl orchestrates, and it is called by the RenderBeginTag() method of WebControl. The WebControl version of Render() executes the following routines in order, with RenderBeginTag() calling AddAttributesToRender():

- RenderBeginTag()
- RenderContents()
- RenderEndTag()

Figure 4-7 shows the relationship graphically.

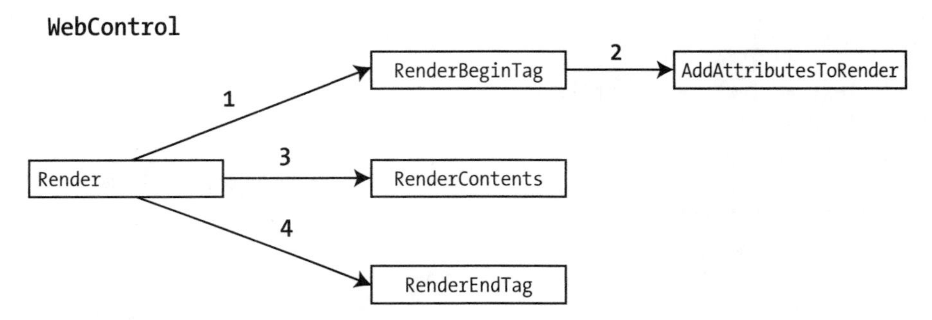

Figure 4-7. *The rendering process in the WebControl class*

Depending on the level of control required, you can overload each step of the process as necessary. The RenderBeginTag()/RenderEndTag() method pairs are less commonly overloaded, because they do the outer tag rendering by looking up the TagKey or TagName property values and emitting the content via HtmlTextWriter.

The key point to remember is that when you override AddAttributesToRender(), you must also call the base WebControl version of the method to ensure that the style properties managed by WebControl are emitted properly:

```
base.AddAttributesToRender(writer);
```

Also, you can use HtmlTextWriter and its AddAttribute() method to add other attributes as necessary:

```
writer.AddAttribute("value",Text);
```

Now that we have covered the basics of inheriting from WebControl, we can move on to add style capabilities to our TextBox control from earlier in this book.

A Styled TextBox Control

In this section, we bring back our favorite TextBox control from chapters past and update it with WebControl capabilities. As you would guess, most of the implementation remains the same. The biggest changes relate to how we handle the rendering process.

The first step in updating TextBox is to inherit from WebControl and set the constructor to create the tag for the outer shell of the control. The following code snippet sets up our WebControl version of the TextBox to render an <input> tag:

```
public class Textbox : WebControl, IPostBackDataHandler
{
   public Textbox() : base(HtmlTextWriterTag.Input)
   {
   }
}
```

The rendering code in this version of TextBox is dramatically smaller than the previous version that inherited from Control. All we have to implement is the AddAttributesToRender() method to set the <input> tag with the appropriate attributes, and we need to call the base class version to add the style properties:

```
override protected void AddAttributesToRender(HtmlTextWriter writer)
{
   writer.AddAttribute("type","text");
   writer.AddAttribute("name",UniqueID);
   writer.AddAttribute("value",Text);

   base.AddAttributesToRender(writer);
}
```

Listing 4-2 shows the full code for the TextBox control.

Listing 4-2. *The TextBox Control*

```
using System;
using System.Web.UI;
using System.Web.UI.WebControls;
using System.Collections.Specialized;
using System.ComponentModel;

namespace ControlsBook2Lib.Ch04
{
  [ToolboxData("<{0}:textbox runat=server></{0}:textbox>"),
  DefaultProperty("Text")]
  public class Textbox : WebControl, IPostBackDataHandler
  {
    public Textbox()
      : base(HtmlTextWriterTag.Input)
    {
    }

    public virtual string Text
    {
      get
```

```
    {
      object text = ViewState["Text"];
      if (text == null)
        return string.Empty;
      else
        return (string)text;
    }
    set
    {
      ViewState["Text"] = value;
    }
  }

  public bool LoadPostData(string postDataKey,
     NameValueCollection postCollection)
  {
    string postedValue = postCollection[postDataKey];
    if (!Text.Equals(postedValue))
    {
      Text = postedValue;
      return true;
    }
    else
      return false;
  }

  public void RaisePostDataChangedEvent()
  {
    OnTextChanged(EventArgs.Empty);
  }

  private static readonly object TextChangedKey = new object();
  public event EventHandler TextChanged
  {
    add
    {
      Events.AddHandler(TextChangedKey, value);
    }
    remove
    {
      Events.RemoveHandler(TextChangedKey, value);
    }
  }
```

```
    protected virtual void OnTextChanged(EventArgs e)
    {
      EventHandler textChangedEventDelegate =
         (EventHandler)Events[TextChangedKey];
      if (textChangedEventDelegate != null)
      {
        textChangedEventDelegate(this, e);
      }
    }

    override protected void AddAttributesToRender(HtmlTextWriter writer)
    {
      writer.AddAttribute("type", "text");
      writer.AddAttribute("name", UniqueID);
      writer.AddAttribute("value", Text);

      base.AddAttributesToRender(writer);
    }
  }
}
```

The Web Control Style Web Form

The Web Control Style web form is a workbench for testing both the Label and the TextBox controls we have created so far in this chapter. It has a set of controls to allow the user to interactively change style properties, rendering the control with its new styles on the web form. Figure 4-8 displays what the web form looks like when displayed in a browser.

The top of the form is the TextBox control with properties that are set in the .aspx tag page to make the TextBox background gray and set its text to Tahoma font with bold and italic features:

```
<apress:textbox id="NameTextbox" runat="server" Font-Bold="True"
BackColor="#E0E0E0" Font-Italic="True" Font-Names="Tahoma"></apress:textbox>
```

Below the web form is a set of server controls that provide a control panel for styling a Label control at the very bottom of the .aspx page, just before the footer:

```
<apress:label id="NameLabel" runat="server" Text="blank"></apress:label><br/>
```

The user can set the following properties: Font-Name, ForeColor, Bold, Italic, and Underline, along with CssClass. In ASP.NET 1.1, the .aspx page had a link to an external style sheet called WebControlStyle. This was useful for exercising the CssClass property, as all the style rules had class selectors:

```
<link href="WebControlStyle.css" type="text/css" rel="stylesheet"/>
```

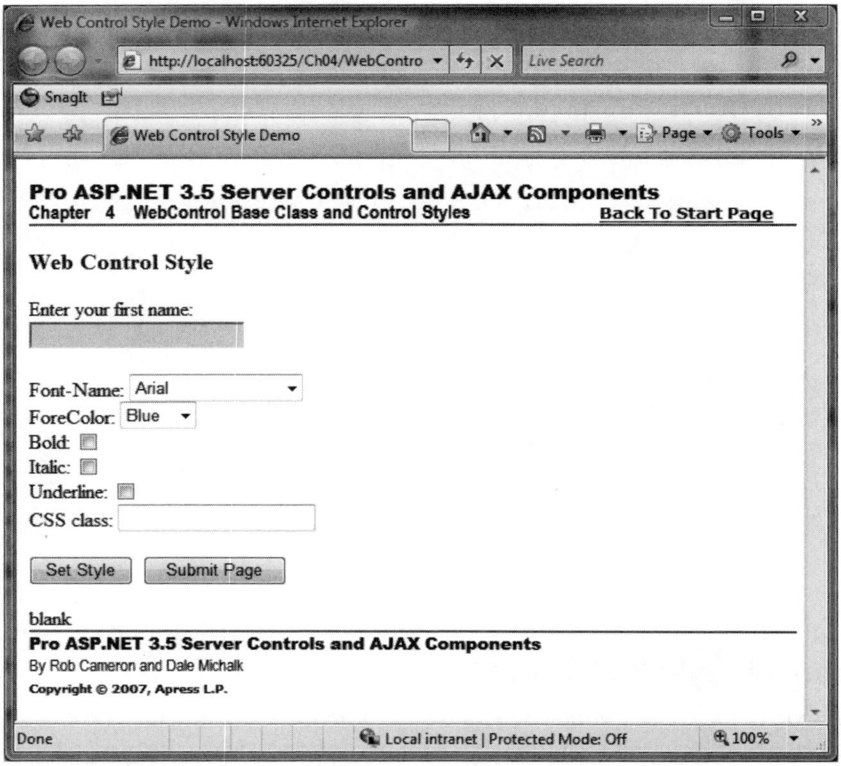

Figure 4-8. *The Web Control Style web form*

In ASP.NET 2.0 and later, when using master pages, a `<link>` tag can be added directly to the `<head>` portion of the `.aspx` page, by adding a content tag to the head section of the master page. Another option is to add the `<link>` tag programmatically as shown here:

```
private void AddCssLinktoHeader()
{
  HtmlLink cssRef = new HtmlLink();
  cssRef.Href = "../Ch04/WebControlStyle.css";
  cssRef.Attributes.Add("rel", "stylesheet");
  cssRef.Attributes.Add("type", "text/css");
  Header.Controls.Add(cssRef);
}
```

Notice that the `Href` value must be provided relative to the directory where the master page exists.

To try applying a CSS class selector via the `CssClass` property, type either **yellowbackground** or **grayborder** in the CSS class text box, and click the Set Style button. You can see the style changes take effect based on the class name you typed. The full listing of the web form is shown in Listings 4-3 and 4-4, and the style sheet is shown in Listing 4-5.

Listing 4-3. *The Web Control Style Web Form .aspx File*

```
<%@ Page Language="C#"
  MasterPageFile="~/MasterPage/ControlsBook2MasterPage.Master"
  AutoEventWireup="true" CodeBehind="WebControlStyle.aspx.cs"
  Inherits="ControlsBook2Web.Ch04.WebControlStyle"
  Title="Web Control Style Demo" %>

<%@ Register TagPrefix="apress" Namespace="ControlsBook2Lib.Ch04"
Assembly="ControlsBook2Lib" %>
<asp:Content ID="Content1" ContentPlaceHolderID="ChapterNumAndTitle" runat="server">
  <asp:Label ID="ChapterNumberLabel" runat="server"
Width="14px">4</asp:Label>  <asp:Label
    ID="ChapterTitleLabel" runat="server" Width="360px">
   WebControl Base Class and Control
Styles</asp:Label>
</asp:Content>
<asp:Content ID="Content2" ContentPlaceHolderID="PrimaryContent" runat="server">
  <h3>
    Web Control Style</h3>
  <span id="Prompt">Enter your first name:</span><br />
  <apress:Textbox ID="NameTextbox" runat="server"
    Font-Bold="True" BackColor="#E0E0E0"
    Font-Italic="True" Font-Names="Tahoma"></apress:Textbox>
  <br />
  <br />
  Font-Name:
  <asp:DropDownList ID="FontDropDownList" runat="server">
    <asp:ListItem Value="Arial">Arial</asp:ListItem>
    <asp:ListItem Value="Courier New">Courier New</asp:ListItem>
    <asp:ListItem Value="Times New Roman">Times New Roman</asp:ListItem>
    <asp:ListItem Value="Monotype Corsiva">Monotype Corsiva</asp:ListItem>
  </asp:DropDownList><br />
  ForeColor:
  <asp:DropDownList ID="ForeColorDropDownList" runat="server">
    <asp:ListItem Value="Blue">Blue</asp:ListItem>
    <asp:ListItem Value="Red">Red</asp:ListItem>
    <asp:ListItem Value="Black">Black</asp:ListItem>
  </asp:DropDownList><br />
  <asp:CheckBox ID="BoldCheckbox" runat="server" Text="Bold: "
TextAlign="Left"></asp:CheckBox><br />
  <asp:CheckBox ID="ItalicCheckbox" runat="server" Text="Italic: " TextAlign="Left">
  </asp:CheckBox><br />
  <asp:CheckBox ID="UnderlineCheckbox" runat="server" Text="Underline: "
    TextAlign="Left">
  </asp:CheckBox><br />
```

```
    CSS class:
    <asp:TextBox ID="CssClassTextBox" runat="server" Text=""></asp:TextBox><br />
    <br />
    <asp:Button ID="SetStyleButton" runat="server" Text="Set Style"
      OnClick="SetStyleButton_Click">
    </asp:Button> 
    <asp:Button ID="SubmitPageButton" runat="server" Text="Submit Page">
   </asp:Button><br />
    <br />
    <apress:Label ID="NameLabel" runat="server" Text="blank"></apress:Label>
    <br />
  </asp:Content>
```

Listing 4-4. *The Web Control Style Web Form Code-Behind Class File*

```
using System;
using System.Drawing;
using System.ComponentModel;
using System.Web.UI.HtmlControls;

namespace ControlsBook2Web.Ch04
{
  public partial class WebControlStyle : System.Web.UI.Page
  {
    protected void Page_Load(object sender, EventArgs e)
    {
      //Add link to css class file
      AddCssLinktoHeader();

    }

    private void AddCssLinktoHeader()
    {
      HtmlLink cssRef = new HtmlLink();
      cssRef.Href = "../Ch04/WebControlStyle.css";
      cssRef.Attributes.Add("rel", "stylesheet");
      cssRef.Attributes.Add("type", "text/css");
      Header.Controls.Add(cssRef);
    }
```

```
    protected void SetStyleButton_Click(object sender, EventArgs e)
    {
      NameLabel.Text = NameTextbox.Text;

      NameLabel.CssClass = CssClassTextBox.Text;

      NameLabel.Font.Name = FontDropDownList.SelectedItem.Value;
      NameLabel.Font.Bold = (BoldCheckbox.Checked == true);
      NameLabel.Font.Italic = (ItalicCheckbox.Checked == true);

      // Use the TypeConverter for the System.Drawing.Color class
      // to get the typed Color value from the string value
      Color c =
         (Color)TypeDescriptor.GetConverter(typeof(Color)).ConvertFromString(
         ForeColorDropDownList.SelectedItem.Value);
      NameLabel.ForeColor = c;

      // set the text-decoration CSS style properties
      // using manual manipulation of the Style property
      string textdecoration = "none";
      if (UnderlineCheckbox.Checked == true)
        textdecoration = "underline";
      NameLabel.Style["text-decoration"] = textdecoration;
    }
  }
}
```

Listing 4-5. *The WebControlStyle.css File*

```
.yellowbackground
{
  background-color: #ffff66;
}

.grayborder
{
  border-right: gray thin groove;
  padding-right: 2px;
  border-top: gray thin groove;
  padding-left: 2px;
  padding-bottom: 2px;
  border-left: gray thin groove;
  padding-top: 2px;
  border-bottom: gray thin groove;
}
```

The Set Style button on the Web Control Style web form is used to programmatically change the style properties of the Label control in the code-behind file. The SetStyleButton_Click routine performs the heavy lifting. The attributes set are fairly easy ones that include the Text- and Font-related properties, along with the CssClass of the control.

A more complicated effort is required to set up the ForeColor property of the control to a value of type System.Drawing.Color. We use the TypeConverter class that is available to perform this conversion from our string value to the exact Color type necessary to set the ForeColor property:

```
// Use the TypeConverter for the System.Drawing.Color class
// to get the typed Color value from the string value
Color c =
   (Color)TypeDescriptor.GetConverter(typeof(Color)).ConvertFromString(
   ForeColorDropDownList.SelectedItem.Value);
NameLabel.ForeColor = c;
```

In Chapter 11, in which we discuss designer support, we show how to build and work with TypeConverter classes.

The final part of the Set Style button click handler is code that uses the Style property to set the underline styling of the Label control. This step is not necessary, as there is an Underline property exposed by the Font object. We do it here to demonstrate the longer version:

```
// set the text-decoration CSS style property
// using manual manipulation of the Style property
string textdecoration = "none";
if (UnderlineCheckbox.Checked == true)
   textdecoration = "underline";
NameLabel.Style["text-decoration"] = textdecoration;
```

The other button on the web form with a Submit Page caption is there to execute a post-back without any server-side code executing. We use it to cycle the values from ViewState to demonstrate that the controls are working with client state properly.

Navigate to the WebControlStyle.aspx page to display the web form in your browser. Enter your first name in the TextBox at the top and click the Set Style button. The display should look similar to Figure 4-9, with the Label control picking up the TextBox Text property value.

The HTML emitted by the TextBox control shows the translation from top-level server control properties to the style attribute on the HTML <input> element:

```
<input type="text" name="NameTextbox" value="" id="NameTextbox"
style="background-color:#E0E0E0;font-family:Tahoma;font-weight:bold;
font-style:italic;" />
```

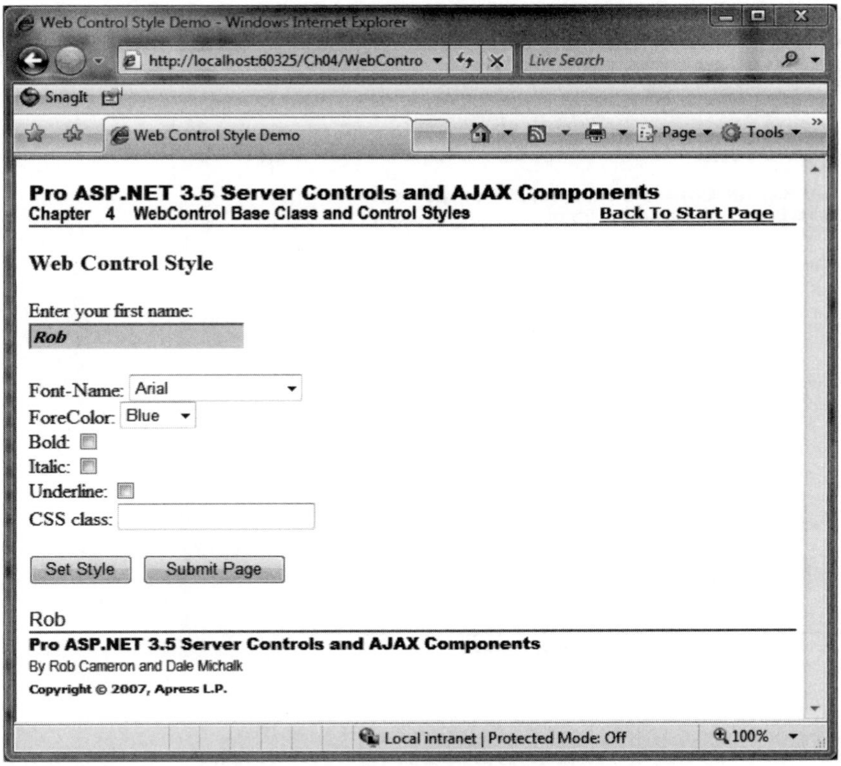

Figure 4-9. *Setting the name and style in the Web Control Style web form*

The same process occurs at the bottom of the web form with the `Label` control. It picks up the style properties we set in HTML:

```
<span id="NameLabel" style="color:Blue;font-family:Arial;
text-decoration:none;">Rob</span>
```

For the next demonstration, we change the `Font-Name` to Monotype Corsiva; select the italic, bold, and underline options; and enter **grayborder** in the `CssClass` `TextBox` control, as shown in Figure 4-10.

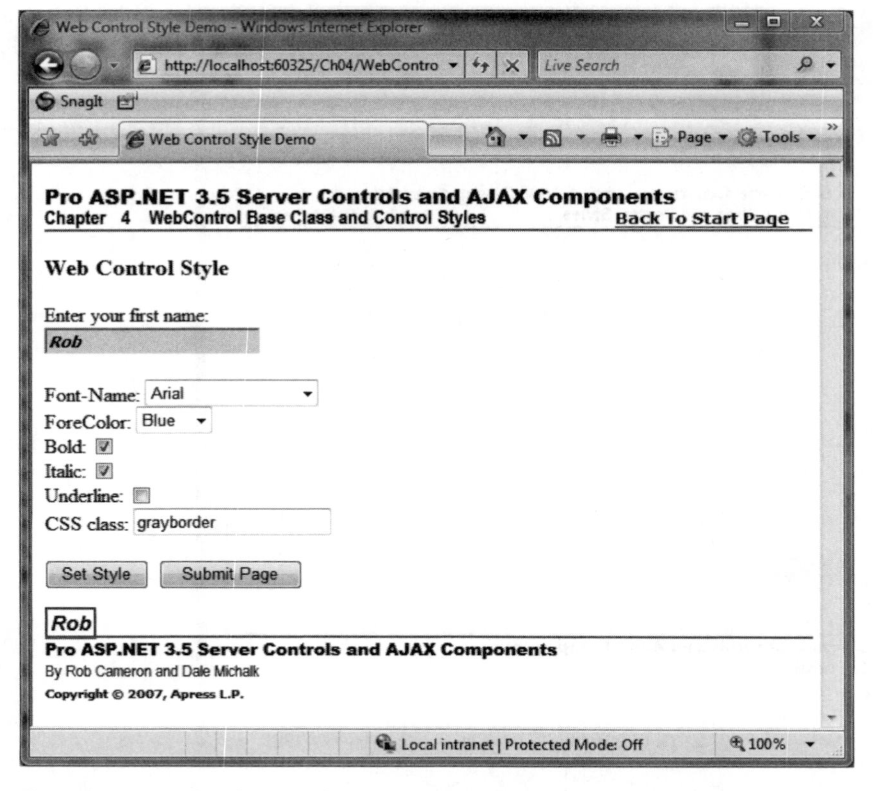

Figure 4-10. *Grayborder CSS class, Monotype Corsiva font, and italic, bold, and underline styles in the Web Control Style web form*

This renders the `Label` in quite a different manner, picking up the color and the font text settings such as italic, bold, and underline. The most prominent feature is the gray border styling picked up by using the `CssClass` attribute in conjunction with the external style sheet, `WebControlStyle.css`. The HTML for the `Label` control is as follows:

```
<span id="NameLabel" class="grayborder" style="color:Blue;font-family:Monotype
Corsiva;font-weight:bold;font-style:italic;text-decoration:underline;">Rob</span>
```

The same settings rendered in Firefox 2.0, shown in Figure 4-11, demonstrate that it displays the style settings with aplomb.

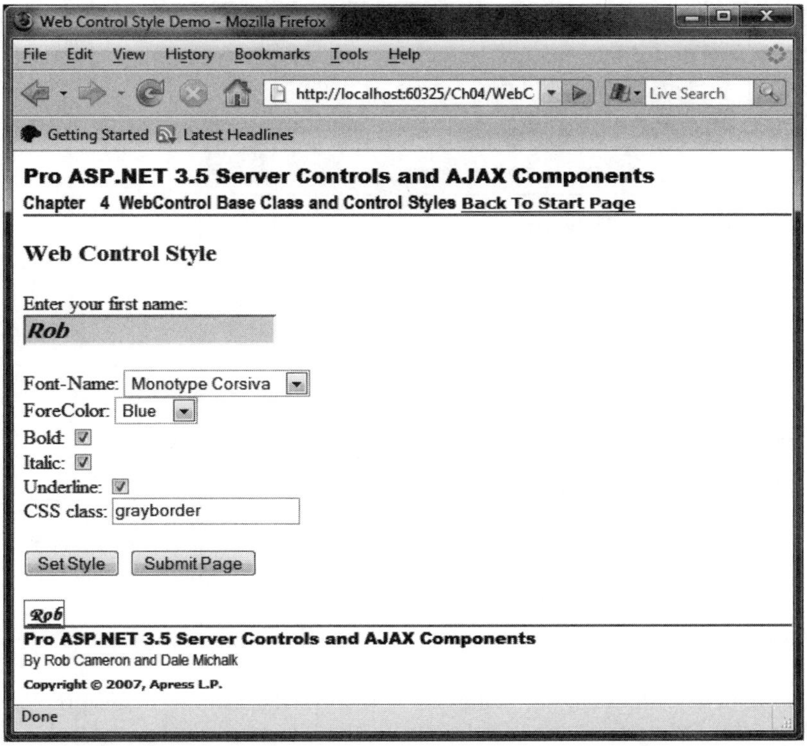

Figure 4-11. *Styles in Firefox 2.0*

Styles, HTML 3.2, and Down-Level Browsers

The styling in ASP.NET is thankfully smart enough to help a browser that only supports HTML 3.2 display the page properly as well. You have two options for testing this: adding the `ClientTarget="downlevel"` attribute to the `@Page` directive at the top of the web form `.aspx` page or finding a browser client that only supports HTML 3.2. The 3.2 browser is a better test, because Internet Explorer (IE) or Netscape will still render styles that are present that don't translate into HTML 3.2 tags.

In order to test this, we downloaded a copy of Netscape 3.04, installing on Windows Vista, just to see how good down-level support really is in ASP.NET 2.0 and later. Running the same web form test with the `Font-Name` set to `Monotype Corsiva`, `CssClass` set to `grayborder`, and the italic, bold, and underline options selected results in the screenshot shown in Figure 4-12.

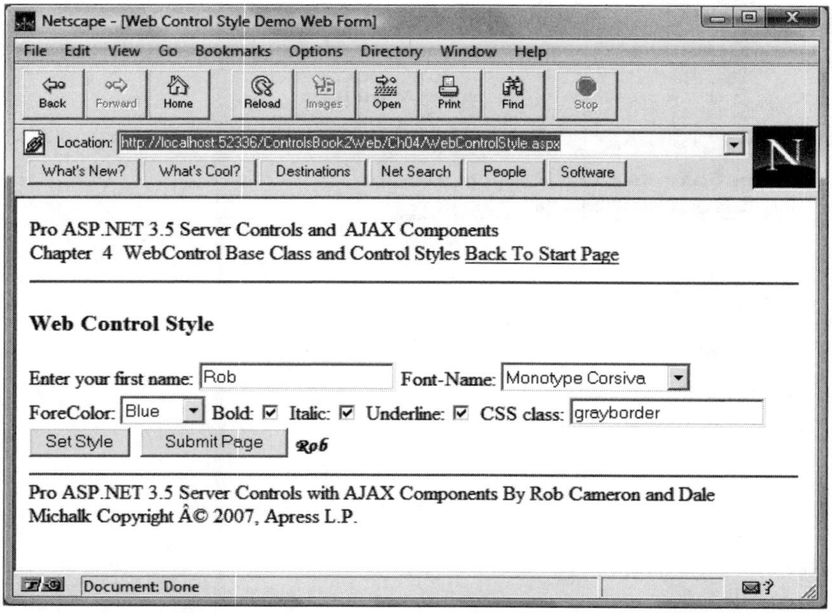

Figure 4-12. *Down-level browser rendering*

Netscape 3.04 does not know how to interpret the `<br/>` tag correctly, resulting in the jumbled output. Changing the tag to `<br>` instead does render the line breaks correctly, but the web form then fails Visual Studio XHTML validation with this error:

```
Cannot switch views: Validation (ASP.Net): Element '' is missing the '>' character
from its closing tag.
```

Besides the issue with the `<br/>` tag, the web form does its best to translate the desired CSS style properties to HTML 3.2 tags for the old Netscape browser. For the most part, it does a good job, especially with text. Viewing the HTML source shows how this compatibility was achieved:

```
<span id="ctl00_ControlsBookContent_NameLabel" class="grayboarder"
style="text-decoration:underline;"><b><i><font face="Monotype Corsiva"
color="Blue">Rob</font></i></b></span>
```

The `style` attribute is still present because we used the `Style` collection for setting the `text-decoration` attribute in the code-behind class. Setting the font to have an underline style using this method is the reason why the `text-decoration` property does not affect the display in HTML 3.2 and why you should be careful when using the `Style` property unless you are only targeting an up-level browser. The `class` attribute is present as well, but it is ignored by the down-level browser, so we won't see a border either. As you can see, building controls that inherit from `WebControl` provides cross-browser support without your having to worry about the details of browser detection and raw HTML output. We next discuss what goes on under the covers with respect to down-level browser support.

Down-Level Browser Style Rendering Behind the Scenes

The style conversion that occurs automatically when the Web Control Style web form is viewed in the down-level Netscape browser is a clever technology built into the ASP.NET framework. When a request is made for an `.aspx` page, ASP.NET parses the header information to determine the capability of the browser. An instance of the `System.Web.HttpBrowserCapabilities` class is attached to the `HttpRequest` class via its `Browser` property.

The `HttpBrowserCapabilities` class has a `TagWriter` property pointing to an instance of the `HtmlTextWriter` class, or a type inherited from it, to inject HTML into the output stream. Up-level browsers such as IE 6.0 and Netscape 7.02 are rendered with an instance of `HtmlTextWriter`, whereas HTML 3.2 and down-level browsers are rendered with an instance of `Html32TextWriter`.

`Html32TextWriter` has a special implementation for handling style information added through `AddStyleAttribute`. When you call `RenderBeginTag`, it converts the style properties into necessary HTML tags such as `<font>`, `<b>`, and `<i>`. Because the interfaces are identical between `HtmlTextWriter` and `Html32TextWriter`, controls are none the wiser and do not need to worry about the differences, which makes developing cross-browser-friendly web pages as well as server controls much easier when inheriting from `WebControl`.

We examine the `HttpBrowserCapabilities` class in more detail in Chapter 8, which is dedicated to integrating client script with control development.

Custom Styling

The `WebControl` base class provides a great start in implementing styling in your control. It offers a base set of style properties that affect the look and feel of the rendered HTML. With that said, sometimes your controls will be more complex than a single HTML tag. Think of how the composite control renders a whole host of child controls by recursively calling `Render()` on each control. Because the child controls are not directly accessible to outside clients, how can you make the individual controls accessible without breaking the composite control object?

The `Style` class that backs the `ControlStyle` property on a `WebControl`-based control can easily be used by the composite control to provide custom style properties for its child controls. Many of the more advanced list controls, such as the `DataGrid` in ASP.NET, provide the ability to stylize different settings—for example, how alternating items or edited items appear through the `ItemStyle`, `AlternateItemStyle`, and `EditItemStyle` properties. The `DataGrid` exposes the `Style` classes through these properties, applying the styles prior to the start of the rendering process. We demonstrate how to manage styles in a composite control in the next section.

The Styled InputBox Control

To demonstrate custom styling, we develop a composite control called `InputBox` that aggregates the controls built so far in this chapter (see Figure 4-13). It consists of a `Label` control and a `TextBox` control placed near each other, as a web developer normally would place them when laying out a web form. To set the styles on each of the child controls, `InputBox` exposes `LabelStyle` and `TextBoxStyle` properties. It also merges the child control styles with the parent styles set via the `ControlStyle` property to provide a consistent appearance.

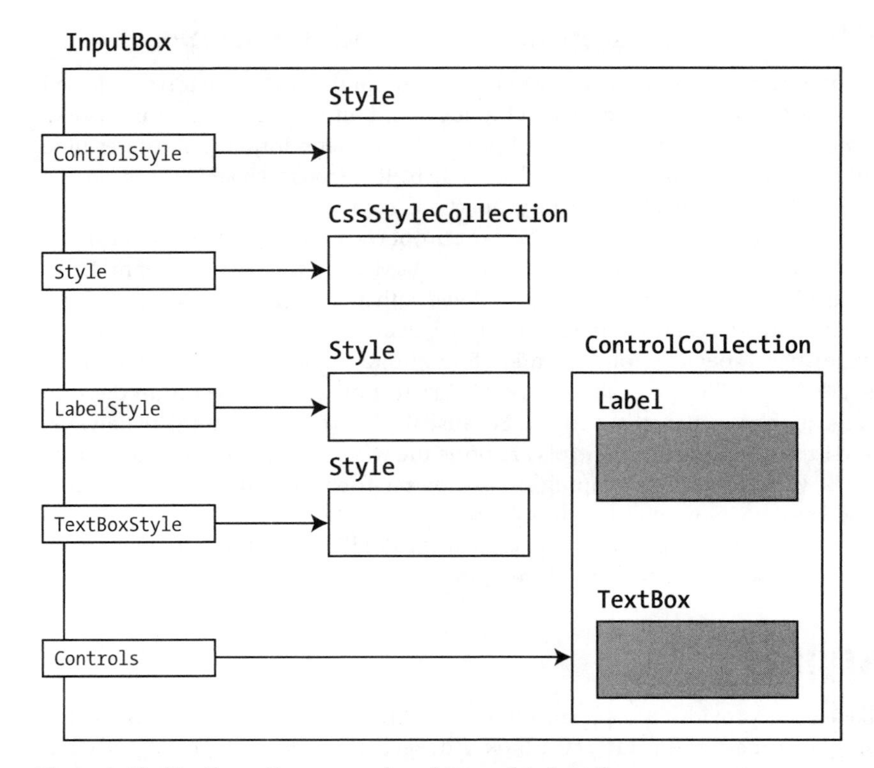

Figure 4-13. *The InputBox control and its multiple styles*

The first step in building our control is to select the tag that represents the outer shell of our custom control. For the `InputBox` we use a `<div>` tag. We pass the tag enumeration value to the base constructor of `WebControl` so that it knows how to render itself:

```
public InputBox() : base(HtmlTextWriterTag.Div)
{
}
```

Because we are building a composite control, we need to override the `CreateChildControls()` method so we can populate the internal `Controls` collection with our child controls. `InputBox` adds the `Label` and `TextBox` controls, in that order:

```
override protected void CreateChildControls()
{
   ControlsBookLib.Ch04.Label label = new ControlsBookLib.Ch04.Label();
   Controls.Add(label);

   ControlsBookLib.Ch04.Textbox textbox = new ControlsBookLib.Ch04.Textbox();
   Controls.Add(textbox);
}
```

The text properties of the child Label and TextBox controls are wired up to top-level properties of our new InputBox control as LabelText and TextBoxText, respectively. The bulk of the code is spent looking up the child controls by position in the Controls collection to set or get the Text property value by casting to the appropriate type:

```
public string LabelText
{
   get
   {
      EnsureChildControls();
      ControlsBookLib.Ch04.Label label =
         (ControlsBookLib.Ch04.Label) Controls[0];
      return label.Text;
   }
   set
   {
      EnsureChildControls();
      ControlsBookLib.Ch04.Label label =
         (ControlsBookLib.Ch04.Label) Controls[0];
      label.Text = value;
   }
}

public string TextboxText
{
   get
   {
      EnsureChildControls();
      ControlsBookLib.Ch04.Textbox textbox =
         (ControlsBookLib.Ch04.Textbox) Controls[1];
      return textbox.Text;
   }
   set
   {
      EnsureChildControls();
      ControlsBookLib.Ch04.Textbox textbox =
         (ControlsBookLib.Ch04.Textbox) Controls[1];
      textbox.Text = value;
   }
}
```

One item to highlight for our new composite control is the EnsureChildControls() method of System.Web.UI.Control, which prevents us from trying to work with a null pointer. EnsureChildControls() checks to see if the child control collection is populated and will cause the CreateChildControls() method to be called if necessary. We do this in our Text routines to ensure that we find the appropriate child control and can safely manipulate its Text property. This is an important step to take before accessing the control hierarchy when working with composite controls.

LabelStyle and TextBoxStyle

Now that we have code to create the child Label and TextBox controls, as well as code to get and set their Text properties, we can move on to demonstrating how to implement custom styles.

Both LabelStyle and TextBoxStyle rely on private instances of the Style class to hold style properties. The private instance is exposed via a read-only property. One of the tasks for this read-only property is to make an instance copy of the configured Style class for each child control available. The other task of the property is to manage ViewState tracking for style settings:

```
Style labelStyle;
public virtual Style LabelStyle
{
   get
   {
      if (labelStyle == null)
      {
         labelStyle = new Style();
         if (IsTrackingViewState)
            ((IStateManager)labelStyle).TrackViewState();
      }
      return labelStyle;
   }
}

Style textboxStyle;
public virtual Style TextboxStyle
{
   get
   {
      if (textboxStyle == null)
      {
         textboxStyle = new Style();
         if (IsTrackingViewState)
            ((IStateManager)textboxStyle).TrackViewState();
      }
      return textboxStyle;
   }
}
```

As discussed in Chapter 3, ViewState is implemented via a StateBag collection that tracks modifications to its collection. Both the Style class and the Control class support ViewState, providing access through implementing the IStateManager interface:

```
interface IStateManager
{
   bool IsTrackingViewState() {  get; }
   void TrackViewState();
   void LoadViewState(object state);
   object SaveViewState();
}
```

The TextBoxStyle and LabelStyle properties' get accessor methods call the IsTrackingViewState() method of the InputBox control to determine if the control is tracking ViewState changes. If it is, the code ensures that state is maintained for the style properties as well.

Customizing ViewState

The WebControl class has facilities to manage ViewState serialization for styles maintained in WebControl's ControlStyle property instance of the Style class. Because we are providing our own style management implementation, we need to customize ViewState persistence mechanisms to include our new styling information, as shown in the following code:

```
override protected object SaveViewState()
{
   object baseState = base.SaveViewState();
   object labelStyleState = (labelStyle != null) ?
((IStateManager)labelStyle).SaveViewState() : null;
   object textboxStyleState = (textboxStyle != null) ?
((IStateManager)textboxStyle).SaveViewState() : null;

   object[] state = new object[3];
   state[0] = baseState;
   state[1] = labelStyleState;
   state[2] = textboxStyleState;

   return state;
}
```

The first thing we do in the code is call WebControl's version of SaveViewState() to ensure we don't break any behavior implemented in the base class. Calling base.SaveViewState() persists state information, including the values in the ControlStyle property. Next, we persist the styling information for the label and text box into ViewState. This is accomplished by casting the Style instances to the IStateManager interface on the Style class so that we gain access to the SaveViewState() method. Finally, we package the three object state binary large objects (BLOBs) into an object array that the ASP.NET framework persists into ViewState.

Retrieving style information from ViewState performs these steps in reverse. Our LoadViewState() method is as follows:

```
override protected void LoadViewState(object savedState)
{
   if (savedState != null)
   {
      object[] state = (object[])savedState;

      if (state[0] != null)
         base.LoadViewState(state[0]);
      if (state[1] != null)
         ((IStateManager)LabelStyle).LoadViewState(state[1]);
      if (state[2] != null)
         ((IStateManager)TextboxStyle).LoadViewState(state[2]);
   }
}
```

LoadViewState() casts the incoming parameter to an object array identical to what we used to persist style information in SaveViewState(). We next call LoadViewSate() for each Style class, checking to ensure that we don't have a null reference before loading state from ViewState. Order matters, so WebControl LoadViewState() goes first followed by the Label and TextBox controls' LoadViewState() routines. At the end of the InputBox LoadViewState() routine, we can be assured that the saved ViewState is retrieved from the postback and is ready to go for rendering.

Rendering the Output

Normally, a composite control leaves the rendering to the base class implementation of Control or WebControl. Because we are doing our own custom style work, we override Render() for the maximum amount of control. In our Render() method override (shown in the following code snippet), we need to call RenderBigTag() to emit the starting <div> tag and the base style properties, we need to call RenderChildren() to have the child controls render their content, and finally, we need to call RenderEndTag() to emit the closing </div> tag. We skip calling RenderContents(), because we took full responsibility for rendering the control, including the inner HTML.

```
override protected void Render(HtmlTextWriter writer)
{
   PrepareControlHierarchy();
   RenderBeginTag(writer);
   RenderChildren(writer);
   RenderEndTag(writer);
}
```

Our implementation of Render() performs some extra work to massage the style information in a helper method named PrepareControlHierarchy() prior to rendering. PrepareControlHierarchy() obtains a reference to each of our child controls so that it can apply style properties:

```
private void PrepareControlHierarchy()
{
   ControlsBookLib.Ch04.Label label =
     (ControlsBookLib.Ch04.Label) Controls[0];
   label.ApplyStyle(LabelStyle);
   label.MergeStyle(ControlStyle);

   ControlsBookLib.Ch04.Textbox textbox =
                    (ControlsBookLib.Ch04.Textbox) Controls[1];
   textbox.ApplyStyle(TextboxStyle);
   textbox.MergeStyle(ControlStyle);
}
```

The ApplyStyle() class method overwrites any existing style properties that are in effect for a control. You can use this to wipe the slate clean, as it replaces all style properties.

The MergeStyle() class method is used to add style properties that are not already set in the Style instance. You have to be careful with what MergeStyle() considers to be set. For a Style attribute such as Font.Italic, it does not consider a false value to be a set value. So, if the existing Style instance has Font.Italic explicitly set to false, MergeStyle() will set Font.Italic to true if the style to be copied has it set to true, as a value of true is considered to be set.

PrepareControlHierachy() uses ApplyStyle() for the custom style properties to load all their attributes. This ensures that the TextBox is decorated with its TextBoxStyle properties and the Label is decorated with its LabelStyle properties. The parent InputBox ControlStyle style is then merged using MergeStyle() to fill in any style properties that are not set by the custom styles. If there aren't any custom style properties selected, the ControlStyle properties will be the default for the two custom controls. Listing 4-6 shows the full listing for InputBox.

Listing 4-6. *The InputBox Custom Control Class File*

```
using System;
using System.Web.UI;
using System.Web.UI.WebControls;
using System.Collections.Specialized;

namespace ControlsBook2Lib.Ch04
{
  [ToolboxData("<{0}:inputbox runat=server></{0}:inputbox>")]
  public class InputBox : WebControl
  {
    public InputBox()
      : base(HtmlTextWriterTag.Div)
    {
    }

    public string LabelText
    {
      get
      {
        EnsureChildControls();
        ControlsBook2Lib.Ch04.Label label =
           (ControlsBook2Lib.Ch04.Label)Controls[0];
        return label.Text;
      }
      set
      {
        EnsureChildControls();
        ControlsBook2Lib.Ch04.Label label =
           (ControlsBook2Lib.Ch04.Label)Controls[0];
        label.Text = value;
      }
    }
```

```
public string TextboxText
{
  get
  {
    EnsureChildControls();
    ControlsBook2Lib.Ch04.Textbox textbox =
       (ControlsBook2Lib.Ch04.Textbox)Controls[1];
    return textbox.Text;
  }
  set
  {
    EnsureChildControls();
    ControlsBook2Lib.Ch04.Textbox textbox =
       (ControlsBook2Lib.Ch04.Textbox)Controls[1];
    textbox.Text = value;
  }
}

Style labelStyle;
public virtual Style LabelStyle
{
  get
  {
    if (labelStyle == null)
    {
      labelStyle = new Style();
      if (IsTrackingViewState)
        ((IStateManager)labelStyle).TrackViewState();
    }
    return labelStyle;
  }
}

Style textboxStyle;
public virtual Style TextboxStyle
{
  get
  {
    if (textboxStyle == null)
    {
      textboxStyle = new Style();
      if (IsTrackingViewState)
        ((IStateManager)textboxStyle).TrackViewState();
    }
```

```
        return textboxStyle;
      }
    }

    override protected void LoadViewState(object savedState)
    {
      if (savedState != null)
      {
        object[] state = (object[])savedState;

        if (state[0] != null)
          base.LoadViewState(state[0]);
        if (state[1] != null)
          ((IStateManager)LabelStyle).LoadViewState(state[1]);
        if (state[2] != null)
          ((IStateManager)TextboxStyle).LoadViewState(state[2]);
      }
    }

    override protected object SaveViewState()
    {
      object baseState = base.SaveViewState();
      object labelStyleState = (labelStyle != null) ?
((IStateManager)labelStyle).SaveViewState() : null;
      object textboxStyleState = (textboxStyle != null) ?
((IStateManager)textboxStyle).SaveViewState() : null;

      object[] state = new object[3];
      state[0] = baseState;
      state[1] = labelStyleState;
      state[2] = textboxStyleState;

      return state;
    }

    override protected void CreateChildControls()
    {

      ControlsBook2Lib.Ch04.Label label = new ControlsBook2Lib.Ch04.Label();
      Controls.Add(label);

      ControlsBook2Lib.Ch04.Textbox textbox = new ControlsBook2Lib.Ch04.Textbox();
      Controls.Add(textbox);
    }
```

```
    public override ControlCollection Controls
    {
      get
      {
        EnsureChildControls();
        return base.Controls;
      }
    }

    private void PrepareControlHierarchy()
    {
      ControlsBook2Lib.Ch04.Label label = (ControlsBook2Lib.Ch04.Label)Controls[0];
      label.ApplyStyle(LabelStyle);
      label.MergeStyle(ControlStyle);

      ControlsBook2Lib.Ch04.Textbox textbox =
(ControlsBook2Lib.Ch04.Textbox)Controls[1];
      textbox.ApplyStyle(TextboxStyle);
      textbox.MergeStyle(ControlStyle);
    }

    override protected void Render(HtmlTextWriter writer)
    {
      PrepareControlHierarchy();
      RenderBeginTag(writer);
      RenderChildren(writer);
      RenderEndTag(writer);
    }
  }
}
```

The InputBox Style Web Form

We now put our new server control to the test with an updated version of the styling workbench from the previous example. The web form example for the InputBox control takes the previous style setting workbench and adds the ability to set styles for the Label and the TextBox as well. Figure 4-14 provides a snapshot of the updated workbench with a panel for styling both child controls.

The control panel for each child control's Style has the same feature set as our previous Web Control Style web form, minus the ability to set the CssClass attribute. It does add a radio button group at the top of the control boxes that allows you to either set or not set the styling for the Label or TextBox control. The full code listings for the web form and the code-behind class file are shown in Listings 4-7 and 4-8, respectively.

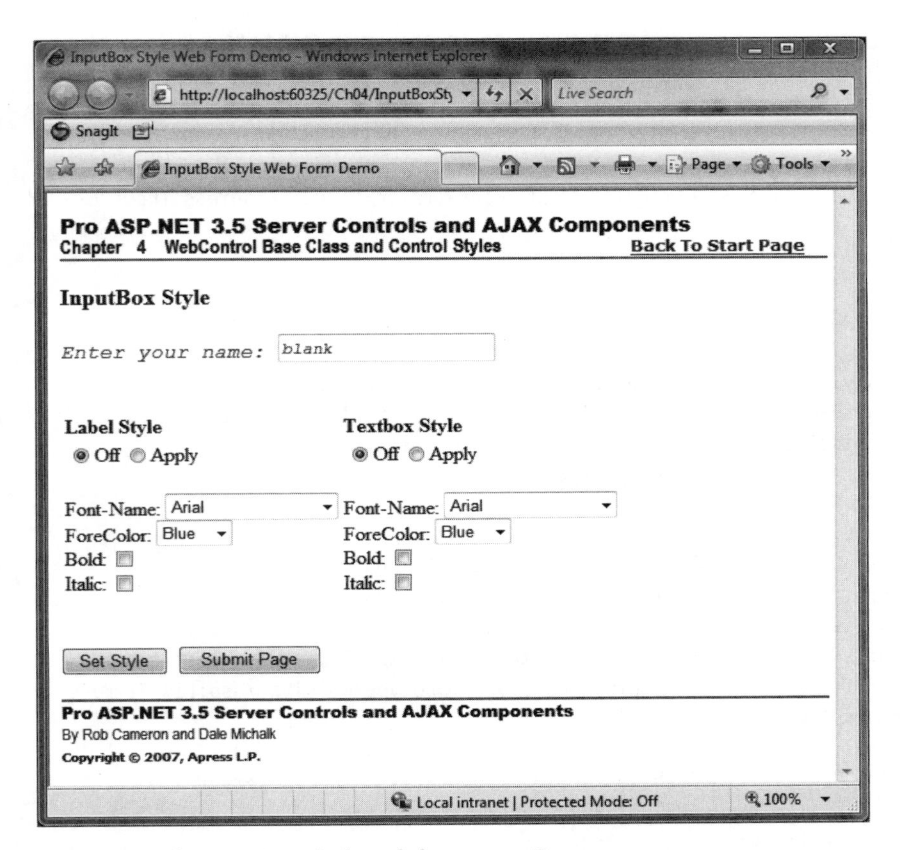

Figure 4-14. *The InputBox Style web form .aspx Page*

Listing 4-7. *The InputBox Style Web Form .aspx Page File*

```
<%@ Page Language="C#"
  MasterPageFile="~/MasterPage/ControlsBook2MasterPage.Master"
  AutoEventWireup="true" CodeBehind="InputBoxStyle.aspx.cs"
  Inherits="ControlsBook2Web.Ch04.InputBoxStyle"
  Title="InputBox Style Web Form Demo" %>

<%@ Register TagPrefix="apress" Namespace="ControlsBook2Lib.Ch04"
Assembly="ControlsBook2Lib" %>
<asp:Content ID="Content1" ContentPlaceHolderID="ChapterNumAndTitle" runat="server">
  <asp:Label ID="ChapterNumberLabel" runat="server"
Width="14px">4</asp:Label>  <asp:Label
    ID="ChapterTitleLabel" runat="server" Width="360px">
    WebControl Base Class and Control Styles</asp:Label>
</asp:Content>
```

```
<asp:Content ID="Content2" ContentPlaceHolderID="PrimaryContent" runat="server">
  <h3>
    InputBox Style</h3>
  <apress:InputBox ID="NameInputBox" runat="server" LabelText="Enter your name: "
  TextboxText="blank"
    Font-Names="Courier New" ForeColor="Red" Font-Italic="True"></apress:InputBox>
  <br />
  <br />
  <table>
    <tr>
      <td>
        <span style="font-weight: bold">Label Style</span><br />
        <asp:RadioButtonList ID="LabelActionList" RepeatColumns="3" runat="server">
          <asp:ListItem Value="Off" Selected="True">Off</asp:ListItem>
          <asp:ListItem Value="Apply">Apply</asp:ListItem>
        </asp:RadioButtonList><br />
        Font-Name:
        <asp:DropDownList ID="LabelFontDropDownList" runat="server">
          <asp:ListItem Value="Arial">Arial</asp:ListItem>
          <asp:ListItem Value="Courier New">Courier New</asp:ListItem>
          <asp:ListItem Value="Times New Roman">Times New Roman</asp:ListItem>
          <asp:ListItem Value="Monotype Corsiva">Monotype Corsiva</asp:ListItem>
        </asp:DropDownList><br />
        ForeColor:
        <asp:DropDownList ID="LabelForeColorDropDownList" runat="server">
          <asp:ListItem Value="Blue">Blue</asp:ListItem>
          <asp:ListItem Value="Red">Red</asp:ListItem>
          <asp:ListItem Value="Black">Black</asp:ListItem>
        </asp:DropDownList><br />
        <asp:CheckBox ID="LabelBoldCheckbox" runat="server" Text="Bold: "
        TextAlign="Left">
        </asp:CheckBox><br />
        <asp:CheckBox ID="LabelItalicCheckbox" runat="server" Text="Italic: "
       TextAlign="Left">
        </asp:CheckBox><br />
      </td>
      <td>
        <span style="font-weight: bold">Textbox Style</span><br />
        <asp:RadioButtonList ID="TextboxActionList" RepeatColumns="3"
        runat="server">
          <asp:ListItem Value="Off" Selected="True">Off</asp:ListItem>
          <asp:ListItem Value="Apply">Apply</asp:ListItem>
        </asp:RadioButtonList><br />
        Font-Name:
```

```
        <asp:DropDownList ID="TextboxFontDropDownList" runat="server">
          <asp:ListItem Value="Arial">Arial</asp:ListItem>
          <asp:ListItem Value="Courier New">Courier New</asp:ListItem>
          <asp:ListItem Value="Times New Roman">Times New Roman</asp:ListItem>
          <asp:ListItem Value="Monotype Corsiva">Monotype Corsiva</asp:ListItem>
        </asp:DropDownList><br />
        ForeColor:
        <asp:DropDownList ID="TextboxForeColorDropDownList" runat="server">
          <asp:ListItem Value="Blue">Blue</asp:ListItem>
          <asp:ListItem Value="Red">Red</asp:ListItem>
          <asp:ListItem Value="Black">Black</asp:ListItem>
        </asp:DropDownList><br />
        <asp:CheckBox ID="TextboxBoldCheckbox" runat="server" Text="Bold: "
       TextAlign="Left">
        </asp:CheckBox><br />
        <asp:CheckBox ID="TextboxItalicCheckbox" runat="server" Text="Italic: "
       TextAlign="Left">
        </asp:CheckBox><br />
      </td>
    </tr>
  </table>
  <br />
  <br />
  <asp:Button ID="SetStyleButton" runat="server" Text="Set Style" Height="23px"
  Width="83px"
    OnClick="SetStyleButton_Click"></asp:Button> 
  <asp:Button ID="SubmitPageButton" runat="server" Text="Submit Page">
 </asp:Button><br />
  <br />
</asp:Content>
```

Listing 4-8. *The InputBox Style Web Form Code-Behind Class File*

```
using System;
using System.Drawing;
using System.ComponentModel;

namespace ControlsBook2Web.Ch04
{
  public partial class InputBoxStyle : System.Web.UI.Page
  {
    protected void Page_Load(object sender, EventArgs e)
    {

    }
```

```
    protected void SetStyleButton_Click(object sender, EventArgs e)
    {
      if (LabelActionList.SelectedIndex > 0)
        SetLabelStyle();

      if (TextboxActionList.SelectedIndex > 0)
        SetTextboxStyle();
    }
    private void SetLabelStyle()
    {
      NameInputBox.LabelStyle.Font.Name = LabelFontDropDownList.SelectedItem.Value;
      NameInputBox.LabelStyle.Font.Bold = (LabelBoldCheckbox.Checked == true);
      NameInputBox.LabelStyle.Font.Italic = (LabelItalicCheckbox.Checked == true);
      Color labelColor =
         (Color)TypeDescriptor.GetConverter(typeof(Color)).ConvertFromString(
         LabelForeColorDropDownList.SelectedItem.Value);
      NameInputBox.LabelStyle.ForeColor = labelColor;
    }

    private void SetTextboxStyle()
    {
      NameInputBox.TextboxStyle.Font.Name =
        TextboxFontDropDownList.SelectedItem.Value;
      NameInputBox.TextboxStyle.Font.Bold = (TextboxBoldCheckbox.Checked == true);
      NameInputBox.TextboxStyle.Font.Italic =
       (TextboxItalicCheckbox.Checked == true);

      // Use the TypeConverter for the System.Drawing.Color class
      // to get the typed Color value from the string value
      Color textboxColor =
         (Color)TypeDescriptor.GetConverter(typeof(Color)).ConvertFromString(
         TextboxForeColorDropDownList.SelectedItem.Value);
      NameInputBox.TextboxStyle.ForeColor = textboxColor;
    }
  }
}
```

The default rendering style of the web form displays our InputBox in a red Courier New font with italic enabled. Both the Label and TextBox controls inside the InputBox pick up the parent-level settings in the .aspx page:

```
<apress:inputbox id="NameInputBox" runat="server" LabelText="Enter your name: "
                 TextboxText="blank" Font-Names="Courier New" ForeColor="Red"
                 Font-Italic="True">
</apress:inputbox>
```

The style properties from the .aspx page render the following HTML tags for the InputBox control:

```
<div id="NameInputBox"
     style="color:Red;font-family: Courier New;font-style:italic;">
   <span style="color:Red;font-family:Courier New;font-style:italic;">
     Enter your name:
   </span>
   <input type="text" name="_ctl1" value="blank"
          style="color:Red;font-family:Courier New;font-style:italic;" />
</div>
```

The HTML snippet shows that the <div>, <span>, and <input> tags all have identical style property strings.

Applying the LabelStyle and TextBoxStyle Settings

Now, it is time to mix things up a little. Go to the Label Style panel, and select the Apply radio button. Check the Bold check box, leaving the rest of the settings for the Label style as they are. Click the Set Style button to post the web form back to the web server, and apply the style changes to the Label child control of the InputBox control:

```
private void SetStyleButton_Click(object sender, System.EventArgs e)
{
   if (LabelActionList.SelectedIndex > 0)
      SetLabelStyle();

   if (TextboxActionList.SelectedIndex > 0)
      SetTextboxStyle();
}
```

The SetStyleButton_Click routine handles the button click activity and is responsible for checking the radio button group for each control to determine whether or not to update the custom styles for the embedded Label and TextBoxStyle controls to the current settings on the web form. In this iteration, only the SetLabelStyle routine is executed, because we set the radio button group to Apply. The code in SetLabelStyle is almost identical to what we discussed in the previous Web Control Style web form example. The web form renders as shown in Figure 4-15.

The HTML for our InputBox control reveals the presence of a different style attribute for the <span> tag representing the Label control:

```
<div id="NameInputBox"
     style="color:Red;font-family:Courier New;font-style:italic;">
   <span style="color:Blue;font-family:Arial;font-weight:bold;font-style:italic;">
     Enter your name:
   </span>
   <input type="text" name="_ctl1" value="Rob"
          style="color:Red;font-family:Courier New;font-style:italic;" />
</div>
```

The <span> tag has a style attribute that reflects the Arial font and bold font weight settings. What is interesting is that the <span> tag still inherits the italic font style from the parent InputBox ControlStyle property settings. This shows how the control method MergeStyle()

will overwrite a `Font.Italic = false` style setting. The code-behind class sets it every time in the following line of code, so it is not an issue of us not accessing the `LabelStyle` property. It is a behavior to be aware of in the current implementation of the ASP.NET style system.

```
NameInputBox.LabelStyle.Font.Italic = (LabelItalicCheckbox.Checked == true);
```

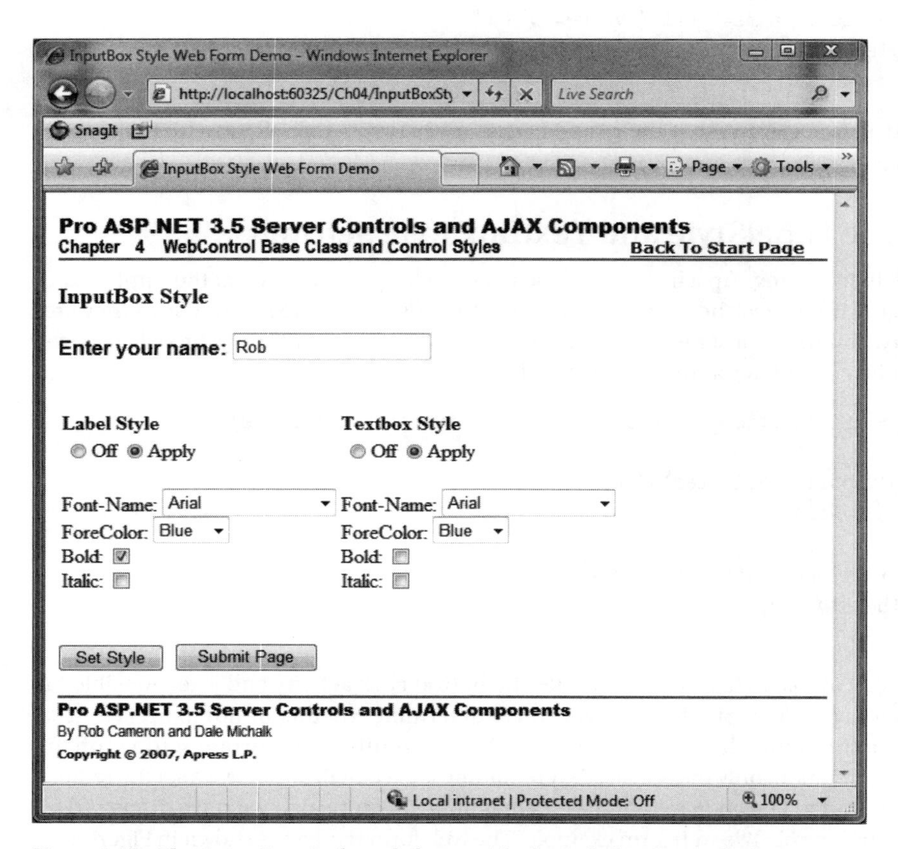

Figure 4-15. *The InputBox Style web form with the Label style applied*

The next step in our demonstration is to exercise the `TextBox Style` settings. Check the Apply radio button for the `TextBoxStyle` box, and then select a different font, such as bold Monotype Corsiva, with a ForeColor of black. Click the Set Style button again to post the web form. The result in Figure 4-16 shows that the two child controls have separate styles, but are both inheriting the italic setting from their parent control via `MergeStyle()`.

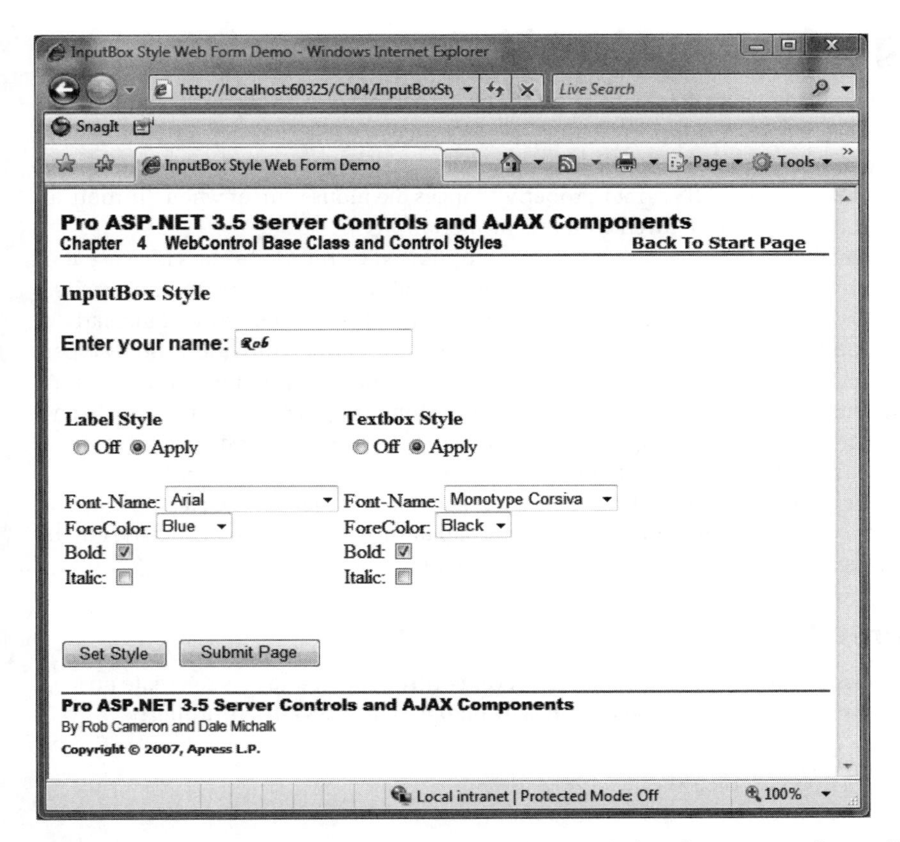

Figure 4-16. *The InputBox Style web form with both Label and TextBox styles applied*

The HTML source confirms the screenshot style view in the browser:

```
<div id="ctl00_ControlsBookContent_NameInputBox"
     style="color:Red;font-family:Courier New;font-style:italic;">
  <span style="color:Blue;font-family:Arial;font-weight:bold;font-style:normal;">
    Enter your name:
  </span>
  <input type="text" name="ctl00$ControlsBookContent$ctl01" value="Rob"
        style="color:Black;font-family:Monotype Corsiva;font-weight:bold;
               font-style:normal;" />
</div>
```

Now that we have covered the basics on styling when inheriting from WebControl, we will move on to cover how to create a custom style class that integrates into the framework while providing additional capabilities.

Creating a Custom Style Class

The Style class that we have worked with so far in this chapter is geared toward a small set of CSS style features. However, IE supports a much larger range of CSS capabilities that allow for some very nice features in your web application. One such attribute is the CSS property named cursor. As you would guess, the CSS cursor property changes the mouse cursor when the mouse passes over HTML elements configured with this property.

One method available to add styles not directly supported by the Style class is to use the Styles collection provided by WebControl and add additional styling using name/value pairs. This option is geared more toward control users. Server control developers should instead provide access to additional styles through custom Style classes, which provide strongly typed access to styling and better designer support with drop-down boxes containing enumeration types or perhaps made available to control users via a custom designer. This is the approach taken by the DataGrid control, which exposes the TableItemStyle via its HeaderStyle, FooterStyle, ItemStyle, AlternatingItemStyle, EditItemStyle, and SelectedItemStyle properties.

Following our own recommendation, we next create a FancyLabelStyle class for our FancyLabel server control that provides a new styling capability that configures how the cursor renders. This takes advantage of the CSS cursor property supported by IE.

The CursorStyle Enumeration

To add our new custom style to the FancyLabel server control, the first task is to create an enumeration that represents the various settings available to the CSS cursor property:

```
public enum CursorStyle
{
   auto,
   hand,
   crosshair,
   help,
   move,
   text,
   wait
}
```

This makes it convenient for us to emit the appropriate text value in the output string using the Enum.Format() method. The next step is to create the FancyLabelStyle class, overriding the constructors from the base Style class:

```
public class FancyLabelStyle : Style
{
   public FancyLabelStyle() : base()
   {
   }

   public FancyLabelStyle(StateBag ViewState) : base(ViewState)
   {
   }
}
```

In the preceding declaration are two constructors. We can either create a Style object that maintains its own ViewState or integrate into the ViewState of the control by calling base(ViewState). For a noncomposite server control, we recommend passing in the control's ViewState and not creating a separate StateBag for a custom Style class in order to maximize performance. We maintain the value of the Cursor's style in ViewState, as shown in the following code:

```
public CursorStyle Cursor
{
   get
   {
      if (ViewState["cursor"]!= null)
      {
         return (CursorStyle)ViewState["cursor"] ;
      }
      else
      {
         return CursorStyle.auto ;
      }
   }
   set
   {
      ViewState["cursor"] = value;
   }
}
```

Style classes add their attributes to a control's output stream by implementing the AddAttributesToRender() method. It takes a reference to the HtmlTextWriter instance the control is using, along with a direct reference to the control itself. Our version of AddAttributesToRender() checks to make sure the Cursor property has been set by checking for the value in ViewState before it adds style properties to HtmlTextWriter:

```
override public void AddAttributesToRender(HtmlTextWriter writer, WebControl owner)
{
   base.AddAttributesToRender(writer, owner); // Ensure base Style class adds its
   // attributes to the output stream
   if (ViewState["cursor"] != null)
   {
      string cursor =
         Enum.Format(typeof(CursorStyle), (CursorStyle)ViewState["cursor"], "G");
      writer.AddStyleAttribute("cursor", cursor);
   }
```

The CursorStyle enumeration is formatted into a string value and added to HtmlTextWriter through its AddStyleAttribute() method. Before we do this, we call the base version of AddAttributesToRender() at the beginning of the method to ensure that the rest of the Style class properties make it into the final output along with our custom property extension.

The Style class also has two overrides available, CopyFrom() and MergeWith(), that allow a control developer to extend the copying and merging of style information. WebControl uses these methods in its ApplyStyle() and MergeStyle() methods. WebControl.MergeStyle() calls Style.MergeWith(), and WebControl.ApplyStyle() calls Style.CopyFrom().

The first method we implement to enhance our custom style class is CopyFrom():

```
override public void CopyFrom(Style style)
{
   base.CopyFrom(style);

   FancyLabelStyle flstyle = style as FancyLabelStyle;
   if (flstyle != null)
      Cursor = flstyle.Cursor;
}
```

CopyFrom() calls the base class version to copy all the standard style properties. It then casts the Style reference passed in to make sure it is of type FancyLabelStyle before it copies the Cursor property. CopyFrom() overwrites Cursor regardless of its current setting.

MergeWith() is similar to CopyFrom(), except it should copy a property only if the value in the Style object has not already been set. Our implementation uses our custom IsEmpty property to determine whether it needs to perform the copy operation. If our current style is set, then IsEmpty returns false and prevents us from overwriting the current setting. It also does a cast to ensure that we are dealing with the correct Style type before copying:

```
override public void MergeWith(Style style)
{
   base.MergeWith(style);

   FancyLabelStyle flstyle = style as FancyLabelStyle;

   //Only merge if inbound style is set and current style is not set
   if ((flstyle != null) && (!flstyle.IsEmpty) && (IsEmpty))
      Cursor = flstyle.Cursor;
}
```

The IsEmpty property follows the pattern of the base Style class. Here is the signature of our version:

```
protected internal new bool IsEmpty
{
   get
   {  //Call base class version to get default behavior
       return base.IsEmpty && (ViewState["cursor"] == null);
   }
}
```

Note that we don't use the override keyword. The base class Style implements this property with the internal keyword, which prevents us from overriding this property. Instead, we use the keyword new to provide our custom replacement. We still call the base version of this method internally, but we also implement custom logic to handle our additional style setting.

The final method we implement is Reset(). This method simply calls the base class version of Reset and removes the cursor value from ViewState:

```
override public void Reset()
{
   base.Reset();

   if (ViewState["cursor"] != null)
   {
      ViewState.Remove("cursor");
   }
}
```

Listing 4-9 presents the complete `FancyLabelStyle` class.

Listing 4-9. *The FancyLabelStyle Class File*

```
using System;
using System.Web.UI;
using System.Web.UI.WebControls;

namespace ControlsBook2Lib.Ch04
{
  public enum CursorStyle
  {
    auto,
    hand,
    crosshair,
    help,
    move,
    text,
    wait
  }

  public class FancyLabelStyle : Style
  {
    public FancyLabelStyle()
      : base()
    {
    }

    public FancyLabelStyle(StateBag ViewState)
      : base(ViewState)
    {
    }

    public CursorStyle Cursor
    {
      get
      {
```

```
        if (ViewState["cursor"] != null)
        {
          return (CursorStyle)ViewState["cursor"];
        }
        else
        {
          return CursorStyle.auto;
        }
      }
      set
      {
        ViewState["cursor"] = value;
      }
    }

    override public void CopyFrom(Style style)
    {
      base.CopyFrom(style);

      FancyLabelStyle flstyle = style as FancyLabelStyle;
      if (flstyle != null)
        Cursor = flstyle.Cursor;
    }

    override public void MergeWith(Style style)
    {
      base.MergeWith(style);

      FancyLabelStyle flstyle = style as FancyLabelStyle;

      //Only merge if inbound style is set and current style is not set
      if ((flstyle != null) && (!flstyle.IsEmpty) && (IsEmpty))
        Cursor = flstyle.Cursor;
    }

    override public void Reset()
    {
      base.Reset();

      if (ViewState["cursor"] != null)
      {
        ViewState.Remove("cursor");
      }
    }
```

```
    // Hide base class version of IsEmpty using the keyword "new"
    //and provide our own
    // The keyword "internal" limits access to within the assembly only,
    //following the pattern
    // established by the base Style class
    protected internal new bool IsEmpty
    {
      get
      { // Call base class version to get default behavior
        return base.IsEmpty && (ViewState["cursor"] == null);
      }
    }

    override public void AddAttributesToRender
                         (HtmlTextWriter writer, WebControl owner)
    {
      base.AddAttributesToRender(writer, owner); // Ensure base Style class adds its
      // attributes to the output stream
      if (ViewState["cursor"] != null)
      {
        string cursor =
           Enum.Format(typeof(CursorStyle), (CursorStyle)ViewState["cursor"], "G");
        writer.AddStyleAttribute("cursor", cursor);
      }
    }
  }
}
```

The FancyLabel Control

The FancyLabel control is our choice for implementing the wonderful cursor capability of the FancyLabelStyle style class. It inherits the code from our Label example earlier in the chapter. We take it into the garage for an overhaul to gain the new style capabilities.

The first upgrade for FancyLabel is overriding the ControlStyle property creation logic. The CreateControlStyle() method override is the recommended way to replace the Style class that is normally associated with ControlStyle to one of your own. We substitute in FancyLabelStyle for the FancyLabel control:

```
protected override Style CreateControlStyle()
{
   FancyLabelStyle style = new FancyLabelStyle(ViewState);
   return style;
}
```

One of the nice features about WebControl is the top-level support it gives to style properties. We mimic this feature set by adding a new top-level property to make it easy to set the cursor styling. It is linked directly to our LabelStyle class instance operating under the ControlStyle property:

```
public CursorStyle Cursor
{
   get
   {
      return ((FancyLabelStyle)ControlStyle).Cursor;
   }
   set
   {
      ((FancyLabelStyle)ControlStyle).Cursor = value;
   }
}
```

The Cursor property accessor must cast ControlStyle to the FancyLabelStyle class via an explicit cast because ControlStyle is defined to be of type of Style. Once this is complete, the Cursor property of the style class is available.

Rendering the FancyLabel Control

The final step is to provide the correct rendering of the new style class in our FancyLabel control. Unfortunately, this step is not the automatic process you might think it would be. The culprit causing the implementation challenge is the design of the Style base class and how WebControl interacts with it.

Both WebControl and the Style class have an implementation of the AddAttributesToRender() method, as Figure 4-17 illustrates. The WebControl version does things such as add utility attributes to the HTML start tag for the control for settings such as Enabled, AccessKey, ToolTip, and TabIndex via the HtmlTextWriter AddAttribute() method. It also walks through the Attributes collection of WebControl, adding those through HtmlTextWriter as well.

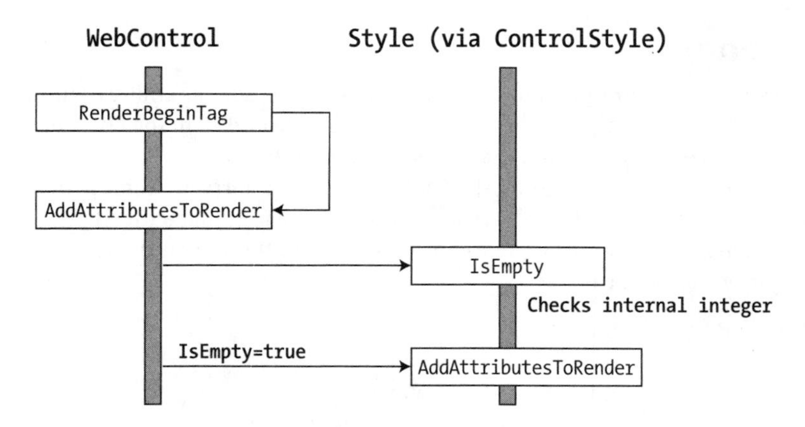

Figure 4-17. *WebControl and Style AddAttributesToRender()*

The Style class instance that is linked to the ControlStyle property is called by WebControl to add its style properties through its version of AddAttributesToRender(). There is one caveat with this call. It is executed only if the Style object signals that its internal state has been modified via the return value of the Style IsEmpty property. In the base Style class, IsEmpty is declared as internal. Because we want our new version of IsEmpty to be called, we hide the base class version by declaring our version of IsEmpty with the new modifier:

```
protected internal new bool IsEmpty
{
   get
   { // Call base class version to get default behavior
      return base.IsEmpty && (ViewState["cursor"] == null);
   }
}
```

Listing 4-10 shows the full control class.

Listing 4-10. *The FancyLabel Control Class File*

```
using System;
using System.Web.UI;
using System.Web.UI.WebControls;
using System.ComponentModel;

namespace ControlsBook2Lib.Ch04
{
  [ToolboxData("<{0}:fancylabel runat=server></{0}:fancylabel>"),
  DefaultProperty("Text")]
  public class FancyLabel : WebControl
  {
    public FancyLabel()
      : base(HtmlTextWriterTag.Span)
    {
    }

    public CursorStyle Cursor
    {
      get
      {
        return ((FancyLabelStyle)ControlStyle).Cursor;
      }
      set
      {
        ((FancyLabelStyle)ControlStyle).Cursor = value;
      }
    }

    public virtual string Text
    {
      get
      {
        object text = ViewState["Text"];
```

```
          if (text == null)
            return string.Empty;
          else
            return (string)text;
        }
        set
        {
          ViewState["Text"] = value;
        }
      }

      protected override Style CreateControlStyle()
      {
        FancyLabelStyle style = new FancyLabelStyle(ViewState);
        return style;
      }

      override protected void RenderContents(HtmlTextWriter writer)
      {
        writer.Write(Text);
      }
    }
  }
```

The FancyLabel Style Web Form

FancyLabel Style is a web form that provides an opportunity to demonstrate our newly minted `FancyLabel Style` class and the containing control, `FancyLabel`. The web form contains eight different `FancyLabel` controls with different `Cursor` properties and one `FancyLabel` without any cursor set to test default behavior. The web form code is provided in full in Listings 4-11 and 4-12.

Listing 4-11. *The FancyLabel Style Web Form .aspx File*

```
<%@ Page Language="C#"
  MasterPageFile="~/MasterPage/ControlsBook2MasterPage.Master"
  AutoEventWireup="true" CodeBehind="FancyLabelStyle.aspx.cs"
  Inherits="ControlsBook2Web.Ch04.FancyLabelStyle"
  Title="FancyLabel Style Demo" %>

<%@ Register TagPrefix="apress" Namespace="ControlsBook2Lib.Ch04"
Assembly="ControlsBook2Lib" %>
<asp:Content ID="Content1" ContentPlaceHolderID="ChapterNumAndTitle" runat="server">
  <asp:Label ID="ChapterNumberLabel" runat="server"
Width="14px">4</asp:Label>  <asp:Label
    ID="ChapterTitleLabel" runat="server" Width="360px">
    WebControl Base Class and Control Styles</asp:Label>
```

```
</asp:Content>
<asp:Content ID="Content2" ContentPlaceHolderID="PrimaryContent" runat="server">
  <h3>
    FancyLabelStyle</h3>
  <apress:FancyLabel ID="DefaultLabel" runat="server" CssClass="grayborder" Text=
   "No cursor set">
  </apress:FancyLabel>
  <br />
  <br />
  <apress:FancyLabel ID="AutoLabel" runat="server" CssClass="grayborder" Text=
   "Auto cursor set">
  </apress:FancyLabel>
  <br />
  <br />
  <apress:FancyLabel ID="CrosshairLabel" runat="server" CssClass="grayborder"
   Text="Crosshair cursor set">
  </apress:FancyLabel>
  <br />
  <br />
  <apress:FancyLabel ID="HandLabel" runat="server" CssClass="grayborder"
   Text="Hand cursor set">
  </apress:FancyLabel>
  <br />
  <br />
  <apress:FancyLabel ID="HelpLabel" runat="server" CssClass="grayborder"
   Text="Help cursor set">
  </apress:FancyLabel>
  <br />
  <br />
  <apress:FancyLabel ID="MoveLabel" runat="server" CssClass="grayborder"
   Text="Move cursor set">
  </apress:FancyLabel>
  <br />
  <br />
  <apress:FancyLabel ID="TextLabel" runat="server" CssClass="grayborder"
   Text="Text cursort set">
  </apress:FancyLabel>
  <br />
  <br />
  <apress:FancyLabel ID="WaitLabel" runat="server" CssClass="grayborder"
  Text="Wait cursor set">
  </apress:FancyLabel>
  <br />
  <br />
  <asp:Button ID="Button1" runat="server" Text="Submit"></asp:Button><br />
</asp:Content>
```

Listing 4-12. *The FancyLabel Style Web Form Code-Behind Class File*

```
using System;
using System.Web.UI.HtmlControls;

namespace ControlsBook2Web.Ch04
{
  public partial class FancyLabelStyle : System.Web.UI.Page
  {
    protected void Page_Load(object sender, EventArgs e)
    {
      AddCssLinktoHeader();
      if (!Page.IsPostBack)
      {
        AutoLabel.Cursor = ControlsBook2Lib.Ch04.CursorStyle.auto;
        CrosshairLabel.Cursor = ControlsBook2Lib.Ch04.CursorStyle.crosshair;
        HandLabel.Cursor = ControlsBook2Lib.Ch04.CursorStyle.hand;
        HelpLabel.Cursor = ControlsBook2Lib.Ch04.CursorStyle.help;
        MoveLabel.Cursor = ControlsBook2Lib.Ch04.CursorStyle.move;
        TextLabel.Cursor = ControlsBook2Lib.Ch04.CursorStyle.text;
        WaitLabel.Cursor = ControlsBook2Lib.Ch04.CursorStyle.wait;
      }
    }

    private void AddCssLinktoHeader()
    {
      HtmlLink cssRef = new HtmlLink();
      cssRef.Href = "../Ch04/WebControlStyle.css";
      cssRef.Attributes.Add("rel", "stylesheet");
      cssRef.Attributes.Add("type", "text/css");
      Header.Controls.Add(cssRef);
    }
  }
}
```

Figure 4-18 shows what the web form looks like when it's rendered.

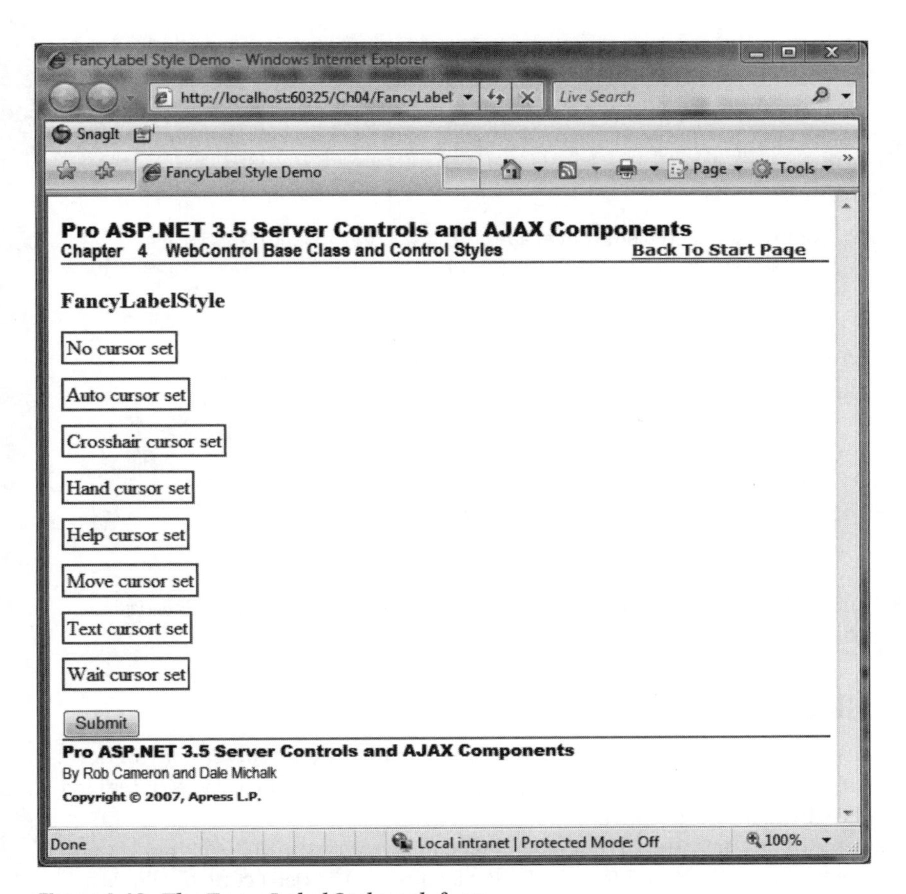

Figure 4-18. *The FancyLabel Style web form*

The following HTML fragment shows the rendered <span> tags and their style attributes for the CSS cursor property:

```
<br/><br/><br/><br/><br/><br/><br/><br/><br/><br/><br/><br/>
<span id="ctl00_ControlsBookContent_AutoLabel" class="grayborder"
      style="cursor:auto;">Auto cursor set</span>
  <br />
  <br />
  <span id="ctl00_ControlsBookContent_CrosshairLabel" class="grayborder"
        style="cursor:crosshair;">Crosshair cursor set</span>
  <br />
  <br />
  <span id="ctl00_ControlsBookContent_HandLabel" class="grayborder"
        style="cursor:hand;">Hand cursor set</span>
```

```
<br />
<br />
<span id="ctl00_ControlsBookContent_HelpLabel" class="grayborder"
      style="cursor:help;">Help cursor set</span>
<br />
<br />
<span id="ctl00_ControlsBookContent_MoveLabel" class="grayborder"
      style="cursor:move;">Move cursor set</span>
<br />
<br />
<span id="ctl00_ControlsBookContent_TextLabel" class="grayborder"
      style="cursor:text;">Text cursort set</span>
<br />
<br />
<span id="ctl00_ControlsBookContent_WaitLabel" class="grayborder"
      style="cursor:wait;">Wait cursor set</span>
<br />
<br />
<input type="submit" name="ctl00$ControlsBookContent$Button1" value="Submit"
       id="ctl00_ControlsBookContent_Button1" /><br />
```

The StyleCollection Class

New in ASP.NET 2.0 and later, the StyleCollection class can be used by server control developers to store and manage Style objects for a control. Style objects stored in a StyleCollection object are applied to different portions of the control.

The best example of how a StyleCollection object can benefit control developers is a hierarchical control, such as the ASP.NET 2.0 and later Menu control. The Menu control allows an ASP.NET developer to define a Style by menu depth in the control. The StyleCollectionDemo web form provides an example of how this works by declaratively providing three Style objects in a LevelMenuItemStyles tag:

```
<LevelMenuItemStyles>
  <asp:MenuItemStyle BackColor="Beige" Font-Italic="True" Font-Names="Verdana"
                     ForeColor="Green" Font-Underline="False" />
  <asp:MenuItemStyle BackColor="Black" Font-Italic="False" Font-Names="Tahoma"
                     ForeColor="Orange" Font-Underline="False" />
  <asp:MenuItemStyle BackColor="Green" Font-Italic="True" Font-Names="Arial"
                     ForeColor="Red" Font-Underline="False" />
</LevelMenuItemStyles>
```

The MenuItemStyle objects declared in the preceding tag are applied in order of level, so the first MenuItemStyle with a BackColor equal to "Beige" is applied to the top-level menu. The second MenuItemStyle applies to the next submenu level, and so on. The declarative syntax makes it very easy to apply styles per menu level. The LevelMenuItemStyles object is also available at runtime and can be altered as shown in the StyleCollectionDemo web form Page_Load event handler:

```
MenuItemStyle alterStyle = new MenuItemStyle();
alterStyle.BackColor = System.Drawing.Color.Navy;
alterStyle.ForeColor = System.Drawing.Color.Gold;

// Remove the last of the three menu item styles. Note that
// since the collection has a zero-based index, the third
// entry has an index value of 2.
MainMenuID.LevelMenuItemStyles.RemoveAt(2);
MainMenuID.LevelMenuItemStyles.Add(alterStyle);
```

Figure 4-19 shows the StyleMenuCollectionDemo web form.

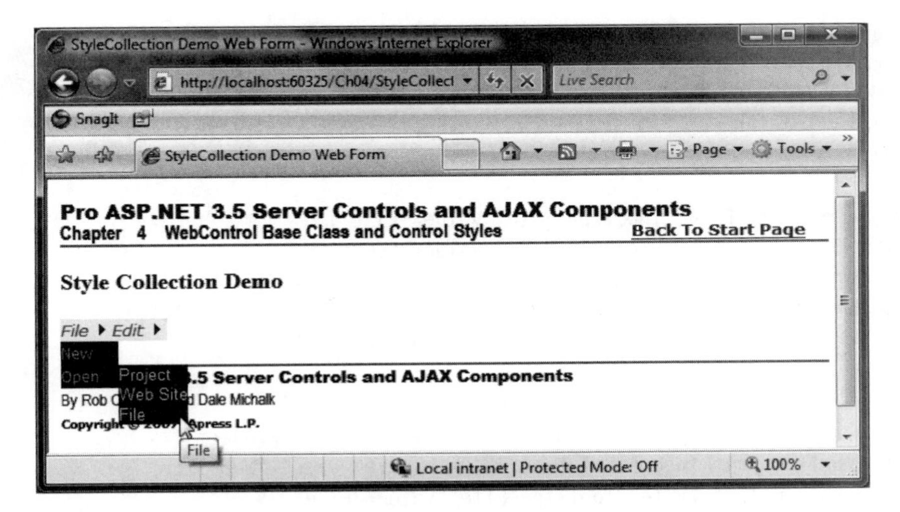

Figure 4-19. *StyleCollectionDemo web form in Action*

In Figure 4-19, you can see the styles applied to the three menu levels, including the dynamically altered style for the third menu level, providing a highly intuitive means to apply styles. Listings 4-13 and 4-14 show the code for the StyleCollectionDemo web form.

Listing 4-13. *The StyleCollectionDemo Web Form .aspx File*

```
<%@ Page Language="C#"
  MasterPageFile="~/MasterPage/ControlsBook2MasterPage.Master"
  AutoEventWireup="true" CodeBehind="StyleCollectionDemo.aspx.cs"
  Inherits="ControlsBook2Web.Ch04.StyleCollectionDemo"
  Title="StyleCollection Demo Web Form" %>

<asp:Content ID="Content1" ContentPlaceHolderID="ChapterNumAndTitle" runat="server">
  <asp:Label ID="ChapterNumberLabel" runat="server"
Width="14px">4</asp:Label>  <asp:Label
    ID="ChapterTitleLabel" runat="server" Width="360px">
   WebControl Base Class and Control Styles</asp:Label>
```

```
</asp:Content>
<asp:Content ID="Content2" ContentPlaceHolderID="PrimaryContent" runat="server">
  <h3>
    Style Collection Demo</h3>
  <asp:Menu ID="MainMenuID" Font-Names="Arial" ForeColor="Blue" runat="server"
   Orientation="Horizontal">
    <LevelMenuItemStyles>
      <asp:MenuItemStyle BackColor="Beige" Font-Italic="True" Font-Names="Verdana"
   ForeColor="Green"
        Font-Underline="False" />
      <asp:MenuItemStyle BackColor="Black" Font-Italic="False" Font-Names="Tahoma"
   ForeColor="Orange"
        Font-Underline="False" />
      <asp:MenuItemStyle BackColor="Green" Font-Italic="True" Font-Names="Arial"
        ForeColor="Red"
        Font-Underline="False" />
    </LevelMenuItemStyles>
    <Items>
      <asp:MenuItem Text="File" ToolTip="File" Value="File">
        <asp:MenuItem Text="New" ToolTip="New" Value="New">
          <asp:MenuItem Text="Project" ToolTip="Project" Value="Project" />
          <asp:MenuItem Text="Web Site" ToolTip="Web Site" Value="Web Site" />
          <asp:MenuItem Text="File" ToolTip="File" Value="File" />
        </asp:MenuItem>
        <asp:MenuItem Text="Open" ToolTip="Open" Value="Open">
          <asp:MenuItem Text="Project" ToolTip="Project" Value="Project" />
          <asp:MenuItem Text="Web Site" ToolTip="Web Site" Value="Web Site" />
          <asp:MenuItem Text="File" ToolTip="File" Value="File" />
        </asp:MenuItem>
      </asp:MenuItem>
      <asp:MenuItem Text="Edit" ToolTip="Edit" Value="Edit">
        <asp:MenuItem Text="Find and Replace" ToolTip="Find and Replace"
         Value="Find and Replace">
          <asp:MenuItem Text="Quick Find" ToolTip="Quick Find" Value="Quick Find" />
          <asp:MenuItem Text="Quick Replace" ToolTip="Quick Replace"
            Value="Quick Replace" />
          <asp:MenuItem Text="Find in Files" ToolTip="Find in Files"
            Value="Find in Files" />
        </asp:MenuItem>
        <asp:MenuItem Text="Advanced" ToolTip="Advanced" Value="Advanced">
          <asp:MenuItem Text="Format Document" ToolTip="Format Document"
           Value="Format Document" />
          <asp:MenuItem Text="Make Uppercase" ToolTip="Make Uppercase"
           Value="Make Uppercase" />
          <asp:MenuItem Text="Make Lowercase" ToolTip="Make Lowercase"
           Value="Make Lowercase" />
```

```
        </asp:MenuItem>
      </asp:MenuItem>
    </Items>
  </asp:Menu>
  <br />
</asp:Content>
```

Listing 4-14. *The StyleCollectionDemo Web Form Code-Behind Class File*

```
using System;
using System.Web.UI.WebControls;

namespace ControlsBook2Web.Ch04
{
  public partial class StyleCollectionDemo : System.Web.UI.Page
  {
    protected void Page_Load(object sender, EventArgs e)
    {
      if (!IsPostBack)
      {
        MenuItemStyle alterStyle = new MenuItemStyle();
        alterStyle.BackColor = System.Drawing.Color.Navy;
        alterStyle.ForeColor = System.Drawing.Color.Gold;

        // Remove the last of the three menu item styles. Note that
        // since the collection has a zero-based index, the third
        // entry has an index value of 2.
        MainMenuID.LevelMenuItemStyles.RemoveAt(2);
        MainMenuID.LevelMenuItemStyles.Add(alterStyle);
      }
    }
  }
}
```

Summary

In this chapter, we started off with a discussion of how HTML documents have two aspects to them: content and appearance. HTML initially promoted tags such as `<font>`, `<b>`, and `<table>` to enhance document appearance. This mixed content with the appearance, increasing code maintenance challenges. We next covered Cascading Style Sheets (CSS). CSS specifies a language to modify the appearance of an HTML document that permits separation of content from appearance. CSS style rules can be declared inline via the `style` attribute, in the document in the `<head>` section via a `<style>` block, or externally via the `<link>` tag.

Then we covered the new rendering model provided by `WebControl`. When you develop your own custom controls, we recommend starting with `WebControl` to leverage the capabilities it brings to the table such as styling and down-level browser support.

WebControl offers explicit support for CSS styling via the ControlStyle class, which exposes the System.Web.UI.WebControls.Style class, and the Style properties, which expose the CssStyleCollection class. WebControl provides top-level style properties that are directly linked to the properties of the Style class exposed by the ControlStyle property for easier access by web developers.

As part of the down-level browser support built into WebControl, ASP.NET is smart enough to choose HtmlTextWriter to emit CSS styles for up-level browsers or to choose Html32TextWriter to use HTML 3.2 style tags for down-level browsers.

Developers can expose multiple Style class instances via custom properties, but they must explicitly manage instance creation, ViewState persistence, and rendering. To implement a custom style class, start with the base Style class and then add additional custom style properties as necessary to meet requirements.

Finally, we provide a quick demonstration of the new StyleCollection object, available in ASP.NET 2.0 and later, that allows server control developers to provide a declarative method of applying multiple styles to different areas of a server control.

CHAPTER 5

Server Control Events

In this chapter, we explore the intricacies of working with server control events. The first part of this chapter is a general discussion of the .NET event architecture. We discuss how to add events to a control, bringing back our favorite `TextBox` control as part of the demonstration. Then, we illustrate how to define custom events and add them to yet another version of our famous `TextBox`. We also examine `System.Web.UI.Control`'s support for maintaining events. Next, we show how to initiate and capture a postback using a `Button` control that we create named `SuperButton`. This section examines `Command` events and event bubbling with an example composite control to demonstrate these concepts. In the final portion of the chapter, we bring it all together with a discussion of the page life cycle, focusing on events. Let's start with a quick overview of events and ASP.NET controls.

Events and ASP.NET Controls

The event-based development paradigm is a well-traveled path on the Windows platform with Visual Basic 6.0 and Visual C++ Microsoft Foundation Classes (MFC) development tools. In this model, developers need not be concerned with the details of how to gather input from hardware or render output to the video card; instead, they can focus on business logic coded in event handlers attached to UI widgets that receive events from the operating system. In ASP.NET, this development model is brought to the Web in much the same way through server controls.

The key technology that sets ASP.NET apart from previous web development paradigms is the use of server-side controls as first-class objects in a similar fashion to Visual Basic or MFC. Server controls provide a rich, object-oriented method of building web content in an environment that is normally spartan in its feature set and procedural in its execution model. A critical aspect of working with objects such as ASP.NET server controls is event-based programming, which we cover in this chapter.

The Need for Events in ASP.NET

In any object-oriented development framework, events are a necessary means of decoupling reusable functionality from the specifics of any given application. This is true in ASP.NET as well. Events allow the encapsulated functionality of a server control, such as a `Button`, to be hooked into the logic of an application without requiring any changes, such as recompilation, to the Button itself.

Events simplify the work of the programmer by providing a consistent protocol for development. Client applications can register their interest in a UI object or control via an event and be notified later by the control when some activity has taken place in the same way regardless of the control. The only thing that changes from control to control is the number or type of events that are available as well as possibly the arguments that a particular event makes available in its method signature. Figure 5-1 presents a comparison between traditional programming and event-based programming.

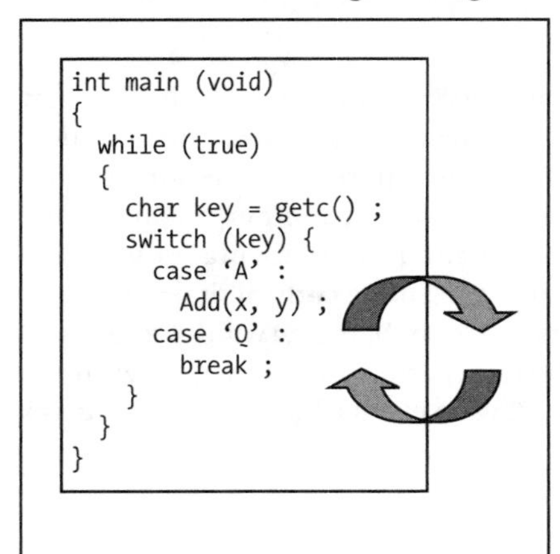

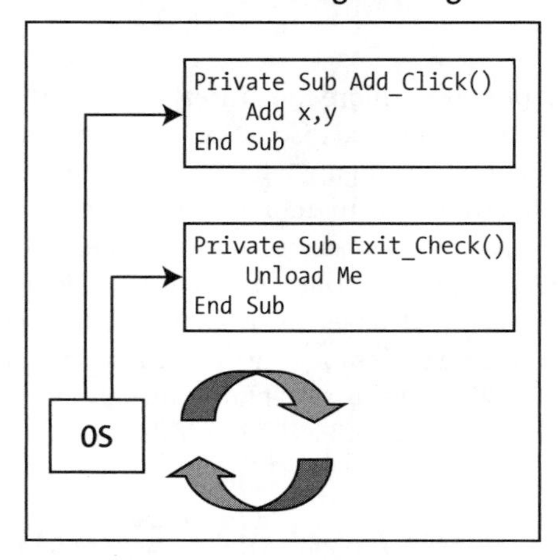

Figure 5-1. *Traditional programming versus event-based programming*

ASP.NET turns on its head the traditional assumption that UI controls are only appropriate for thick-client applications. Through clever use of client-side state and the HTTP `POST` protocol, ASP.NET server controls appear as if they maintain memory on the client and react to user interaction by raising events. Server controls do this without having to resort to a bunch of client-side tricks such as applets or ActiveX controls. Even browsing devices that don't support JavaScript on the client can raise events through HTML form actions.

Figure 5-2 illustrates how a control can raise events and make it look like ASP.NET has turned the browser into an interactive thick-client application. The `TextBox` exposes the `TextChanged` event, while the `Button` notifies interested clients through a `Click` event. All event-handling code for the `TextChanged` and `Click` events is located on the server where the ASP.NET processing occurs. In Chapter 9, we cover how you can take this a step further via ASP.NET 1.0 AJAX, where only a portion of the page is updated instead of causing a full postback, so the web page behaves even more like a thick-client application.

For the event code to react to changes the user makes with the `TextBox` on the web form in the browser, the control must shift execution from the browser back to the web server. The `Button` control is responsible for handling this by generating a form postback when it is clicked.

`Buttons` automatically generate a form postback, but other server controls can also generate a postback using JavaScript. Changing the `AutoPostBack` property for a control that supports it, such as `BulletedList`, `CheckBox`, `ListControl`, and `TextBox`, from the default value of `false` to `true` will cause the control to emit the appropriate JavaScript, taking advantage of client-side events to cause postback.

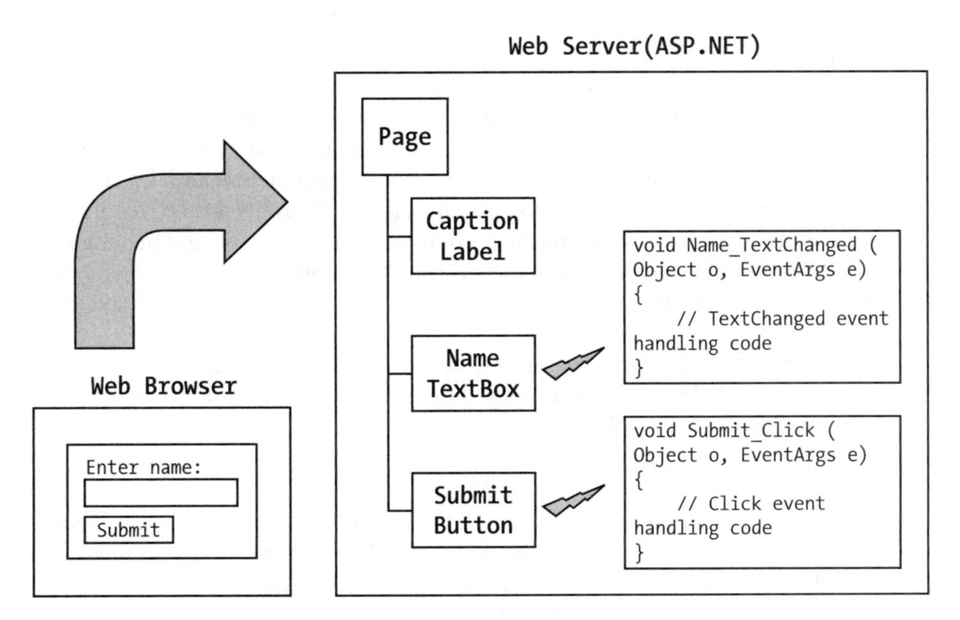

Figure 5-2. *Server-side control events in ASP.NET*

When a user clicks a `Button` in a web form and the browser performs an HTTP `POST` back to the web server, ASP.NET builds the page control tree on the server to dynamically handle the postback request. As discussed in Chapter 3, ASP.NET gives each control in the control tree that has `ViewState` enabled a chance to examine posted data through its `LoadPostData` method. In this method, the control can examine the user input on the server via the posted data and compare it to what was previously stored in `ViewState`. If the data has indeed changed, and if the control has an event that can be fired in response to the data change, the control should return `true` to ASP.NET in `LoadPostData`. Later on in the page life cycle, ASP.NET will call the `RaisePostDataChangedEvent` member for each server control that returned `true` in `LoadPostData` so that the control can, in turn, raise the appropriate event and execute any business logic implemented via an event handler written by the developer. This is the ASP.NET page life cycle that repeats during each postback for state (data) changes and event firing. Before we dive into writing events for ASP.NET, we first provide a high-level overview of events in the .NET Framework in the next section.

The .NET Framework Event Model

Events are generally used in UI development to notify the appropriate object that the user has made a selection, but events can be used for any asynchronous communication need. Whether you're developing desktop Windows applications using Windows Forms or web applications using ASP.NET, classes as objects need a mechanism to communicate with each other. The .NET Framework provides a first-class event model based on delegates, which we discuss in this section.

Delegates

Delegates are similar to interfaces—they specify a contract between the publisher and the subscriber. Although an interface is generally used to specify a set of member functions, a delegate specifies the signature of a single function. To create an instance of a delegate, you must create a function that matches the delegate signature in terms of parameters and data types.

Delegates are often described as safe function pointers; however, unlike function pointers, delegates call more than one function at a time and can represent both static and instance methods. Also unlike function pointers, delegates provide a type-safe callback implementation and can be secured through code access permissions as part of the .NET Framework security model.

Delegates have two parts in the relationship: the delegate declaration and the delegate instance or static method. The delegate declaration defines the function signature as a reference type. Here is how a delegate is declared:

```
public delegate int PrintStatusNotify (object printer, object document) ;
```

Delegates can be declared either outside a class definition or as part of a class through the use of the `delegate` keyword. The .NET Framework `Delegate` class and the .NET Framework `MulticastDelegate` class serve as the base classes for delegates, but neither of these classes is creatable by developers; instead, developers use the `delegate` keyword. As background, the `MulticastDelegate` base class maintains a linked list of delegates that are invoked in order of declaration when the delegate is fired, as you will see in our example in the next section.

In .NET Framework 2.0 and later, anonymous delegates are supported. Anonymous delegates allow a developer to skip the `delegate` declaration and instead define the delegate using more of an inline syntax, to borrow a term from C++. Let's borrow some code from the .NET Framework 2.0 anonymous delegate sample to serve as an example; the borrowed code is available on MSDN Online (search for "Anonymous Delegates Sample"). The example declares a delegate as expected:

```
// Define the delegate method.
delegate decimal CalculateBonus(decimal sales);
```

Next, an object (in this sample an `Employee` class) is declared that has an event declared of type `CalculateBonus` like this:

```
public CalculateBonus calculation_algorithm;
```

After that, declare a named method; the way to define a delegate implementation in .NET Framework 1.1 is like this:

```
static decimal CalculateStandardBonus(decimal sales)
{
    return sales / 10;
}
```

Next, a standard bonus delegate that uses the named method listed previously is defined:

```
CalculateBonus standard_bonus =
new CalculateBonus(CalculateStandardBonus);
```

The preceding code declares a new delegate and passes in the named method (CalculateStandardBonus) for the event method. Things get interesting in the next delegate declaration, which declares the anonymous delegate listed here:

```
CalculateBonus enhanced_bonus =
delegate(decimal sales) { return multiplier * sales / 10; };
```

Instead of using new and passing in a method name, it uses the delegate keyword and declares an unnamed function that takes a parameter named sales of type decimal and returns a calculation of type decimal. The compiler infers the delegate type by the type of the variable (enhanced_bonus of type CalculateBonus). From a runtime perspective, named delegates and anonymous delegates are equivalent, but we would be remiss not to mention this new .NET Framework 2.0 and later syntax.

One question that arises with delegates is what happens if an invoked method throws an exception. Does the delegate continue processing the methods in the invocation list? Actually, if an exception is thrown, the delegate stops processing methods in the invocation list. It does not matter whether or not an exception handler is present. This makes sense, because odds are that if an invoked method throws an exception, methods that follow may throw an exception as well, but it is something to keep in mind.

Working with Delegates

In this section we create a console-based application to demonstrate how delegates work. In our example, we declare a very simple delegate that takes one parameter:

```
delegate void SimpleMulticastDelegate(int i);
```

We next declare a class that contains two class instance methods and one static method. These methods match the signature of the previous delegate declaration:

```
public class DelegateImplementorClass
{
    public void ClassMethod(int i)
    {
        Console.WriteLine("You passed in " + i.ToString() +"
                          to the class method");
    }

    static public void StaticClassMethod(int j)
    {
        Console.WriteLine("You passed in "+ j.ToString() +"
         to the static class method");
    }

    public void YetAnotherClassMethod(int k)
    {
        Console.WriteLine("You passed in " + k.ToString() +"
        to yet another class method");
    }
}
```

In method `Main`, the entry point of any console application in .NET, we put the delegate to work. Here we declare an instance of `DelegateImplementorClass`, as we will add instance methods from this class as subscribers to our delegate:

```
DelegateImplementorClass ImpClass = new DelegateImplementorClass();
```

We next declare an instance of our delegate, adding an instance method to the delegate invocation list that will be called when the delegate instance executes:

```
SimpleMulticastDelegate d = new SimpleMulticastDelegate(ImpClass.ClassMethod);
```

Firing the delegate is simply a matter of calling the delegate instance function:

```
d(5);
```

The rest of method `Main` adds additional methods to the delegate's invocation list. Listing 5-1 is the full code listing. Figure 5-3 shows the output. Notice how each subsequent call to the delegate reflects this in the output. Each time the delegate fires, it passes the parameter value to each subscriber in its invocation list, taking advantage of multicasting behavior.

Listing 5-1. *Delegates in Action*

```
using System;

namespace ControlsBook2.Ch05
{
  delegate void SimpleMulticastDelegate(int i);

  public class DelegateImplementorClass
  {
    public void ClassMethod(int i)
    {
      Console.WriteLine("You passed in " + i.ToString() + " to the class method");
    }

    static public void StaticClassMethod(int j)
    {
      Console.WriteLine("You passed in " + j.ToString() +
      " to the static class method");
    }

    public void YetAnotherClassMethod(int k)
    {
      Console.WriteLine("You passed in " + k.ToString() +
                        " to yet another class method");
    }
  }
```

```
    class Program
    {
        static void Main(string[] args)
        {
            DelegateImplementorClass ImpClass = new DelegateImplementorClass();

            SimpleMulticastDelegate d = new SimpleMulticastDelegate(ImpClass.ClassMethod);
            d(5);
            Console.WriteLine("");

            d += new SimpleMulticastDelegate(DelegateImplementorClass.StaticClassMethod);
            d(10);
            Console.WriteLine("");

            d += new SimpleMulticastDelegate(ImpClass.YetAnotherClassMethod);
            d(15);
            Console.Read();
        }
    }
}
```

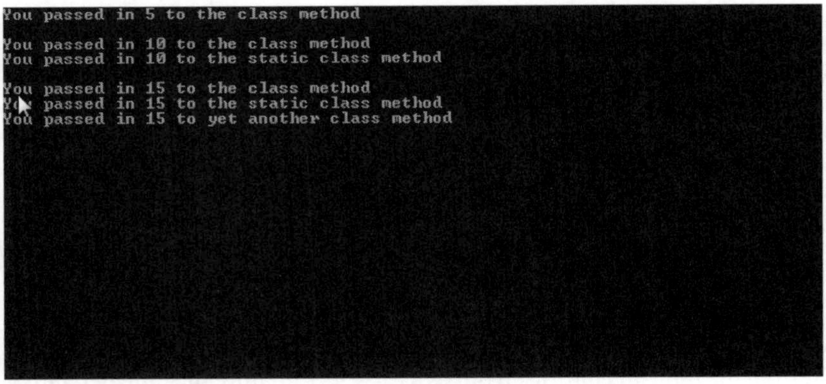

```
You passed in 5 to the class method

You passed in 10 to the class method
You passed in 10 to the static class method

You passed in 15 to the class method
You passed in 15 to the static class method
You passed in 15 to yet another class method
```

Figure 5-3. *Output from our work with delegates*

Stepping back for a minute, you can see how delegates quite successfully fulfill the requirements of the publisher/subscriber model. Here we have the member function `Main` using an instance of the delegate to send messages to subscribing methods in the `DelegateImplementorClass` class. As long as the subscribing methods match the delegate signature, the delegate is happy to add those methods to its invocation list, and it promptly processes this list each time it is invoked with a call to `d()`.

If you step through this code with the debugger, you will notice that methods on the delegate's invocation list are synchronously called in the order that they are added to the invocation list. The syntax for adding a delegate to the invocation list may seem strange at first, because what we are really adding is something more akin to function pointers than, say, an integer. The magic behind this is the keyword delegate and the .NET infrastructure provided by the System.Delegate and System.Delegate.MulticastDelegate classes. The result is that the language compiler simplifies things by providing a keyword that developers use to plug into the delegate infrastructure.

Events

As you may have guessed by now, delegates are the heart and soul of event handling in .NET. They provide the underlying infrastructure for asynchronous callbacks and UI events in web applications under ASP.NET. In addition to the delegate keyword, there is also the event keyword in C#. The event keyword lets you specify a delegate that will fire upon the occurrence of some event in your code. The delegate associated with an event can have one or more client methods in its invocation list that will be called when the object indicates that an event has occurred, as is the case with a MulticastDelegate.

We can declare an event using the event keyword followed by a delegate type and the name of the event. The following event declaration creates a Click event with public accessibility that would be right at home on a Button control:

```
public event EventHandler Click;
```

The name of the event should be a verb signifying that some action has taken place. Init, Click, Load, Unload, and TextChanged are all good examples of such verbs used in the ASP.NET framework.

The event declaration causes the C# compiler to emit code that adds a private field to the class named Click, along with add and remove methods for working with the events hooked in from clients. The nice thing about the event declaration and the code it generates is that it happens under the covers without your having to worry about it. Later on in this chapter, we discuss how to optimize event registration with respect to storage for controls that publish a large number of events, but only a small fraction of them are likely to be subscribed to for a given control instance.

System.EventHandler Delegate

The common denominator of the event declarations with .NET controls is the delegate class System.EventHandler. All the built-in controls in ASP.NET use its signature or some derivative of it to notify their clients when events occur. We recommend that you leverage this infrastructure, because it reduces the amount of custom event development required. In addition, the signature of EventHandler permits server controls in the .NET Framework and their clients to interoperate:

```
delegate void EventHandler(Object o, EventArgs e);
```

The first parameter to EventHandler is an object reference to the control that raised the event. The second parameter to the delegate, EventArgs, contains data pertinent to the event. The base EventArgs class doesn't actually hold any data; it's more of an extensibility point for custom events to override. The EventArgs class does have a read-only static field named Empty that returns an instance of the class that's syntactically convenient to use when raising an event that doesn't require any special arguments or customization.

Invoking an Event in a Control

After you add an event to a control, you need to raise the event in some manner. Instead of calling the event directly, a good design pattern followed by all the prebuilt server controls in ASP.NET is to add a virtual protected method that invokes the event with a prefix of On attached to the name of the method. This provides an additional level of abstraction that allows controls that derive from a base control to easily override the event-raising mechanism to run additional business logic or suppress event invocation altogether. The following code shows an OnClick protected method used to provide access to the Click event of class:

```
protected virtual void OnClick(EventArgs e)
{
   if (Click != null)
      Click(this, e);
}
```

The first thing the protected method does is check to see if any client methods have registered themselves with the Click event instance. The event field will have a null value if no clients have registered a method onto the delegate's invocation list. If clients have subscribed to the Click event with a method having a matching signature, the event field will contain an object reference to a delegate that maintains the invocation list of all registered delegates. The OnClick routine next invokes the event using the function call syntax along with the name of the event. The parameters passed in are a reference to the control raising the event and the event arguments passed into the routine.

Adding an Event to the TextBox Control

The TextBox control that we started in Chapter 3 had the beginnings of a nice clone of the ASP.NET System.Web.UI.WebControls.TextBox control. It saves its values to ViewState, emits the correct HTML to create a text box in the browser, and handles postback data correctly. The control is well on its way to becoming a respectable member of the family.

We next enhance our TextBox control by adding the capability to raise an event when the Text property of the control has changed, as detected by comparing the value currently stored in ViewState with postback data.

Enhancing the TextBox Control with a TextChanged Event

The next step in our TextBox journey is to add a TextChanged event to help bring its functionality more in line with that of the built-in ASP.NET text controls. This necessitates adding an event declaration and enhancing the implementation of the IPostBackDataHandler interface in our control. The most important upgrade is the addition of the TextChanged event field and a protected OnTextChanged method to invoke it:

```
protected virtual void OnTextChanged(EventArgs e)
{
   if (TextChanged != null)
      TextChanged(this, e);
}
public event EventHandler TextChanged;
```

The second upgrade is the logic enhancement to the LoadPostData and RaisePostDataChanged methods. In LoadPostData, the ViewState value of the Text property is checked against the incoming value from postback for any differences. If there is a difference, the Text property is changed to the new value in ViewState, and true is returned from the routine. This guarantees that the event is raised when RaisePostDataChangedEvent is called by ASP.NET 2.0 and later further on in the page life cycle.

```
public bool LoadPostData(string postDataKey, NameValueCollection postCollection)
{
   string postedValue = postCollection[postDataKey];
   if (!Text.Equals(postedValue))
   {
      Text = postedValue;
      return true;
   }
   else
      return false;
}
```

The upgrade to the RaisePostDataChangedEvent method is the addition of a single line. Instead of being blank, it calls on our newly created OnTextChanged method to invoke the TextChanged event. We use the static field Empty of the EventArgs class to create an instance of EventArgs for us, as we don't need to customize EventArgs in this case:

```
public void RaisePostDataChangedEvent()
{
   OnTextChanged(EventArgs.Empty);
}
```

The code in Listing 5-2 is full text of the control after the modifications required to add the TextChanged event.

Listing 5-2. *The Improved TextBox Control with Events Using System*

```
using System.Web;
using System.Web.UI;
using System.Collections.Specialized;
using System.ComponentModel;

namespace ControlsBook2Lib.Ch05
{
  [ToolboxData("<{0}:textbox runat=server></{0}:textbox>"),
  DefaultProperty("Text")]
  public class TextBox : Control, IPostBackDataHandler
  {
    public string Text
    {
```

```
    get
    {
      object text = ViewState["Text"];
      if (text == null)
        return string.Empty;
      else
        return (string)text;
    }
    set
    {
      ViewState["Text"] = value;
    }
  }

  public bool LoadPostData(string postDataKey,
     NameValueCollection postCollection)
  {
    string postedValue = postCollection[postDataKey];
    if (!Text.Equals(postedValue))
    {
      Text = postedValue;
      return true;
    }
    else
      return false;
  }

  public void RaisePostDataChangedEvent()
  {
    OnTextChanged(EventArgs.Empty);
  }

  protected virtual void OnTextChanged(EventArgs e)
  {
    if (TextChanged != null)
      TextChanged(this, e);
  }

  public event EventHandler TextChanged;

  protected override void Render(HtmlTextWriter writer)
  {
    base.Render(writer);
    Page.VerifyRenderingInServerForm(this);
    // write out the <INPUT type="text"> tag
    writer.Write("<INPUT type=\"text\" name=\"");
    writer.Write(this.UniqueID);
    writer.Write("\" value=\"" + this.Text + "\" />");
```

```
        }
    }
}
```

Using the TextBox Control on a Web Form

The TextBox web form shown in the Design view in Figure 5-4 hosts the newly minted TextBox control with its TextChanged event capabilities.

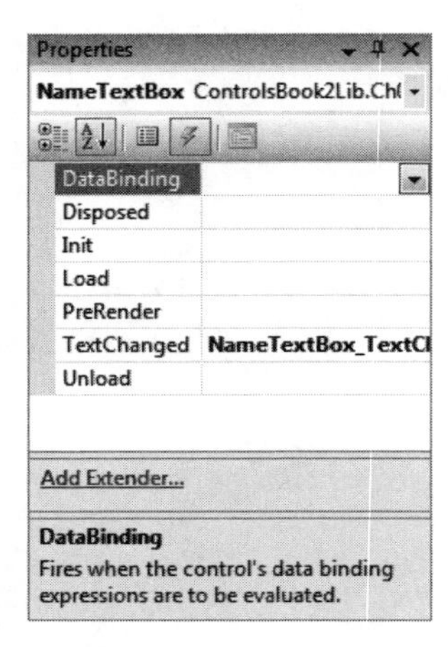

Figure 5-4. *Server-side control events in ASP.NET*

The web form contains an instance of our TextBox control named NameTextBox, along with a Label control named ChangeLabel that is used to indicate the raising of TextChanged event. The label is programmatically set to a value of "No change!" along with the current time by default during the loading of the web form. Raising the TextChanged event causes the event-handling code to set the label's value to "Changed" along with the current time. This allows you to recycle the control several times to verify that the event is working properly.

The TextChanged event of the NameTextBox control is visible when you select the control in the Design view of Visual Studio and look at it in the Properties window, as shown in Figure 5-4. Click the lightning bolt icon to categorize the properties by events and you will see TextChanged. We used an event handler called Name_TextChanged as a client subscriber to the TextChanged event. The full extent of our code work is shown in Listings 5-3 and 5-4.

Listing 5-3. *The TextBox Web Form .aspx File*

```
<%@ Page Language="C#"
MasterPageFile="~/MasterPage/ControlsBook2MasterPage.Master"
  AutoEventWireup="true" CodeBehind="TextBox.aspx.cs"
Inherits="ControlsBook2Web.Ch05.TextBox"   Title="Untitled Page" %>
```

```
<%@ Register TagPrefix="apress" Namespace="ControlsBook2Lib.Ch05"
Assembly="ControlsBook2Lib" %>
<asp:Content ID="Content1" ContentPlaceHolderID="ChapterNumAndTitle" runat="server">
  <asp:Label ID="ChapterNumberLabel" runat="server"
  Width="14px">5</asp:Label>  <asp:Label
    ID="ChapterTitleLabel" runat="server" Width="360px">
   Server Control Events</asp:Label></asp:Content>
<asp:Content ID="Content2" ContentPlaceHolderID="PrimaryContent" runat="server">
  <h3>
    TextBox</h3>
  Enter your name:<br />
  <apress:TextBox ID="NameTextBox" runat="server"
  OnTextChanged="NameTextBox_TextChanged">
  </apress:TextBox>
  <br />
  <br />
  <asp:Button ID="SubmitPageButton" runat="server" Text="Submit Page">
  </asp:Button><br />
  <br />
  <asp:Label ID="ChangeLabel" runat="server" Text=""></asp:Label><br />
</asp:Content>
```

Listing 5-4. *The TextBox Web Form Code-Behind Class File*

```
using System;
using System.Web.UI;
using System.Web.UI.WebControls;

namespace ControlsBook2Web.Ch05
{
  public partial class TextBox : System.Web.UI.Page
  {
    protected void Page_Load(object sender, EventArgs e)
    {
      ChangeLabel.Text = DateTime.Now.ToLongTimeString() + ": No change.";
    }

    protected void NameTextBox_TextChanged(object sender, EventArgs e)
    {
      ChangeLabel.Text = DateTime.Now.ToLongTimeString() + ": Changed!";
    }
  }
}
```

In ASP.NET 1.1, the event wiring is conducted, usually by the Visual Studio .NET 2003 designer, inside the InitializeComponent routine:

```
private void InitializeComponent()
{
   this.NameTextBox.TextChanged += new System.EventHandler(this.Name_TextChanged);
   this.Load += new System.EventHandler(this.Page_Load);
}
```

In ASP.NET 2.0 and later, the syntax is much more streamlined; you simply declare the event handler as an attribute on the server control tag:

```
<apress:textbox id="NameTextBox" runat="server"
OnTextChanged="NameTextBox_TextChanged">
```

Notice the attribute OnTextChanged is assigned the method name in the code-behind file, simplifying the page model greatly. Behind the scenes in ASP.NET 2.0 and later, just like in ASP.NET 1.1, the Name_TextChanged method is wrapped by a System.EventHandler delegate and then passed to the TextChanged event of our custom TextBox control to add it to its delegate invocation list. The execution of the web form during the initial page request results in the UI output of Figure 5-5. The ViewState rendered by the control into this web form shows the Text property as a blank value. We entered a name into the TextBox as well, but we haven't clicked the button to submit the web form via postback.

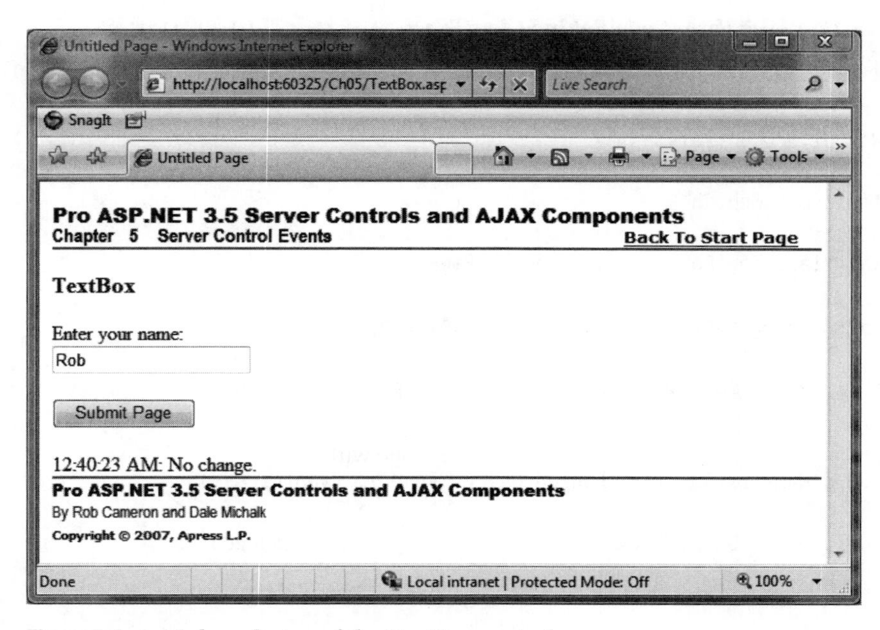

Figure 5-5. *Initial rendering of the TextBox control*

Upon clicking the button to execute a postback to the web server, the TextBox control will read the blank value from ViewState and find the name value "Rob" when the ASP.NET invokes LoadPostData. Because the posted data is different from the current ViewState value, it calls its internal OnTextChanged method to raise events to all registered delegate subscribers. This results in the Name_TextChanged event handler method firing, and the code that changes the label to reflect the new value executes:

```
private void Name_TextChanged(object sender, System.EventArgs e)
{
   ChangeLabel.Text = DateTime.Now.ToLongTimeString() + ": Changed!";
}
```

The result is that ChangeLabel displays the text containing the current time and the word "Changed!" as shown in Figure 5-6.

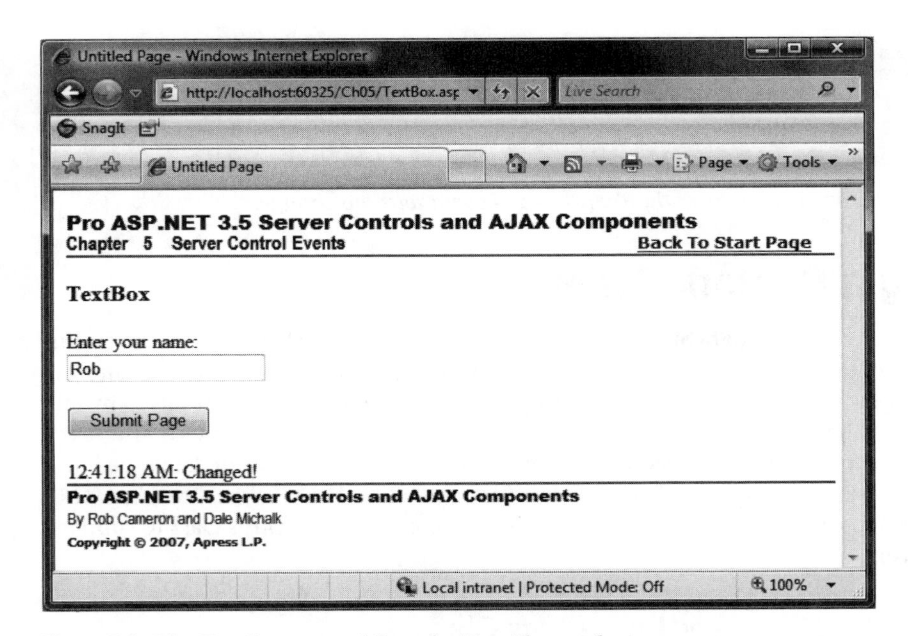

Figure 5-6. *The TextBox control fires the TextChanged event.*

The next step in this demonstration is to recycle the page without changing the value in the TextBox control by simply clicking the Submit Page button. Because the ViewState and the control's text post data contain the same value of "Rob," no event is raised. The increment of the timestamp in the label in Figure 5-7 confirms that the page was processed successfully. Our control is able to react appropriately to changes of its Text property.

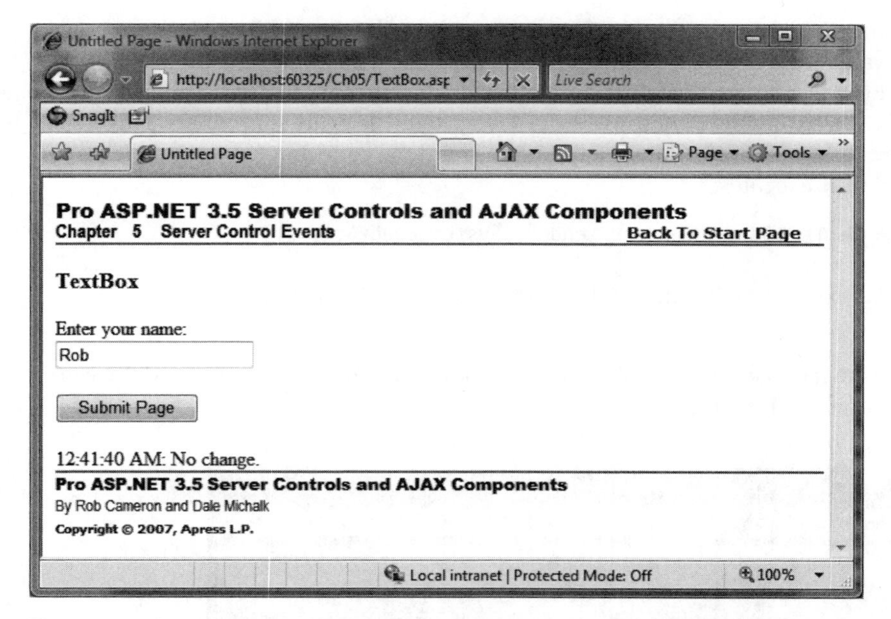

Figure 5-7. *The TextBox control fires the TextChanged event with no change.*

Creating a Custom Event

If an event does not provide data but is merely a signal that something has happened, you can take advantage of the `EventHandler` delegate class and its empty `EventArgs` implementation. However, we want to provide additional information in the `TextChanged` event raised by our `TextBox` control. The newly minted event will track both before and after values of the `Text` property between postback submissions. The control loads the `oldValue` from data saved in `ViewState`; the `newValue` value loads from the data received in the `<INPUT type="text">` HTML element through postback. We now move on to create our custom `EventArgs` class to support our custom event.

Creating a TextChangedEventArgs Class

The first requirement is to create an enhanced `EventArgs`-based class that holds the event data. We create a new class derived from `EventArgs` that exposes two read-only properties to clients, `OldValue` and `NewValue`, as shown in the following code:

```
public class TextChangedEventArgs : EventArgs
{
   private string oldValue;
   private string newValue;
```

```
   public TextChangedEventArgs(string oldValue, string newValue)
   {
      this.oldValue = oldValue;
      this.newValue = newValue;
   }

   public string OldValue
   {
      get
      {
         return oldValue;
      }
   }

   public string NewValue
   {
      get
      {
         return newValue;
      }
   }
}
```

The class created is fairly straightforward. The two properties have only `get` accessors to make them read-only, making the constructor the only way to populate the internal fields with their values.

Creating a TextChangedEventHandler Delegate

Delegate creation is the next step in defining our custom event. There is not an inheritance chain that must be followed with delegates, as all delegate types are created using the keyword `delegate`. Instead, we choose to follow the method signature used by other controls in ASP.NET to build on a successful design pattern.

The signature of the delegate has two parameters and a `void` return value. The first parameter remains of type `object`, and the second parameter must be of type `EventArgs` or derived from it. Because we already created the `TextChangedEventArgs` class, we use that as our second parameter to take advantage of its `OldValue` and `NewValue` properties.

The name used in the declaration of the following delegate is also important. The pattern for ASP.NET controls is to add the word "EventHandler" to the end of the event of the delegate. In this case, we add "TextChanged" to "EventHandler" to get `TextChangedEventHandler` as our name.

Both the `TextChangedEventArgs` class and the `TextChangedEventHandler` delegate are put into a file named `TextChanged.cs` that is part of the `ControlsBook2Lib` library project for reference by our new control, as shown in Listing 5-5.

Listing 5-5. *The TextChanged.cs Class File for the TextChangedEventArgs Class and TextChangedEventHandler Delegate Definitions*

```
using System;

namespace ControlsBook2Lib.Ch05
{
   public delegate void
         TextChangedEventHandler(object o, TextChangedEventArgs tce);

   public class TextChangedEventArgs : EventArgs
   {
      private string oldValue;
      private string newValue;

      public TextChangedEventArgs(string oldValue, string newValue)
      {
         this.oldValue = oldValue;
         this.newValue = newValue;
      }

      public string OldValue
      {
         get
         {
            return oldValue;
         }
      }

      public string NewValue
      {
         get
         {
            return newValue;
         }
      }
   }
}
```

Adding an Event to the CustomEventTextBox Control

To demonstrate the newly minted `TextChangedEventHandler` delegate, we take our `TextBox` control and copy its contents into a class named `CustomEventTextBox`. Another option would be to customize the behavior in an object-oriented manner by overriding the necessary methods in a derived class. However, in this chapter, we choose the route of separate classes so that we can more clearly isolate the two `TextBox` control examples and highlight the different design decisions embodied in them.

Replacing the event declaration is the easiest part. The control starts with an EventHandler delegate but is changed to take a TextChangedEventHandler delegate:

```
public event TextChangedEventHandler TextChanged;
```

The second change is the replacement of the OnTextChanged event invocation method to take TextChangedEventArgs as the single parameter to the method, as shown in the following code. This is one of the reasons for having the On-prefixed methods in controls as an abstraction layer. It makes it a simpler code change to augment or replace the event mechanism.

```
protected virtual void OnTextChanged(TextChangedEventArgs tce)
{
   if (TextChanged != null)
      TextChanged(this, tce);
}
```

The next step is to add logic to track the before and after values. A private string field named oldText is added to the class and is given its value inside LoadPostData. This gives us a chance to load TextChangedEventArgs properly when we raise the event. Here is a snippet of the code change from LoadPostData that does the work:

```
if (!Text.Equals(postedValue))
{
   oldText = Text;
   Text = postedValue;
   return true;
}
```

The last step is to replace all routines that call OnTextChanged. We have only one: RaisePostDataChanged. It takes the before and after values from the oldText field and the Text property in LoadPostData and creates a new TextChangedEventArgs class instance:

```
public void RaisePostDataChangedEvent()
{
   OnTextChanged(new TextChangedEventArgs(oldText, Text));
}
```

Our control is now ready for testing on a web form to display its dazzling event capabilities. Listing 5-6 contains the full source code.

Listing 5-6. *The CustomEventTextBox Control Class File*

```
using System;
using System.Web;
using System.Web.UI;
using System.Collections.Specialized;
using System.ComponentModel;
```

```
namespace ControlsBook2Lib.Ch05
{
  [ToolboxData("<{0}:customeventtextbox runat=server></{0}:customeventtextbox>"),
  DefaultProperty("Text")]
  public class CustomEventTextBox : Control, IPostBackDataHandler
  {
    private string oldText;

    public virtual string Text
    {
      get
      {
        object text = ViewState["Text"];
        if (text == null)
          return string.Empty;
        else
          return (string)text;
      }
      set
      {
        ViewState["Text"] = value;
      }
    }

    public bool LoadPostData(string postDataKey,
       NameValueCollection postCollection)
    {
      string postedValue = postCollection[postDataKey];
      if (!Text.Equals(postedValue))
      {
        oldText = Text;
        Text = postedValue;
        return true;
      }
      else
        return false;
    }

    public void RaisePostDataChangedEvent()
    {
      OnTextChanged(new TextChangedEventArgs(oldText, Text));
    }

    protected virtual void OnTextChanged(TextChangedEventArgs tce)
    {
      if (TextChanged != null)
        TextChanged(this, tce);
    }
```

```
    public event TextChangedEventHandler TextChanged;

    protected override void Render(HtmlTextWriter writer)
    {
      base.Render(writer);
      Page.VerifyRenderingInServerForm(this);
      // write out the <INPUT type="text"> tag
      writer.Write("<INPUT type=\"text\" name=\"");
      writer.Write(this.UniqueID);
      writer.Write("\" value=\"" + this.Text + "\" />");
    }
  }
}
```

Using the CustomEventTextBox Control on a Web Form

After building our new control, we are ready to put it to use in the CustomEventTextBox web form. This web form has the CustomEventTextBox control plus a button and two labels named BeforeLabel and AfterLabel that are used to track the before and after values of the control when the custom TextChanged event is raised.

Creating the event mapping in Visual Studio is performed in the same manner as the previous TextChanged event in the preceding TextBox demonstration. We use the Properties window, as shown in Figure 5-8, to wire up the event to the NameCustom_TextChanged handling method in the code-behind class.

The web form starts out with the labels displaying blank values, as shown in Figure 5-9. We enter Rob's name to cause the next form submit to raise the event. Listings 5-7 and 5-8 contain the source code for the CustomEventTextBox web form.

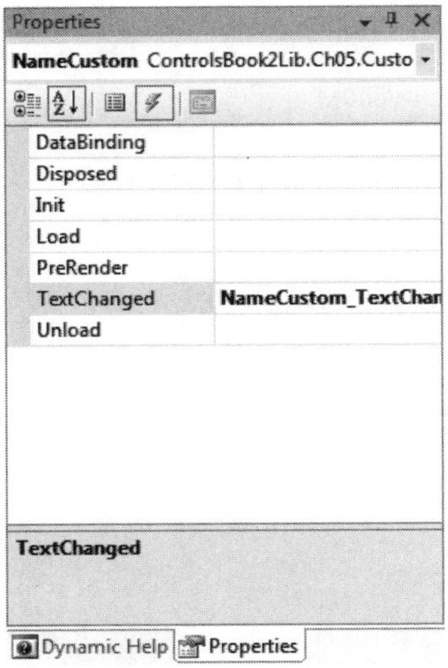

Figure 5-8. *The Properties window view of our custom TextChanged event*

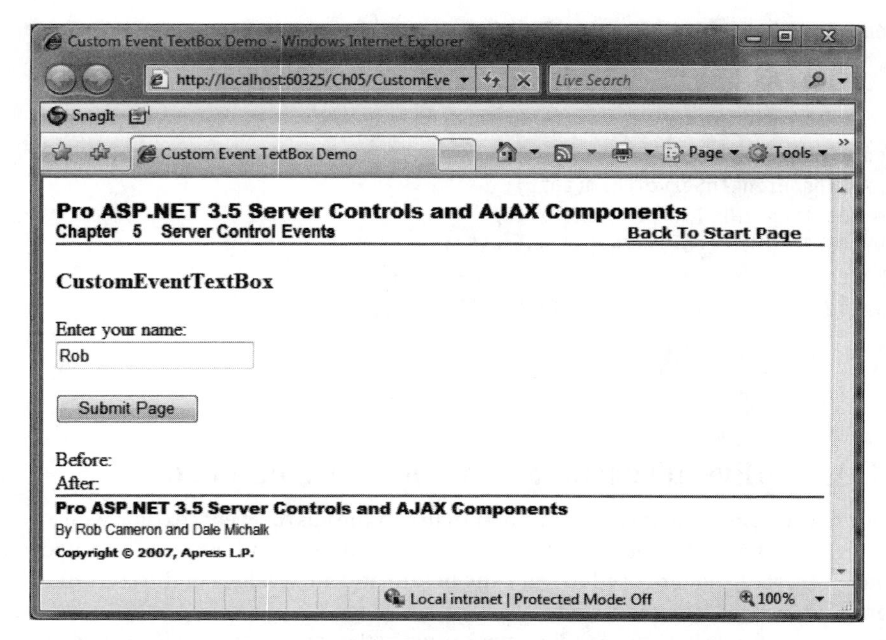

Figure 5-9. *Initial page request with the CustomEventTextBox web form*

Listing 5-7. *The CustomEventTextBox Web Form .aspx File*

```
<%@ Page Language="C#"
MasterPageFile="~/MasterPage/ControlsBook2MasterPage.Master"
  AutoEventWireup="true" CodeBehind="CustomEventTextBox.aspx.cs"
  Inherits="ControlsBook2Web.Ch05.CustomEventTextBox"
  Title="Custom Event TextBox Demo" %>

<%@ Register TagPrefix="apress" Namespace="ControlsBook2Lib.Ch05"
  Assembly="ControlsBook2Lib" %>
<asp:Content ID="Content1" ContentPlaceHolderID="ChapterNumAndTitle" runat="server">
  <asp:Label ID="ChapterNumberLabel" runat="server"
Width="14px">5</asp:Label>  <asp:Label
    ID="ChapterTitleLabel" runat="server" Width="360px">Server Control Events
   </asp:Label>
</asp:Content>
<asp:Content ID="Content2" ContentPlaceHolderID="PrimaryContent" runat="server">
  <h3>
    CustomEventTextBox</h3>
```

```
  Enter your name:<br />
  <apress:CustomEventTextBox ID="NameCustom" runat="server"
  OnTextChanged="NameCustom_TextChanged">
  </apress:CustomEventTextBox>
  <br />
  <br />
  <asp:Button ID="SubmitPageButton" runat="server" Text="Submit Page"></asp:Button>
  <br />
  <br />
  Before:<asp:Label ID="BeforeLabel" runat="server" Text=""></asp:Label><br />
  After:<asp:Label ID="AfterLabel" runat="server" Text=""></asp:Label><br />
</asp:Content>
```

Listing 5-8. *The CustomEventTextBox Web Form Code-Behind Class File*

```
using System;
using System.Web.UI;
using System.Web.UI.WebControls;

namespace ControlsBook2Web.Ch05
{
  public partial class CustomEventTextBox : System.Web.UI.Page
  {
    protected void Page_Load(object sender, EventArgs e)
    {
      BeforeLabel.Text = NameCustom.Text;
      AfterLabel.Text = NameCustom.Text;
    }

    protected void NameCustom_TextChanged(object o,
   ControlsBook2Lib.Ch05.TextChangedEventArgs tce)
    {
      BeforeLabel.Text = tce.OldValue;
      AfterLabel.Text = tce.NewValue;
    }
  }
}
```

We exercise the custom event by submitting the page by clicking the Submit Page button. This causes the `AfterLabel` control to change to “Rob,” whereas the `BeforeLabel` keeps the old blank value, as shown in Figure 5-10.

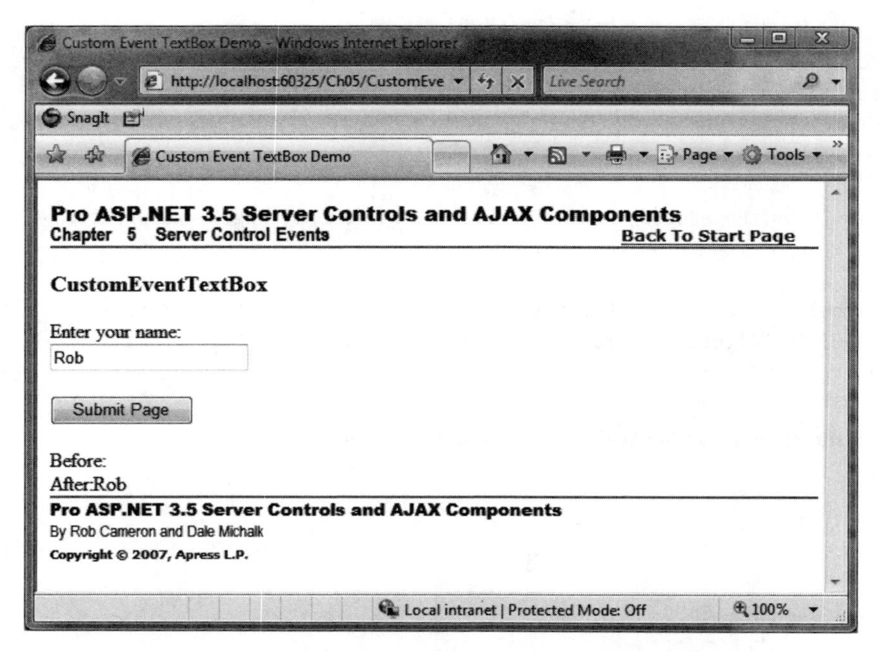

Figure 5-10. *The page after submitting the CustomEventTextBox web form*

The Visual Studio Properties window did its job in wiring up to the custom event. It was smart enough to realize we had to use `TextChangedEventHandler` as a delegate to wrap the `NameCustom_TextChanged` event-handling method. This behavior by the Designer is one more reason we recommend sticking to the event model design pattern implemented in .NET. As mentioned previously, the resulting wire-up code appears in the `.aspx` page as an attribute on the server control:

```
<apress:CustomEventTextBox id="NameCustom" runat="server"
OnTextChanged="NameCustom_TextChanged"></apress:CustomEventTextBox>
```

The following definition of `NameCustom_TextChanged` shows it is connected to `TextChanged` correctly, taking `TextChangedEventArgs` as its second parameter. The parameter named `tce` is the conduit to the information added to the `BeforeLabel` and `AfterLabel` `Text` values:

```
private void NameCustom_TextChanged(object o,
                        ControlsBook2Lib.Ch05.TextChangedEventArgs tce)
{
   BeforeLabel.Text = tce.OldValue;
   AfterLabel.Text = tce.NewValue;
}
```

Figure 5-11 shows what happens if we type a second name in the `CustomEventTextBox` control input box and click the Submit Page button to generate another postback. The control successfully remembers what the previous input was.

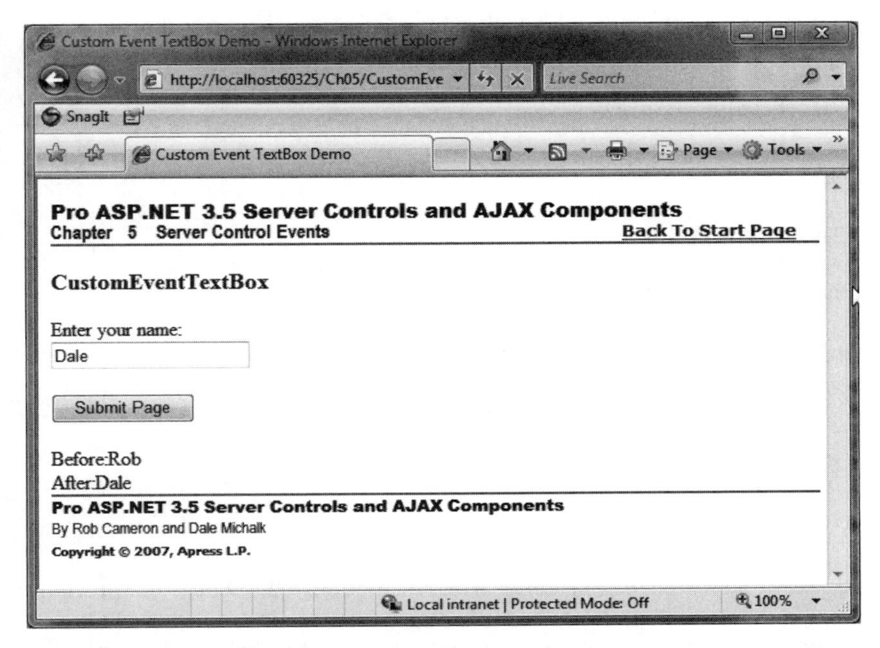

Figure 5-11. *The second request with a new name on the CustomEventTextBox web form*

Capturing Postback with the Button Control

The `TextBox` control does a great job in gathering input and raising state change events to their clients, but sometimes we need controls that provide action and post data back to the server. A perfect example of this type of control in the ASP.NET framework is the `System.Web.UI.WebControls.Button` control. The `Button` control exists for one reason: to post the page back to the server and raise events.

We would be remiss if we only reverse-engineered the ASP.NET `TextBox` control and left out the `Button` control, so our next task is to build our own version of the `Button` control. We add some bells and whistles along the way, such as the capability for the control to display itself as a `Button` or as a hyperlink similar to the `LinkButton` control in ASP.NET. This new, amazing `Button` server control will be named `SuperButton` for all its rich functionality.

Rendering the Button

The first decision we have to make when building our button relates to how it will render. Because we decided to render either as an `<INPUT type="submit">` or an `<A>` tag, we choose to use a strongly-typed enumeration as a means to configure its display output. We call this enumeration `ButtonDisplay` and give it values that reflect how our button can appear in a web form:

```
public enum ButtonDisplay
{
   Button = 0,
   Hyperlink = 1
}
```

The ButtonDisplay enumeration is exposed from our control through a Display property. It defaults to a Button value if nothing is passed into the control:

```
public virtual ButtonDisplay Display
{
   get
   {
      object display = ViewState["Display"];
      if (display == null)
         return ButtonDisplay.Button;
      else
         return (ButtonDisplay) display;
   }
   set
   {
      ViewState["Display"] = value;
   }
}
```

We also have a Text property that has an identical representation in the code to our previous examples. It will appear as text on the surface of the button or as the text of the hyperlink.

The button-rendering code needs to have an if/then construct to switch the display based on the enumeration value set by the developer/user. It also needs a way to submit the page back to the web server when using the hyperlink display mode. The hyperlink is normally used for navigation and is not wired into the postback mechanism that buttons get for free.

When updating the code from .NET Framework 1.1 server control to .NET Framework 2.0 and later, this warning message appeared:

```
'System.Web.UI.Page.GetPostBackClientHyperlink(System.Web.UI.Control, string)' is
obsolete: 'The recommended alternative is ClientScript.GetPostBackClientHyperlink.
```

Page.ClientScript.GetPostBackClientHyperlink is the replacement for System.Web.UI. Page.GetPostBackClientHyperlink. The Page.ClientScript object is of type ClientScriptManager, which is a new class introduced in ASP.NET 2.0 and later that defines methods for managing client-side scripts in web applications.

The ClientScriptManager class comes to the rescue in this instance. It has a static method named GetPostBackClientHyperlink that registers the JavaScript necessary to submit the web form via an HTTP POST. In the web form example that hosts our SuperButton control, we examine the HTML output to see how it is integrated into the postback process. Here is the code that hooks into the postback mechanism:

```
override protected void Render(HtmlTextWriter writer)
{
   base.Render(writer);
   Page.VerifyRenderingInServerForm(this);

   if (Display == ButtonDisplay.Button)
```

```
{
   writer.Write("<INPUT type=\"submit\"");
   writer.Write(" name=\"" + this.UniqueID + "\"");
   writer.Write(" id=\"" + this.UniqueID + "\"");
   writer.Write(" value=\"" + Text + "\"");
     writer.Write(" />");
}
else if (Display == ButtonDisplay.Hyperlink)
{
   writer.Write("<A href=\"");
   writer.Write(Page.ClientScript.GetPostBackClientHyperlink(this,""));
   writer.Write("\">" + Text + "</A>");
}
}
```

Exposing a Click Event and the Events Collection

The first event we add to our SuperButton control is a Click event. This is your garden-variety System.EventHandler delegate type event, but our actual event implementation will be different this time around. Instead of adding an event field to the control class, we reuse a mechanism given to all controls from the System.Web.UI.Control base class.

The Events read-only property inherited from the Control class provides access to an event collection of type System.ComponentModel.EventHandlerList. EventHandlerList provides access to delegates that represent the invocation list for each event the control exposes. This means that the only memory taken up to handle event delegates is by those events that have a client event handler method registered, unlike the previous technique, which takes a hit for each event, regardless of any clients using it. This can potentially save a fair amount of memory on a control that exposes many events. Figure 5-12 graphically depicts the benefits of using the Events collection.

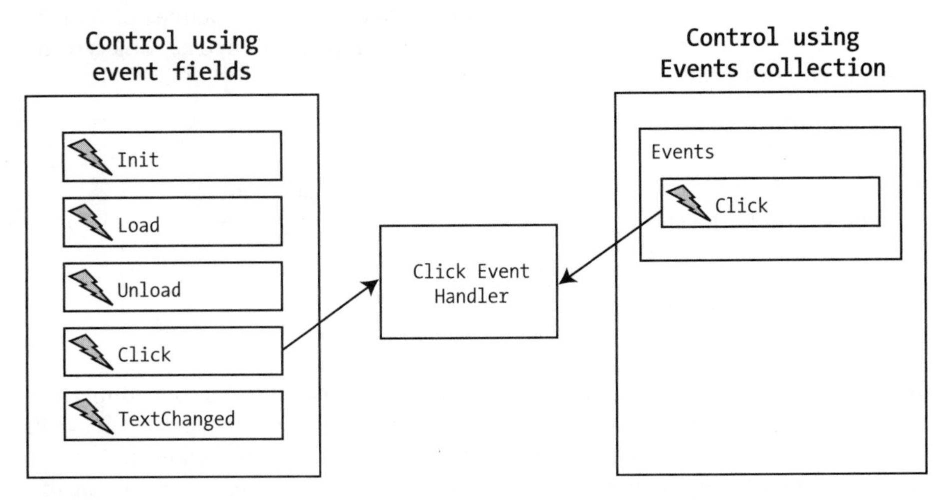

Figure 5-12. *The difference between using an event field and using the Events collection*

The first thing we need to do for an event using this new model is provide a key for the delegate that is used to store it inside the Events collection. We add this at the top of our class by creating a generic static, read-only object to represent the key for our click-related delegate:

```
private static readonly object ClickEvent = new object();
```

The second step is to use the syntax C# provides for custom delegate registration with our Click event. It is an expansion of the event declaration used previously that includes add and remove code blocks. It is similar to the get and set code blocks that programmers can use to define properties in C#. The result is the following Click event:

```
public event EventHandler Click
{
   add
   {
      Events.AddHandler(ClickEvent, value);
   }
   remove
   {
      Events.RemoveHandler(ClickEvent, value);
   }
}
```

The first thing to notice is the event declaration itself. It is declared with an event keyword, delegate type, name, and accessibility modifier as before. The new functionally is added via code blocks below the declaration. The add and remove code blocks handle the delegate registration process in whatever manner they see fit. In this case, these code blocks are passed the delegate reference via the value keyword to accomplish their assigned tasks.

The code in our Click event uses the Events collection to add the delegate via AddHandler or to remove the delegate via RemoveHandler. ClickEvent is the access key used to identify the Click delegates in our Events collection, keeping like event handlers in separate buckets.

After we declare our event with its event subscription code, we need to define our OnClick method to raise the event. The code uses the Events collection and our defined key object to get the Click delegate and raise the event to subscribers:

```
protected virtual void OnClick(EventArgs e)
{
   EventHandler clickEventDelegate = (EventHandler)Events[ClickEvent];
   if (clickEventDelegate != null)
   {
      clickEventDelegate(this, e);
   }
}
```

The first step is to pull the delegate of type EventHandler from the Events collection. Our second step as before is to check it for a null value to ensure that we actually need to invoke it. The invocation code on the delegate is the same as we used previously with our event in the TextBox demonstrations. We invoke the delegate using function call syntax with the name of the delegate. At this point, our Click event is ready to go—all we need to do is raise it when a postback occurs.

Command Events and Event Bubbling

The second event exposed by our SuperButton control is a command event. The command event is a design pattern borrowed from the controls in the System.Web.UI.WebControls namespace that makes event handling in list controls easier.

One example for this scenario is the DataGrid control, which can have buttons embedded in a column for edit and delete operations. The buttons activate edit or delete functionality respectively in the DataGrid control, as long as the command events exposed by these buttons have the correct CommandName property in the CommandEventArgs class as part of the event. If the button is set with a CommandName of "Delete", it kicks off delete activity. If the button is set with a CommandName of "Edit", it starts edit functions in the DataGrid control. Controls that raise command events that are not in those expected by the DataGrid control are wrapped into an ItemCommand event exposed by the control.

The capabilities provided by a command event are an implementation of event bubbling. Event bubbling is a technique that allows a child control to propagate command events up its control hierarchy, allowing the event to be handled in a more convenient location. Figure 5-13 provides a graphical depiction of event bubbling. This technique allows the DataGrid control to take a crack at handling the button events despite the fact that the buttons are several layers deep inside of its control hierarchy.

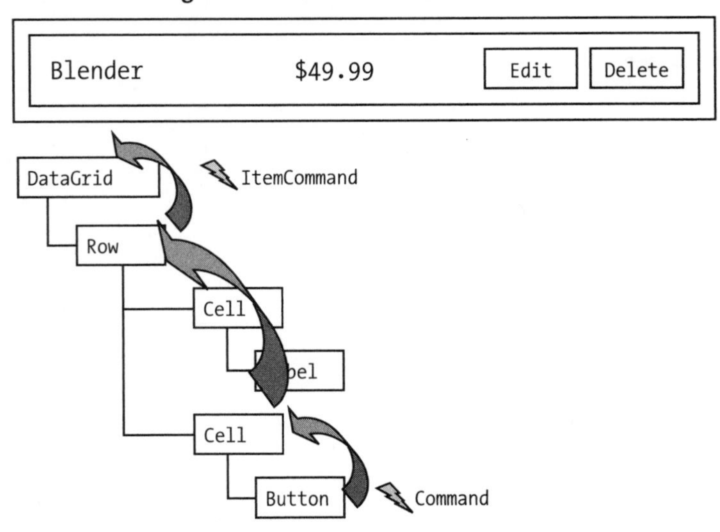

Figure 5-13. *Event bubbling*

Exposing the Command Event

The techniques used to expose a command event on our control are similar to those used with the Click event. As before, an important preliminary task to creating the event declaration is the need for an object to provide a "key" that gives access to the event in the Events collection. The CommandEvent field handles this chore:

```
private static readonly object CommandEvent = new object();
```

The event declaration for the Command event is almost identical to the Click event except for the delegate type used. It exposes the CommandEventHandler delegate, which provides data through the CommandEventArgs parameter to clients registered to process the event:

```
public event CommandEventHandler Command
{
   add
   {
      Events.AddHandler(CommandEvent, value);
   }
   remove
   {
      Events.RemoveHandler(CommandEvent, value);
   }
}
```

The CommandEventArgs class provides two properties: CommandName and CommandArgument. A control is expected to maintain these values as part of a command event bubbling protocol. These values are copied directly into the CommandEventArgs class when the command event is raised. Command controls expose these values through the CommandName and CommandArgument public properties, respectively:

```
public virtual string CommandName
{
   get
   {
      object name = ViewState["CommandName"];
      if (name == null)
         return string.Empty;
      else
         return (string) name;
   }
   set
   {
      ViewState["CommandName"] = value;
   }
}

public virtual string CommandArgument
{
   get
   {
      object arg = ViewState["CommandArgument"];
      if (arg == null)
         return string.Empty;
```

```
      else
         return (string) arg;
   }
   set
   {
      ViewState["CommandArgument"] = value;
   }
}
```

The final step in working with a command event is to raise the event. The OnCommand method in our class holds this important code. It pulls back the appropriate delegate type from the Events collection and invokes it in a similar manner to the OnClick method we reviewed earlier:

```
protected virtual void OnCommand(CommandEventArgs ce)
{
   CommandEventHandler commandEventDelegate =
      (CommandEventHandler) Events[CommandKey];
   if (commandEventDelegate != null)
   {
      commandEventDelegate(this, ce);
   }

   RaiseBubbleEvent(this, ce);
}
```

The new code that stands out is the RaiseBubbleEvent method call at the end of the OnCommand method. This code takes advantage of the internal event-bubbling plumbing that all controls receive just by inheriting from System.Web.UI.Control.

RaiseBubbleEvent takes an object reference and a System.EventArgs reference for its two parameters. This permits all events, even those not related to command event functionality, to take advantage of event bubbling. Naturally, the primary concern of event bubbling in ASP.NET is with command events.

At this point in our design, we have successfully exposed both the Click event and the command event for our control using the Events collection. One of the limitations of the Events collection is its implementation as a linked list. Given the nature of the linked list data structure, it can cause a performance problem in certain scenarios when many delegate nodes are traversed in order to find the correct event delegate. As background, you are free to use other System.Collections types to hold event delegates. One alternative to using a linked list is to implement the events collection as a Hashtable, which can speed access.

Capturing the Postback via IPostBackEventHandler

As part of our design, we had the requirement of rendering the button as either a normal button or as a specially configured hyperlink to submit the web form. With events in hand, we now move on to hooking the button click into the postback process through implementation of the IPostBackEventHandler interface. To achieve this, we next implement the single method of the postback interface, RaisePostBackEvent:

```
public void RaisePostBackEvent(string argument);
```

RaisePostBackEvent takes a single argument as a means to retrieve a value from the form submission. When a Button submits a web form, it always passes a blank value for this argument to RaisePostBackEvent. Our hyperlink-rendering code has a choice of what information to pass via the Page.ClientScript.GetPostBackClientHyperlink method call. The following code snippet submits a blank value to keep things in line with our button rendering:

```
writer.Write("<A href=\"");
writer.Write(Page.ClientScript.GetPostBackClientHyperlink(this,""));
writer.Write("\">" + Text + "</A>");
```

The RaisePostBackEvent implementation in our SuperButton control has very little work to do, as we encapsulated the bulk of our event-generating code in the OnClick and OnCommand methods:

```
public void RaisePostBackEvent(string argument)
{
   OnCommand(new CommandEventArgs(CommandName, CommandArgument));
   OnClick(EventArgs.Empty);
}
```

Completing the RaisePostBackEvent method brings our SuperButton control to fruition. Listing 5-9 is the class file for the control and its related enumeration. The control needs a using import for the System.Web.UI.WebControls namespace, because it takes advantage of Command events.

Listing 5-9. *The SuperButton Control Class File*

```
using System;
using System.Web.UI;
using System.Web.UI.WebControls;

namespace ControlsBook2Lib.Ch05
{
  public enum ButtonDisplay
  {
    Button = 0,
    Hyperlink = 1
  }

  [ToolboxData("<{0}:superbutton runat=server></{0}:superbutton>")]
  public class SuperButton : Control, IPostBackEventHandler
  {
    public virtual ButtonDisplay Display
    {
      get
      {
        object display = ViewState["Display"];
        if (display == null)
          return ButtonDisplay.Button;
```

```
      else
        return (ButtonDisplay)display;
    }
    set
    {
      ViewState["Display"] = value;
    }
  }

  public virtual string Text
  {
    get
    {
      object text = ViewState["Text"];
      if (text == null)
        return string.Empty;
      else
        return (string)text;
    }
    set
    {
      ViewState["Text"] = value;
    }
  }

  private static readonly object ClickKey = new object();

  public event EventHandler Click
  {
    add
    {
      Events.AddHandler(ClickKey, value);
    }
    remove
    {
      Events.RemoveHandler(ClickKey, value);
    }
  }

  protected virtual void OnClick(EventArgs e)
  {
    EventHandler clickEventDelegate =
       (EventHandler)Events[ClickKey];
    if (clickEventDelegate != null)
    {
      clickEventDelegate(this, e);
    }
  }
```

```
private static readonly object CommandKey = new object();

public event CommandEventHandler Command
{
  add
  {
    Events.AddHandler(CommandKey, value);
  }
  remove
  {
    Events.RemoveHandler(CommandKey, value);
  }
}

public virtual string CommandName
{
  get
  {
    object name = ViewState["CommandName"];
    if (name == null)
      return string.Empty;
    else
      return (string)name;
  }
  set
  {
    ViewState["CommandName"] = value;
  }
}

public virtual string CommandArgument
{
  get
  {
    object arg = ViewState["CommandArgument"];
    if (arg == null)
      return string.Empty;
    else
      return (string)arg;
  }
  set
  {
    ViewState["CommandArgument"] = value;
  }
}
```

```
    protected virtual void OnCommand(CommandEventArgs ce)
    {
      CommandEventHandler commandEventDelegate =
         (CommandEventHandler)Events[CommandKey];
      if (commandEventDelegate != null)
      {
        commandEventDelegate(this, ce);
      }

      RaiseBubbleEvent(this, ce);
    }

    public void RaisePostBackEvent(string argument)
    {
      OnCommand(new CommandEventArgs(CommandName, CommandArgument));
      OnClick(EventArgs.Empty);
    }

    protected override void Render(HtmlTextWriter writer)
    {
      base.Render(writer);
      Page.VerifyRenderingInServerForm(this);

      if (Display == ButtonDisplay.Button)
      {
        writer.Write("<INPUT type=\"submit\"");
        writer.Write(" name=\"" + this.UniqueID + "\"");
        writer.Write(" id=\"" + this.UniqueID + "\"");
        writer.Write(" value=\"" + Text + "\"");
        writer.Write(" />");
      }
      else if (Display == ButtonDisplay.Hyperlink)
      {
        writer.Write("<A href=\"");
        writer.Write(Page.ClientScript.GetPostBackClientHyperlink(this, ""));
        writer.Write("\">" + Text + "</A>");
      }
    }
  }
}
```

Using the SuperButton Control on a Web Form

The SuperButton web form hosts two `SuperButton` controls: one of the button variety and the other of the hyperlink persuasion. It also has a label that is set according to event handlers for each button. The first request to the web form generates the page shown in Figure 5-14. Listings 5-10 and 5-11 provide the source code for this web form.

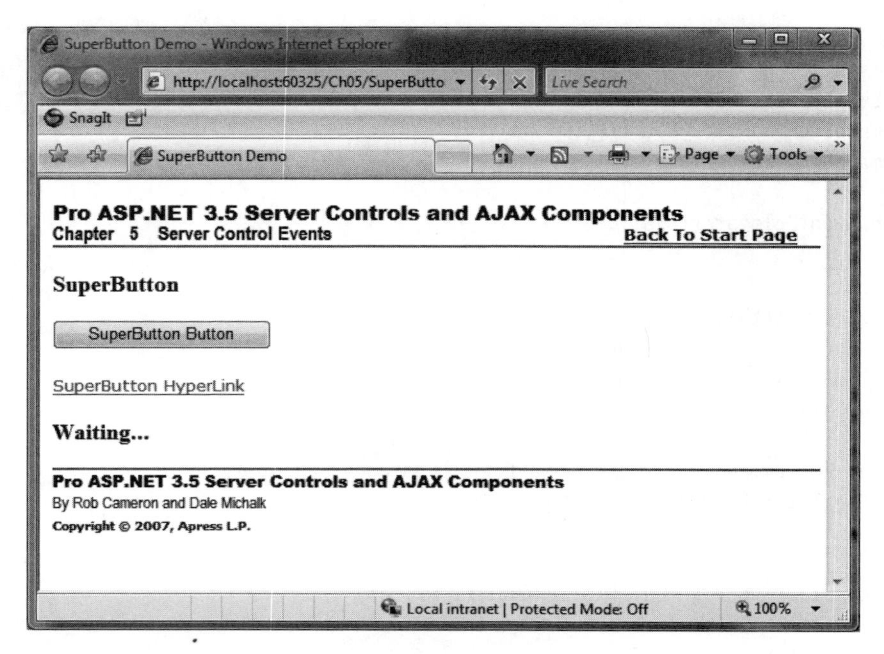

Figure 5-14. *The SuperButton web form rendering its first request*

Listing 5-10. *The SuperButton Web Form .aspx File*

```
<%@ Page Language="C#"
MasterPageFile="~/MasterPage/ControlsBook2MasterPage.Master"
  AutoEventWireup="true" CodeBehind="SuperButton.aspx.cs"
Inherits="ControlsBook2Web.Ch05.SuperButton"
  Title="SuperButton Demo" %>

<%@ Register TagPrefix="apress" Namespace="ControlsBook2Lib.Ch05"
Assembly="ControlsBook2Lib" %>
<asp:Content ID="Content1" ContentPlaceHolderID=
                   "ChapterNumAndTitle" runat="server">
  <asp:Label ID="ChapterNumberLabel" runat="server" Width="14px">5</asp:Label>
    <asp:Label
    ID="ChapterTitleLabel" runat="server" Width="360px">
   Server Control Events</asp:Label></asp:Content>
<asp:Content ID="Content2" ContentPlaceHolderID="PrimaryContent" runat="server">
  <h3>
    SuperButton</h3>
  <apress:SuperButton ID="superbtn" runat="server"
```

```
  Text="SuperButton Button" OnClick="superbtn_Click">
  </apress:SuperButton>
  <br />
  <br />
  <apress:SuperButton Display="hyperlink" ID="superlink" runat="server"
        Text="SuperButton HyperLink"
    OnClick="superlink_Click">
  </apress:SuperButton>
  <br />
  <br />
  <h3>
    <asp:Label ID="ClickLabel" runat="server">Waiting...</asp:Label></h3>
</asp:Content>
```

Listing 5-11. *The SuperButton Web Form Code-Behind Class File*

```
using System;
using System.Web.UI;
using System.Web.UI.WebControls;

namespace ControlsBook2Web.Ch05
{
  public partial class SuperButton : System.Web.UI.Page
  {
    protected void Page_Load(object sender, EventArgs e)
    {
      ClickLabel.Text = "Waiting...";
    }

    protected void superbtn_Click(object sender, EventArgs e)
    {
      ClickLabel.Text = "superbtn was clicked!";
    }

    protected void superlink_Click(object sender, EventArgs e)
    {
      ClickLabel.Text = "superlink was clicked!";
    }
  }
}
```

Clicking the button generates the output shown in Figure 5-15. Clicking the hyperlink generates the output shown in Figure 5-16.

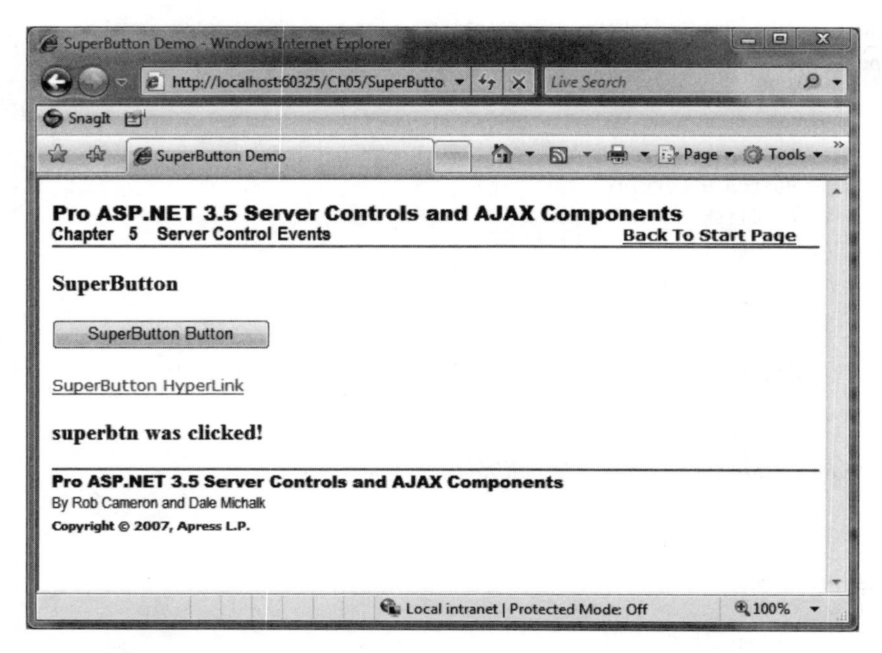

Figure 5-15. *The SuperButton web form after a button click*

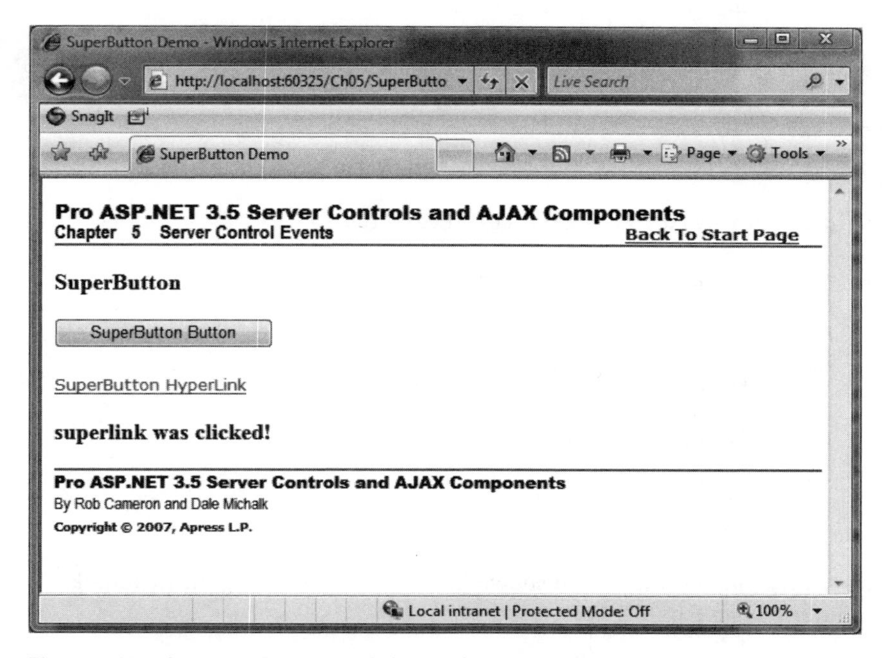

Figure 5-16. *The SuperButton web form after a hyperlink click*

Of more interest is what is rendered on the HTML page that represents the web form. Listing 5-12 shows the HTML.

Listing 5-12. *The SuperButton Web Form's Rendered HTML*

```
<!DOCTYPE html PUBLIC "-//W3C//DTD XHTML 1.0 Transitional//EN"
"http://www.w3.org/TR/xhtml1/DTD/xhtml1-transitional.dtd">
<html xmlns="http://www.w3.org/1999/xhtml">
<head><title>SuperButton Demo</title>
<link href="../css/ControlsBook2Master.css" rel="stylesheet" type="text/css" />
    <link href="../css/SkinnedControl.css" rel="stylesheet" type="text/css" />
  </head>
<body>
  <form name="aspnetForm" method="post" action="SuperButton.aspx" id="aspnetForm">
<div>
<input type="hidden" name="__EVENTTARGET" id="__EVENTTARGET" value="" />
<input type="hidden" name="__EVENTARGUMENT" id="__EVENTARGUMENT" value="" />
<input type="hidden" name="__VIEWSTATE" id="__VIEWSTATE" value=
"/wEPDwUKMTk1NzAxNTA4OQ9kFgJmD2QWAgIDD2QWAgIND2QWAgIF
     Dw8WAh4EVGV4dAUKV2FpdGluZy4uLmRkZCVrMj4twiLopSQe2Bv49Qt4I2Me" />
</div>

<script type="text/javascript">
//<![CDATA[
var theForm = document.forms['aspnetForm'];
if (!theForm) {
    theForm = document.aspnetForm;
}
function __doPostBack(eventTarget, eventArgument) {
    if (!theForm.onsubmit || (theForm.onsubmit() != false)) {
        theForm.__EVENTTARGET.value = eventTarget;
        theForm.__EVENTARGUMENT.value = eventArgument;
        theForm.submit();
    }
}
//]]>
</script>


<script src="/WebResource.axd?d=puMa8Av1AilWiuWD8_1Zng2
&amp;t=633213291362029098" type="text/javascript"></script>

<script src="/ScriptResource.axd?d=0oc1BWZd820Y0xgUreI6u7sW71ZA_JJlVHJD
   bjlwydjgePxXiP4o8bnwriUWSGvMmu3bfGm7GGOYOkZOpjk1i_0-3o
  X6tEF2F-Ad4yqjb1I1&amp;t=633213301364593098"
  type="text/javascript"></script>
<script type="text/javascript">
//<![CDATA[
if (typeof(Sys) === 'undefined') throw new Error(
     'ASP.NET Ajax client-side framework failed to load.');
//]]>
</script>
```

```
<script src="/ScriptResource.axd?d=Ooc1BWZd82OYOxgUreI6u7sW71ZA_JJlV
HJDbjlwydjgePxXiP4o8bnwriUWSGvMq_aVE3uFzkIcPnHrB6A2BVXqGLckRO
G1AUsyomgWNBg3Fxr9HCw9umLH5BqubMkkO&amp;t=
633213301364593098" type="text/javascript"></script>
<script src="../ch09/hoverbutton.js" type="text/javascript"></script>
  <div id="HeaderPanel">
    <script type="text/javascript">
//<![CDATA[
Sys.WebForms.PageRequestManager._initialize('ctl00$ControlsBook2ScriptManager',
document.getElementById('aspnetForm'));
Sys.WebForms.PageRequestManager.getInstance()._updateControls([], [], [], 90);
//]]>
</script>

    <span id="ctl00_Label2" class="TitleHeader"
    style="display:inline-block;height:18px;width:604px;">
Pro ASP.NET 3.5 Server Controls and AJAX Components</span><br />
    <div id="ChapterInfo" class="Chapter">
      <span id="ctl00_label1">Chapter</span>  

  <span id="ctl00_ChapterNumAndTitle_ChapterNumberLabel" style=
  "display:inline-block;width:14px;">5</span>  <span
  id="ctl00_ChapterNumAndTitle_ChapterTitleLabel"
  style="display:inline-block;width:360px;">Server Control Events</span>
      <a id="ctl00_DefaultPage" href="../Default.aspx">Back To Start Page</a><br />
      <img id="ctl00_Image1" src="../img/blueline.jpg" style="border-width:0px;" />
      <br />
    </div>

  <h3>
    SuperButton</h3>

  <INPUT type="submit" name="ctl00$PrimaryContent$superbtn"
   id="ctl00$PrimaryContent$superbtn" value="SuperButton Button" />
  <br />
  <br />

  <A href="javascript:__doPostBack('ctl00$PrimaryContent$superlink','')">
                      SuperButton HyperLink</A>
  <br />
  <br />
  <h3>
    <span id="ctl00_PrimaryContent_ClickLabel">Waiting...</span></h3>

    <div id="FooterPanel">
      <img id="ctl00_Image2" src="../img/blueline.jpg" style="border-width:0px;" />
      <br />
```

```
        <span id="ctl00_Label5" class="TitleFooter">
            Pro ASP.NET 3.5 Server Controls and AJAX Components</span><br />
        <span id="ctl00_Label6" class="Author">By Rob Cameron and Dale Michalk</span>
        <br />
        <span id="ctl00_Label7" class="Copyright">Copyright © 2007, Apress L.P.</span>
</div>
  </div>


<script type="text/javascript">
//<![CDATA[
Sys.Application.initialize();
//]]>
</script>
</form>
</body>
</html>
```

The first thing to examine is how our hyperlink generates a postback:

```
<A href="javascript:__doPostBack('ctl00$ControlsBookContent$superlink','')">
SuperButton HyperLink</A><br/>
```

It uses a JavaScript function named `__doPostBack`, which actually sends the page back to the server. This JavaScript invocation is added by our `Page.ClientScript.GetPostBackClientHyperlink` call in the `Render` method of `SuperButton`. The `__doPostBack` JavaScript routine is emitted into the HTML by the ASP.NET framework as a result of this method call:

```
<div>
<input type="hidden" name="__EVENTTARGET" value="" />
<input type="hidden" name="__EVENTARGUMENT" value="" />
<div/>
<script language="javascript">
<!--
var theForm = document.forms['aspnetForm'];
if (!theForm) {
    theForm = document.aspnetForm;
}
function __doPostBack(eventTarget, eventArgument) {
    if (!theForm.onsubmit || (theForm.onsubmit() != false)) {
        theForm.__EVENTTARGET.value = eventTarget;
        theForm.__EVENTARGUMENT.value = eventArgument;
        theForm.submit();
    }
}
// -->
</script>
```

The JavaScript code programmatically submits the form and sets two hidden variables to give ASP.NET enough information about what control was responsible for causing the postback. It doesn't need this extra step when rendering the <INPUT type="submit"> button, but the step is mandatory for hyperlinks. You can also see that the purpose of the second parameter in Page.ClientScript.GetPostBackClientHyperlink is to pass an eventArgument, which makes its way back to the RaisePostBack method invocation on the server-side control implementation as the string parameter named argument.

Composing the SuperButton Control into a Composite Pager Control

Our SuperButton control is capable of raising command events through the event-bubbling mechanism. To capture these bubbled events, we use a composite control named Pager. Pager recognizes bubbled command events from its children and raises a PageCommand event to its event clients. This is similar to the event bubbling performed by the DataGrid list control when it grabs all command events from child controls and exposes them via a single ItemCommand event. We next describe the design of the Pager control, starting with how the control is constructed.

Building the Pager Child Control Hierarchy

Composite control development begins with creating a child control hierarchy. The Pager control uses a private method named CreateChildControlHierarchy that is called from the overridden protected CreateChildControls method inherited from the Control class. Listing 5-13 provides the source code for CreateChildControlHierarchy. CreateChildControls is called by the ASP.NET Framework to allow composite controls to build up their structure prior to rendering.

Listing 5-13. *The Pager Implementation of CreateChildControlHierarchy*

```
private SuperButton buttonLeft ;
private SuperButton buttonRight;
private void CreateChildControlHierarchy()
{
   LiteralControl tableStart = new
      LiteralControl("<table border=1><tr><td>");
   Controls.Add(tableStart);

      buttonLeft = new SuperButton();
   buttonLeft.ID = "buttonLeft";
   if (Context != null)
   {
      buttonLeft.Text = Context.Server.HtmlEncode("<") + " Left";
   }
   else
   {
      buttonLeft.Text = "< Left";
   }
```

```
    buttonLeft.CommandName = "Page";
    buttonLeft.CommandArgument = "Left";
    Controls.Add(buttonLeft);

    LiteralControl spacer = new LiteralControl("  ");
    Controls.Add(spacer);

    buttonRight = new SuperButton();
    buttonRight.ID = "buttonRight";
    buttonRight.Display = Display;
    if (Context != null)
    {
        buttonRight.Text = "Right " + Context.Server.HtmlEncode(">");
    }
    else
    {
        buttonRight.Text = "Right  >";
    }
    buttonRight.CommandName = "Page";
    buttonRight.CommandArgument = "Right";
    Controls.Add(buttonRight);

    LiteralControl tableEnd = new
        LiteralControl("</td></tr></table>");
    Controls.Add(tableEnd);
}
```

The child control collection created by the Pager control includes a set of SuperButton controls representing left and right direction arrows that are wrapped inside an HTML table. The Left direction SuperButton includes the text "< Left", and the Right direction SuperButton uses "Right >". The Text property uses HtmlEncode to properly render the special characters. Otherwise, CreateChildControlHierarchy renders straight text when Context is not available at design time.

```
if (Context != null)
{
    buttonLeft.Text = Context.Server.HtmlEncode("<") + " Left";
}
else
{
    buttonLeft.Text = "< Left";
}
```

The most important settings in CreateChildControlHierarchy are the Command properties. The CommandName value chosen for the SuperButton controls is Page. This lets the Pager know that it is receiving Command events from its specially configured SuperButton controls. CommandArgument tells the Pager whether it is the left or right control emitting the event:

```
buttonLeft.CommandName = "Page";
buttonLeft.CommandArgument = "Left";
...
buttonRight.CommandName = "Page";
buttonRight.CommandArgument = "Right";
```

The final rendering feature is the Display property passed on to the SuperButton controls. Our Pager can display its left and right UI elements as either buttons or hyperlinks. The implementation of the Display property in Pager is as follows. It calls EnsureChildControls and then gets or sets the Display property on the child controls. The SuperButton server control defaults to a Display value of Button, which becomes the default for Pager as well if the value is not set.

```
public virtual ButtonDisplay Display
{
   get
   {
      EnsureChildControls();
      return buttonLeft.Display ;
   }
   set
   {
      EnsureChildControls();
      buttonLeft.Display  = value;
      buttonRight.Display = value;
   }
}
```

Defining the PageCommand Event

The Pager control exposes a custom PageCommand event to let its client know whether it is moving in the left or right direction. The PageDirection enumeration provides a finite way to specify this in code:

```
public enum PageDirection
{
   Left = 0,
   Right = 1
}
```

The PageCommandEventArgs class uses this enumeration as the data type for its Direction property exposed as part of an EventArgs replacement for the PageCommand delegate. The complete PageCommand event–related code is grouped in the PageCommand class file shown in Listing 5-14.

Listing 5-14. *The PageCommand Class File*

```
using System;

namespace ControlsBook2Lib.Ch05
{
  public enum PageDirection
  {
    Left = 0,
    Right = 1
  }

  public delegate void PageCommandEventHandler(object o,
  PageCommandEventArgs pce);

  public class PageCommandEventArgs
  {
    public PageCommandEventArgs(PageDirection direction)
    {
      this.direction = direction;
    }

    PageDirection direction;
    public PageDirection Direction
    {
      get { return direction; }
    }
  }
}
```

Exposing the PageCommand Event from the Pager Control

The Pager control uses the PageCommandEventHandler delegate to declare its event-handling code. As with the SuperButton, we use the Events property technique for handling delegate registration:

```
private static readonly object PageCommandKey = new object();
public event PageCommandEventHandler PageCommand
{
   add
   {
      Events.AddHandler(PageCommandKey, value);
   }
   remove
   {
      Events.RemoveHandler(PageCommandKey, value);
   }
}
```

We also add an OnPageCommand method to raise the event. This method uses the custom PageCommandEventArgs class we defined earlier to invoke the PageCommandEventHandler delegate:

```
protected virtual void OnPageCommand(PageCommandEventArgs pce)
{
   PageCommandEventHandler pageCommandEventDelegate =
             (PageCommandEventHandler) Events[PageCommandEvent];
   if (pageCommandEventDelegate != null)
   {
      pageCommandEventDelegate(this, pce);
   }
}
```

OnPageCommand is the last bit of code required to raise events associated with the PageCommand event type. The next task is to capture the bubbled Command events and turn them into PageCommand events.

Capturing the Bubbles via OnBubbleEvent

The OnBubbleEvent method inherited from System.Web.UI.Control is the counterpart to the RaiseBubbleEvent method used inside the SuperButton control. It allows a control to hook into the stream of bubbled events from child controls and process them accordingly:

```
protected override bool OnBubbleEvent(object source, EventArgs e);
```

The method definition for OnBubbleEvent specifies the ubiquitous System.EventHandler method signature, with one difference. It takes an object reference and an EventArgs reference but returns a bool. The bool return value indicates whether or not the control has processed the bubble event. A value of false indicates that the bubble event should continue bubbling up the control hierarchy; a value of true indicates a desire to stop the event in its tracks, because it has been handled. If a control does not implement OnBubbleEvent, the default implementation passes the event on up to parent controls.

The Pager control implements its OnBubbleEvent as shown in Listing 5-15.

Listing 5-15. *The Pager Implementation of OnBubbleEvent*

```
protected override bool OnBubbleEvent(object source, EventArgs e)
{
   bool result = false;
   CommandEventArgs ce = e as CommandEventArgs;

   if (ce != null)
   {
      if (ce.CommandName.Equals("Page"))
      {
         PageDirection direction;
         if (ce.CommandArgument.Equals("Right"))
            direction = PageDirection.Right;
```

```
         else
            direction = PageDirection.Left;

         PageCommandEventArgs pce =
            new PageCommandEventArgs(direction);

         OnPageCommand(pce);
         result = true;
      }
   }
   return result;
}
```

The result variable holds the return value of OnBubbleEvent for the Pager control. It is set to false, assuming failure until success. The first check is to cast the EventArgs reference to ensure we receive a Command event of the proper type. The code performs this check using the as keyword in C# to cast the reference to the desired type, which returns null if the cast fails.

If the type cast succeeds, the next check is to ensure the proper CommandName is set to "Page". After the checks pass, the OnBubbleEvent code can create a PageCommandEventArgs class and set the Direction property according to the CommandArgument value. The final task is to raise the PageCommand event by calling OnPageCommand. Finally, the function returns the value of result to tell the ASP.NET framework whether or not the event was handled.

The INamingContainer Interface

When a composite control builds up its child control tree, it sets each control's identification via the ID property. For example, the Pager control sets the left SuperButton child control ID property value in the following single line of code:

```
buttonLeft.ID = "buttonLeft";
```

The problem with using just the ID value to uniquely identify child controls is that multiple Pager controls could be used on a web form, and the emitted button or hyperlink ID values would conflict. To protect against name collisions, each composite control creates a unique namespace that prefixes the ID of a control with the parent control's ID (and the parent control's parent's ID and so on) and a dollar sign or underscore. The INamingContainer interface tells ASP.NET to do this. INamingContainer is a marker interface (i.e., an interface without any defined methods) used by ASP.NET to identify the parent in a composite control to ensure unique names or IDs for child controls as they are dynamically created during the page-rendering process.

Implementing the INamingContainer interface in the Pager server control activates this mechanism, causing ASP.NET to prefix the ID of a control with the parent control's ID and a colon. The previous left button in a Pager control named "pagerbtn" would therefore have an ID value of "buttonLeft" but a UniqueID value of "pagerbtn$buttonLeft". Listing 5-16 contains the full code listing for the Pager control.

Listing 5-16. *The Pager Control Class File*

```
using System;
using System.ComponentModel;
using System.Web.UI;
using System.Web.UI.WebControls;
using ControlsBook2Lib.Ch11.Design;

namespace ControlsBook2Lib.Ch05
{
  [ToolboxData("<{0}:pager runat=server></{0}:pager>")]
  public class Pager : CompositeControl
  {
    private static readonly object PageCommandKey = new object();
    public event PageCommandEventHandler PageCommand
    {
      add
      {
        Events.AddHandler(PageCommandKey, value);
      }
      remove
      {
        Events.RemoveHandler(PageCommandKey, value);
      }
    }

    protected virtual void OnPageCommand(PageCommandEventArgs pce)
    {
      PageCommandEventHandler pageCommandEventDelegate =
         (PageCommandEventHandler)Events[PageCommandKey];
      if (pageCommandEventDelegate != null)
      {
        pageCommandEventDelegate(this, pce);
      }
    }

    protected override bool OnBubbleEvent(object source, EventArgs e)
    {
      bool result = false;
      CommandEventArgs ce = e as CommandEventArgs;

      if (ce != null)
      {
        if (ce.CommandName.Equals("Page"))
        {
          PageDirection direction;
          if (ce.CommandArgument.Equals("Right"))
            direction = PageDirection.Right;
```

```
      else
        direction = PageDirection.Left;

      PageCommandEventArgs pce =
         new PageCommandEventArgs(direction);

      OnPageCommand(pce);
      result = true;
    }
  }
  return result;
}

public ButtonDisplay Display
{
  get
  {
    EnsureChildControls();
    return buttonLeft.Display;
  }
  set
  {
    EnsureChildControls();
    buttonLeft.Display = value;
    buttonRight.Display = value;
  }
}

protected override void CreateChildControls()
{
  Controls.Clear();
  CreateChildControlHierarchy();
}

public override ControlCollection Controls
{
  get
  {
    EnsureChildControls();
    return base.Controls;
  }
}

private SuperButton buttonLeft;
private SuperButton buttonRight;
```

```
    private void CreateChildControlHierarchy()
    {
      LiteralControl tableStart = new
         LiteralControl("<table border=1><tr><td>");
      Controls.Add(tableStart);

      buttonLeft = new SuperButton();
      buttonLeft.ID = "buttonLeft";
      if (Context != null)
      {
        buttonLeft.Text = Context.Server.HtmlEncode("<") + " Left";
      }
      else
      {
        buttonLeft.Text = "< Left";
      }
      buttonLeft.CommandName = "Page";
      buttonLeft.CommandArgument = "Left";
      Controls.Add(buttonLeft);

      LiteralControl spacer = new LiteralControl("  ");
      Controls.Add(spacer);

      buttonRight = new SuperButton();
      buttonRight.ID = "buttonRight";
      buttonRight.Display = Display;
      if (Context != null)
      {
        buttonRight.Text = "Right " + Context.Server.HtmlEncode(">");
      }
      else
      {
        buttonRight.Text = "Right  >";
      }
      buttonRight.CommandName = "Page";
      buttonRight.CommandArgument = "Right";
      Controls.Add(buttonRight);

      LiteralControl tableEnd = new
         LiteralControl("</td></tr></table>");
      Controls.Add(tableEnd);
    }
  }
}
```

Using the Pager Control on a Web Form

The Pager Event Bubbling web form demonstrates the Pager control in both its button and hyperlink display motifs. A single label represents the PageCommand activity generated by the two controls. The first request for the page appears in the browser, as shown in Figure 5-17. Listings 5-17 and 5-18 provide the .aspx and code-behind files for this web form.

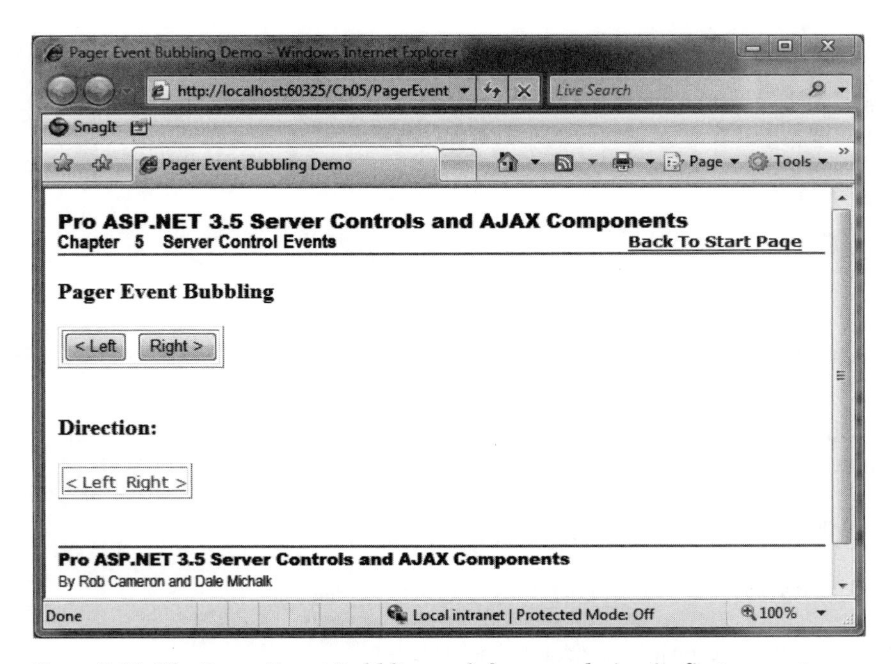

Figure 5-17. *The Pager Event Bubbling web form rendering its first request*

Listing 5-17. *The Pager Event Bubbling Web Form .aspx File*

```
<%@ Page Language="C#"
MasterPageFile="~/MasterPage/ControlsBook2MasterPage.Master"
  AutoEventWireup="true" CodeBehind="PagerEventBubbling.aspx.cs"
  Inherits="ControlsBook2Web.Ch05.PagerEventBubbling"
  Title="Pager Event Bubbling Demo" %>

<%@ Register TagPrefix="apress" Namespace="ControlsBook2Lib.Ch05"
  Assembly="ControlsBook2Lib" %>
<asp:Content ID="Content1" ContentPlaceHolderID="ChapterNumAndTitle" runat="server">
  <asp:Label ID="ChapterNumberLabel" runat="server" Width="14px">5</asp:Label>
         <asp:Label
        ID="ChapterTitleLabel" runat="server" Width="360px">
       Server Control Events</asp:Label>
</asp:Content>
```

```
<asp:Content ID="Content2" ContentPlaceHolderID="PrimaryContent" runat="server">
  <h3>
    Pager Event Bubbling</h3>
  <apress:Pager ID="pager1" Display="Button" runat="server"
OnPageCommand="Pagers_PageCommand">
  </apress:Pager>
  <br />
  <br />
  <h3>
    Direction: <asp:Label ID="DirectionLabel" runat="server"></asp:Label></h3>
  <apress:Pager ID="pager2" runat="server" Display="Hyperlink"
OnPageCommand="Pagers_PageCommand">
  </apress:Pager>
  <br />
  <br />
</asp:Content>
```

Listing 5-18. *The Pager Event Bubbling Web Form Code-Behind Class File*

```
using System;
using System.Web.UI;
using System.Web.UI.WebControls;

namespace ControlsBook2Web.Ch05
{
  public partial class PagerEventBubbling : System.Web.UI.Page
  {
    protected void Page_Load(object sender, EventArgs e)
    {

    }

    protected void Pagers_PageCommand(object o,
   ControlsBook2Lib.Ch05.PageCommandEventArgs pce)
    {
      DirectionLabel.Text = ((Control)o).ID + ": " +
        Enum.GetName(typeof(ControlsBook2Lib.Ch05.PageDirection), pce.Direction);
    }
  }
}
```

The Pager controls are wired to the same event handler in the code-behind class named Pagers_PageCommand in the .aspx file web form.

```
ControlsBook2LibControlsBook2LibOnPageCommand="Pagers_PageCommand"
```

Pagers_PageCommand has an all-important second parameter of type PageCommandEventArgs. We use it along with the System.Enum class's static GetName method to produce a textual representation of the PageDirection enumeration value for display in the DirectionLabel Text property:

```
private void Pagers_PageCommand(object o, C
                          ontrolsBookLib.Ch05.PageCommandEventArgs pce)
{
   DirectionLabel.Text =
      Enum.GetName(typeof(ControlsBook2Lib.Ch05.PageDirection),
            pce.Direction);
}
```

Click the Left button of the top Pager control to verify that it is working. The result should look something like Figure 5-18.

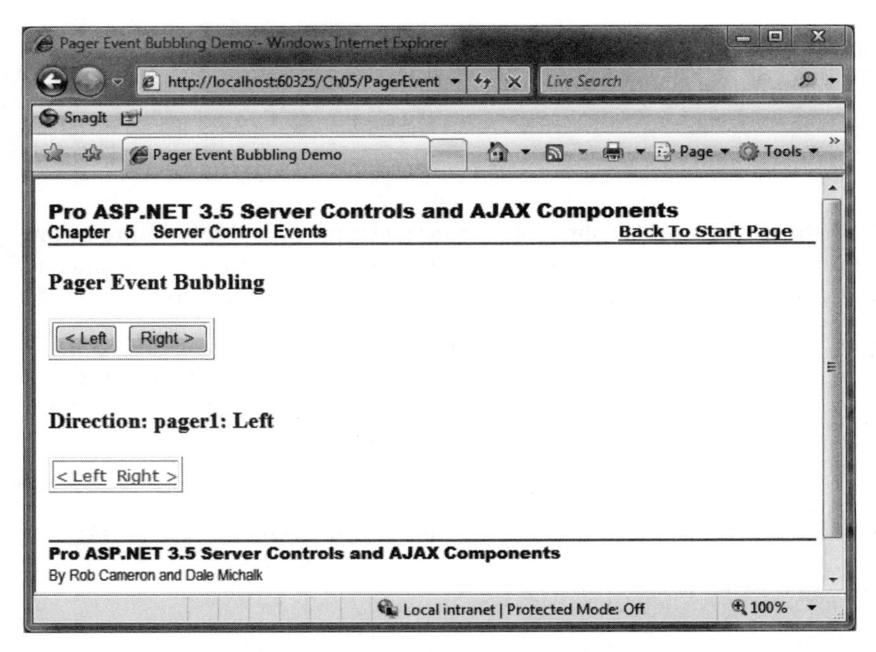

Figure 5-18. *The Page Event Bubbling web form after clicking the Left hyperlink button*

Try the Right button with the bottom Pager, which is in a hyperlink form, and you should get output similar to Figure 5-19.

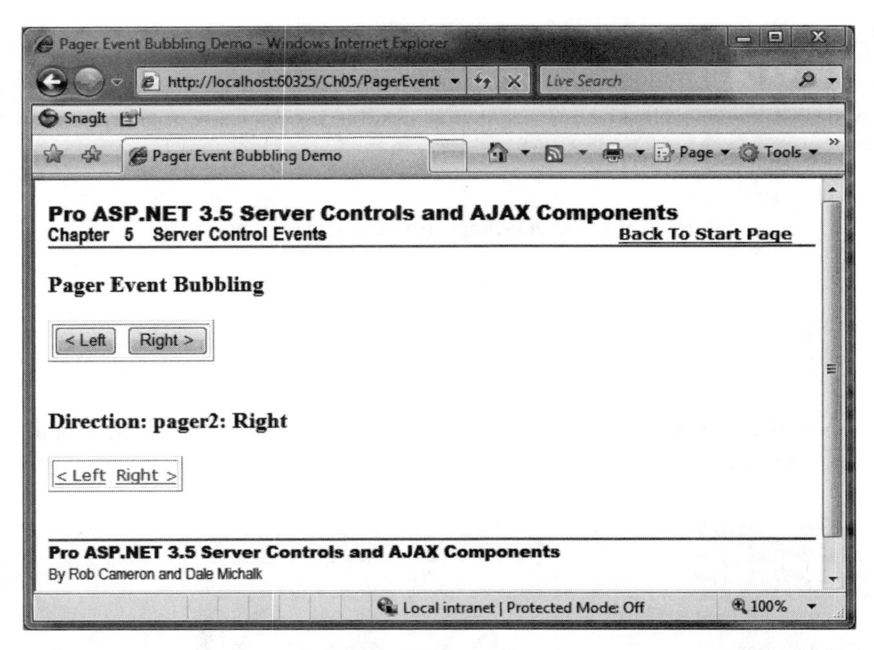

Figure 5-19. *The Page Event Bubbling web form after clicking the Right hyperlink button*

A snippet from the rendered HTML shows that the `pager1` and `pager2` `Pager` controls from the Pager Event Bubbling web form have their child controls identified in a nested fashion due to the `INamingContainer` interface with ASP.NET generating the `UniqueID` property:

```
<INPUT type="submit" name="ctl00$ControlsBookContent$pager1$buttonLeft"
id="ctl00$ControlsBookContent$pager1$buttonLeft" value="&lt; Left" />  
<INPUT type="submit" name="ctl00$ControlsBookContent$pager1$buttonRight"
id="ctl00$ControlsBookContent$pager1$buttonRight" value="Right &gt;"
/></td></tr></table><br/>
 <br/>
 <h3>Direction: <span id="ctl00_ControlsBookContent_DirectionLabel">pager2:
Right</span></h3>
 <table border=1><tr><td><A
href="javascript:__doPostBack
('ctl00$ControlsBookContent$pager2$buttonLeft','')">&lt;
Left</A>  <A href="javascript:__doPostBack
('ctl00$ControlsBookContent$pager2$buttonRight','')">
Right &gt;</A></td></tr></table><br/>
```

In the final section of this chapter, we review the control life cycle, which provides orderly processing to the busy life of server controls.

Control Life Cycle

The examples so far have demonstrated the use of server-side events to coordinate the activities of an ASP.NET application as part of an .aspx page. Each HTTP request/response cycle that the page executes follows a well-defined process known as the control execution life cycle. The Page server control orchestrates these activities on behalf of all the server controls in the Page's control tree. Control developers need to understand the flow of execution to ensure that their custom controls perform as expected as part of an ASP.NET web form. Figure 5-20 provides a high-level view of the page life cycle.

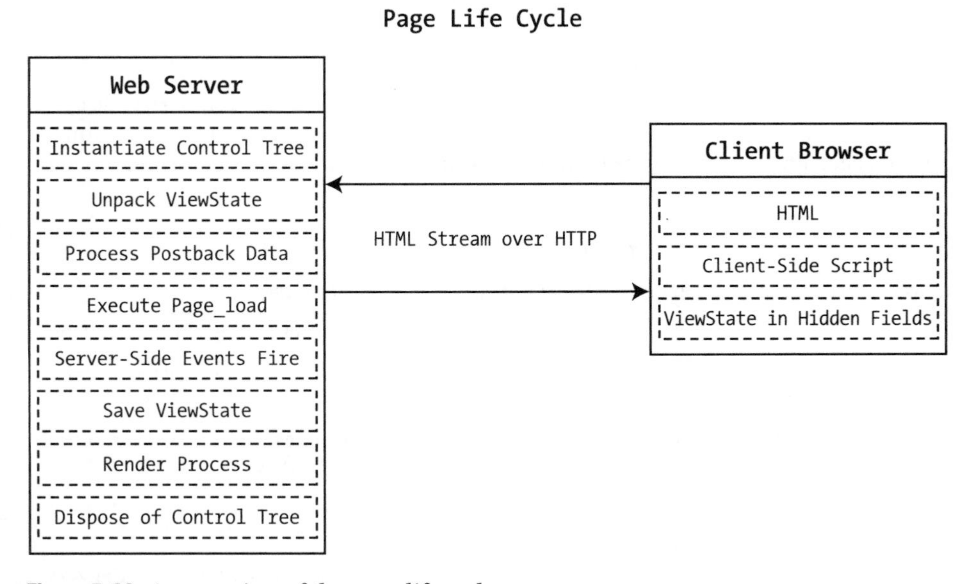

Figure 5-20. *An overview of the page life cycle*

After the initial page request as an HTTP GET, each subsequent HTTP POST page request/response cycle generally consists of the following steps:

1. Instantiate the control tree, creating each server control object.
2. Unpack ViewState, which includes control state in ASP.NET 2.0 and later, for each server control object.
3. Set the state from the previous server-side processing cycle for each object in the tree.
4. Process postback data.
5. Handle the Page_Load event.
6. Let controls know that data changed through postback, updating control state as necessary.
7. Execute server-side events based on data changes from postback.

8. Persist state back to ViewState, which includes control state in ASP.NET 2.0 and later.
9. Execute the render process for each server control.
10. Unload the page and its control tree.

This process is what provides the illusion of a stateful application to the end user. During each request/response round-trip, state is unpacked, changes are processed, the UI is updated, and the page is sent back to the user's browser with its new state values embedded in a hidden form field as ViewState, ready for the next request/response cycle. We next examine what events are available to controls as the page life cycle executes on the server side.

Plugging Into the Life Cycle

Server controls have a well-defined behavior pattern that coincides with the overall page life cycle. The ASP.NET framework provides a series of events that server controls can override to customize behavior during each phase of the life cycle. Table 5-1 provides an overview of these events.

Table 5-1. *Server Control Events Related to the Control Execution Life Cycle*

Server Control Event	Page Life Cycle Phase	Description
Init	Initialization	Initializes settings for the control.
LoadViewState	Unpack ViewState	Populates the state values of the control from ViewState.
LoadControlState	Unpack control state	Populates the state values of the control from control state.
LoadPostData	Handle form postback	Updates control's state values from data posted data.
Load	Page_Load event	Executes code common to every page request/response cycle.
TrackViewState	Track ViewState	Causes IsTrackingViewState property to return true when called.
RaisePostDataChangedEvent	Initialization for server-side events	Notifies control that newly posted data changed its state.
RaisePostBackEvent	Execute server-side events	Goes hand-in-hand with previous events listed in this table. Server-side events fire as a result of changes found in posted data for a particular control.
PreRender	Render process	Allows each control a chance to update state values before rendering.
SaveViewState	Save ViewState	Persists a control's updated state through the ViewState mechanism.

Table 5-1. *Server Control Events Related to the Control Execution Life Cycle*

Server Control Event	Page Life Cycle Phase	Description
SaveControlState	Save control state	Persists a control's updated control state through the ViewState mechanism
Render	Render process	Generates HTML reflecting the control's state and settings.
Dispose	Dispose of control tree	Releases any resources held by the control before teardown.

As Table 5-1 shows, ASP.NET provides each server control the capability to finely tune each phase in the life cycle. You can choose to accept default behavior, or you can customize a particular phase by overriding the appropriate event.

The Lifecycle Server Control

Now that we have covered the basics of the control execution life cycle, we are going to examine this process in more detail by overriding all available events in a server control named Lifecycle. The overridden methods generally fall into two camps: those that raise defined events exposed by a control and those that are not events but perform a necessary action for the control.

OnInit, OnLoad, OnPreRender, and OnUnload are events defined in System.Web.UI.Control that a control developer can override as required for a particular control. LoadViewState, LoadControlState, LoadPostData, RaisePostDataChangedEvent, RaisePostBackEvent, TrackViewState, SaveControlState, SaveViewState, and Render are all events that perform necessary actions for the control to maintain its state and event processing.

Caution As with most object-oriented class hierarchies, it is usually (though not always) necessary to call the base class's version of an overridden method in the descendent class to ensure consistent behavior. If the base method is not called in the descendent class, class instances will most likely fail to behave as expected—or worse, they could cause instability.

The implementation of Dispose deviates from the previous description for overridden methods. The Control class does expose a Dispose event, but it does not have an OnDispose method to raise it. Instead, providing a Dispose method follows the design pattern for objects that work with scarce resources, implementing the IDisposable interface.

Life Cycle and the HTTP Protocols GET and POST

The page life cycle differs based on whether the web form is requested for the first time via an HTTP GET or instead is initiated as part of a postback resulting from an HTTP POST generated by a control element on the page submitting the web form back to the server. The HTTP POST generally causes more life cycle activities because of the requirement to process data posted by the client back to the web server, raising events associated with state changes.

Figure 5-21 shows the two variants (initial GET versus initial POST) of the web form life cycle and the names of the phases we discuss in detail shortly.

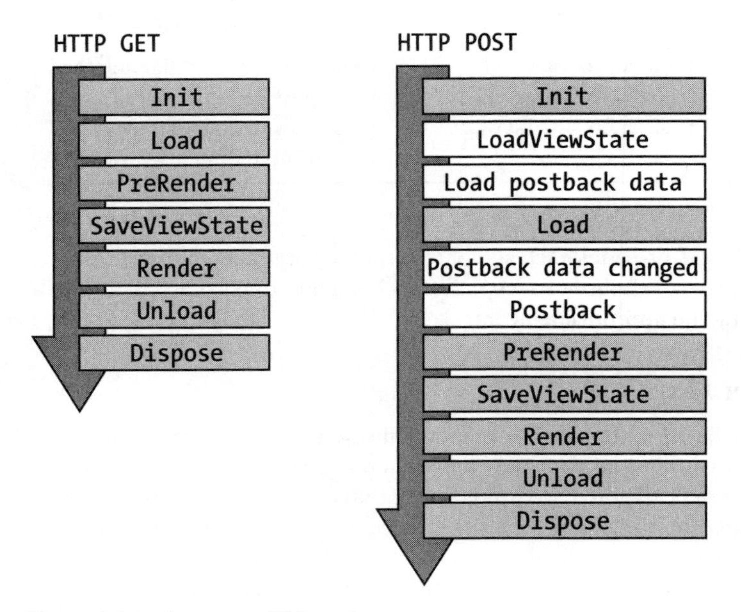

Figure 5-21. *The control life cycle*

In order to discuss the control life cycle, we use a control that overrides the methods necessary to track the execution of each of the life cycle events as they occur. Listing 5-19 provides the class file for the `Lifecycle` control that handles this task. The implementation of each overridden method is quite simple, with a call to the trace function notifying us that the method is executing.

Listing 5-19. *The Lifecycle Control Class File*

```
using System;
using System.Web.UI;
using System.Collections.Specialized;
using System.Diagnostics;

namespace ControlsBook2Lib.Ch05
{
  [ToolboxData("<{0}:lifecycle runat=server></{0}:lifecycle>")]
  public class Lifecycle : Control, IPostBackEventHandler, IPostBackDataHandler
  {
```

```
// Init Event
protected override void OnInit(System.EventArgs e)
{
  Trace("Lifecycle: Init Event.");
  base.OnInit(e);
}

protected override void TrackViewState()
{
  Trace("Lifecycle: Track ViewState.");
  base.TrackViewState();
}

// Load ViewState Event
protected override void LoadViewState(object savedState)
{
  Trace("Lifecycle: Load ViewState Event.");
  base.LoadViewState(savedState);
}

protected override void LoadControlState(object savedState)
{
  Trace("Lifecycle: Load ControlState Event.");
  base.LoadControlState(savedState);
}

public override void DataBind()
{
  Trace("Lifecycle: DataBind Event.");
  base.DataBind();
}

// Load Postback Data Event
public bool LoadPostData(string postDataKey,
   NameValueCollection postCollection)
{
  Trace("Lifecycle: Load PostBack Data Event.");
  Page.RegisterRequiresRaiseEvent(this);
  return true;
}

// Load Event
protected override void OnLoad(System.EventArgs e)
{
  Trace("Lifecycle: Load Event.");
  base.OnLoad(e);
}
```

```
// Post Data Changed Event
public void RaisePostDataChangedEvent()
{
  Trace("Lifecycle: Post Data Changed Event.");
}

// Postback Event
public void RaisePostBackEvent(string argument)
{
  Trace("Lifecycle: PostBack Event.");
}

// PreRender Event
protected override void OnPreRender(System.EventArgs e)
{
  Trace("Lifecycle: PreRender Event.");
  Page.RegisterRequiresPostBack(this);
  base.OnPreRender(e);
}

// Save ViewState
protected override object SaveViewState()
{
  Trace("Lifecycle: Save ViewState.");
  return base.SaveViewState();
}

// Save ControlState
protected override object SaveControlState()
{
  Trace("Lifecycle: Save ControlState.");
  return base.SaveControlState();
}

// Render Event
protected override void Render(HtmlTextWriter writer)
{
  base.Render(writer);
  Trace("Lifecycle: Render Event.");
  writer.Write("<h3>LifeCycle Control</h3>");
}

// Unload Event
protected override void OnUnload(System.EventArgs e)
{
  Trace("Lifecycle: Unload Event.");
  base.OnUnload(e);
}
```

```
    // Dispose Event
    public override void Dispose()
    {
      Trace("Lifecycle: Dispose Event.");
      base.Dispose();
    }

    private void Trace(string info)
    {
      if (Context != null)
      {
        Context.Trace.Warn(info);
        Debug.WriteLine(info);
      }
    }
  }
}
```

Listings 5-20 and 5-21 outline the web form that hosts the control, with the ASP.NET tracing mechanism turned on. The UI appearance is a single button on the web form with trace output turned on.

Listing 5-20. *The Life Cycle Web Form .aspx Page File*

```
<%@ Page Trace="true" Language="C#"
MasterPageFile="~/MasterPage/ControlsBook2MasterPage.Master"
  AutoEventWireup="true" CodeBehind="LifeCycle.aspx.cs"
Inherits="ControlsBook2Web.Ch05.LifeCycle"
  Title="LifeCycle Demo" %>

<%@ Register TagPrefix="apress" Namespace="ControlsBook2Lib.Ch05"
                         Assembly="ControlsBook2Lib" %>
<asp:Content ID="Content1" ContentPlaceHolderID="ChapterNumAndTitle" runat="server">
  <asp:Label ID="ChapterNumberLabel" runat="server"
Width="14px">5</asp:Label>  <asp:Label
ID="ChapterTitleLabel" runat="server" Width="360px">
Server Control Events</asp:Label>
</asp:Content>
<asp:Content ID="Content2" ContentPlaceHolderID="PrimaryContent" runat="server">
  <h3>
    LifeCycle</h3>
  <apress:Lifecycle ID="life1" runat="server" />
  <asp:Button ID="Button1" runat="server" Text="Button"></asp:Button>
</asp:Content>
```

Listing 5-21. *The Life Cycle Web Form Code-Behind Class File*

```
using System;
using System.Web.UI;
using System.Web.UI.WebControls;

namespace ControlsBook2Web.Ch05
{
  public partial class LifeCycle : System.Web.UI.Page
  {
    protected void Page_Load(object sender, EventArgs e)
    {

    }
  }
}
```

The first execution of the Life Cycle web form results in an HTTP GET protocol request and generates the life cycle events shown in the ASP.NET trace output shown in Figure 5-22.

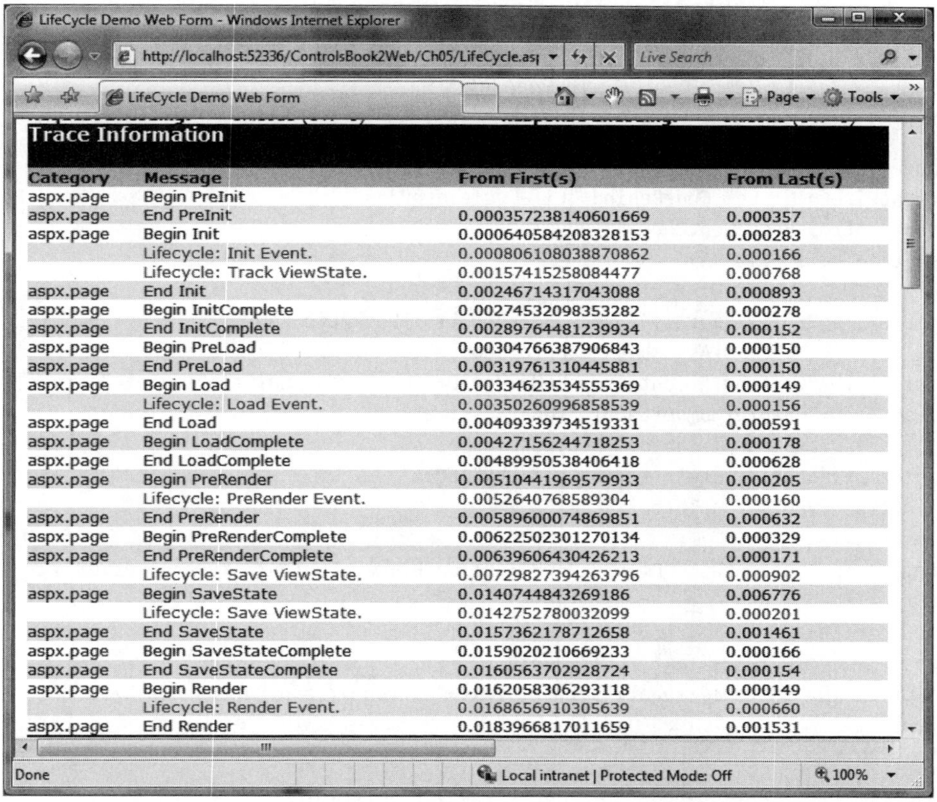

LifeCycle Demo Web Form - Windows Internet Explorer

http://localhost:52336/ControlsBook2Web/Ch05/LifeCycle.asp

Trace Information

Category	Message	From First(s)	From Last(s)
aspx.page	Begin PreInit		
aspx.page	End PreInit	0.000357238140601669	0.000357
aspx.page	Begin Init	0.000640584208328153	0.000283
	Lifecycle: Init Event.	0.000806108038870862	0.000166
	Lifecycle: Track ViewState.	0.00157415258084477	0.000768
aspx.page	End Init	0.00246714317043088	0.000893
aspx.page	Begin InitComplete	0.00274532098353282	0.000278
aspx.page	End InitComplete	0.00289764481239934	0.000152
aspx.page	Begin PreLoad	0.00304766387906843	0.000150
aspx.page	End PreLoad	0.00319761310445881	0.000150
aspx.page	Begin Load	0.00334623534555369	0.000149
	Lifecycle: Load Event.	0.00350260996858539	0.000156
aspx.page	End Load	0.00409339734519331	0.000591
aspx.page	Begin LoadComplete	0.00427156244718253	0.000178
aspx.page	End LoadComplete	0.00489950538406418	0.000628
aspx.page	Begin PreRender	0.00510441969579933	0.000205
	Lifecycle: PreRender Event.	0.0052640768589304	0.000160
aspx.page	End PreRender	0.00589600074869851	0.000632
aspx.page	Begin PreRenderComplete	0.00622502301270134	0.000329
aspx.page	End PreRenderComplete	0.00639606430426213	0.000171
	Lifecycle: Save ViewState.	0.00729827394263796	0.000902
aspx.page	Begin SaveState	0.0140744843269186	0.006776
	Lifecycle: Save ViewState.	0.0142752780032099	0.000201
aspx.page	End SaveState	0.0157362178712658	0.001461
aspx.page	Begin SaveStateComplete	0.0159020210669233	0.000166
aspx.page	End SaveStateComplete	0.0160563702928724	0.000154
aspx.page	Begin Render	0.0162058306293118	0.000149
	Lifecycle: Render Event.	0.0168656910305639	0.000660
aspx.page	End Render	0.0183966817011659	0.001531

Done | Local intranet | Protected Mode: Off | 100%

Figure 5-22. *The Lifecycle.aspx trace output from an HTTP GET request*

We next cover the life cycle events that occur when an HTTP GET request occurs, starting with the Init event.

Init Event

The first phase processed by the control is the Init event. We are notified of this phase by overriding the protected OnInit method inherited from the base class System.Web.UI.Control:

```
override protected void OnInit(System.EventArgs e)
{
   base.OnInit();
   Trace("Lifecycle:  Init Event.");
}
```

The code in the OnInit method uses a private utility method called Trace that sends status information to the Trace class via the control's Context property available to ASP.NET server controls:

```
private void Trace(string info)
{
   Page.Trace.Warn(info);
   Debug.WriteLine(info);
}
```

This class method also sends output to the debug stream via the System.Diagnostics.Debug class and its WriteLine method. The reason for this extra step is to view Unload and Dispose event execution, which occurs after the web form is finished writing out its content via the Render method and the ASP.NET trace tables have been generated. You can view debug stream information in the Output window of Visual Studio when debugging.

The Init event is an opportunity for the control to initialize any resources it needs to service the page request. A control can access any child controls in this method if necessary; however, peer- and parent-level controls are not guaranteed to be accessible at this point in the life cycle.

Overriding methods such as OnInit from the base class System.Web.UI.Control requires that we call the base version of this method to ensure proper functioning of the event. The base class implementation of OnInit actually raises the Init event exposed by the root Control class to clients.

If you override OnInit but do not call the base class version of this event, the event will not be raised to clients that are registered to receive it. This applies to the other On-prefixed methods such as OnLoad, OnPreRender, and OnUnload, which are part of the life cycle process, as well as other non-life-cycle-specific event methods such as OnDataBinding and OnBubbleEvent.

TrackViewState Method

The TrackViewState method executes immediately after initialization and marks the beginning of ViewState processing, and state tracking, in the control life cycle. If you have attribute values that you do not want to save in ViewState across page round-trips for efficiency purposes, you should set these values in the OnInit method. Otherwise, all control property value modifications performed after this method executes will persist to ViewState.

If desired, you can make modifications to state values in this method that won't be marked as dirty as long as you do so before executing the inherited base.TrackViewState method or before calling the encapsulated StateBag.TrackViewState method.

Load Event

The Load event should be quite familiar to you, because we have leveraged this convenient location for common page code in our web forms in previous examples. It is a handy place to put page initialization logic, because you are guaranteed that all controls in the Page's control tree are created and all state-loading mechanisms have restored each control's state back to where it was at the end of the previous request/ response page round-trip. This event also occurs before any controls in the Page's control tree fire their specific events resulting from value changes in postback data. To customize control behavior in this phase, override the OnLoad method.

PreRender Event

The PreRender event is a phase in the control life cycle that represents the last-ditch chance for a control to do something before it is rendered. This is the location to put code that must execute before rendering but after the Load event, state management methods, and postback events have occurred. Controls can override the OnPreRender method for this special situation. Note that changes made to a control's state at this point in the life cycle will persist to ViewState.

SaveViewState Method

The SaveViewState method saves the ViewState dictionary by default without any additional action by you. Overriding this method is only necessary when a control needs to customize state persistence in ViewState. This method is called only when the EnableViewState property inherited from Control is set to true. The object instance that is returned from this method is serialized by ASP.NET into the final ViewState string that is emitted into the page's __VIEWSTATE hidden field. Be aware that SaveViewState is called twice in our sample code as a result of enabling page tracing, which makes a call to SaveViewState to gather information for tracing purposes. With tracing disabled during normal page execution, SaveViewState is called only once.

SaveControlState Method

The SaveControlState method saves the control state changes to ViewState. Overriding this method is only necessary when a control needs to customize state persistence in control state. Control state may or may not be used by a server control. In contrast to ViewState, control state cannot be disabled by the developer user. Control state is stored using the same mechanism of ViewState, but it cannot be turned off like ViewState.

Render Method

You are, by now, very familiar with overriding the Render method in a custom control to generate a control's UI. The HtmlTextWriter class does the bulk of the work here, writing out the control as HTML and script where applicable to the HTTP response stream. Note that any changes to a control's state made within this method will render into the UI but will not be saved as part of ViewState.

Unload Event

The Page class implements this method to perform cleanup. Overriding the OnUnload method from the base control class allows the control to hook into this event. Although the Unload event is an opportunity for a control to release any resources that it has obtained in earlier control events such as Init or Load, it is recommended that you release resources in its Dispose method.

The trace output from the ASP.NET page does not display any information pertaining to this event, because it fires after Render executes, but we can use the debug stream output from the Output window when debugging the web form in Visual Studio to see the result:

```
Lifecycle: Init Event.
Lifecycle: Track ViewState.
Lifecycle: Load Event.
Lifecycle: PreRender Event.
Lifecycle: Save ViewState.
Lifecycle: Save ViewState.
Lifecycle: Render Event.
Lifecycle: Unload Event.
Lifecycle: Dispose Event.
```

Dispose Method

Dispose is the recommended location for cleaning up resources. Implementing a Dispose method is recommended in .NET Framework programming when unmanaged resources (such as a connection to SQL Server) are acquired by a control and need to be safely released within the garbage collection architecture. The pattern is based on the IDispose interface that gives a way for clients to tell an object to clean up its unmanaged resources:

```
Interface IDispose
{
   void Dispose();
}
```

Once a client is finished working with an object, the client notifies the object that it is finished by calling the object's Dispose method. This gives the object immediate confirmation that it can clean up its resources instead of waiting for its Finalize method to be called during garbage collection. Because Dispose is the design pattern common in .NET, it is recommended that you implement cleanup in Dispose instead of Unload to release unmanaged resources.

HTTP POST Request via Postback

Additional events and methods of the control life cycle are exercised once we execute a postback of the Life Cycle web form by clicking the button. The output of the trace is much larger, so the screen shot in Figure 5-23 is filled by that table.

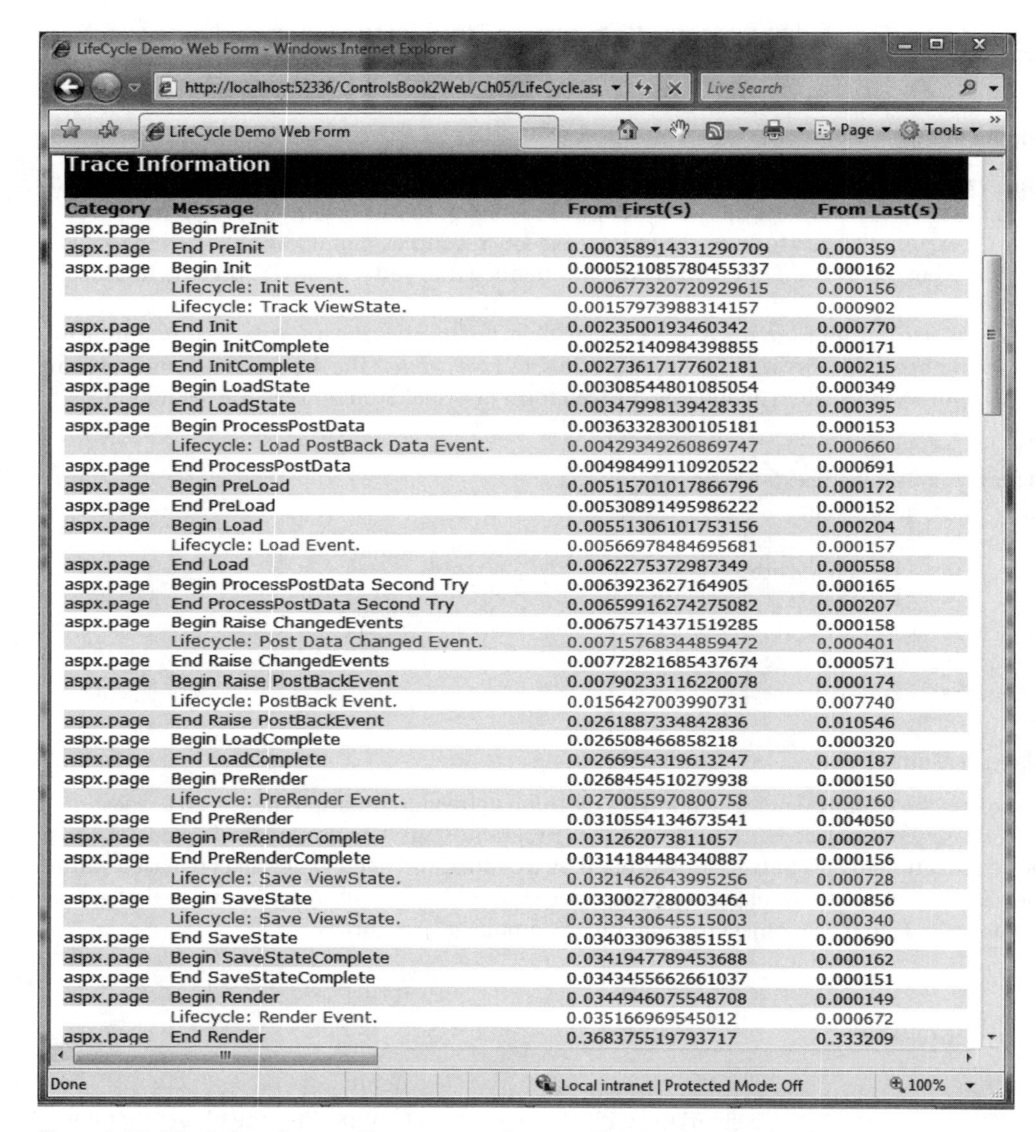

Trace Information

Category	Message	From First(s)	From Last(s)
aspx.page	Begin PreInit		
aspx.page	End PreInit	0.000358914331290709	0.000359
aspx.page	Begin Init	0.000521085780455337	0.000162
	Lifecycle: Init Event.	0.000677320720929615	0.000156
	Lifecycle: Track ViewState.	0.00157973988314157	0.000902
aspx.page	End Init	0.0023500193460342	0.000770
aspx.page	Begin InitComplete	0.00252140984398855	0.000171
aspx.page	End InitComplete	0.00273617177602181	0.000215
aspx.page	Begin LoadState	0.00308544801085054	0.000349
aspx.page	End LoadState	0.00347998139428335	0.000395
aspx.page	Begin ProcessPostData	0.00363328300105181	0.000153
	Lifecycle: Load PostBack Data Event.	0.00429349260869747	0.000660
aspx.page	End ProcessPostData	0.00498499110920522	0.000691
aspx.page	Begin PreLoad	0.00515701017866796	0.000172
aspx.page	End PreLoad	0.00530891495986222	0.000152
aspx.page	Begin Load	0.00551306101753156	0.000204
	Lifecycle: Load Event.	0.00566978484695681	0.000157
aspx.page	End Load	0.0062275372987349	0.000558
aspx.page	Begin ProcessPostData Second Try	0.0063923627164905	0.000165
aspx.page	End ProcessPostData Second Try	0.00659916274275082	0.000207
aspx.page	Begin Raise ChangedEvents	0.00675714371519285	0.000158
	Lifecycle: Post Data Changed Event.	0.00715768344859472	0.000401
aspx.page	End Raise ChangedEvents	0.00772821685437674	0.000571
aspx.page	Begin Raise PostBackEvent	0.00790233116220078	0.000174
	Lifecycle: PostBack Event.	0.0156427003990731	0.007740
aspx.page	End Raise PostBackEvent	0.0261887334842836	0.010546
aspx.page	Begin LoadComplete	0.026508466858218	0.000320
aspx.page	End LoadComplete	0.0266954319613247	0.000187
aspx.page	Begin PreRender	0.0268454510279938	0.000150
	Lifecycle: PreRender Event.	0.0270055970800758	0.000160
aspx.page	End PreRender	0.0310554134673541	0.004050
aspx.page	Begin PreRenderComplete	0.031262073811057	0.000207
aspx.page	End PreRenderComplete	0.0314184484340887	0.000156
	Lifecycle: Save ViewState.	0.0321462643995256	0.000728
aspx.page	Begin SaveState	0.0330027280003464	0.000856
	Lifecycle: Save ViewState.	0.0333430645515003	0.000340
aspx.page	End SaveState	0.0340330963851551	0.000690
aspx.page	Begin SaveStateComplete	0.0341947789453688	0.000162
aspx.page	End SaveStateComplete	0.0343455662661037	0.000151
aspx.page	Begin Render	0.0344946075548708	0.000149
	Lifecycle: Render Event.	0.035166969545012	0.000672
aspx.page	End Render	0.368375519793717	0.333209

Figure 5-23. *The Lifecycle.aspx Trace output from an HTTP POST postback*

The output from the Visual Studio Debug window confirms the sequence of events as well:

```
Lifecycle: Init Event.
Lifecycle: Track ViewState.
Lifecycle: Load Event.
Lifecycle: PreRender Event.
Lifecycle: Save ViewState.
Lifecycle: Save ViewState.
Lifecycle: Render Event.
Lifecycle: Unload Event.
```

```
Lifecycle: Dispose Event.
Lifecycle: Init Event.
Lifecycle: Track ViewState.
Lifecycle: Load PostBack Data Event.
Lifecycle: Load Event.
Lifecycle: Post Data Changed Event.
Lifecycle: PostBack Event.
Lifecycle: PreRender Event.
Lifecycle: Save ViewState.
Lifecycle: Save ViewState.
Lifecycle: Render Event.
Lifecycle: Unload Event.
Lifecycle: Dispose Event.
```

LoadViewState Method

Overriding the `LoadViewState` method is necessary if a control has previously overridden `SaveViewState` to customize `ViewState` serialization. Customization of the `ViewState` persistence mechanism is commonly performed by developers in more complex controls that have complex properties such as a reference type or a collection of objects. The decision to customize `ViewState` really comes down to whether or not a control's state can be easily or efficiently reduced to a string representation.

LoadControlState Method

Overriding the `LoadControlState` method is necessary if a control has previously overridden `SaveControlState` to customize `ControlState` serialization. Customization of the `ControlState` persistence mechanism is commonly performed by developers in more complex controls that have properties that must always be available even if `ViewState` is not available.

LoadPostBackData Method

In the previous chapter, we discussed how to retrieve client form post data via implementation of the `IPostBackDataHandler` interface. The `LoadPostData` routine is given the opportunity to process the postback data and to update the control's state. It also allows the control to notify ASP.NET that it wishes to raise an event at a later time in order to permit clients a chance to process the state change. For our purposes, the `Lifecycle` control always returns `true`, so the change event is always raised.

Keen observers will notice that we really should not be receiving the form post information, because we did not emit an HTML tag such as `<INPUT>`. However, we greased the wheels in the ASP.NET framework by calling `Page.RegisterRequiresPostBack` in `OnPreRender`:

```
override protected void OnPreRender(System.EventArgs e)
{
   base.OnPreRender(e);
   Trace("Lifecycle: PreRender Event.");
   Page.RegisterRequiresPostBack(this);
}
```

This makes it possible to receive a call to our LoadPostData method by ASP.NET. We perform a similar task in LoadPostData to ensure we receive the PostBack event by calling Page.RegisterRequiresRaiseEvent:

```
public bool LoadPostData(string postDataKey, NameValueCollection postCollection)
{
   Trace("Lifecycle: Load PostBack Data Event.");
   Page.RegisterRequiresRaiseEvent(this);
   return true;
}
```

RaisePostDataChangedEvent Method

For controls that have state changes reflected in postback data, these controls most likely need to raise server-side events. These events are raised from within the RaisePostDataChangedEvent method of each respective control. Following this design guideline ensures that control state is restored from ViewState and updated from postback data before the various events begin to fire. Raising server-side events from within any other control method can cause hard-to-debug side effects for event consumers. This routine is called only if the LoadPostData returns true.

RaisePostBackEvent Method

Implementing RaisePostBackEvent ensures that the server control notifies ASP.NET that the state of the control has changed. To participate in postback processing, a control must implement the IPostBackEventHandler interface. Controls implement this interface and emit some sort of HTML to submit the web form back to the server, whether via a button or an HTML element with JavaScript code to submit the form programmatically.

In our sample Lifecycle control, we rigged the system by calling Page.RegisterRequiresRaiseEvent in the LoadPostData method. Our SuperButton control sample in this chapter demonstrates how to execute this properly. We use this shortcut to hook into this event for purposes discussing the control life cycle.

Summary

In this chapter, we discussed how to implement events in the ASP.NET framework. Event-based programming is a critical aspect of ASP.NET development, making web development more like developing with Visual Basic on the Windows desktop. We also discussed how to bubble events up the control hierarchy and we explored the control life cycle.

System.EventHandler is the default delegate type for events in ASP.NET. Inherit from this type when you create custom event handlers so that your controls behave in a similar manner to the built-in controls.

Events are generally invoked in a control through a virtual protected method that prefixes the word "On" to the event name to create a method name such as OnClick and OnTextChanged. Custom events implement their own delegate type with the name suffixed by "EventHandler". Custom events can also implement a custom EventArgs-derived class to provide event data tailored to the particular situation. The simplest way for a control to expose an event is to declare one as a public field of a custom control class.

Controls can use the Events collection inherited from System.Web.UI.Control to efficiently manage events in a sparse collection instead of the one-field-per-event model. Using the Events collection along with custom event registration code can potentially save a large amount of memory for a control with many events that are not all normally implemented.

Command events are a special event type used by list controls in ASP.NET to simplify handling buttons as child controls. Command events expose CommandName and CommandArgument properties to communicate their intentions to the parent control.

Event bubbling is a concept in ASP.NET whereby a control can raise an event through its parent control hierarchy. RaiseBubbleEvent starts the event in motion. Parent controls can catch the event by overriding OnBubbleEvent. RaisePostBackEvent is the method in IPostBackEventHandler that allows a control to capture a postback generated by a change in data.

INamingContainer is used by a composite control to ensure that its child controls have a unique name on the page even if the composite control is used several times on the page via the UniqueID property.

Controls follow a well-defined life cycle execution process to help coordinate events and activities. Understanding the control life cycle will ensure your custom controls behave as expected. The complete control life cycle for an HTTP GET request includes these events in order: Init, TrackViewState, Load, PreRender, SaveViewState, SaveControlState, Render, Unload, and Dispose. The complete control life cycle for an HTTP POST request includes these events in order: Init, TrackViewState, LoadViewState, LoadControlState, LoadPostData, Load, RaisePostDataChangedEvent, PostBack, PreRender, SaveViewState, Render, Unload, and Dispose.

CHAPTER 6

Server Control Templates

Starting in ASP.NET 2.0, adding templates and data binding to server controls requires much less code than in previous versions of ASP.NET. The examples in this chapter take advantage of these improvements.

Templates allow customization of how server controls or HTML elements display data. Templates and data binding generally are brought together in more advanced controls, such as the ASP.NET `GridView` or `Repeater` server controls, making database-driven web development quick and easy. Pull a piece of data from the database via ADO.NET, bind it to a server control, configure its style properties and templates, and web developers can build a very appealing HTML display that appears to act like a Visual Basic form with data paging, alternate colors, and so on. The server control handles all the heavy lifting that would normally require a large amount of hand coding in plain old ASP. We cover combining data binding with templates in the next chapter.

In this chapter, we focus on adding support for templates to server controls. We start the examples with a template control named `TemplateMenu`; this example shows you how to build a server control that lets you apply templates to hyperlinks. The next example control builds demonstrates how to treat content tags as data to build out control content.

Customized Control Content

HTML is a combination of content and appearance. The previous chapter showed how server controls customize the appearance of content through the use of style attributes that modify features such as font, color, size, or even placement of the HTML. In this chapter, we discuss how to modify the core content of the Web Form through two incredibly useful techniques: templates and data binding.

Templates allow web developers to specify the HTML elements and server controls that render as part of the main server control's output. The server control provides templates that are placeholders for content insertion, as illustrated in Figure 6-1. Templates allow customization of how a control renders simply by editing the `.aspx` page. Server control developers should look to add template functionality to custom controls to provide this level of flexibility when it makes sense to allow the developer user to customize the UI of the server control.

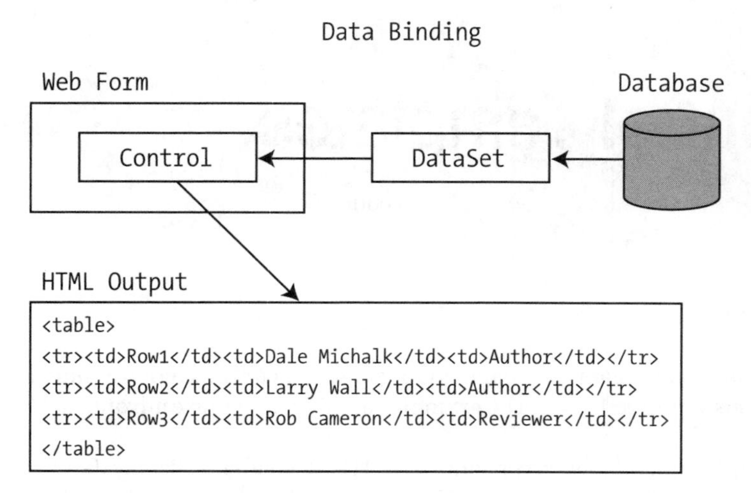

Figure 6-1. *Templates with server controls*

Using Control Templates

An ASP.NET template is a mix of HTML elements and ASP.NET controls that make up the layout for a particular area of a control. Templates increase the level of flexibility in a control and allow the developer/user to customize the graphical presentation of control content. The following code snippet is a hypothetical MyTemplate template:

```
<MyTemplate>
   <span>Raw HTML</span>
   <asp:Label id="Label1" runat="server" Text="My Server Control Label" />
</MyTemplate>
```

The template has begin and end tags with some content consisting of raw HTML intermixed with ASP.NET server controls. You normally specify the content declaratively, but you can load it from a file or instantiate it from a prebuilt template class at runtime for dynamic template use, as we show in Chapter 7 when we test our version of the Repeater control.

In some ways, ASP.NET's support for templates partially removes the look-and-feel burden from the control developer. The control developer can focus on plumbing while the control user, or the graphic designer working in concert with the control user, can build pleasing templates that lay inside the control. Of course, the control developer can provide custom designers that can help with template creation, but this is not required (we cover design-time functionality in Chapter 11.)

The ParseChildren Attribute

A control that provides support for templates must indicate to the ASP.NET page parser that it wishes to manage its child content by adding the ParseChildren attribute to its class declaration.

This attribute instructs the page parser to handle child elements as control properties. For controls that inherit from `System.Web.UI.WebControls.WebControl` or a descendent class, this functionality comes for free via inheritance. You must add the attribute manually to controls based on `System.Web.UI.Control`.

The `ParseChildren` attribute has a property named `ChildrenAsProperties` that configures the parsing behavior. `WebControl` sets the `ChildrenAsProperties` property of the `ParseChildren` attribute to true by default, as shown in the following line of code. If you need to use a different value for a server control based on `WebControl`, remember to set the attribute explicitly to override the default behavior.

```
ParseChildrenAttribute(ChildrenAsProperties = true)
```

`ParseChildrenAttribute` also takes a shortened version to set the `ChildrenAsProperties` property:

```
ParseChildren(true)
```

The presence of the `ParseChildren` attribute set to true for `ChildrenAsProperties` causes the ASP.NET page parser to map top-level XML elements or tags under the server control directly to its exposed properties. The server control is responsible for providing the appropriate mapping, as illustrated in Figure 6-2.

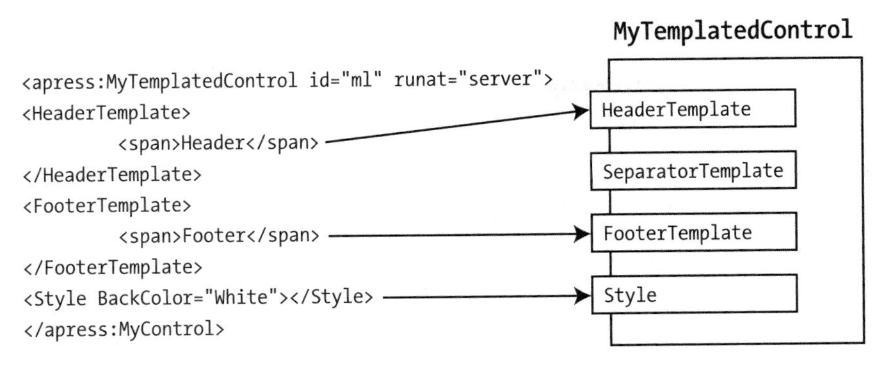

Figure 6-2. *The ParseChildren attribute with ChildrenAsProperties=true*

If the `ChildrenAsProperties` property value is set to false instead of true, ASP.NET attempts to process the child content of the outer control tags as embedded server controls, as shown in Figure 6-3. The default implementation of a control's `IParserAccessor` interface and its single `AddParsedSubObject` method adds those child server controls to the parent control's `Controls` collection. Literal text in between the tags becomes a `LiteralControl` server control instance.

[ParseChildren(ChildrenAsProperties=false)]

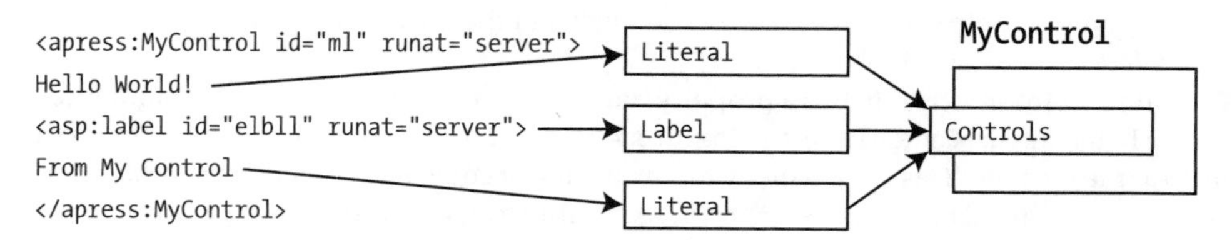

Figure 6-3. *The ParseChildren attribute with ChildrenAsProperties=false*

A Menu Control with Templates

The menu control implemented back in Chapter 2 displayed a simple list of HTML hyperlinks. We revisit its design to illustrate the use of UI templates. The hyperlinks will be retained while we provide several custom templates to render the output.

We build the `TemplateMenu` control as a composite control with three templates: `HeaderTemplate`, `FooterTemplate`, and `SeparatorTemplate` (see Figure 6-4). As you would guess, `HeaderTemplate` and `FooterTemplate` allow developers to customize the top and bottom portions of the menu control. `SeparatorTemplate` provides customization of the content between hyperlinks. To keep things simple, the control uses an internal data source to provide content for rendering each hyperlink in the menu.

TemplateMenu Control

HeaderTemplate

SeparatorTemplate

Authors Book Site <>Apress<>Microsoft<>GotDotNet

To Browse To

FooterTemplate

Figure 6-4. *The TemplateMenu control templates*

The first step in building our composite control is to inherit from `CompositeControl`. This will use a `<DIV>` tag as the enclosing tag as well as implement `INamingContainer`, which is required for template controls, because you will embed controls in templates that may conflict in their ID values.

`CompositeControl` is one of the new base classes, listed in Chapter 2, that provide additional useful functionality for the control developer. The primary benefit of inheriting from `CompositeControl` is the associated designer `CompositeControlDesigner`, which provides basic design-time support for composite control developers.

The following code shows our server control declaration:

```
[ToolboxData("<{0}:templatemenu
runat=server></{0}:templatemenu>"),Designer(typeof(TemplateMenuDesigner))]
public class TemplateMenu : CompositeControl
    private ArrayList menuData;
   public TemplateMenu() : base(HtmlTextWriterTag.Div)
   {
      menuData = new ArrayList();
      menuData.Add(new MenuItemData("Authors Book Site","","",""));
      menuData.Add(new MenuItemData("Apress","http://www.apress.com","",""));
      menuData.Add(new MenuItemData("Microsoft","http://www.microsoft.com","",""));
      menuData.Add(new MenuItemData("GotDotNet","http://asp.net","",""));
   }
...
}
```

Notice the attributes applied to the `TemplateMenu` class. The `ToolBoxData` attribute provides a means to customize the initial HTML, such as initial or default values, when the control is dragged from the Visual Studio Toolbox and placed on the design surface.

Since we want to be able to edit the templates using the Visual Studio design-time environment, we override the default `CompositeControlDesigner` and add our own custom designer via the `Designer` attribute. We cover how to create custom designer classes in Chapter 11, but we use it here to demonstrate its functionality.

The constructor for our control fills a private `ArrayList` collection that holds the title and URL of each of the hyperlinks in the menu. Hard-coding the data in the control is replaced in later examples where the link data is provided via nested child tags.

`MenuItemData` is the type held in the private `ArrayList`. It has properties for the title of the hyperlink, the URL it directs the browser to, the URL to display it as an image instead of text, and the `Target` property to direct a particular frame to load the address from the hyperlink. We use it to store hyperlink data in all our menu examples.

The Template Properties

Because `WebControl` parses the child content into properties, we need to give the ASP.NET page parser a target that matches up with properties on our control when it encounters the child `HeaderTemplate`, `FooterTemplate`, and `SeparatorTemplate` tags in the `.aspx` page. The control does this by exposing `ITemplate` type properties of those exact names:

```
private ITemplate headerTemplate;
[Browsable(false),Description("The header template"),
PersistenceMode(PersistenceMode.InnerProperty),
TemplateContainer(typeof(BasicTemplateContainer))]
public ITemplate HeaderTemplate
{
   get
   {
      return headerTemplate;
   }
```

```
      set
      {
         headerTemplate = value;
      }
   }
```

The preceding snippet is the portion of the control that implements the HeaderTemplate property and its storage. The HeaderTemplate property does a set and get on the private ITemplate type field named headerTemplate. ASP.NET is smart enough to query the type of the property and realize that it is working with ITemplate. It then follows a set of steps to instantiate a Template class and assign it to the property. The code for the FooterTemplate and SeparatorTemplate properties is identical to that of the HeaderTemplate property.

The final item that a template property needs is a TemplateContainer attribute to tell ASP.NET what type of control will contain the template. This step wires up the control content inside the template to its outside container and allows value-added features such as data binding to occur.

The HeaderTemplate property uses the BasicTemplateContainer type to do this. BasicTemplateContainer is a very simple WebControl shell that renders a <SPAN> tag. The full class definition is as follows:

```
public class BasicTemplateContainer : WebControl, INamingContainer
{
  public BasicTemplateContainer() : base(HtmlTextWriterTag.Span)
  {
    this.BorderWidth = 2;
    this.BorderStyle = BorderStyle.Outset;
  }
}
```

The template container itself can be customized as shown previously by modifying the BorderWidth and BorderStyle attributes. The separator template would not look good with the modified border attributes, so it uses the SeperatorTemplateContainer, which renders as an empty HTML Span tag:

```
public class SeperatorTemplateContainer : WebControl, INamingContainer
{
  public SeperatorTemplateContainer() : base(HtmlTextWriterTag.Span)
  {
  }
}
```

Creating the Header Section

The TemplateMenu control is a composite control, so it needs to override the CreateChildControls method to add child controls to its Controls collection. The control abstracts this process by using a CreateControlHierarchy helper method to do the child creation work. CreateControlHierarchy contains code to add the templates and the hyperlinks as child controls:

```
override protected void CreateChildControls()
{
   Controls.Clear();
   CreateControlHierarchy();
}
```

CreateControlHierarchy starts out by working with the HeaderTemplate template. The first item that must always be checked is whether the template property has a value. This is detected by examining the template property for a null value:

```
if (HeaderTemplate != null)
{
   BasicTemplateContainer header = new BasicTemplateContainer();
   HeaderTemplate.InstantiateIn(header);
   Controls.Add(header);
   Controls.Add(new LiteralControl("<br>"));
}
```

If the template property is null, a common feature of server controls is to render a generic default HTML template so the output is consistent. The ASP.NET DataGrid control does this by rendering a simple, plain HTML table when it is bound to a data source without templates. For the HeaderTemplate template, we ignore the template and display nothing if it is null.

After the code checks for a null value of the template property, it next instantiates the container that will serve as the host for the template content. The TemplateMenu control wraps all templates into a <SPAN> HTML element via the use of a custom BasicTemplateContainer control based on System.Web.UI.WebControls.WebControl. To load the template content into the BasicTemplateContainer control, the ITemplate interface provides an InstantiateIn method that takes the container as a parameter, as shown in Figure 6-5.

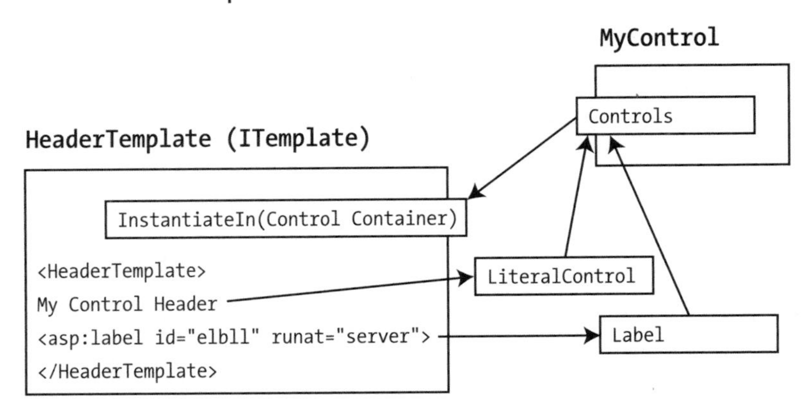

Figure 6-5. *ITemplate and InstantiateIn*

The use of InstantiateIn completes the work required for the header control container. The control code next adds the header to its child Controls collection. We also add a LiteralControl object that renders a <BR> tag to make the separation of the header from the hyperlinks a mandatory feature of the UI rendering of the TemplateMenu control.

Creating the Footer Section

The code for the FooterTemplate at the end of CreateControlHierarchy is almost identical to that of the HeaderTemplate. The only real difference besides a different template property is that it adds the <BR> tag before it adds the template content:

```
if (FooterTemplate != null)
{
   Controls.Add(new LiteralControl("<br>"));
   BasicTemplateContainer footer = new BasicTemplateContainer();
   FooterTemplate.InstantiateIn(footer);
   Controls.Add(footer);
}
```

Creating the Hyperlink Section

The middle of the code for the CreateControlHierarchy method adds the items in the menu using the ASP.NET HyperLink control. The data for the process is provided by the ArrayList collection exposed by the private menuData field that we instantiated in the constructor for our control.

The first task in building each hyperlink is iterating through the menuData ArrayList. We use a loop and a counter to help us track when we need to apply the MenuSeparatorTemplate template to separate the hyperlinks. The loop drives retrieval of the instances of the MenuItemData class from the collection and the execution of the CreateMenuItem helper method:

```
int count = menuData.Count;
for (int index = 0; index < count; index++)
{
   MenuItemData itemdata = (MenuItemData) menuData[index];
   CreateMenuItem(itemdata.Title, itemdata.Url,itemdata.ImageUrl, itemdata.Target);

   if (index != count-1)
   {
      if (SeparatorTemplate != null)
      {
         SeperatorTemplateContainer separator = new SeperatorTemplateContainer ();
         SeparatorTemplate.InstantiateIn(separator);
         Controls.Add(separator);
      }
      else
      {
         Controls.Add(new LiteralControl(" | "));
      }
   }
}
```

CreateMenuItem creates an ASP.NET HyperLink control and adds it to the TemplateMenu control child controls:

```
private void CreateMenuItem(string title, string url,
                                                string target, string imageurl)
{
   HyperLink link = new HyperLink();
   link.Text = title;
   link.NavigateUrl = url;
   link.ImageUrl = imageurl;
   link.Target = target;
   Controls.Add(link);
}
```

The SeparatorTemplate uses a different template container, the SeperatorTemplateContainer, but otherwise, the code follows the lead of the FooterTemplate and HeaderTemplate templates. What is unique in this piece of code is the addition of code to render a sensible separator via LiteralControl should the user decide not to wire in a SeparatorTemplate value in the .aspx page.

When you build a server control that supports templates, it is recommended that you ensure the control functions properly, or at least degrades gracefully, with a basic default template if templates are not specified.

The full version of the TemplateMenu control is shown in Listing 6-1.

Listing 6-1. *The TemplateMenu Control*

```
using System;
using System.Web;
using System.Web.UI;
using System.Web.UI.WebControls;
using System.Collections;
using System.ComponentModel;
using ControlsBook2Lib.Ch11.Design;

namespace ControlsBook2Lib.Ch06
{
  [ToolboxData("<{0}:templatemenu runat=server></{0}:templatemenu>"),
  Designer(typeof(TemplateMenuDesigner))]
  public class TemplateMenu : CompositeControl
  {
    private ArrayList menuData;
    public TemplateMenu()
      : base()
    {
      menuData = new ArrayList()
     //Uses new C# 3.0 Object and Collection Initializers
      {
        new MenuItemData{Title="Apress", Url="http://www.apress.com"},
        new MenuItemData{Title="Microsoft", Url="http://www.microsoft.com"},
        new MenuItemData{Title="ASP.Net", Url="http://asp.net"}
```

```
    };
  }

  private ITemplate headerTemplate;
  [Browsable(false), Description("The header template"),
  PersistenceMode(PersistenceMode.InnerProperty),
  TemplateContainer(typeof(BasicTemplateContainer))]
  public ITemplate HeaderTemplate
  {
    get
    {
      return headerTemplate;
    }
    set
    {
      headerTemplate = value;
    }
  }

  private ITemplate footerTemplate;
  [Browsable(false), Description("The footer template"),
  PersistenceMode(PersistenceMode.InnerProperty),
  TemplateContainer(typeof(BasicTemplateContainer))]
  public ITemplate FooterTemplate
  {
    get
    {
      return footerTemplate;
    }
    set
    {
      footerTemplate = value;
    }
  }

  private ITemplate separatorTemplate;
  [Browsable(false), Description("The separator template"),
  PersistenceMode(PersistenceMode.InnerProperty),
 TemplateContainer(typeof(SeperatorTemplateContainer))]
  public ITemplate SeparatorTemplate
  {
    get
    {
      return separatorTemplate;
    }
```

```
  set
  {
    separatorTemplate = value;
  }
}

private void CreateControlHierarchy()
{
  if (HeaderTemplate != null)
  {
    BasicTemplateContainer header = new BasicTemplateContainer();
    HeaderTemplate.InstantiateIn(header);
    Controls.Add(header);
  }

  int count = menuData.Count;
  for (int index = 0; index < count; index++)
  {
    MenuItemData itemdata = (MenuItemData)menuData[index];

    HyperLink link = new HyperLink() { Text = itemdata.Title,
    NavigateUrl = itemdata.Url, ImageUrl = itemdata.ImageUrl,
    Target = itemdata.Target };
    Controls.Add(link);

    if (index != count - 1)
    {
      if (SeparatorTemplate != null)
      {
        SeperatorTemplateContainer separator = new SeperatorTemplateContainer();
        SeparatorTemplate.InstantiateIn(separator);
        Controls.Add(separator);
      }
      else
      {
        Controls.Add(new LiteralControl(" | "));
      }
    }
  }

  if (FooterTemplate != null)
  {
    BasicTemplateContainer footer = new BasicTemplateContainer();
    FooterTemplate.InstantiateIn(footer);
    Controls.Add(footer);
  }
}

override protected void CreateChildControls()
```

```
    {
      Controls.Clear();
      CreateControlHierarchy();
    }

    public override ControlCollection Controls
    {
      get
      {
        EnsureChildControls();
        return base.Controls;
      }
    }

    public override void DataBind()
    {
      CreateChildControls();
      ChildControlsCreated = true;

      base.DataBind();
    }
  }
}
```

The new C# 3.0 object initialization and collection initialization features are put to use when menuArray is instantiated in Listing 6-1. The source file for the templates, TemplateContainers.cs, is shown in Listing 6-2. Listing 6-3 contains the MenuItemData data class used to populate the menu hyperlinks.

Listing 6-2. *TheTemplateContainers Code File*

```
using System;
using System.Web;
using System.Web.UI;
using System.Web.UI.WebControls;

namespace ControlsBook2Lib.Ch06
{
   public class BasicTemplateContainer : WebControl, INamingContainer
   {
      public BasicTemplateContainer() : base(HtmlTextWriterTag.Span)
      {
        this.BorderWidth = 2;
        this.BorderStyle = BorderStyle.Outset;
      }
   }
```

```
  public class SeperatorTemplateContainer : WebControl, INamingContainer
  {
    public SeperatorTemplateContainer() : base(HtmlTextWriterTag.Span)
    {
    }
  }
}
```

Listing 6-3. *The MenuItemData Data Class*

```
using System;
using System.ComponentModel;

namespace ControlsBook2Lib.Ch06
{
  [TypeConverter(typeof(ExpandableObjectConverter))]
  public class MenuItemData
  {
    public MenuItemData()
    {

    }

    //Override this method to display just MenuItemData
    //instead of fully qualified type
    //in the custom collection editor
    public override string ToString()
    {
      return "MenuItemData";
    }

    [NotifyParentProperty(true)]
    public string Title {get; set; }

    [NotifyParentProperty(true)]
    public string Url { get; set; }

    [NotifyParentProperty(true)]
    public string ImageUrl {get; set; }

    [NotifyParentProperty(true)]
    public string Target { get; set; }
  }
}
```

Viewing the TemplateMenu Control

The web form created for viewing the TemplateMenu control could not be simpler. It consists of a single control on the form—that's it. The following templates exercise the UI customization features of the control:

```
<apress:TemplateMenu id="menu1" runat="server" height="43px" width="224px">
  <SeparatorTemplate> | </SeparatorTemplate>
  <HeaderTemplate>
    <span style="FONT-WEIGHT: bold; COLOR: white;
BACKGROUND-COLOR: blue">Please follow the link of interest</span>
  </HeaderTemplate>
  <FooterTemplate>
    <span style="FONT-WEIGHT: bold; COLOR: white;
BACKGROUND-COLOR: red">Thanks for visiting this site</span>
  </FooterTemplate>
</apress:TemplateMenu><br/><br/>
```

We can edit the templates for the web form by clicking the HTML tab in Visual Studio. The .NET Framework also provides the ability to visually edit templates, and the Designer(typeof(TemplateMenuDesigner))] attribute applied to the TemplateMenu class provides this support for the TemplateMenu server control.

This custom designer, which we cover in detail in Chapter 11, adds an Edit Templates menu item to the task list for the control. Click the task arrow when the control is selected in the designer; click Edit Template; and then choose the template you want to edit. This brings up a visual UI for the template, where you can drag and drop other ASP.NET controls, such as an image control for the separator template, and edit the style for the template in the Properties tool window. Figure 6-6 shows the results of our control after customizing its templates. Listings 6-4 and 6-5 contain the .aspx file and code-behind class for the TemplateMenu web form, respectively.

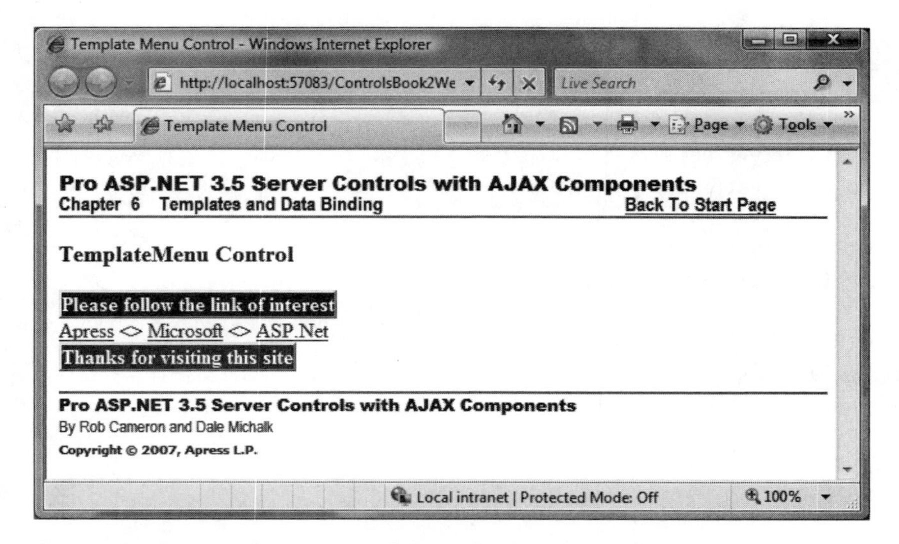

Figure 6-6. *The TemplateMenu web form displayed in a browser*

Listing 6-4. *The TemplateMenu Web Form .aspx File*

```
<%@ Page Language="C#"
MasterPageFile="~/MasterPage/ControlsBook2MasterPage.Master"
  AutoEventWireup="true" CodeBehind="TemplateMenu.aspx.cs"
Inherits="ControlsBook2Web.Ch06.TemplateMenu"
  Title="Template Menu Control Demo" %>

<%@ Register TagPrefix="apress" Namespace="ControlsBook2Lib.Ch06"
Assembly="ControlsBook2Lib" %>
<asp:Content ID="Content1" ContentPlaceHolderID="ChapterNumAndTitle"
             runat="server">
  <asp:Label ID="ChapterNumberLabel" runat="server"
  Width="14px">6</asp:Label>  <asp:Label
    ID="ChapterTitleLabel" runat="server" Width="360px">
    Server Control Templates</asp:Label>
</asp:Content>
<asp:Content ID="Content2" ContentPlaceHolderID="PrimaryContent"
            runat="server">
  <h3>
    TemplateMenu Control</h3>
  <apress:TemplateMenu ID="menu1" runat="server" Height="43px" Width="224px">
    <SeparatorTemplate>
      &lt;&gt;
    </SeparatorTemplate>
    <HeaderTemplate>
      <div style="font-weight: bold; color: white; background-color: blue">
        Please follow the link of interest</div>
    </HeaderTemplate>
    <FooterTemplate>
      <div style="font-weight: bold; color: white; background-color: red">
        Thanks for visiting this site</div>
    </FooterTemplate>
  </apress:TemplateMenu>
  <br />
  <br />
</asp:Content>
```

Listing 6-5. *The TemplateMenu Web Form Code-Behind Class File*

```
using System;

namespace ControlsBook2Web.Ch06
{
  public partial class TemplateMenu : System.Web.UI.Page
  {
    protected void Page_Load(object sender, EventArgs e)
    {
```

```
      }
    }
  }
```

Checking the Rendered HTML

The HTML rendered by the `TemplateMenu` control verifies that the control has successfully included the templates in its output:

```
<div id="ctl00_ControlsBookContent_menu1" style="height:43px;width:224px;">
  <span style="display:inline-block;border-width:2px;border-style:Outset;">
    <span style="FONT-WEIGHT: bold; COLOR: white; BACKGROUND-COLOR: blue">
    Please follow the link of interest
    </span>
  </span><br>
   <a href="http://www.apress.com">Apress</a><span> &lt;&gt; </span>
  <a href="http://www.microsoft.com">Microsoft</a><span> &lt;&gt; </span>
  <a href="http://asp.net">ASP.Net</a><br>
  <span style="display:inline-block;border-width:2px;border-style:Outset;">
    <span style="FONT-WEIGHT: bold; COLOR: white; BACKGROUND-COLOR: red">
     Thanks for visiting this site
    </span>
  </span>
</div>
```

The `HeaderTemplate` and `FooterTemplate` templates go into the final HTML verbatim. The code that builds the hyperlinks correctly inserts the `SeparatorTemplate` template with the <> characters as well. The next section discusses how to store data as child tags that are part of a server control.

Parsing Data from the Control Tags

The `TemplateMenu` control has one major limitation. The data it uses to display the hyperlinks is hard-coded in its constructor. A user of this control must have the source code to modify what is displayed. This is not the best way to go about building controls that are flexible and adaptable. Giving web developers a way to pass in the necessary data is a much better approach and is what we cover in the sections that follow.

The approach that we take to add customizable data to the control is to use child tags that pass in the data to the control. This is similar to the method used by the ASP.NET list controls, such as `DropDownList` and `CheckBoxList`, which support the use of the `asp:listitem` tag to pass in data declaratively. The server control we build in the next section uses the `ParseChildren` attribute. In the following section, we build a server control that shows how to customize this process further using a `ControlBuilder` class.

The TagDataMenu Control

The `TagDataMenu` control is an example control we create in this section that reads its child tag values to build its collection of data for hyperlinks. It does this by taking advantage of a feature of the ParseChildren attribute that tells the ASP.NET page parser to treat child content as items to be added to a collection.

The following attribute shows the ChildrenAsProperties property being set on the ParseChildren attribute, along with a DefaultProperty property:

```
[ParseChildren(ChildrenAsProperties=true, DefaultProperty="MenuItems")]
```

The following shorthand code does the same thing:

```
[ParseChildren(true, "MenuItems")]
```

Setting the DefaultProperty property in the ParseChildren attribute causes the ASP.NET page parser to look at all the child XML content of the server control as items in a collection. The items are created by the page parser and added to the collection specified by the MenuItems property. The type of the item in the collection is determined by the name of the child tag. ASP.NET looks for that type name in the project and creates an object for it, filling in its properties according to the tag attributes.

TagDataMenu configures itself for using the MenuItems collection by setting up its ParseChildren attribute accordingly:

```
[ParseChildren(true, "MenuItems")]
[ToolboxData("<{0}:TagDataMenu runat=server></{0}:TagDataMenu>")]
public class TagDataMenu : CompositeControl
{
   public TagDataMenu() : base(HtmlTextWriterTag.Div)
   {
   }
...
}
```

Figure 6-7 illustrates the relationship between the TagDataMenu control and its MenuItems collection.

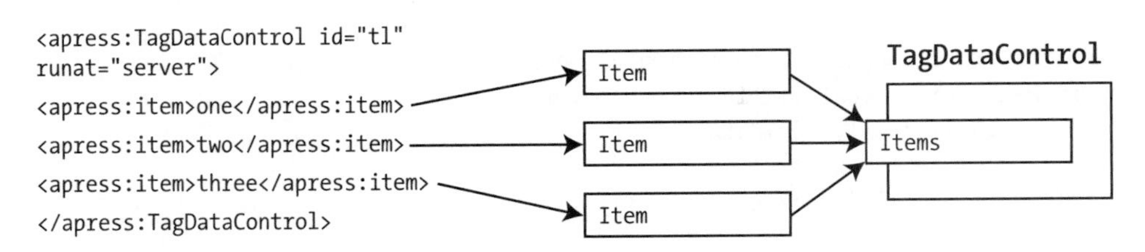

Figure 6-7. *The ParseChildren attribute with the Default property*

The read-only MenuItems property exposed by the control takes advantage of generics by implementing a List like this: List<MenuItemData>. This collection is populated by ASP.NET based on the control's child tag data:

```
private MenuItemDataCollection menuData;
[DesignerSerializationVisibility(DesignerSerializationVisibility.Content),
Description("Collection of MenuItemData objects for display"),
PersistenceMode(PersistenceMode.InnerDefaultProperty),NotifyParentProperty(true)]
public MenuItemDataCollection MenuItems
    {
      get
      {
         if (menuData == null)
         {
            menuData = new MenuItemDataCollection();
         }
         return menuData;
      }
}
```

Permitting data entry in child tags has one trade-off: a lack of template support. ASP.NET assumes that all the child tags go into the `DefaultProperty` collection, and it will not parse if it sees templates. For controls as simple as `TagDataMenu`, this is a reasonable trade-off. More advanced controls, such as the `Repeater` control we build in Chapter 7, will expose a property that allows web developers to set the data source programmatically.

The slimmed-down `CreateControlHierarchy` method doesn't have to worry about template building. We're able to reuse `CreateMenuItem` from the `TemplateMenu` control. For menu link separation, we use the pipe character (`|`) as the separator this time around:

```
override protected void CreateChildControls()
{
   Controls.Clear();
   CreateControlHierarchy();
}

private void CreateControlHierarchy()
{
   int count = menuData.Count;
   for (int index = 0; index < count; index++)
   {
      MenuItemData itemdata = (MenuItemData) menuData[index];
      CreateMenuItem(itemdata.Title, itemdata.Url,
         itemdata.ImageUrl, itemdata.Target);

      if ((count > 1) && (index < count -1))
      {
         Controls.Add(new LiteralControl(" | "));
      }
   }
}
```

Listing 6-6 presents the full code for the TagDataMenu control.

Listing 6-6. *The TagDataMenu Control Class File*

```
using System;
using System.Web;
using System.Web.UI;
using System.Web.UI.WebControls;
using System.Collections.Generic;
using System.ComponentModel;
using ControlsBook2Lib.Ch11.Design;

namespace ControlsBook2Lib.Ch06
{
  // PaseChildren attribute tells the ASP.NET page parser to treat
  // child content as items to be added to a collection.
  [ParseChildren(true, "MenuItems")]
  [ToolboxData("<{0}:tagdatamenu runat=server></{0}:tagdatamenu>")]
  public class TagDataMenu : CompositeControl
  {
    public TagDataMenu()
      : base()
    {
    }

    private List<MenuItemData> menuData = new List<MenuItemData>();

    // This collection is automatically populated by ASP.NET because of the
    // ParseChildren attribute on the class
    [DesignerSerializationVisibility(DesignerSerializationVisibility.Content),
    Description("Collection of MenuItemData objects for display"),
    PersistenceMode(PersistenceMode.InnerDefaultProperty),
    NotifyParentProperty(true)]
    public List<MenuItemData> MenuItems
    {
      get
      {
        if (menuData == null)
        {
          menuData = new List<MenuItemData>();
        }
        return menuData;
      }
    }
```

```
    private void CreateMenuItem(string title, string url, string
    target, string imageUrl)
    {
      HyperLink link = new HyperLink();
      link.Text = title;
      link.NavigateUrl = url;
      link.ImageUrl = imageUrl;
      link.Target = target;
      Controls.Add(link);
    }

    override protected void CreateChildControls()
    {
      Controls.Clear();
      CreateControlHierarchy();
    }

    private void CreateControlHierarchy()
    {
      int count = MenuItems.Count;
      for (int index = 0; index < count; index++)
      {
        MenuItemData itemdata = (MenuItemData)MenuItems[index];
        CreateMenuItem(itemdata.Title, itemdata.Url,
       itemdata.ImageUrl, itemdata.Target);

        if ((count > 1) && (index < count - 1))
        {
          Controls.Add(new LiteralControl(" | "));
        }
      }
    }

    public override ControlCollection Controls
    {
      get
      {
        EnsureChildControls();
        return base.Controls;
      }
    }
  }
}
```

We mentioned previously that the MenuItems property uses generics and is declared as a List. This removes the need to create a custom collection. This type provides us with the ability to add a collection editor at design time to permit editing of menu item data via a dialog box in much the same way as the built-in ASP.NET server controls that have InnerDefaultProperty persistence.

By default, ASP.NET provides a UI type editor for design-time editing of the MenuItems. As background, for properties that we do not want to be visible in the Visual Studio Properties tool window, we add this attribute:

```
[Browsable(false)]
```

For collection properties that we do not want to be serialized as data, we add this attribute:

```
[DesignerSerializationVisibility(DesignerSerializationVisibility.Hidden)]
```

The DesignerSerializationVisibility attribute indicates whether the value for a property is Visible and should be persisted in initialization code; or whether it is Hidden and should not be persisted in initialization code; or whether it consists of Content, which should have initialization code generated for each public, not hidden property of the object assigned to the property. The default value if the attribute is not present is Visible, and the Visual Studio Designer, at design time, will attempt to serialize the property based on the property's type. The MenuItems property on the TagDataMenu class is an example of a property with visibility set to Content:

```
[DesignerSerializationVisibility(DesignerSerializationVisibility.Content),
PersistenceMode(PersistenceMode.InnerDefaultProperty),NotifyParentProperty(true)]
public MenuItemDataCollection MenuItems
   {

   }
...
}
```

We now move on to discuss how to customize the parsing process using a ControlBuilder class. This option provides for complete customization of the parsing process, as you will see in the next section.

The BuilderMenuControl

The BuilderMenu control demonstrates a second technique for reading the child tags and creating the menu data. It uses a feature of ASP.NET that allows for complete customization of the control parsing process by implementing a custom ControlBuilder class. The implementation of the BuilderMenu control will be identical to that of the TagDataMenu control, except for the ability to manage the tag parsing process.

The normal default ControlBuilder that is linked to classes that derive from the base System.Web.UI.Control class performs the following tasks:

- Parses the child XML content into control types
- Creates the child control
- Calls on the IParserAccessor interface method AddParsedSubObject to add the child control to the server control's Controls collection, as shown in Figure 6-8

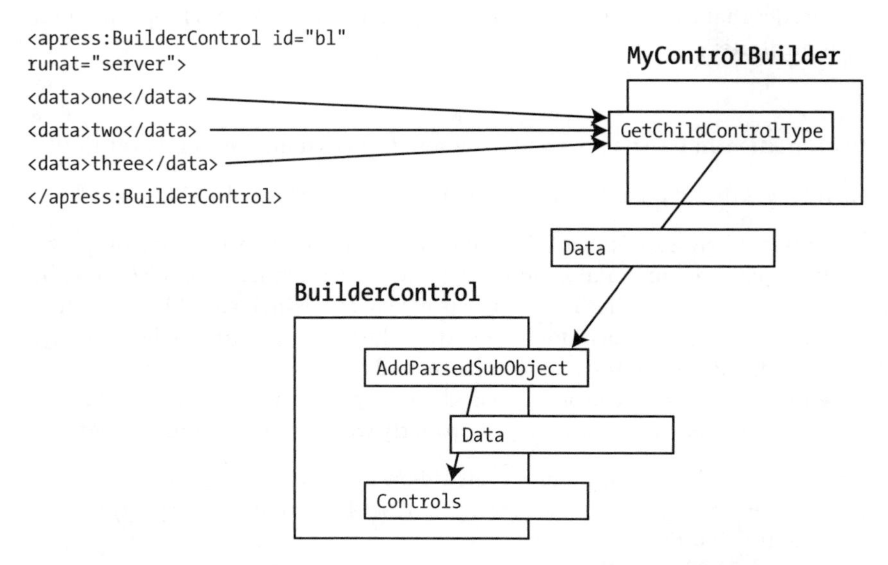

Figure 6-8. *ControlBuilder and the IParserAccessor.AddParsedSubObject default*

A custom ControlBuilder gets the opportunity to completely customize the way the ASP.NET page parser parses the child content. This is configured by adding the ControlBuilder attribute. The class declaration portion of the BuilderMenu control looks like this:

```
[ParseChildren(false)]
[ControlBuilder(typeof(MenuControlBuilder))]
[ToolboxData("<{0}:BuilderMenu runat=server></{0}:BuilderMenu>")]
public class BuilderMenu : CompositeControl
{
   public BuilderMenu() : base()
   {

   }
...
}
```

The first thing to note is that the ParseChildren attribute is set to false. This means that we want the ControlBuilder to make the decisions on how the child XML tags are handled. The attribute of interest is the ControlBuilder attribute, which is passed the System.Type reference of the MenuControlBuilder class.

MenuControlBuilder derives from the System.Web.UI.ControlBuilder class and overrides two methods to customize the parsing process. The most common reason to create your own ControlBuilder is to override the GetChildControlType method so that the control to which the builder is applied can determine how to map between a child tag and the class that needs to be created to represent the child tag during server-side processing:

```
public class MenuControlBuilder : ControlBuilder
{
public override Type GetChildControlType(String tagName, Dictionary attributes)
{
   if (String.Compare(tagName, "data", true) == 0)
   {
      return typeof(MenuItemData);
   }

   return null;
}
```

MenuControlBuilder looks for child tags with a name of "data". If it finds a match, it returns the MenuItemData type back to the BuilderMenu control to which it is linked. This assumes that the data tag has the appropriate attributes that map to the MenuItemData type's properties.

The other method that the MenuControlBuilder class overrides is AppendLiteralString. We give this method an empty implementation to ignore the literal content that is between the tags that hold the data.

```
public override void AppendLiteralString(string s)
{
   // Ignores literals between tags
}
```

There are other features of ControlBuilder parsing that we left out in this demonstration. For example, ControlBuilders can parse the raw string content between the server control's parent tags and provide support for nested ControlBuilders to process child control content. Please refer to the .NET Framework documentation for more information.

Going back to the BuilderMenu control, let's look at the implementation of IParserAccessor and the AddParsedSubObject method. The following code simply adds the data object passed into its internal ArrayList collection exposed by the menuData field. The only check it performs is a type check to ensure the right type instance is being passed from the ControlBuilder associated with the control.

```
protected override void AddParsedSubObject(Object obj)
{
   if (obj is MenuItemData)
   {
      menuData.Add(obj);
   }
}
```

Listings 6-7 and 6-8 show the final listing of BuilderMenu and its helper MenuControlBuilder.

Listing 6-7. *The BuilderMenu Control Class File*

```
using System;
using System.Web.UI;
using System.Web.UI.WebControls;
using System.Collections;
using System.ComponentModel;
using ControlsBook2Lib.Ch11.Design;

namespace ControlsBook2Lib.Ch06
{
  [ParseChildren(false)]
  [ControlBuilder(typeof(MenuControlBuilder))]
  [ToolboxData("<{0}:buildermenu runat=server></{0}:buildermenu>")]
  public class BuilderMenu : CompositeControl
  {
    public BuilderMenu()
      : base()
    {
    }

    private ArrayList menuData = new ArrayList();
    public ArrayList MenuItems
    {
      get
      {
        return menuData;
      }
    }

    protected override void AddParsedSubObject(Object obj)
    {
      if (obj is MenuItemData)
      {
        menuData.Add(obj);
      }
    }

    private void CreateMenuItem(string title, string url, string
   target, string imageUrl)
    {
      HyperLink link = new HyperLink();
      link.Text = title;
      link.NavigateUrl = url;
      link.ImageUrl = imageUrl;
      link.Target = target;
      Controls.Add(link);
    }
```

```
    private void CreateControlHierarchy()
    {
      int count = menuData.Count;
      for (int index = 0; index < count; index++)
      {
        MenuItemData itemdata = (MenuItemData)menuData[index];
        CreateMenuItem(itemdata.Title, itemdata.Url,
           itemdata.ImageUrl, itemdata.Target);

        if ((count > 1) && (index < count - 1))
        {
          Controls.Add(new LiteralControl(" | "));
        }
      }
    }

    override protected void CreateChildControls()
    {
      CreateControlHierarchy();
    }

    public override ControlCollection Controls
    {
      get
      {
        EnsureChildControls();
        return base.Controls;
      }
    }
  }
}
```

Listing 6-8. *The MenuControlBuilder Control Builder Class File*

```
using System;
using System.Web;
using System.Web.UI;
using System.Collections;

namespace ControlsBook2Lib.Ch06
{
   public class MenuControlBuilder : ControlBuilder
   {
      public override Type GetChildControlType(String tagName,
         IDictionary attributes)
      {
```

```
         if (String.Compare(tagName, "data", true) == 0)
         {
            return typeof(MenuItemData);
         }

         return null;
      }

      public override void AppendLiteralString(string s)
      {
         s.Trim();
         // Ignores literals between tags.
      }
   }
}
```

Viewing the Tag Parsing Menu Controls

The Tag Parsing Menu web form demonstrates both of our declaratively loaded menu controls in action. In Visual Studio, if you click the `TagDataMenu` control and select the `MenuItems` property, you will see a button that, if clicked, will bring up a UI collection editor for the `MenuItemData` collection. For the `TagDataMenu` control, the child tags take the name of the `MenuItemData` hyperlink data class:

```
<apress:tagdatamenu id="menu1" runat="server">
  <apress:MenuItemData title="Apress" url="http://www.apress.com" imageurl=""
            target="" />
  <apress:MenuItemData title="Microsoft" url="http://www.microsoft.com"
            imageurl="" target="" />
  <apress:MenuItemData title="GotDotNet" url="http://www.gotdotnet.com"
            imageurl="" target="" />
</apress:tagdatamenu>
```

The `BuilderMenu` control needs tags with the “data” name so that the `MenuControlBuilder` grabs each item and passes it into the control:

```
<apress:buildermenu id="menu2" runat="server">
  <data title="Apress" url="http://www.apress.com" imageurl="" target="" />
  <data title="Microsoft" url="http://www.microsoft.com" imageurl="" target="" />
  <data title="GotDotNet" url="http://www.gotdotnet.com" imageurl="" target="" />
</apress:buildermenu>
```

Figure 6-9 shows that the final result for the two controls in the browser after they are rendered is identical.

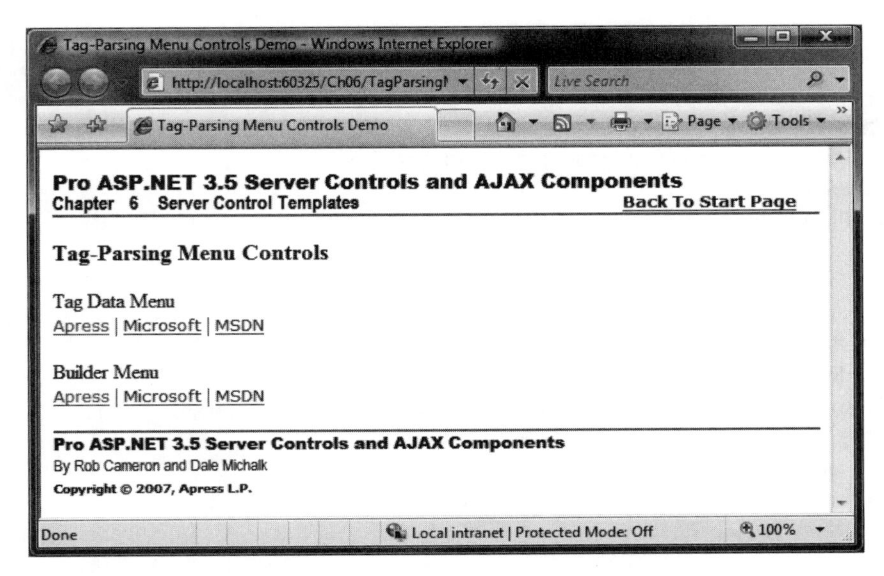

Figure 6-9. *The Tag Parsing Menu web form displayed in a browser*

Listings 6-9 and 6-10 contain the full code for the web form.

Listing 6-9. *The TagParsingMenus Web Form .aspx File*

```
<%@ Page Language="C#"
MasterPageFile="~/MasterPage/ControlsBook2MasterPage.Master"
  AutoEventWireup="true" CodeBehind="TagParsingMenu.aspx.cs"
Inherits="ControlsBook2Web.Ch06.TagParsingMenu"
  Title="Tag-Parsing Menu Controls Demo" %>

<%@ Register TagPrefix="apress" Namespace="ControlsBook2Lib.Ch06"
Assembly="ControlsBook2Lib" %>
<asp:Content ID="Content1" ContentPlaceHolderID=
        "ChapterNumAndTitle" runat="server">
  <asp:Label ID="ChapterNumberLabel" runat="server"
  Width="14px">6</asp:Label>  <asp:Label
    ID="ChapterTitleLabel" runat="server" Width="360px">
    Server Control Templates</asp:Label></asp:Content>
<asp:Content ID="Content2" ContentPlaceHolderID=
      "PrimaryContent" runat="server">
  <h3>
    Tag-Parsing Menu Controls</h3>
  <div id="TagDataMenu">
    Tag Data Menu<br />
    <apress:TagDataMenu ID="TagDataMenu1" runat="server">
      <apress:MenuItemData Title="Apress" ImageUrl=""
                Url="http://www.apress.com" Target="">
      </apress:MenuItemData>
```

```
      <apress:MenuItemData Title="Microsoft" ImageUrl=""
                 Url="http://www.microsoft.com"
        Target=""></apress:MenuItemData>
      <apress:MenuItemData Title="MSDN" ImageUrl=""
                Url="http://msdn.microsoft.com" Target="">
      </apress:MenuItemData>
    </apress:TagDataMenu>
  </div>
  <br />
  <div id="Builder Menu">
    Builder Menu<br />
    <apress:BuilderMenu ID="BuilderMenu1" runat="server">
      <data title="Apress" url="http://www.apress.com" imageurl="" target="" />
      <data title="Microsoft" url=http://www.microsoft.com
     imageurl="" target="" />
      <data title="MSDN" url="http://msdn.microsoft.com" imageurl="" target="" />
    </apress:BuilderMenu>
  </div>
  <br />
</asp:Content>
```

Listing 6-10. *The Tag Parsing Menus Web Form Code-Behind Class File*

```
using System;

namespace ControlsBook2Web.Ch06
{
  public partial class TagParsingMenu : System.Web.UI.Page
  {
    protected void Page_Load(object sender, EventArgs e)
    {

    }
  }
}
```

Summary

Templates are one of the two primary ways to modify the graphical content of an ASP.NET web form. Templates provide a way for developers to declaratively insert raw HTML through server controls into the output of a prebuilt control. Templates can be loaded dynamically through `Page.LoadTemplate` or instantiated by classes that implement the `ITemplate` interface.

The `ParseChildren` attribute determines if ASP.NET parses a server control's inner tag content in an `.aspx` page as child controls or child properties. The `ControlBuilder` attribute allows a control to redirect the tag parsing process to a custom `ControlBuilder` class.

In the next chapter, we continue our discussion of template-based control by adding databinding to the mix.

CHAPTER 7

■ ■ ■

Server Control Data Binding

The vast majority of web sites that provide dynamic content do so by rendering HTML that represents a data source to a database back-end system. A common task for web developers is to retrieve data and format it for output manually or through technology like ASP.NET data binding. Starting in ASP.NET 2.0, adding templates and data binding to server controls requires much less code than in previous versions of ASP.NET. We take advantage of these improvements in the examples in this chapter.

Data binding dynamically merges a collection of data with a server control at runtime to produce HTML content representing the data source, as shown in Figure 7-1.

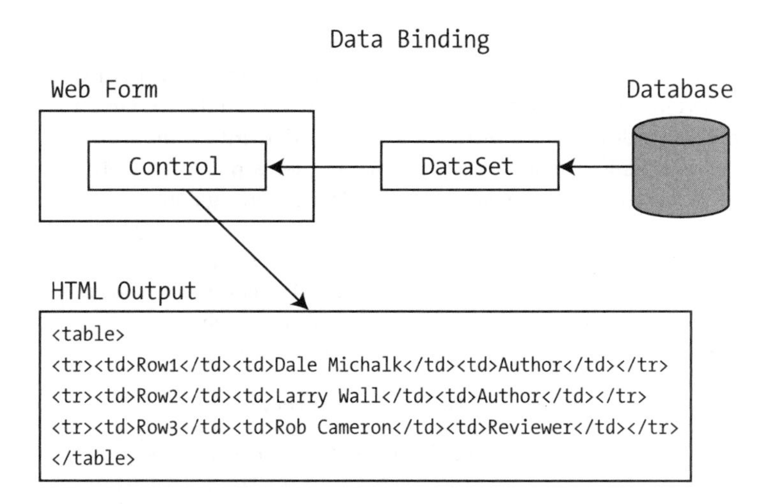

Figure 7-1. *Data binding with server controls*

Templates and data binding are naturally complementary. Data binding efficiently brings data into the control, and templates allow customization of how server controls or HTML elements display the data. Templates and data binding generally are brought together in more advanced controls, such as the ASP.NET `GridView` or `Repeater` server controls, making database-driven web development quick and easy. Pull a piece of data from the database via ADO.NET or an `IDataSource`-based control, bind it to a server control, configure its style properties and templates resulting in a very appealing HTML display that appears to act like a Visual Basic form with data paging, alternate colors, and so on. The server control handles all the heavy lifting that would normally require a large amount of hand coding in plain old ASP.

In this chapter, we start off the examples with a clone of the ASP.NET `Repeater` control that puts templates and data binding in action together. We next examine how to interact with the rich features of our `Repeater` control and demonstrate how to load templates dynamically from disk and create them programmatically. We close the chapter with a sample that inherits from one of the new base server control classes introduced in .NET Framework 2.0 called `DataBoundCompositeControl`. The `EnhancedSpreadSheetControl` sample takes the `SimpleSpreadSheetControl` sample from the documentation and adds `IDataSource` binding support, header row functionality, and other UI enhancements, as well as additional design-time features to make it a more useful control.

Customized Control Content

HTML is a combination of content and appearance. Chapter 5 showed how server controls customize the appearance of content through the use of style attributes that modify features such as font, color, size, or even placement of the HTML. In Chapter 6, we discussed how to modify the core content of the web form through two incredibly useful techniques: templates and tag parsing. In this chapter, we cover how to add data binding support.

Control Data Binding

Using server control tags is a convenient way to declaratively configure simple server controls such as the menu controls we developed. For complex, dynamically loaded data, we need to take a more sophisticated path. The tried-and-true approach to passing data into a server control is through data binding, which we cover in this section. This is a complex topic, but we present plenty of code in the following subsections to help you get started with adding data binding capabilities to your own controls.

Data binding comes in several different forms. Simple data binding occurs when a data-binding expression is evaluated to a single value and that value is used to set the property of a server control. The following code snippet binds the result of a method named `MyDataBoundMethod` on a web form to the `Text` property of an ASP.NET server control:

```
<asp:Label id="MyLabel" runat="server" Text="<%= MyDataBoundMethod() %> />
```

Repeated or complex data binding occurs when a collection of multirow data is bound to a list control that iterates through its contents to generate HTML output. The classic example of this is binding a `DataSet` to an ASP.NET `DataGrid` control to generate an HTML table representing the data. This is also the case when we take a simple collection such as an `ArrayList` full of strings and bind it to a `DropDownList` control. The next subsection covers the data binding base class options available in the .NET Framework.

DataBinding Base Class Options

There are several useful base classes that can simplify writing data bound controls. The .NET Framework documentation is helpful in suggesting where to start with the base classes and provides sample implementations. Here is a list of these specialized base classes:

- System.Web.UI.WebControls.DataBoundControl: This can serve as a base class when displaying data in list or tabular form. The designer DataBoundControlDesigner class is configured on this base class via the Designer attribute.
- System.Web.UI.WebControls.CompositeDataBoundControl: This class inherits from DataBoundControl and can serve as the base class for tabular data bound controls that are composed of other server controls.
- System.Web.UI.WebControls.HierarchicalDataBoundControl: This one can serve as a base class to create data bound controls that work with classes that implement the IHierarchicalDataSource interface and classes that derive from the HierarchicalDataSourceControl and HierarchicalDataSourceView classes.

There certainly may be scenarios where complete control is required and the preceding base classes are limiting in some way, in which case a control developer can always simply inherit from Control or WebControl. Otherwise, we recommend that developers consider these base classes as a first option, since inheriting from them can save time. In the next section, we take a look at a sample control that inherits from the DataBoundControl base class.

The Repeater Control

The case study we present to help explain data binding creates a replica of the Repeater control built into ASP.NET. The Repeater control is a data-bound server control that takes advantage of templates to generate the display for the data source. It is a complex control that requires a fair amount of source code, but this effort is worth the ease of use data binding provides to the user of a data bindable server control.

The Repeater control includes five templates: HeaderTemplate, FooterTemplate, SeparatorTemplate, ItemTemplate, and AlternatingItemTemplate. We provided the first three templates types in our TemplateMenu control. For clarity, those three templates do not take advantage of data binding. We are adding data binding capabilities to the ItemTemplate and AlternatingItemTemplate templates.

The ItemTemplate and AlternatingItemTemplate templates are applied to each row of data retrieved from the data source based on an alternating pattern. The SeparatorTemplate template is placed between the item templates to keep things looking nice. The diagram in Figure 7-2 shows how the templates determine the output of the control rendering process.

Our Repeater control implements a fairly sophisticated system of events that provide rich functionality: ItemCommand, ItemCreated, and ItemDataBound. ItemCommand is an event raised by our Repeater control that aggregates bubbled command events raised by subordinate command controls such as an ASP.NET Button control. We discuss these events in detail in the section titled "Repeater Control Event Management" later in this chapter.

The ItemCreated event is raised each time a RepeaterItem control is created. This gives the client of the event an opportunity to modify or change the final control output in the template dynamically. ItemDataBound gives the same opportunity, except it is raised *after* any data binding has been performed on a template. This event is limited to the ItemTemplate and AlternatingItemTemplate templates, because the header and footer templates do not support data binding.

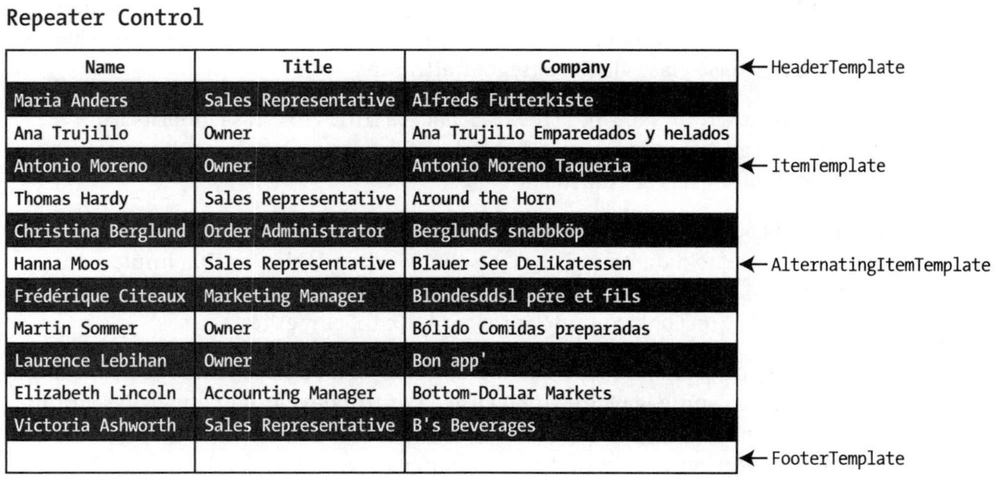

Repeater Control

Name	Title	Company
Maria Anders	Sales Representative	Alfreds Futterkiste
Ana Trujillo	Owner	Ana Trujillo Emparedados y helados
Antonio Moreno	Owner	Antonio Moreno Taqueria
Thomas Hardy	Sales Representative	Around the Horn
Christina Berglund	Order Administrator	Berglunds snabbköp
Hanna Moos	Sales Representative	Blauer See Delikatessen
Frédérique Citeaux	Marketing Manager	Blondesddsl pére et fils
Martin Sommer	Owner	Bólido Comidas preparadas
Laurence Lebihan	Owner	Bon app'
Elizabeth Lincoln	Accounting Manager	Bottom-Dollar Markets
Victoria Ashworth	Sales Representative	B's Beverages

HeaderTemplate
ItemTemplate
AlternatingItemTemplate
FooterTemplate

Figure 7-2. *The Repeater control and its templates*

The RepeaterItem Container Control

RepeaterItem is a building block used by the Repeater control to create its content. It is based on the System.Web.UI.Control base class and serves as the primary container for instantiating templates and working with events.

The following code snippet shows how the RepeaterItem control is declared, inheriting from Control and implementing the INamingContainer interface to prevent name collisions on child controls:

```
public class RepeaterItem : Control, INamingContainer
{
...
   public RepeaterItem(int itemIndex, ListItemType itemType, object dataItem)
   {
      this.itemIndex = itemIndex;
      this.itemType = itemType;
      this.dataItem = dataItem;
   }
...
...
}
```

The private data members are instantiated by the constructor. These fields are exposed as public properties as well:

```
private object dataItem;
public object DataItem
{
```

```
   get
   {
      return dataItem;
   }
   set
   {
      dataItem = value;
   }
}

private int itemIndex;
public int ItemIndex
{
   get
   {
      return itemIndex;
   }
}

private ListItemType itemType;
public ListItemType ItemType
{
   get
   {
      return itemType;
   }
}
```

ItemIndex exposes the relative position of the RepeaterItem control with respect to its siblings underneath the parent Repeater control. ItemType borrows the ListItemType enumeration from the System.Web.UI.WebControl namespace to identify the purpose of the RepeaterItem control. The following code shows a reproduction of the enumeration definition in the System.Web.UI.WebControls namespace:

```
enum ListItemType
{
   Header,
   Footer,
   Item,
   AlternatingItem,
   SelectedItem,
   EditItem,
   Separator,
   Pager
}
```

The last property exposed by the RepeaterItem class is DataItem. For RepeaterItem child controls that are bound to a data source (i.e., ItemTemplate or AlternatingItemTemplate

RepeaterItems), DataItem will reference a particular row in the collection that makes up the data source. This permits us to use the Container.DataItem syntax in a data-binding expression:

```
<ItemTemplate>
   <% Container.DataItem[Name] %>
</ItemTemplate>
```

Command Events and the RepeaterItem Control

The RepeaterItem control plays a key role in ensuring that Command events are bubbled up to the parent Repeater control so that it can raise an ItemCommand event to the outside world. The following code takes Command events that are bubbled and wraps the events in a custom RepeaterCommandEventArgs object to provide additional information on the event's source:

```
protected override bool OnBubbleEvent(object source, EventArgs e)
{
   CommandEventArgs ce = e as CommandEventArgs;

   if (ce != null)
   {
      RepeaterCommandEventArgs rce = new
                           RepeaterCommandEventArgs(this, source, ce);
      RaiseBubbleEvent(this, rce);

      return true;
   }
   else
      return false;
}
```

The OnBubbleEvent member function performs a typecast to validate that it is indeed a Command event, instantiates a RepeaterCommandEventArgs class, and then sends it on up to the Repeater control through the RaiseBubbleEvent method. The return value of true indicates to ASP.NET that the event was handled. Later on, we show the code in Repeater that handles the bubbled event and raises its own Command event.

We create a custom EventArgs class to make working with the Repeater control easier, as shown in Listing 7-1. Instead of having to search through all the controls that are in the Repeater's Control collection, we can narrow it down to just the RepeaterItem control of interest.

Listing 7-1. *The RepeaterCommand Event Class File*

```
using System;
using System.Web.UI.WebControls;

namespace ControlsBook2Lib.Ch07
{
   public delegate void RepeaterCommandEventHandler(object o,
                                          RepeaterCommandEventArgs rce);
```

```
   public class RepeaterCommandEventArgs : CommandEventArgs
   {
      public RepeaterCommandEventArgs(RepeaterItem item, object commandSource,
         CommandEventArgs originalArgs) : base(originalArgs)
      {
         this.item = item;
         this.commandSource = commandSource;
      }

      private RepeaterItem item;
      public RepeaterItem Item
      {
         get
         {
            return item;
         }
      }

      private object commandSource;
      public object CommandSource
      {
         get
         {
            return commandSource;
         }
      }
   }
}
```

The source of the event is available in the RepeaterCommandEventArgs class via the CommandSource property. The RepeaterItem container control that houses the CommandSource property is reachable through the Item property. It allows us to identify and programmatically manipulate the exact block of content that was the source of the event. Our code for this control also defines a delegate named RepeaterCommandEventHandler to work with the custom EventArgs class. Listing 7-2 shows the full listing for the RepeaterItem control.

Listing 7-2. *The RepeaterItem Control Class File*

```
using System;
using System.ComponentModel;
using System.Web;
using System.Web.UI;
using System.Web.UI.WebControls;

namespace ControlsBook2Lib.Ch07
{
```

```
public class RepeaterItem : Control, INamingContainer
{
   [ToolboxItem(false)]
   public RepeaterItem(int itemIndex, ListItemType itemType, object dataItem)
   {
      this.itemIndex = itemIndex;
      this.itemType = itemType;
      this.DataItem = dataItem;
   }

   public object DataItem { get; set; }

   private int itemIndex;
   public int ItemIndex
   {
      get
      {
         return itemIndex;
      }
   }

   private ListItemType itemType;
   public ListItemType ItemType
   {
      get
      {
         return itemType;
      }
   }

   protected override bool OnBubbleEvent(object source, EventArgs e)
   {
      CommandEventArgs ce = e as CommandEventArgs;

      if (ce != null)
      {
         RepeaterCommandEventArgs rce = new
        RepeaterCommandEventArgs(this, source, ce);
         RaiseBubbleEvent(this, rce);

         return true;
      }
      else
         return false;
   }
}
```

```
   public delegate void RepeaterItemEventHandler(object o,
   RepeaterItemEventArgs rie);

   public class RepeaterItemEventArgs : EventArgs
   {
      public RepeaterItemEventArgs(RepeaterItem item)
      {
         this.item = item;
      }

      private RepeaterItem item;
      public RepeaterItem Item
      {
         get
         {
            return item;
         }
      }
   }
}
```

In the next section, we discuss the implementation details of our version of the Repeater server control.

The Repeater Control Architecture

Now that we have the main building block of our Repeater control ready for action, we can move on to the core logic of our control. As shown in the following code, Repeater inherits from System.Web.UI.WebControls.DataBoundControl and implements INamingContainer to prevent control ID conflicts like its RepeaterItem sibling. The ParseChildren attribute set to true on the Repeater class enables the use of template properties. PersistChildren is set to false to prevent child controls from being persisted as nested inner controls; they are instead persisted as nested elements. The Designer attribute associates a custom designer named RepeaterDesigner that provides template editing design-time support. We discuss RepeaterDesigner further in Chapter 11.

```
[ToolboxData("<{0}:repeater runat=server></{0}:repeater>"), ParseChildren(true),
PersistChildren(false),
 Designer(typeof(ControlsBook2Lib.Ch11.Design.RepeaterDesigner))]
  public class Repeater : DataBoundControl, INamingContainer
  {
```

The heart of the architecture behind Repeater is two methods: CreateChildControls and PerformDataBinding. Both of these member functions create the control hierarchy for Repeater, but each does so as a result of two fundamentally different scenarios. First, here is the code for the DataBind method:

```
public override void DataBind()
{
  this.PerformSelect();
}
```

Starting in ASP.NET 2.0, the PerformSelect method performs the work to load the data as listed here:

```
protected override void PerformSelect()
{
  if (!IsBoundUsingDataSourceID)
  {
    OnDataBinding(EventArgs.Empty);
  }

  GetData().Select(CreateDataSourceSelectArguments(),
      OnDataSourceViewSelectCallback);

  RequiresDataBinding = false;
  MarkAsDataBound();

  OnDataBound(EventArgs.Empty);
}
```

Depending on whether the control is bound using an IDataSource control introduced in ASP.NET 2.0 or any other DataSource control determines how PerformSelect executes. The OnDataBinding call must occur before the GetData call if not bound with an IDataSource-based control, which is where the check on IsBoundUsingDataSourceID is necessary at the beginning of the method. The GetData method retrieves the DataSourceView object from the IDataSource associated with the data-bound control so OnDataBinding is called prior to GetData. Finally, the DataBound event is raised.

The method GetData is called within PerformSelect and takes a callback method as a parameter. The callback method is OnDataSourceViewSelectCallback, which calls PerformDataBinding to build out the control via the CreateControlHierarchy method. Once again, whether the control is bound to an IDataSource-based control or not determines how the control tree is built by passing in different parameters to CreateControlHierarchy.

As you would guess, DataBind takes precedence as a control-loading mechanism when binding to a data source. It is called on the web form after the data source has been linked to the control.

The first task of DataBind is to fire the data-binding event OnDataBinding. If the Repeater control is binding to a design-time data source, firing this event in DataBind is required for the control to see the selected design-time data source at runtime.

Next, DataBind starts with a clean slate, clearing the current set of controls and any ViewState values that are lingering, after which the control is ready to track ViewState. As shown in the preceding code, once the table has been set, DataBind builds the child control hierarchy based on the data source through the CreateControlHierarchy method. It then sets the ChildControlsCreated property to true to let ASP.NET know that the control is populated. This prevents the framework from calling CreateChildControls after DataBind.

We next discuss how CreateChildControls handles control creation. Here is the code for CreateChildControls:

```
override protected void CreateChildControls()
{
   Controls.Clear();
   if (ViewState["ItemCount"] != null)
   {
      CreateControlHierarchy(false);
   }
    ClearChildViewState();
}
```

You have already encountered CreateChildControls in all the composite controls samples so far in the book. It is called whenever the control needs to render itself outside of a DataBind. The code implementation uses the CreateControlHierarchy helper method to do the dirty work as in the DataBind method. The single difference is that the code in CreateChildControls checks the ViewState ItemCount property. If ItemCount is not null, this indicates that we need to re-create the control hierarchy using postback control ViewState values. Figure 7-3 illustrates the difference between DataBind and CreateChildControls.

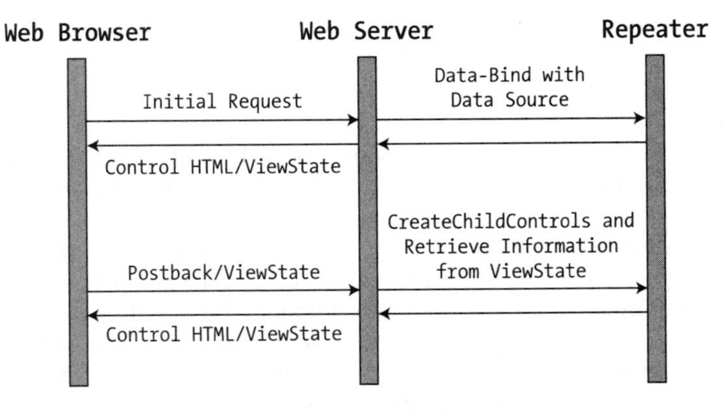

Figure 7-3. *DataBind versus CreateChildControls*

We pass a Boolean value to CreateControlHierarchy to indicate whether it needs to use the data source to build up the control hierarchy or whether it should try to rebuild the control hierarchy from ViewState at the beginning of a postback cycle. For CreateChildControls, we pass in false to CreateChildHierarchy if ItemCount is present in ViewState.

The data binding process is controlled by three properties: DataSourceID, DataMember, and DataSource. Notice that none of these properties are declared directly in our custom Repeater control. Our Repeater control inherits from DataBoundControl, where much of the data binding functionality is handled by the base class itself. The DataSourceID is set as the DataSource when using an IDataSource-based control first introduced in ASP.NET 2.0, such as the SqlDataSource class. DataSourceID appears in the Properties window, but DataSource does not, though DataSource is still a public property that can be set in code.

In the next section, we dissect CreateControlHierarchy by breaking the code into bite-sized chunks as part of the discussion.

The CreateControlHierarchy Method

CreateControlHierarchy contains the most complicated logic in the Repeater control. It has logic that covers creating the header and footer section of the control, along with the data-bound item content. The first part of CreateControlHierarchy creates the header section of the control:

```
private void CreateControlHierarchy(bool useDataSource)
{
   items = new ArrayList();
   IEnumerable ds = null;

   if (HeaderTemplate != null)
   {
      RepeaterItem header = CreateItem(-1, ListItemType.Header, false, null);
   }
```

The preceding code checks for the presence of a HeaderTemplate template, and if it exists, it creates a header RepeaterItem via CreateItem. CreateItem is the code that handles the actual RepeaterItem creation and adds it to the Repeater's Controls collection.

The items field is an ArrayList containing the RepeaterItem collection for the RepeaterControl. It is declared as a private field under the Repeater class:

```
private ArrayList items = null;
```

You can think of this as a secondary collection of child controls like the Controls collection but one that is filtered to include just the RepeaterItem containers that represent data from the data source.

After the header is created, CreateControlHierarchy creates the core data-oriented RepeaterItem child controls. The first step in the process is resolving the DataSource. If CreateControlHierarchy is called from the PerformDataBinding method, the useDataSource Boolean parameter will be set to true and the usingIDataSource parameter will be false or true depending on whether the control is bound to an IDataSource-based control. Otherwise, if CreateControlHierarchy is called from CreateChildControls, useDataSource and usingIDataSource will be set to false:

```
private void CreateControlHierarchy(bool useData, bool
     usingIDataSource, IEnumerable data)
```

We now move on to discuss how the Repeater control resolves its data source and builds up its control hierarchy as it data binds.

The DataSourceHelper Class and Data Binding

When building the control hierarchy as a result of data binding, we use a helper class named DataSourceHelper to resolve the DataSource to something that supports the IEnumerable interface. You can use this code directly to perform the same task in your data-bound custom server controls.

The ResolveDataSource method of the DataSourceHelper class detects the interfaces supported by the data source and will walk into the DataMember field of the DataSource if necessary. For collections such as arrays based on System.Array, ArrayList, and the DataReader classes of ADO.NET, ResolveDataSource performs a simple cast to IEnumerable.

Complex IListSource data collections such as the DataSet account for the bulk of the work in ResolveDataSource. For DataSet, we need to drill down into its child collections based on the DataMember passed into the control. Here is how DataSet is declared:

```
public class DataSet : MarshalByValueComponent, IListSource,
                       ISupportInitialize, ISerializable
```

The IListSource interface implemented by the DataSet provides a way to determine if there are multiple DataTable child collections by checking the value of the Boolean ContainsListCollection property. If the class implementing IListSource supports a bindable list, we need to use the ITypedList interface to bind to it at runtime. The DataViewManager class provides just such a bindable list for the DataTables that make up a DataSet. DataViewManager has the following declaration:

```
public class DataViewManager : MarshalByValueComponent,
   IBindingList, IList, ICollection, IEnumerable, ITypedList
```

The GetList method of the IListSource interface implemented by the DataSet class returns an instance of the ITypedList interface implemented by the DataViewManager class through casting to the appropriate interface. We use the ITypedList interface to dynamically bind to the correct data source. Figure 7-4 provides a diagram of the process required to handle an ITypedList data source such as a DataSet.

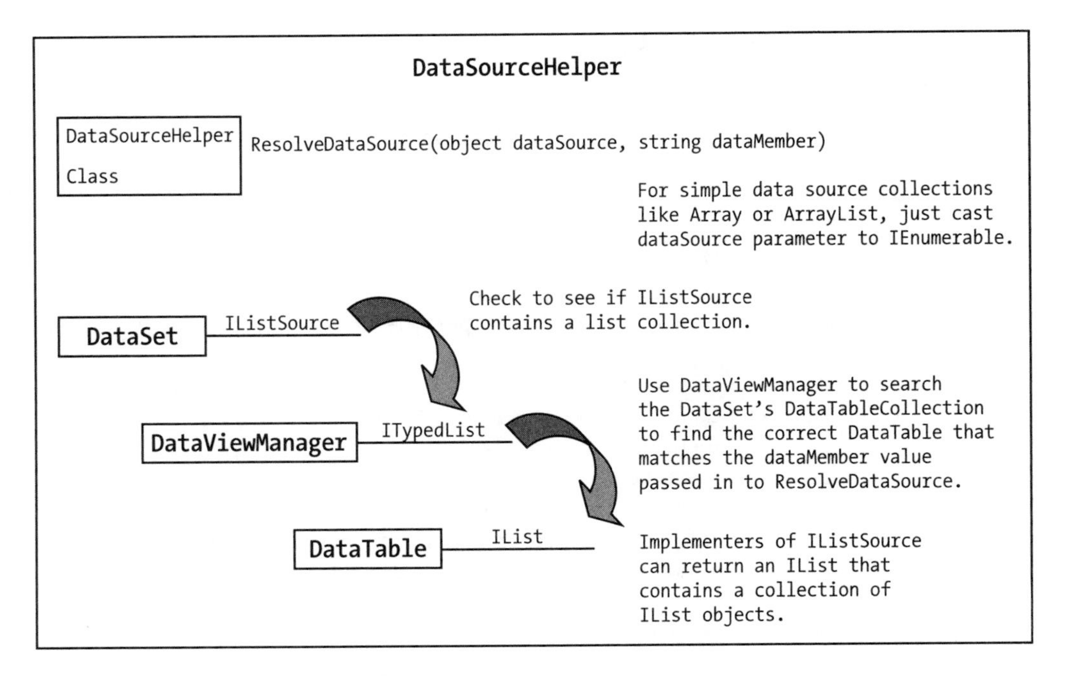

Figure 7-4. *Resolving IListSource data sources*

ITypedList gives us the ability to dynamically find properties exposed by a class. DataViewManager, as part of its ITypedList implementation, exposes the DataTables as properties in its DataViewSettingCollection. The code checks the dynamic properties of DataViewManager to see if it can retrieve the DataViewSetting property that matches the DataMember passed into the Repeater control. If the DataMember is blank, we choose the first DataTable in the DataSet. Listing 7-3 presents the full source code for the DataSourceHelper class.

Listing 7-3. *The DataSourceHelper Class File*

```
using System;
using System.Collections;
using System.ComponentModel;

namespace ControlsBook2Lib.Ch07
{
  public class DataSourceHelper
  {
    public static object ResolveDataSource(object dataSource, string dataMember)
    {
      if (dataSource == null)
        return null;

      if (dataSource is IEnumerable)
      {
        return (IEnumerable)dataSource;
      }
      else if (dataSource is IListSource)
      {
        IList list = null;
        IListSource listSource = (IListSource)dataSource;
        list = listSource.GetList();
        if (listSource.ContainsListCollection)
        {
          ITypedList typedList = (ITypedList)list;
          PropertyDescriptorCollection propDescCol =
             typedList.GetItemProperties(new PropertyDescriptor[0]);

          if (propDescCol.Count == 0)
            throw new Exception("ListSource without DataMembers");

          PropertyDescriptor propDesc = null;
          //Check to see if dataMember has a value, if not, default to first
          //property (DataTable) in the property collection (DataTableCollection)
          if ((dataMember == null) || (dataMember.Length < 1))
          {
            propDesc = propDescCol[0];
          }
```

```
          else //If dataMember is set, try to find it in the property collection
            propDesc = propDescCol.Find(dataMember, true);

          if (propDesc == null)
            throw new Exception("ListSource missing DataMember");

          object listitem = list[0];

          //Get the value of the property (DataTable) of interest
          object member = propDesc.GetValue(listitem);

          if ((member == null) || !(member is IEnumerable))
            throw new Exception("ListSource missing DataMember");

          return (IEnumerable)member;
        }
        else
          return (IEnumerable)list;
      }
      return null;
    }
  }
}
```

The end result is a PropertyDescriptor that allows us to dynamically retrieve the appropriate data for binding. For the DataSet, this gives us a reference to a DataTable. We cast the result to IEnumerable and return it to the control so that we can continue the data binding process.

PropertyDescriptor, PropertyDescriptorCollection, and IListSource are all members of the System.ComponentModel namespace. This namespace plays a critical role in performing dynamic lookups and enhancing the design-time experience of controls. We focus on the design time support, including data binding design time support, in Chapter 11.

The DummyDataSource Class and Postback

If CreateControlHierarchy is not in the midst of a DataBind, it needs to determine whether or not it is in a postback environment. We can check this by looking for the ItemCount variable in ViewState. If it is present, we create a DummyDataSource object that is appropriately named, because it serves as a placeholder to rehydrate the control state that was originally rendered and sent back to the web server via postback. Listing 7-4 provides the class source code for DummyDataSource.

Listing 7-4. *The DummyDataSource Class File*

```
using System;
using System.Collections;
using System.ComponentModel;
```

```
namespace ControlsBook2Lib.Ch07
{
   internal sealed class DummyDataSource : ICollection
   {
      public DummyDataSource(int dataItemCount)
      {
         this.Count = dataItemCount;
      }

      public int Count { get; set; }

      public bool IsReadOnly
      {
         get
         {
            return false;
         }
      }

      public bool IsSynchronized
      {
         get
         {
            return false;
         }
      }

      public object SyncRoot
      {
         get
         {
            return this;
         }
      }

      public void CopyTo(Array array, int index)
      {
         for (IEnumerator e = this.GetEnumerator(); e.MoveNext();)
            array.SetValue(e.Current, index++);
      }

      public IEnumerator GetEnumerator()
      {
         return new DummyDataSourceEnumerator(Count);
      }
```

```
      private class DummyDataSourceEnumerator : IEnumerator
      {
         private int count;
         private int index;

         public DummyDataSourceEnumerator(int count)
         {
            this.count = count;
            this.index = -1;
         }

         public object Current
         {
            get
            {
               return null;
            }
         }

         public bool MoveNext()
         {
            index++;
            return index < count;
         }

         public void Reset()
         {
            this.index = -1;
         }
      }
   }
}
```

DummyDataSource implements the necessary collection interfaces to be compatible with the rendering logic in Repeater. The key ingredients are implementation of the IEnumerable and IEnumeration interfaces. As an example of how this works, this code snippet enumerates a string array:

```
string[] numbers = new string[] { one,two,three };
foreach (string number in numbers)
{
   // action
}
```

IEnumerable signifies that the collection supports enumeration via constructs, such as the foreach statement in C#. The method to get the enumerator from an IEnumerable collection is GetEnumerator. It returns an IEnumerator interface.

Client code uses the IEnumerator interface to move around the collection. MoveNext advances the cursor, and the Current property allows the client to grab the item pointed to by the cursor in the collection. The following code shows what really goes on when you use foreach in C#:

```
IEnumerator enum = numbers.GetEnumerator();
string number = null;
while (enum.MoveNext())
{
   number = enum.Current;
   // action
}
```

DummyDataSource implements its enumerator as a private nested class named DummyDataSourceEnumerator. It returns an instance of this class from its GetEnumerator method. Figure 7-5 illustrates the role that the DummyDataSource class plays during postback.

The dummy collection source is initialized by passing in the count of items to the DummyDataSource constructor. When a client retrieves the enumerator, it will iterate through that count of items, returning a null value. This may seem pointless, but it is enough to prime the pump inside CreateControlHierarchy to rehydrate the RepeaterItem controls from ViewState during postback. Once the controls are added, each RepeaterItem control can retrieve its former contents using ViewState and postback data. We now move on to how the Repeater control creates its content when data binding to a data source.

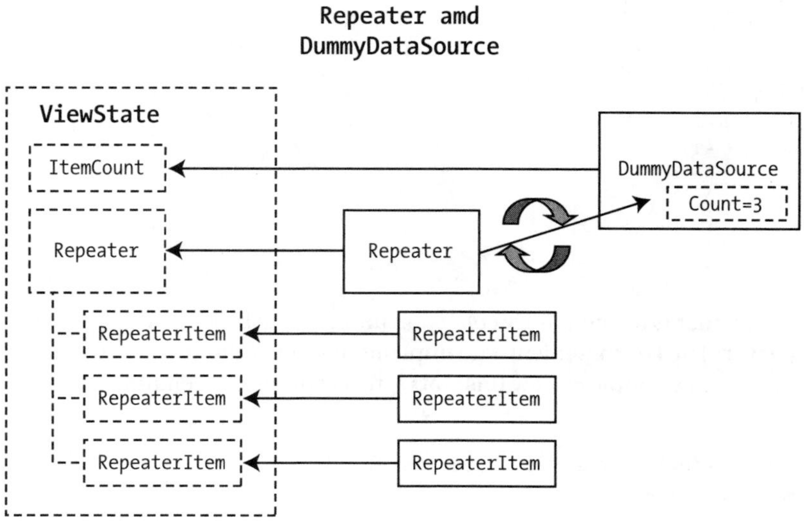

Figure 7-5. *Using DummyDataSource*

Creating the Middle Content

Once we have a valid object in the DataSource property, we can continue the task of creating the RepeaterItem controls in CreateControlHierarchy, as shown in the following code. If the previous step failed, the DataSource will be null, and no content gets rendered. However, if the call to ResolveDataSource is successful, the code loops through the DataSource named ds using a foreach construct to create RepeaterItem controls. Like the header section of the Repeater control, the CreateItem method does the bulk of work in configuring each RepeaterItem.

```
if (ds != null)
{
  int index = 0;
  count = 0;
  RepeaterItem item;
  ListItemType itemType = ListItemType.Item;

  foreach (object dataItem in (IEnumerable)ds)
  {
    if (index != 0)
    {
      RepeaterItem separator = CreateItem(-1, ListItemType.Separator, false, null);
    }

    item = CreateItem(index, itemType, useData, dataItem);
    items.Add(item);
    index++;
    count++;

    if (itemType == ListItemType.Item)
      itemType = ListItemType.AlternatingItem;
    else
      itemType = ListItemType.Item;
  }
}
```

The looping code also keeps track of the index of the RepeaterItem and the total count of controls added to the Controls collection. It meets our specification of having an item, an alternating item, and a separator by alternating between ItemTemplate and AlternatingItemTemplate, as well as including a RepeaterItem control implementing SeparatorTemplate between each data item.

The final section of CreateControlHierarchy is the portion that creates the footer for our Repeater implementation:

```
if (FooterTemplate != null)
{
   RepeaterItem footer = CreateItem(-1, ListItemType.Footer, false, null);
}

if (useData)
{
   ViewState["ItemCount"] = ((ds != null) ? count : -1);
}
```

The last if-then construct stores the count of RepeaterItem controls in ViewState so we can rehydrate DummyDataSource on postback. We drill into the CreateItem method in the next section.

Creating the RepeaterItem Control in CreateItem

Much of the previous code in CreateControlHierarchy offloaded work to CreateItem. CreateItem is tasked with doing quite a few things beyond just creating a RepeaterItem control: it handles template instantiation and raises the ItemDataBound and ItemCreated events.

The first portion of CreateItem checks the ListItemType so that it can determine the right enumeration to use with the RepeaterItem control:

```
private RepeaterItem CreateItem(int itemIndex, ListItemType itemType,
bool dataBind, object dataItem)
{
  ITemplate selectedTemplate;

  switch (itemType)
  {
    case ListItemType.Header:
      selectedTemplate = headerTemplate;
      break;
    case ListItemType.Item:
      selectedTemplate = itemTemplate;
      break;
    case ListItemType.AlternatingItem:
      selectedTemplate = alternatingItemTemplate;
      break;
    case ListItemType.Separator:
      selectedTemplate = separatorTemplate;
      break;
    case ListItemType.Footer:
      selectedTemplate = footerTemplate;
      break;
    default:
      selectedTemplate = null;
      break;
  }

  if ((itemType == ListItemType.AlternatingItem) &&
     (alternatingItemTemplate == null))
  {
    selectedTemplate = itemTemplate;
    itemType = ListItemType.Item;
  }
```

```
  RepeaterItem item = new RepeaterItem(itemIndex, itemType, dataItem);

  if (selectedTemplate != null)
  {
    selectedTemplate.InstantiateIn(item);
  }

  OnItemCreated(new RepeaterItemEventArgs(item));

  Controls.Add(item);

  if (dataBind)
  {
    item.DataBind();
    OnItemDataBound(new RepeaterItemEventArgs(item));
  }
  return item;
}
```

The code next instantiates a RepeaterItem control with the index of the object, the ListItemType, and a reference to the data source. For RepeaterItem instances that are based on the HeaderTemplate, FooterTemplate, and SeparatorTemplate templates, the dataItem parameter will be null. Only the ItemTemplate- and AlternatingItemTemplate-based RepeaterItem controls are linked to a row in the data source:

```
RepeaterItem item = new RepeaterItem(itemIndex, itemType, dataItem);

if (selectedTemplate != null)
{
   selectedTemplate.InstantiateIn(item);
}

OnItemCreated(new RepeaterItemEventArgs(item));

Controls.Add(item);
```

At this point in CreateItem, the RepeaterItem control is fully populated, and we raise the ItemCreated event through the OnItemCreated method to allow interested clients to react to the creation process. They can then add additional controls to our RepeaterItem to customize its content if necessary. After this event is raised, we add the RepeaterItem control to the Controls collection of the Repeater class.

If we are data binding, the code calls DataBind on the RepeaterItem to resolve its data binding expressions to the piece of data attached to its DataItem property. We also raise an event via OnItemDataBound, as shown in the following code. This causes any data binding expressions in the templates to resolve to the particular row in the data source and get needed data for the final render process.

```
   if (dataBind)
   {
      item.DataBind();
      OnItemDataBound(new RepeaterItemEventArgs(item));
   }
   return item;
}
```

The last step is to return the RepeaterItem so that the calling code can add it to the items ArrayList maintained by Repeater.

Accessing RepeaterItem Instances After Creation

CreateControlHierarchy, along with CreateItem, does a great job of creating RepeaterItem instances and adding them to the Controls collection and the items generic List, providing access to a read-only collection to give access to the RepeaterInfo instances without having to create a custom collection class of RepeaterItems.

The Items property on Repeater uses a collection of type generic List<> to allow easy access to the RepeaterItems. Note that items is a private field for the Items property that we also use in CreateControlHierarchy. We now move on to discuss the various events that the Repeater control implements.

Repeater Control Event Management

Repeater exposes an ItemCommand event, an ItemCreated event, and an ItemDataBound event. We use the Events collection provided by System.Web.UI.Control to track registered client delegates. The following code for the ItemCommand event is reproduced in a similar manner for the ItemCreated and ItemDataBound events:

```
private static readonly object ItemCommandKey = new object();
public event RepeaterCommandEventHandler ItemCommand
{
   add
   {
      Events.AddHandler(ItemCommandKey, value);
   }
   remove
   {
      Events.RemoveHandler(ItemCommandKey, value);
   }
}
```

The On-prefixed protected methods use standard event techniques to notify the delegates that subscribe to the event when it is fired. The following OnItemCommand is mirrored by OnItemDataBound and OnItemCreated:

```
protected virtual void OnItemCommand(RepeaterCommandEventArgs rce)
{
   RepeaterCommandEventHandler repeaterCommandEventDelegate =
      (RepeaterCommandEventHandler) Events[ItemCommandKey];
```

```
   if (repeaterCommandEventDelegate != null)
   {
      repeaterCommandEventDelegate(this, rce);
   }
}
```

ItemCommand requires an extra step to handle the RepeaterCommand events bubbled up from child RepeaterItem controls. To wire into the event bubbling, it implements OnBubbleEvent:

```
protected override bool OnBubbleEvent(object source, EventArgs e)
{
   RepeaterCommandEventArgs rce = e as RepeaterCommandEventArgs;

   if (rce != null)
   {
      OnItemCommand(rce);
      return true;
   }
   else
      return false;
}
```

OnBubble traps the RepeaterCommand events and raises them as ItemCommand events to event subscribers. Listing 7-5 shows the final source code for the Repeater control class.

Listing 7-5. *The Repeater Control Class File*

```
using System;
using System.Web;
using System.Web.UI;
using System.Web.UI.WebControls;
using System.Web.UI.Design.WebControls;
using System.Collections;
using System.Collections.Generic;
using System.ComponentModel;
using ControlsBook2Lib.Ch11.Design;

namespace ControlsBook2Lib.Ch07
{
  [ToolboxData("<{0}:repeater runat=server></{0}:repeater>"),
 ParseChildren(true), PersistChildren(false),
 Designer(typeof(ControlsBook2Lib.Ch11.Design.RepeaterDesigner))]
  public class Repeater : DataBoundControl, INamingContainer
  {
    #region Template Code
    private ITemplate headerTemplate;
    [Browsable(false), TemplateContainer(typeof(RepeaterItem)),
    PersistenceMode(PersistenceMode.InnerProperty)]
    public ITemplate HeaderTemplate
```

```
{
  get
  {
    return headerTemplate;
  }

  set
  {
    headerTemplate = value;
  }
}

private ITemplate footerTemplate;
[Browsable(false), TemplateContainer(typeof(RepeaterItem)),
PersistenceMode(PersistenceMode.InnerProperty)]
public ITemplate FooterTemplate
{
  get
  {
    return footerTemplate;
  }

  set
  {
    footerTemplate = value;
  }
}

private ITemplate itemTemplate;
[Browsable(false), TemplateContainer(typeof(RepeaterItem)),
PersistenceMode(PersistenceMode.InnerProperty)]
public ITemplate ItemTemplate
{
  get
  {
    return itemTemplate;
  }

  set
  {
    itemTemplate = value;
  }
}
```

```
private ITemplate alternatingItemTemplate;
[Browsable(false), TemplateContainer(typeof(RepeaterItem)),
PersistenceMode(PersistenceMode.InnerProperty)]
public ITemplate AlternatingItemTemplate
{
  get
  {
    return alternatingItemTemplate;
  }

  set
  {
    alternatingItemTemplate = value;
  }
}

private ITemplate separatorTemplate;
[Browsable(false), TemplateContainer(typeof(RepeaterItem)),
PersistenceMode(PersistenceMode.InnerProperty)]
public ITemplate SeparatorTemplate
{
  get
  {
    return separatorTemplate;
  }

  set
  {
    separatorTemplate = value;
  }
}

private RepeaterItem CreateItem(int itemIndex, ListItemType
itemType, bool dataBind, object dataItem)
{
  ITemplate selectedTemplate;

  switch (itemType)
  {
    case ListItemType.Header:
      selectedTemplate = headerTemplate;
      break;
```

```
        case ListItemType.Item:
          selectedTemplate = itemTemplate;
          break;
        case ListItemType.AlternatingItem:
          selectedTemplate = alternatingItemTemplate;
          break;
        case ListItemType.Separator:
          selectedTemplate = separatorTemplate;
          break;
        case ListItemType.Footer:
          selectedTemplate = footerTemplate;
          break;
        default:
          selectedTemplate = null;
          break;
      }

      if ((itemType == ListItemType.AlternatingItem) &&
         (alternatingItemTemplate == null))
      {
        selectedTemplate = itemTemplate;
        itemType = ListItemType.Item;
      }

      RepeaterItem item = new RepeaterItem(itemIndex, itemType, dataItem);

      if (selectedTemplate != null)
      {
        selectedTemplate.InstantiateIn(item);
      }

      OnItemCreated(new RepeaterItemEventArgs(item));

      Controls.Add(item);

      if (dataBind)
      {
        item.DataBind();
        OnItemDataBound(new RepeaterItemEventArgs(item));
      }
      return item;
    }
    #endregion
```

```
[Browsable(false)]
public List<RepeaterItem> Items
{
  get
  {
    EnsureChildControls();
    return items;
  }
}

protected override void PerformSelect()
{
  // Call OnDataBinding here if bound to a data source using the
  // DataSource property (instead of a DataSourceID), because the
  // databinding statement is evaluated before the call to GetData.
  if (!IsBoundUsingDataSourceID)
  {
    OnDataBinding(EventArgs.Empty);
  }

  // The GetData method retrieves the DataSourceView object from
  // the IDataSource associated with the data-bound control.
  GetData().Select(CreateDataSourceSelectArguments(),
      OnDataSourceViewSelectCallback);

  // The PerformDataBinding method has completed.
  RequiresDataBinding = false;
  MarkAsDataBound();

  // Raise the DataBound event.
  OnDataBound(EventArgs.Empty);
}

private void OnDataSourceViewSelectCallback(IEnumerable retrievedData)
{

  // Call OnDataBinding only if it has not already been
  // called in the PerformSelect method.
  if (IsBoundUsingDataSourceID)
  {
    OnDataBinding(EventArgs.Empty);
  }
  // The PerformDataBinding method binds the data in the
  // retrievedData collection to elements of the data-bound control.
  PerformDataBinding(retrievedData);
}
```

```
protected override void PerformDataBinding(IEnumerable data)
{
  base.PerformDataBinding(data);

  Controls.Clear();
  ClearChildViewState();
  TrackViewState();

  if (IsBoundUsingDataSourceID)
    CreateControlHierarchy(true, true, data);
  else
    CreateControlHierarchy(true, false, data);
  ChildControlsCreated = true;
}


protected override void ValidateDataSource(object dataSource)
{
  if (((dataSource != null) && !(dataSource is IListSource)) &&
      (!(dataSource is IEnumerable) && !(dataSource is IDataSource)))
  {
    throw new InvalidOperationException();
  }
}

public override void DataBind()
{
  this.PerformSelect();
}

private List<RepeaterItem> items;  //private collection backing Items property
private void CreateControlHierarchy(bool useData, bool
usingIDataSource, IEnumerable data)
{
  items = new List<RepeaterItem>();
  IEnumerable ds = null;

  if (HeaderTemplate != null)
  {
    RepeaterItem header = CreateItem(-1, ListItemType.Header, false, null);
  }
```

```
int count = -1;
if (useData)
{
  if (!usingIDataSource)
    ds = (IEnumerable)DataSourceHelper.ResolveDataSource(DataSource,
     DataMember);
  else
    ds = data;
}
else
{
  count = (int)ViewState["ItemCount"];
  if (count != -1)
  {
    ds = new DummyDataSource(count);
  }
}

if (ds != null)
{
  int index = 0;
  count = 0;
  RepeaterItem item;
  ListItemType itemType = ListItemType.Item;

  foreach (object dataItem in (IEnumerable)ds)
  {
    if (index != 0)
    {
      RepeaterItem separator = CreateItem(-1,
     ListItemType.Separator, false, null);
    }

    item = CreateItem(index, itemType, useData, dataItem);
    items.Add(item);
    index++;
    count++;

    if (itemType == ListItemType.Item)
      itemType = ListItemType.AlternatingItem;
    else
      itemType = ListItemType.Item;
  }
}
```

```
  if (FooterTemplate != null)
  {
    RepeaterItem footer = CreateItem(-1, ListItemType.Footer, false, null);
  }

  if (useData)
  {
    ViewState["ItemCount"] = ((ds != null) ? count : -1);
  }
}

override protected void CreateChildControls()
{
  Controls.Clear();
  if (ViewState["ItemCount"] != null)
  {
    CreateControlHierarchy(false, false, null);
  }
  ClearChildViewState();
}

public override ControlCollection Controls
{
  get
  {
    EnsureChildControls();
    return base.Controls;
  }
}

private static readonly object ItemCommandKey = new object();
public event RepeaterCommandEventHandler ItemCommand
{
  add
  {
    Events.AddHandler(ItemCommandKey, value);
  }
  remove
  {
    Events.RemoveHandler(ItemCommandKey, value);
  }
}
```

```
private static readonly object ItemCreatedKey = new object();
public event RepeaterItemEventHandler ItemCreated
{
  add
  {
    Events.AddHandler(ItemCreatedKey, value);
  }
  remove
  {
    Events.RemoveHandler(ItemCreatedKey, value);
  }
}

private static readonly object ItemDataBoundKey = new object();
public event RepeaterItemEventHandler ItemDataBound
{
  add
  {
    Events.AddHandler(ItemDataBoundKey, value);
  }
  remove
  {
    Events.RemoveHandler(ItemDataBoundKey, value);
  }
}

protected override bool OnBubbleEvent(object source, EventArgs e)
{
  RepeaterCommandEventArgs rce = e as RepeaterCommandEventArgs;

  if (rce != null)
  {
    OnItemCommand(rce);
    return true;
  }
  else
    return false;
}

protected virtual void OnItemCommand(RepeaterCommandEventArgs rce)
{
  RepeaterCommandEventHandler repeaterCommandEventDelegate =
     (RepeaterCommandEventHandler)Events[ItemCommandKey];
```

```
        if (repeaterCommandEventDelegate != null)
        {
          repeaterCommandEventDelegate(this, rce);
        }
      }

      protected virtual void OnItemCreated(RepeaterItemEventArgs rie)
      {
        RepeaterItemEventHandler repeaterItemEventDelegate =
           (RepeaterItemEventHandler)Events[ItemCreatedKey];
        if (repeaterItemEventDelegate != null)
        {
          repeaterItemEventDelegate(this, rie);
        }
      }

      protected virtual void OnItemDataBound(RepeaterItemEventArgs rie)
      {
        RepeaterItemEventHandler repeaterItemEventDelegate =
           (RepeaterItemEventHandler)Events[ItemDataBoundKey];
        if (repeaterItemEventDelegate != null)
        {
          repeaterItemEventDelegate(this, rie);
        }
      }
    }
  }
```

Now that we have covered the construction of our version of the Repeater control, in the next section we put it to the test to see if it behaves in a similar manner to the built-in ASP.NET Repeater server control.

Data Binding with the Repeater Control

Our long journey to build a Repeater control replica is complete. Now, we need to take it for a test drive with a variety of .NET collection types and a design-time DataSet to prove that the core feature set works as advertised.

The Databound Repeater web form has five Repeater controls that are attached to five different collection types: Array, ArrayList, SqlDataReader, DataSet, and an IDataSource-based control. The form also has a button on it to exercise the postback capabilities of the Repeater control to show how the control remembers its previous content without having to perform an additional data bind. The UI for the web form is shown in Figure 7-6.

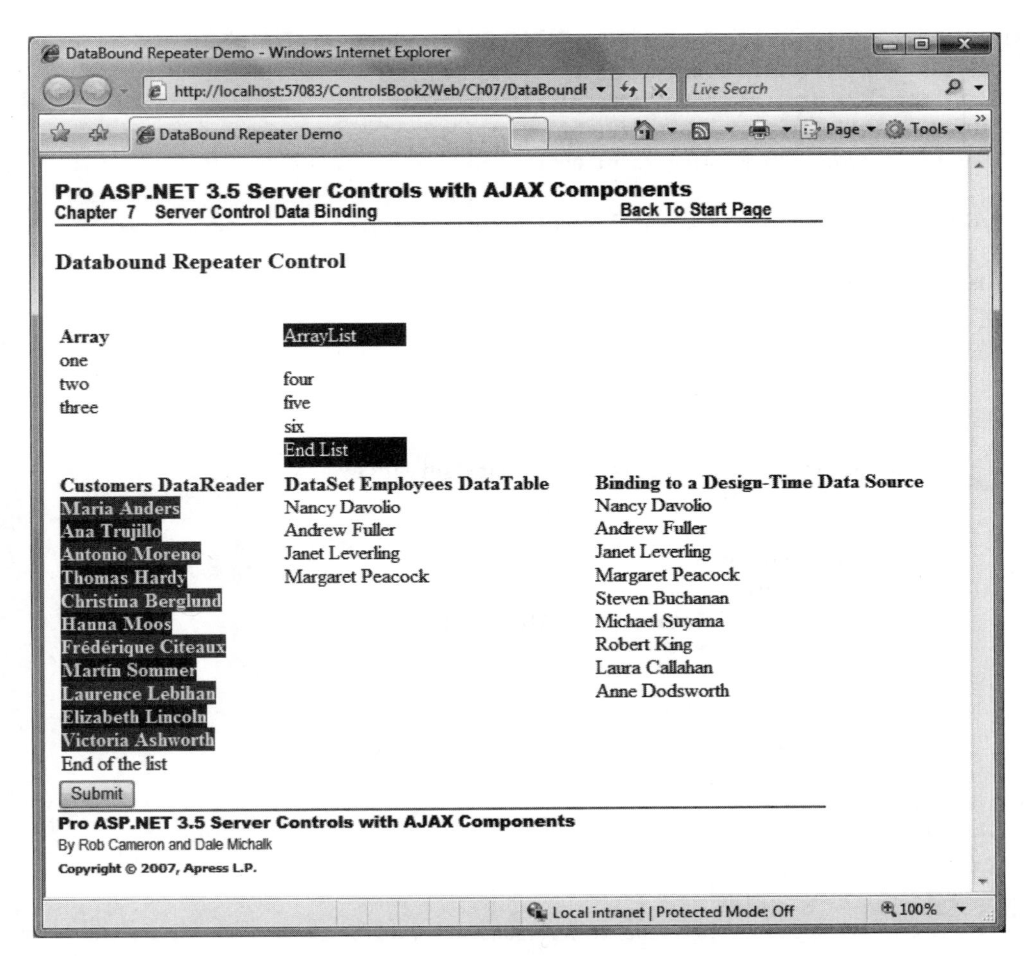

Figure 7-6. *The rendered Databound Repeater web form*

Listings 7-6 and 7-7 show the full code for the web form.

Listing 7-6. *The DataboundRepeater Web Form .aspx File*

```
<%@ Page Language="C#"
MasterPageFile="~/MasterPage/ControlsBook2MasterPage.Master"
  AutoEventWireup="true" CodeBehind="DataBoundRepeater.aspx.cs"
Inherits="ControlsBook2Web.Ch07.DataBoundRepeater"
  Title="DataBound Repeater Demo" %>

<%@ Register TagPrefix="apress" Namespace="ControlsBook2Lib.Ch07"
Assembly="ControlsBook2Lib" %>
```

```
<asp:Content ID="Content1" ContentPlaceHolderID="ChapterNumAndTitle" runat="server">
  <asp:Label ID="ChapterNumberLabel" runat="server"
  Width="14px">7</asp:Label>  <asp:Label
    ID="ChapterTitleLabel" runat="server" Width="360px">
    Server Control Data Binding</asp:Label>
</asp:Content>
<asp:Content ID="Content2" ContentPlaceHolderID="PrimaryContent" runat="server">
  <h3>
    Databound Repeater Control</h3>
  <br />
  <table>
    <tbody>
      <tr valign="top">
        <td>
          <apress:Repeater ID="repeaterA" runat="server">
            <HeaderTemplate>
              <b>Array</b><br />
            </HeaderTemplate>
            <ItemTemplate>
              <%# Container.DataItem %></ItemTemplate>
            <SeparatorTemplate>
              <br />
            </SeparatorTemplate>
          </apress:Repeater>
          <br />
        </td>
        <td>
            </td>
        <td class="style1">
          <apress:Repeater ID="repeaterAl" runat="server">
            <HeaderTemplate>
              <div>
                <asp:Label ID="Label1" runat="server"
                BackColor="Maroon"
                ForeColor="White" Text="ArrayList"
                  Width="96px"></asp:Label></div>
              <br />
            </HeaderTemplate>
            <ItemTemplate>
            </ItemTemplate>
            <SeparatorTemplate>
              <br />
            </SeparatorTemplate>
            <FooterTemplate>
              <div style="color: white; height: 24px; background-color: navy">
              </div>
            </FooterTemplate>
```

```
      </apress:Repeater>
      <br />
    </td>
  </tr>
  <tr valign="top">
    <td>
      <apress:Repeater ID="repeaterRdrCust" runat="server">
        <HeaderTemplate>
          <b>Customers DataReader</b><br />
        </HeaderTemplate>
        <ItemTemplate>
          <div style="display: inline; font-weight: bold;
          color: yellow; background-color: red">
            <%# DataBinder.Eval(Container.DataItem,"ContactName") %></div>
        </ItemTemplate>
        <AlternatingItemTemplate>
          <div style="display: inline; font-weight: bold;
          color: yellow; background-color: blue">
            <%# DataBinder.Eval(Container.DataItem,"ContactName") %></div>
        </AlternatingItemTemplate>
        <SeparatorTemplate>
          <br />
        </SeparatorTemplate>
        <FooterTemplate>
          <br />
          End of the list
        </FooterTemplate>
      </apress:Repeater>
    </td>
    <td>
    </td>
    <td class="style1">
      <apress:Repeater ID="repeaterDtEmp" runat="server">
        <HeaderTemplate>
          <b>DataSet Employees DataTable</b><br />
        </HeaderTemplate>
        <ItemTemplate>
          <%# DataBinder.Eval(Container.DataItem,"FirstName") %>
          <%# DataBinder.Eval(Container.DataItem,"LastName") %>
        </ItemTemplate>
        <SeparatorTemplate>
          <br />
        </SeparatorTemplate>
      </apress:Repeater>
    </td>
    <td>
      <apress:Repeater ID="RepeaterDesignTime" runat="server"
```

```
            DataSourceID="EmployeeDataSource">
            <HeaderTemplate>
              <b>Binding to a Design-Time Data Source</b><br />
            </HeaderTemplate>
            <ItemTemplate>
              <%# DataBinder.Eval(Container.DataItem,"FirstName") %>
              <%# DataBinder.Eval(Container.DataItem,"LastName") %>
            </ItemTemplate>
            <SeparatorTemplate>
              <br />
            </SeparatorTemplate>
          </apress:Repeater>
        </td>
      </tr>
    </tbody>
  </table>
  <asp:Button ID="Button1" runat="server" Text="Submit"></asp:Button> 
  <asp:SqlDataSource ID="EmployeeDataSource" runat="server" ConnectionString=
   "<%$ ConnectionStrings:NorthWindDB %>"
    ProviderName="<%$ ConnectionStrings:NorthWindDB.ProviderName %>"
SelectCommand="SELECT [FirstName], [LastName], [Title] FROM [Employees]">
  </asp:SqlDataSource>
</asp:Content>
<asp:Content ID="Content3" runat="server" ContentPlaceHolderID="HeadSection">
  <style type="text/css">
    .style1
    {
      width: 207px;
    }
  </style>
</asp:Content>
```

Listing 7-7. *The DataboundRepeater Code-Behind Class File*

```
using System;
using System.Data;
using System.Data.Common;
using System.Data.SqlClient;
using System.Collections;
using System.Web.Configuration;

namespace ControlsBook2Web.Ch07
{
```

```
public partial class DataBoundRepeater : System.Web.UI.Page
{
  protected System.Data.SqlClient.SqlDataAdapter dataAdapterEmp;
  protected System.Data.SqlClient.SqlCommand sqlSelectCommand1;
  protected DataSetEmp dataSetEmp;

  protected void Page_Load(object sender, EventArgs e)
  {
    if (!Page.IsPostBack)
    {
      string[] array = new String[] { "one", "two", "three" };
      repeaterA.DataSource = array;
      repeaterA.DataBind();

      ArrayList list = new ArrayList();
      list.Add("four");
      list.Add("five");
      list.Add("six");
      repeaterAl.DataSource = list;
      repeaterAl.DataBind();

      SqlDataReader dr = GetCustomerDataReader();
      repeaterRdrCust.DataSource = dr;
      repeaterRdrCust.DataBind();
      dr.Close();

      DataSet ds = new DataSet();
      FillEmployeesDataSet(ds);

      repeaterDtEmp.DataSource = ds;
      repeaterDtEmp.DataMember = "Employees";
      repeaterDtEmp.DataBind();
    }
  }

  private SqlDataReader GetCustomerDataReader()
  {
    SqlConnection conn =
       new SqlConnection(WebConfigurationManager.ConnectionStrings["NorthWindDB"]
.ConnectionString);
    conn.Open();
```

```
      SqlCommand cmd =
         new SqlCommand("SELECT CustomerID, ContactName, ContactTitle,
         CompanyName FROM Customers WHERE CustomerID LIKE '[AB]%'",
         conn);
      SqlDataReader dr = cmd.ExecuteReader(CommandBehavior.CloseConnection);
      return dr;
    }

    private void FillEmployeesDataSet(DataSet ds)
    {
      SqlConnection conn =
         new SqlConnection(WebConfigurationManager.ConnectionStrings["NorthWindDB"]
.ConnectionString);
      conn.Open();

      SqlDataAdapter da =
         new SqlDataAdapter("SELECT EmployeeID, FirstName, LastName,
         Title FROM Employees WHERE EmployeeID < 5",
         conn);
      da.Fill(ds, "Employees");

      conn.Close();
    }
  }
}
```

In the next section, we test the events published by the Replica Repeater server control we created in this chapter.

Advanced Interaction with the Repeater Control

The previous web form demonstrates that our Repeater control is capable of binding to a variety of data sources. The Advanced Repeater web form takes this a few steps further. Instead of just binding a SqlDataReader to a Repeater control, the Advanced Repeater web form hooks into the ItemCreated and ItemDataBound events of our Repeater control to dynamically alter its output.

The Advanced Repeater web form dynamically adds an ASP.NET Label control to each RepeaterItem row in its ItemCreated handler:

```
protected void repeaterRdrCust_ItemCreated(object o,
ControlsBook2Lib.Ch07.RepeaterItemEventArgs rie)
{
  ControlsBook2Lib.Ch07.RepeaterItem item = rie.Item;
  if (item.ItemType == ListItemType.Item)
  {
    Label lblID = new Label();
    lblID.ID = "lblID";
    item.Controls.Add(lblID);
    item.Controls.Add(new LiteralControl(" "));
  }
```

Once the control data binds, it changes the value of the added `Label` control to the `CustomerID` value of the current row in the `SqlDataReader`:

```
protected void repeaterRdrCust_ItemDataBound(object o,
ControlsBook2Lib.Ch07.RepeaterItemEventArgs rie)
{
  ControlsBook2Lib.Ch07.RepeaterItem item = rie.Item;
  DbDataRecord row = (DbDataRecord)item.DataItem;
  string ID = (string)row["CustomerID"];
  Label lblID = (Label)item.FindControl("lblID");
  lblID.Text = ID;
}
```

The result of the event handling during creation and data binding is the browser output shown in Figure 7-7.

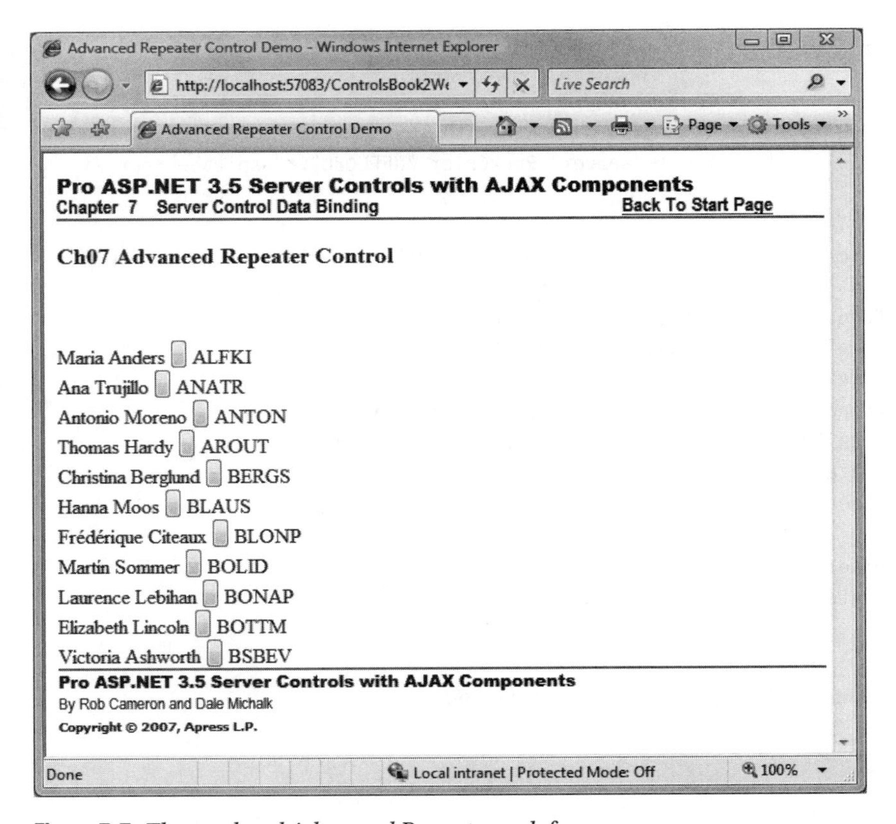

Figure 7-7. *The rendered Advanced Repeater web form*

Listings 7-8 and 7-9 present the full code for the web form.

Listing 7-8. *The AdvancedRepeater .aspx Page File*

```
<%@ Page Language="C#"
MasterPageFile="~/MasterPage/ControlsBook2MasterPage.Master"
  AutoEventWireup="true" CodeBehind="AdvancedRepeater.aspx.cs"
Inherits="ControlsBook2Web.Ch07.AdvancedRepeater"
  Title="Advanced Repeater Control Demo" %>

<%@ Register TagPrefix="apress" Namespace="ControlsBook2Lib.Ch07"
Assembly="ControlsBook2Lib" %>
<asp:Content ID="Content1" ContentPlaceHolderID="ChapterNumAndTitle" runat="server">
  <asp:Label ID="ChapterNumberLabel" runat="server"
   Width="14px">7</asp:Label>  <asp:Label
   ID="ChapterTitleLabel" runat="server" Width="360px">
   Server Control Data Binding</asp:Label>
</asp:Content>
<asp:Content ID="Content2" ContentPlaceHolderID="PrimaryContent" runat="server">
  <h3>
    Ch07 Advanced Repeater Control</h3>
  <b>
    <asp:Label ID="status" runat="server" BackColor="#FFC080"></asp:Label><br />
  </b>
  <br />
  <apress:Repeater ID="repeaterRdrCust" runat="server"
   OnItemCommand="repeaterRdrCust_ItemCommand"
   OnItemDataBound="repeaterRdrCust_ItemDataBound"
   OnItemCreated="repeaterRdrCust_ItemCreated">
    <ItemTemplate>
      <%# DataBinder.Eval(Container.DataItem,"ContactName") %>
      <asp:Button ID="contact1" runat="server"></asp:Button>
    </ItemTemplate>
    <SeparatorTemplate>
      <br />
    </SeparatorTemplate>
  </apress:Repeater>
</asp:Content>
```

Listing 7-9. *The AdvancedRepeater Code-Behind Class File*

```
using System;
using System.Data;
using System.Data.Common;
using System.Data.SqlClient;
using System.Web.UI;
using System.Web.UI.WebControls;
using ControlsBook2Lib.Ch07;
using System.Web.Configuration;
```

```
namespace ControlsBook2Web.Ch07
{
  public partial class AdvancedRepeater : System.Web.UI.Page
  {
    protected void Page_Load(object sender, EventArgs e)
    {
      status.Text = "";
      if (!Page.IsPostBack)
      {
        SqlDataReader dr = GetCustomerDataReader();
        repeaterRdrCust.DataSource = dr;
        repeaterRdrCust.DataBind();
        dr.Close();
      }
    }

    private SqlDataReader GetCustomerDataReader()
    {
      SqlConnection conn =
         new SqlConnection(WebConfigurationManager.ConnectionStrings["NorthWindDB"].
                ConnectionString);
      conn.Open();

      SqlCommand cmd ='
         new SqlCommand("SELECT CustomerID, ContactName, ContactTitle,
               CompanyName FROM Customers WHERE CustomerID LIKE '[AB]%'",
         conn);
      SqlDataReader dr = cmd.ExecuteReader(CommandBehavior.CloseConnection);
      return dr;
    }

    protected void repeaterRdrCust_ItemCommand(object o,
ControlsBook2Lib.Ch07.RepeaterCommandEventArgs rce)
    {
      ControlsBook2Lib.Ch07.RepeaterItem item = rce.Item;
      Label lblID = (Label)item.FindControl("lblID");
      status.Text = lblID.Text + " was clicked!";
    }

    protected void repeaterRdrCust_ItemDataBound(object o,
ControlsBook2Lib.Ch07.RepeaterItemEventArgs rie)
    {
      ControlsBook2Lib.Ch07.RepeaterItem item = rie.Item;
      DbDataRecord row = (DbDataRecord)item.DataItem;
      string ID = (string)row["CustomerID"];
      Label lblID = (Label)item.FindControl("lblID");
      lblID.Text = ID;
    }
```

```
    protected void repeaterRdrCust_ItemCreated(object o,
ControlsBook2Lib.Ch07.RepeaterItemEventArgs rie)
    {
      ControlsBook2Lib.Ch07.RepeaterItem item = rie.Item;
      if (item.ItemType == ListItemType.Item)
      {
        Label lblID = new Label();
        lblID.ID = "lblID";
        item.Controls.Add(lblID);
        item.Controls.Add(new LiteralControl(" "));
      }
    }
  }
}
```

More work remains for the AdvancedDataRepeater after rendering—specifically, firing events. The web form is wired into the ItemCommand event raised by the Repeater control. This is triggered by the ASP.NET Button control that is a part of each row rendered in conjunction with the data from the Customers table in the Northwind database:

```
protected void repeaterRdrCust_ItemCommand(object o,
ControlsBook2Lib.Ch07.RepeaterCommandEventArgs rce)
{
  ControlsBook2Lib.Ch07.RepeaterItem item = rce.Item;
  Label lblID = (Label)item.FindControl("lblID");
  status.Text = lblID.Text + " was clicked!";
}
```

The RepeaterCommand method that handles the ItemCommand event uses RepeaterCommandEventArgs and its Item property to retrieve the RepeaterItem control that contains the row where the button was clicked. It uses this control reference along with the FindControl method to locate the dynamically added Label control. The Text property value of the Label control is the same as the CustomerID value from the database. RepeaterCommand displays this information in the status Label control at the top the web form. Figure 7-8 shows what happens when we click the first row's button.

As shown in the examples, our Repeater copy fires its events as one would expect of any of the built-in list controls. We next demonstrate how our Repeater is capable of loading templates dynamically, just like the built-in one.

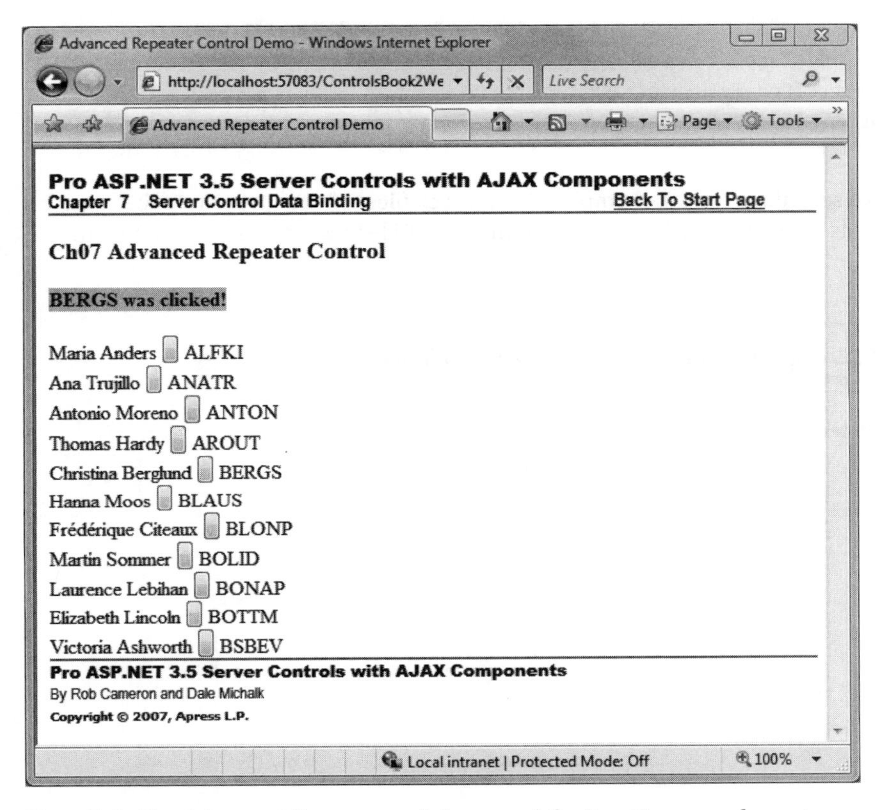

Figure 7-8. *The Advanced Repeater web form and the ItemCommand event*

Using Dynamic Templates

The templates used in the `Menu` and `Repeater` demonstrations to this point were statically declared in an `.aspx` page. Sometimes, web developers must generate the templates on the fly to modify the output of the templated control. ASP.NET lends a helping hand with two techniques: loading from file via the `LoadTemplate` method of the `Page` class and creating a prebuilt class that implements the `ITemplate` interface. We discuss these techniques in the following sections.

The Dynamic Templates Web Form

The Dynamic Templates web form demonstrates how to dynamically load templates into an instance of the `Repeater` control built in this chapter. The `Repeater` control on the web form looks like the typical `Repeater` bound to a `SqlDataReader`. The difference is the `DropDownList` control that is used to select which template to apply to the `Repeater` control when it is loaded:

```
<asp:DropDownList id="templateList" Runat="server" AutoPostBack="True">
  <asp:ListItem>FileTemplate.ascx</asp:ListItem>
  <asp:ListItem>CustCodeTemplate</asp:ListItem>
  <asp:ListItem>CustFileTemplate.ascx</asp:ListItem>
</asp:DropDownList>
```

The first two selections load the template from `.ascx` files that are present in the same virtual directory as the web form. The default template is `FileTemplate.ascx`, as shown in Figure 7-9.

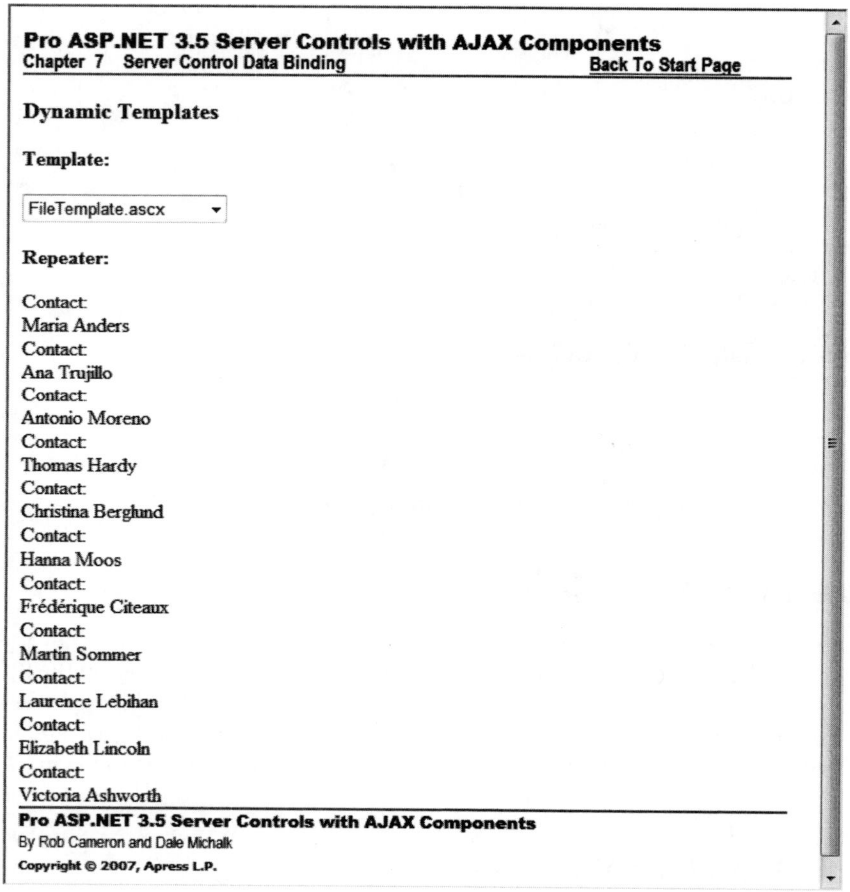

Figure 7-9. *The Dynamic Templates web form and FileTemplate.ascx*

The actual code for the `.ascx` file is shown in Listing 7-10. Notice that we did not have to include the `<ITEMTEMPLATE>` container tags.

Listing 7-10. *The FileTemplate and CustFileTemplate .ascx Files*

```
<%@ Control Language="C#" AutoEventWireup="true"
   CodeBehind="FileTemplate.ascx.cs"
    Inherits="ControlsBook2Web.Ch07.FileTemplate" %>
Contact:<br>
<span> <%# DataBinder.Eval(Container, "DataItem.ContactName") %> </span>
<br/>
<%@ Control Language="C#" AutoEventWireup="true"
CodeBehind="CustFileTemplate.ascx.cs"
  Inherits="ControlsBook2Web.Ch07.CustFileTemplate" %>
Contact:<br />
<input type="text" value="<%# DataBinder.Eval(Container,
 "DataItem.ContactName") %>" />
<br />
```

Because the DropDownList control has the AutoPostBack property set to true, changing the template used by the Repeater control is as easy as selecting a different template in the DropDownList control. This causes a postback to occur and executes the code in LoadRepeater that is responsible for finding the right template and binding it to the Repeater control:

```
string templateName = templateList.SelectedItem.Text;
if (templateName.IndexOf(".ascx") > 0)
{
   repeaterRdrCust.ItemTemplate = Page.LoadTemplate(templateName);
}
```

The first thing the code does is check for the .ascx file extension to determine whether this is a file-based template. Next, the code calls Page.LoadTemplate to load the template from disk. At that point, it can assign the ITemplate reference to the ItemTemplate property of the Repeater server control and continue with the rest of the data-binding process. Figure 7-10 demonstrates a different layout with the template CustFileTemplate.ascx.

Selecting the CustCodeTemplate option from the DropDownList control executes a different code path that programmatically instantiates templates and assigns them to the Repeater control:

```
else
{
   repeaterRdrCust.HeaderTemplate = new CustCodeHeaderTemplate();

   repeaterRdrCust.ItemTemplate = new CustCodeItemTemplate(true);

   repeaterRdrCust.AlternatingItemTemplate = new CustCodeItemTemplate(false);

   repeaterRdrCust.FooterTemplate = new CustCodeFooterTemplate();
}
```

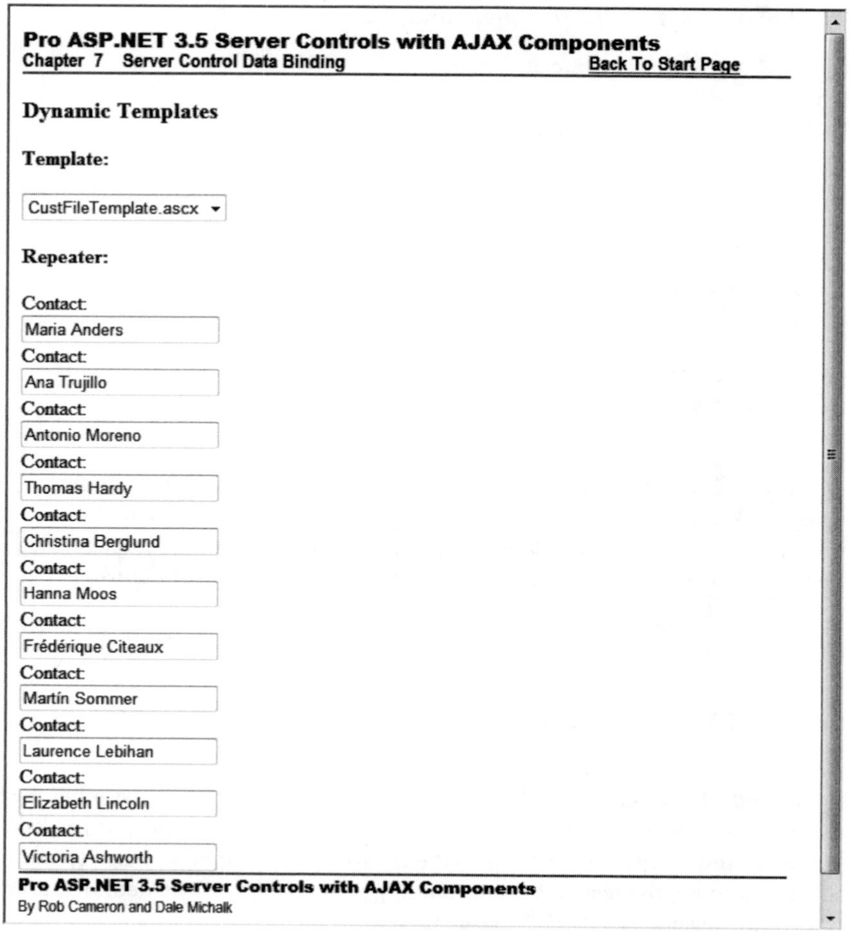

Pro ASP.NET 3.5 Server Controls with AJAX Components
Chapter 7 Server Control Data Binding Back To Start Page

Dynamic Templates

Template:

CustFileTemplate.ascx

Repeater:

Contact: Maria Anders
Contact: Ana Trujillo
Contact: Antonio Moreno
Contact: Thomas Hardy
Contact: Christina Berglund
Contact: Hanna Moos
Contact: Frédérique Citeaux
Contact: Martín Sommer
Contact: Laurence Lebihan
Contact: Elizabeth Lincoln
Contact: Victoria Ashworth

Pro ASP.NET 3.5 Server Controls with AJAX Components
By Rob Cameron and Dale Michalk

Figure 7-10. *The Dynamic Templates web form and CustFileTemplate.ascx*

Three custom template classes are used to affect the output of `Repeater`: `CustCodeHeaderTemplate`, `CustCodeItemTemplate`, and `CustCodeFooterTemplate`. The `CustCodeItemTemplate` class does double duty by implementing both the `ItemTemplate` and `AlternatingItemTemplate` templates for the `Repeater` control. The Boolean value passed to the `CustCodeItemTemplate` templates' constructor in the web form's code behind file ensures they have unique colors to make the output easy to read, as shown in Figure 7-11.

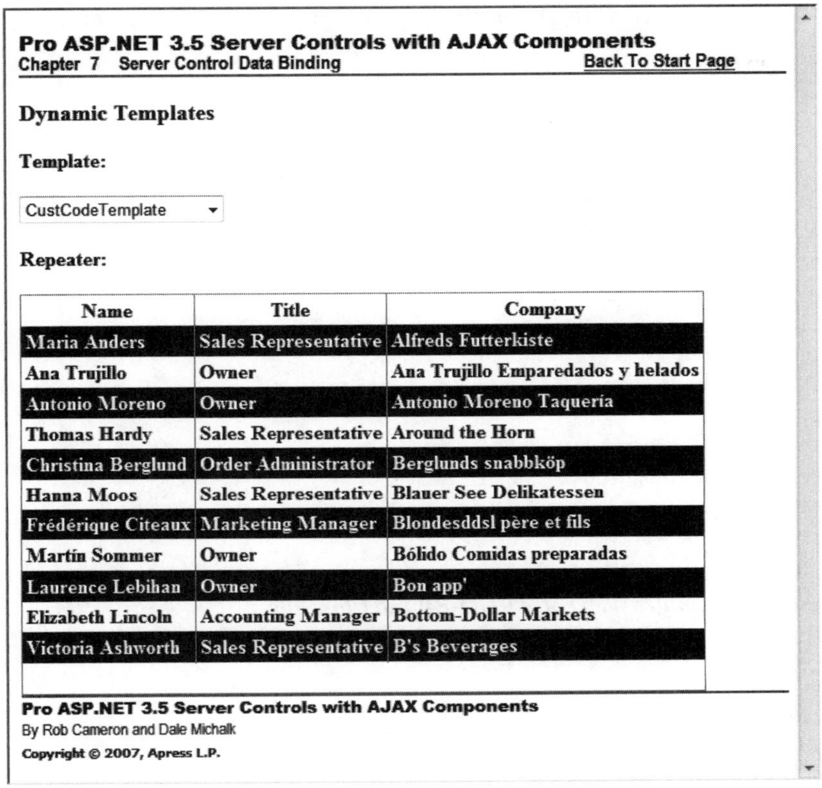

Pro ASP.NET 3.5 Server Controls with AJAX Components
Chapter 7 Server Control Data Binding Back To Start Page

Dynamic Templates

Template:

CustCodeTemplate

Repeater:

Name	Title	Company
Maria Anders	Sales Representative	Alfreds Futterkiste
Ana Trujillo	Owner	Ana Trujillo Emparedados y helados
Antonio Moreno	Owner	Antonio Moreno Taquería
Thomas Hardy	Sales Representative	Around the Horn
Christina Berglund	Order Administrator	Berglunds snabbköp
Hanna Moos	Sales Representative	Blauer See Delikatessen
Frédérique Citeaux	Marketing Manager	Blondesddsl père et fils
Martín Sommer	Owner	Bólido Comidas preparadas
Laurence Lebihan	Owner	Bon app'
Elizabeth Lincoln	Accounting Manager	Bottom-Dollar Markets
Victoria Ashworth	Sales Representative	B's Beverages

Pro ASP.NET 3.5 Server Controls with AJAX Components
By Rob Cameron and Dale Michalk
Copyright © 2007, Apress L.P.

Figure 7-11. *The Dynamic Templates web form and CustCodeTemplates.cs*

Listings 7-11 and 7-12 show the full code for the web form.

Listing 7-11. *The DynamicTemplates .aspx Page File*

```
<%@ Page Language="C#"
MasterPageFile="~/MasterPage/ControlsBook2MasterPage.Master"
  AutoEventWireup="true" CodeBehind="DynamicTemplates.aspx.cs
" Inherits="ControlsBook2Web.Ch07.DynamicTemplates"
  Title="Dynamic Templates Demo" %>

<%@ Register TagPrefix="apress" Namespace="ControlsBook2Lib.Ch07
Assembly="ControlsBook2Lib" %>
<asp:Content ID="Content1" ContentPlaceHolderID="ChapterNumAndTitle"
                              runat="server">
  <asp:Label ID="ChapterNumberLabel" runat="server"
    Width="14px">7</asp:Label><asp:Label
    ID="ChapterTitleLabel" runat="server" Width="360px">
          Server Control Data Binding</asp:Label>
</asp:Content>
```

```
<asp:Content ID="Content2" ContentPlaceHolderID="PrimaryContent" runat="server">
  <h3>
    Dynamic Templates</h3>
  <b>Template: </b>
  <br />
  <br />
  <asp:DropDownList ID="templateList" runat="server" AutoPostBack="True">
    <asp:ListItem>FileTemplate.ascx</asp:ListItem>
    <asp:ListItem>CustCodeTemplate</asp:ListItem>
    <asp:ListItem>CustFileTemplate.ascx</asp:ListItem>
  </asp:DropDownList>
  <br />
  <br />
  <b>Repeater:</b><br />
  <br />
  <apress:Repeater ID="repeaterRdrCust" runat="server">
  </apress:Repeater>
</asp:Content>
```

Listing 7-12. *The DynamicTemplates Web Form Code-Behind Class File*

```
using System;
using System.Data;
using System.Data.SqlClient;
using System.Web.UI.WebControls;
using ControlsBook2Lib.Ch07;
using System.Web.Configuration;

namespace ControlsBook2Web.Ch07
{
  public partial class DynamicTemplates : System.Web.UI.Page
  {
    protected void Page_Load(object sender, EventArgs e)
    {
      LoadRepeater();
    }

    private void LoadRepeater()
    {
      string templateName = templateList.SelectedItem.Text;
      if (templateName.IndexOf(".ascx") > 0)
      {
        repeaterRdrCust.ItemTemplate = Page.LoadTemplate(templateName);
      }
      else
      {
        repeaterRdrCust.HeaderTemplate = new CustCodeHeaderTemplate();
```

```
        repeaterRdrCust.ItemTemplate = new CustCodeItemTemplate(true);

        repeaterRdrCust.AlternatingItemTemplate = new CustCodeItemTemplate(false);

        repeaterRdrCust.FooterTemplate = new CustCodeFooterTemplate();
      }

      SqlDataReader dr = GetCustomerDataReader();
      repeaterRdrCust.DataSource = dr;
      repeaterRdrCust.DataBind();
      dr.Close();
    }

    private SqlDataReader GetCustomerDataReader()
    {
      SqlConnection conn =
         new SqlConnection(WebConfigurationManager.ConnectionStrings["NorthWindDB"]
.ConnectionString);
      conn.Open();

      SqlCommand cmd =
         new SqlCommand("SELECT CustomerID, ContactName, ContactTitle,
         CompanyName FROM Customers WHERE CustomerID LIKE '[AB]%'",
         conn);
      SqlDataReader dr = cmd.ExecuteReader(CommandBehavior.CloseConnection);

      return dr;
    }
  }
}
```

Our Repeater class does a pretty good job of mimicking the built-in Repeater class, and we hope you agree that it provides a nice example of inheriting from the DataBoundControl base class. We covered the basics of using templates in Chapter 6, and in the next section, we dig a bit deeper with a discussion of the template implementation in the Repeater server control.

Implementing the ITemplate Interface

The ITemplate interface requires that only a single method named InstantiateIn be implemented by a control. The template code gets a reference to its container as the sole parameter and is free to add control content to the container.

The TemplateMenu sample in Chapter 6 shares its templates with the Dynamic Templates sample from the previous section, and both are implemented in the CustomCodeTemplates class. The following implementation of InstantiateIn in the CustCodeHeaderTemplate template shows that its job is to set up the Literal control that emits an HTML table header. CustCodeFooterTemplate does much the same for closing out the HTML table.

```
public void InstantiateIn(Control container)
{
   LiteralControl table =
      new LiteralControl(
      "<table cellspacing=\"0\" cellpadding=\"3\" " +
      "rules=\"cols\" bordercolor=\"#999999\" border=\"1\" " +
      "style=\"background-color:White;border-color:#999999;" +
      "border-width:1px;border-style:None;" +
      "border-collapse:collapse;\">" +
      "<th>Name</th><th>Title</th><th>Company</th>"
      );
   container.Controls.Add(table);
}
```

CustCodeItemTemplate is a bit more complex, because it adds Label controls representing the ContactName, ContactTitle, and CompanyName columns into the mix. These tags go hand in hand with the necessary <TR> and <TD> tags to build the rows in the HTML table.

We also wire in the capability for this template class to serve as an ItemTemplate or AlternatingItemTemplate template via a Boolean parameter that is passed to its constructor:

```
public class CustCodeItemTemplate : ITemplate
{
   bool isItem = false;

   public CustCodeItemTemplate(bool IsItem)
   {
      isItem = IsItem;
}
```

CustCodeItemTemplate also has Color and BackgroundColor properties that generate a blue or white color string, depending on the Boolean value of isItem:

```
public string BackgroundColor
{
   get
   {
      if (isItem)
         return "blue";
      else
         return "white";
   }
}

public string Color
{
   get
   {
```

```
      if (isItem)
         return "white";
      else
         return "blue";
   }
}
```

This customization provides a nice alternating blue and white color scheme in the table output for the control using the templates. InstantiateIn makes use of the property to set up the <TR> tag with the right CSS style properties. It also adds the necessary LiteralControl controls that will bind the data to its source:

```
public void InstantiateIn(Control container)
{
   LiteralControl row =
      new LiteralControl("<tr style=\"color:" + Color +
      ";background-color:" + BackgroundColor +
      ";font-weight:bold;\">");
   container.Controls.Add(row);

   LiteralControl contactName = new LiteralControl();
   contactName.DataBinding += new EventHandler(BindContactName);
   container.Controls.Add(contactName);

   LiteralControl contactTitle = new LiteralControl();
   contactTitle.DataBinding += new EventHandler(BindContactTitle);
   container.Controls.Add(contactTitle);

   LiteralControl companyName = new LiteralControl();
   companyName.DataBinding += new EventHandler(BindCompanyName);
   container.Controls.Add(companyName);

   row = new LiteralControl("</tr>");
   container.Controls.Add(row);
}
```

To make the data binding process work properly, the template has built-in data binding event handlers wired to each LiteralControl instance representing a column in the data source. During data binding, each template data binds, and the LiteralControls inside of the template data bind as well, firing events that the template handles by casting to the RepeaterItem container and accessing the current data source row to fill in the Text property of the LiteralControl controls. The code for ContactName is as follows:

```
private void BindContactName(object source, EventArgs e)
{
   LiteralControl contactName = (LiteralControl) source;
   RepeaterItem item = (RepeaterItem) contactName.NamingContainer;
```

```
    contactName.Text = "<td>" +
       DataBinder.Eval(item.DataItem, "ContactName")
       + "</td>";
}
```

Listing 7-13 contains the full code for all the custom-coded templates.

Listing 7-13. *The CustCodeTemplates.cs Template Class File*

```
using System;
using System.Web.UI;

namespace ControlsBook2Lib.Ch07
{
  public class CustCodeHeaderTemplate : ITemplate
  {
    public void InstantiateIn(Control container)
    {
      LiteralControl table =
         new LiteralControl(
         "<table cellspacing=\"0\" cellpadding=\"3\" " +
         "rules=\"cols\" bordercolor=\"#999999\" border=\"1\" " +
         "style=\"background-color:White;border-color:#999999;" +
         "border-width:1px;border-style:None;" +
         "border-collapse:collapse;\">" +
         "<th>Name</th><th>Title</th><th>Company</th>"
         );
      container.Controls.Add(table);
    }
  }

  public class CustCodeItemTemplate : ITemplate
  {
    bool isItem = false;

    public CustCodeItemTemplate(bool IsItem)
    {
      isItem = IsItem;

    }

    public string BackgroundColor
    {
      get
      {
```

```
    if (isItem)
      return "blue";
    else
      return "white";
  }
}

public string Color
{
  get
  {
    if (isItem)
      return "white";
    else
      return "blue";
  }
}

public void InstantiateIn(Control container)
{
  LiteralControl row =
     new LiteralControl("<tr style=\"color:" + Color +
     ";background-color:" + BackgroundColor +
     ";font-weight:bold;\">");
  container.Controls.Add(row);

  LiteralControl contactName = new LiteralControl();
  contactName.DataBinding += new EventHandler(BindContactName);
  container.Controls.Add(contactName);

  LiteralControl contactTitle = new LiteralControl();
  contactTitle.DataBinding += new EventHandler(BindContactTitle);
  container.Controls.Add(contactTitle);

  LiteralControl companyName = new LiteralControl();
  companyName.DataBinding += new EventHandler(BindCompanyName);
  container.Controls.Add(companyName);

  row = new LiteralControl("</tr>");
  container.Controls.Add(row);
}

private void BindContactName(object source, EventArgs e)
{
  LiteralControl contactName = (LiteralControl)source;
  RepeaterItem item = (RepeaterItem)contactName.NamingContainer;
  contactName.Text = "<td>" +
```

```
            DataBinder.Eval(item.DataItem, "ContactName")
            + "</td>";
    }

    private void BindContactTitle(object source, EventArgs e)
    {
      LiteralControl contactTitle = (LiteralControl)source;
      RepeaterItem item = (RepeaterItem)contactTitle.NamingContainer;
      contactTitle.Text = "<td>" +
         DataBinder.Eval(item.DataItem, "ContactTitle")
         + "</td>";
    }

    private void BindCompanyName(object source, EventArgs e)
    {
      LiteralControl companyName = (LiteralControl)source;
      RepeaterItem item = (RepeaterItem)companyName.NamingContainer;
      companyName.Text = "<td>" +
         DataBinder.Eval(item.DataItem, "CompanyName")
         + "</td>";
    }
  }

  public class CustCodeFooterTemplate : ITemplate
  {
    public void InstantiateIn(Control container)
    {
      LiteralControl table = new LiteralControl("<tr>
      <td colspan=3> </td></tr></table>");
      container.Controls.Add(table);
    }
  }
}
```

In the next subsection, we cover how to write a control that inherits from the CompositeDataBoundControl base class.

CompositeDataBoundControl

In the previous section, we inherited from the base class DataBoundControl for Repeater to leverage its built-in features. In this section, we investigate the CompositeDataBoundControl base class.

In the .NET Framework documentation, there is a sample listed in the documentation for the CompositeDataBoundControl base class called the SimpleSpreadsheetControl. When first examining the sample to see how it worked, the control did not data bind correctly to a SqlDataSource if DataSourceMode is configured as DataSet. Instead of returning the data values for each row in the table, it simply wrote out the ToString() value for the System.Data.DataRowView class.

The code where the data binding occurs in the SimpleSpreadsheetControl checks for DbDataRecord and then writes out the data. If the data object is not of type DbDataRecord, it simply writes out the string value for the object using ToString(), which is why System.Data.DataRowView is rendered for each row instead of the data from the SqlDataSource. This issue provided us an excuse to improve the implementation resulting in the EnhancedSpreadSheet control. First, let's take a look at how the CompositeDataBoundControl works.

CompositeDataBoundControl Mechanics

In general, composite control rendering is centered around the CreateChildControls method that is inherited from the base Control class. The Render method is not overridden in a composite server control, because the child controls perform their own rendering. By simply creating the child controls, a composite server control achieves rendering its contents.

When inheriting from CompositeDataBoundControl, it is required to override this method:

```
CreateChildControls(IEnumerable dataSource,Boolean dataBinding)
```

When initially loading the page, a dataSource is passed in based on how the control is configured for data binding and dataBinding is set to true. The rows are built out with data from the configured data source and rendered to the browser. Upon postback, the value for the dataSource parameter is an array of null objects that has a count that matches the number of rows added to the HTML Table's Rows collection. The value of dataBinding is false, since the values will be retrieved from ViewState unless the data binding configuration was altered programmatically by the developer. For postback, the control creates an empty (but not null) TableRow object for the header and a set of empty EnhancedSpreadsheetRow objects as place holders for the values stored in ViewState.

The EnhancedSpreadsheetControl

This section covers the improvements made to the SimpleSpreadsheetControl in our new control called the EnhancedSpreadsheetControl. The first improvement provided in the EnhancedSpreadsheetControl is to allow the control to data bind to a SqlDataSource by also checking to see if the data source object is of type DataRowView. If it is, the code writes out the data values associated with the data source. Here is a snippet from the server control class's EnhancedSpreadsheetRow.RenderContents method:

```
if (datarow is DataRowView)
{
  DataRow temp = ((DataRowView)datarow).Row;

  for (int i = 0; i < temp.Table.Columns.Count; ++i)
  {
    cellData = new TableCell();
    row.Cells.Add(cellData);
    cellData.Text = temp[i].ToString();
  }
```

In addition to adding a border and other visual configuration to the containing Table object, one other enhancement is the addition of a header row that reads the schema of the first data row to determine the column names using this code:

```
if (dataRow is DbDataRecord)
{
  DbDataRecord temp = (DbDataRecord)dataRow;
  for (int i = 0; i < temp.FieldCount; ++i)
  {
    columnName = new TableCell();
    headerRow.Cells.Add(columnName);
    columnName.Text = temp.GetName(i);
  }
}

if (dataRow is DataRowView)
{
  DataRowView drv = (DataRowView)dataRow;
  for (int i = 0; i < drv.Row.Table.Columns.Count; ++i)
  {
    columnName = new TableCell();
    headerRow.Cells.Add(columnName);
    columnName.Text = drv.Row.Table.Columns[i].Caption;
  }
}
```

Listings 7-14 and 7-15 have the source code for EnhancedSpreadsheetControl and EnhancedSpreadsheetRow respectively.

Listing 7-14. *The EnhancedSpreadsheetControl Control*

```
using System;
using System.Data;
using System.Drawing;
using System.ComponentModel;
using System.Collections;
using System.Data.Common;
using System.Web.UI;
using System.Web.UI.WebControls;

namespace ControlsBook2Lib.Ch07
{
  [ToolboxData("<{0}:EnhancedSpreadsheetControl
   runat=server></{0}:EnhancedSpreadsheetControl>")]
  public class EnhancedSpreadsheetControl : CompositeDataBoundControl
  {
```

```
protected Table table = new Table();

[Browsable(false)]
public virtual TableRowCollection Rows
{
  get
  {
    EnsureChildControls();
    return table.Rows;
  }
}

public Color HeaderRowBackColor
{
  get
  {
    object headerRowBackColor = ViewState["HeaderRowBackColor"];
    if (headerRowBackColor == null)
      return Color.White;
    else
      return (Color)headerRowBackColor;
  }
  set
  {
    ViewState["HeaderRowBackColor"] = value;
  }
}

public Color HeaderRowForeColor
{
  get
  {
    object headerRowForeColor = ViewState["HeaderRowForeColor"];
    if (headerRowForeColor == null)
      return Color.Black;
    else
      return (Color)headerRowForeColor;
  }
  set
  {
    ViewState["HeaderRowForeColor"] = value;
  }
}
```

```
protected override int CreateChildControls(IEnumerable dataSource,
bool dataBinding)
{
  int count = 0;
  if (dataSource != null)
  {
    table = new Table();
    Controls.Add(table);

    table.Attributes.Add("border", "1");
    table.Attributes.Add("cellpadding", "2");

    if (dataBinding)
    {
      EnhancedSpreadsheetRow row;
      TableCell cellData;
      IEnumerator e = dataSource.GetEnumerator();
      e.MoveNext();
      //Populate Header Row based on datasource schema for first data item
      BuildHeaderRow(e.Current, dataBinding);
      ++count;  //Increment for header row

      do
      {
        object datarow = e.Current;
        row = new EnhancedSpreadsheetRow(count, datarow, dataBinding);
        this.Rows.Add(row);
        if (datarow is DbDataRecord)
        {
          DbDataRecord temp = (DbDataRecord)datarow;
          for (int i = 0; i < temp.FieldCount; ++i)
          {
            cellData = new TableCell();
            row.Cells.Add(cellData);
            cellData.Text = temp.GetValue(i).ToString();
          }
        }
        if (datarow is DataRowView)
        {
          DataRow temp = ((DataRowView)datarow).Row;
```

```
          for (int i = 0; i < temp.Table.Columns.Count; ++i)
          {
            cellData = new TableCell();
            row.Cells.Add(cellData);
            cellData.Text = temp[i].ToString();
          }
        }
        row.HorizontalAlign = HorizontalAlign.Center;
        ++count;
      }
      while (e.MoveNext());
    }
    else  //Not databinding, values come from ViewState
    {
      //Add TableRow row as placeholder for
      //header row ViewState
      TableRow headerRow = new TableRow();
      this.Rows.Add(headerRow);
      IEnumerator e = dataSource.GetEnumerator();
      e.MoveNext();
      ++count; //increment since header row handled

      //Add correct number of EnhancedSpreadsheetRows
      //as placeholder for data row ViewState
      EnhancedSpreadsheetRow row;
      while (e.MoveNext())
      {
        row = new EnhancedSpreadsheetRow(count,e.Current,dataBinding);
        row.HorizontalAlign = HorizontalAlign.Center;
        this.Rows.Add(row);
        ++count;
      }
    }
  }
  return count;
}

private void BuildHeaderRow(object dataRow, bool dataBinding)
{
  //Add header row with column names:
  TableRow headerRow = new TableRow();
  this.Rows.Add(headerRow);

  TableCell columnName;
```

```
        if (dataRow is DbDataRecord)
        {
          DbDataRecord temp = (DbDataRecord)dataRow;
          for (int i = 0; i < temp.FieldCount; ++i)
          {
            columnName = new TableCell();
            headerRow.Cells.Add(columnName);
            columnName.Text = temp.GetName(i);
          }
        }

        if (dataRow is DataRowView)
        {
          DataRowView drv = (DataRowView)dataRow;
          for (int i = 0; i < drv.Row.Table.Columns.Count; ++i)
          {
            columnName = new TableCell();
            headerRow.Cells.Add(columnName);
            columnName.Text = drv.Row.Table.Columns[i].Caption;
          }
        }

        headerRow.HorizontalAlign = HorizontalAlign.Center;
        headerRow.BackColor = HeaderRowBackColor;
        headerRow.ForeColor = HeaderRowForeColor;
      }
    }
}
```

Listing 7-15. *The EnhancedSpreadsheetRow Control*

```
using System;
using System.ComponentModel;
using System.Collections.Generic;
using System.Text;
using System.Web.UI;
using System.Web.UI.WebControls;

namespace ControlsBook2Lib.Ch07
{
  public class EnhancedSpreadsheetRow : TableRow, IDataItemContainer
  {
    private object data;
    private int _itemIndex;
```

```
    public EnhancedSpreadsheetRow(int itemIndex, object o, bool dataBinding)
    {
      if (dataBinding)
      {
        data = o;
        _itemIndex = itemIndex;
      }
    }

    public virtual object Data
    {
      get
      {
        return data;
      }
    }

    object IDataItemContainer.DataItem
    {
      get
      {
        return Data;
      }
    }

    int IDataItemContainer.DataItemIndex
    {
      get
      {
        return _itemIndex;
      }
    }

    int IDataItemContainer.DisplayIndex
    {
      get
      {
        return _itemIndex;
      }
    }
  }
}
```

The EnhancedSpreadsheetControl is demonstrated in the EnhancedSpreadsheetControl.aspx web form, shown in Figure 7-12.

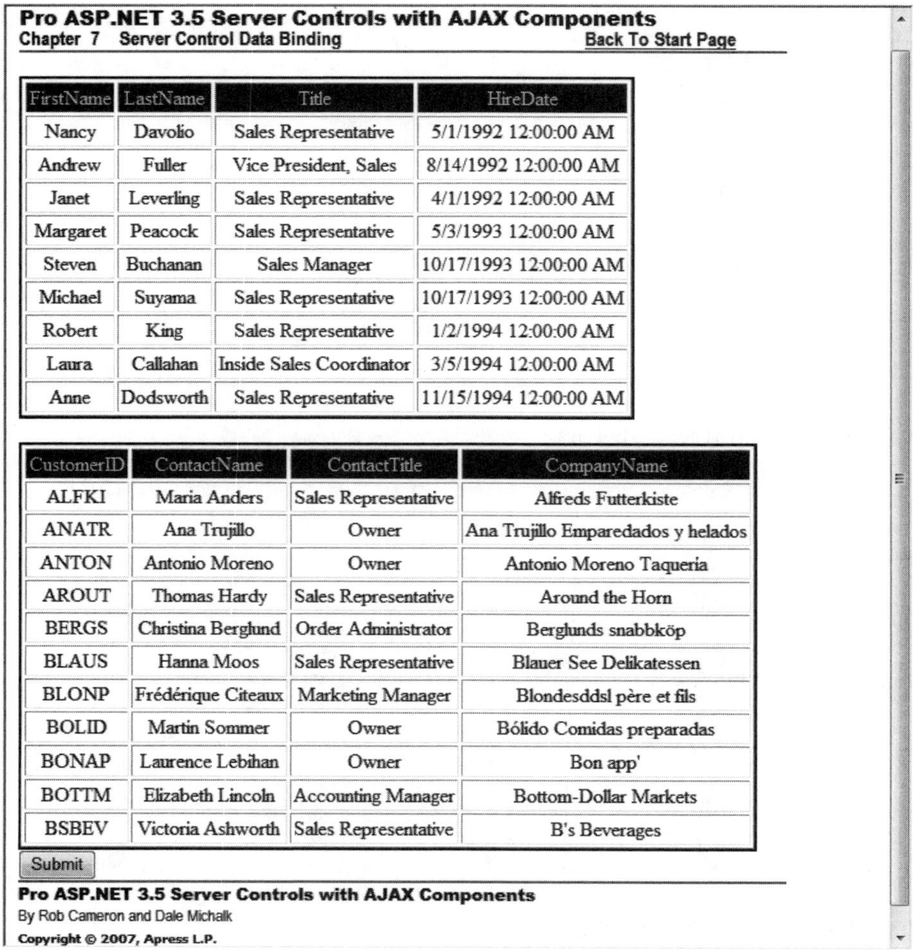

Pro ASP.NET 3.5 Server Controls with AJAX Components
Chapter 7 Server Control Data Binding Back To Start Page

FirstName	LastName	Title	HireDate
Nancy	Davolio	Sales Representative	5/1/1992 12:00:00 AM
Andrew	Fuller	Vice President, Sales	8/14/1992 12:00:00 AM
Janet	Leverling	Sales Representative	4/1/1992 12:00:00 AM
Margaret	Peacock	Sales Representative	5/3/1993 12:00:00 AM
Steven	Buchanan	Sales Manager	10/17/1993 12:00:00 AM
Michael	Suyama	Sales Representative	10/17/1993 12:00:00 AM
Robert	King	Sales Representative	1/2/1994 12:00:00 AM
Laura	Callahan	Inside Sales Coordinator	3/5/1994 12:00:00 AM
Anne	Dodsworth	Sales Representative	11/15/1994 12:00:00 AM

CustomerID	ContactName	ContactTitle	CompanyName
ALFKI	Maria Anders	Sales Representative	Alfreds Futterkiste
ANATR	Ana Trujillo	Owner	Ana Trujillo Emparedados y helados
ANTON	Antonio Moreno	Owner	Antonio Moreno Taqueria
AROUT	Thomas Hardy	Sales Representative	Around the Horn
BERGS	Christina Berglund	Order Administrator	Berglunds snabbköp
BLAUS	Hanna Moos	Sales Representative	Blauer See Delikatessen
BLONP	Frédérique Citeaux	Marketing Manager	Blondesddsl père et fils
BOLID	Martin Sommer	Owner	Bólido Comidas preparadas
BONAP	Laurence Lebihan	Owner	Bon app'
BOTTM	Elizabeth Lincoln	Accounting Manager	Bottom-Dollar Markets
BSBEV	Victoria Ashworth	Sales Representative	B's Beverages

Submit

Pro ASP.NET 3.5 Server Controls with AJAX Components
By Rob Cameron and Dale Michalk
Copyright © 2007, Apress L.P.

Figure 7-12. *The EnhancedSpreadsheetControl demonstration web form*

Listings 7-16 and 7-17 have the code for the EnhancedSpreadSheetControl demonstration web form.

Listing 7-16. *The EnhancedSpreadSheetControl Web Form .aspx File*

```
<%@ Page Language="C#"
MasterPageFile="~/MasterPage/ControlsBook2MasterPage.Master"
  AutoEventWireup="true" CodeBehind="EnhancedSpreadSheetControl.aspx.cs"
Inherits="ControlsBook2Web.Ch07.EnhancedSpreadSheetControl"
  Title="Enhanced Spreadsheet Control Demo" %>
```

```
<%@ Register TagPrefix="apress" Namespace="ControlsBook2Lib.Ch07"
Assembly="ControlsBook2Lib" %>
<asp:Content ID="Content1" ContentPlaceHolderID="ChapterNumAndTitle"
    runat="server">
  <asp:Label ID="ChapterNumberLabel" runat="server"
  Width="14px">7</asp:Label>  <asp:Label
    ID="ChapterTitleLabel" runat="server" Width="360px">
                 Server Control Data Binding</asp:Label>
</asp:Content>
<asp:Content ID="Content2" ContentPlaceHolderID="PrimaryContent" runat="server">
  <br />
  <apress:EnhancedSpreadsheetControl ID="EnhancedSpreadsheetControl1"
        runat="Server"
    DataMember="DefaultView" DataSourceID="SqlDataSource1" BorderWidth="2px"
HeaderRowColor="Gainsboro"
    HeaderRowBackColor="Navy" HeaderRowForeColor="Gold" />
  <asp:SqlDataSource ID="SqlDataSource1" runat="server"
  ConnectionString="<%$ ConnectionStrings:NorthWindDB %>"
    SelectCommand=
        "SELECT [FirstName], [LastName], [Title], [HireDate] FROM [Employees]">
  </asp:SqlDataSource>
  <br />
  <br />
  <apress:EnhancedSpreadsheetControl ID="EnhancedSpreadsheetControl2"
       runat="server"
    BorderWidth="2px" HeaderRowColor="Gainsboro"
    HeaderRowBackColor="Navy" HeaderRowForeColor="Gold" />
  <br />
  <asp:Button ID="Button1" runat="server" Text="Submit" />
  <br />
</asp:Content>
```

Listing 7-17. *The EnhancedSpreadSheetControl Code-Behind Class File*

```
using System;
using System.Data;
using System.Data.SqlClient;
using System.Configuration;
using System.Web.Configuration;

namespace ControlsBook2Web.Ch07
{
  public partial class EnhancedSpreadSheetControl : System.Web.UI.Page
  {
    protected void Page_Load(object sender, EventArgs e)
    {
        EnhancedSpreadsheetControl1.DataBind();
```

```
            SqlDataReader dr = GetCustomerDataReader();
            EnhancedSpreadsheetControl2.DataSource = dr;
            EnhancedSpreadsheetControl2.DataBind();
            dr.Close();
        }

        private SqlDataReader GetCustomerDataReader()
        {
          SqlConnection conn =
             new SqlConnection(WebConfigurationManager.
                     ConnectionStrings["NorthWindDB"].ConnectionString);
          conn.Open();

          SqlCommand cmd =
             new SqlCommand("SELECT CustomerID, ContactName, ContactTitle,
                 CompanyName FROM Customers WHERE CustomerID LIKE '[AB]%'",
             conn);
          SqlDataReader dr = cmd.ExecuteReader(CommandBehavior.CloseConnection);
          return dr;
        }

        private void FillEmployeesDataSet(DataSet ds)
        {
          SqlConnection conn =
             new SqlConnection(WebConfigurationManager.
                      ConnectionStrings["NorthWindDB"].ConnectionString);
          conn.Open();

          SqlDataAdapter da =
             new SqlDataAdapter("SELECT EmployeeID, FirstName, LastName, Title
                    FROM Employees WHERE EmployeeID < 5",
             conn);
          da.Fill(ds, "Employees");
          conn.Close();
        }
    }
}
```

Summary

Data binding simplifies the task of rendering data intermixed with HTML for web developers by rendering a control according to the information in the data source that is bound to the control. Data-bound controls should strive to support a variety of data sources by implementing both IEnumerable and IListSource.

Templates and data binding are the two primary ways to modify the graphical content of an ASP.NET web form. Templates provide a way for developers to declaratively insert raw HTML through server controls into the output of a prebuilt control. Templates can be loaded dynamically through Page.LoadTemplate or instantiated by classes that implement the ITemplate interface. The Repeater control built in this chapter demonstrates how to combine templates with data binding for a rich user experience.

The built-in base classes for data binding such as DataBoundControl inherited by our Repeater and the DataBoundCompositeControl inherited by the EnhancedSpreadsheetControl can greatly simplify data binding tasks.

CHAPTER 8

Integrating Client-Side Script

Software development, like any other engineering discipline, requires trade-offs between competing issues such as browser reach versus platform features, client-side interactivity versus server-side processing and its necessary round-trips, and time required to build versus rich user interactivity. This chapter focuses on how these trade-offs come into play with respect to integrating client-side scripts into your ASP.NET server control development efforts.

Although the .NET Framework provides top-notch support for server-side development through its rich object model, ASP.NET server controls are an excellent way to facilitate development of web applications with a rich client-side UI. ASP.NET provides the means to encapsulate client-side script complexity within the confines of a server control and build a reusable UI widget library that can be consumed by developers building web applications.

In ASP.NET 3.5, AJAX functionality is well integrated into the ASP.NET server control model, which we cover in the next chapter. The functionality enabled by ASP.NET AJAX is based on the capabilities we discuss in this chapter. Also, there may be situations where you want to quickly add scripts to a server control, which we also cover in this chapter.

To start off, we describe the various features that client-side scripting can provide to a web application, and after that, we dive into the details of how to integrate those client-side features into custom server controls.

Client-Side Script Server Control Scenarios

In this chapter, we cover the gamut of client-side features. Here are the highlights of the topics we cover:

- *Handling client-side events:* This script executes when a client activity occurs, such as when the user clicks with the mouse, moves the mouse, or presses a key. You handle these events by adding script code to HTML tag attributes on the page.
- *Handling the* `Page_Load` *event in the browser:* You add this script code to the bottom of an HTML page that executes on page load in the browser. It usually performs initialization tasks.
- *Running scripts when a page form is submitted:* This consists of adding a script to handle verification or validation tasks before posting back to the web server. You accomplish this through JavaScript form submission code or by handling the `onsubmit` event of the `<form>` tag.

- *Integrating client- and server-side events:* This script ensures client-side events and data are appropriately mapped to server-side code operations when the form is posted back to the web server.
- *Using the web resource system introduced in ASP.NET 2.0 for managing content:* This allows scripts and other file resources to be compiled into an assembly. Script and file resources can then be rendered from the web server via the `WebResource.axd` handler without the extra deployment step of copying loose file content.
- *Using ASP.NET 2.0 (or later) client callbacks:* A new feature introduced in ASP.NET 2.0 provides a structured way for client-side scripts to invoke server-side functionality to retrieve data or content from the server without executing a full-page postback and refresh of the HTML page in the browser.

We feel the best way to cover these client-side script scenarios is to develop a set of server controls that demonstrates the listed capabilities. The controls we build in this chapter include an image control that performs client-side image mouse rollovers, a control that confirms the user's action when clicking a link button, and an up/down numeric control similar to its desktop cousin that can work with or without JavaScript support. In the last example, we show how to use client callbacks as part of a server control that fetches data from an MSN Money stock news feed without requiring a postback when the requested stock symbol is changed by the user.

Handling Client-Side Events

The web browser has its own object model representing the HTML tags and events that occur when the user is interacting with them. This event system within the browser has been around for a while and is completely different from the server-side event mechanism we discussed in detail in Chapter 5.

Client-side events fired in the browser window are added to HTML tags via attributes with names such as `onclick`, `onblur`, `onmouseover`, `onmouseout`, and so on. The value of the event-handling attribute contains the script that you want to execute when the event is raised. The following HTML snippet shows a `<SPAN>` tag with an inline `onclick` event handler that pops up an alert message box:

```
<span id="TopLabel" tabindex="1" onclick="alert('TopLabel clicked!');">
TopLabel</span>
```

The browser is perfectly happy to execute this JavaScript when the `<span>` tag is clicked. The first server control example demonstrates how to add script code to an ASP.NET server control to handle a client-side click event like the previous one. As an ASP.NET developer, you have two options available to add the `onclick` event code to the server control:

- You can add it declaratively via an attribute on the control's tag in the `.aspx` page.
- You can add it programmatically to the `Attributes` collection of the server control in the code-behind class.

Adding the code to the `.aspx` page is the simpler of the two options. Another way to add a client-side click event handler is to encapsulate the script into a server control. The following code shows how to generate the `<span>` content with an `onclick` event handler using an ASP.NET

Label server control and adding an onclick attribute. The page parser is responsible for ensuring this becomes part of the control's final output.

```
<asp:Label ID="TopLabel" Runat="server" Text="TopLabel"
tabIndex=1 onclick="alert('TopLabel clicked!');">TopLabel</asp:Label>
```

The following code shows the second option: adding the attribute to the HTML element via the Attributes collection of the server control in the code-behind class. The recommended place to put this type of code is in the Page_Load event because the control is fully initialized.

```
BottomLabel.Attributes.Add("onclick", "alert('BottomLabel clicked!');");
```

The two preceding techniques add the client-side script code via external manipulation of the server control. You can add the same attribute-handling code internally to a server control just as easily. Listing 8-1 shows a server control that inherits from the ASP.NET Label control and adds code to an override of the OnPreRender method that generates an onclick attribute to the final output of our new custom Label control, ClickLabel.

Listing 8-1. *The ClickLabel Server Control*

```
using System;
using System.Web.UI;
using System.Web.UI.WebControls;
using System.ComponentModel;

namespace ControlsBook2Lib.Ch08
{
  [ToolboxData("<{0}:ClickLabel runat=server></{0}:ClickLabel>"),
  DefaultProperty("ClickText")]
  public class ClickLabel : Label
  {
    public virtual string ClickText
    {
      get
      {
        return (string)ViewState["ClickText"];
      }
      set
      {
        ViewState["ClickText"] = value;
      }
    }

    protected override void OnPreRender(EventArgs e)
    {
      base.OnPreRender(e);

      // Add the onclick client-side event handler to
      // display a JavaScript alert box
```

```
      Attributes.Add("onclick", "alert('" + ClickText + "');");
    }
  }
}
```

This ensures that the control's `Attributes` collection is loaded before the `Render` method is called. A `ClickText` property is provided to make the control easily configurable as to what text message displays in the JavaScript alert pop-up. Though this is a trivial example, it does demonstrate one way to make client-side script capabilities available through a server control to the developer/user without the developer having to know how to write the JavaScript. In the next section, we present a web form that demonstrates these options.

The Click Web Form

The following Click web form example demonstrates all three techniques for emitting client-side event handlers. The web form renders with three `Label` controls that all generate the same JavaScript alert pop-up when clicked. The following HTML code shows the `<span>` tags and their inline client-side JavaScript:

```
<span id="TopLabel" onclick="alert('TopLabel clicked!');">Click the TopLabel</span>
<br>
<span id="MiddleLabel" onclick="alert('MiddleLabel clicked!');">
Click the MiddleLabel</span>
<br>
<span id="BottomLabel" onclick="alert('BottomLabel clicked!');">
Click the BottomLabel</span>
```

Figure 8-1 shows what happens when the middle `ClickLabel` text output is clicked.

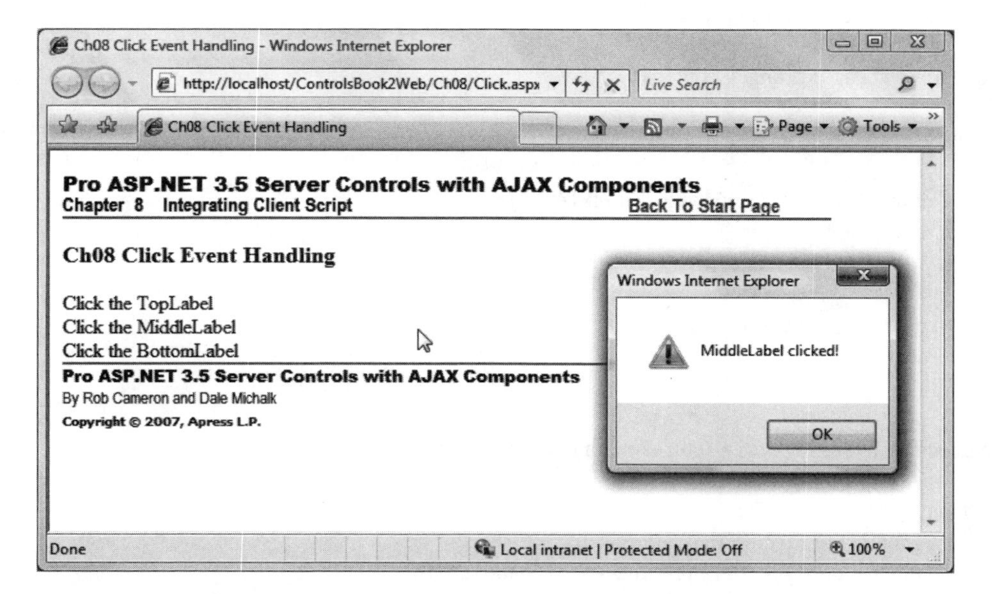

Figure 8-1. *The Click web form after the middle label is clicked*

The full code for the web form is shown in Listings 8-2 and 8-3.

Listing 8-2. *The Click Web Form .aspx Page File*

```
<%@ Page Language="C#"
MasterPageFile="~/MasterPage/ControlsBook2MasterPage.Master"
  AutoEventWireup="true" CodeBehind="Click.aspx.cs"
Inherits="ControlsBook2Web.Ch08.Click"  Title="Click Demo" %>

<%@ Register Assembly="ControlsBook2Lib" Namespace=
             "ControlsBook2Lib.Ch08" TagPrefix="apress" %>
<asp:Content ID="Content1" ContentPlaceHolderID=
             "ChapterNumAndTitle" runat="server">
  <asp:Label ID="ChapterNumberLabel" runat="server"
Width="14px">8</asp:Label>  <asp:Label
    ID="ChapterTitleLabel" runat="server" Width="360px">
                      Integrating Client-Side Script</asp:Label>
</asp:Content>
<asp:Content ID="Content2" ContentPlaceHolderID="PrimaryContent" runat="server">
  <h3>
    Ch08 Click Event Handling</h3>
  <asp:Label ID="TopLabel" runat="server" Text=
                "Click the TopLabel" onclick="alert('TopLabel clicked!');" />
  <br />
  <apress:ClickLabel ID="ClickLabel1" runat="server" Text=
                  "Click the MiddleLabel" ClickText="MiddleLabel clicked!" />
  <br />
  <asp:Label ID="BottomLabel" runat="server" Text="Click the BottomLabel" />
</asp:Content>
```

Listing 8-3. *The Click Web Form Code-Behind Class File*

```
using System;
using System.Collections.Generic;
using System.Web.UI;

namespace ControlsBook2Web.Ch08
{
  public partial class Click : System.Web.UI.Page
  {
    protected void Page_Load(object sender, EventArgs e)
    {
      BottomLabel.Attributes.Add("onclick",
             "alert('BottomLabel clicked!');");
    }
  }
}
```

Controls such as Button, LinkButton, and ImageButton have additional support for click handling that goes beyond the preceding sample. The OnClientClick attribute can be set on these controls in either the .aspx page or in the code-behind class as a property to achieve the same effect that we showed with the Label controls.

Now that we have introduced how to add client-side script to a server control, we move on to a more interesting example of providing image rollovers within a server control by integrating client-side scripts.

Handling Mouse Events for Image Rollovers

Although the ASP.NET Image control makes it easy to assign image URL information through its Designer property support, its distinct lack of rich functionality provides ample room for improvement. A nice extension to this control would be the capability to perform client-side image mouse rollovers. As we demonstrate in Chapter 3 with the TextBox3d control, the object-oriented nature of ASP.NET makes it easy to take existing controls and inherit from them to add additional features. RolloverImageLink is a server control that we build next that inherits the full feature set of the ASP.NET Image server control while adding client-side rollover capability and hyperlink navigation.

As shown in the following code, RolloverImageLink adds an OverImageUrl property that stores the location of the rollover image file and a NavigationalUrl property that stores the hyperlink location. The EnableClientScript property allows the user to turn on or off the client JavaScript functionality on demand.

```
[ToolboxData("<{0}:RolloverImageLink runat=server></{0}:RolloverImageLink>"),
DefaultProperty("NavigateUrl")]
public class RolloverImageLink : Image
{
   public virtual bool EnableClientScript
   {
      get
      {
         object script = ViewState["EnableClientScript"];
         return (script == null) ? true : (bool) script;
      }
      set
      {
         ViewState["EnableClientScript"] = value;
      }
   }

   public string NavigateUrl
   {
      get
      {
         object url = ViewState["NavigateUrl"];
         return (url == null) ? "" : (string) url;
      }
```

```
      set
      {
         ViewState["NavigateUrl"] = value;
      }
   }

   public string OverImageUrl
   {
      get
      {
         object url = ViewState["OverImageUrl"];
         return (url == null) ? "" : (string) url;
      }
      set
      {
         ViewState["OverImageUrl"] = value;
      }
   }

   public bool PreLoadImages
   {
      get
      {
         object pre = ViewState["PreLoadImages"];
         return (pre == null) ? true : (bool) pre;
      }
      set
      {
         ViewState["PreLoadImages"] = value;
      }
   }
```

RolloverImageLink also supports preloading the images pointed to by the ImageUrl and OverImageUrl properties, so you don't have to write the time-consuming JavaScript that makes the rollover effect much more responsive in the browser. If the user sets the PreLoadImages property of the control to true, this generates extra JavaScript that loads the images when the page is loaded into the browser.

JavaScript Detection

The RolloverImageLink control is a good citizen in that it detects the browser support for JavaScript before it generates the client script to render the rollover images. The DetermineRenderClientScript method encapsulates the verification logic and sets a private bool named renderClientScript, depending on the outcome:

```
private bool renderClientScript = false;
protected void DetermineRenderClientScript()
{
   if (EnableClientScript &&
      Context.Request.Browser. EcmaScriptVersion.Major >=1)
      renderClientScript = true;
}
```

The JavaScript capability is checked by examining an instance of the HttpBrowserCapabilities class that is taken from the Browser property of the current request context. For now, all we use is the EcmaScriptVersion property, but there are a variety of other detection-specific attributes one can use to tailor the output of a server control if desired, and these can be found in the documentation for the class.

Rendering Client Script Code

RolloverImageLink takes advantage of most of the features built into ASP.NET via the ClientScriptManager class that is attached to the Page class as a static ClientScript property for emitting JavaScript into the HTML output in a modular manner. This capability includes a registration system that ensures only a single instance of a block of script code is emitted in the final HTML output, despite the presence of multiple instances of a server control that need it on a web form. The ClientScriptManager replaces the now-obsolete methods that hang off the Page class directly as static methods and consolidates client interaction in one class. Table 8-1 summarizes the script-related feature set of ClientScriptManager.

Table 8-1. *ASP.NET ClientScriptManager Class Script Registration Methods*

Method	Description
RegisterClientScriptBlock	Emits the specified JavaScript code at the top of the HTML form to allow all of the controls on the page rendered after it to reference it.
IsClientScriptBlockRegistered	Checks to see if a previous control has registered a JavaScript block at the top of the HTML form.
RegisterStartupScript	Emits the specified JavaScript code at the bottom of the HTML form to be able to access any of the controls on the web form from the script block.
IsStartupScriptRegistered	Checks to see if a previous control has registered a start-up JavaScript block at the bottom of the HTML form.
RegisterArrayDeclaration	Emits an array value to the specified JavaScript array name at the bottom of the HTML form. This method can be called repeatedly from multiple controls. The values are aggregated in the same array.
RegisterOnSubmitStatement	Emits JavaScript code that is executed in the context of an onsubmit event handler on the HTML <form> element.
IsOnSubmitStatementRegistered	Checks to see if a previous control has registered an onsubmit event handler on the HTML <form> element.

Table 8-1. *ASP.NET ClientScriptManager Class Script Registration Methods*

Method	Description
`RegisterClientScriptInclude`	Emits a JavaScript script block that includes the script file specified in a URL parameter in the function.
`IsClientScriptIncludeRegistered`	Checks to see if a previous control has registered to emit a similar script block include for a script file.
`RegisterClientScriptResource`	Emits a JavaScript script block that includes script content from compiled resources inside an assembly served via the `WebResource.axd` HTTP handler.
`GetWebResourceUrl`	Provides a URL with content from compiled resources inside an assembly served via the `WebResource.axd` HTTP handler.
`GetPostBackEventReference`	Emits a JavaScript that allows a control to initiate a postback to the server.
`GetCallbackEventReference`	Emits a JavaScript that allows a client-side script to initiate an out-of- band call to the server to retrieve data or content without requiring a full postback of the browser page.

The bulk of the JavaScript creation occurs in the `OnPreRender` method of the `RolloverImageLink` control:

```
protected override void OnPreRender(EventArgs e)
{
    base.OnPreRender(e);

     DetermineRenderClientScript();

    if (renderClientScript)
    {
        // register the image-swapping JavaScript
        // if it is not already registered
        if (!Page.ClientScript.IsClientScriptBlockRegistered(
            typeof(RolloverImageLink),"SWAP_SCRIPT"))
        {
            Page.ClientScript.RegisterClientScriptBlock(
                typeof(RolloverImageLink),
               "SWAP_SCRIPT",
               SWAP_SCRIPT,
               true);
        }

        if (this.PreLoadImages)
        {
            // add image names to the
            // array of rollover images to be preloaded
```

```
            Page.ClientScript.RegisterArrayDeclaration(
                SWAP_ARRAY,
               "'" + ResolveUrl(this.ImageUrl) + "'," +
               "'" + ResolveUrl(this.OverImageUrl) + "'");

            // register the image, preloading JavaScript
            // if it is not already registered
            if (!Page.ClientScript.IsStartupScriptRegistered(
                typeof(RolloverImageLink),"PRELOAD_SCRIPT"))
            {
                Page.ClientScript.RegisterStartupScript(
                   typeof(RolloverImageLink),
                   "PRELOAD_SCRIPT",
                   PRELOAD_SCRIPT.Replace("{arrayname}", SWAP_ARRAY),
                   true);
            }
        }
    }
}
```

The first client script feature we use in RolloverImageLink is the capability to render a script function that swaps the images for rollover effect at the top of the HTML document. The server control code uses the ClientScriptManager method RegisterClientScriptBlock in conjunction with the constant string named SWAP_SCRIPT, as shown in the following code. This string constant uses the "at" symbol (@) to enable verbatim strings that allow for easy formatting and maintenance inside the server control. Before we register the client script, we check to see if the script block has already been registered by another instance of the control on the page with a call to IsClientScriptBlockRegistered. Note that if we were to call RegisterClientScript twice, the content of the second invocation would replace the script generated by the first call.

```
protected const string SWAP_SCRIPT = @"
function __Image_Swap(sName, sSrc)
{
document.images[sName].src = sSrc;
}
";
```

RegisterClientScriptBlock takes four parameters: a type definition that scopes the script registration on a Page, a unique ID that identifies the script block for that Type, the string value of the script to be emitted, and a Boolean value that tells the control system to include enclosing <script> tags around the script content.

If we are preloading the images, we register the necessary information using a data-oriented approach to the script processing. We can easily do this—ASP.NET makes it simple to emit JavaScript arrays. The RegisterArrayDeclaration method of the Page object allows us to add all the image names to the HTML document as an array that our PRELOAD_SCRIPT script block can iterate over when loading images. Unlike the swap script function, this script is emitted near the end of the document.

The image preloading script comes from a constant string like the one for swapping images. It is a little different because it has a placeholder, {arrayname}, for the array that is emitted into the output:

```
protected const string PRELOAD_SCRIPT = @"
for (index = 0; index < {arrayname}; index++)
{
loadimg = new Image();
loadimg.src = {arrayname}[index];
}
";
```

The OnPreRender code replaces the array name correctly from the script template and passes it to the RegisterStartupScript method of the Page class. This will emit it at the very bottom of the HTML form, after any registered JavaScript arrays. Of course, we also check to see if the script was registered by a previous control with a call to IsStartupScriptRegistered provided by the Page class.

Rendering the HTML Code

The RolloverImageLink control overrides the rendering process of the inherited image control so that it can add the hyperlink and JavaScript code. The main task is to wrap the <img> tag generation process of the base Image control with an enclosing <a> tag.

■ **Note** Because generating the link (<a> tag) is an HTML operation, it is not affected by the value of the EnableClientScript property on the server control. This functionality is present on the server regardless of JavaScript capabilities.

Before we do this, we call the Page method named VerifyRenderingInServerForm, as shown in the following code. This method raises an exception if the control is not rendering within the confines of a <form runat="server"> tag required for the web form environment. It is a good habit to put this call into the Render phase of a control, especially if the control is emitting client-side script that performs a postback to the web server.

```
protected override void Render(HtmlTextWriter writer)
{
   // ensure the control is used inside <form runat="server">
   Page.VerifyRenderingInServerForm(this);

   // set up attributes for the enclosing hyperlink
   // <a href></a> tag pair that go around the <img> tag
   writer.AddAttribute("href",this.NavigateUrl);
```

```
    // we have to create an ID for the <a> tag so that it
    // doesn't conflict with the <img> tag generated by
    // the base Image control
    writer.AddAttribute("name",this.UniqueID + "_href");

    // emit onmouseover/onmouseout attributes that handle
    // client events and invoke our image-swapping JavaScript
    // code if client supports it
    if (renderClientScript)
    {
       writer.AddAttribute("onmouseover",
          SWAP_FUNC + "('" + this.UniqueID + "','" +
          ResolveUrl(this.OverImageUrl) + "');");
       writer.AddAttribute("onmouseout",
          SWAP_FUNC + "('" + this.UniqueID + "','" +
          ResolveUrl(this.ImageUrl) + "');");

    }
    writer.RenderBeginTag(HtmlTextWriterTag.A);

    // use name attribute to identify HTML <img> element
    // for older browsers
    writer.AddAttribute("name",this.UniqueID);

    base.Render(writer);

    writer.RenderEndTag();
}
```

The first section of our Render override adds attributes to help generate the <a> hyperlink, including the href attribute that is linked to NavigateUrl. Notice that we create a unique name attribute for the <a> tag to prevent any naming conflicts with other tags on the page, including a potential conflict with the <img> tag of the inherited Image control.

The next step in working with the <a> tag is to add the onmouseover and onmouseout event-handling attributes. Render puts values in the attributes to call the image-swapping JavaScript function. This is done using the SWAP_FUNC constant that points to the actual JavaScript function name. After the <a> tag attributes are added to the HtmlTextWriter stream, we render the beginning <a> tag.

The next step is to prepare for the base Image class to render the <img> tag. To make the script friendlier to browsers that favor the name attribute in JavaScript, we add a name attribute to the HtmlTextWriter stream before we call on the base Image class's Render method. The RolloverImageLink override of Render ends by emitting the closing </a> tag.

At this point, the control is fully implemented, as shown in Listing 8-4.

Listing 8-4. *The RolloverImageLink Server Control*

```
using System;
using System.Web.UI;
using System.Web.UI.WebControls;
using System.ComponentModel;

namespace ControlsBook2Lib.Ch08
{
  [ToolboxData("<{0}:RolloverImageLink runat=server></{0}:RolloverImageLink>"),
  DefaultProperty("NavigateUrl")]
  public class RolloverImageLink : Image
  {
    public virtual bool EnableClientScript
    {
      get
      {
        object script = ViewState["EnableClientScript"];
        return (script == null) ? true : (bool)script;
      }
      set
      {
        ViewState["EnableClientScript"] = value;
      }
    }

    public string NavigateUrl
    {
      get
      {
        object url = ViewState["NavigateUrl"];
        return (url == null) ? "" : (string)url;
      }
      set
      {
        ViewState["NavigateUrl"] = value;
      }
    }

    public string OverImageUrl
    {
      get
      {
        object url = ViewState["OverImageUrl"];
        return (url == null) ? "" : (string)url;
      }
```

```
    set
    {
      ViewState["OverImageUrl"] = value;
    }
  }

  public bool PreLoadImages
  {
    get
    {
      object pre = ViewState["PreLoadImages"];
      return (pre == null) ? true : (bool)pre;
    }
    set
    {
      ViewState["PreLoadImages"] = value;
    }
  }

  protected const string SWAP_FUNC = "__Image_Swap";
  protected const string SWAP_ARRAY = "__Image_Swap_Array";

  //@ symbol in front of the string preserves the layout of the string content
  protected const string SWAP_SCRIPT = @"
        function __Image_Swap(sName, sSrc)
        {
          document.images[sName].src = sSrc;
        }
        ";

  protected const string PRELOAD_SCRIPT = @"
        for (index = 0; index < {arrayname}; index++)
        {
          loadimg = new Image();
          loadimg.src = {arrayname}[index];
        }
        ";

  private bool renderClientScript = false;
  protected void DetermineRenderClientScript()
  {
    if (EnableClientScript &&
       Context.Request.Browser.EcmaScriptVersion.Major >= 1)
      renderClientScript = true;
  }
```

```
protected override void OnPreRender(EventArgs e)
{
  base.OnPreRender(e);

  DetermineRenderClientScript();

  if (renderClientScript)
  {
    // register the image-swapping JavaScript
    // if it is not already registered
    if (!Page.ClientScript.IsClientScriptBlockRegistered(
        typeof(RolloverImageLink), "SWAP_SCRIPT"))
    {
      Page.ClientScript.RegisterClientScriptBlock(
          typeof(RolloverImageLink),
         "SWAP_SCRIPT",
         SWAP_SCRIPT,
         true);
    }

    if (this.PreLoadImages)
    {
      // add image names to the
      // array of rollover images to be preloaded
      Page.ClientScript.RegisterArrayDeclaration(
          SWAP_ARRAY,
         "'" + ResolveUrl(this.ImageUrl) + "'," +
         "'" + ResolveUrl(this.OverImageUrl) + "'");

      // register the image, preloading JavaScript
      // if it is not already registered
      if (!Page.ClientScript.IsStartupScriptRegistered(
          typeof(RolloverImageLink), "PRELOAD_SCRIPT"))
      {
        Page.ClientScript.RegisterStartupScript(
           typeof(RolloverImageLink),
           "PRELOAD_SCRIPT",
           PRELOAD_SCRIPT.Replace("{arrayname}", SWAP_ARRAY),
           true);
      }
    }
  }
}
```

```
    protected override void Render(HtmlTextWriter writer)
    {
      // ensure the control is used inside <form runat="server">
      Page.VerifyRenderingInServerForm(this);

      // set up attributes for the enclosing hyperlink
      // <a href></a> tag pair that go around the <img> tag
      writer.AddAttribute("href", this.NavigateUrl);

      // we have to create an ID for the <a> tag so that it
      // doesn't conflict with the <img> tag generated by
      // the base Image control
      writer.AddAttribute("name", this.UniqueID + "_href");

      // emit onmouseover/onmouseout attributes that handle
      // client events and invoke our image-swapping JavaScript
      // code if client supports it
      if (renderClientScript)
      {
        writer.AddAttribute("onmouseover",
           SWAP_FUNC + "('" + this.UniqueID + "','" +
           ResolveUrl(this.OverImageUrl) + "');");
        writer.AddAttribute("onmouseout",
           SWAP_FUNC + "('" + this.UniqueID + "','" +
           ResolveUrl(this.ImageUrl) + "');");
      }
      writer.RenderBeginTag(HtmlTextWriterTag.A);

      // use name attribute to identify HTML <img> element
      // for older browsers
      writer.AddAttribute("name", this.UniqueID);

      base.Render(writer);

      writer.RenderEndTag();
    }
  }
}
```

The RolloverImage Web Form

The RolloverImage web form demonstrates the RolloverImageLink server control by adding two controls linked to large numeric images (1 and 2), as shown in Figure 8-2.

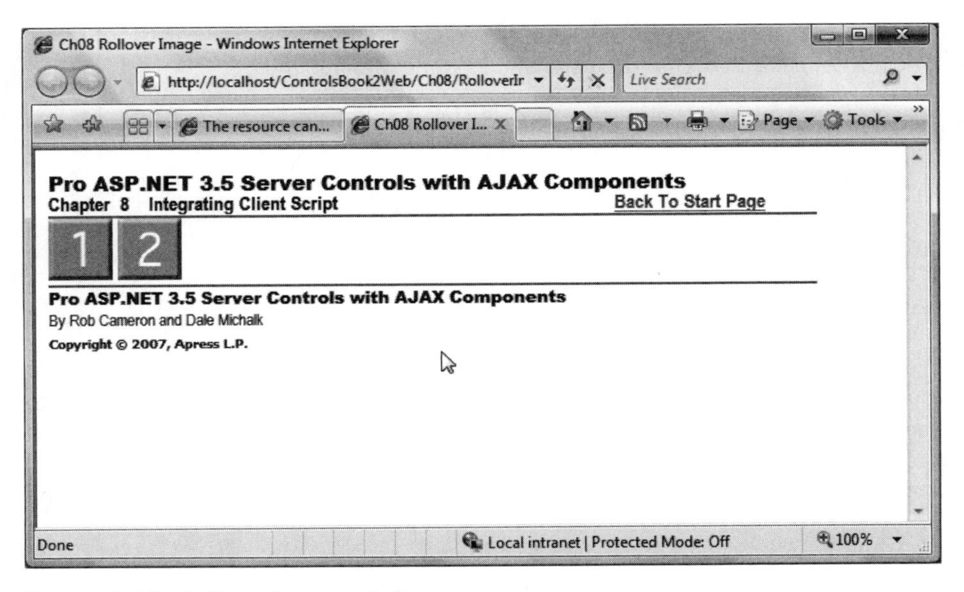

Figure 8-2. *The RolloverImage web form*

When you hover over a button with the mouse, the image changes to a pushed down version, providing the nice effect shown in Figure 8-3.

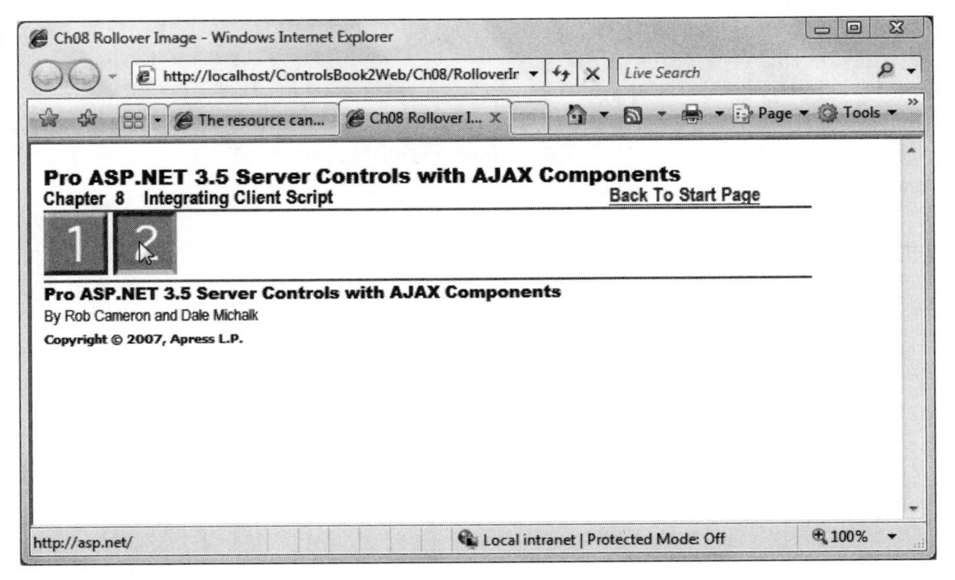

Figure 8-3. *The RolloverImage web form on rollover*

If you click an image, the page will navigate either to the publisher's site or to the ASP.NET web site. The full code for the web form is shown in Listings 8-5 and 8-6.

Listing 8-5. *The RolloverImage Web Form .aspx Page File*

```
<%@ Page Language="C#"
MasterPageFile="~/MasterPage/ControlsBook2MasterPage.Master"
  AutoEventWireup="true" CodeBehind="RolloverImage.aspx.cs"
Inherits="ControlsBook2Web.Ch08.RolloverImage"
  Title="RolloverImage Demo" %>

<%@ Register Assembly="ControlsBook2Lib" Namespace=
                                        "ControlsBook2Lib.Ch08" TagPrefix="apress" %>
<asp:Content ID="Content1" ContentPlaceHolderID="HeadSection" runat="server">
</asp:Content>
<asp:Content ID="Content2" ContentPlaceHolderID="ChapterNumAndTitle"
               runat="server">
  <asp:Label ID="ChapterNumberLabel" runat="server"
  Width="14px">8</asp:Label>  <asp:Label
    ID="ChapterTitleLabel" runat="server" Width="360px">
                      Integrating Client-Side Script</asp:Label>
</asp:Content>
<asp:Content ID="Content3" ContentPlaceHolderID="PrimaryContent" runat="server">
  <apress:RolloverImageLink ID="image1" runat="server"
  ImageUrl="ex1.gif" OverImageUrl="ex1_selected.gif"
    NavigateUrl="http://www.apress.com" />
  <apress:RolloverImageLink ID="image2" runat="server" ImageUrl="ex2.gif"
       OverImageUrl="ex2_selected.gif"
       NavigateUrl="http://asp.net" EnableClientScript="True" /><br />
</asp:Content>
```

Listing 8-6. *The RolloverImage Web Form Code-Behind Class File*

```
using System;

namespace ControlsBook2Web.Ch08
{
  public partial class RolloverImage : System.Web.UI.Page
  {
    protected void Page_Load(object sender, EventArgs e)
    {

    }
  }
}
```

Analyzing the Rollover HTML Output

The rollover functionality lives in the emitted hyperlink tags in the HTML output. The top of the HTML form also contains the image-swapping function called by the onmouseover and onmouseout client event handlers attached to the hyperlinks, as shown here:

```
<script type="text/javascript">
<!--

          function __Image_Swap(sName, sSrc)
          {
            document.images[sName].src = sSrc;
          }
          // -->
</script>
```

The Image control output shows the <img> tags wrapped by an <a> tag and the client-script event mappings for onmouseover and onmouseout:

```
<a href="http://www.apress.com" name="ctl00$ControlsBookContent$image1_href"
onmouseover="__Image_Swap('ctl00$ControlsBookContent$image1',
'/ControlsBook2Web/Ch08/ex1_selected.gif');" onmouseout=
"__Image_Swap('ctl00$ControlsBookContent$image1',
'/ControlsBook2Web/Ch08/ex1.gif');"><img name="ctl00$ControlsBookContent$image1"
id="ctl00_ControlsBookContent_image1" src="ex1.gif" style="border-width:0px;" /></a>
<a href="http://asp.net" name="ctl00$ControlsBookContent$image2_href"
onmouseover="__Image_Swap('ctl00$ControlsBookContent$image2',
     '/ControlsBook2Web/Ch08/ex2_selected.gif');" onmouseout=
     "__Image_Swap('ctl00$ControlsBookContent$image2',
     '/ControlsBook2Web/Ch08/ex2.gif');"><img name=
     "ctl00$ControlsBookContent$image2"
id="ctl00_ControlsBookContent_image2" src="ex2.gif" style="border-width:0px;" /></a>
```

At the bottom of the HTML document is the code to preload the images. It creates the Image JavaScript object and sets the src attribute to complete its task. One script block is emitted for each control to initialize its images:

```
<script type="text/javascript">
<!--
var __Image_Swap_Array =  new Array('/ControlsBook2Web/Ch08/ex1.gif','/
ControlsBook2Web/Ch08/ex1_selected.gif',
'/ControlsBook2Web/Ch08/ex2.gif',
'/ControlsBook2Web/Ch08/ex2_selected.gif');
// -->
</script>
<script type="text/javascript">
<!--
```

```
          for (index = 0; index < __Image_Swap_Array; index++)
          {
            loadimg = new Image();
            loadimg.src = __Image_Swap_Array[index];
          }
// -->
</script>
```

Running a Client Script When a Form Is Submitted

The previous section showed how to run client script at load time of the HTML document via the `RegisterStartupScript` method in the `ClientScriptManager` class. In this section, we discuss how to execute a client script just after postback is initiated by the end user, whether through a button click or through a JavaScript-based method. We create two custom server controls to assist in presenting the concepts required to execute client script when a form is submitted. The first server control we discuss is the `FormConfirmation` control.

The FormConfirmation Control

`FormConfirmation` is a server control designed to display a message when the browser is ready to submit the HTML document back to the web server. We inherit from `System.Web.UI.Control`, because we do not have a UI to display and, therefore, do not need the styling and device-rendering features of `System.Web.UI.WebControls.WebControl`.

Listing 8-7 provides the source code for the `FormConfirmation` server control. ASP.NET allows you to add code to the `onsubmit` event attribute of the `<form>` tag generated by the web form via the `RegisterOnSubmitStatement` method in the `ClientScriptManager` class. This hooks into the normal HTTP posting mechanism, as we describe in Chapter 5.

Listing 8-7. *The FormConfirmation Server Control*

```
using System;
using System.Web;
using System.Web.UI;
using System.ComponentModel;

namespace ControlsBook2Lib.Ch08
{
  [ToolboxData("<{0}:FormConfirmation runat=server></{0}:FormConfirmation>"),
  DefaultProperty("Message")]
  public class FormConfirmation : Control
  {
    public virtual string Message
    {
      get
      {
        return (string)ViewState["Message"];
      }
```

```
      set
      {
        ViewState["Message"] = value;
      }
    }

    protected override void OnPreRender(EventArgs e)
    {
      if (Context.Request.Browser.EcmaScriptVersion.Major >= 1)
      {
        string script = "return (confirm('" + this.Message + "'));";

        // register JavaScript code for onsubmit event
        // of the HTML <form> element
        Page.ClientScript.RegisterOnSubmitStatement(typeof(FormConfirmation),
            "FormConfirmation", script);
      }
    }

    protected override void Render(HtmlTextWriter writer)
    {
      // make sure the control is rendered inside
      // <form runat=server> tags
      Page.VerifyRenderingInServerForm(this);

      base.Render(writer);
    }
  }
}
```

FormConfirmation exposes a Message property to allow web developers to customize the JavaScript confirmation prompt to the end user. This simple control takes advantage of the ClientScriptManager class's RegisterOnSubmitStatement method we described previously to properly inject the script into the HTML stream loaded in the browser. Just drop the control on a web form, and voilà! You can confirm that the user is ready to proceed with submitting the form back to the server. If the user does not affirm the form submission, the script cancels the action by returning false. The other item to highlight for this control is the Render override for the purposes of ensuring the control is located inside a web form via the Page class's VerifyRenderingInServerForm method.

In the next section, we discuss an interesting variation on this theme of confirming navigation away from a page by adding the capability of checking whether a user wants to move on to a new page or stay on the current web form.

The ConfirmedLinkButton Control

The ConfirmedLinkButton button prompts with a custom message that will not navigate if the user cancels the action. ConfirmedLinkButton does not use the RegisterOnSubmitStatement of the ClientScriptManager class; rather, it uses the client-side postback system of ASP.NET.

We use this control on a web form in conjunction with the previously created FormConfirmation control to show how the two mechanisms interact.

The source code for the ConfirmedLinkButton server control is provided in Listing 8-8. ConfirmedLinkButton exposes a Message property like FormConfirmation, but it differs in that it inherits from the LinkButton control. LinkButton renders as a hyperlink but submits the web form via JavaScript.

Listing 8-8. *The ConfirmedLinkButton Server Control*

```
using System;
using System.Web;
using System.Web.UI;
using System.Web.UI.WebControls;
using System.Text;
using System.ComponentModel;

namespace ControlsBook2Lib.Ch08
{
  [ToolboxData("<{0}:ConfirmedLinkButton runat=server></{0}:ConfirmedLinkButton>"),
  DefaultProperty("Message")]
  public class ConfirmedLinkButton : LinkButton
  {
    private string message = "";
    public virtual string Message
    {
      get { return message; }
      set { message = value; }
    }

    protected override void AddAttributesToRender(HtmlTextWriter writer)
    {
      // enhance the LinkButton by replacing its
      // href attribute while leaving the rest of the
      // rendering process to the base class
      if (Context != null && Context.Request.Browser.EcmaScriptVersion.Major >= 1 &&
        this.Message != "")
      {
        StringBuilder script = new StringBuilder();
        script.Append("javascript: if (confirm('");
        script.Append(this.Message);
        script.Append("')) {");
        // get the ASP.NET JavaScript that does a form
        // postback and have this control submit it
        script.Append(Page.ClientScript.GetPostBackEventReference(this, ""));
        script.Append("}");
        writer.AddAttribute(HtmlTextWriterAttribute.Href,
           script.ToString());
```

```
            }
        }
    }
}
```

We override the AddAttributesToRender method so that we can change the normal href attribute content to add a call to the JavaScript confirm method instead. Because we override the href attribute, we use the GetPostBackEventReference method to set up postback; otherwise, the form submission mechanism will not fire. GetPostBackEventReference obtains a reference to a client-side script function that causes the server to post back to the page.

Because this control is inheriting from an existing WebControl, we do not need to call Page.VerifyRenderingInServerForm, because this call is already performed by the base class implementation of LinkButton. In the next section, we test the behavior of the ConfirmedLinkButton and FormConfirmation server controls in the Confirm web form demonstration .aspx page.

The Confirm Web Form

The interaction between the client form submission event and the code emitted by controls to perform JavaScript postbacks for ASP.NET is not as integrated as we would like. The core problem is that the onsubmit client event is not fired if the HTML form is submitted programmatically via JavaScript. To demonstrate the need for better integration, the Confirm web form hosts a set of form posting controls.

On the Confirm web form are a regular ASP.NET Button that does a traditional HTML form post and an ASP.NET LinkButton that uses JavaScript from ASP.NET to cause a postback. We also have our FormConfirmation and ConfirmedLinkButton server controls to show how they provide confirmation on form submit in their own unique manner. Figure 8-4 shows the static web form display output.

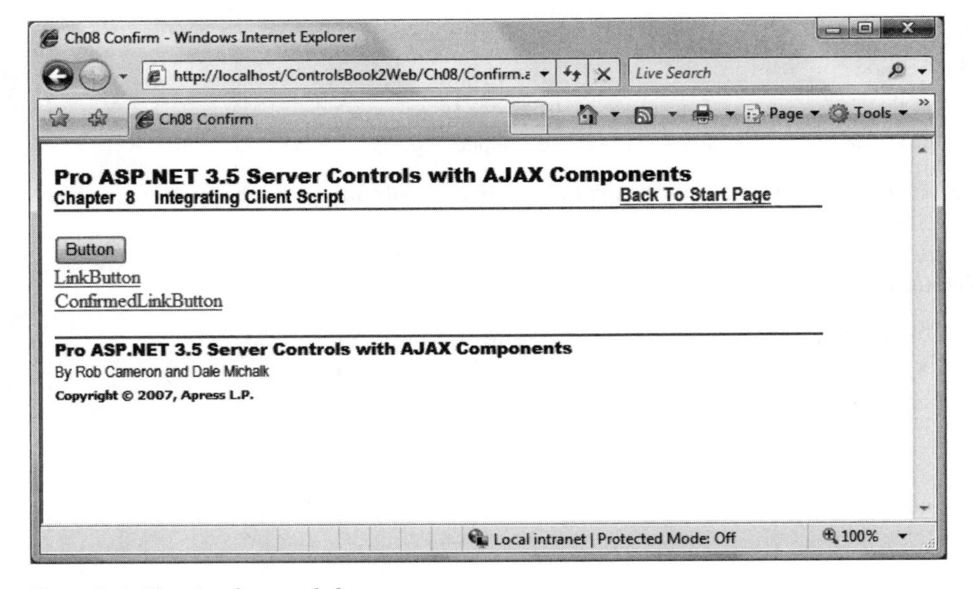

Figure 8-4. *The Confirm web form*

The code-behind web form class has logic to announce which control was responsible for the postback to help us see what is going on. The first control we exercise is the regular ASP.NET Button on the form. This Button causes the form to post, but we plugged into this mechanism with the FormConfirmation server control. When this button is clicked, it kicks off the FormConfirmation server control's JavaScript code according to the setting on its Message property, as shown in Figure 8-5. Click the Reset Status button to return the form to its original state.

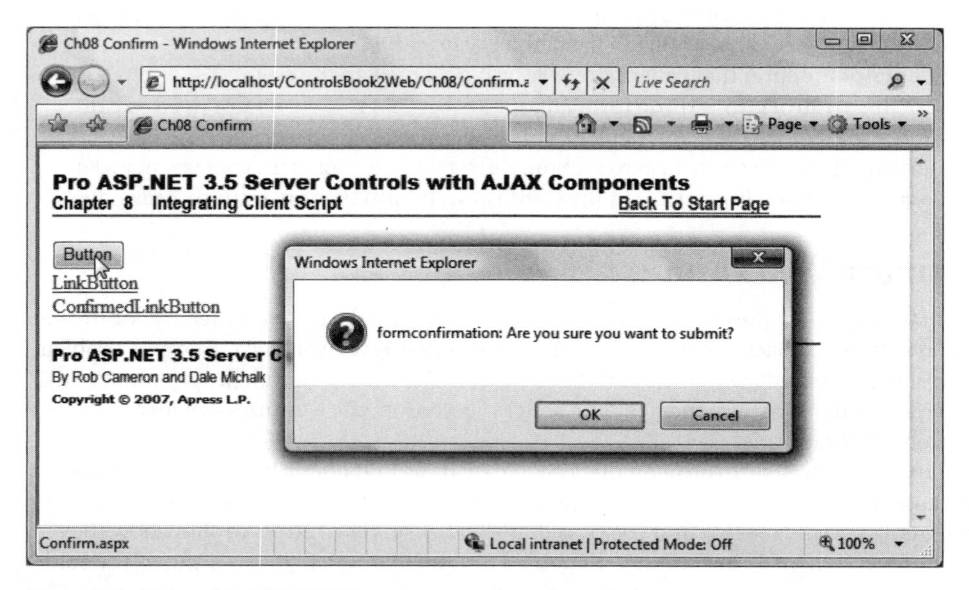

Figure 8-5. *Using the ASP.NET Button control on the web form*

The HTML generated by the web form shows the emission of the onsubmit JavaScript handler on the <form> tag:

```
<form name="aspnetForm" method="post" action="Confirm.aspx" onsubmit=
"javascript:return WebForm_OnSubmit();" id="aspnetForm">
```

The next iteration of the Confirm web form in Figure 8-6 shows what happens when the ASP.NET LinkButton is clicked.

This control executes the __doPostback JavaScript method emitted by ASP.NET to programmatically submit the web form:

```
<a id="ctl00_ControlsBookContent_linkbutton1"href="javascript:__doPostBack
('ctl00$ControlsBookContent$linkbutton1','')">LinkButton</a>
```

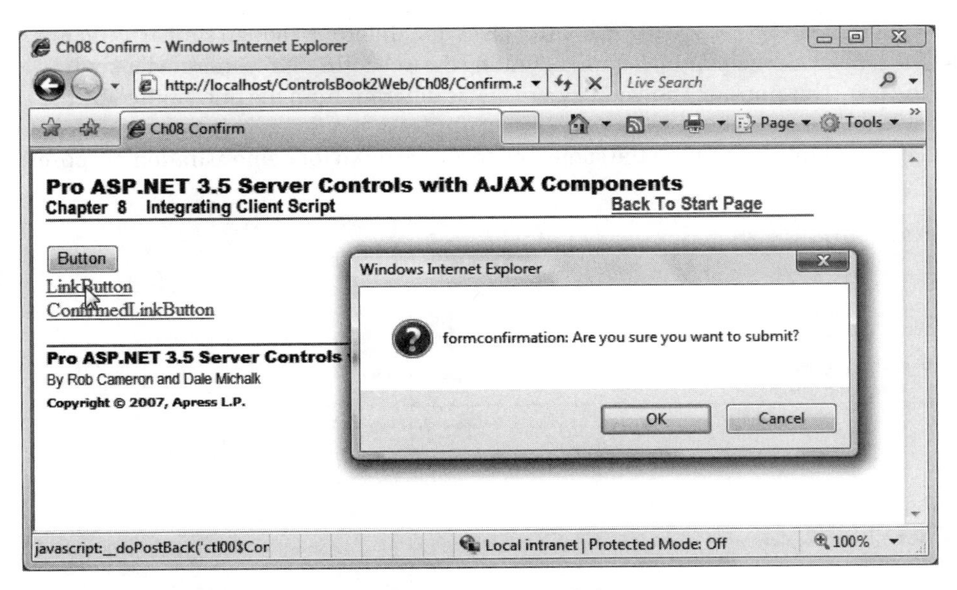

Figure 8-6. *Using the ASP.NET LinkButton on the web form*

`__doPostBack` is emitted by the core ASP.NET Framework when a control registers to initiate a client-side postback via JavaScript. If you select View ➤ Source in the browser, you can see how the script works. It locates the HTML `<form>` tag and calls its `Submit` method:

```
<script type="text/javascript">
<!--
var theForm = document.forms['aspnetForm'];
if (!theForm) {
    theForm = document.aspnetForm;
}
function __doPostBack(eventTarget, eventArgument) {
    if (!theForm.onsubmit || (theForm.onsubmit() != false)) {
        theForm.__EVENTTARGET.value = eventTarget;
        theForm.__EVENTARGUMENT.value = eventArgument;
        theForm.submit();
    }
}
// -->
</script>
```

This results in the web form submitting with a customized JavaScript alert box popping up and hooking into the form submission process with the `FormConfirmation` control.

The use of the ConfirmedLinkButton control gives us a different, though similar, outcome. It executes its own JavaScript pop-up before submitting the web form with "confirmedlinkbutton" as part of the text. This pop-up, shown in Figure 8-7, is different from the one emitted by the FormConfirmation control. The FormConfirmation control also renders a dialog, so normally, you would not use both controls on the same web form; we do so for demonstration purposes.

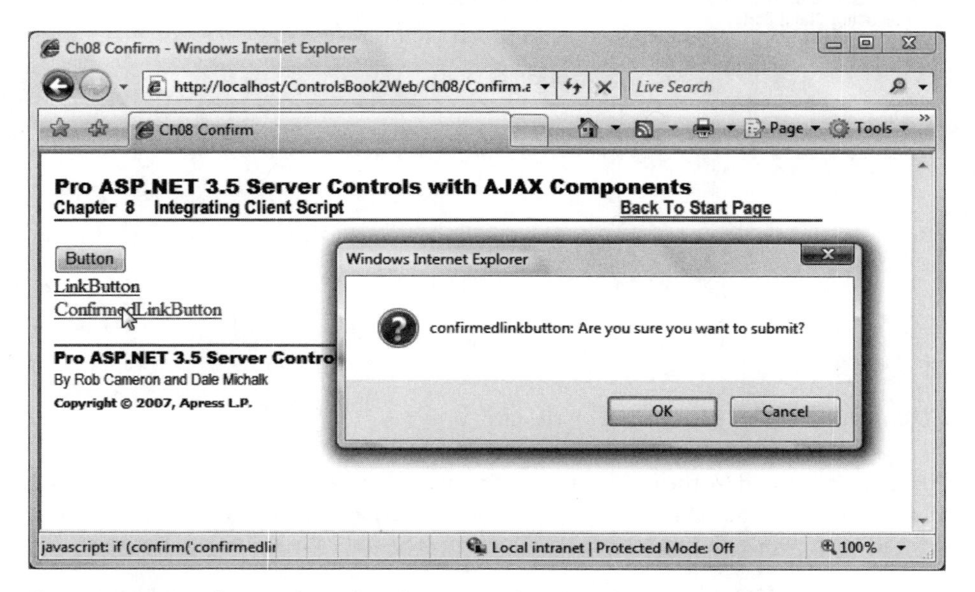

Figure 8-7. *Using the ConfirmedLinkButton control on the web form*

ConfirmedLinkButton emits a hyperlink that is similar to the LinkButton hyperlink, but it tacks on extra JavaScript to confirm the form submission before calling __doPostBack:

```
<a href="javascript: if (confirm('confirmedlinkbutton:
Are you sure you want to submit?'))
{__doPostBack('ctl00$ControlsBookContent$confirmlink1','')}">
ConfirmedLinkButton</a>
```

The point of this discussion is to show you what mechanisms are available to server controls to cause postback and how to plug into the architecture. The full Confirm web form is shown in Listings 8-9 and 8-10.

Listing 8-9. *The Confirm Web Form .aspx Page File*

```
<%@ Page Language="C#"
MasterPageFile="~/MasterPage/ControlsBook2MasterPage.Master"
  AutoEventWireup="true" CodeBehind="Confirm.aspx.cs"
 Inherits="ControlsBook2Web.Ch08.Confirm"
  Title="Confirm Demo" %>
```

```
<%@ Register Assembly="ControlsBook2Lib" Namespace=
 "ControlsBook2Lib.Ch08" TagPrefix="apress" %>
<asp:Content ID="Content1" ContentPlaceHolderID="ChapterNumAndTitle" runat="server">
  <asp:Label ID="ChapterNumberLabel" runat="server" Width="14px">8</asp:Label> 
 <asp:Label      ID="ChapterTitleLabel" runat="server" Width="360px">
Integrating Client-Side Script</asp:Label>
</asp:Content>
<asp:Content ID="Content2" ContentPlaceHolderID="PrimaryContent" runat="server">
  <apress:FormConfirmation ID="confirm1" runat="server" Message=
  "formconfirmation: Are you sure you want to submit?" />
  <br />
  <asp:Button ID="button1" runat="server" Text="Button" OnClick="Button_Click" />
  <br />   <asp:LinkButton ID="linkbutton1" runat="server" Text="LinkButton"
  OnClick="LinkButton_Click" /><br />
  <apress:ConfirmedLinkButton ID="confirmlink1" runat="server"
  Message="confirmedlinkbutton: Are you sure you want to submit?"
    OnClick="ConfirmLinkButton_ClickClick">ConfirmedLinkButton
    </apress:ConfirmedLinkButton>
  <br />
  <br />
  <br />
  <asp:Button ID="Button2" runat="server" Text="Reset Status"
    onclick="Button2_Click" />
  <asp:Label ID="status" runat="server" Text="Click a button."/>
</asp:Content>
```

Listing 8-10. *The Confirm Web Form Code-Behind Class File*

```
using System;

namespace ControlsBook2Web.Ch08
{
  public partial class Confirm : System.Web.UI.Page
  {
    protected void Page_Load(object sender, EventArgs e)
    {

    }

    protected void Button_Click(object sender, System.EventArgs e)
    {
      status.Text = "Regular Button Clicked! - " + DateTime.Now;
    }

    protected void LinkButton_Click(object sender, System.EventArgs e)
    {
      status.Text = "LinkButton Clicked! - " + DateTime.Now;
    }
```

```
    protected void ConfirmLinkButton_ClickClick(object sender, System.EventArgs e)
    {
      status.Text = "ConfirmLinkButton Clicked! - " + DateTime.Now;
    }

    protected void Button2_Click(object sender, EventArgs e)
    {
      status.Text = "Click a button.";
    }
  }
}
```

So far in this chapter, we have covered how to integrate client-side script in general, how to execute client script on page load, and how to execute client script during form submission or as part of navigation. In the next section, we explore how to integrate client- and server-side events to provide graceful degradation if client-side script support is not available.

Integrating Client-Side and Server-Side Events

The event processing that occurs in the client browser is separate from the ASP.NET activity that occurs on the server to generate HTML output and respond to server-side events. In this section, we build an example server control that provides seamless integration of the two event models in a similar manner to the built-in ASP.NET `Validator` controls' client-side and server-side functionality. We discuss `Validator` controls in Chapter 10. The control we build in this chapter is similar in functionality to the `NumericUpDown` Windows Forms control.

Control developers who extend or create a server control that uses client-side features need to ensure that the client activities are smoothly integrated with the feature set of ASP.NET and do not contradict or interfere with mechanisms such as `ViewState` or postback. It is also recommended that developers build controls that integrate client-side scripts to degrade gracefully when the client viewing the generated HTML content does not support advanced features. A good example of this is the `Validator` class of controls, which emit client-side JavaScript validation routines only if the browser supports JavaScript. Let's now dive into creating the `UpDown` custom server control.

The UpDown Server Control

To demonstrate integration between client-side programming and server controls along with graceful down-level client rendering, we construct a server control that mimics the `NumericUpDown` control from the Windows Forms desktop .NET development environment; our control is shown in Figure 8-8.

The `UpDown` server control takes the form of a composite control with a `TextBox` to hold the value and two `Buttons` with the captions + and - to represent up and down incrementing clicks. Although the UI is not spectacular, it permits us to show how to wire up client script with server events.

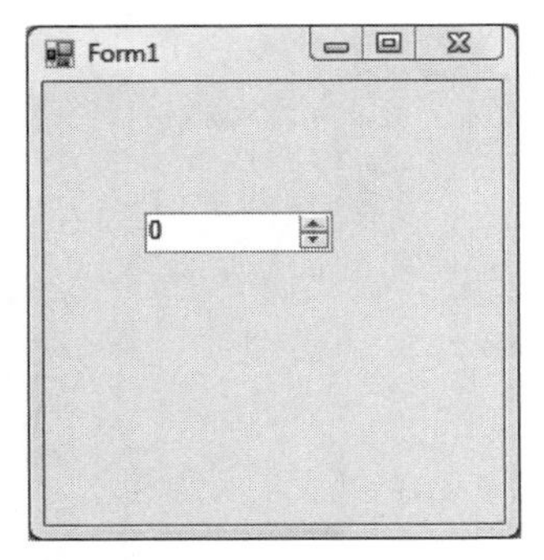

Figure 8-8. *The UpDown Windows Forms desktop control*

If the browser supports it, the UpDown server control emits JavaScript that increments or decrements the value in the TextBox in the local environment of the browser without having to make a round-trip to the web server to perform these operations. Client-side operations include the same functionality available in the server-side events, such as range checking, though we simply display a message notifying the user of the input error while in the server-side events we throw an ArgumentOutOfRangeException. The UpDown server control has a number of important properties that we discuss in the next section.

Key Properties: MinValue, MaxValue, Increment, and Value

The UpDown server control exposes four properties that allow developers to configure its behavior in the Visual Studio Designer: MinValue, MaxValue, Increment, and Value. The property handlers perform data validation tasks to ensure the number set for the Value property falls between the MinValue and MaxValue property range. We default to System.Int.MaxRange for the MaxValue property to prevent an exception if the value is too large. Here's how these properties are declared within the UpDown server control:

```
public virtual int MinValue
{
   get
   {
      EnsureChildControls();
      object min = ViewState["MinValue"];
      return (min == null) ? 0 : (int) min;
   }
   set
   {
      EnsureChildControls();
      if (value < MaxValue)
         ViewState["MinValue"] = value;
      else
         throw new ArgumentException(
"MinValue must be less than MaxValue.","MinValue");
   }
}
```

```
public virtual int MaxValue
{
   get
   {
      EnsureChildControls();
      object max = ViewState["MaxValue"];
      return (max == null) ? System.Int32.MaxValue : (int) max;
   }
   set
   {
      EnsureChildControls();
      if (value > MinValue)
         ViewState["MaxValue"] = value;
      else
         throw new ArgumentException(
"MaxValue must be greater than MinValue.","MaxValue");
   }
}

public int Value
{
   get
   {
      EnsureChildControls();
      object value = (int)ViewState["value"];
      return (value != null) ? (int)value : 0;
   }
   set
   {
      EnsureChildControls();
      if ((value <= MaxValue) &&
         (value >= MinValue))
      {
         valueTextBox.Text = value.ToString();
         ViewState["value"] = value ;
      }
      else
      {
         throw new ArgumentOutOfRangeException("Value",
         "Value must be between MinValue and MaxValue.");
      }
   }
}
```

```
public int Increment
{
   get
   {
      EnsureChildControls();
      object inc = ViewState["Increment"];
      return (inc == null) ? 1 : (int) inc;
   }
   set
   {
      EnsureChildControls();
      if (value > 0)
         ViewState["Increment"] = value;
   }
}
```

When you view the UpDown.aspx file in the Visual Studio Designer, if you select the updown1 control and try to give it a value that is either above MaxValue or below MinValue, you will get a message dialog box reporting the error. Likewise, if you set MaxValue to a number that is less than MinValue, or vice versa, you will get an error dialog box. This design-time behavior is a good way to help developers understand how the control works and what errors to catch in exception handler blocks when working with the control at runtime.

In the next section, we move on to describe how the control is constructed.

Accessing UpDown Child Controls

UpDown is a composite server control that declares private controls of type TextBox to render an <INPUT type="text"> tag and two Button controls to render <INPUT type="button"> tags. It adds these controls by overriding the CreateChildControls method from WebControl, and it wires up their events to the parent control's events.

Because our control will emit JavaScript that needs to know the fully qualified name of each child control in order to work properly on the client, we implement the INamingContainer interface to ensure generation of unique names and use the UniqueID property from each of our private control declarations. In the following code, we access the UniqueID of the valueTextBox that holds the value of the UpDown control:

```
scriptInvoke = DOWN_FUNC + "('" + valueTextBox.UniqueID
```

Now that we have presented an overview of how the control is constructed, we can jump into a discussion in the next section of how the control renders itself to support client-side and server-side event integration.

Preparing the Script for Rendering

Like any good client-side script-rendering server control, UpDown checks to see if the browser can support client-side script prior to rendering. DetermineRenderClientScript is similar to what we looked at for the Focus control—it checks for Document Object Model (DOM) Level 1 compliance and JavaScript features. Our client script is not very demanding, as we use only the document.getElementById method, but this method could be extended to perform additional checking if you want to support other browsers:

```
protected void DetermineRenderClientScript()
{
    if (EnableClientScript)
    {
        if ((Page != null) && (Page.Request != null))
        {
            HttpBrowserCapabilities caps = Context.Request.Browser;

            // require JavaScript and DOM Level 1
            // support to render client-side code
            // (IE 5+ and Netscape 6+)
            if (caps.EcmaScriptVersion.Major >= 1 &&
               caps.W3CDomVersion.Major >= 1)
            {
                renderClientScript = true;
            }
        }
    }
}
```

The OnPreRender method calls DetermineRenderClientScript to guide its JavaScript emissions. In UpDown, we take a different approach from previous server controls in the chapter if we get the green light that we can take advantage of client script. The Web Resource system that is new to ASP.NET 2.0 allows what formerly required loose script files installed in folders like aspnet_client on the web server to actually have them originate from the compiled assembly itself as embedded resources. The embedded resources are retrieved by browser clients using special URLs created by ASP.NET that point back to the WebResource.axd handler for a web site. We will use it for JavaScript functionality with the UpDown control, but it can also be employed to embed images, style sheets, or other loose content for easy deployment and maintenance.

The Web Resource system is enabled by two primary steps for marking resources:

- Setting the Build Action for a file in Visual Studio to Embedded Resource
- Adding a WebResource attribute at the assembly level for the embedded resource

The control source code has the following attribute for the UpDown.js script file in the project:

```
[assembly: WebResource("ControlsBook2Lib.Ch08.UpDown.js", "text/javascript")]
```

The parameters to the WebResource attribute include a fully qualified name to the resource file in a project that accounts for folder depth and the MIME type of the resource being embedded in the assembly.

After the web resources have been embedded and made visible via the WebResource attribute, the control needs to emit something to link in the URL for it. This can be done with either the GetWebResourceUrl method of the ClientScriptManager class for generic content or the more applicable RegisterClientScriptResource call for our UpDown control, which emits a script block with the src attribute pointing at the web resource URL.

```
Page.ClientScript.RegisterClientScriptResource(typeof(UpDown),
            "ControlsBook2Lib.Ch08.UpDown.js");
```

The rest of the prerendering functionality wires up the appropriate client events using the function names in the UpDown.js file:

```
protected override void OnPreRender(EventArgs e)
{
    base.OnPreRender(e);

    DetermineRenderClientScript();

    // textbox script that validates the textbox when it
    // loses focus after input
    string scriptInvoke = "";
    if (renderClientScript)
    {
        scriptInvoke = this.CHECK_FUNC + "('" +
        valueTextBox.UniqueID +
           "'," + this.MinValue + "," + this.MaxValue + ")";
        valueTextBox.Attributes.Add("onblur", scriptInvoke);
    }

    // add the '+' button client script function that
    // manipulates the textbox on the client side
    if (renderClientScript)
    {
        scriptInvoke = UP_FUNC + "('" + valueTextBox.UniqueID +
           "'," + this.MinValue + "," + this.MaxValue + "," + this.Increment
           + "); return false;";
        upButton.Attributes.Add("onclick", scriptInvoke);
    }

    // add the '-' button client script function that
    // manipulates the textbox on the client side
    if (renderClientScript)
    {
        scriptInvoke = DOWN_FUNC + "('" + valueTextBox.UniqueID +
           "'," + this.MinValue + "," + this.MaxValue + "," + this.Increment
           + "); return false;";
        downButton.Attributes.Add("onclick", scriptInvoke);
    }

    // register to ensure we receive postback handling
    // to properly handle child input controls
    Page.RegisterRequiresPostBack(this);
```

```
    if (renderClientScript)
    {
        // register the <script> block that does the
        // client-side handling
        Page.ClientScript.RegisterClientScriptResource(typeof(UpDown),
            "ControlsBook2Lib.Ch08.UpDown.js");
    }
}
```

First, we add a script to the valueTextBox TextBox to check its value when the user tabs out or otherwise exits the control. The onblur client-side event is triggered anytime a user enters a value in the text box and switches the focus from that element on the web page to some other element. The CHECK_FUNC constant points to __UpDown_Check in UpDown.js. Here is the code for __UpDown_Check:

```
function __UpDown_Check(boxid, min, max)
{
   var box = document.getElementById(boxid);

   if (isNaN(parseInt(box.value)))
      box.value = min;
   if (box.value > max)
      box.value = max;
   if (box.value < min)
      box.value = min;
}
```

We have to pass in the exact ID of the control on the client side, as well as our minimum and maximum values for validation purposes. The client script checks for nonnumeric values and resets to the minimum value if they are found. The next part of OnPreRender configures client-side script for the plus and minus buttons:

```
// add the '+' button client script function that
// manipulates the textbox on the client side
if (renderClientScript)
{
   scriptInvoke = UP_FUNC + "('" + valueTextBox.UniqueID +
      "'," + this.MinValue + "," + this.MaxValue + "," +
      this.Increment + "); return false;";
   upButton.Attributes.Add("onclick",scriptInvoke);
}

// add the '-' button client script function that
// manipulates the textbox on the client side
```

```
if (renderClientScript)
{
   scriptInvoke = DOWN_FUNC + "('" + valueTextBox.UniqueID +
      "'," + this.MinValue + "," + this.MaxValue + "," +
      this.Increment + "); return false;";
   downButton.Attributes.Add("onclick",scriptInvoke);
}
```

The client-side script for the up and down buttons is virtually identical. The script function for the up button is as follows:

```
function __UpDown_Up(boxid, min, max, howmuch)
{
   var box = document.getElementById(boxid);

   var newvalue = parseInt(box.value) + howmuch;
   if ((newvalue <= max) && (newvalue >= min))
      box.value = newvalue;
}
```

It takes the ID of the text box and the minimum, maximum, and increment values from the server control's properties. We check for valid numbers within the range of the minimum and maximum values on the client. We display an alert message box if a constraint is violated. This makes sure client-side operations are validated as they are as part of server-side validation.

In the next section, we get into the nitty-gritty of how the control is constructed, starting with an examination of the `CreateChildControls` method.

Creating the Child Controls

We covered the supporting methods and prerendering steps. Now, we can dive into `CreateChildControls` and see how it sets things up. At the top of the class file, we declare our child controls:

```
private TextBox valueTextBox ;
private Button upButton ;
private Button downButton ;
```

We use these references in `CreateChildControls` when building up the control hierarchy in our composite control:

```
protected override void CreateChildControls()
{
   Controls.Clear();

   // add the textbox that holds the value
   valueTextBox = new TextBox();
   valueTextBox.ID = "InputText";
   valueTextBox.Width = 40;
   valueTextBox.Text = "0";
   Controls.Add(valueTextBox);
```

```
   // add the '+' button
   upButton = new Button();
   upButton.ID = "UpButton";
   upButton.Text = " + ";
   upButton.Click += new System.EventHandler(this.UpButtonClick);
   Controls.Add(upButton);

   // add the '-' button
   downButton = new Button();
   downButton.ID = "DownButton";
   downButton.Text = " - ";
   downButton.Click += new System.EventHandler(this.DownButtonClick);
   Controls.Add(downButton);
}
```

The first thing we do is clear out the control tree so we start with a clean slate. We set the downButton Button to the same size as the upButton Button to improve our UI just a bit. We add server-side event handlers to both upButton and downButton, in case we need them because either the client-side script is not enabled or the browser does not support the level of DOM access required. In the next section, we discuss how the UpDown control provides a smooth experience to the end user with a discussion of how the server control monitors for value changes.

The ValueChanged Event

Our server control makes it easy to monitor the UpDown control and be notified only when it changes value through a server-side event named ValueChanged. The ValueChanged event is raised when it detects a difference between the Value property of the control from ViewState and what is received from the client after a postback:

```
public event EventHandler ValueChanged
{
   add
   {
      Events.AddHandler(ValueChangedKey, value);
   }
   remove
   {
      Events.RemoveHandler(ValueChangedKey, value);
   }
}

protected virtual void OnValueChanged(EventArgs e)
{
   EventHandler valueChangedEventDelegate =
      (EventHandler) Events[ValueChangedKey];
```

```
   if (valueChangedEventDelegate != null)
   {
      valueChangedEventDelegate(this, e);
   }
}
```

ValueChanged follows the basic pattern of the System.EventHandler delegate for its event declaration, so we can reuse the System.EventArgs class that goes with it. We also leverage the built-in Events property from System.Web.Control to efficiently store our subscribing delegates. We covered event-handling mechanisms in Chapter 5.

Now, we have a way to generate events based on the value being changed. In the next section, we discuss how to retrieve the old and new value to enforce the UI logic.

Retrieving the Data

The ValueChanged event does us little good if we cannot retrieve the value of the form at postback. Instead of relying on the default value and event handling of the TextBox control, we take matters into our own hands for our composite control to ensure that we are notified during the form postback processing. We set things up by calling Page.RegisterRequiresPostback in OnPreRender. We finish the task by implementing the methods of IPostBackDataHandler.

In the following code, LoadPostData uses knowledge of the TextBox control's UniqueID property to index into the posted data collection. Once we retrieve the value, we can validate that it is a number with the Parse function of the System.Int32 type. We include a try-catch, so we can handle problems with parsing if it is not an integer:

```
bool IPostBackDataHandler.LoadPostData(string postDataKey,
   NameValueCollection postCollection)
{
   bool changed = false;

   // grab the value posted by the textbox
   string postedValue = postCollection[valueTextBox.UniqueID];
   int postedNumber = 0;

   try
   {
      postedNumber = System.Int32.Parse(postedValue);

      if (!Value.Equals(postedNumber))
         changed = true;

      Value = postedNumber;
   }
   catch (FormatException fe)
   {
      changed = false;
   }
   return changed;
}
```

If the value is an integer, we can assign it to the Value property. We perform range checking in the property declaration. Before we do assign the value, we first check the Value property's ViewState value to see if there was indeed a change. If this is the case, we return true from the function. Returning true causes RaisePostChangedEvent to be invoked and, in turn, raise our ValueChanged event via the OnValueChanged helper method, as shown in the following code:

```
void IPostBackDataHandler.RaisePostDataChangedEvent()
{
   OnValueChanged(EventArgs.Empty);
}
```

Because our control publishes just a single event, the corresponding RaisePostDataChangedEvent is also simple. In the next section, we drill down into how child button clicks that change the value are handled by the composite control and how the control dynamically determines whether or not to fire server-side events.

Handling Child Control Events

We glossed over the fact that we mapped the button-click events to server-side handlers in our composite UpDown control. They are not necessary if we assume the browser can handle the client-side script. The client-side onclick event fully handles the clicking of the up and down buttons and never needs to post back to the web server. Of course, this is not a good situation if you have a down-level client. If this is the case, you can fall back on the natural capability of the buttons to execute a postback by virtue of being located on a web form. We assign the server-side events to our buttons in CreateChildControls in case they are required.

The UpDown control can make several assumptions when the server reaches its handlers for the buttons. The first is that the Value property is loaded with the number in the TextBox. We discussed the LoadPostData handling that did this in the previous section. The second is that all other events have fired. Remember that buttons and other controls initiating postback always let other events fire before getting their turn.

The implementation of UpButtonClick takes the Increment property, applies it to the Value property, and makes sure its stays in bounds, as shown in the following code. Because it knows that a change has occurred, it raises the OnValueChanged event. DownButtonClick is identical except for subtracting the Increment value:

```
protected void UpButtonClick(object source, EventArgs e)
{
   int newValue = Value + Increment;
   if ((newValue <= MaxValue) && (newValue >= MinValue))
   {
      Value = newValue;
      OnValueChanged(EventArgs.Empty);
   }
}
```

At this point, our data loading and event raising tasks are complete. Our control is prepared to render in the browser. Listing 8-11 presents the full source code for the UpDown control. Listing 8-12 contains the UpDown.js JavaScript file.

Listing 8-11. *The UpDown Server Control*

```
using System;
using System.Collections.Specialized;
using System.ComponentModel;
using System.Web;
using System.Web.UI;
using System.Web.UI.WebControls;

[assembly: WebResource("ControlsBook2Lib.Ch08.UpDown.js", "text/javascript")]

namespace ControlsBook2Lib.Ch08
{
   [ToolboxData("<{0}:UpDown runat=server></{0}:UpDown>"),
   DefaultProperty("Value")]
   public class UpDown : WebControl, IPostBackDataHandler, INamingContainer
   {
      protected const string UP_FUNC = "__UpDown_Up";
      protected const string DOWN_FUNC = "__UpDown_Down";
      protected string CHECK_FUNC = "__UpDown_Check";


      private TextBox valueTextBox ;
      private Button upButton ;
      private Button downButton ;
      private bool renderClientScript;
      private static readonly object ValueChangedKey = new object();

      public UpDown() : base(HtmlTextWriterTag.Div)
      {
         renderClientScript = false;
      }

      public virtual bool EnableClientScript
      {
         get
         {
            EnsureChildControls();
            object script = ViewState["EnableClientScript"];
            if (script == null)
               return true;
            else
               return (bool) script;
         }
```

```
      set
      {
         EnsureChildControls();
         ViewState["EnableClientScript"] = value;
      }
   }

   public virtual int MinValue
   {
      get
      {
         EnsureChildControls();
         object min = ViewState["MinValue"];
         return (min == null) ? 0 : (int) min;
      }
      set
      {
         EnsureChildControls();
         if (value < MaxValue)
            ViewState["MinValue"] = value;
         else
            throw new ArgumentException(
            "MinValue must be less than MaxValue.","MinValue");
      }
   }

   public virtual int MaxValue
   {
      get
      {
         EnsureChildControls();
         object max = ViewState["MaxValue"];
         return (max == null) ? System.Int32.MaxValue : (int) max;
      }
      set
      {
         EnsureChildControls();
         if (value > MinValue)
            ViewState["MaxValue"] = value;
         else
            throw new ArgumentException(
            "MaxValue must be greater than MinValue.","MaxValue");
      }
   }

   public int Value
   {
```

```
        get
        {
            EnsureChildControls();
            object value = (int)ViewState["value"];
            return (value != null) ? (int)value : 0;
        }
        set
        {
            EnsureChildControls();
            if ((value <= MaxValue) &&
                (value >= MinValue))
            {
                valueTextBox.Text = value.ToString();
                ViewState["value"] = value ;
            }
            else
            {
                throw new ArgumentOutOfRangeException("Value",
                "Value must be between MinValue and MaxValue.");
            }
        }
    }

    public int Increment
    {
        get
        {
            EnsureChildControls();
            object inc = ViewState["Increment"];
            return (inc == null) ? 1 : (int) inc;
        }
        set
        {
            EnsureChildControls();
            if (value > 0)
                ViewState["Increment"] = value;
        }
    }

    // LoadPostData is overridden to get the data
    // back from the textbox and set up the
    // ValueChanged event if necessary
    bool IPostBackDataHandler.LoadPostData(string postDataKey,
        NameValueCollection postCollection)
    {
        bool changed = false;
```

```
        // grab the value posted by the textbox
        string postedValue = postCollection[valueTextBox.UniqueID];
        int postedNumber = 0;

        try
        {
            postedNumber = System.Int32.Parse(postedValue);

            if (!Value.Equals(postedNumber))
              changed = true;

            Value = postedNumber;
        }
        catch (FormatException)
        {
            changed = false;
        }
        return changed;
    }

    void IPostBackDataHandler.RaisePostDataChangedEvent()
    {
        OnValueChanged(EventArgs.Empty);
    }

    public event EventHandler ValueChanged
    {
        add
        {
            Events.AddHandler(ValueChangedKey, value);
        }
        remove
        {
            Events.RemoveHandler(ValueChangedKey, value);
        }
    }

    protected virtual void OnValueChanged(EventArgs e)
    {
        EventHandler valueChangedEventDelegate =
            (EventHandler) Events[ValueChangedKey];
        if (valueChangedEventDelegate != null)
        {
            valueChangedEventDelegate(this, e);
        }
    }
```

```
// up/down button click handling when client-side
// script functionality is not enabled
protected void UpButtonClick(object source, EventArgs e)
{
   int newValue = Value + Increment;
   if ((newValue <= MaxValue) && (newValue >= MinValue))
   {
      Value = newValue;
      OnValueChanged(EventArgs.Empty);
   }
}

protected void DownButtonClick(object source, EventArgs e)
{
   int newValue = Value - Increment;
   if ((newValue <= MaxValue) && (newValue >= MinValue))
   {
         Value = newValue;
      OnValueChanged(EventArgs.Empty);
   }
}

protected void DetermineRenderClientScript()
{
   if (EnableClientScript)
   {
      if ((Page != null) && (Page.Request != null))
      {
         HttpBrowserCapabilities caps = Context.Request.Browser;

         // require JavaScript and DOM Level 1
         // support to render client-side code
         // (IE 5+ and Netscape 6+)
         if (caps.EcmaScriptVersion.Major >= 1 &&
            caps.W3CDomVersion.Major >= 1)
         {
            renderClientScript = true;
         }
      }
   }
}
```

```
protected override void OnPreRender(EventArgs e)
{
   base.OnPreRender(e);

   DetermineRenderClientScript();

   // textbox script that validates the textbox when it
   // loses focus after input
   string scriptInvoke = "";
   if (renderClientScript)
   {
      scriptInvoke = this.CHECK_FUNC + "('" +
      valueTextBox.UniqueID +
         "'," + this.MinValue + "," + this.MaxValue + ")";
      valueTextBox.Attributes.Add("onblur",scriptInvoke);
   }

   // add the '+' button client script function that
   // manipulates the textbox on the client side
   if (renderClientScript)
   {
      scriptInvoke = UP_FUNC + "('" + valueTextBox.UniqueID +
         "'," + this.MinValue + "," + this.MaxValue + "," + this.Increment
         + "); return false;";
      upButton.Attributes.Add("onclick",scriptInvoke);
   }

   // add the '-' button client script function that
   // manipulates the textbox on the client side
   if (renderClientScript)
   {
      scriptInvoke = DOWN_FUNC + "('" + valueTextBox.UniqueID +
         "'," + this.MinValue + "," + this.MaxValue + "," + this.Increment
         + "); return false;";
      downButton.Attributes.Add("onclick",scriptInvoke);
   }

   // register to ensure we receive postback handling
   // to properly handle child input controls
   Page.RegisterRequiresPostBack(this);
```

```
         if (renderClientScript)
         {
            // register the <script> block that does the
            // client-side handling
             Page.ClientScript.RegisterClientScriptResource(typeof(UpDown),
                 "ControlsBook2Lib.Ch08.UpDown.js");
         }
      }

      public override ControlCollection Controls
      {
         get
         {
            EnsureChildControls();
            return base.Controls;
         }
      }

      protected override void CreateChildControls()
      {
         Controls.Clear();

         // add the textbox that holds the value
         valueTextBox = new TextBox();
         valueTextBox.ID = "InputText";
         valueTextBox.Width = 40;
         valueTextBox.Text = "0";
        Controls.Add(valueTextBox);

         // add the '+' button
         upButton = new Button();
         upButton.ID = "UpButton";
         upButton.Text = " + ";
         upButton.Click += new System.EventHandler(this.UpButtonClick);
         Controls.Add(upButton);

         // add the '-' button
         downButton = new Button();
         downButton.ID = "DownButton";
         downButton.Text = " - ";
         downButton.Click += new System.EventHandler(this.DownButtonClick);
        Controls.Add(downButton);
      }
   }
}
```

Listing 8-12. *The UpDown JavaScript File*

```
function __UpDown_Check(boxid, min, max)
{
  var box = document.getElementById(boxid);

  if (isNaN(parseInt(box.value)))
    box.value = min;
  if (box.value > max)
  {
    alert('Value cannot be greater than the Maximum allowed.');
    box.value = max;
  }
  if (box.value < min)
  {
    alert('Value cannot be less than the Minimum.');
    box.value = min;
  }
}

function __UpDown_Up(boxid, min, max, howmuch)
{
  var box = document.getElementById(boxid);

  var newvalue = parseInt(box.value) + howmuch;
  if ((newvalue <= max) && (newvalue >= min))
    box.value = newvalue;
}

function __UpDown_Down(boxid, min, max, howmuch)
{
  var box = document.getElementById(boxid);

  var newvalue = parseInt(box.value) - howmuch;
  if ((newvalue <= max) && (newvalue >= min))
    box.value = newvalue;
}
```

In the next section, we move on to the web form demonstration of our newly minted UpDown custom server control, testing that it correctly implements the expected UI logic.

The UpDown Web Form

To test the UpDown control, we place it on a web form named UpDown and take it for a test drive, as shown in Figure 8-9. Clicking the buttons shows that the time label isn't advancing.

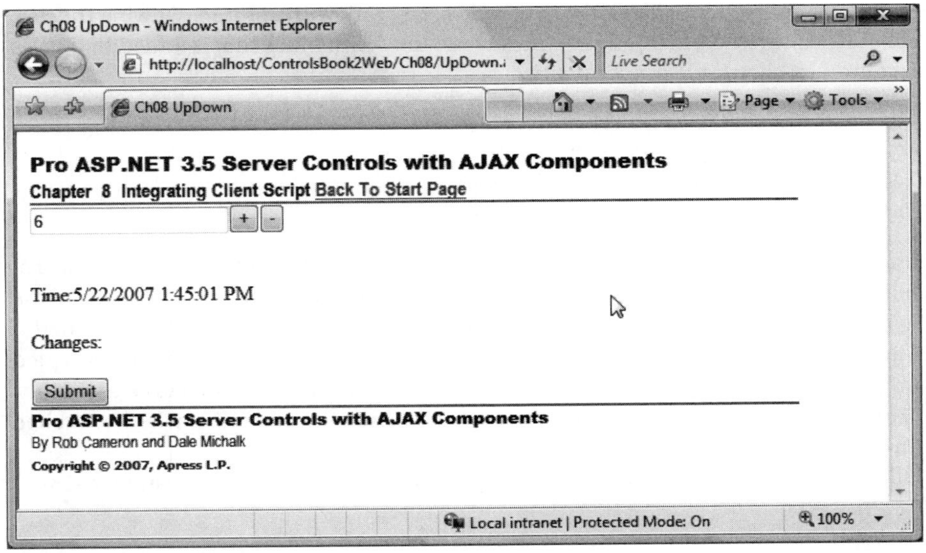

Figure 8-9. *The UpDown control in action on a web form*

If you add the following name/value pair to the @Page directive of the web form, it will force the control to stop emitting JavaScript:

```
ClientTarget="downlevel"
```

The result in Figure 8-10 shows the time label changing on each button click because a server postback occurs.

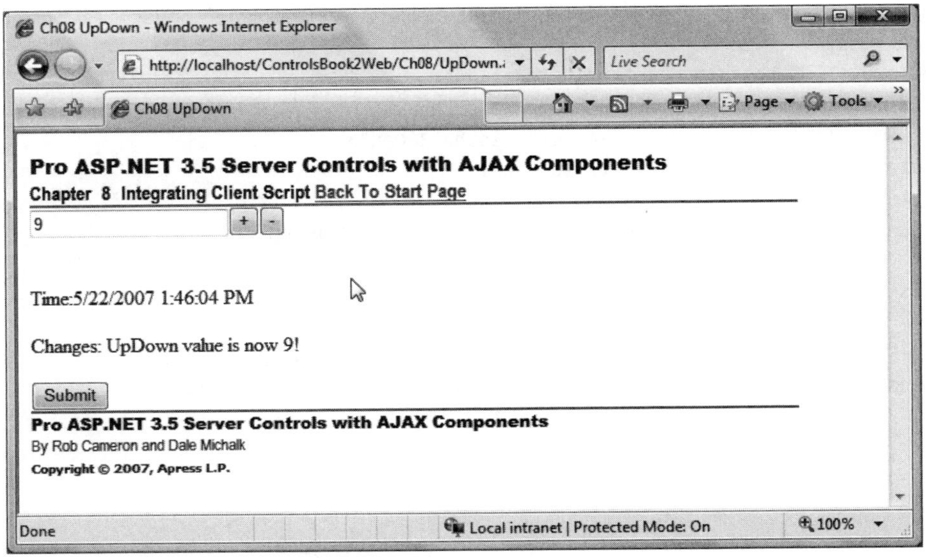

Figure 8-10. *The UpDown control with EnableClientScript = "False"*

As you can see, both client-side and server-side code work with aplomb. Viewing the source code that is rendered into the form one can see the script block that is added that gives the UpDown control its client side functionality:

```
<script src="/ControlsBook2Web/ WebResource.axd?d=
SkYTaYYXk75i231OYwPL35uNSpiWvrGd4PWPmHoFkkJW-
MP7oRKUTQnH3nGbezsIQoLucMZWprW1QVh2mXqhrQ2&amp;t=
633154197040000000" type="text/javascript"></script>
```

The RegisterScriptResource call to ClientScriptManager emits a <script> tag with a src attribute pointing to the WebResource.axd handler that has d and t parameters. If one used the GetWebResourceUrl of ClientScriptManager a similar parameterized URL would be returned but would have required manual rendering of the <script> tag. The d parameter is an encrypted value that represents the identifier for the resource annotated by the WebResource assembly attribute. The t parameter is a timestamp, which helps the browser determine whether cached content returned from a resource handler has changed.

The full source code for the web form and code-behind class is shown in Listings 8-13 and 8-14.

Listing 8-13. *The UpDown Web Form .aspx Page File*

```
<%@ Page Language="C#"
MasterPageFile="~/MasterPage/ControlsBook2MasterPage.Master"
  AutoEventWireup="true" CodeBehind="UpDown.aspx.cs"
 Inherits="ControlsBook2Web.Ch08.UpDown"
  Title="UpDown Demo" %>

<%@ Register Assembly="ControlsBook2Lib" Namespace=
"ControlsBook2Lib.Ch08" TagPrefix="apress" %>
<asp:Content ID="Content1" ContentPlaceHolderID="ChapterNumAndTitle"
          runat="server">
    <asp:Label ID="ChapterNumberLabel" runat="server"
    Width="14px">8</asp:Label>  <asp:Label
    ID="ChapterTitleLabel" runat="server" Width="360px">
    Integrating Client-Side Script</asp:Label>
</asp:Content>
<asp:Content ID="Content2" ContentPlaceHolderID="PrimaryContent"
          runat="server">
    <apress:UpDown ID="updown1" runat="server" MinValue="1"
          MaxValue="15" Increment="3"
    Value="6" OnValueChanged="updown1_ValueChanged" Width="98px"
        EnableClientScript="True"></apress:UpDown>
  <br />
  <br />
  Time:<asp:Label ID="timelabel" runat="server" /><br />
  <br />
```

```
  Changes:<asp:Label ID="changelabel" runat="server" /><br />
  <br />
  <asp:Button ID="submitbtn" runat="server" Text="Submit" />
</asp:Content>
```

Listing 8-14. *UpDown Web Form Code-Behind Class File*

```
using System;

namespace ControlsBook2Web.Ch08
{
  public partial class UpDown : System.Web.UI.Page
  {
    protected void Page_Load(object sender, EventArgs e)
    {
      timelabel.Text = DateTime.Now.ToString();
      changelabel.Text = "";
    }

    protected void updown1_ValueChanged(object sender, System.EventArgs e)
    {
      changelabel.Text = " UpDown value is now " + updown1.Value + "!";
    }
  }
}
```

Client Callbacks

The normal client server interaction in ASP.NET is driven by the postback process, which shuttles HTML form and `ViewState` data for processing to the server and causes the subsequent refresh of the results in the browser once they are sent back. While making life simpler from a web development perspective and the foundation of the ASP.NET control model, it impacts the end-user experience in negative ways. At a minimum, the flashing of the HTML can be annoying for the user, and the entire experience may be perceived as unresponsive if there is significant latency observed when communicating across the network for even the smallest UI change.

Client callbacks are a feature added to the ASP.NET 2.0 release that provide a standardized way to make requests for pieces of data or content from client-side scripts without the need to build the underlying plumbing to make such a call or change the ASP.NET web form model significantly.

This feature set was a precursor to the more complete ASP.NET AJAX Extensions feature set we discuss later in the book but still has value when more limited client-side functionality is needed with a controls feature set without requiring the complete deployment of the entire ASP.NET Ajax Extensions framework. The one thing they do share in common is the use of the `XmlHttpRequest` object introduced by Internet Explorer that gives client-side script the ability to make network calls back to a server. We will leave the plumbing discussion for later chapters on Ajax technologies and focus on the high level API gives the web developer in ASP.NET.

Client Callbacks API

The client callback system is anchored on the server side by the ICallbackEventHandler interface implemented by a web form or a server control that wishes to be the target of a client script call. The interface defines two functions that are executed in sequence to receive the parameters from the client through the RaiseCallbackEvent method and then send the response content back via a GetCallbackResult method.

```
void RaiseCallbackEvent(string eventArgument)
string GetCallbackResult()
```

The argument sent to RaiseCallbackEvent and the response sent back from GetCallbackResult are both of type string and require the appropriate translation between the world of JavaScript and .NET. The splitting of the API into two calls also means the web form or control needs to maintain internal state between the two invocations to store execution results and then return them.

In order for client side script to invoke the ICallbackEventHandler interface, it needs the support of the ClientScriptManager method GetCallbackEventReference to create a JavaScript function call stub that links to a client side script library pulled in to support the process. A variety of other method overloads are provided for additional support, such as making the call synchronous or asynchronous, as well as providing a user side error handling function if something goes awry. We take the simplest form to show in our examples:

```
public string GetCallbackEventReference ( Control control, string argument,
  string clientCallback, string context)
```

The control parameter is the web form or server control that implements ICallbackEventHandler, the argument parameter is the JavaScript variable on the client side that is being passed to the RaiseCallbackEvent method, and the clientCallBack parameter is the client-side function that will be invoked with the results of the server call. context is a parameter placeholder for JavaScript code that is executed before the callback code is invoked and its result value is returned to the JavaScript code specified via the clientCallback parameter as a like named context parameter to that JavaScript function. This feature set is not used by our samples, so it will be set to null.

The Callback Web Form

The Callback web form in Figure 8-11 shows an example of the client callback feature when implemented via code on a web form. The somewhat contrived example shows a DropDownList control holding vehicle category data linked in a parent-child hierarchy with a ListBox control displaying vehicles from several manufacturers. Changes to the category in the DropDownList refresh the vehicles displayed in the ListBox according to that category. The top set of controls uses the traditional approach to the solution with an automatic postback control with server-side data binding changes while the bottom set uses client-side callback features to refresh the data without a postback. The clock at the top of the page confirms whether a postback was incurred or not.

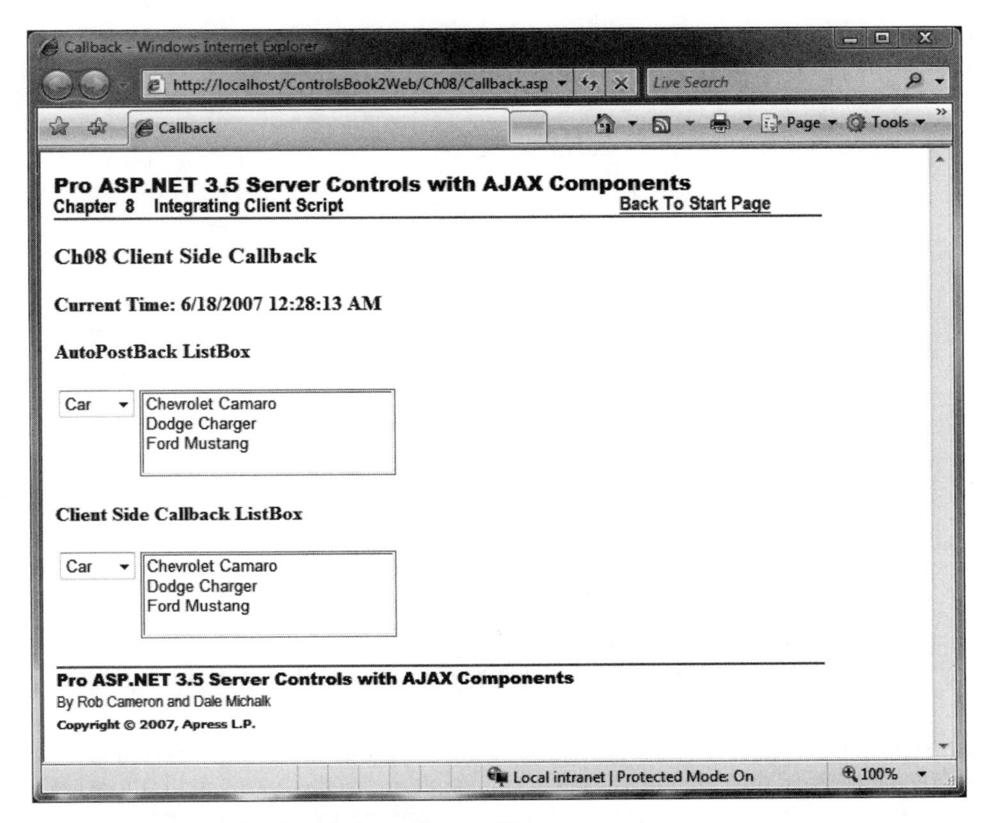

Figure 8-11. *The Callback web form client callback example*

The key function in the web form code is a utility function named `RenderScripts`. The first thing it does is add client-side JavaScript code to detect a `select` element change from the rendered `DropDownList` named `CbCategoryDrp` and then tie its selected value to an invocation of a function named `GetVehicles`.

```
CbCategoryDrp.Attributes.Add("onChange",
 "GetVehicles(this.options[this.selectedIndex].value)");
```

`GetVehicles` is a small wrapper over the `GetCallbackEventReference` stub that is registered for inclusion into the HTML content via `RegisterClientScriptBlock`.

```
string callBack = Page.ClientScript.GetCallbackEventReference(
    this, "category", "LoadVehicles", null);

string clientCallFunc = "function GetVehicles(category)
{ " + callBack + "; }";
Page.ClientScript.RegisterClientScriptBlock(this.GetType(),
    "GetVehicles", clientCallFunc, true);
```

The key parameters to the `GetCallBackEventReference` include the category JavaScript variable that is defined by `GetVehicles`, which takes the selected value of the `select` element generated by the DropDownList control. The other parameter of interest is the LoadVehicles that is also defined in the server-side RenderScripts method.

```
        string clientRecFunc = @"
            function LoadVehicles(results, context)
            {
                var vehLst = document.getElementById('$list');
                vehLst.innerHTML = '';

                var cars = results.split(';');
                for (var i = 0; i < cars.length-1; i++)
                {
                    var values = cars[i].split(':');
                    var option = document.createElement('option');
                    option.value = values[0];
                    option.innerHTML = values[1];
                    vehLst.appendChild(option);
                }
            }";

        Page.ClientScript.RegisterClientScriptBlock(this.GetType(),
            "LoadVehicles", clientRecFunc.Replace("$list",CbVehicleLst.ClientID),
             true);
```

LoadVehicles takes the results from the server-side callback as well as a context parameter and uses the data to load the data into the client side rendering of the CbVehicleList ListBox control. The script text has a placeholder for the name of the control; it is replaced at registration time with the actual ClientID property of the ListBox.

The other interesting item of note is the encoding mechanism used to send vehicle data to the client, which is best understood by looking at the web form's implementation of ICallbackEventHandler.

```
    public void RaiseCallbackEvent(string eventArgument)
    {
        cbVehicles = GetVehiclesByCategory(eventArgument);
    }

    public string GetCallbackResult()
    {
        string result = "";
        foreach (Vehicle veh in cbVehicles)
        {
            result += veh.Name + ":" + veh.Description + ";";
        }
        return result;
    }
```

The Vehicle class has two properties named Name and Description, which are serialized into a string. The properties are separated with a colon and returned instances are separated by semicolons. We will delve into the more elegant means of doing such serialization with a more natural JavaScript syntax called JavaScript Object Notation (JSON) later in this book, when we focus on ASP.NET Ajax Extensions.

Looking at the final rendering of the code in the browser, you can see the linkup between the client script in `GetVehicle` and a `WebForm_DoCallback` method that is brought in along with other callback JavaScript method support via a script `include`. An interesting side trip for the user is to follow the reference to the included script and see the use of `XmlHttpRequest` and `iframe` techniques to implement the callback.

```
<script src="/ControlsBook2Web/WebResource.axd?d=5DxW5OyyTz6vxBRQ_8ouAg2&amp;t=
633160590894162000" type="text/javascript"></script>

<script type="text/javascript">
<!--
            function LoadVehicles(results, context)
            {
                var vehLst = document.getElementById(
                'ctl00_ControlsBookContent_CbVehicleLst');
                vehLst.innerHTML = '';

                var cars = results.split(';');
                for (var i = 0; i < cars.length-1; i++)
                {
                    var values = cars[i].split(':');
                    var option = document.createElement('option');
                    option.value = values[0];
                    option.innerHTML = values[1];
                    vehLst.appendChild(option);
                }
            }

function GetVehicles(category)
{
                WebForm_DoCallback('__Page',category,LoadVehicles,null,null,false);
            }
// -->
</script>
```

The full code for the Callback web form is show in Listings 8-15 and 8-16.

Listing 8-15. *The Callback Web Form .aspx Page File*

```
<%@ Page Language="C#"
MasterPageFile="~/MasterPage/ControlsBook2MasterPage.Master"
  AutoEventWireup="true" CodeBehind="Callback.aspx.cs"
Inherits="ControlsBook2Web.Ch08.Callback"
  Title="Callback Demo" %>
```

```
<asp:Content ID="Content1" ContentPlaceHolderID="ChapterNumAndTitle" r
unat="server">
  <asp:Label ID="ChapterNumberLabel" runat="server"
  Width="14px">8</asp:Label>  <asp:Label
    ID="ChapterTitleLabel" runat="server" Width="360px">
    Integrating Client-Side Script</asp:Label>
</asp:Content>
<asp:Content ID="Content2" ContentPlaceHolderID="PrimaryContent" runat="server">
  <h3>
    Ch08 Client Side Callback</h3>
  <h4>
    Current Time:
    <%= DateTime.Now %>
  </h4>
  <h4>
    AutoPostBack ListBox</h4>
  <table>
    <tr valign="top">
      <td>
        <asp:DropDownList ID="CategoryDrp" runat="server" AutoPostBack="true"
        OnSelectedIndexChanged="CategoryDrp_SelectedIndexChanged">
          <asp:ListItem Selected="true">Car</asp:ListItem>
          <asp:ListItem>Truck</asp:ListItem>
          <asp:ListItem>SUV</asp:ListItem>
        </asp:DropDownList>
      </td>
      <td>
        <asp:ListBox ID="VehicleLst" Width="200" runat="server"
          DataTextField="Description"
          DataValueField="Name"></asp:ListBox>
      </td>
    </tr>
  </table>
  <h4>
    Client Side Callback ListBox</h4>
  <table>
    <tr valign="top">
      <td>
        <asp:DropDownList ID="CbCategoryDrp" runat="server">
          <asp:ListItem Selected="true">Car</asp:ListItem>
          <asp:ListItem>Truck</asp:ListItem>
          <asp:ListItem>SUV</asp:ListItem>
        </asp:DropDownList>
      </td>
      <td>
```

```
        <asp:ListBox ID="CbVehicleLst" Width="200" runat="server"
         DataTextField="Description"
          DataValueField="Name"></asp:ListBox>
      </td>
    </tr>
  </table>
  <br />
</asp:Content>
```

Listing 8-16. *Callback Web Form Code-Behind Class File*

```
using System;
using System.Collections.Generic;
using System.Web.UI;

namespace ControlsBook2Web.Ch08
{
  public partial class Callback : System.Web.UI.Page, ICallbackEventHandler
  {
    private List<Vehicle> cbVehicles;

    protected void Page_Load(object sender, EventArgs e)
    {
      if (!Page.IsPostBack)
      {
        LoadVehicleListBoxes();
      }
    }

    private void RenderScripts()
    {

      CbCategoryDrp.Attributes.Add("onChange",
       "GetVehicles(this.options[this.selectedIndex].value)");

      string clientRecFunc = @"
            function LoadVehicles(results, context)
            {
                var vehLst = document.getElementById('$list');
                vehLst.innerHTML = '';

                var cars = results.split(';');
```

```
                for (var i = 0; i < cars.length-1; i++)
                {
                    var values = cars[i].split(':');
                    var option = document.createElement('option');
                    option.value = values[0];
                    option.innerHTML = values[1];
                    vehLst.appendChild(option);
                }
            }";

      Page.ClientScript.RegisterClientScriptBlock(this.GetType(),
      "LoadVehicles", clientRecFunc.Replace(
     "$list", CbVehicleLst.ClientID), true);

      string callBack = Page.ClientScript.GetCallbackEventReference(
          this, "category", "LoadVehicles", null);

      string clientCallFunc = "function GetVehicles(category)
      { " + callBack + "; }\n";
      Page.ClientScript.RegisterClientScriptBlock(this.GetType(),
          "GetVehicles", clientCallFunc, true);
    }

    private void LoadVehicleListBoxes()
    {
      VehicleLst.DataSource = GetVehiclesByCategory(CategoryDrp.SelectedValue);
      VehicleLst.DataBind();

      CbVehicleLst.DataSource = GetVehiclesByCategory(CbCategoryDrp.SelectedValue);
      CbVehicleLst.DataBind();

      RenderScripts();
    }

    protected void CategoryDrp_SelectedIndexChanged(object sender, EventArgs e)
    {
      LoadVehicleListBoxes();
    }


    private List<Vehicle> GetVehiclesByCategory(string category)
    {
      List<Vehicle> vehicles = new List<Vehicle>();
```

```
    switch (category)
    {
      case "Car":
        vehicles.Add(new Vehicle("Camaro", "Chevrolet Camaro"));
        vehicles.Add(new Vehicle("Charger", "Dodge Charger"));
        vehicles.Add(new Vehicle("Mustang", "Ford Mustang"));
        break;
      case "Truck":
        vehicles.Add(new Vehicle("Silverado", "Chevrolet Silverado"));
        vehicles.Add(new Vehicle("Ram", "Dodge"));
        vehicles.Add(new Vehicle("F150", "Ford F150"));
        break;
      case "SUV":
        vehicles.Add(new Vehicle("Yukon", "Chevrolet Yukon"));
        vehicles.Add(new Vehicle("Durango", "Dodge Durango"));
        vehicles.Add(new Vehicle("Expedition", "Ford Expedition"));
        break;
    }
    return vehicles;
  }
  #region ICallbackEventHandler Members

  public string GetCallbackResult()
  {
    string result = "";
    foreach (Vehicle veh in cbVehicles)
    {
      result += veh.Name + ":" + veh.Description + ";";
    }
    return result;
  }

  public void RaiseCallbackEvent(string eventArgument)
  {
    cbVehicles = GetVehiclesByCategory(eventArgument);
  }
  #endregion
}

public class Vehicle
{
  public Vehicle(string name, string description)
  {
    Name = name;
    Description = description;
  }
```

```
    public string Name {get; set;}

    public string Description {get; set;}
  }
}
```

The StockNews Callback Control

Most web developers would prefer for controls to hide the details of the client-side callback process and not have to wire it up themselves like in our first example. The ASP.NET control library itself follows this strategy with the `TreeView` control and its use of the callback feature set to implement an on-demand population of child tree view nodes without requiring a full page refresh.

We will follow the same callback strategy with a server control that fetches the news for a stock symbol from the MSN Money stock news RSS feed. The UI of this custom composite control includes a `DropDownList` control that contains the stock symbols and a `div` element below it that contains the rendered contents of the RSS feed. Figure 8-12 shows the results of putting the control on a web form.

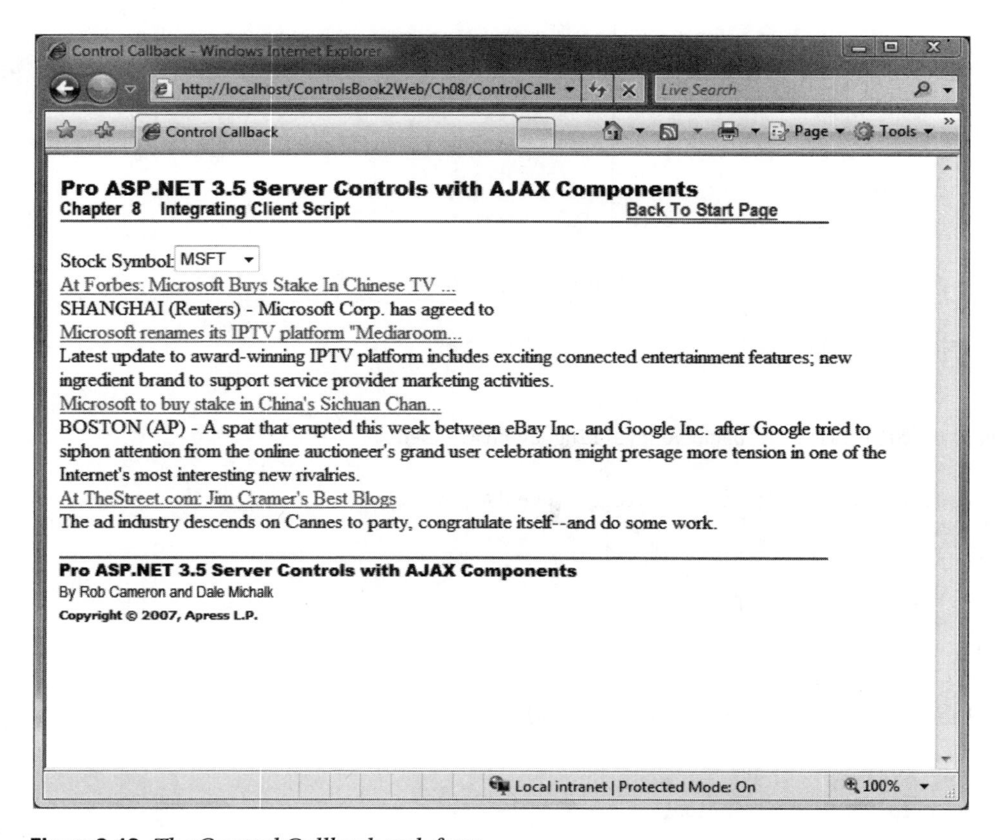

Figure 8-12. *The Control Callback web form*

The StockNews control derives from the CompositeDataBoundControl abstract control base class to handle the bulk of its server control overhead. The control creation implementation in CreateChildControls takes an IEnumerable collection of strings that represent the stock symbols and loads them into a DropDownList control. It also invokes a helper method named CreateClientScript to generate the client side functionality.

```
protected override int CreateChildControls(
System.Collections.IEnumerable dataSource, bool dataBinding)
        {
            int count = 0;
            if (dataSource != null)
            {
                LiteralControl txt = new LiteralControl("Stock Symbol:");
                Controls.Add(txt);

                list = new DropDownList();
                Controls.Add(list);

                div = new HtmlGenericControl("div");
                Controls.Add(div);

                if (dataBinding)
                {
                    IEnumerator e = dataSource.GetEnumerator();
                    while(e.MoveNext())
                    {
                        string symbol = e.Current.ToString();
                        ListItem item = new ListItem(symbol, symbol);
                        list.Items.Add(item);
                        count++;

                    }
                }
                else
                {
                    IEnumerator e = dataSource.GetEnumerator();
                    while (e.MoveNext())
                    {
                        ListItem item = new ListItem("","");
                        list.Items.Add(item);
                        count++;
                    }
                }
                CreateClientScript();
            }
            return count;
        }
```

CreateClientScript builds the callback script logic and wires it with the appropriate client-side interactivity of the DropDownList control. The GetNews and LoadNews functions are similar in functionality to the previous web form callback example.

```
private void CreateClientScript()
{
    list.Attributes.Add("onChange",
        "GetNews(this.options[this.selectedIndex].value)");

    string clientRecFunc = @"
    function LoadNews(results, context)
    {
        var newsDiv = document.getElementById('$div');
        newsDiv.innerHTML = results;
    }";
    Page.ClientScript.RegisterClientScriptBlock(this.GetType(),
        "LoadNews", clientRecFunc.Replace("$div",div.ClientID),
        true);

    string callBack = Page.ClientScript.GetCallbackEventReference(
        this, "symbol", "LoadNews", null);
    string clientCallFunc = "function GetNews(symbol){ " +
        callBack + "; }";
    Page.ClientScript.RegisterClientScriptBlock(this.GetType(),
        "GetNews", clientCallFunc, true);
}
```

A bigger difference in the control callback implementation is evident in the code that handles the callback invocation in the control server-side code. The result returned is sent back in HTML form for the client to insert into the div element below the DropDownList control. The call to GetNewsItem does all the work to retrieve and parse the RSS feed into a generic List collection of NewsItem-based objects that are serialized into the HTML string.

```
public void RaiseCallbackEvent(string eventArgument)
{
    items = GetNewsItems(eventArgument);
}

public string GetCallbackResult()
{
    StringBuilder sb = new StringBuilder();
    if (items != null)
    {
        foreach (NewsItem item in items)
        {
            sb.Append("<span><a href='");
            sb.Append(item.Link);
            sb.Append("'>");
```

```
                sb.Append(item.Title);
                sb.Append("</a><span>");
                sb.Append("<br />");
                sb.Append("<span>");
                sb.Append(item.Description);
                sb.Append("</span>");
                sb.Append("<br />");
            }
        }
        return sb.ToString();
    }
```

Another interesting implementation note in `StockNews` control is the use of the `PreRender` overload to prime the initial content of the HTTP GET request to the form with the symbol selected by the `DropDownList` control. This timing in the control life cycle not only ensures an initial value in the control but also aligns nicely with any postback that might occur with other controls on the form and lets `ViewState` work its magic to keep our client side activities in sync with the normal server side functionality of a postback.

```
protected override void OnPreRender(EventArgs e)
{
   base.OnPreRender(e);
   RaiseCallbackEvent(list.SelectedValue);
   div.InnerHtml = GetCallbackResult();
}
```

The other code of interest that is specific to .NET 3.5 is the Language Integrated Query (LINQ) code that iterates over the feed data, creates a collection of anonymous types that contain the data from the field, and then uses object initialization to create the feed items for rendering to the browser. You can find this code in the `GetNewsItems` method in Listing 8-17. In the source code included in this book, the `StockNews.cs` code file includes the "old way" to do this using an `XPathNavigator` for comparison purposes. The full code listing for both the server control and its related web form are in Listings 8-17, 8-18, and 8-19.

Listing 8-17. *StockNews Control Class File*

```
using System;
using System.Web.UI;
using System.Web.UI.HtmlControls;
using System.Web.UI.WebControls;
using System.ComponentModel;
using System.Collections;
using System.Collections.Generic;
using System.Text;
using System.Net;
using System.Linq;
using System.Xml.Linq;
```

```
namespace ControlsBook2Lib.Ch08
{
  [ToolboxData("<{0}:StockNews runat=server></{0}:StockNews>"),
  DefaultProperty("Symbols")]
  public class StockNews : CompositeDataBoundControl, ICallbackEventHandler
  {
    protected DropDownList list = new DropDownList();
    protected HtmlGenericControl div;
    private List<NewsItem> items;

    [Browsable(false)]
    public virtual ListItemCollection Symbols
    {
      get
      {
        EnsureChildControls();
        return list.Items;
      }
    }

    protected override int CreateChildControls(System.Collections.IEnumerable
     dataSource, bool dataBinding)
    {
      int count = 0;
      if (dataSource != null)
      {
        LiteralControl txt = new LiteralControl("Stock Symbol:");
        Controls.Add(txt);

        list = new DropDownList();
        Controls.Add(list);

        div = new HtmlGenericControl("div");
        Controls.Add(div);

        if (dataBinding)
        {
          IEnumerator e = dataSource.GetEnumerator();
          while (e.MoveNext())
          {
            string symbol = e.Current.ToString();
            ListItem item = new ListItem(symbol, symbol);
            list.Items.Add(item);
            count++;

          }
        }
```

```
    else
    {
      IEnumerator e = dataSource.GetEnumerator();
      while (e.MoveNext())
      {
        ListItem item = new ListItem("", "");
        list.Items.Add(item);
        count++;
      }
    }
    CreateClientScript();
  }
  return count;
}

protected override void OnPreRender(EventArgs e)
{
  base.OnPreRender(e);
  RaiseCallbackEvent(list.SelectedValue);
  div.InnerHtml = GetCallbackResult();
}

private void CreateClientScript()
{
  list.Attributes.Add("onChange",
      "GetNews(this.options[this.selectedIndex].value)");

  string clientRecFunc = @"
        function LoadNews(results, context)
        {
            var newsDiv = document.getElementById('$div');
            newsDiv.innerHTML = results;
        }";
  Page.ClientScript.RegisterClientScriptBlock(this.GetType(),
      "LoadNews", clientRecFunc.Replace("$div", div.ClientID),
      true);

  string callBack = Page.ClientScript.GetCallbackEventReference(
      this, "symbol", "LoadNews", null);
  string clientCallFunc = "function GetNews(symbol){ " +
      callBack + "; }";
  Page.ClientScript.RegisterClientScriptBlock(this.GetType(),
      "GetNews", clientCallFunc, true);

}
```

```
public string GetCallbackResult()
{
  StringBuilder sb = new StringBuilder();
  if (items != null)
  {
    foreach (NewsItem item in items)
    {
      sb.Append("<span><a href='");
      sb.Append(item.Link);
      sb.Append("'>");
      sb.Append(item.Title);
      sb.Append("</a><span>");
      sb.Append("<br />");
      sb.Append("<span>");
      sb.Append(item.Description);
      sb.Append("</span>");
      sb.Append("<br />");
    }
  }
  return sb.ToString();
}

public void RaiseCallbackEvent(string eventArgument)
{
  items = GetNewsItems(eventArgument);
}

private List<NewsItem> GetNewsItems(string symbol)
{
  List<NewsItem> Feeditems = new List<NewsItem>();
  string url = "http://moneycentral.msn.com/community/rss/generate_feed.aspx" +
      "?feedType=0&symbol=" + symbol;
  XDocument rssFeed = XDocument.Load(url);
  var posts = from item in rssFeed.Descendants("item")
              select new
              {
                Title = item.Element("title").Value,
                Description = item.Element("description").Value,
                Link = item.Element("link").Value,
              };

  var stockPosts = from item in posts
                   select item;
```

```
      foreach (var item in stockPosts)
      {
        Feeditems.Add(new NewsItem { Title = item.Title, Description =
        item.Description, Link = item.Link });
      }
      return Feeditems;
    }
  }

  class NewsItem
  {
    public string Title;
    public string Description;
    public string Link;
  }
}
```

Listing 8-18. *The Callback Web Form .aspx Page File*

```
<%@ Page Language="C#"
MasterPageFile="~/MasterPage/ControlsBook2MasterPage.Master"
  AutoEventWireup="true" CodeBehind="ControlCallback.aspx.cs"
Inherits="ControlsBook2Web.Ch08.ControlCallback"
  Title="Untitled Page" %>

<%@ Register Assembly="ControlsBook2Lib" Namespace="ControlsBook2Lib.Ch08"
TagPrefix="apress" %>
<asp:Content ID="Content1" ContentPlaceHolderID="ChapterNumAndTitle" runat="server">
  <asp:Label ID="ChapterNumberLabel" runat="server"
  Width="14px">8</asp:Label>  <asp:Label
    ID="ChapterTitleLabel" runat="server" Width="360px">
    Integrating Client-Side Script</asp:Label>
</asp:Content>
<asp:Content ID="Content2" ContentPlaceHolderID="PrimaryContent" runat="server">
  <br />
  <apress:StockNews ID="stockNews" runat="server" />
  <br />
</asp:Content>
```

Listing 8-19. *Callback Web Form Code-Behind Class File*

```
using System;

namespace ControlsBook2Web.Ch08
{
  public partial class ControlCallback : System.Web.UI.Page
  {
    protected void Page_Load(object sender, EventArgs e)
    {
      if (!Page.IsPostBack)
      {
        LoadSymbols();
      }
    }

    private void LoadSymbols()
    {
      stockNews.DataSource = new string[] { "MSFT", "IBM", "GOOG", "ORCL" };
      stockNews.DataBind();
    }
  }
}
```

Summary

Client-side scripts can make a web application more appealing, interactive, and scalable. ASP.NET allows encapsulation of the client-side script code to reduce some of the inherent complexity client script can bring to web development projects. Controls support adding client-side event attributes to the .aspx page declaratively and programmatically via the Attributes collection. Also, the ClientScriptManager class that is tied to the Page.ClientScript property supports several options for registering client-side scripts: RegisterClientScriptBlock for the top of the form, RegisterStartupScript for the bottom of the form, RegisterArrayDeclaration for adding an array, and RegisterOnSubmitStatement for hooking into the onsubmit event of the form.

Client-side detection is done through an instance of the HttpBrowserCapabilities class. An instance is provided by the Page.Request.Browser class. Controls should provide graceful degradation wherever possible, in case a client doesn't support client-side functionality to the level required.

Be careful when you map to the onsubmit event of an HTML form. It will fire when a control such as LinkButton uses the client-side JavaScript form submission code provided by ASP.NET.

Client callbacks are a great way to pull data or content from the server to the client without requiring a postback or refreshing of the browser page. They also make deployment easy by being integrated directly into the ASP.NET 2.0 or later Framework feature set.

CHAPTER 9

■ ■ ■

ASP.NET AJAX Controls and Extenders

Up to this chapter, we have provided the necessary background to create powerful ASP.NET server controls that support custom styling, templating, data binding, and client-side scripts. While the existing client-side script integration is useful in ASP.NET, ASP.NET AJAX takes it to the next level by providing a powerful client-side script library that integrates well with the server-side programming model and design-time support that ASP.NET developers know and love.

In this chapter, we bridge the gap to client-side integration when building custom server controls via ASP.NET AJAX. We provide an overview of ASP.NET AJAX extensibility points followed by step-by-step examples on how to create AJAX-enabled server controls as well as ASP.NET AJAX extenders and client-side behaviors.

ASP.NET AJAX

ASP.NET AJAX enables developers to quickly create web pages that include a rich user experience with responsive and familiar UI elements, quite often without writing a single line of JavaScript. In addition, ASP.NET AJAX includes a client script library that incorporates cross-browser ECMAScript (JavaScript) and dynamic HTML (DHTML) technologies. ASP.NET AJAX integrates the JavaScript library with the ASP.NET to provide a powerful tool set that can help developers improve the user experience and the efficiency of web applications without giving up the server-side programming model they love.

Note We will show all the configuration steps and, of course, all of the code in this chapter, but we don't provide complete background on all ASP.NET AJAX functionality. That would take an entire book.

There are two primary ways to leverage the ASP.NET AJAX framework. There is a client-site option that is more familiar to anyone who has hand-coded AJAX in JavaScript, and there is also a server-side option that performs partial page updates on the client as you would expect with AJAX but still executes the full server-side page life cycle. No matter what route you choose, any page that wants to leverage the ASP.NET AJAX functionality must include a `ScriptManager` control on the page to include the required underlying plumbing. In the next section, we cover partial page updates.

Partial Page Updates

Partial page updates are driven by the ASP.NET AJAX UpdatePanel server control. The UpdatePanel is a container control where developers can drag regular ASP.NET server controls and HTML into the designer and have the contents of the UpdatePanel updated without causing a full page postback. Upon the first HTTP GET, the entire page is sent to the browser as expected. This is where the magic occurs: if any of the controls within the UpdatePanel cause a server postback, or a Trigger in the UpdatePanel is configured to cause the postback, only the UI contained within the UpdatePanel control is updated, eliminating the full postback flicker so familiar to end users. It results in a reduced amount of data flowing over the network, helping to conserve bandwidth while not sacrificing the benefits of what we know and love about ASP.NET, such as the server-side event execution model and design-time control configuration.

Taking advantage of the UpdatePanel is extremely simple. Add an ASP.NET AJAX ScriptManager nonvisual server control to your page, add an UpdatePanel, and drag controls into the UpdatePanel that you want to update independently from the rest of the page.

SimpleUserControlAJAX Demonstration

The UpdatePanel is a great tool to add AJAX functionality to an ASP.NET application with minimal effort. To demonstrate this, we took the SimpleUserControl example from Chapter 2 and converted into the SimpleUserControlAJAX example by adding an UpdatePanel to the user control to encapsulate the GridView control.

By simply adding an UpdatePanel around the GridView, paging, sorting, and so forth in the GridView no longer causes a full web form postback. Since this is dynamic in nature, screen shots are not included, so please download and run the sample to see the benefits of the UpdatePanel. Listing 9-1 shows the source code for SimpleUserControlAJAX.ascx.

Listing 9-1. *The SimpleUserControlAJAX User Control*

```
<%@ Control Language="C#" AutoEventWireup="true"
CodeBehind="SimpleUserControlAJAX.ascx.cs"
Inherits="ControlsBook2Web.Ch09.SimpleUserControlAJAX" %>
<asp:UpdatePanel ID="UpdatePanel1" runat="server">
  <ContentTemplate>
    <asp:GridView ID="GridView1" runat="server" AllowPaging="True"
      AllowSorting="True" AutoGenerateColumns="False" CellPadding="4"
      DataKeyNames="ID" DataSourceID="ApressBooksds"
      EmptyDataText="There are no data records to display." Font-Names="Arial"
      Font-Size="X-Small" ForeColor="#333333" GridLines="None">
      <Columns>
        <asp:commandfield ShowSelectButton="True" />
        <asp:boundfield DataField="ID" HeaderText="ID" ReadOnly="True"
          SortExpression="ID" Visible="False" />
        <asp:boundfield DataField="ISBN" HeaderText="ISBN" SortExpression="ISBN" />
        <asp:boundfield DataField="Author" HeaderText="Author"
```

```
          SortExpression="Author" />
        <asp:boundfield DataField="Title" HeaderText="Title"
        SortExpression="Title" />
        <asp:boundfield DataField="Description" HeaderText="Description"
          SortExpression="Description" />
        <asp:boundfield DataField="DatePublished" HeaderText="DatePublished"
          SortExpression="DatePublished" />
        <asp:boundfield DataField="NumPages" HeaderText="NumPages"
          SortExpression="NumPages" />
        <asp:boundfield DataField="TOC" HeaderText="TOC" SortExpression="TOC" />
        <asp:boundfield DataField="Price" HeaderText="Price"
       SortExpression="Price" />
      </Columns>
      <FooterStyle BackColor="#990000" Font-Bold="True" ForeColor="White" />
      <RowStyle BackColor="#FFFBD6" ForeColor="#333333" />
      <SelectedRowStyle BackColor="#FFCC66" Font-Bold="True" ForeColor="Navy" />
      <PagerStyle BackColor="#FFCC66" ForeColor="#333333"
      HorizontalAlign="Center" />
      <HeaderStyle BackColor="#990000" Font-Bold="True" ForeColor="White" />
      <AlternatingRowStyle BackColor="White" />
    </asp:GridView>
    <asp:AccessDataSource ID="ApressBooksds" runat="server"
      DataFile="..\App_Data\ApressBooks.mdb" SelectCommand="SELECT * FROM [Books]">
    </asp:AccessDataSource>
  </ContentTemplate>
</asp:UpdatePanel>
```

Listings 9-2 and 9-3 have the source code for the SimpleUserControlAjaxDemo web form and code-behind file.

Listing 9-2. *The SimpleUserControlAJAX Web Form .aspx Page File*

```
<%@ Page Language="C#"
MasterPageFile="~/MasterPage/ControlsBook2MasterPage.Master"
  AutoEventWireup="true" CodeBehind="SimpleUserControlAJAXDemo.aspx.cs"
  Inherits="ControlsBook2Web.Ch09.SimpleUserControlAJAXDemo1"
  Title="Simple user Control AJAX Demo" %>

<%@ Register Src="SimpleUserControlAJAX.ascx" TagName=
"SimpleUserControlAJAX" TagPrefix="apressuc" %>
<asp:Content ID="Content1" ContentPlaceHolderID="ChapterNumAndTitle" runat="server">
  <asp:Label ID="ChapterNumberLabel" runat="server"
  Width="14px">9</asp:Label>  <asp:Label
    ID="ChapterTitleLabel" runat="server" Width="360px">
   ASP.NET AJAX Controls and Extenders</asp:Label>
</asp:Content>
<asp:Content ID="Content2" ContentPlaceHolderID="PrimaryContent" runat="server">
  <apressuc:SimpleUserControlAJAX ID="SimpleUserControlAJAX1" runat="server" />
</asp:Content>
```

Listing 9-3. *The SimpleUserControlAJAX Web Form Code-Behind Class File*

```
using System;

namespace ControlsBook2Web.Ch02
{
  public partial class SimpleUserControlDemo : System.Web.UI.Page
  {
    protected void Page_Load(object sender, EventArgs e)
    {

    }
  }
}
```

We won't cover the UpdatePanel control any further. Next, we cover the ASP.NET AJAX infrastructure, where we demonstrate extending ASP.AJAX functionality with custom controls and extenders.

ASP.NET AJAX Extensibility

ASP.NET AJAX provides a set of ASP.NET namespaces as well as base classes and services via the System.Web.Extensions assembly. Table 9-1 provides an overview of the namespaces either extended or added originally by ASP.NET AJAX 1.0 and now included in .NET Framework 3.5.

Table 9-1. *ASP.NET AJAX-Related Namspaces*

Namespace	Description
System.Web.Configuration	This namespace is extended by ASP.NET AJAX to support declarative and programmatic access to ASP.NET AJAX configuration elements. Example classes are ScriptingJsonSerializationSection and ScriptingSectionGroup.
System.Web.Script.Serialization	This namespace was added to ASP.NET to support JavaScript Object Notation (JSON) serialization as well as provide extensibility features to customize serialization.
System.Web.Script.Services	This namespace was added to ASP.NET to provide attributes for customizing web service support in ASP.NET AJAX. Example classes are ScriptServiceAttribute and ScriptMethodAttribute.
System.Web.UI	This namespace is extended by ASP.NET AJAX to provide classes and interfaces that enable client-server communication and rich UI. Example classes are ExtenderControl, ScriptControl, and UpdatePanel.
System.Web.UI.Design	This namespace is extended by ASP.NET AJAX to provide design-time support for Microsoft ASP.NET AJAX. Example classes are UpdatePanelDesigner, TimeDesigner, and UpdateProgressDesigner.
System.Web.Handlers	This namespace is extended by ASP.NET AJAX to provide the necessary HTTP handler (ScriptResourceHandler) and HTTP module (ScriptModule) to support ASP.NET AJAX.

In this chapter, we focus on the classes that support extending ASP.NET AJAX functionality for custom server controls. Table 9-2 provides an overview of the important base classes in ASP.NET AJAX for use when creating ASP.NET AJAX controls and extenders.

Table 9-2. *Important ASP.NET AJAX Classes and Interfaces*

Base Class	Description
`ExtenderControl`	This is the abstract base class implemented when creating an ASP.NET AJAX extender control. This class inherits from `Control` and implements `IExtenderControl`.
`IExtenderControl`	Implement this interface to build an extender control that does not require a `ScriptManager`. The `IExtenderControl` interface registers the script libraries for a control by calling the `GetScriptReferences()` method, and it registers `ScriptDescriptor` objects by calling the `GetScriptDescriptors(Control)` method.
`IScriptControl`	Implement this interface to add ASP.NET AJAX support to a custom server control. The methods of the `IScriptControl` interface provide references to script libraries that define client components and script descriptors that represent instances of client types required to add script control functionality in an ASP.NET Server control. It's found in the `System.Web.UI` namespace.
`ScriptControl`	This is the abstract base class implemented when creating an ASP.NET server control that includes ASP.NET AJAX functionality. This class inherits from `WebControl` and implements `IScriptControl`.
`ScriptReference`	This class registers an `ECMAScript (JavaScript)` file for use on a web page.

The two primary items in the Table 9-2 are the `ExtenderControl` class and `IScriptControl` interface. Add the `IScriptControl` interface to a custom server control that will include ASP.NET AJAX functionality. You create controls that inherit from `ExtenderControl` when you want to encapsulate client-side functionality (e.g., DHTML behavior) that is applied to other server controls, such as built-in the `TextBox` or `Button` server controls. Both `ExtenderControl` and `IScriptControl` require implementation of two methods:

- `GetScriptReferences`
- `GetScriptDescriptors`

These two methods are at the heart of wiring up server-side ASP.NET with the client-side ASP.NET AJAX script library and custom behaviors. We cover these two methods next in preparation for creating both a custom ASP.NET AJAX server control and a custom ASP.NET AJAX Extender later in this chapter.

The GetScriptReferences Method

In order to add AJAX functionality to a custom server control, some `JavaScript` code is probably required. It is a good convention to create a `.js` file that has the same name as the custom server control to help keep things organized. This script file must be made available to the control at runtime.

The GetScriptReferences method adds references to the required script files at runtime so that they are available to the custom AJAX server control. You can certainly include multiple script files as part of a server control to help keep things organized. For this reason, the GetScriptReferences returns a collection of ScriptReference objects, one for each script. There are two ways to obtain a script reference. One way is to provide a reference to the script based on the script's relative location to the web page via the ScriptReference object's .Path property.

The other way is to obtain a reference to a script included in an assembly as an embedded resource via the ScriptReference.Assembly property, which is our preferred method to ship JavaScript files with an ASP.NET AJAX custom server control. Here is an example implementation of the GetScriptReferences method:

```
protected virtual IEnumerable<ScriptReference> GetScriptReferences()
{
  ScriptReference reference = new ScriptReference();
  //Load script from embedded resource
  reference.Assembly = "ControlsBook2Lib";
  reference.Name = "ControlsBook2Lib.Ch09.HighlightedHyperLink.js";

  return new ScriptReference[] { reference };
}
```

For the preceding code to succeed, a couple of steps must be taken:

- The script file named HighlightedHyperLink.js must have its Build Action property set to Embedded Resource so that the script is included in the compiled assembly as a resource.
- The other step is to add a WebResource attribute to the assembly like this:

```
[assembly: WebResource("ControlsBook2Lib.Ch09.HighlightedHyperLink.js",
"text/javascript")]
```

The WebResourceAttribute defines the metadata attribute that enables an embedded resource in an assembly to be available. At runtime, ASP.NET dynamically creates a script file for the resource that is downloaded to the client just like a normal JavaScript file referenced by a URL. In the next section, we cover the GetScriptDescriptors method.

The GetScriptDescriptors Method

The allure of ASP.NET AJAX is having AJAX functionality without losing the server-side programming model or losing the ability to configure server controls in Visual Studio at design time. For this to work, there must be a means to convert server-side configuration to client-side configuration and functionality. Thankfully, ASP.NET AJAX provides the plumbing to make this happen, and the GetScriptDescriptors method is the means to plug into the infrastructure.

The GetScriptDescriptors method returns one or more ScriptDescriptor objects via a ScriptDescriptor collection. Each ScriptDescriptor object has information about a client-side component that is required. The ScriptDescriptor includes the client type to create, the properties to assign, and the events to add handlers for. Here is an example implementation of the GetScriptDescriptors method:

```
protected virtual IEnumerable<ScriptDescriptor> GetScriptDescriptors()
{
  ScriptControlDescriptor descriptor = new ScriptControlDescriptor
("ControlsBook2Lib.Ch09.HighlightedHyperlink", this.ClientID);

  descriptor.AddProperty("highlightCssClass", this.HighlightCssClass);
  descriptor.AddProperty("nohighlightCssClass", this.NoHighlightCssClass);

  return new ScriptDescriptor[] { descriptor };
}
```

The preceding code creates a client-side component called `ControlsBook2Lib.Ch09.HighlightedHyperlink` in the constructor for the `ScriptBehaviorDescriptor` object. The constructor also provides the client-side name of the server control that the client-side component interacts with via the `this.ClientID` property. Since AJAX extender server controls apply behaviors via client-side components to other ASP.NET server controls, `this.ClientID` would not be used. Instead, for an extender control, the value passed in would be `targetControl.ClientID`.

After the new `ScriptBehaviorDescriptor` object is created, methods are called to set properties (via `AddProperty`), event handler names (via `AddEvent`), and so forth on the client-side component created in the constructor.

Implementing an ASP.NET AJAX custom server control requires a bit more work, which we describe later in this chapter. First, we dive in with example code that leverages the ASP.NET AJAX client library functionality in the next section.

ASP.NET AJAX Client Script

The ASP.NET AJAX client script provides numerous advantages over plain old JavaScript. The script library adds object-oriented-like capabilities to JavaScript code to increase code reuse, flexibility, and maintainability. There are many extensions that reduce development time by wrapping common functionality, such as making cross-browser-compatible `XmlHttp` calls. For example, instead of making calls to `XmlHttp` objects directly, there is a `Sys.Net.WebRequest` object that greatly enhances `XmlHttp` functionality through a higher level, cross-browser programming model.

The ASP.NET AJAX client script supports reflection to examine the structure and components of client script at runtime. It adds enumerations to provide an easily readable alternative to integer representations. There are debugging extensions and a trace feature for faster and more informative debugging than with traditional JavaScript debugging techniques, as well as the ability to create debug and retail versions of script files that are automatically managed by ASP.NET. Let's take a look at a simple example of a client-side control called `HoverButton` to further examine the ASP.NET AJAX client script library.

HoverButton Example

The `HoverButton` example is based on the example in the ASP.NET AJAX documentation with some minor modifications, and it's very useful in helping you understand the ASP.NET AJAX client script library. Understanding how to write JavaScript client-side controls using the ASP.NET AJAX client-side library is critical to writing ASP.NET AJAX-enabled custom server controls.

The web form HoverButton.aspx is pretty simple in that it declares a plain old HTML <button> and a <div> tag. HoverButton.aspx has event handlers for the HoverButton client control as well as start-up code. The file HoverButton.js has the actual declaration of the HoverButton client component that manages the behavior. Let's start by going through the JavaScript in the web form HoverButton.aspx. The JavaScript starts out with this code:

```
var app = Sys.Application;
app.add_load(applicationLoadHandler);
```

The add_load method provides a delegate function that is called when the Application.load event occurs. The load event is raised after all scripts have been loaded and the objects in the application have been created and initialized. Here is the event handler for load from HoverButton.aspx:

```
function applicationLoadHandler(sender, args)
{
  $create(ControlsBook2Lib.Ch09.HoverButton,
    {text: 'A HoverButton Control',  //properties
        element: {style: {fontWeight: "bold", borderWidth: "2px"}}},  //properties
    {click: doClick, hover: doSomethingOnHover,
    unhover: doSomethingOnUnHover}, //events
    null, //references (none in this case)
    $get('Button1')); //element where the behavior is applied
}
```

The $create method is a shortcut to the Sys.Component.Create method in the ASP.NET AJAX client library. Here is the syntax of the call:

```
$create(type, properties, events, references, element);
```

From the preceding example, the type is ControlsBook2Lib.Ch09.HoverButton found in HoverButton.js. The type parameter is mandatory. The properties, events, references, and element parameters are optional but will most likely be present if the component is going to do something useful. The value must be in JavaScript Object Notation (JSON) format for the properties, events, references, and element parameters, which explains why the syntax is not very familiar (but the comments in the text just before this paragraph identify the parameters). For more information on JSON, please refer to the ASP.NET AJAX client-side library documentation.

The third parameter, events, is interesting since the rest of the JavaScript in HoverButton.aspx contains the event handlers mapped in the $create call. We see that the click event is mapped to the doClick function located in HoverButton.aspx, the hover event handler is the doSomethingOnHover function, and the unhover event handler is the doSomethingOnUnHover function. When you run the page HoverButton.aspx, you see that all events fire with the <div id="HoverLabel"> element having text set and cleared based on whether or not the mouse is hovering over the button. When the HTML <button id="Button1"> is clicked, the doClick event fires, displaying the alert message. Listings 9-4 and 9-5 provide the source code for HoverButton.aspx and HoverButton.aspx.cs, respectively.

Listing 9-4. *The HoverButton Web Form .aspx Page File*

```
<%@ Page Language="C#" MasterPageFile="~/MasterPage/ControlsBook2MasterPage.Master"
AutoEventWireup="true" CodeBehind="HoverButton.aspx.cs"
Inherits="ControlsBook2Web.Ch09.HoverButton"
Title="HoverButton Client Control Demo" %>

<asp:Content ID="Content1" ContentPlaceHolderID="HeadSection" runat="server">
  <style type="text/css">
    button
    {
      border: solid 1px black;
    }
    #HoverLabel
    {
      color: blue;
    }
  </style>
</asp:Content>
<asp:Content ID="Content2" ContentPlaceHolderID="ChapterNumAndTitle" runat="server">
  <asp:Label ID="ChapterNumberLabel" runat="server"
  Width="14px">9</asp:Label>  <asp:Label
    ID="ChapterTitleLabel" runat="server" Width="360px">
   ASP.NET AJAX Controls and Extenders</asp:Label>
</asp:Content>
<asp:Content ID="Content3" ContentPlaceHolderID="PrimaryContent" runat="server">

  <script type="text/javascript">
    var app = Sys.Application;
    app.add_load(applicationLoadHandler);

    function applicationLoadHandler(sender, args)
    {
        $create(ControlsBook2Lib.Ch09.HoverButton,
          {text: 'A HoverButton Control',  //properties
          element: {style: {fontWeight: "bold", borderWidth: "2px"}}},
        //properties (continued)
        {click: doClick, hover:
        doSomethingOnHover, unhover: doSomethingOnUnHover},
        //events
           null, //references (none in this case)
          $get('Button1'));
      //element where the behavior is applied
      //(in this case, the HTML button Button1)
    }
```

```
    function doSomethingOnHover(sender, args)
    {
        hoverMessage = "The mouse is over the button."
        $get('HoverLabel').innerHTML = hoverMessage;
    }

    function doSomethingOnUnHover(sender, args)
    {
       $get('HoverLabel').innerHTML = "";
    }

    function doClick(sender, args)
    {
       alert("The client-side JavaScript function
       doClick handled the HoverButton click event.");
    }
  </script>

  <br />
  <br />
  <button type="button" id="Button1">
  </button>
   
  <div id="HoverLabel">
  </div>
  <br />
  <br />
</asp:Content>
```

Listing 9-5. *The HoverButton Web Form Code-Behind Class File*

```
using System;

namespace ControlsBook2Web.Ch09
{
  public partial class HoverButton : System.Web.UI.Page
  {
    protected void Page_Load(object sender, EventArgs e)
    {

    }
  }
}
```

We now dive into the contents of `HoverButton.js`, which contains the `HoverButton` client control. The ASP.NET AJAX client script library provides support for namespaces via the `Type.registerNamespace` call, which helps to keep things organized.

Writing object-oriented-like JavaScript using the ASP.NET AJAX library is fairly straightforward but requires a deeper level understanding of the JavaScript language. An excellent MSDN article that provides great background can be found here:

http://msdn.microsoft.com/msdnmag/issues/07/05/JavaScript/default.aspx

In `HoverButton.js`, you find a `HoverButton` constructor function, a `HoverButton` prototype, and a call that registers the `HoverButton` class into the client-side framework. The constructor does what you would expect; that is, it initializes the class through a call to `initializeBase` and then sets the event handlers to null. Through the client-side framework, when the developer user creates a `HoverButton` client control as in `HoverButton.aspx`, `initializeBase` is called when the page is run, which then calls `initialize` on the `HoverButton` prototype. The prototype provides the meat of the class, wiring up event handlers, and so on, as well as clean-up via a `dispose` method. Listing 9-6 contains the JavaScript from `HoverButton.js`.

Listing 9-6. *The HoverButton.js Script File*

```
Type.registerNamespace("ControlsBook2Lib.Ch09");

//HoverButton Constructor
ControlsBook2Lib.Ch09.HoverButton = function(element)
{
    ControlsBook2Lib.Ch09.HoverButton.initializeBase(this, [element]);

    this._clickDelegate = null;
    this._hoverDelegate = null;
    this._unhoverDelegate = null;
}

//HoverButton Prototype
ControlsBook2Lib.Ch09.HoverButton.prototype =
{
    // text property accessors.
    get_text: function()
    {
        return this.get_element().innerHTML;
    },
    set_text: function(value)
    {
        this.get_element().innerHTML = value;
    },

    // Bind and unbind to click event.
    add_click: function(handler)
    {
        this.get_events().addHandler('click', handler);
    },
```

```
    remove_click: function(handler)
    {
        this.get_events().removeHandler('click', handler);
    },

    // Bind and unbind to hover event.
    add_hover: function(handler)
    {
        this.get_events().addHandler('hover', handler);
    },
    remove_hover: function(handler)
    {
        this.get_events().removeHandler('hover', handler);
    },

    // Bind and unbind to unhover event.
    add_unhover: function(handler)
    {
        this.get_events().addHandler('unhover', handler);
    },
    remove_unhover: function(handler)
    {
        this.get_events().removeHandler('unhover', handler);
    },

    // Release resources before control is disposed.
    dispose: function()
    {
        var element = this.get_element();

        if (this._clickDelegate)
        {
            Sys.UI.DomEvent.removeHandler(element, 'click', this._clickDelegate);
            delete this._clickDelegate;
        }

        if (this._hoverDelegate)
        {
            Sys.UI.DomEvent.removeHandler(element, 'focus', this._hoverDelegate);
            Sys.UI.DomEvent.removeHandler(element, 'mouseover',
            this._hoverDelegate);
            delete this._hoverDelegate;
        }
```

```
        if (this._unhoverDelegate)
        {
            Sys.UI.DomEvent.removeHandler(element, 'blur', this._unhoverDelegate);
            Sys.UI.DomEvent.removeHandler(element, 'mouseout',
            this._unhoverDelegate);
            delete this._unhoverDelegate;
        }
        ControlsBook2Lib.Ch09.HoverButton.callBaseMethod(this, 'dispose');
    },

    initialize: function()
    {
        var element = this.get_element();

        if (!element.tabIndex) element.tabIndex = 0;

        if (this._clickDelegate === null)
        {
            this._clickDelegate = Function.createDelegate(this, this._clickHandler);
        }
        Sys.UI.DomEvent.addHandler(element, 'click', this._clickDelegate);

        if (this._hoverDelegate === null)
        {
            this._hoverDelegate = Function.createDelegate(this, this._hoverHandler);
        }
        Sys.UI.DomEvent.addHandler(element, 'mouseover', this._hoverDelegate);
        Sys.UI.DomEvent.addHandler(element, 'focus', this._hoverDelegate);

        if (this._unhoverDelegate === null)
        {
            this._unhoverDelegate =
           Function.createDelegate(this, this._unhoverHandler);
        }
        Sys.UI.DomEvent.addHandler(element, 'mouseout', this._unhoverDelegate);
        Sys.UI.DomEvent.addHandler(element, 'blur', this._unhoverDelegate);

        ControlsBook2Lib.Ch09.HoverButton.callBaseMethod(this, 'initialize');

    },

    _clickHandler: function(event)
    {
        var h = this.get_events().getHandler('click');
        if (h) h(this, Sys.EventArgs.Empty);
    },
```

```
        _hoverHandler: function(event)
        {
            var h = this.get_events().getHandler('hover');
            if (h) h(this, Sys.EventArgs.Empty);
        },

        _unhoverHandler: function(event)
        {
            var h = this.get_events().getHandler('unhover');
            if (h) h(this, Sys.EventArgs.Empty);
        }
}

//Register the new class
ControlsBook2Lib.Ch09.HoverButton.registerClass('ControlsBook2Lib.Ch09.HoverButton',
Sys.UI.Control);

// Since this script is not loaded by System.Web.Handlers.ScriptResourceHandler
// invoke Sys.Application.notifyScriptLoaded to notify ScriptManager
// that this is the end of the script.
if (typeof(Sys) !== 'undefined') Sys.Application.notifyScriptLoaded();
```

This concludes our background work in preparing to write ASP.NET AJAX server controls. In the next section, we cover how to write an ASP.NET AJAX extender server control as well as an ASP.NET custom server control that integrates ASP.NET AJAX functionality.

ASP.NET AJAX Server Controls

As we mentioned previously, there are generally two types of ASP.NET AJAX server controls: extender controls, which apply client-side behavior to a different ASP.NET server control without requiring any modification of the other ASP.NET server control, and ASP.NET AJAX server controls, which are simply server controls that integrate ASP.NET AJAX functionality, adding script to its own capabilities. In the next section, we create an ASP.NET AJAX extender server control.

The TextCaseExtender Control

Quite often, applications require input in a particular case, such as lowercase or uppercase text. While there are lots of ways to enforce case, in this section, we demonstrate an extender control that enforces three types of case: lowercase, uppercase, and title case. We define "title case" as text in which the first letter of every word is capitalized. The server control inherits from `System.Web.UI.ExtenderControl`, as you would expect, since it is an extender control.

The associated client-side component named `TextCaseBehavior` is located in `ControlsBook2Lib.Ch09.TextCaseBehavior.js`. The client-side component is accessible as an embedded resource through the implementation of `GetScriptReferences` and `Assembly:WebResource` attributes, as described in the "The GetScriptReferences Method" section.

The control declares an enumeration type TextCaseStyle with three possible values: LowerCase, TitleCase, and UpperCase. TextCaseStyle is the type for the CaseStyle property of the extender server control. The CaseStyle property is configured to use ViewState as you would expect and also is decorated with the Bindable, Category, DefaultValue, and Localizable attributes.

In the GetScriptDescriptors method, the CaseStyle property is set on the client-side component so that it knows how to enforce the case on the target control. For more information on the GetScriptDescriptors see the "The GetScriptDescriptors Method" section. Listing 9-7 has the full listing of the TextCaseExtender server control.

Listing 9-7. *The TextCaseExtender Class File*

```
using System;
using System.Collections.Generic;
using System.ComponentModel;
using System.Web.UI;
using System.Web.UI.WebControls;

//Attribute required to make embedded resource script files available at run time.
[assembly: WebResource("ControlsBook2Lib.Ch09.TextCaseBehavior.js",
"text/javascript")]

public enum TextCaseStyle
{
  LowerCase,
  TitleCase,
  UpperCase
}

namespace ControlsBook2Lib.Ch09
{
  [TargetControlType(typeof(Control))]
  [ToolboxData("<{0}:textcaseextender runat=server></{0}:textcaseextender>")]
  public class TextCaseExtender : ExtenderControl
  {
    [Bindable(true)]
    [Category("Appearance")]
    [DefaultValue("LowerCase")]
    [Localizable(true)]
    public TextCaseStyle CaseStyle
    {
      get
      {
        return (TextCaseStyle)ViewState["CaseStyle"];
      }
```

```
      set
      {
        ViewState["CaseStyle"] = value;
      }
    }

    protected override IEnumerable<ScriptReference> GetScriptReferences()
    {
      ScriptReference reference = new ScriptReference();
      //Load script from embedded resource
      reference.Assembly = "ControlsBook2Lib";
      reference.Name = "ControlsBook2Lib.Ch09.TextCaseBehavior.js";

      return new ScriptReference[] { reference };
    }

    protected override IEnumerable<ScriptDescriptor> GetScriptDescriptors
   (Control targetControl)
    {
      ScriptBehaviorDescriptor descriptor = new
ScriptBehaviorDescriptor("ControlsBook2Lib.Ch09.TextCaseBehavior",
targetControl.ClientID);
      descriptor.AddProperty("caseStyle", this.CaseStyle.ToString());
      return new ScriptDescriptor[] { descriptor };
    }
  }
}
```

In the next section, we describe the TextCaseBehavior client-side component.

The TextCaseBehavior Client-Side Component

Every ASP.NET AJAX server control and extender control has a component to specify client-side behavior. For the TextCaseExtender extender server control, it is the TextCaseBehavior client-side component.

The TextCaseBehavior component has one property called caseStyle that is set by the TextCaseExtender extender server control in the GetScriptDescriptors method. TextCaseBehavior adds a handler for the key-up event named onKeyUp to the target control where the extender control should be applied. onKeyUp checks the caseStyle setting and enforces the desired text case, as shown in Listing 9-8.

Listing 9-8. *The TextCaseBehavior JavaScript File*

```
Type.registerNamespace('ControlsBook2Lib.Ch09');

// Define the behavior properties.
ControlsBook2Lib.Ch09.TextCaseBehavior = function(element)
{
```

```
    ControlsBook2Lib.Ch09.TextCaseBehavior.initializeBase(this, [element]);

    this._caseStyle = null;
}

// Create the prototype for the behavior
ControlsBook2Lib.Ch09.TextCaseBehavior.prototype =
{
    initialize : function()
    {
        ControlsBook2Lib.Ch09.TextCaseBehavior.callBaseMethod(this, 'initialize');

        $addHandlers(this.get_element(),
                     { 'keyup' : this._onKeyUp},
                    //Note onkeyups => 'keyup' when adding handlers
                     this);
    },

    dispose : function()
    {
        $clearHandlers(this.get_element());
        ControlsBook2Lib.Ch09.TextCaseBehavior.callBaseMethod(this, 'dispose');
    },

    _onKeyUp: function(e)
    {
        if (this.get_element() && !this.get_element().disabled)
        {
            switch(this._caseStyle)
            {
            case 'LowerCase':
              this.get_element().value=this.get_element().value.toLowerCase();
              break
            case 'UpperCase':
              this.get_element().value=this.get_element().value.toUpperCase();
              break
            case 'TitleCase':
              this.get_element().value=this.get_element().value.toLowerCase();
              this.get_element().value=this.get_element().value.toTitleCase();
              break
            }
        }
    },
```

```
    // Behavior property
     get_caseStyle : function()
     {
        return this._caseStyle;
    },

    set_caseStyle : function(value)
    {
        if (this._caseStyle !== value)
        {
            this._caseStyle = value;
            this.raisePropertyChanged('caseStyle');
        }
    }
}

// Optional descriptor for JSON serialization.
ControlsBook2Lib.Ch09.TextCaseBehavior.descriptor =
{
    properties: [ {name: 'caseStyle', type: String} ]
}

// Register the class as a type that inherits from Sys.UI.Control.
ControlsBook2Lib.Ch09.TextCaseBehavior.registerClass('ControlsBook2Lib.Ch09.
TextCaseBehavior', Sys.UI.Behavior);

//Create toTitleCase() prototype
String.prototype.toTitleCase = function ()
{
  var str = "";
  var str2 = "" ;
  var tokens = this.split(' ');
  for(key in tokens)
  {
    str2 = tokens[key].substr(0,1).toUpperCase()
   + tokens[key].substr(1,tokens[key].length);

    //Don't add space if on last token in string
    if (key != (tokens.length-1))
      str += str2+' ';
     else
      str+=str2;
  }
   return str;
}

if (typeof(Sys) !== 'undefined') Sys.Application.notifyScriptLoaded();
```

Notice the call toTitleCase used to enforce the TitleCase configuration. This is not a built-in function on strings. It is added via the String.prototype.toTitleCase function shown in Listing 9-8. The client-side component TextCaseBehavior enforces the text case configuration as each character is typed. The TextCaseExtender is enforced on an ASP.NET TextBox control in the TextCaseExtender web form shown in Listings 9-9 and 9-10.

Listing 9-9. *The TextCaseExtender Web Form .aspx Page File*

```
<%@ Page Language="C#"
MasterPageFile="~/MasterPage/ControlsBook2MasterPage.Master"
  AutoEventWireup="true" CodeBehind="TextCaseExtender.aspx.cs"
Inherits="ControlsBook2Web.Ch09.TextCaseExtenderControl"
  Title="TextCaseExtender Demo" %>

<%@ Register TagPrefix="apress" Namespace="ControlsBook2Lib.Ch09"
Assembly="ControlsBook2Lib" %>
<asp:Content ID="Content1" ContentPlaceHolderID="HeadSection" runat="server">
</asp:Content>
<asp:Content ID="Content2" ContentPlaceHolderID="ChapterNumAndTitle"
        runat="server">
  <asp:Label ID="ChapterNumberLabel" runat="server"
Width="14px">9</asp:Label>  <asp:Label
    ID="ChapterTitleLabel" runat="server" Width="360px">
ASP.NET AJAX Controls and Extenders</asp:Label>
</asp:Content>
<asp:Content ID="Content3" ContentPlaceHolderID="PrimaryContent" runat="server">
  <br />
  <asp:TextBox ID="TextBox1" runat="server" Width="300px"></asp:TextBox><br />
  <br />
  <br />
  <asp:Label ID="Label1" runat="server" Text=
  "Set case in the DropDownList, click Submit, and then type some text."
    CssClass="Chapter"></asp:Label><br />
  <asp:DropDownList ID="DropDownList1" runat="server" Height="21px" Width="148px">
    <asp:ListItem Text="LowerCase" Value="lowercase" Selected="True" />
    <asp:ListItem Text="TitleCase" Value="TitleCase" />
    <asp:ListItem Text="UpperCase" Value="UPPERCASE" />
  </asp:DropDownList><br />
  <asp:Button ID="Button1" runat="server" Text="Submit" OnClick="Button1_Click" />
  <apress:TextCaseExtender ID="TextCaseExtender1" runat="server"
  TargetControlID="TextBox1"
    CaseStyle="LowerCase" />
</asp:Content>
```

Listing 9-10. *The TextCaseExtender Web Form Code-Behind Class File*

```
using System;

namespace ControlsBook2Web.Ch09
{
  public partial class TextCaseExtenderControl : System.Web.UI.Page
  {
    protected void Page_Load(object sender, EventArgs e)
    {

    }

    protected void Button1_Click(object sender, EventArgs e)
    {
      //Convert selected value to TextCaseStyle and then update TextCaseExtender
      TextCaseExtender1.CaseStyle = (TextCaseStyle)Enum.Parse(typeof(TextCaseStyle),
      DropDownList1.SelectedValue, true);
      //Reset page
      TextBox1.Text = "";
      this.SetFocus(TextBox1);
    }
  }
}
```

The form has a DropDownList box with case settings and a submit button that performs a postback to enforce the setting configured in the DropDownList. It seems a bit silly to have a server-side postback to enforce a client-side setting, but it demonstrates how the server-side configuration is enforced on the client-side behavior. This concludes our discussion of the TextCaseExtender control. In the next section, we create an ASP.NET server control that integrates ASP.NET AJAX functionality.

The HighlightedHyperLink ASP.NET AJAX Server Control

In this section, we cover the custom ASP.NET AJAX server control HighlightedHyperLink that includes a client-side behavior that applies a custom CSS style to an HTTP hyperlink when the user moves the mouse over the hyperlink, providing nice visual cuing over which link will be clicked if the primary mouse button is clicked.

Since HighlightedHyperLink is just a customization of the ASP.NET HyperLink control, it inherits from HyperLink but implements IScriptControl to bring in the ASP.NET AJAX functionality. The associated client-side component HighlightedHyperLink is contained in an embedded resource ControlsBook2Lib.Ch09.HighlightedHyperLink.js file. As before, the script is marked as embedded, and an Assembly:WebResource attribute is used to make it available via the GetScriptReferences method.

To ensure proper behavior in HighlightedHyperlink, since it implements the IScriptControl interface directly, the OnPreRender method is overridden to check for the presence of a ScriptManager control. In addition, even though this control inherits from an existing ASP.NET control (HyperLink), it overrides the Render method to make the required call to ScriptManager.RegisterScriptDescriptors to wire up the client-script with the ASP.NET client-script engine.

The HighlightedHyperLink ASP.NET AJAX server control has to properties to configure the client-side component behavior called HighlightCssClass and NoHighlightCssClass. These properties backed by ViewState are configured on the client-side component via the GetScriptDescriptors method. Listing 9-11 has the full code of the HighlightedHyperlink server control.

Listing 9-11. *The HighlightedHyperLink Class File*

```
using System;
using System.Collections.Generic;
using System.ComponentModel;
using System.Web;
using System.Web.UI;
using System.Web.UI.WebControls;

//Attribute required to make embedded resource script files available at run time
[assembly: WebResource("ControlsBook2Lib.Ch09.HighlightedHyperLink.js"
, "text/javascript")]

namespace ControlsBook2Lib.Ch09
{
  [DefaultProperty("HighlightCssClass")]
  [ToolboxData(
  "<{0}:highlightedhyperLink runat=server></{0}:highlightedhyperLink>")]
  public class HighlightedHyperLink : HyperLink, IScriptControl
  {
    private ScriptManager sm;

    [Bindable(false)]
    [Category("Target Control Appearance")]
    [DefaultValue("")]
    [Localizable(true)]
    public string HighlightCssClass
    {
      get
      {
        return (string)ViewState["HighlightCssClass"];
      }
      set
      {
        ViewState["HighlightCssClass"] = value;
      }
    }
```

```
[Bindable(false)]
[Category("Target Control Appearance")]
[DefaultValue("")]
[Localizable(true)]
public string NoHighlightCssClass
{
  get
  {
    return (string)ViewState["NoHighlightCssClass"];
  }
  set
  {
    ViewState["NoHighlightCssClass"] = value;
  }
}

protected override void OnPreRender(EventArgs e)
{
  if (!this.DesignMode)
  {
    // Test for ScriptManager and register if it exists
    sm = ScriptManager.GetCurrent(Page);

    if (sm == null)
      throw new HttpException(
      "A ScriptManager control must exist on the current page.");

    sm.RegisterScriptControl(this);
  }

  base.OnPreRender(e);
}

protected override void Render(HtmlTextWriter writer)
{
  if (!this.DesignMode)
    sm.RegisterScriptDescriptors(this);

  base.Render(writer);
}

protected virtual IEnumerable<ScriptReference> GetScriptReferences()
{
  ScriptReference reference = new ScriptReference();
  //Load script from embedded resource
  reference.Assembly = "ControlsBook2Lib";
  reference.Name = "ControlsBook2Lib.Ch09.HighlightedHyperLink.js";
```

```
      return new ScriptReference[] { reference };
    }

    protected virtual IEnumerable<ScriptDescriptor> GetScriptDescriptors()
    {
      ScriptControlDescriptor descriptor = new ScriptControlDescriptor
     ("ControlsBook2Lib.Ch09.HighlightedHyperlink", this.ClientID);
      descriptor.AddProperty("highlightCssClass", this.HighlightCssClass);
      descriptor.AddProperty("nohighlightCssClass", this.NoHighlightCssClass);

      return new ScriptDescriptor[] { descriptor };
    }

    IEnumerable<ScriptReference> IScriptControl.GetScriptReferences()
    {
      return GetScriptReferences();
    }

    IEnumerable<ScriptDescriptor> IScriptControl.GetScriptDescriptors()
    {
      return GetScriptDescriptors();
    }
  }
}
```

In the next section, we describe the HighlightedHyperLink client-side component.

The HighlightedHyperlink Client-Side Component

Every ASP.NET AJAX server control and extender control has a client-side behavior. For our ASP.NET AJAX server control, the name of the client-side behavior is HighlightedHyperlink to match the name of the server control.

The HighlightedHyperlink component has two properties, highlightCssClass and nohighlightCssClass, that are set by the HighlightedHyperLink server control in the GetScriptDescriptors method. HighlightedHyperLink adds two event handlers for the mouseover and mouseout events named _onMouseover and _onMouseOut respectively. It is in these event handlers where the HighlightCssClass and NoHighlightCssClass properties configured on the HighlightedHyperLink ASP.NET AJAX server control are applied to the control on the client side. Listing 9-12 contains the HighlightedHyperlink client-side component JavaScript.

Listing 9-12. *The HighlightedHyperlink JavaScript File*

```
Type.registerNamespace('ControlsBook2Lib.Ch09');

// Define the control properties.
ControlsBook2Lib.Ch09.HighlightedHyperlink = function(element)
{
```

```
    ControlsBook2Lib.Ch09.HighlightedHyperlink.initializeBase(this, [element]);

    this._highlightCssClass = null;
    this._nohighlightCssClass = null;
}

// Create the prototype for the control
ControlsBook2Lib.Ch09.HighlightedHyperlink.prototype =
{
    initialize : function()
    {
        ControlsBook2Lib.Ch09.HighlightedHyperlink.
        callBaseMethod(this, 'initialize');

        this._onMouseOver = Function.createDelegate(this, this._onMouseOver);
        this._onMouseOut = Function.createDelegate(this, this._onMouseOut);

        $addHandlers(this.get_element(),
                     { 'mouseover' : this._onMouseOver,
                       'mouseout' : this._onMouseOut },
                     this);
        this.get_element().className = this._nohighlightCssClass;
    },

    dispose : function()
    {
        $clearHandlers(this.get_element());

        ControlsBook2Lib.Ch09.HighlightedHyperlink.callBaseMethod(this, 'dispose');
    },

    // Event delegates
    _onMouseOver : function(e)
    {
        if (this.get_element() && !this.get_element().disabled)
        {
            this.get_element().className = this._highlightCssClass;
        }
    },

    _onMouseOut : function(e)
    {
        if (this.get_element() && !this.get_element().disabled)
        {
            this.get_element().className = this._nohighlightCssClass;
        }
    },
```

```
    // Control properties
    get_highlightCssClass : function()
    {
        return this._highlightCssClass;
    },

    set_highlightCssClass : function(value)
    {
        if (this._highlightCssClass !== value)
        {
            this._highlightCssClass = value;
            this.raisePropertyChanged('highlightCssClass');
        }
    },

    get_nohighlightCssClass : function()
    {
        return this._nohighlightCssClass;
    },

    set_nohighlightCssClass : function(value)
    {
        if (this._nohighlightCssClass !== value)
        {
            this._nohighlightCssClass = value;
            this.raisePropertyChanged('nohighlightCssClass');
        }
    }
}

// Optional descriptor for JSON serialization.
ControlsBook2Lib.Ch09.HighlightedHyperlink.descriptor =
{
    properties: [   {name: 'highlightCssClass', type: String},
                    {name: 'nohighlightCssClass', type: String} ]
}

// Register the class as a type that inherits from Sys.UI.Control.
ControlsBook2Lib.Ch09.HighlightedHyperlink.registerClass('ControlsBook2Lib.Ch09.
HighlightedHyperlink', Sys.UI.Control);

if (typeof(Sys) !== 'undefined') Sys.Application.notifyScriptLoaded();
```

Notice that the `HighlightedHyperlink` client-side component doesn't need to know the CSS class names in advance. The client-side component also contains an optional descriptor for JSON serialization support. Figure 9-1 shows `HighlightedHyperLink` ASP.NET AJAX-enabled server control in action in the `HighlightedHyperLink` web form.

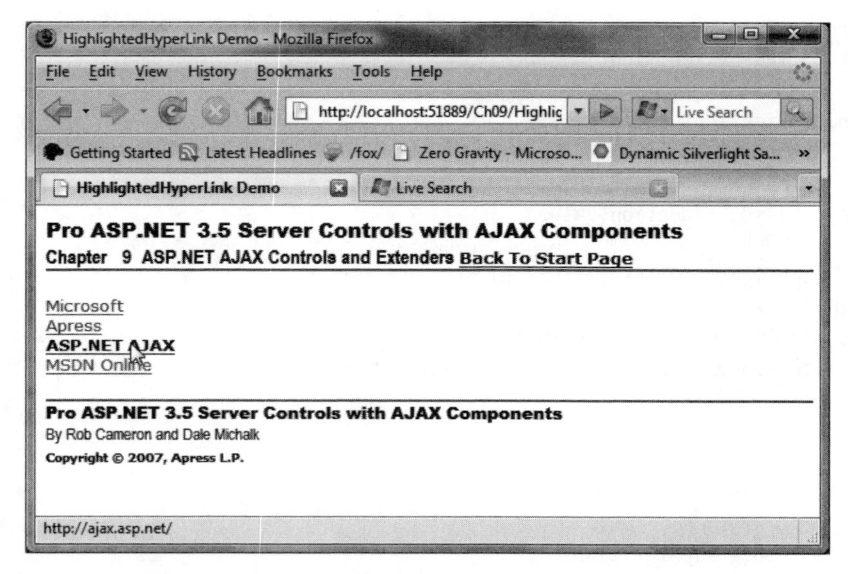

Figure 9-1. *The rendered HighlightedHyperLink web form in Firefox*

The source code for the `HighlightedHyperLink` web form and code-behind file is shown in Listings 9-13 and 9-14.

Listing 9-13. *The HighlightedHyperLink Web Form .aspx Page File*

```
<%@ Page Language="C#"
MasterPageFile="~/MasterPage/ControlsBook2MasterPage.Master"
  AutoEventWireup="true" CodeBehind="HighlightedHyperlink.aspx.cs"
Inherits="ControlsBook2Web.Ch09.HighlightedHyperlink"
  Title="HighlightedHyperLink Demo" %>

<%@ Register TagPrefix="apress" Namespace="ControlsBook2Lib.Ch09"
Assembly="ControlsBook2Lib" %>
<asp:Content ID="Content1" ContentPlaceHolderID="HeadSection" runat="server">
  <style type="text/css">
    .Highlight
    {
      color: navy;
      font-weight: bolder;
    }
    .NoHighlight
    {
      color: Green;
      font-weight: lighter;
    }
  </style>
</asp:Content>
```

```
<asp:Content ID="Content2" ContentPlaceHolderID="ChapterNumAndTitle" runat="server">
  <asp:Label ID="ChapterNumberLabel" runat="server
Width="14px">9</asp:Label>  <asp:Label
    ID="ChapterTitleLabel" runat="server" Width="360px">
  ASP.NET AJAX Controls and Extenders</asp:Label>
</asp:Content>
<asp:Content ID="Content3" ContentPlaceHolderID="PrimaryContent" runat="server">
  <br />
  <apress:HighlightedHyperLink ID="HighlightedHyperLink1"
    HighlightCssClass="Highlight"
    NoHighlightCssClass="NoHighlight" runat="server"
NavigateUrl="http://www.microsoft.com">Microsoft
   </apress:HighlightedHyperLink><br />
  <apress:HighlightedHyperLink ID="HighlightedHyperLink2"
    HighlightCssClass="Highlight"
    NoHighlightCssClass="NoHighlight" runat="server"
    NavigateUrl="http://apress.com">Apress
    </apress:HighlightedHyperLink><br />
  <apress:HighlightedHyperLink ID="HighlightedHyperLink3"
    HighlightCssClass="Highlight"
    NoHighlightCssClass="NoHighlight" runat="server"
    NavigateUrl="http://ajax.asp.net">
    ASP.NET AJAX</apress:HighlightedHyperLink><br />
  <apress:HighlightedHyperLink ID="HighlightedHyperLink4"
    HighlightCssClass="Highlight"
    NoHighlightCssClass="NoHighlight" runat="server"
    NavigateUrl="http://msdn.microsoft.com">
    MSDN Online</apress:HighlightedHyperLink><br />
  <br />
</asp:Content>
```

Listing 9-14. *The HighlightedHyperLink Web Form Code-Behind Class File*

```
using System;

namespace ControlsBook2Web.Ch09
{
  public partial class HighlightedHyperlink : System.Web.UI.Page
  {
    protected void Page_Load(object sender, EventArgs e)
    {

    }
  }
}
```

This concludes our discussion of the `HighlightedHyperLink` ASP.NET AJAX server control.

Summary

In this chapter, we provided an overview of ASP.NET AJAX, both the server-side and client-side functionality. ASP.NET AJAX includes a powerful client-side script library that provides cross-browser compatibility, as well as a powerful client-side programming model that mimics object-oriented behavior in JavaScript.

We covered the server-side programming model that requires implementation of the GetScriptDescriptors and GetScriptReferences methods. We also explained how the server-side configuration is passed to the client-side component utilizing the ScriptBehaviorDescriptor class. Finally, we demonstrated how to implement both an ASP.NET AJAX server control by implementing IScriptControl, as well as how to implement an extender control by inheriting from the ExtenderControl base class.

For additional examples of ASP.NET AJAX server controls and extenders, we recommend downloading and reviewing the ASP.NET AJAX Control Toolkit available at http://asp.net/ajax/ajaxcontroltoolkit/samples/.

CHAPTER 10

Other Server Controls

Up to this chapter, we have focused on providing the necessary background to create powerful ASP.NET server controls that support custom styling, templating, data binding, client-side script, and ASP.NET AJAX. These development techniques and features can be put to work in many different ways. In this part of the book, we begin to move on to advanced topics such web part development and design-time support.

In this chapter, we begin our advanced topic journey by covering web part development and adaptive control programming. We will start off with a discussion on building web parts for both ASP.NET and Microsoft Office SharePoint Server 2007. Next, we will focus on adaptive control development, including the mobile controls for devices. In the next section, we begin our journey with web parts.

Note For information on building custom validator controls, the MSDN documentation contains a nice set of cross-browser validator control samples that also comply with the WWW Consortium DOM Level 1 specification; the samples are located here: `http://msdn2.microsoft.com/en-us/library/aa719624(VS.71).aspx`.

Web-Part-Based Web Site Development

This chapter won't attempt to provide a complete overview of the web part infrastructure and development model available in ASP.NET, because the documentation does a very good job of explaining what functionality is available. What I will do is provide a discussion on various web part topics encountered while building out the example web parts in this chapter to help you understand the moving parts available when building web parts. If you find that you need more background information on a particular area, here is the top-level link to the ASP.NET web parts documentation at MSDN Online:

`http://msdn2.microsoft.com/en-us/library/e0s9t4ck(VS.90).aspx`

From the preceding link, you can navigate to these sections for more detail on a particular topic:

- ASP.NET Web Parts Overview
- Web Parts Control Set Overview

- Web Parts Page Display Modes
- Web Parts Personalization
- Web Parts Connections Overview

For an idea of what's possible, look no further than Microsoft Office SharePoint Server (MOSS) 2007, which is built on top of ASP.NET and the web part infrastructure. A public-facing Internet site built on top of MOSS with custom web parts is `http://www.glu.com`. Here is a link to the first of a three-part series on how this site was built by Allin Consulting on MOSS and ASP.NET web parts:

`http://blogs.msdn.com/sharepoint/archive/2007/06/14/`
`moss-has-got-game-glu-mobile-s-website-www-glu-com-how-we-did-it-part-1-of-3.aspx`

With that background out of the way, we'll dive into a discussion on web part development in the next section.

Web Part Development

Web parts have existed in SharePoint for many years. Initially, the web part development model was based on VBScript, which is not what most developers would call their favorite development language or environment. In SharePoint Server 2003, Microsoft more closely integrated SharePoint with ASP.NET, providing namespaces for supporting web part development in .NET. With .NET Framework 2.0, the ASP.NET team integrated the web part infrastructure and development model within ASP.NET itself. However, the two web part models remained separate. Building web parts that targeted both ASP.NET 2.0 and SharePoint Server 2003 required custom compilation, since different namespaces and base classes where required. In Microsoft Office SharePoint Server (MOSS) 2007, SharePoint is completely integrated with and built on ASP.NET 2.0. This means that you can build web parts for MOSS using the ASP.NET `WebPart` base class.

■ **Note** Microsoft recommends inheriting from the ASP.NET `WebPart` base class whether developing for pure ASP.NET or SharePoint.

The next section provides a brief overview of the ASP.NET web part infrastructure to set the state for building web parts that take advantage of this framework.

Web Part Infrastructure

One of the features of `WebPart`-based applications is personalization. `WebParts` can have attributes configured with the `PersonalizableAttribute` so that a user can create a unique view on the page. Personalization for an ASP.NET web site requires that the SQL personalization provider is configured for the site.

Note Personalization requires that the `<trust level="" />` element is configured for `Medium` in order to access members in the `SqlClient` namespace.

The `SqlPersonalizationProvider` class is used to configure the personalization in SQL Server.

The ASP.NET SQL Server Registration Tool (`Aspnet_regsql.exe`) can be used to set up the database location for web part personalization, among other databases such as the ASP.NET membership database. The tool is located at `\%windir%\Microsoft.NET\Framework\v2.0.50727`, or at the same location for a later version of the framework.

There is a section in the `web.config` file to declaratively configure web part personalization via the `WebPartsPersonalization` class under `<system.web> <WebParts> <personalization. . . >` that can be used to configure the web part environment. Refer to the MSDN documentation for more information on the `WebPartsPersonalization` class.

Web parts are hosted within the rich web part infrastructure, so as you would expect, there are additional customizations available for web part developers. Table 10-1 provides a list of the most common overrides when creating a `WebPart` server control.

Table 10-1. *WebPart Common Overrides*

WebPart Member	Overview
`"Allow" properties`	These are behavior-focused properties that control developers may want to manage for the logic of their custom `WebPart` control. Examples are `AllowClose`, `AllowConnect`, and `AllowEdit`.
`CreateChildControls`	It is quite common to build web parts based on composite server controls to encapsulate chunks of functionality as a `WebPart` control.
`CreateEditorParts`	Web parts can have custom editor web parts based on `EditorPart` to enable users to edit custom web part properties. Override `CreateEditorParts` to incorporate the custom `EditorPart` control.
`PersonalizableAttribute`	This attribute is applied to properties of the custom web part that the user may want to save unique settings to.
Rendering methods	As with custom server controls, sometimes you may need to override `Render` or `RenderContents` to completely change the outputted HTML or to simply customize it by also calling the base method.
`Verbs`	Add custom `WebPartVerb` objects to the `Verbs` collection to allow custom menu actions to appear along with the standard verbs such as close or minimize.

With that background out of the way, let's move on to creating web parts in the next section.

Creating Web Parts

In this section, we create two server controls and demonstrate them in a basic ASPX page. Next, we convert the server controls to web parts and then demonstrate them in a web part portal page.

This may seem like the long road to building web parts, but we believe it is more realistic. In many situations, developers will create server controls and statically code the page layout and what server controls appear on a page as part of an application. Initially, there are perhaps just a couple of server controls, but after a couple of cycles where users ask for additional functionality or views on data, developers may find themselves with a library of server controls with different users requesting multiple combinations of server controls, resulting in multiple, hand-coded, statically linked and created web forms. At this point, the developer may ask, "Why not create a web part portal page where users can pick which controls display on the page, how the controls are laid out, and which controls are linked?"

Regarding what type of scenario may fit this model, a reporting web portal or business intelligence application comes to mind, so our focus for this demonstration is providing a reporting page focused on the famous `Northwind` database with NorthWind customers as the theme for the site.

In the next section, we build the server controls web form with two server controls reporting NorthWind customer data.

The Server Controls

As mentioned in the previous section, we start out by creating server control versions of the web parts and then show how to turn them into web parts in the next section. The two server controls retrieve data from the `NorthWind` database. The first server control displays a list of customers and allows editing of existing customers but not insertion or deletion. The second server control takes a customer ID and displays invoice highlights for the customer based on the provided customer ID. Both server controls allow sorting and paging, as well as provide a simple style to show row highlighting.

If you have read this book straight through, you can probably guess that each of the two server controls detailed here is a composite control containing a `GridView` and a `DataSource` control and inheriting from `CompositeControl`. All of those guesses would be correct. Listing 10-1 contains the `CustomerList` custom server control.

Listing 10-1. *The CustomerList Server Control*

```
using System;
using System.Drawing;
using System.Web.UI;
using System.Web.UI.WebControls;

namespace ControlsBook2Lib.Ch10
{
  [ToolboxData("<{0}:CustomerList runat=server></{0}:CustomerList>")]
  public class CustomerList : CompositeControl
  {
    private const string strSelectCmd = @"Select * from [Customers]";
    private const string strUpdateCmd = @"UPDATE [Customers] SET " +
      @"[CompanyName] = @CompanyName, [ContactName] = @ContactName, " +
      @"[Phone] = @Phone WHERE [CustomerID] = @CustomerID";
```

```
public CustomerList()
{
}

public String CustomerID
{
  get
  {
    object customerID = ViewState["CustomerID"];
    if (customerID == null)
      return String.Empty;
    else
      return (String)customerID;
  }
  set
  {
    ViewState["CustomerID"] = value;
  }
}

// Allow page developers to set the connection string.
public String ConnectionString
{
  get
  {
    object connectionString = ViewState["ConnectionString"];
    if (connectionString == null)
      return String.Empty;
    else
      return (String)connectionString;
  }
  set
  {
    ViewState["ConnectionString"] = value;
  }
}

public Boolean AllowCustomerEditing
{
  get
  {
    object allowEditing = ViewState["AllowCustomerEditing"];
    if (allowEditing == null)
      return false;
    else
      return (Boolean)allowEditing;
  }
```

```
    set
    {
      ViewState["AllowCustomerEditing"] = value;
    }
  }

  protected override void CreateChildControls()
  {
    Controls.Clear();

    SqlDataSource ds = new SqlDataSource(this.ConnectionString, strSelectCmd);
    ds.ID = "dsCustomers";
    ds.DataSourceMode = SqlDataSourceMode.DataSet;
    ds.UpdateCommandType = SqlDataSourceCommandType.Text;
    ds.UpdateCommand = strUpdateCmd;
    ParameterCollection updateParams = new ParameterCollection();
    updateParams.Add(_createParameter("CustomerID", TypeCode.String));
    updateParams.Add(_createParameter("CompanyName", TypeCode.String));
    updateParams.Add(_createParameter("ContactName", TypeCode.String));
    updateParams.Add(_createParameter("Phone", TypeCode.String));

    Controls.Add(ds);

    Label title = new Label();
    title.Text = "Customer list";
    Controls.Add(title);

    LiteralControl br = new LiteralControl("<br/>");
    Controls.Add(br);

    GridView grid = new GridView();
    grid.ID = "customerGrid";
    grid.Font.Size = 8;
    grid.AllowPaging = true;
    grid.AllowSorting = true;
    grid.AutoGenerateColumns = false;
    String[] fields = { "CustomerID" };
    grid.DataKeyNames = fields;
    grid.DataSourceID = "dsCustomers";
    CommandField controlButton = new CommandField();

    //Only show Edit button if control configured to allow it
    if (AllowCustomerEditing)
      controlButton.ShowEditButton = true;
```

```
    controlButton.ShowSelectButton = true;
    grid.Columns.Add(controlButton);
    BoundField customerID = _createBoundField("CustomerID");
    customerID.ReadOnly = true;
    grid.Columns.Add(customerID);
    grid.Columns.Add(_createBoundField("CompanyName"));
    grid.Columns.Add(_createBoundField("ContactName"));
    grid.Columns.Add(_createBoundField("Phone"));
    grid.SelectedRowStyle.BackColor = Color.AntiqueWhite;

    grid.SelectedIndexChanged += new EventHandler(SelectedIndexChanged);
    grid.PageIndexChanged += new EventHandler(PageIndexChanged);
    Controls.Add(grid);
    Style.Add(HtmlTextWriterStyle.FontFamily, "arial");
    BorderStyle = BorderStyle.Solid;
    BorderColor = Color.LightBlue;
  }

  protected void SelectedIndexChanged(object sender, EventArgs e)
  {
    GridViewRow row = ((GridView)(sender)).SelectedRow;
    CustomerID = row.Cells[1].Text;
  }

  protected void PageIndexChanged(object sender, EventArgs e)
  {
    ((GridView)(sender)).SelectedIndex = -1;
  }

  private BoundField _createBoundField(String fieldName)
  {
    BoundField field = new BoundField();
    switch (fieldName)
    {
      case "CompanyName": field.HeaderText = "Company Name";
        break;
      case "ContactName": field.HeaderText = "Contact Name";
        break;
      case "PhoneName": field.HeaderText = "Phone Name";
        break;
      case "CustomerID": field.HeaderText = "Customer ID";
        break;
      default: field.HeaderText = fieldName; break;
    }
```

```
      field.SortExpression = fieldName;
      field.DataField = fieldName;
      return field;
    }

    private Parameter _createParameter(String paramName, TypeCode dataTypeCode)
    {
      Parameter theParm = new Parameter(paramName, dataTypeCode);
      return theParm;
    }
  }
}
```

The CustomerID property is used to store the selected row's CustomerID value from the customer list. The ConnectionString is a public property for the SqlDataSource control that is part of the server control hierarchy to use to connect to the database. The CustomerList server control allows editing of the customer list. The AllowCustomerEditing property is used to control whether the editing is permitted for a particular instance of the control on a web form.

As with all composite server controls, CreateChildControls does all of the heavy lifting to build out the server control hierarchy. The controls include a Label for the title, a LiteralControl to contain a br tag, a SqlDataSource, and, of course, the GridView control.

The CreateChildControls override attaches two events to the GridView control, one for the SelectedIndexChanged event and the other for the PageIndexChanged event. The SelectedIndexChanged event sets the CustomerID property to the CustomerID value from the GridView. The PageIndexChanged event resets the SelectedIndex to -1 so that a row is not selected after the page is changed. The CustomerInvoices server control is similar to the CustomerList server control, except that it is based on a database view instead of a table and so does not allow editing. Listing 10-2 shows the source code for the CustomerInvoices server control.

Listing 10-2. *The CustomerInvoices Server Control*

```
using System;
using System.Drawing;
using System.Web.UI;
using System.Web.UI.WebControls;

namespace ControlsBook2Lib.Ch10
{
  [ToolboxData("<{0}:CustomerInvoices runat=server></{0}:CustomerInvoices>")]
  public class CustomerInvoices : CompositeControl
  {
    private const string strSelectCmd = @"Select * from [Invoices] where "+
      "CustomerID = '{0}'";
```

```
public CustomerInvoices()
{
}

public String CustomerID
{
  get
  {
    object customerID = ViewState["CustomerID"];
    if (customerID == null)
      return String.Empty;
    else
      return (String)customerID;
  }
  set
  {
    ViewState["CustomerID"] = value;
  }
}

// Allow page developers to set the connection string.
public String ConnectionString
{
  get
  {
    object connectionString = ViewState["ConnectionString"];
    if (connectionString == null)
      return String.Empty;
    else
      return (String)connectionString;
  }
  set
  {
    ViewState["ConnectionString"] = value;
  }
}
protected override void CreateChildControls()
{
  Controls.Clear();

  SqlDataSource ds = new SqlDataSource(this.ConnectionString,
  String.Format(strSelectCmd,CustomerID));
  ds.ID = "dsCustomerInvoices";
  ds.DataSourceMode = SqlDataSourceMode.DataSet;
  Controls.Add(ds);
```

```
    Label title = new Label();
    title.Text = "Customer Invoices - "+ CustomerID;
    Controls.Add(title);

    LiteralControl br = new LiteralControl("<br/>");
    Controls.Add(br);

    GridView grid = new GridView();
    grid.ID = "customerInvoicesGrid";
    grid.Font.Size = 8;
    grid.AllowPaging = true;
    grid.PageSize = 5;
    grid.AllowSorting = true;
    grid.AutoGenerateColumns = false;
    String[] fields = { "CustomerID" };
    grid.DataKeyNames = fields;
    grid.DataSourceID = "dsCustomerInvoices";
    CommandField controlButton = new CommandField();
    controlButton.ShowSelectButton = true;
    grid.Columns.Add(controlButton);
    grid.Columns.Add(_createBoundField("OrderID"));
    grid.Columns.Add(_createBoundField("RequiredDate"));
    grid.Columns.Add(_createBoundField("ShippedDate"));
    grid.Columns.Add(_createBoundField("ProductName"));
    grid.Columns.Add(_createBoundField("Quantity"));
    grid.SelectedRowStyle.BackColor = Color.AntiqueWhite;

    grid.SelectedIndexChanged += new EventHandler(SelectedIndexChanged);
    grid.PageIndexChanged += new EventHandler(PageIndexChanged);

    Controls.Add(grid);
    Style.Add(HtmlTextWriterStyle.FontFamily, "arial");
    BorderStyle = BorderStyle.Solid;
    BorderColor = Color.LightBlue;
  }

  protected void SelectedIndexChanged(object sender, EventArgs e)
  {
    GridViewRow row = ((GridView)(sender)).SelectedRow;
  }
```

```
    protected void PageIndexChanged(object sender, EventArgs e)
    {
      ((GridView)(sender)).SelectedIndex = -1;
    }

    private BoundField _createBoundField(String fieldName)
    {
      BoundField field = new BoundField();
      switch (fieldName)
      {
        case "Order ID": field.HeaderText = "Order ID";
          break;
        case "RequiredDate": field.HeaderText = "Required Date";
          break;
        case "ShippedDate": field.HeaderText = "Shipped Date";
          break;
        case "ProductName": field.HeaderText = "Product Name";
          break;
        case "Quanity": field.HeaderText = "Quantity Ordered";
          break;
        default: field.HeaderText = fieldName; break;
      }
      field.DataField = fieldName;
      field.SortExpression = fieldName;
      return field;
    }

    private Parameter _createParameter(String paramName, TypeCode dataTypeCode)
    {
      Parameter theParm = new Parameter(paramName, dataTypeCode);
      return theParm;
    }
  }
}
```

Both controls have two helper methods for building out the control hierarchy; they are named `_createBoundField` and `_createParameter`, and they help to create the bound fields and parameters for the `GridView` control. The demonstration web form for the two server controls is `CustomerInfo.aspx`. The source code is shown in Listings 10-3 and 10-4.

Listing 10-3. *The Customer Information Web Form .aspx Page File*

```
<%@ Page Language="C#"
MasterPageFile="~/MasterPage/ControlsBook2MasterPage.Master"
AutoEventWireup="true" CodeBehind="CustomerInfo.aspx.cs"
Inherits="ControlsBook2Web.Ch10.CustomerInfo"
Title="Customer Info Demo Web Form" %>
<%@ Register assembly="ControlsBook2Lib" namespace="ControlsBook2Lib.Ch10"
tagprefix="apress" %>
<asp:Content ID="Content1" ContentPlaceHolderID="HeadSection" runat="server">
</asp:Content>
<asp:Content ID="Content2" ContentPlaceHolderID="ChapterNumAndTitle" runat="server">
</asp:Content>
<asp:Content ID="Content3" ContentPlaceHolderID="PrimaryContent" runat="server">
  <br />
  <br />
  <apress:CustomerList ID="CustomerList1" runat="server"
  ConnectionString = "<%$ ConnectionStrings:NorthWindDB %>"
    AllowCustomerEditing="True" />
  <br /> <br />
  <apress:CustomerInvoices ID="CustomerInvoices1" runat="server"  CustomerID="VINET"
  ConnectionString = "<%$ ConnectionStrings:NorthWindDB %>" />
  <br /> <br />
</asp:Content>
```

Listing 10-4. *The Customer Information Web Form Code-Behind Class File*

```
using System;

namespace ControlsBook2Web.Ch10
{
  public partial class CustomerInfo : System.Web.UI.Page
  {
    protected void Page_Load(object sender, EventArgs e)
    {

    }
  }
}
```

Figure 10-1 shows how the customer information web form application appears in the browser.

We could wire up these controls by bubbling up the SelectedIndexChanged event for the GridView to the CustomerList parent control as shown in Chapter 5, so that we can get the customer ID and then pass it to the CustomerInvoices control, but we want to link the controls using the web part, which we cover in the next section when we convert the server controls into web parts.

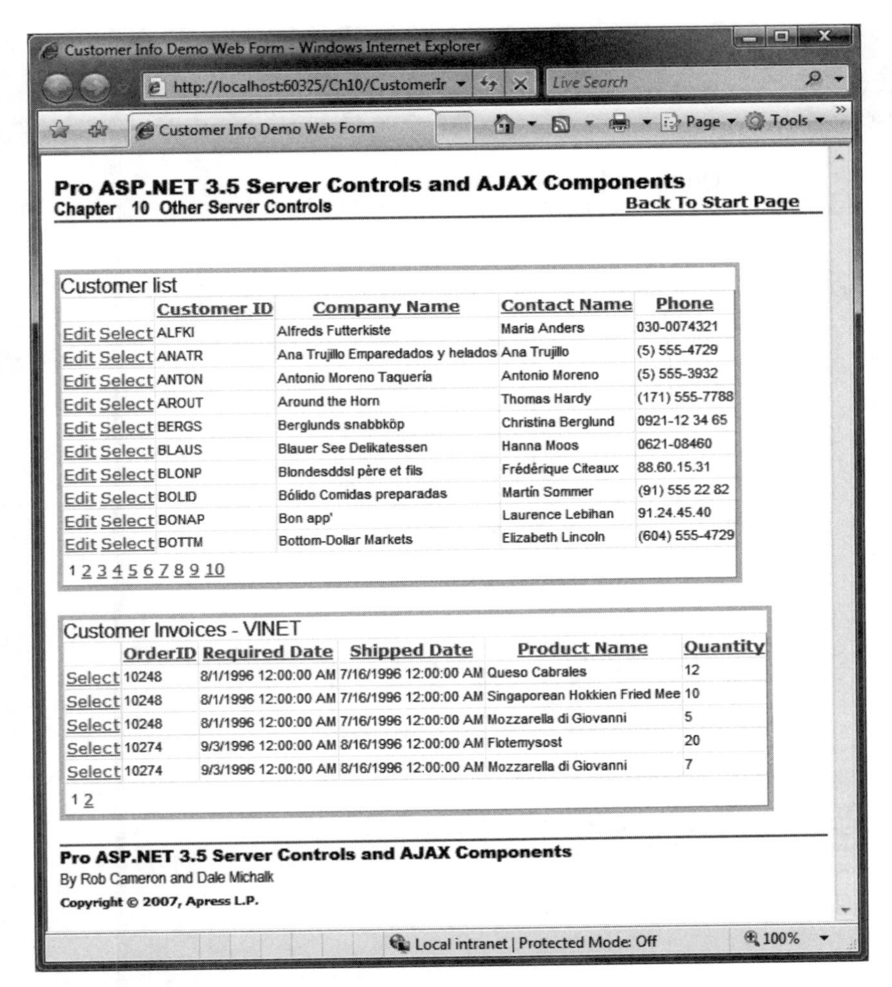

Figure 10-1. *The Customer Info web form in the browser*

Converting to WebPart Controls

To start the conversion, we copied the `CustomerList` and `CustomerInvoices` server control to new class files with the same names but with the term "`WebPart`" appended. To start, `System.Web.UI.WebControls.WebParts` was added to the class files, and the base control changed from `CompositeControl` to `WebPart`.

At this point, the project compiles. As a test, we begin by creating the test form to see if the web parts will host in a `WebPartZone` control. We added a page, `CustomerInfoWebPart.aspx`, to the web project. Next, we added `WebPartZone` and `ZoneTemplate` controls to contain the two web parts. A required step is to add a `WebPartManager` control to the page to enable web part functionality. Figure 10-2 shows the results of this minimalist effort.

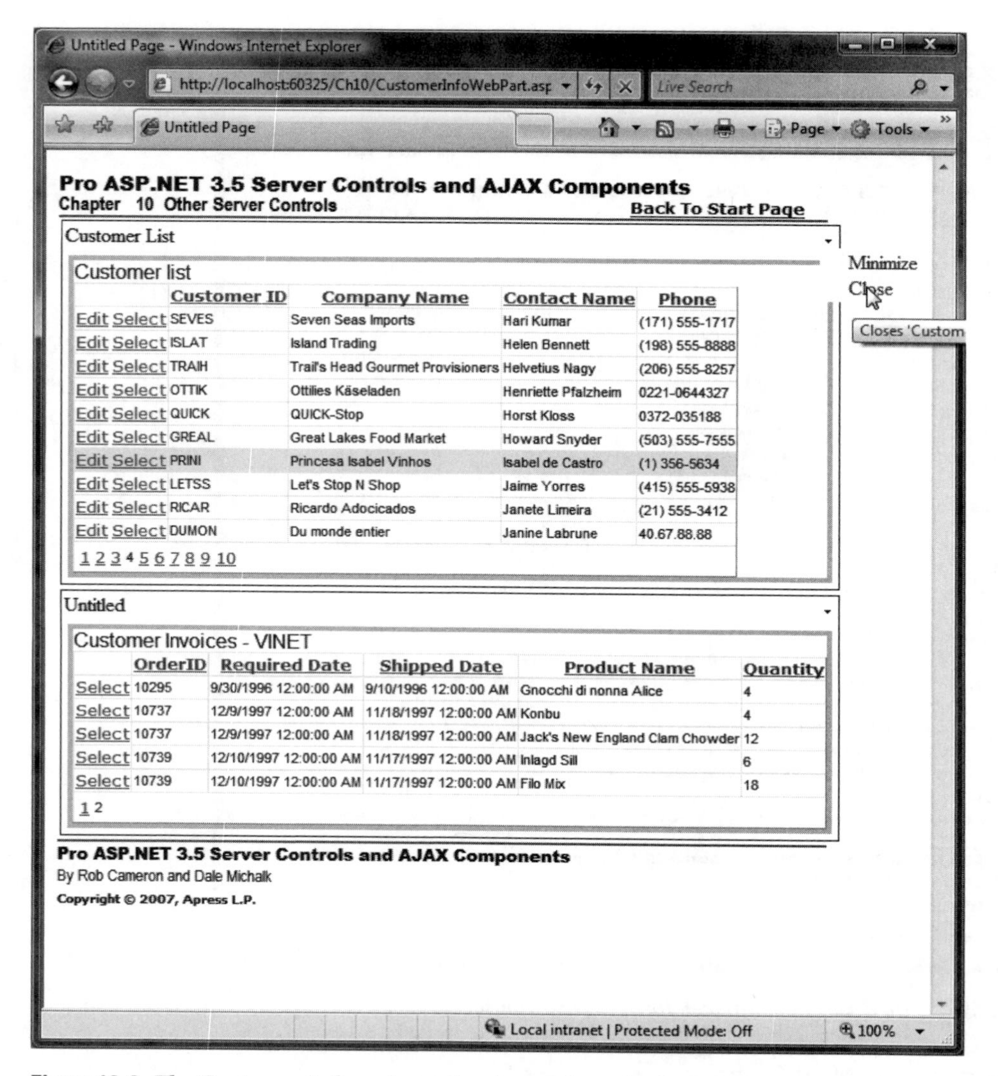

Figure 10-2. *The Customer Info web part basic web form in the browser*

The web form renders with the additional chrome of the web parts around the controls, including the basic web part menu containing just the Minimize and Close commands, but this version of the web page is not much different from the server control version. We next discuss how to enable different web part modes, such as design.

The WebPartPageController Server Control

Part of the allure of web forms with web parts is the ability to provide to end users design-time functionality normally in the hands of developers. The `WebPartPageController` server control provides a menu to do this by plugging into the web part page functionality. One example behavior is the ability to move the location of web parts by entering design mode for the page. Once finished designing the page, the end user can choose browse mode in the drop-down menu. The `WebPartPageController` control also allows the user to choose whether to save personalization data at the User or Shared scope. One consideration would be to apply role checking on this setting if only certain users should be able to select the Shared scope. Figure 10-3 shows `WebpartPageController` in action.

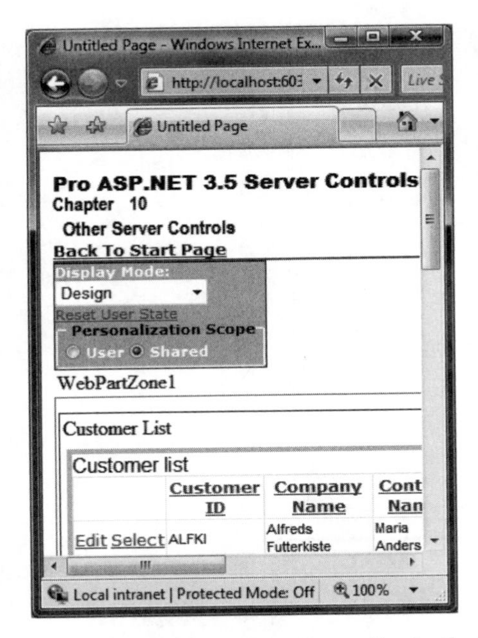

Figure 10-3. *WebpartPageController in the browser*

Figure 10-4 shows the form in design mode with the mouse dragging `CustomerInvoicesWebPart` to the top of the web part zone within the browser.

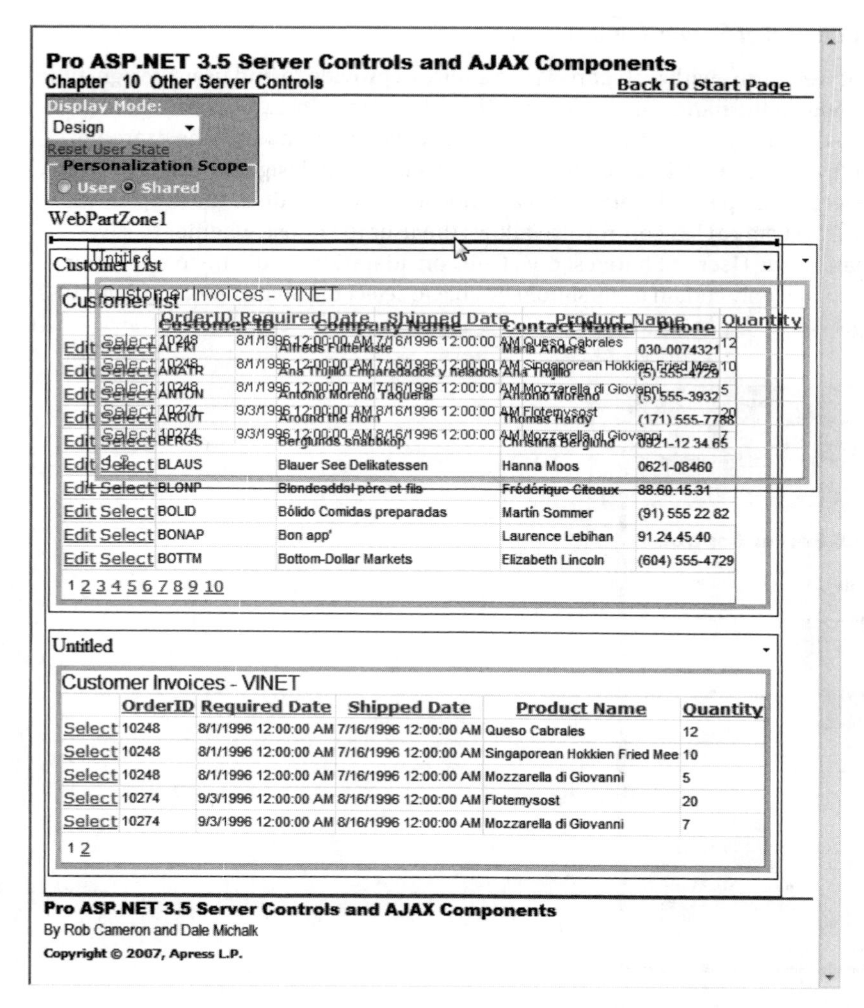

Figure 10-4. *The Customer Info web part web form in design mode*

What is handy about this server control is that just by dropping it on to the web-part-enabled web form, you get immediate customization functionality. Listing 10-5 provides the source code for the `WebPartController` server control.

Listing 10-5. *The WebPartPageController Server Control*

```
using System;
using System.ComponentModel;
using System.Web.UI;
using System.Web.UI.HtmlControls;
using System.Web.UI.WebControls;
using System.Web.UI.WebControls.WebParts;
```

```
namespace ControlsBook2Lib.Ch10
{
  [DefaultProperty("DisplayModeText")]
  [ToolboxData("<{0}:WebPartPageController runat=server>
</{0}:WebPartPageController>")]
  public class WebPartPageController : CompositeControl
  {
    WebPartManager _currentWebPartManager;

    Label displayMode;
    DropDownList displayModeDropDown;
    RadioButton userRB;
    RadioButton sharedRB;
    Panel personalizationScopePanel;

    #region Properties
    [Bindable(true), Category("Appearance"), DefaultValue("Display Mode"),
    Localizable(true), Description(
    "Sets the text on the caption for the web part state dropdown.")]
    public string DisplayModeText
    {
      get
      {
        object displayModeText = ViewState["DisplayModeText"];
        if (displayModeText == null)
          return string.Empty;
        else
          return (string)displayModeText;
      }

      set
      {
        ViewState["DisplayModeText"] = value;
      }
    }

    [Bindable(true), Category("Appearance"), DefaultValue("Reset User State"),
    Localizable(true), Description(
    "Configures the text on the link button to reset state.")]
    public string ResetStateText
    {
      get
      {
        object resetStateText = ViewState["ResetStateText"];
        if (resetStateText == null)
          return string.Empty;
```

```
      else
        return (string)resetStateText;
    }

    set
    {
      ViewState["ResetStateText"] = value;
    }
  }

  [Bindable(true), Category("Appearance"), Localizable(true),
  DefaultValue("Reset the current user's personalization data for the page."),
  Description("Configures the tooltip for the link button to reset state.")]
  public string ResetStateToolTip
  {
    get
    {
      object resetStateToolTip = ViewState["ResetStateToolTip"];
      if (resetStateToolTip == null)
        return string.Empty;
      else
        return (string)resetStateToolTip;
    }

    set
    {
      ViewState["ResetStateToolTip"] = value;
    }
  }

  #endregion

  #region Overrides
  protected override void OnInit(EventArgs e)
  {
    base.OnInit(e);

    _currentWebPartManager =
     WebPartManager.GetCurrentWebPartManager(Page);
  }

  protected override void OnPreRender(EventArgs e)
  {
    base.OnPreRender(e);

    String browseModeName = WebPartManager.BrowseDisplayMode.Name;
```

```
    //Reset items collection on dropdown
    displayModeDropDown.Items.Clear();

    // Fill the DropDown with the names of supported display modes.
    foreach (WebPartDisplayMode mode
    in _currentWebPartManager.SupportedDisplayModes)
    {
      String modeName = mode.Name;
      // Make sure a mode is enabled before adding it.
      if (mode.IsEnabled(_currentWebPartManager))
      {
        ListItem item = new ListItem(modeName, modeName);
        displayModeDropDown.Items.Add(item);
      }
    }

    // If shared scope is allowed for this user, display the scope-switching
    // UI and select the appropriate radio button for the current user scope.
    if (_currentWebPartManager.Personalization.CanEnterSharedScope)
    {
      personalizationScopePanel.Visible = true;
      if (_currentWebPartManager.Personalization.Scope
      == PersonalizationScope.User)
        userRB.Checked = true;
      else
        sharedRB.Checked = true;
    }

    ListItemCollection items = displayModeDropDown.Items;
    int selectedIndex =
      items.IndexOf(items.FindByText(_currentWebPartManager.DisplayMode.Name));
    displayModeDropDown.SelectedIndex = selectedIndex;
  }

  public override ControlCollection Controls
  {
    get
    {
      EnsureChildControls();
      return base.Controls;
    }
  }

  public override Unit Height
  {
```

```
    get
    {
      return base.Height;
    }
    set
    {
      EnsureChildControls();
      Unit min = new Unit(87);
      if (value.Value > min.Value)
        base.Height = value;
      else
        base.Height = min;
    }
  }

  public override Unit Width
  {
    get
    {
      return base.Width;
    }
    set
    {
      EnsureChildControls();
      Unit min = new Unit(167);
      if (value.Value >= min.Value)
        base.Width = value;
      else
        base.Width = min;
    }
  }

  protected override void CreateChildControls()
  {
    Controls.Clear();
    CreateChildControlHierarchy();
  }

  #endregion

  private void CreateChildControlHierarchy()
  {
    Panel rootPanel = new Panel
    {
      ID = "rootPanel",
      BorderWidth = 1,
      BackColor = this.BackColor,
```

```
  ForeColor = this.ForeColor
};
rootPanel.Font.Names = new string[] { "Verdana", "Arial", "Sans Serif" };

rootPanel.Width = this.Width;
rootPanel.Height = this.Height;
Controls.Add(rootPanel);

displayModeDropDown = new DropDownList
{
  ID = "displayModeDropDown",
  AutoPostBack = true,
  Width = 120
};
displayModeDropDown.SelectedIndexChanged += new
EventHandler(displayModeDropDown_SelectedIndexChanged);

displayMode = new Label
{
  ID = "displayMode",
  Text = DisplayModeText,
  AssociatedControlID = "DisplayModeDropDown"
};
displayMode.Font.Bold = true;
displayMode.Font.Size = 8;

//Add in order of desired rendering
rootPanel.Controls.Add(displayMode);
HtmlGenericControl div1 = new HtmlGenericControl("div");
div1.Controls.Add(displayModeDropDown);
rootPanel.Controls.Add(div1);

LinkButton resetUserState = new LinkButton
{
  ID = "resetUserState",
  Text = ResetStateText,
  ToolTip = ResetStateToolTip
};
resetUserState.Font.Size = 8;
resetUserState.Click += new EventHandler(resetUserState_Click);
HtmlGenericControl div2 = new HtmlGenericControl("div");
div2.Controls.Add(resetUserState);
rootPanel.Controls.Add(div2);
personalizationScopePanel = new Panel
{
  ID = "personalization Scope",
  GroupingText = "Personalization Scope",
```

```
    Width = 165
  };
  personalizationScopePanel.Font.Size = 8;
  personalizationScopePanel.Font.Bold = true;
  rootPanel.Controls.Add(personalizationScopePanel);

  userRB = new RadioButton
  {
    ID = "userRB",
    Text = "User",
    AutoPostBack = true,
    GroupName = "Scope"
  };
  userRB.CheckedChanged += new EventHandler(userRB_CheckedChanged);
  personalizationScopePanel.Controls.Add(userRB);

  sharedRB = new RadioButton
  {
    ID = "sharedRB",
    Text = "Shared",
    AutoPostBack = true,
    GroupName = "Scope"
  };
  sharedRB.CheckedChanged += new EventHandler(sharedRB_CheckedChanged);
  personalizationScopePanel.Controls.Add(sharedRB);
}

#region Control Events
void sharedRB_CheckedChanged(object sender, EventArgs e)
{
  if (_currentWebPartManager.Personalization.CanEnterSharedScope &&
        _currentWebPartManager.Personalization.Scope
       == PersonalizationScope.User)
    _currentWebPartManager.Personalization.ToggleScope();
}

void userRB_CheckedChanged(object sender, EventArgs e)
{
  if (_currentWebPartManager.Personalization.Scope
  == PersonalizationScope.Shared)
    _currentWebPartManager.Personalization.ToggleScope();
}

void resetUserState_Click(object sender, EventArgs e)
{
  _currentWebPartManager.Personalization.ResetPersonalizationState();
}
```

```
    void displayModeDropDown_SelectedIndexChanged(object sender, EventArgs e)
    {
      String selectedMode = displayModeDropDown.SelectedValue;

      WebPartDisplayMode mode =
      _currentWebPartManager.SupportedDisplayModes[selectedMode];
      if (mode != null)
        _currentWebPartManager.DisplayMode = mode;
    }
    #endregion
  }
}
```

Now that we have good control over the web part page functionality, we next take care of a little bit of code cleanup to make the web parts look better before moving on to discuss how to enable connections between web parts.

Connecting Web Parts

In the previous sections, we created server controls and then converted them to web parts. We also added a handy web page controller web part to expose web part page functionality to end users. In the server control versions of the web parts, we added a border and a label to contain a title for the control. If you view the screen shots in Figures 10-1 to 10-4, you see that the `CustomerListWebPart` control has the title set to Customer List, resulting in the phrase "Customer List" appearing twice. The `CustomerInvoicesWebPart` has a title of Untitled. Web parts include their own border and title functionality, so we first need to remove the blue border functionality from the server controls. Next, we'll start the work on connecting the web parts.

First, we create an interface for passing the customer ID from the `CustomerListWebPart` to the `CustomerInvoicesWebPart` called `ICustomerID`. We add the `[Personalizable()]` attribute to the `CustomerID` property on the `CustomerListWebPart` control so that the value of `CustomerID` is saved as part of the persistence service and will be available the next time the page is loaded.

Next, we add a new method to the `CustomerListWebPart` called `ProvideICustomerID` that returns an `ICustomerID` object. The new method is decorated with the `ConnectionProvider` attribute so that the web part infrastructure is aware of how to connect this web part.

For the `CustomerInvoicesWebPart`, we add a private variable called `customerIDProvider` of type `ICustomerID` to hold a reference. We also add a `GetICustomerID` method that takes a parameter of type `ICustomerID` and assigns it to the private variable `customerIDProvider`. Finally, we override `OnPreRender` for the `CustomerInvoicesWebPart` so that the `CustomerID` can be retrieved from the provider and set on the `CustomerInvoicesWebPart`'s `CustomerID` property.

Wiring Up the Page

To allow connections between the web parts, we first add a `ConnectionZone` web control to the `CustomerInfoWebPart.aspx` markup and add verbs such as connect, configure, disconnect, and so on to the `ConnectionZone` control. We also override `OnPreRender` in `CustomerInfoWebPart.aspx.cs` and set properties for the connection verbs and UI to customize the connection functionality. This completes the work necessary to wire up our server controls and link them the web-part way.

To test this functionality, run the page, and select the new Connect option that appears as a Display mode. This menu item is available because the `WebPartPageController` server control dynamically reads what modes are supported by the `WebPartManager` control on the page. Figure 10-5 shows the web form in Connect mode.

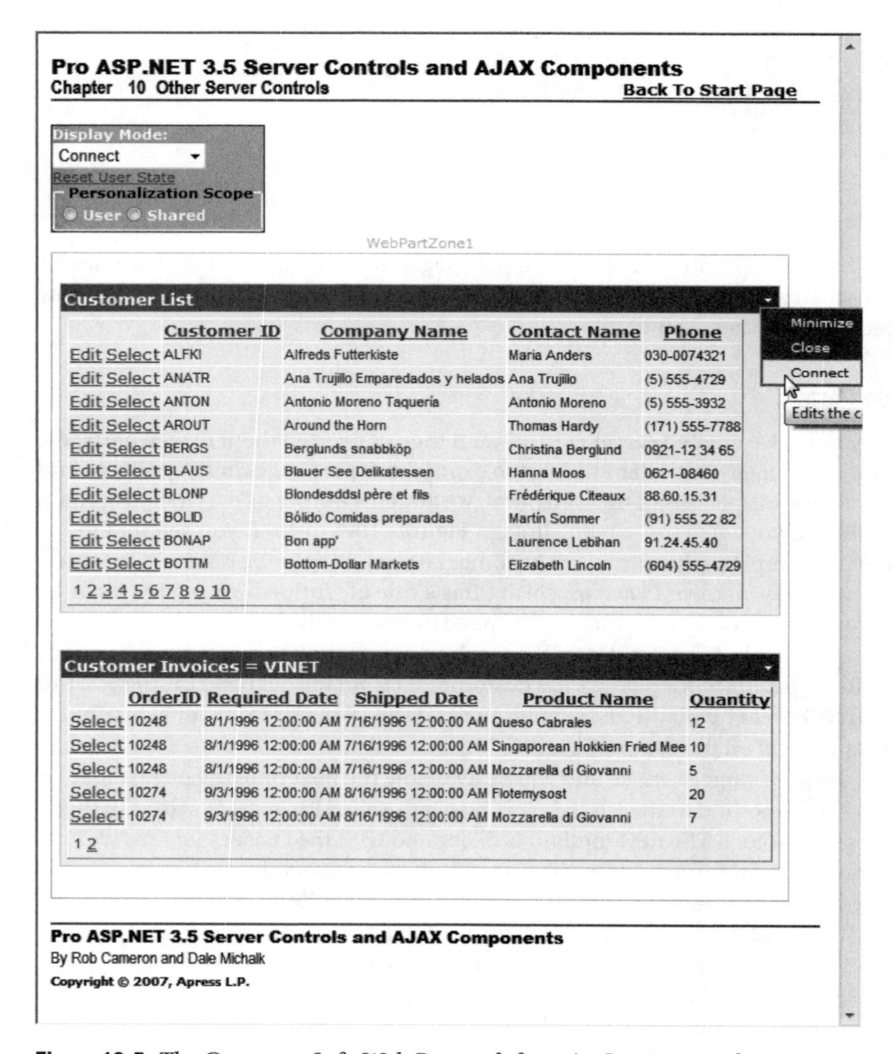

Figure 10-5. *The Customer Info Web Part web form in Connect mode*

After clicking Connect as shown in Figure 10-5, Figure 10-6 shows a screen shot of the Create and Manage Connections functionality, as well as the Close Zone button to cancel out creating a connection.

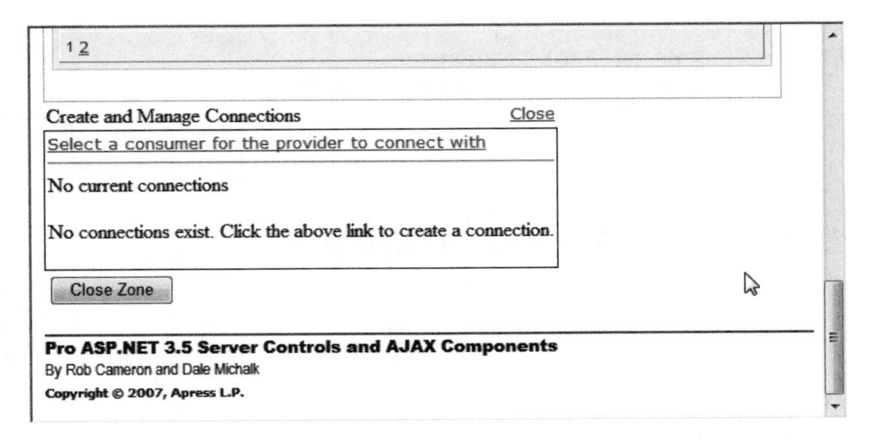

Figure 10-6. *The Create and Manage Connections UI without any connections*

Figure 10-7 shows the UI after clicking the "Select a consumer" link with the `CustomerInvoices` web part selected for the To value.

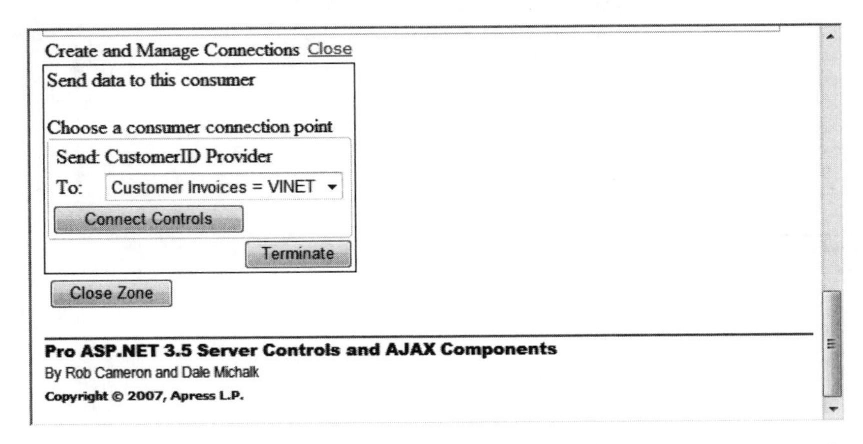

Figure 10-7. *The Create and Manage Connections UI after connecting the web parts*

After clicking the Connect Controls button and selecting Browse mode in `WebPartPageController`, the controls are now linked. Selecting a row in the `CustomerList` web part filters the `CustomerInvoices` web part to invoices for the selected customer based on the `CustomerID` passed via the web part connection, as shown in Figure 10-8 where `CustomerID` `BLAUS` is selected and the customer's invoices display below in the `CustomerInvoices` web part.

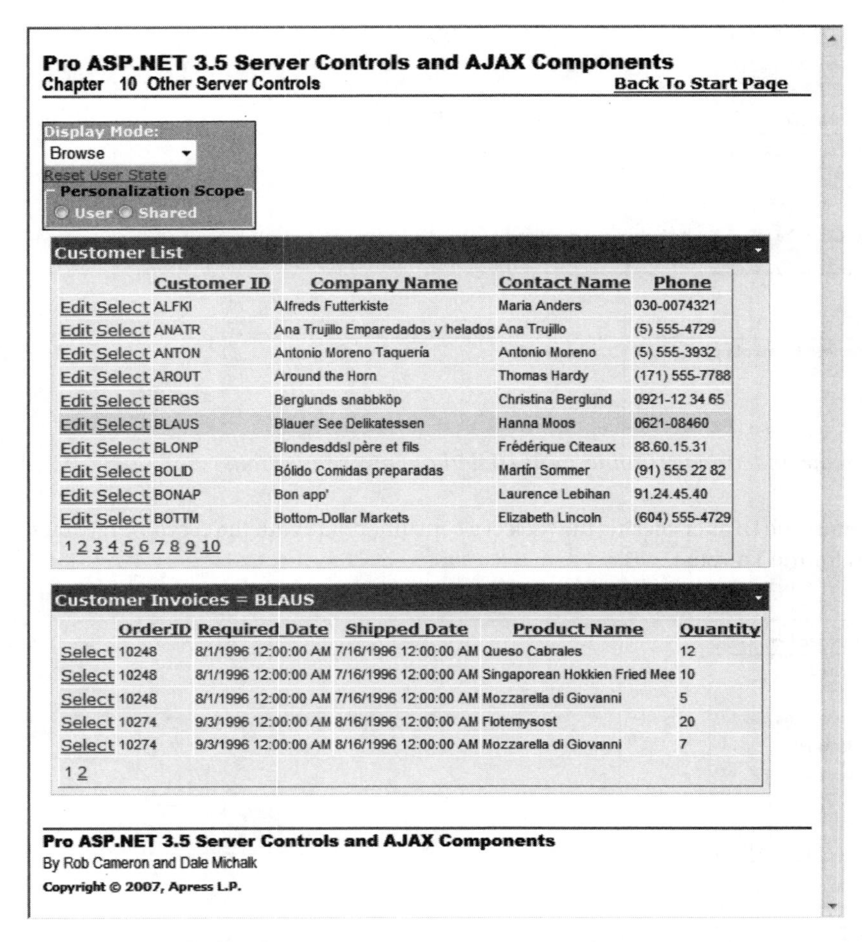

Figure 10-8. *Linked web parts*

This concludes our web part walkthrough. The final web part source code for the `CustomerListWebPart` and `CustomerInvoicesWebPart` web parts as well as the final `CustomerInfoWebPart` web form are provided in Listings 10-6, 10-7, 10-8, and 10-9 respectively.

Listing 10-6. *The CustomerListWebPart Server Control*

```
using System;
using System.Drawing;
using System.Web.UI;
using System.Web.UI.WebControls;
using System.Web.UI.WebControls.WebParts;

namespace ControlsBook2Lib.Ch10
{
  [ToolboxData("<{0}:CustomerListWebPart runat=server></{0}:CustomerListWebPart>")]
```

```
public class CustomerListWebPart : WebPart, ICustomerID
{
  private const string strSelectCmd = @"Select * from [Customers]";
  private const string strUpdateCmd = @"UPDATE [Customers] SET " +
    @"[CompanyName] = @CompanyName, [ContactName] = @ContactName, " +
    @"[Phone] = @Phone WHERE [CustomerID] = @CustomerID";

  public CustomerListWebPart()
  {
  }

  [Personalizable()]
  public virtual String CustomerID
  {
    get
    {
      object customerID = ViewState["CustomerID"];
      if (customerID == null)
        return String.Empty;
      else
        return (String)customerID;
    }
    set
    {
      ViewState["CustomerID"] = value;
    }
  }

  //This callback method returns the provider.
  [ConnectionProvider("CustomerID Provider", "CustomerIDProvider")]
  public ICustomerID ProvideICustomerID()
  {
    return this;
  }

  // Allow page developers to set the connection string.
  public String ConnectionString
  {
    get
    {
      object connectionString = ViewState["ConnectionString"];
      if (connectionString == null)
        return String.Empty;
      else
        return (String)connectionString;
    }
```

```
    set
    {
      ViewState["ConnectionString"] = value;
    }
  }

  public Boolean AllowCustomerEditing
  {
    get
    {
      object allowEditing = ViewState["AllowCustomerEditing"];
      if (allowEditing == null)
        return false;
      else
        return (Boolean)allowEditing;
    }
    set
    {
      ViewState["AllowCustomerEditing"] = value;
    }
  }

  protected override void CreateChildControls()
  {
    Controls.Clear();

    SqlDataSource ds = new SqlDataSource(this.ConnectionString, strSelectCmd);
    ds.ID = "dsCustomers";
    ds.DataSourceMode = SqlDataSourceMode.DataSet;
    ds.UpdateCommandType = SqlDataSourceCommandType.Text;
    ds.UpdateCommand = strUpdateCmd;
    ParameterCollection updateParams = new ParameterCollection();
    updateParams.Add(_createParameter("CustomerID", TypeCode.String));
    updateParams.Add(_createParameter("CompanyName", TypeCode.String));
    updateParams.Add(_createParameter("ContactName", TypeCode.String));
    updateParams.Add(_createParameter("Phone", TypeCode.String));

    Controls.Add(ds);

    GridView grid = new GridView();
    grid.ID = "customerGrid";
    grid.Font.Size = 8;
    grid.AllowPaging = true;
    grid.AllowSorting = true;
    grid.AutoGenerateColumns = false;
    String[] fields = { "CustomerID" };
    grid.DataKeyNames = fields;
```

```
  grid.DataSourceID = "dsCustomers";
  CommandField controlButton = new CommandField();

  //Only show Edit button if control configured to allow it
  if (AllowCustomerEditing)
    controlButton.ShowEditButton = true;

  controlButton.ShowSelectButton = true;
  grid.Columns.Add(controlButton);
  BoundField customerID = _createBoundField("CustomerID");
  customerID.ReadOnly = true;
  grid.Columns.Add(customerID);
  grid.Columns.Add(_createBoundField("CompanyName"));
  grid.Columns.Add(_createBoundField("ContactName"));
  grid.Columns.Add(_createBoundField("Phone"));
  grid.SelectedRowStyle.BackColor = Color.AntiqueWhite;

  grid.SelectedIndexChanged += new EventHandler(SelectedIndexChanged);
  grid.PageIndexChanged += new EventHandler(PageIndexChanged);
  Controls.Add(grid);
  Style.Add(HtmlTextWriterStyle.FontFamily, "arial");
}

protected void SelectedIndexChanged(object sender, EventArgs e)
{
  GridViewRow row = ((GridView)(sender)).SelectedRow;
  CustomerID = row.Cells[1].Text;
}

protected void PageIndexChanged(object sender, EventArgs e)
{
  ((GridView)(sender)).SelectedIndex = -1;
}

private BoundField _createBoundField(String fieldName)
{
  BoundField field = new BoundField();
  switch (fieldName)
  {
    case "CompanyName": field.HeaderText = "Company Name";
      break;
    case "ContactName": field.HeaderText = "Contact Name";
      break;
    case "PhoneName": field.HeaderText = "Phone Name";
      break;
```

```
          case "CustomerID": field.HeaderText = "Customer ID";
            break;
          default: field.HeaderText = fieldName; break;
        }
        field.SortExpression = fieldName;
        field.DataField = fieldName;
        return field;
      }

      private Parameter _createParameter(String paramName, TypeCode dataTypeCode)
      {
        Parameter theParm = new Parameter(paramName, dataTypeCode);
        return theParm;
      }
    }
}
```

Listing 10-7. *The CustomerListWebPart Server Control*

```
using System;
using System.Drawing;
using System.Web.UI;
using System.Web.UI.WebControls;
using System.Web.UI.WebControls.WebParts;

namespace ControlsBook2Lib.Ch10
{
  [ToolboxData("<{0}:CustomerInvoicesWebPart
  runat=server></{0}:CustomerInvoicesWebPart>")]
  public class CustomerInvoicesWebPart : WebPart
  {
    private const string strSelectCmd = @"Select * from [Invoices] where " +
      "CustomerID = '{0}'";
    private ICustomerID _customerIDProvider;

    public CustomerInvoicesWebPart()
    {
    }

    public String CustomerID
    {
      get
      {
        object customerID = ViewState["CustomerID"];
        if (customerID == null)
          return String.Empty;
```

```
      else
        return (String)customerID;
    }
    set
    {
      ViewState["CustomerID"] = value;
    }
  }

  //The ConnectionConsumer attribute identifies
  //this method as the mechanism for connecting with
  // the provider.
  [ConnectionConsumer("CustomerID Consumer", "CustomerIDConsumer")]
  public void GetICustomerID(ICustomerID Provider)
  {
    _customerIDProvider = Provider;
  }

  protected override void OnPreRender(EventArgs e)
  {
    base.OnPreRender(e);

    if (this._customerIDProvider != null)
    {
      CustomerID = _customerIDProvider.CustomerID.Trim();
    }
    Title = "Customer Invoices = " + CustomerID;
  }

  // Allow page developers to set the connection string.
  public String ConnectionString
  {
    get
    {
      object connectionString = ViewState["ConnectionString"];
      if (connectionString == null)
        return String.Empty;
      else
        return (String)connectionString;
    }
    set
    {
      ViewState["ConnectionString"] = value;
    }
  }
```

```
protected override void CreateChildControls()
{
  Controls.Clear();

  SqlDataSource ds = new SqlDataSource(this.ConnectionString,
  String.Format(strSelectCmd, CustomerID));
  ds.ID = "dsCustomerInvoicesWebPart";
  ds.DataSourceMode = SqlDataSourceMode.DataSet;
  Controls.Add(ds);

  GridView grid = new GridView();
  grid.ID = "CustomerInvoicesWebPartGrid";
  grid.Font.Size = 8;
  grid.AllowPaging = true;
  grid.PageSize = 5;
  grid.AllowSorting = true;
  grid.AutoGenerateColumns = false;
  String[] fields = { "CustomerID" };
  grid.DataKeyNames = fields;
  grid.DataSourceID = "dsCustomerInvoicesWebPart";
  CommandField controlButton = new CommandField();
  controlButton.ShowSelectButton = true;
  grid.Columns.Add(controlButton);
  grid.Columns.Add(_createBoundField("OrderID"));
  grid.Columns.Add(_createBoundField("RequiredDate"));
  grid.Columns.Add(_createBoundField("ShippedDate"));
  grid.Columns.Add(_createBoundField("ProductName"));
  grid.Columns.Add(_createBoundField("Quantity"));
  grid.SelectedRowStyle.BackColor = Color.AntiqueWhite;

  grid.SelectedIndexChanged += new EventHandler(SelectedIndexChanged);
  grid.PageIndexChanged += new EventHandler(PageIndexChanged);

  Controls.Add(grid);
  Style.Add(HtmlTextWriterStyle.FontFamily, "arial");
}

protected void SelectedIndexChanged(object sender, EventArgs e)
{
  GridViewRow row = ((GridView)(sender)).SelectedRow;
}

protected void PageIndexChanged(object sender, EventArgs e)
{
  ((GridView)(sender)).SelectedIndex = -1;
}
```

```
    private BoundField _createBoundField(String fieldName)
    {
      BoundField field = new BoundField();
      switch (fieldName)
      {
        case "Order ID": field.HeaderText = "Order ID";
          break;
        case "RequiredDate": field.HeaderText = "Required Date";
          break;
        case "ShippedDate": field.HeaderText = "Shipped Date";
          break;
        case "ProductName": field.HeaderText = "Product Name";
          break;
        case "Quanity": field.HeaderText = "Quantity Ordered";
          break;
        default: field.HeaderText = fieldName; break;
      }
      field.DataField = fieldName;
      field.SortExpression = fieldName;
      return field;
    }

    private Parameter _createParameter(String paramName, TypeCode dataTypeCode)
    {
      Parameter theParm = new Parameter(paramName, dataTypeCode);
      return theParm;
    }
  }
}
```

Listing 10-8. *The Customer Information Web Part Web Form .aspx Page File*

```
<%@ Page Language="C#" MasterPageFile="~/MasterPage/ControlsBook2MasterPage.Master"
AutoEventWireup="true"
CodeBehind="CustomerInfoWebPart.aspx.cs"
Inherits="ControlsBook2Web.Ch10.CustomerInfoWebPart"
Title="Customer Info Web Part Demo Web Form" %>
<%@ Register TagPrefix="apress" Namespace="ControlsBook2Lib.Ch10"
 Assembly="ControlsBook2Lib" %>

<asp:Content ID="Content1" ContentPlaceHolderID="HeadSection" runat="server">
</asp:Content>
<asp:Content ID="Content2" ContentPlaceHolderID="ChapterNumAndTitle" runat="server">
<asp:Label ID="ChapterNumberLabel" runat="server"
Width="14px">10</asp:Label>  <asp:Label
    ID="ChapterTitleLabel" runat="server" Width="360px">Other Server Controls
    </asp:Label>
```

```
</asp:Content>
<asp:Content ID="Content3" ContentPlaceHolderID="PrimaryContent" runat="server">
  <div>
  <br />
    <asp:WebPartManager ID="WebPartManager1" runat="server">
    </asp:WebPartManager>
    <apress:WebPartPageController ID="options" runat="server"  DisplayModeText=
    "Display Mode:"
        ResetStateText="Reset User State"

        ResetStateToolTip=
        "Reset the current user's personalization data for the page."
        Height="87px" Width="167px" BackColor="Silver" ForeColor="White" />
  <asp:webpartzone id="WebPartZone1" runat="server" BorderColor="#CCCCCC"
      Font-Names="Verdana" Padding="6" >
    <EmptyZoneTextStyle Font-Size="0.8em" />
    <PartStyle Font-Size="0.8em" ForeColor="#333333" />
    <TitleBarVerbStyle Font-Size="0.6em" Font-Underline="False" ForeColor="White" />
    <MenuLabelHoverStyle ForeColor="#E2DED6" />
    <MenuPopupStyle BackColor="#5D7B9D" BorderColor="#CCCCCC" BorderWidth="1px"
      Font-Names="Verdana" Font-Size="0.6em" />
    <MenuVerbStyle BorderColor="#5D7B9D" BorderStyle="Solid" BorderWidth="1px"
      ForeColor="White" />
    <PartTitleStyle BackColor="#5D7B9D" Font-Bold="True" Font-Size="0.8em"
      ForeColor="White" />
    <zonetemplate>
      <apress:CustomerListWebPart id="CustomerListWebPart" runat="server"
         ConnectionString = "<%$ ConnectionStrings:NorthWindDB %>"
        Title="Customer List" AllowEdit="False" AllowCustomerEditing="True" />
      <apress:CustomerInvoicesWebPart ID="CustomerInvoicesWebPart1" runat="server"
      CustomerID="VINET"
      ConnectionString = "<%$ ConnectionStrings:NorthWindDB %>"
      Title="Customer Invoices"/>
    </zonetemplate>
    <MenuVerbHoverStyle BackColor="#F7F6F3" BorderColor="#CCCCCC"
      BorderStyle="Solid" BorderWidth="1px" ForeColor="#333333" />
    <PartChromeStyle BackColor="#F7F6F3" BorderColor="#E2DED6" Font-Names="Verdana"
      ForeColor="White" />
    <HeaderStyle Font-Size="0.7em" ForeColor="#CCCCCC" HorizontalAlign="Center" />
    <MenuLabelStyle ForeColor="White" />
  </asp:webpartzone>
  <asp:connectionszone id="connectionsZone1" runat="server" >
    <cancelverb text="Terminate" />
    <closeverb text="Close Zone" />
    <configureverb text="Configure" />
    <connectverb text="Connect Controls" />
    <disconnectverb text="End Connection" />
```

```
  </asp:connectionszone>
  <br />
  </div>
</asp:Content>
```

Listing 10-9. *The Customer Information Web Part Web Form Code-Behind Class File*

```
using System;

namespace ControlsBook2Web.Ch10
{
  public partial class CustomerInfoWebPart : System.Web.UI.Page
  {
    protected void Page_Load(object sender, EventArgs e)
    {

    }

    protected override void OnPreRender(EventArgs e)
    {
      base.OnPreRender(e);

      // Set properties on verbs.
      connectionsZone1.CancelVerb.Description =
        "Terminates the connection process";
      connectionsZone1.CloseVerb.Description =
        "Closes the connections UI";
      connectionsZone1.ConfigureVerb.Description =
        "Configure the transformer for the connection";
      connectionsZone1.ConnectVerb.Description =
        "Connect two WebPart controls";
      connectionsZone1.DisconnectVerb.Description =
        "End the connection between two controls";

      // Set properties for UI text strings.
      connectionsZone1.ConfigureConnectionTitle =
        "Configure";
      connectionsZone1.ConnectToConsumerInstructionText =
        "Choose a consumer connection point";
      connectionsZone1.ConnectToConsumerText =
        "Select a consumer for the provider to connect with";
      connectionsZone1.ConnectToConsumerTitle =
        "Send data to this consumer";
      connectionsZone1.ConnectToProviderInstructionText =
        "Choose a provider connection point";
      connectionsZone1.ConnectToProviderText =
        "Select a provider for the consumer to connect with";
```

```
      connectionsZone1.ConnectToProviderTitle =
        "Get data from this provider";
      connectionsZone1.ConsumersInstructionText =
        "WebPart controls that receive data from providers";
      connectionsZone1.ConsumersTitle = "Consumer Controls";
      connectionsZone1.GetFromText = "Receive from";
      connectionsZone1.GetText = "Retrieve";
      connectionsZone1.HeaderText =
       "Create and Manage Connections";
      connectionsZone1.InstructionText =
       "Manage connections for the selected WebPart control";
      connectionsZone1.InstructionTitle =
        "Manage connections for consumers or providers";
      connectionsZone1.NoExistingConnectionInstructionText =
        "No connections exist. Click the above link to create "
        + "a connection.";
      connectionsZone1.NoExistingConnectionTitle =
        "No current connections";
      connectionsZone1.ProvidersInstructionText =
        "WebPart controls that send data to consumers";
      connectionsZone1.ProvidersTitle = "Provider controls";
    }
  }
}
```

For further testing, close the web form and reopen it. You should see that your previous settings, such as the selected customer and the connection, are restored. This is a result of the personalization configuration on the web part and in the web form UI based on the `WebPartPageController` settings. Click Reset User State, and the connection and currently selected value will reset to the default values. You can again build the connection between the two server controls by selecting Connect for the `WebPartPageController` Display Mode `DropDownList` and clicking Connect on the web part menu to reconnect the web parts' link.

Web Part Development Tips

In the preceding sections, we covered the details of creating web parts and enabling web part functionality. An item to consider when building web part pages with multiple web parts is performance. On a web part page with five or six web parts, each calling either a web service or making one or more database calls, performance can suffer depending on application load and similar considerations. If you find that performance is an issue, an excellent way to improve performance is to perform tasks such as calling a web service or retrieving data from a database on separate threads. The article "Asynchronous Web Parts" by Fritz Onion, available at the following URL, provides an excellent reference on how to do this:

`http://msdn.microsoft.com/msdnmag/issues/06/07/ExtremeASPNET/default.aspx`

If you intend to make extensive use of web parts, the `OnPreRender` code in Listing 10-9 for the `CustomerInfoWebPart.aspx.cs` page could be added to a master page that contains the desired web part zones, including `ConnectionZone`. In addition, `WebPartPageController` could also be added as part of a master page. This would standardize a site on a single web part page template with the boilerplate code added to the master page.

This concludes our coverage of web part development. In the next section, we cover adaptive control behavior.

Adaptive Control Behavior

With versions after .NET Framework 1.0, Microsoft shipped an add-on called the Mobile Internet Toolkit. In .NET Framework 1.1, the toolkit was fully incorporated into the .NET Framework. These extensions to ASP.NET are called mobile controls and are located under the `System.Web.UI.MobileControls` namespace. Fortunately, the mobile web page framework is based on the same fundamental model as ASP.NET, with the web form construct and server control model, providing for a short learning curve to develop mobile web applications.

When the .NET Framework 2.0 was in beta, the product team shared information about the new control adapter framework that was going to be introduced. Initially, there was talk of the control adapter framework replacing the device adapters for mobile controls that became part of .NET Framework 1.1, but the product team backed off this concept. When you think about it, not trying to do this makes a lot of sense because of the limitations of mobile device capabilities. In general, mobile browsers have limited capabilities, such as small screen size and limited navigation, though that is changing with each new generation of phones. Also, from an application design perspective, it would not make sense to have full parity with a desktop web application in most cases due to the limited bandwidth available and smaller screen size. Most mobile applications are designed to provide streamlined access to the most important application processes.

What is exciting is that the control adapter framework remained in .NET Framework 2.0 and later to provide web developers the ability to modify the HTML output of the built-in server controls.

For mobile web development, the ASP.NET mobile controls live on in the .NET Framework 3.5, which we cover later in this chapter. However, first we provide an overview of the adaptive behavior framework including steps to build a custom control adapter in the next section.

Nonmobile Adaptive Behavior

Starting in .NET Framework 2.0, ASP.NET includes the ability to change rendering for a web server control such as the built-in `TreeView` server control. The adaptive rendering functionality provides for multiple ways to modify control behavior:

- Use declarative device markup or browser filtering to affect how control properties are set based on device filter definitions.
- Configure a web application to render multiple markups depending on the browser device.
- Create a custom `TextWriter` class to render output.
- Use the `XhtmlTextWriter` or `ChtmlTextWriter` classes to customize control tags and attributes.
- Develop a custom control adapter that substitutes an adapter life cycle method for the default life cycle method for an existing server control.

In addition to controlling rendering, server control behavior can be modified for a target browsing device as follows:

- Prevent a custom control from being adapted, which may be desirable for server control developers.
- Alter `ViewState` management.
- Alter how postback data is processed.

Refer to the ASP.NET documentation for details on how to take advantage of the adapter control framework in general. In the next section, we focus on building control adapters.

Control Adapters

The adaptive control behavior framework allows the control developer to substitute custom rendering behavior at key life cycle stages of a server control, without actually modifying or inheriting from the target control. A single instance of the control adapter is mapped into a page to modify behavior of all server control instances of the target server control type.

What happens is that when a page request is made, the ASP.NET page processing pipeline checks to see if there is an associated adapter for a control in the page's control tree and calls the adapter's associated method, instead of the target control's method. So, instead of calling the control's `Render` method, the control adapter's `Render` method is called instead. Quite often, the control adapter will refer to the control's version of the method, so it is not necessary to reimplement every bit of a control's functionality in the control adapter, which is one of the reasons why this architecture is so appealing. Control developers have to implement only what is needed. The relevant namespace for control adapters are `System.Web.UI.Adapters` and `System.Web.UI.WebControls.Adapters`, when targeting nonmobile scenarios.

■ Note There is also a `ControlAdapter` class in the `System.Web.UI.MobileControls.Adapters` namespace for mobile scenarios that we cover later in this chapter.

There are many built-in adapters listed in the .NET Framework documentation in the `System.Web.UI.Adapters` namespace, such as the `DataBoundControlAdapter` and `HideDisabledControlAdapter` classes. Table 10-2 lists the key base classes and role in the adaptive framework.

Table 10-2. *Key Classes in the Adaptive Control Framework*

Class	Description
`ControlAdapter`	Base class for all control adapters
`WebControlAdapter`	Base class for adaptively rendering server controls that inherit from the `WebControl` class
`PageAdapter`	Base class for adaptively rendering a web form

The ControlAdapter class is abstract, providing base methods for adaptive functionality such as representative methods of the control life cycle like the following:

- OnInit
- OnLoad
- OnPreRender
- OnUnload
- Render
- RenderChildren

These methods are implemented by custom control adapters to alter the corresponding target control's behavior in the control life cycle. So, to modify Render in the target server control, the control adapter would override method to implement the new functionality. Not every method must be implemented in order to create a control adapter. In the next section, we briefly discuss page adapters.

The PageAdapter Base Class

The PageAdapter class is an abstract class that can be implemented to adapt a web page for a specific class of browsers as well as to alter ASP.NET web form behavior. Before implementing a custom PageAdapter class, instead consider implementing a custom text writer class that derivers from HtmlTextWriter as a means to provide the desired functionality.

The example in the documentation called CustomPageAdapter overrides the RenderBeginHyperlink method in order to add a src attribute that points to the current page for all hyperlink controls on the page. This is an example of creating a PageAdapter for a reason beyond targeting a specific class of browsers.

Another example available on the Internet demonstrates a PageAdapter class that alters the way ASP.NET handles ViewState. There are two ways to do this with a very small amount of code, and both require that session state is enabled. The first method is to override PageAdapter.LoadPageStateFromPersistenceMedium and PageAdpater.SavePageStateToPersistenceMedium to store the state in session state. The second method is to override PageAdapter.GetStatePersister so that it returns a SessionPageStatePersister. With the second technique, you can run into issues if a user creates multiple browser windows within the same session. Therefore, with any technique that provides this type of deep behavior modification, testing is always a good idea.

For further examples, search the Internet for the text "PageAdapter" and numerous posts with examples will pop up.

I should add that both methods require a .browsers file in the App_Browsers folder for the web site so that the custom PageAdapter is picked up by ASP.NET. The file would contain a small amount of configuration code like this:

```
<browsers>
  <browser refID="Default">
    <controlAdapters>
      <adapter controlType="System.Web.UI.Page"
       adapterType="PageSessionStateAdapter" />
    </controlAdapters>
  </browser>
</browsers>
```

The adapter element in the preceding code designates the target control in the controlType attribute and the custom PageAdapter in the adapterType attribute. This concludes our discussion of PageAdapters. In the next section, we cover the WebControlAdapter base class as well as provide an example control adapter.

The WebControlAdapter Base Class

So far, we have provided background on the adaptive control behavior architecture and discussed how it works. In this section, we go a bit deeper and implement two simple custom control adapters: one that inherits from the ControlAdapter base class and another that inherits from the WebControlAdapter base class.

Our simple adapters essentially perform the same functionality in changing the output from a <span> HTML tag to a <div> HTML tag for the StatefulLabel and FancyLabel server controls created earlier in this book. As you might guess, the StatefulLabel custom adapter class name is StatefulLabelAdapter, following the naming convention in the .NET Framework of appending "Adapter" to the target control's class name. Likewise, the FancyLabel adapter is named FancyLabelAdapter.

Both adapters override the Render method to output an HTML <div> tag instead of the standard <span> tag. Naturally, the custom adapters need to know what value to output, so each uses a Control property that points to the target control to obtain the value of the Text property found on both controls. Listings 10-10 and 10-11 contain the custom control adapters' source code.

Listing 10-10. *The StatefulLabelAdapter Control Adapter*

```
using System.Web.UI.Adapters;
using ControlsBook2Lib.Ch03;

namespace ControlsBook2Lib.Ch10
{
  class StatefulLabelAdapter : ControlAdapter
  {
    protected override void Render(System.Web.UI.HtmlTextWriter writer)
    {
      //base.Render(writer);  Don't want default rendering so comment out

      //Change rendering from a span to a div
      writer.RenderBeginTag(HtmlTextWriterTag.Div);
      //Get a reference to the target control to determine what value to write out
      writer.Write(((StatefulLabel)this.Control).Text);
      writer.RenderEndTag();
    }
  }
}
```

Listing 10-11. *The FancyLabelAdapter Control Adapter*

```
using System.Web.UI;
using System.Web.UI.WebControls.Adapters;
using ControlsBook2Lib.Ch04;

namespace ControlsBook2Lib.Ch10
{
  class FancyLabelAdapter : WebControlAdapter
  {
    protected override void Render(System.Web.UI.HtmlTextWriter writer)
    {
      //base.Render(writer);  Don't want default rendering so comment out

      //Change rendering from a span to a div
      writer.RenderBeginTag(HtmlTextWriterTag.Div);
      //Get a reference to the target control to determine what value to write out
      writer.Write(((FancyLabel)this.Control).Text);
      writer.RenderEndTag();
    }
  }
}
```

Note that, since the `StatefulLabel` custom server control inherits from `Control`, the `StatefulLabelAdapter` control adapter must inherit from `ControlAdapter`. Likewise, since the `FancyLabel` custom server control inherits from `WebControl`, the `FancyLabelAdapter` control adapter must inherit from `WebControlAdapter`.

For the control adapters to be picked up by ASP.NET, an ASP.NET folder must be added to the web project by right-clicking the web project and selecting Add ➤ Add ASP.NET Folder ➤ App_Browsers. In this folder, create a file with any name and with the file extension of `.browser`. If you right-click App_Browsers and select Add ➤ New Item, you can select Browser File in the Add New Item dialog box to provide a starting file. Listing 10-12 contains our simple `.browser` file, named `NonMobileAdapter.browser`.

Listing 10-12. *The NonMobileAdapters.browser File*

```
<browsers>
  <browser refID="Default">
    <controlAdapters>
      <adapter controlType="ControlsBook2Lib.Ch03.StatefulLabel"
               adapterType="ControlsBook2Lib.Ch10.StatefulLabelAdapter" />
      <adapter controlType="ControlsBook2Lib.Ch04.FancyLabel"
               adapterType="ControlsBook2Lib.Ch10.FancyLabelAdapter" />
    </controlAdapters>
  </browser>
</browsers>
```

The adapter elements are commented out when you first unpack the source code so that the samples from Chapters 3 and 4 run correctly and render the span tag. We tried putting the `App_Browsers` folder in the web site's `Ch10` folder to have adapters apply only in that folder, but ASP.NET does not pick up the `.browser` file unless `App_Browsers` is in the root web folder.

Once you go through these simple examples, we highly recommend downloading the `CSSFriendlyTutorial` sample provided by Microsoft. This high-quality sample provides numerous control adapters that output CSS style tags for rendering a number of built-in server controls, such as `GridView`, `Login`, `Menu`, and `TreeView` to name a few. The download includes the adapter source code as well as a sample web site to test out the adapters. It is available here:

```
http://www.asp.net/cssadapters/Default.aspx
```

As you can see from the discussion of control and page adapters, ASP.NET provides a very pluggable model that allows the developer to control just about any aspect of page and server control rendering for precise HTML output that can make any CSS-focused web designer happy. In addition, if a server control is not quite outputting correctly for a particular browser, the tools are available to modify the HTML output as needed.

In the next section, we dive into device-specific rendering for mobile applications.

Mobile Controls Overview

The ability to build web applications that target mobile devices in addition to traditional desktop HTML browsers is becoming an important web application feature as more and more users are browsing the Internet using a mobile device. An example of this is the fact that Microsoft produces several versions of Internet Explorer: Pocket Internet Explorer for the Windows Mobile Professional and Windows Mobile Standard editions, as well as the traditional desktop Internet Explorer product.

Mobile phones sold today support a variety of client markup technology, such as Wireless Markup Language (WML), compact HTML (cHTML), and Extensible Hypertext Markup Language (XHTML). Mobile devices present a great opportunity for delivering web content, especially when combined with the ever-increasing bandwidth available through wireless carrier networks. In addition, many devices sport wireless network adapters, allowing web surfing through relatively high-speed 802.11x wireless networks.

Developing mobile web applications has traditionally been a complex and tedious undertaking due to the need to address the plethora of device capabilities and ever-changing content markup specifications. Devices have different methods of sizing, positioning, and coloring information and of maintaining state on the client. Attempting to address these variations with custom code or XSLT scripts quickly becomes a maintenance nightmare. Add to that the task of keeping up with the actual content or business logic, and mobile web development can quickly become very costly to create and maintain. Having a powerful, flexible framework that provides an abstraction layer between application design and device-specific rendering can mean the difference between success and failure for a mobile development project.

Working in Visual Studio 2008

The mobile controls framework shipped soon after .NET Framework 1.0 as the Mobile Internet Toolkit and was later incorporated into .NET Framework 1.1. The mobile web forms and mobile controls have been brought forward with each new version of the .NET Framework. For Visual

Studio 2008, please review the following MSDN blog post on working with the mobile controls for more information:

```
http://blogs.msdn.com/webdevtools/archive/2007/09/17/
tip-trick-asp-net-mobile-development-with-visual-studio-2008.aspx
```

The blog post has a download containing project and item templates for the mobile controls so that you can work with the mobile controls in Visual Studio 2005 or Visual Studio 2008.

To get started with a new project in Visual Studio 2008, follow the instructions at the preceding link as well as the instructions in the download to set up the templates. After the templates are installed, create an ASP.NET web application project by launching Visual Studio 2008 and selecting File ➤ New ➤ Project and then selecting Web Application. Delete the `default.aspx` and `web.config` files that are automatically created. Right-click the project, and select Add ➤ New Item followed by Mobile Web Configuration File. This adds a `web.config` that has a bunch of device filters defined. Perform the same step to select to add a Mobile Web Form or Mobile Web User Control.

In the next section, we provide an overview of the mobile controls available in ASP.NET.

Mobile Controls Quick Primer

ASP.NET mobile web applications are created using a descendent of the `Page`. The `MobilePage` class inherits from `System.Web.UI.Page`. After downloading the templates described in the previous section, a Mobile Web Form item is available in Visual Studio in the My Templates section in the Add New Item dialog shown in Figure 10-9.

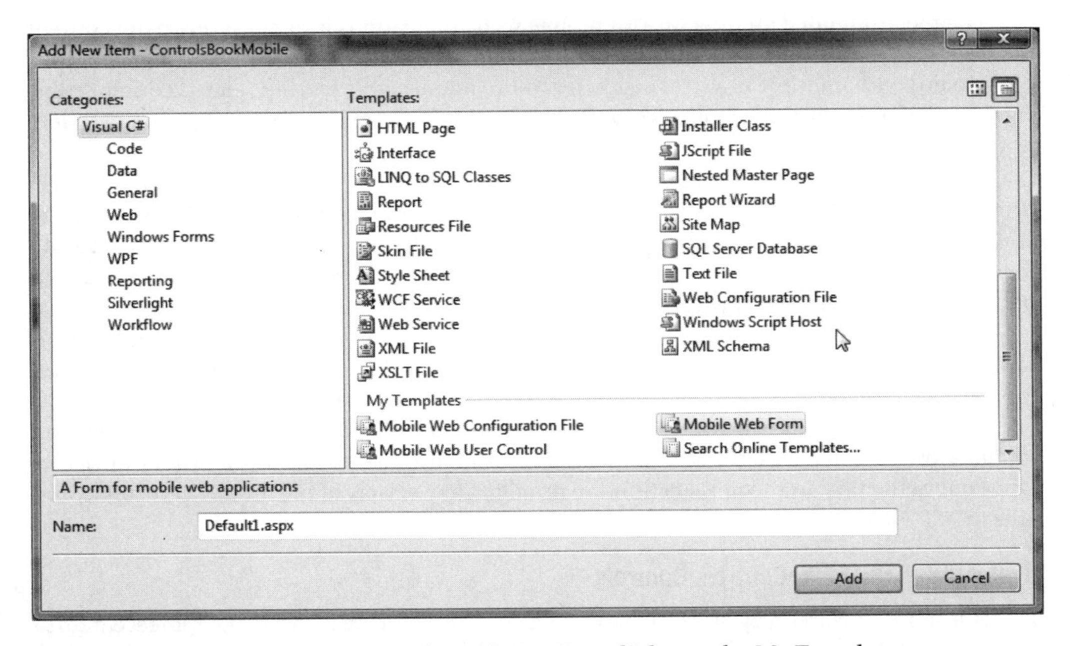

Figure 10-9. *The mobile web items in the Add New Item dialog under My Templates*

This new MobilePage web page class is necessary because of how .aspx pages are constructed to support mobile development. The differences that spring to mind when comparing a regular ASP.NET web form with a mobile web form are that mobile application namespaces and tag prefixes are brought in by the topmost Register directive. The controls and the mobile web form import from the System.Web.UI.MobileControls namespace.

Another noticeable difference is that there is more than one web form tag in the .aspx page. The mobile .aspx page XML schema permits multiple mobile web forms on a single physical file to simplify the process of designing mobile web applications. Figure 10-10 shows the inheritance tree for the mobile Form class.

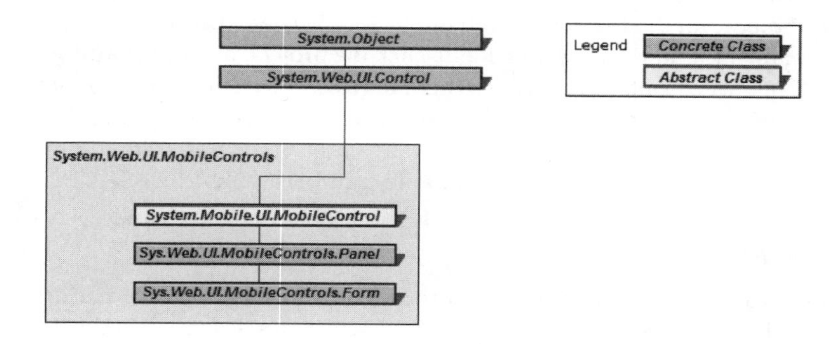

Figure 10-10. *The mobile Form class inheritance tree*

The recommended architecture for mobile web applications is to break down the content into bite-sized chunks that are compatible with small screen displays. Although you could achieve this with multiple physical pages, it is more manageable to keep related content cohesively together on a single .aspx page, with a single MobilePage class, but in separate mobile web forms.

Another benefit of this design choice is that it mirrors the WML deck/card format that is prevalent on many mobile phones: the deck itself has multiple cards, or forms, that contain the content and is downloaded as a single entity. This allows for a fair amount of navigation and manipulation on the device without having to go back to the server over the generally scarce bandwidth of the wireless carrier network.

Only the current, active mobile web form is rendered, even when browsing a mobile web form using a traditional HTML browser. Also, despite multiple form tags within an .aspx page, mobile web form technology fully supports code-behind and server-side event handling.

The unification of these two completely different display models demonstrates how the mobile web form technology automatically accounts for the vast majority of display device types out of the box. In the next section, we provide an overview of the mobile controls available in ASP.NET.

System.Web.UI.MobileControls Controls

In this section, we start off by discussing the various text controls available in the MobileControls namespace. As you would guess, we need a way to navigate through our mobile web forms, and that is the topic of the section titled "Transfer Controls" in this section. We then dive into an example .aspx page to demonstrate these controls in action. After this, we cover list, rich, validation, and pagination mobile server controls, sprinkling in example demonstrations along the way.

After you read this section, you will have a strong sense of what's available in the `MobileControls` namespace and how mobile controls work, as compared to regular server controls. We start off with a discussion of text controls.

Text Controls

The workhorses of the ASP.NET mobile controls namespace are the controls that emit the textual content. Table 10-3 outlines the text-based control options in `System.Web.UI.MobileControls`.

Table 10-3. *Simple Mobile Controls*

Name	HTML Tag	WML Tag	Description
`Label`	`text`	`text`	Displays text
`TextBox`	`<INPUT type="text">` or `<INPUT type="password">`	`<INPUT type="text">` or `<INPUT type="password">`	Gathers text input
`TextView`	`text`, `<a>`, `<b>`, `<i>`, and ` `	`text`, `<a>`, `<b>`, `<i>`, and ` `	Displays text with formatting, navigation, and pagination

The previous example, `MobileBasics.aspx`, demonstrated the `Label` and `TextBox` controls in action. `Label` simply emits the text straight into the output stream without modification or processing. `TextBox` supports the ability to gather text input from a device, including a `Password` option that masks input.

The `TextView` is a supercharged version of the `Label` control that supports pagination to break up its content via the `<p>` or `<br>` tag, offers navigation via the `<a>` tag, and provides additional support for font-related tags, such as `<b>` and `<i>`, in a similar manner to literal text within a `Form` tag.

Transfer Controls

Transfer controls support navigation and are listed in Table 10-4. The `Link` control is used in `MobileBasics.aspx` to navigate among the mobile web forms on the mobile page. The `Link` control can also be used to navigate to a new end-point URL. The `PhoneCall` control is for use with devices that have a wireless radio stack in them; it allows such a device to activate the dialing software. If the device doesn't support that, it will substitute either a text message or a clickable URL.

Table 10-4. *Transfer Mobile Controls*

Name	HTML Tag	WML Tag	Description
`Link`	`<a href="">`	`<go>`	Links to a URL
`Command`	`<INPUT type="Submit">`	`<GO type="submit">`	Posts to a URL
`PhoneCall`	`<a href="">`	`<do>` and `<go>`	Initiates a phone call or links to a URL

The Command control posts back the current web form to the web server for processing form data. Once the content is at the server, you can redirect it to a new URL or to one of the mobile web forms on a page by setting the Page.ActiveForm property.

List Controls

The list controls are best used to display data in mobile device applications and are described in Table 10-5. Like their cousins in WebControl, the list controls make it simple to bind to a data source and display the information in an easily accessible format. As you would expect, these controls take into account the limited screen size of the majority of mobile phones. The controls do differ in their capability to paginate themselves, have static information linked to them, and provide a detailed view of the data they are linked to.

Table 10-5. *List Mobile Controls*

Name	Description	Static/Dynamic	Pagination
List	Renders a list of items	Both	Yes
SelectionList	Renders a list of items Similar to ListBox or ComboBox	Both	No
ObjectList	Renders a list of items with multiple properties and item commands	Dynamic only	Yes

The list controls are very useful for data binding and can provide a master/detail type of navigation.

The Image, AdRotator, and Calendar Controls

The Image and AdRotator controls support the capability to display an image in the mobile device browser. The difference between the two controls is whether the choice is static or dynamic based on who is visiting for advertisement purposes. We have added the Calendar control to this discussion, because this topic is as good as any to cover it in. It is probably the richest control in the mobile space outside of ObjectList. Table 10-6 describes these three controls.

Table 10-6. *Image Mobile Controls*

Name	HTML Tag	WML Tag	Description
Image	<a href="">	<do> and <go>	Links to a new URL or deck
AdRotator	<a href="">	<do> and <go>	Links to a new URL or deck
Calendar	<TABLE>	<DO>, <go>, and <select>	Permits the selection of a date

In the next section, we move on to cover container controls and pagination. Pagination is an especially important topic, because most WML mobile phone devices are limited to displaying four lines of content at a time.

Container Controls and Pagination

The controls discussed previously in this chapter display information. The controls covered in this section, however, provide content management via containment. Table 10-7 summarizes the container controls. You are already familiar with the Form control as a means of grouping together mobile server controls in a nice package on a MobilePage web page. The Panel control is an option for containing controls within a mobile web form.

Using a Panel control within a form is a handy way to group controls together. For instance, you may want to make a group of controls visible or not visible, en masse. Setting the Visible property on a Panel control to false will cause the controls contained by the Panel control to have the same value for their Visible property. In general, controls placed in a Panel control inherit style properties from the Panel container, although a control can override a particular style property if desired.

Table 10-7. *Container Mobile Controls*

Name	HTML Tag	WML Tag	Description
Form	<a href="">	<do> and <go>	Links to a new URL or deck
Panel	<a href="">	<do> and <go>	Links to a new URL or deck

Pagination is an important capability in mobile server controls, because most WML devices only support anywhere from two to ten lines of content onscreen, with each line containing just a few characters.

Controls that support pagination inherit from PagedControl instead of MobileControl. For example, the List, ObjectList, and LiteralText classes all inherit from PagedControl. When you build your own custom mobile server controls, consider inheriting form PagedControl if your control is capable of rendering a large amount of text.

The Form and Panel controls are containers that support pagination of their child control content. For example, the Paginate property of the Panel mobile server control is a suggestion to the ASP.NET runtime to keep the controls on the Panel together when paginating a mobile web form. Likewise, enabling pagination on a Form control provides support to mobile devices with limited screen area by permitting content to be spread across multiple views.

Browsing Mobile Web Forms

Although it is convenient to browse a mobile web form in a desktop browser for basic testing, serious mobile web applications must be tested with all possible browsing devices. At the very least, a mobile web application should be tested with a sampling of device capabilities such as HTML, WML, and XHTML.

Using actual devices is ideal; however, testing with an emulator is the next best thing. Many of the popular mobile phone device manufacturers and other vendors provide an SDK with a phone emulator for testing purposes. It is possible to use an emulator for testing ASP.NET mobile web applications too. To display a mobile web form using the Pocket PC emulator, a wireless application protocol (WAP) emulator, or an XHTML emulator, simply start the emulator, launch the web browser (if necessary), and enter the URL.

Once you have the desired emulators installed, you have a couple of options for debugging a mobile web application. One option is to simply run the web application using Internet Explorer. Once the browser loads, minimize it, and launch the desired emulator by entering the URL for the mobile web application. Because the application is in debug mode, you will hit breakpoints when viewing the web application in the emulator. When you have finished, close Internet Explorer to stop debugging.

Another option is to integrate the emulator into Visual Studio .NET so that the emulator launches when you click Start Debug. To do this, right-click a mobile web form `.aspx` page, and select Browse With from the context menu. Next, click Add; click Browse to locate the emulator executable; click OK; provide a friendly name; and then click OK to return to the Browse With dialog box. Then, select the newly added emulator, and click Set As Default. Note that if the emulator takes a command-line argument, you can provide the URL as a parameter with this syntax:

```
"C:\pathToEmulator\emulator.exe %URL"
```

To have the emulator launch by default, you will need to change a project setting. Right-click the project in Solution Explorer, and select Properties. Next, click the Web tab, and select "Start external program." This allows you to set the path to the emulator, provide command-line arguments, and set the working directory. Note that if the emulator does not take a command-line parameter, you will have to manually enter the URL once the emulator is running. Once the emulator starts browsing the web application, the mobile web application will be in debug mode and will hit any breakpoints that are set and enabled.

This completes our overview of the mobile controls available and development model in ASP.NET. Next, we move on to covering how to build custom mobile controls as the final lap around mobile web development.

Customizing and Implementing Mobile Controls

ASP.NET mobile server controls provide a rich, extensible framework for delivering content viewable on a wide array of mobile devices. In the previous section, we looked at out-of-the-box controls and the feature set available in the .NET Framework as a means to examine mobile server control technology. In this section, we drill down into extensibility and customization mechanisms available to mobile server control developers. The extensibility hooks fall into the following categories:

- The `StyleSheet` control
- Templates
- Device-specific UI choices
- User controls
- Custom controls
- Device adapters

The `StyleSheet` class can provide a consistent look and feel in terms of styling objects, such as `Font`, across a set of controls or any number of mobile forms. Templates provide a mechanism to customize how content renders, such as what controls display content using the techniques discussed in Chapter 6. Device-specific UI customization is available with both of these techniques, as is customizing the attributes of a control based on the target device. Developers have the option to stay within the abstraction layer provide by the Framework, or they can specify alternate content to render on specific devices if it's desired or required. The flexible detection engine built into ASP.NET makes this magic happen, greatly simplifying mobile web development without giving up fine-grained control.

The final two sections of this chapter cover the custom control opportunities discussed earlier in this book for traditional ASP.NET development: user controls and custom controls. Both techniques are available for mobile server control development, with the addition of mobile device capability management. The section covering mobile controls in this chapter examines how mobile controls emit device-specific output with the help of device adapters.

The StyleSheet Control

A couple of options are available to apply styles to controls in the mobile control framework. One option is to configure style attributes on individual controls. This results in increased maintenance as the number of individually configured controls increases, which is not optimal. The other option is the `StyleSheet` control, which provides a method to attach a consistent look and feel across multiple controls, centralizing style maintenance to one location. ASP.NET provides a default `StyleSheet` control with three styles elements named `error`, `subcommand`, and `title`. Table 10-8 shows how each is configured.

Table 10-8. *Default StyleSheet Styles Provided by ASP.NET*

Style	Configuration
`error`	`ForeColor=red`
`subcommand`	`FontSize=small`
`title`	`Font-Bold=true`, or `FontSize=large`

As with other, similar style-handling mechanisms such as CSS, the `StyleSheet` class simplifies maintenance by providing a named `Style` element that represents a collection of style attributes. Due to widely varying device capabilities, `StyleSheet Style` elements provide access to common features that apply across a wide range of devices, particularly those relating to textual display.

Every mobile control contains an internal `Style` object inherited from the `MobileControl` class that is not directly accessible. Instead, `Style` attributes on the internal `Style` object can be customized through public properties:

- `Font` (`Bold`, `Italic`, `Name`, or `Size`)
- `Background` (color)
- `Foreground` (color)
- `Alignment` (`Left`, `Center`, `Right`, or `NotSet`)
- `Wrapping` (`Wrap`, `NoWrap`, or `NotSet`)
- `DeviceSpecific`

Other controls, or your own custom mobile server controls, can have custom Style classes that inherit from the base Style class. For example, the Form class has a custom style class named PagerStyle that inherits from the default Style class to provide access to additional styling customization with respect to pagination. The ability to provide custom style classes to support custom control development is similar to traditional ASP.NET development, as covered in Chapter 4.

After configuring a few styles on the StyleSheet object, we can apply these styles to controls. Controls gain access to StyleSheet styles through the StyleReference property inherited from MobileControl. The StyleReference drop-down list automatically populates with the default styles in addition to the custom styles we defined in the StyleSheet control.

Mobile controls apply configured styles during the rendering process with the help of device adapters, which we discuss later in this chapter. If a control is configured with a style that will not render on a particular device requesting the page, such as a WML browser that does not support color styles, the style will be ignored. This approach ensures that content is returned to the requesting device, albeit with less style.

As we mentioned previously, a control can accept the default style provided by MobileControl, or a control can require a custom style class in order to provide additional customization options for the control user. As an example, the mobile web form takes a custom style class named PagerStyle that provides an easy way for the control user to customize pagination behavior. PagerStyle provides the following attributes to customize the multipage navigation UI:

- NextPageText
- PageLabel
- PreviousPageText

These attributes permit you to customize the UI. For example, if you are programmatically creating a form with Next and Previous links to the appropriate pages, you can override the text for these links by setting the value of the properties previously mentioned. You can use methods such as GetNextPageText, GetPreviousPageText, or GetPageLabel to retrieve the current value of the properties. This chapter's StyleSheetInline.aspx Mobile Web Page demonstration web form in the source code that accompanies this book provides an example of using the StyleSheetInline control. We next discuss a method to store the StyleSheet control in an external file.

The StyleSheetExternal Mobile Web Page

In the previous example, we embedded a StyleSheet control into the mobile web page to make Style attributes available to mobile forms and controls. This model of embedding a style sheet into the mobile web page requires maintenance on each mobile page's StyleSheet object to keep all the mobile web pages in a web application consistent. A better model would be to maintain a single StyleSheet control instance that is shared by all of the mobile web pages in a web application.

The ASP.NET framework provides a method to store a StyleSheet instance in an external file. We provide an example of this in the StyleSheetExternal mobile web page. Instead of embedding a StyleSheet control hosting Style objects, the StyleSheet control references an external user control file. This is what the StyleSheet control looks like in the StyleSheetExternal mobile web page:

```
<mobile:StyleSheet id="ExternalStyleSheet" runat="server"
ReferencePath="ExternalStyleSheetClass.ascx" />
```

The file named `ExternalStyleSheetClass.ascx` is a mobile user control file that is similar to user controls in traditional ASP.NET development that is available for review in the `Chapter 10` folder. The next section provides an overview of templates and device-specific choices.

Templates and Device-Specific Choices

As we discussed in Chapter 6, HTML or markup is a combination of content and appearance. In the previous section, we discussed how to modify appearance using styles. In this section, we discuss how to modify the document skeleton, or scaffold, on which control content hangs. Mobile templates offer similar capabilities as demonstrated in Chapter 6 to enhance the display of a mobile control or surround its data with markup that is driven via data binding. Mobile controls have the additional capability to select a template for rendering in a device-specific manner. This is a feature unique to mobile controls and is what we focus on in this chapter, as we covered the basics of templates and their incorporation in controls in Chapter 6.

The DeviceSpecific.aspx Mobile Web Page

The `DeviceSpecific.aspx` mobile web page demonstrates the use of templates and device-specific rendering to display a multiform web page that modifies its display based on the browsing device capabilities. The default web form activated on the mobile web page renders an input box for performing a search on the `NorthWind` database's `Customers` table by `ContactName`, as we demonstrated previously in the book.

If you run the `DeviceSpecific.aspx` web form, notice that we have a label that displays the user agent string obtained from the `Request` headers collection from the current request:

```
AgentLabel.Text = HttpContext.Current.Request.Headers["User-Agent"];
```

The value for our HTML browser is

```
Mozilla/2.0 (compatible; MSIE 3.02; Windows CE; PPC; 240x320)
```

For a WML browser, we see

```
OWG1 UP/4.1.20a UP.Browser/4.1.20a-XXXX UP.Link/4.1.HTTP-DIRECT
```

The code for the web form displays the value from the `MobileCapabilities` object in two label values:

```
MobileCapabilities caps = (MobileCapabilities)
   HttpContext.Current.Request.Browser;
if (caps != null) //Cast succeeds
{
   PrefRendLabel.Text = caps.PreferredRenderingType.ToString();
   PrefImageLabel.Text = caps.PreferredImageMime.ToString();
}
```

MobileCapabilities inherits from HttpBrowserCapabilities. This allows us to cast the Browser object to the MobileCapabilities type. We next populate the labels with values based on the current request. The value of PreferredImageMIME for the HTML browser is

```
image/gif
```

The WML browser value for PreferredImageMIME is

```
image/vnd.wap.wbmp
```

The value of PreferredRenderingType for the HTML browser is

```
html32
```

The WML browser value for PreferredRenderingType is

```
wml11
```

If you run the sample in both a Windows Mobile device emulator and a WML device emulator, the device-detection engine succeeds in identifying Pocket Internet Explorer and the WML emulator and rendering the content appropriately. In the next sections, we cover how this process works in detail. We start off with a discussion on templates.

Templates

The easiest part of this example to understand is the templated content, especially if you are familiar with the concepts we discussed in Chapter 6. ObjectList has the following templates that you can override:

- HeaderTemplate
- FooterTemplate
- ItemTemplate
- AlternatingItemTemplate
- ItemDetailsTemplate
- SeparatorTemplate

The ObjectList control in the DeviceSpecific.aspx file has two sets of templates. One set of templates targets the textual WML display, and the other set of templates targets richer, HTML-oriented output. The mobile control template mechanism allows us to set up any number of templates for a control, with one getting chosen at runtime based on decisions made by the capability targeting engine.

The default template set with its ItemTemplate demonstrates how data-binding techniques used previously for regular ASP.NET controls function similarly in the mobile control world. The ItemTemplate data-binding expressions are careful to cast to the appropriate data type—in this case, the ObjectListItem class that represents each item in the ObjectList:

```
<ItemTemplate>
Name:<%#((ObjectListItem)Container)["ContactName"]%>  
Title:<%#((ObjectListItem)Container)["ContactTitle"]%>  
Company:<%#((ObjectListItem)Container)["CompanyName"]%>
<br />
</ItemTemplate>
```

Because of the ItemTemplate override, the ObjectList display is limited to our templated list. We forego the master/detail template that the ObjectList adheres to by default, which we examined in previous examples. Notice that there is not a link to a second page that displays the details of each item, because we took things into our own hands. If you want to stick with the default list and just need to override the details page, the template you should target is ItemDetailsTemplate.

The DeviceSpecific and Choice Elements

The templates attached to the ObjectList control are not placed directly under the control's topmost element in the .aspx page, as would be typical for an ASP.NET control. The mobile controls embed templates inside DeviceSpecific and Choice constructs under the ObjectList control.

The DeviceSpecific and Choice tags permit you to specify which templates to render in a device-specific manner. This feature is what sets mobile controls apart from their counterparts in traditional ASP.NET development with respect to templates. DeviceSpecific and Choice elements can do the following:

- Modify the text displayed for a control and text properties. For example, you may want message text to be short on a WML device but longer on a device with a larger display.
- Customize the styles applied, depending on detected device capabilities.
- Specify alternate image types that match detected device capabilities. We do this for the Image1 image mobile control in the next example.

This fine-grained tuning available also allows you to override control properties through the DeviceSpecific/Choice element mechanism. An example of this in the DeviceSpecific.aspx mobile web page is the Image control that overrides its ImageURL property:

```
<mobile:Image id="Image1" ImageUrl="../Ch10/mslogo.bmp" Runat="server">
  <DeviceSpecific>
    <Choice Filter="prefersWBMP" ImageUrl="../Ch10/mslogo.wbmp"></Choice>
  </DeviceSpecific>
</mobile:Image>
```

The default value is the .bmp file; however, there is a choice filter that states that a device that prefers a .wbmp file should use the .wbmp file in place of the .bmp file.

Any control that inherits from MobileControl can contain one—and only one—DeviceSpecific element. DeviceSpecific is a container element that hosts one or more Choice elements. The Choice element has a filter attribute that plugs into the device capability decision engine that is part of the mobile ASP.NET architecture.

In the case of the preceding Image control snippet of code, the Image control takes advantage of the built-in WML rendering features via the prefersWBMP filter attribute value to look for devices that prefer to render .wbmp bitmaps. The ObjectList control's Choice element has an isHTML32 filter value to ensure that the targeted device supports HTML 3.2 as a browsing language:

```
<DeviceSpecific>
   <Choice Filter="isHTML32">
      <HeaderTemplate>
         <table>
...
```

If the filter attribute looking for isHTML32 devices is satisfied, the Choice element selects the HeaderTemplate, ItemTemplate, AlternatingItemTemplate, and FooterTemplate templates for rendering by the ObjectList control. If not, the default Choice element is selected.

```
<Choice>
  <ItemTemplate>
    Name:<%#((ObjectListItem)Container)["ContactName"]%>  
Title:<%#((ObjectListItem)Container)["ContactTitle"]%>  
    Company:<%#((ObjectListItem)Container)["CompanyName"]%>
    <br />
  </ItemTemplate>
</Choice>
```

There can be many Choice elements with filters within a DeviceSpecific tag underneath a mobile control, each targeting a different filter or device capability. The first filter to match will stop the searching process for the appropriate Choice element. If there isn't a match, the Choice element without a filter attribute is selected as the default, and its child content is applied to the output.

In the example, the default Choice element is selected for the ObjectList control if the device filter for isHTML32 never hits. There can be only one default Choice element within a DeviceSpecific element. Because the filter mechanism stops searching at the first match, it is recommended that you put the default Choice element last.

Filter Attribute and deviceFilters Configuration

At this point, you may be wondering how device detection is linked to the DeviceSpecific/Choice element with its filter attribute in the mobile control. The filter attribute refers to a set of XML elements added to the standard web.config file when you select an ASP.NET mobile web application in Visual Studio .NET. You can also manually add these elements to an existing web.config file. The additional configuration section in web.config is appropriately named deviceFilters, as shown in the web.config for the ControlsBook2Mobile project.

The filter XML element represents the comparison rules that controls link to for making their rendering choices. Each filter element has three main properties:

- name
- compare
- argument

Name is used to uniquely identify the filter and is what the Choice element within a mobile control is matched against. The compare attribute is the name of the property of the MobileCapabilities object to test. The argument attribute is the value that should be matched to the capability property listed in the compare attribute. This is a simple Boolean comparison: if the compare attribute points to a capability property value that matches the argument attribute value, the filter is true, and the Choice element on the control is picked.

Earlier we noted that the Image control was looking for prefersWBMP, whereas the ObjectList control wanted isHTML32. You can see from the preceding code listing that we need to see the PreferredRenderingType capability property set to a value of html32, and we need the PreferredImageMIME capability property equal to image/vnd.wap.wbmp for the Choice elements to match.

From a generic standpoint, the capability properties we have discussed need to come from somewhere concrete in ASP.NET, so in the next section, we move on to discuss the MobileCapabilities class and the important role it plays.

MobileCapabilities, browserCaps, and Device Update 2

MobileCapabilities is a class from the System.Web.Mobile namespace that inherits from HttpBrowserCapabilities with strongly typed properties that represent device capabilities for traditional browsers and for a wide variety of mobile devices. It is mainly the receiver of gifts, as it is populated by the ASP.NET request mechanism when a client browser requests a page.

When a client requests a page, ASP.NET creates an instance of the HttpRequest class that exposes a browser property that exposes the MobileCapabilities object for that request. The MobileCapabilities object stores the device capabilities of the requestor. ASP.NET parses the request headers and uses a regular expression to match the HTTP_USER_AGENT contained in the headers. If a match is found, ASP.NET populates the MobileCapabilities object with information from the matching device in the browserCapabilities section of either web.config or machine.config, depending on where a match was found.

Adding support for a new device that accepts an existing rendering or markup technology, such as WML or cHTML, is a matter of adding a <case> to the <browserCaps> element and populating the attributes. The device manufacturer should have information on the capabilities of a particular device; however, rudimentary testing such as sending raw markup and testing with various mobile control configurations on a mobile page can assist in identifying capabilities.

Updates can include support for additional devices compatible with existing rendering technology and updates for additional devices compatible with new rendering or markup technology. For example, Device Update 2 included support for XHTML markup.

The second type of update—support for new rendering technology—not only updates configuration files but also provides one or more additional device adapter assemblies. We discuss device adapter technology later in this chapter. Suffice it to say that support for a new rendering or markup technology requires a new device adapter.

For a device update, changes can be made to the following sections of the machine.config file:

- <assemblies>
- <browserCaps>
- <mobileControls>

If a device update does not include adding support for new rendering or markup technology, only the <browserCaps> section is modified.

■ **Tip** Because of configuration file inheritance or precedence rules, if you make application-specific customizations in an application's web.config file, these settings will take precedence if there are conflicts with settings in machine.conifig. Be sure to verify application-specific customizations after installing a device update.

When you install a device update to the .NET Framework, the device update adds a file reference to the existing <browserCaps> section to a file named deviceUpdate.config. If you make customizations to the <browserCaps> section, these changes are preserved. With the .NET Framework, you have additional options for further customizing the <browserCaps> section:

- Place custom changes in the deviceUpdate.config file. This file is placed at *systemdrive*\WindowsPath\Microsoft.NET\Framework\V2.0.x.
- Create a custom .config file such as deviceCustom.config, and add additional <browserCaps> entries to machine.config. Order matters, so files appearing later in this list take precedence, for example:

```
<file src="deviceUpdate.config" />
<file src="deviceCustom.config />
```

If support for a new device adapter is included in a device update, changes are made to the <assemblies> section of machine.config. Changes are also made to the <mobileControls> section of machine.config. This ensures that mobile controls use the correct device adapter to support the new rendering technology.

Custom Device Adapters and Mobile Controls

If you create or obtain a custom device adapter for a device that is not included with a Microsoft device update, you have two options. You can use the adapter provided in the device update, or you can manually update the references in the <mobileControls> section in machine.config after installing the device update.

For your custom mobile controls, device updates should not affect how they render with existing browsers. For new browsing clients added by a device update, your custom mobile controls should still render correctly, as long as the browser is compatible with your controls' requirements. The key takeaway point is that you should test your custom mobile controls when a new device update is released to ensure compatibility.

New Capabilities in MobileCapabilities

As we mentioned in the last section, the `System.Web.Mobile.MobileCapabilities` class inherits from `HttpBrowserCapabilities`, so by default, it supports the capabilities we discussed earlier in this chapter. Table 10-9 recaps the base class properties.

Table 10-9. *HttpBrowserCapabilities Properties*

Property	Description
`ActiveXControls`	Browser support for ActiveX controls.
`AOL`	Is the browser an AOL version?
`BackgroundSounds`	Browser support for playing sounds.
`Beta`	Is the browser a beta version?
`Browser`	Full browser string from the request headers.
`CDF`	Browser support for Channel Definition Format (CDF).
`ClrVersion`	Version of the .NET CLR supported by browser.
`Cookies`	Browser support for cookies.
`Crawler`	Is the browser a web site crawler for search engines?
`EcmaScriptVersion`	Version of ECMAScript (JavaScript) supported by browser.
`Frames`	Browser support for frames.
`JavaApplets`	Browser support for Java applets.
`JavaScript`	Browser support for JavaScript.
`MajorVersion`	Major version of the browser.
`MinorVersion`	Minor version of the browser.
`MSDomVersion`	Microsoft version of the DOM supported by the browser.
`Platform`	Operating system (OS) platform that the browser is running on.
`Tables`	Browser support for tables.
`TagWriter`	Class used to emit HTML content from the control.
`Type`	Browser name and major version in a single string.
`VBScript`	Browser support for VBScript.
`Version`	`Major.Minor` version of the browser in single string.
`W3CDomVersion`	W3C version of the DOM supported by the browser.
`Win16`	Is the OS the browser is running on Win16 based?
`Win32`	Is the OS the browser is running on Win32 based?

This list is fairly short when compared to the MobileCapabilities class's properties. MobileCapabilities adds the new properties shown in Table 10-10.

Table 10-10. *MobileCapabilities Additional Properties*

Property	Description
CanCombineFormsInDeck	Indicates that the browser on the device can handle decks that contain multiple forms, as separate cards.
CanInitiateVoiceCall	Indicates whether the device is capable of initiating a voice call.
CanRenderAfterInputOrSelectElement	Indicates whether the device can render a card that contains elements after an input or select element.
CanRenderEmptySelects	Indicates whether a device can render empty select markup statements.
CanRenderInputAndSelectElementsTogether	Indicates whether a device can render the <input> and <select> elements together.
CanRenderMixedSelects	Indicates whether the browser on the device can handle <select> tags that include <option> elements with both onpick and value attributes.
CanRenderOneventAndPrevElementsTogether	Indicates whether a device can handle <onevent> and <do type="prev" label="Back"></prev></do> elements when combined together.
CanRenderPostBackCards	Indicates whether a device supports postback cards.
CanRenderSetvarZeroWithMultiSelectionList	Indicates whether a device can accept WML <setvar> elements with the value attribute set to zero for the select/option construct of the multiselection list control.
CanSendMail	Indicates whether the browser supports the mailto tag for e-mail addresses.
DefaultSubmitButtonLimit	Stores the default number of soft keys for a device.
GatewayMajorVersion	Stores the major version number of the wireless gateway used by the mobile device to access a web application.
GatewayMinorVersion	Stores the minor version number of the wireless gateway used by the mobile device to access a web application.
GatewayVersion	Stores the version number of the wireless gateway used by the mobile device to access a web application.
HasBackButton	Indicates whether a device browser has a dedicated Back button.

Table 10-10. *MobileCapabilities Additional Properties (Continued)*

Property	Description
HidesRightAlignedMultiselectScrollbars	Indicates whether the scrollbar of a right-aligned <select multiple> element is obscured by the scrollbar for the page.
InputType	Indicates the type of input supported on a device. The possible values are virtualKeyboard, telephoneKeypad, and keyboard.
IsColor	Indicates whether a device has a color display.
IsMobileDevice	Indicates whether a device is recognized as a mobile device.
MaximumRenderedPageSize	Stores the maximum length of a page, in bytes, that the device can display.
MaximumSoftkeyLabelLength	Stores the maximum length of text that a soft key label can display.
MobileDeviceManufacturer	Stores the name of the device manufacturer.
MobileDeviceModel	Stores the model name of the device, if available.
NumberOfSoftkeys	Stores the number of soft keys available on a device.
PreferredImageMime	Returns the MIME type preferred for images on a device.
PreferredRenderingMime	Returns the MIME type preferred for content on a device.
PreferredRenderingType	Returns the general name for the preferred type of content.
PreferredRenderingTypeChtml10	Static-source identifier to use for compact HTML 1.0.
PreferredRenderingTypeHtml32	Static-source identifier to use for HTML 3.2.
PreferredRenderingTypeWml11	Static-source identifier to use for WML 1.1.
PreferredRenderingTypeWml12	Static-source identifier to use for WML 1.2.
RendersBreakBeforeWmlSelectAndInput	Indicates whether a device inserts an additional break before rendering a WML <select> or <input> element.
RendersBreaksAfterHtmlLists	Indicates whether a device already renders breaks after HTML list tags.
RendersBreaksAfterWmlAnchor	Indicates whether a device or browser produces a break after a stand-alone anchor.
RendersBreaksAfterWmlInput	Returns whether a device automatically renders a break after input elements have been received.

Table 10-10. *MobileCapabilities Additional Properties (Continued)*

Property	Description
RendersWmlDoAcceptsInline	Indicates whether a device renders a WML <do>-based form-accept construct as an inline button instead of a soft key.
RendersWmlSelectsAsMenuCards	Indicates whether a device renders the <select> tag constructs as menu cards instead of a DropDownList.
RequiredMetaTagNameValue	Returns a metatag, which some devices require.
RequiresAttributeColonSubstitution	Indicates whether colons in tag name attributes need to substitute a different character for rendering.
RequiresContentTypeMetaTag	Indicates whether the device requires the content-type metatag.
RequiresDBCSCharacter	Indicates whether a device requires a double-byte character set (DBCS) character.
RequiresHtmlAdaptiveErrorReporting	Indicates whether the HTML device should receive a default ASP.NET error message or an adaptive one for non-HTML devices such as WML.
RequiresLeadingPageBreak	Indicates that an additional break should render.
RequiresNoBreakInFormatting	Indicates that formatting tags should not include break ( ) tags.
RequiresOutputOptimization	Indicates that adapters should try to generate minimal output.
RequiresPhoneNumbersAsPlainText	Indicates whether a device supports phone dialing based on only plain text, instead of special markup.
RequiresSpecialViewStateEncoding	Indicates whether a device requires special encoding for generated ViewState.
RequiresUniqueFilePathSuffix	Indicates whether a unique file path suffix is required so that WAP-cached pages process submitted forms correctly.
RequiresUniqueHtmlCheckboxNames	Indicates whether a device requires that the check box HTML <input> tag contain unique name attribute values.
RequiresUniqueHtmlInputNames	Indicates whether a device requires that HTML <input> tags contain unique name attribute values.
RequiresUrlEncodedPostfieldValues	Indicates whether a device encodes text in the value attribute of a posted field during postback.
ScreenBitDepth	Stores the display depth in bits per pixel of a device's display.

Table 10-10. *MobileCapabilities Additional Properties (Continued)*

Property	Description
ScreenCharactersHeight	Stores the height of the display in character lines.
ScreenCharactersWidth	Stores the screen width in characters.
ScreenPixelsHeight	Stores the height of the display in pixels.
ScreenPixelsWidth	Stores the width of the display in pixels.
SupportsAccessKeyAttribute	Indicates that a device can handle the AccessKey attribute for the <a> and <input> tags.
SupportsBodyColor	Indicates whether a device supports the bgcolor attribute on the <body> tag.
SupportsBold	Indicates whether a device supports bold text as specified through the <b> tag.
SupportsCacheControlMetaTag	Indicates whether a device supports the <meta> tag Cache-Control.
SupportsCss	Indicates whether a device supports CSS for styling.
SupportsDivAlign	Indicates whether a device supports the align attribute within the <div> tag.
SupportsDivNoWrap	Indicates whether a device supports the nowrap attribute within the <div> tag.
SupportsEmptyStringInCookieValue	Indicates whether a device supports an empty string for the value of a cookie.
SupportsFontColor	Indicates whether a device supports the color attribute for the <font> tag.
SupportsFontName	Indicates whether a device supports the name attribute for the <font> tag.
SupportsFontSize	Indicates whether a device supports the size attribute for the <font> tag.
SupportsImageSubmit	Indicates that a device can handle images submitting the form.
SupportsIModeSymbols	Indicates that a device supports i-Mode symbols.
SupportsInputIStyle	Indicates that a device supports the istyle attribute for the <input> tag.
SupportsInputMode	Indicates that a device supports attribute mode for the <input> tag.
SupportsItalic	Indicates that a device supports the <i> tag.
SupportsJPhoneMultiMediaAttributes	Indicates whether a device supports J-Phone multimedia attributes.
SupportsJPhoneSymbols	Indicates whether a device supports picture symbols specific to the J-Phone.

Table 10-10. *MobileCapabilities Additional Properties (Continued)*

Property	Description
SupportsQueryStringInFormAction	Indicates whether a device supports a query string in the action attribute of a <form> tag.
SupportsRedirectWithCookie	Indicates whether a device honors the Set-Cookie header when the cookie is sent in conjunction with a redirect.
SupportsSelectMultiple	Indicates whether a device supports the multiple attribute for HTML select tags.
SupportsUncheck	Indicates whether a device returns the unselected status for an unchecked check box in posted data.

HttpBrowserCapabilities targets World Wide Web Consortium (W3C) standards that traditional desktop web browsers adhere to pretty well, keeping this class fairly simple. As you can see from Table 10-10, device capabilities vary widely in the mobile web application market, and standards are fractious. This size of this table demonstrates the challenges that arise when developers attempt to hand-code applications that target more than a couple of mobile devices.

The ASP.NET mobile controls framework lends a helping hand by abstracting device differences while providing an extensible architecture that allows developers to add support for new devices as they become available.

The groundwork is laid to permit us to move on to control development. Mobile user controls are very similar to their cousins in traditional ASP.NET targeting desktop browsers. In the next section, we discuss mobile user controls, and then we round out this chapter with a discussion of custom server control development and device adapters.

User Controls

The ASP.NET mobile web application development system provides for modularity in control content in the same way as ASP.NET targets desktop browsers. User controls play an important role in this architecture. Here is a list of important characteristics of user controls:

- User controls are a great way to package HTML and modularize web development. They are also a means of replacing the use of IIS include files.
- User controls support properties and methods that can be set either in the HTML as attributes or in the code-behind page of the hosting .ascx page.
- User controls can be cached in the ASP.NET cache based on a number of different parameters to speed web application performance (as detailed in the ASP.NET documentation).
- Certain tags are not permitted in a user control—specifically, the <html>, <head>, <body>, and <form> tags. Using these tags would interfere with the functioning of the hosting .aspx page.
- User control tag declarations should appear between the hosting .aspx page's beginning and ending form tags to ensure proper operation.

In the next section, we build two user controls that mimic the header and footer user controls present in the traditional ASP.NET samples.

Mobile User Controls

Generally, the display constraints of mobile devices and the limited bandwidth available for data communication dictate that content take precedence over style or aesthetics. Mobile web applications tend to be more esoteric when compared to web applications that target desktop browsers.

With the efforts by wireless operators to upgrade their data bandwidth capacity and the release of more powerful mobile devices such as the Pocket PC Phone Edition and the smartphone, this is changing. Designing mobile web applications that can grow as bandwidth and device capability improves warrants consideration.

Because mobile user controls provide a high degree of page modularity, they can help in this effort just as they can when targeting a desktop browser. For example, including header, footer, and left and right pane user controls in a web application is pretty easy to do up front. The application page template simply includes those user controls as part of normal development. User controls can act as placeholders for enriching the page experience as bandwidth and device capacity improve.

For instance, an esoteric one-line copyright statement in the footer could eventually be replaced with a footer you would expect to see in a traditional web application, with contact information, graphic logos, and so on. It is in this vein that we demonstrate mobile user controls.

Our example mobile page, `UserControlHost.aspx`, is a replica of the `DeviceSpecific.aspx` page that we discussed earlier in this chapter, except for the addition of two mobile user controls: a header user control and a footer user control. We wanted the mobile header and footer user controls to resemble their cousins designed for the desktop but take into account mobile device considerations.

Miniaturizing the Header and Footer

To start the conversion process, we add two mobile user control files named `ControlsBook2MobileFooter.ascx` and `ControlsBook2MobileHeader.ascx`. As you can see, the file extension for mobile user controls is the same. Next, we copy and paste the code from the desktop versions of the controls into the mobile versions, changing tag prefixes from `asp:` to `mobile:` and removing all HTML formatting so that we end up with four mobile `Label` controls on the header and three on the footer.

Mobile `Label` controls span the width of the mobile form—you can't put two of these controls side by side on a mobile form. Our first change, then, is to combine the `Label` containing "Chapter" and the placeholder `Label` containing the "Chapter Number" into a single `Label` to conserve one line on a mobile device.

Next, we modify `Label` styling to a size of `Small` and not `Bold` in an effort to make the displayed information compact. Because `<hr>` tags do not have a WML equivalent, we switch to a `.bmp` image for `HTML32` devices and a `.wbmp` file for WML devices to display horizontal line separators in the header and footer controls. The results of our changes can be viewed in the `ControlsBook2Mobile` project's user controls named `ControlsBook2MobileHeader.ascx` and `ControlsBook2MobileFooter.ascx`.

We now focus our discussion on the header user control; it includes the functionality in the footer user control but with a few additional wrinkles.

If you look at the header user control .aspx file, you will see a DeviceSpecific/Choice construct for each mobile Label. The default behavior is to display all three labels. However, if a WML11 device is detected, the user control displays only the first Label for the book title on the header control and the copyright Label for the footer control.

The other Labels have their Visible property set to false to prevent these labels from rendering. A .wbmp file is rendered for a WML11 device using a DeviceSpecific/Choice construct as well.

Next, we explore the mobile page that hosts our new mobile user controls.

Hosting the Header and Footer User Controls

The example mobile page, aptly named UserControlHost.aspx, is a copy of the DeviceSpecific.aspx page from the example earlier in this chapter. To add the header and footer user controls, we drag the user control files and drop them into the appropriate spot (top or bottom) on each mobile form. This results in the addition of the following lines to the .aspx page:

```
<%@ Register TagPrefix="ApressUCMobile" TagName="ControlsBook2MobileHeader"
Src="ControlsBook2MobileHeader.ascx" %>
<%@ Register TagPrefix="ApressUCMobile" TagName="ControlsBook2MobileFooter"
Src="ControlsBook2MobileFooter.ascx" %>
```

We changed the tag prefix from uc1 to ApressUCMobile. Also notice that we had to add the user controls to each mobile form. Here is what the tag declaration for the header control looks like:

```
<ApressUCMobile:ControlsBook2MobileHeader id="ControlsBook2MobileHeader1"
ChapterNumber="10" ChapterTitle="Other Server Controls"
     runat="server"></ApressUCMobile:ControlsBook2MobileHeader>
```

Here is what the tag declaration for the footer control looks like:

```
  <ApressUCMobile:ControlsBook2MobileFooter id="ControlsBook2MobileFooter1"
runat="server"></ApressUCMobile:ControlsBook2MobileFooter>
```

Refer to the UserControlHost.aspx file in the sample code to review the tag declaration. Now that we have covered mobile user controls with an example, we spend the rest of this chapter exploring custom mobile control development issues and device adapters. Much of control development process is the same as when you build mobile controls. Therefore, in the next section, we focus on what is unique to custom mobile control development and develop an example to illustrate the differences between the two development models.

Custom Controls

Mobile server controls are developed in much the same manner as server controls designed for traditional ASP.NET web applications. In this section, we reinforce the similarities and identify the differences between them, starting with a discussion on mobile control rendering.

Rendering the Mobile Control

The level of standardization that exists in the desktop browser market, though not perfect by any means, is much better than what exists in the mobile device world in terms of device capabilities and markup technology.

There are a plethora of devices and more than a few rendering technologies, such as cHTML, WML, XHTML, and so on. This coupled with the rapidly growing and changing mobile device market means that a flexible architecture that isolates device and markup differences is required. Otherwise, the maintenance required to target multiple devices will prove cost prohibitive.

Luckily, ASP.NET provides a pluggable and extendible mobile-control-rendering architecture that isolates device-specific rendering into device adapters while maintaining the fundamental server control architecture, as covered so far in this book.

Device Adapters

Mobile server controls encapsulate logic, events, and properties just like traditional server controls, but mobile controls do not render themselves. Instead of managing their own rendering, like regular server controls, mobile controls offload that portion of the server control life cycle to helper classes or objects called device adapters.

Device adapters provide a nice abstraction layer between server control technology and the many devices and varied markup technology available. Each mobile server control can have several device adapters to render its content on supported devices. Likewise, when a new rendering technology becomes available, a new device adapter set is required for a mobile server control to render to that device, as described in Table 10-11.

Table 10-11. *Device Adapter Set*

Adapter	Description
Control adapter base class	Base class that all device adapters inherit from
Page adapter	Adapter for the mobile page
Form adapter	Adapter for each mobile form on the mobile page
Control adapter	Adapter for each mobile control available
Text writer	Writer that inherits from `MobileTextWriter` with device-specific methods

.NET Framework ASP.NET mobile controls include device adapter sets for the following types of devices:

- `HtmlDeviceAdapters`
- `ChtmlDeviceAdapters`
- `WmlDeviceAdapters`
- `XhtmlAdapters`

So, based on Table 10-11, the following device adapters handle rendering for WML devices that access a given mobile page:

- `WmlControlAdapter`
- `WmlFormAdapter`
- `WmlPageAdapter`
- `WmlMobileTextWriter`

`WmlControlAdapter` provides the base class for specific mobile control adapter classes. For each mobile server control, there is a class that inherits from `WmlControlAdapter` named `WmlControlNameAdapter`, where `ControlName` is something like `Image`, `Label`, `List`, and so on. These device adapters provide WML rendering services for the corresponding control.

All device adapters implement the `IControlAdapter` interface. Table 10-12 details this interface.

Table 10-12. *IControlAdapter Interface*

Members	Description
`Control`	Stores a reference to the associated control
`CreateTemplatedUI`	Creates a templated UI when called by base classes
`HandlePostBackEvent`	Returns true if the event is handled
`ItemWeight`	Stores the approximate weight of an item in the associated control
`LoadAdapterState`	Loads the adapter's private `ViewState`
`LoadPostData`	Returns true if the adapter loads posted data
`OnInit`	Called after a form or page initializes
`OnLoad`	Loads data for the control, page, or device adapter
`OnPreRender`	Performs adapter-specific logic prior to rendering
`OnUnload`	Unloads data for the control, page, or device adapter
`Page`	Stores a reference to the page associated with the device adapter
`Render`	Called by the associated control's `Render` method
`SaveAdapterState`	Saves the adapter's private `ViewState`
`VisibleWeight`	Stores the approximate weight of the control in characters

`ItemWeight` and `VisibleWeight` are two of the more interesting members of the `IControlAdapter` interface. The pagination system in ASP.NET mobile controls uses a weighting system to determine what controls to render on a page and how many items to render per page.

■Note The default unit system in ASP.NET mobile controls is based on a single line equal to 100 units based on the `DefaultWeight` static read-only property on the `ControlPager` class. The default `ItemWeight` is also the same value at 100 units.

Device adapters implementing `IControlAdapter` maintain a reference to a specific control instance in its `Control` property. Device adapter instances are not shared among controls, as a device adapter can maintain instance-specific information or state.

The Mobile Control Life Cycle

The mobile control life cycle inherits the same general life cycle of regular server controls with a few twists related to rendering with device adapters and `ViewState` management. In Chapter 5, we stated that after the initial page request as an HTTP GET, each subsequent HTTP POST page request/response cycle generally consists of the following steps:

1. Instantiate the control tree, creating each server control object.
2. Unpack `ViewState` for each server control object.
3. Set the state from the previous server-side processing cycle for each object in the tree.
4. Process postback data.
5. Handle the `Page_Load` event.
6. Let controls know that data changed through postback, updating control state as necessary.
7. Execute server-side events based on data changes from postback.
8. Persist state back to `ViewState`.
9. Execute the render process for each server control.
10. Unload page and its control tree.

This process provides the illusion of a state-full application to the end user. During each request/response cycle, state is unpacked, changes are processed, and the UI is updated and rendered back to the client device. Because of the varied device capabilities in the mobile web world, two major differences exist in the mobile control life cycle—namely, rendering and `ViewState` management.

Mobile Control and Adapter Interaction

As we mentioned previously, mobile server controls do not render themselves. Mobile server control rendering is handled by device adapters. We also mentioned that each device type and/or markup technology has its own set of adapters ready to go when called into action. We describe exactly how this takes place next.

For each client request, ASP.NET populates the `HttpContext` object's `HttpRequest.Browser` property. This property maintains a reference to an object of type `MobileCapabilities`, which we discussed earlier in this chapter with respect to device detection.

As you may surmise, device detection leads to device adapter set selection. During the initialization phase of the mobile page's life cycle, ASP.NET maps information in the `MobileCapabilities` object to the device mappings in the `<mobileControls>` section of the `web.config` file. Once device adapters are selected and device-specific customizations are applied, the page life cycle continues. Table 10-13 details the mobile control specifics related to the server control life cycle.

Table 10-13. *Mobile Server Control Events Related to the Control Execution Life Cycle*

Server Control Event	Page Life Cycle Phase	Mobile Control Specifics
`Init`	Initialize	`MobileControl.Init` is called. `Adapter.Init` is called.
`LoadViewState`	Unpack `ViewState`	`MobileControl.LoadPrivateViewState` is called. `Adapter.LoadAdapterState` is called.
`LoadPostData`	Handle form postback data	`MobileControl.LoadPostData` is called.
`Load`	`Page_Load` event	`MobileControl.Load` is called. `Adapter.Load` is called.
`RaisePostDataChangedEvent`	Notifies the page that the state of the control has changed.	`MobileControl.RaisePostDataChangedEvent` is called.
`RaisePostBackEvent`	Execute server-side events	`MobileControl.RaisePostBackEvent` is called. Possibly call `Adapter.RaisePostBackEvent` if events can vary based on the client device.
`PreRender`	Render process	`MobileControl.PreRender` is called. `Adapter.PreRender` is called.
`SaveViewState`	Save `ViewState`	`MobileControl.SavePrivateViewState` is called. `Adapter.SaveAdapterState` is called.
`Render`	Render process	`MobileControl.Render` is called, which calls `Adapter.Render`. `MobileTextWriter` is called to actually output the required markup.
`Unload`	Unload process	`MobileControl.Unload` is called. `Adapter.Unload` is called.
`Dispose`	Dispose of control tree	`MobileControl.Dispose` is called.

As you can see, the mobile server control object and device adapter object are tightly coupled from the time that the life cycle starts all the way through rendering. Figure 10-11 illustrates the entire device detection and rendering process.

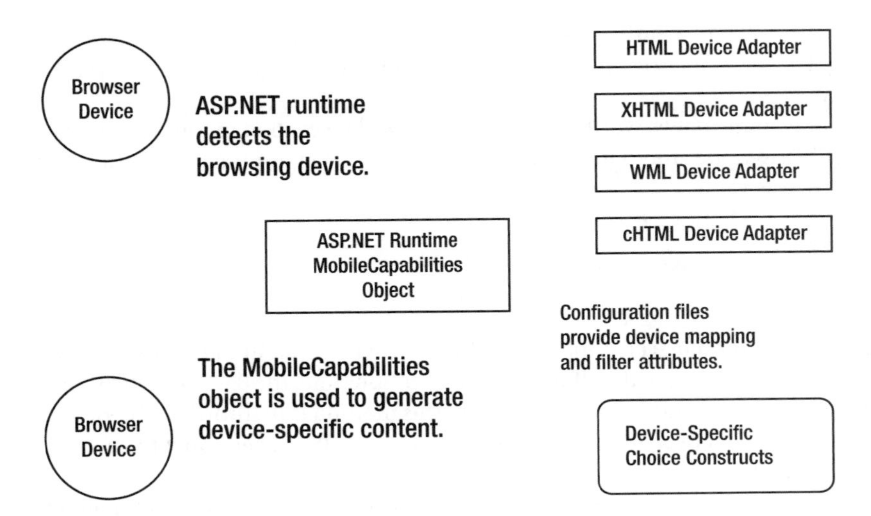

Figure 10-11. *The capability detection and device-specific rendering process*

Managing ViewState

Because of varied mobile device display capabilities and limited bandwidth available to mobile devices, the normal `ViewState` storage mechanism that uses a hidden form field on the client is not a viable option.

Instead, the mobile web application stores `ViewState` data into the `Session` object. Storing `ViewState` in the `Session` object provides a performance boost, because `ViewState` is not transmitted over the wire during each postback cycle. However, this does incur additional memory demands on the server, which is something to keep in mind when you tune your mobile web applications.

Once a client device establishes a session with the web application, the session ID is embedded into the URL of the web application. For example, for the `UserControlHost.aspx` page, the client performs the initial HTTP GET with this URL:

```
http://localhost/ControlsBook2Mobile/ch11/usercontrolhost.aspx
```

When the page loads, a URL similar to this is returned:

```
http://localhost/ControlsBook2Mobile/(sttxgl55ofwsrl45by2l2i55)/Ch11/
UserControlHost.aspx
```

Notice the "(sttxgl55ofwsrl45by2l2i55)" string embedded into the URL. This string links the page to the session ID for the browsing device and is what associates the page's `ViewState` with the current session.

Because the `ViewState` is not physically stored with the page and given the stateless nature of HTTP, it is possible for a page to become out of sync with its current state. For instance, the user can click the Back button when viewing the latest page to bring up the previous page. The most recent `ViewState` on the server would be for the most recent page viewed—not the previous page brought up by the user clicking the Back button.

To alleviate this, the ASP.NET runtime keeps track of a limited number of ViewState pages in a ViewState history. The identifier in the preceding URL indicates what page the user is currently viewing in the history.

You can specify how many pages worth of ViewState should be cached in the web.config file, which can override the value stored in the machine.config file. On our machines, the machine.config file has this value:

```
<mobileControls
          sessionStateHistorySize="6"
...
```

ViewState can expire in mobile web applications because it is stored in the user's current session. If a page does not post back within the session expiration time, the OnViewStateExpire method fires for the page. The default implementation of this method is to throw an exception. An application has the option of overriding this method to prevent the exception if the application can restore ViewState manually.

As with traditional ASP.NET applications, each mobile control is responsible for managing its own ViewState. As we have alluded to, mobile controls differ from traditional server controls with respect to rendering and ViewState. We cover rendering in the next section, but for now, it suffices to say that when a mobile control renders, it has help from device adapters to render its content appropriately for the device currently making the request.

One difference with server controls of type MobileControl is PrivateViewState. Mobile controls have an additional state-management mechanism in PrivateViewState that cannot be disabled as ViewState can be by setting EnableViewState to a value of false. To use PrivateViewState, a control overrides the LoadPrivateViewState and SavePrivateViewState methods.

PrivateViewState is stored in the page sent to the client, so state placed in PrivateViewState should be kept to a minimum due to both limited bandwidth and device capabilities. The main function of PrivateViewState is to make state information available across multiple pages. Here are some reasons why you would want to use PrivateViewState:

- To store the currently active form on a page
- To store pagination information about a form
- To store device-specific decisions made by a control's adapter

The device adapter object is closely tied to its associated mobile control instance, storing ViewState specific to the device adapter in addition to the mobile control's ViewState. All device adapters inherit from the IControlAdapter interface, which includes the following methods:

- LoadAdapterState
- SaveAdapterState

LoadAdapterState is called by the mobile control's LoadPrivateViewState method during the control's life cycle. Likewise, the mobile control's SavePrivateViewState method calls the device adapter's SaveAdapterState method. This extension of ViewState storage to the device adapter provides an opportunity for the device adapter to manage additional state with respect to control UI management. This is a great example of the flexibility this architecture provides.

Now that we have covered the differences between traditional server controls and mobile controls and have discussed the mobile control life cycle, we can move to discuss actually implementing mobile server controls. It is possible to create mobile server controls using the same techniques for traditional server control development, including

- Inheritance (Inherit from an existing control)
- Composition
- Inheriting from `MobileControl`, the base class for all mobile controls, to create a new control

We cover these options in the next sections.

Inheritance

Customizing an existing server control through inheritance is an excellent option, especially for mobile controls because of the increased complexity with rendering. Unless you override the `Render` method in an inherited control, the base mobile control will still handle its own rendering.

Because inheritance in mobile server control development is performed in the same manner as with traditional server control development, we do not provide an example here. Instead, we refer you to Chapter 2, where we implemented an inherited control named `TextBox3d`.

Composition

Building composite mobile server controls is performed in a similar manner to developing traditional mobile control composite controls. As with inheritance, composition generally does not require any additional work due to the differences in rendering technology with mobile controls.

Composition in both traditional and mobile server control development relies on child controls to handle their own rendering. Also, there may be situations in which a composite control's behavior and appearance can be enhanced by altering the contained child controls in a device-specific manner. You can create a device-specific control adapter class that renders a device-specific control tree.

When you build composite mobile server controls, we recommend inheriting from `Panel` instead of `MobileControl`. This is similar to inheriting from a `<div>` tag in traditional composite control development, as it provides a nice container for the control. With composite mobile controls, this is especially important because the .NET Framework mobile architecture attempts to keep controls within a `Panel` displayed as a unit and not split controls in a `Panel` across pages whenever possible.

Because composite mobile control development is similar to building composite controls in traditional ASP.NET development, we do not provide an example but rather refer you to earlier chapters that include composite control samples, such as Chapter 8 with the `UpDown` composite control.

Inheriting from MobileControl

Now that you have a firm grasp of the inner workings of mobile server controls, you can see how similar in design they are to traditional ASP.NET server controls. You should now have a good understanding of what is unique to mobile server controls. We now move on to implementing a simple mobile server control that targets WML and HTML browsers.

The MCTextBox Control

The mobile control TextBox control, or MCTextBox sample, is a duplicate of the TextBox sample from Chapter 5. We first copied the TextBox control source code, changed the namespace to ControlsBookLib.Ch11, and changed the class name to MCTextBox. We also added a using statement for System.Web.UI.MobileControls and changed the inherited class from Control to MobileControl.

For our example, we keep the postback-handling code and continue to use the TextChangedEventHandler class from Chapter 5. We add the property customizations listed in Table 10-14 to round out our mobile control implementation.

Table 10-14. *Added Property Customizations*

Property	Description
MaxLength	Maximum length permitted for the Text property
Numeric	Boolean value that indicates whether the Text property takes only numbers
Password	Boolean value that indicates whether the password characters are displayed
Size	Indicates the estimated size of Text property
Title	Stores the Title value for the control

Listing 10-13 is the code for our mobile control.

Listing 10-13. *The MCTextBox.cs File*

```
using System;
using System.Collections.Specialized;
using System.ComponentModel;
using System.Web.UI;
using System.Web.UI.MobileControls;

namespace ControlsBook2Lib.Ch10
{
  [ToolboxData("<{0}:MCTextBox runat=server></{0}:MCTextBox>"),
  DefaultProperty("Text")]
  public class MCTextBox : MobileControl, IPostBackDataHandler
  {
    public string Text
    {
      get
      {
        object text = ViewState["text"];
```

```
      if (text == null)
        return string.Empty;
      else
        return (string)text;
    }
    set
    {
      ViewState["text"] = value;
    }
  }

  public string Title
  {
    get
    {
      object title = ViewState["title"];
      if (title == null)
        return string.Empty;
      else
        return (string)title;
    }
    set
    {
      ViewState["title"] = value;
    }
  }

  public int MaxLength
  {
    get
    {
      object maxLength = ViewState["maxLength"];
      if (maxLength == null)
        return 0;
      else
        return (int)maxLength;
    }
    set
    {
      ViewState["maxLength"] = value;
    }
  }

  public int Size
  {
```

```
    get
    {
      object size = ViewState["size"];
      if (size == null)
        return 0;
      else
        return (int)size;
    }
    set
    {
      ViewState["size"] = value;
    }
  }

  public bool Password
  {
    get
    {
      object password = ViewState["password"];
      if (password == null)
        return false;
      else
        return (bool)password;
    }
    set
    {
      ViewState["password"] = value;
    }
  }

  public bool Numeric
  {
    get
    {
      object numeric = ViewState["numeric"];
      if (numeric == null)
        return false;
      else
        return (bool)numeric;
    }
    set
    {
      ViewState["numeric"] = value;
    }
  }
```

```
    public event EventHandler TextChanged;

    public bool LoadPostData(string postDataKey,
       NameValueCollection postCollection)
    {
      string postedValue = postCollection[postDataKey];
      if (!Text.Equals(postedValue))
      {
        Text = postedValue;
        return true;
      }
      else
        return false;
    }

    public void RaisePostDataChangedEvent()
    {
      OnTextChanged(EventArgs.Empty);
    }

    protected virtual void OnTextChanged(EventArgs e)
    {
      if (TextChanged != null)
        TextChanged(this, e);
    }
  }
}
```

As we discussed previously, mobile controls do not render themselves. Instead, mobile controls are associated with device adapters to handle rendering tasks. In our example, we implement two device adapters: one for HTML devices and the other for WML devices.

The HTML Device Adapter

This device adapter is pretty easy to create, because the rendering code is essentially the same as the sample server control in Chapter 5. Device adapters follow a naming convention of `RenderingTechnologyControlNameAdapter`, which translates to `HtmlMCTextBoxAdapter` for our sample. Listing 10-14 contains the source code for the HTML device adapter.

Listing 10-14. *The HtmlMCTextBoxAdapter Source File*

```
using System.Web.UI.MobileControls.Adapters;

namespace ControlsBook2Lib.Ch10.Adapters
{
  public class HtmlMCTextBoxAdapter : HtmlControlAdapter
  {
    protected new MCTextBox Control
```

```
    {
      get
      {
        return (MCTextBox)base.Control;
      }
    }

    public override void Render(HtmlMobileTextWriter writer)
    {
      // write out the HTML tag

      writer.Write("<input name=\"" + Control.UniqueID + "\" ");
      writer.Write("value=\"" + Control.Text + "\" ");
      if (Control.Password)
      {
        writer.Write("type=\"password\" ");
      }
      if (Control.Size != 0)
      {
        writer.Write("size=\"" + Control.Size + "\" ");
      }
      writer.Write("/>");

      if (Control.BreakAfter)
      {
        writer.Write("<br>");
      }
    }
  }
}
```

The device adapter inherits from `HtmlControlAdapter` and implements two methods. We replace the `Control` property using the `new` keyword with a strongly typed `Control` read-only property. ASP.NET populates this property with the associated `MCTextBox` control at runtime.

`Render` is the other method we implement, and it has a few enhancements when compared to the original rendering code from the `TextBox` control in Chapter 5. We have logic to add a `<br>` tag if the `BreakAfter` property has a value of `true`. Similarly, we render the input tag as of type password if the `Password` property is set to true.

We also set the size for the `<input>` tag. The `Size` property does not enforce a rule, but it does set the initial width in characters for the control. Following the convention for the mobile control `TextBox`, we ignore the `Numeric` and `Title` properties' settings when rendering HTML.

One difference from the rendering logic in Chapter 5 is that instead of using the `this` reference, we use the strongly typed reference stored in the `Control` property to get control data for rendering. Also, the writer parameter is a reference to `HtmlMobileTextWriter` to handle markup output.

The WML Device Adapter

The WML device adapter is nearly identical to the HTML device adapter, except, of course, for the Render method. Listing 10-15 presents the code for WmlMCTextBoxAdapter.

Listing 10-15. *The WmlMCTextBoxAdapter.cs Source File*

```
using System.Web.UI.MobileControls.Adapters;

namespace ControlsBook2Lib.Ch10.Adapters
{
  public class WmlMCTextBoxAdapter : WmlControlAdapter
  {
    protected new MCTextBox Control
    {
      get
      {
        return (MCTextBox)base.Control;
      }
    }

    public override void Render(WmlMobileTextWriter writer)
    {
      string Format;

      if (Control.Numeric)
      {
        Format = "*N"; //Set format to any number of numeric characters
      }
      else
      {
        Format = "*M"; //Set format to any number of characters
      }
      writer.RenderTextBox(Control.UniqueID, Control.Text, Format, Control.Title,
    Control.Password, Control.Size, Control.MaxLength, false, Control.BreakAfter);
    }
  }
}
```

The Render method takes advantage of a method on the WmlMobileTextWriter writer named RenderTextBox. This method takes a series of parameters for customizing the output. Table 10-15 lists the parameters for RenderTextBox.

When you compare the parameters of this method with the properties on the mobile TextBox and MCTextBox controls, you can see that the Numeric and Title properties are geared toward WML-capable devices.

Table 10-15. *WmlMobileTextWriter.RenderTextBox Parameters*

Parameter	Description
breakAfter	Indicates whether a tag should be rendered after the <input> tag
format	Permits application of WML-specific formatting options
generateRandomID	Indicates whether the identifier for the control should be encrypted
id	Identifier of the associated mobile control
maxLength	Stores the maximum length permitted for the string
password	Indicates if the data should be masked with the password character *
size	Stores the size of the string
title	Stores the title for the text box
value	Value to initialize the control

The other logic in the Render method for the WmlMCTextBoxAdapter class modifies the format parameter for this method, setting it to *N for unlimited numeric characters or *M for unlimited any type of characters. These settings come from the WML specification for the <input> tag. Table 10-16 details the available values for the format setting.

Table 10-16. *Permitted Settings for the WML <input> Tag format Value*

Format	Description
A	Punctuation or uppercase alphabetic characters.
a	Punctuation or lowercase alphabetic characters.
M	All characters permitted.
m	All characters permitted.
N	Numeric characters only.
X	Uppercase characters only.
x	Lowercase characters only.
nf	n indicates a number between 1 and 9 for the number of characters permitted. Replace f with one of the preceding letters to specify what characters are legal.
*f	* indicates any number of characters permitted. Replace f with one of the preceding letters to specify what characters are legal.

Creating device adapters requires a deep understanding of the nuances of the markup language. (Either that or a good reference close at hand!)

Mapping Device Adapters

Now that we have created our mobile server control and device adapters, it is time to modify a configuration file so that the ASP.NET runtime can select the correct device adapter to render the mobile control.

We can inherit from the `machine.config` file and create a new device mapping in the `web.config` file, or we can modify the `machine.config` file. The section of the configuration file we need to customize is the `<mobileControls>` element. For a given device target, we need to map the mobile control to a device adapter. Here is the syntax to map a mobile server control to a device adapter:

```
<control name= "controlName, assembly" adapter="adapterName, assembly" />
```

If the assembly is registered in the GAC, you can omit the assembly name. For our sample, we chose to modify the `<mobileControls>` tag in `web.config` by adding the following section:

```
<mobileControls cookielessDataDictionaryType=
"System.Web.Mobile.CookielessData">
<device name="ControlsBookHtml" inheritsFrom="HtmlDeviceAdapters">
    <control name=
   "ControlsBookLib.Ch11.MCTextBox,ControlsBookLib" adapter=
   "ControlsBookLib.Ch11.Adapters.HtmlMCTextBoxAdapter,ControlsBookLib" />
</device>
<device name="ControlsBookWml" inheritsFrom="WmlDeviceAdapters">
   <control name=
   "ControlsBookLib.Ch11.MCTextBox,ControlsBookLib" adapter=
   "ControlsBookLib.Ch11.Adapters.WmlMCTextBoxAdapter,ControlsBookLib" />
</device>
</mobileControls>
```

In the preceding section, we inherit from the standard device mappings listed in `machine.config` and can simply make the modifications we need for our control. This method makes it easy to add server controls to device adapter mappings.

Testing MCTextBox

Now that we have everything set up, we can put our new control through its paces. The sample mobile page is very similar to the sample in Chapter 5. Because the new control keeps the code the same as much as possible, it handles postback data and generates server-side events if the data changes in the `MCTextBox`. Listings 10-16 and 10-17 provide the source for `MCTextBoxDemo.aspx` and its code-behind file.

Listing 10-16. *The MCTextBoxDemo.aspx File*

```
<%@ Page Language="c#" CodeBehind="MCTextBoxDemo.aspx.cs"
Inherits="ControlsBook2Mobile.Ch10.MCTextBox"
  AutoEventWireup="True" %>
```

```
<%@ Register TagPrefix="mobile" Namespace="System.Web.UI.MobileControls"
Assembly="System.Web.Mobile" %>
<%@ Register TagPrefix="ApressMC" Namespace="ControlsBook2Lib.Ch10"
Assembly="ControlsBook2Lib" %>
<head>
  <meta content="Microsoft Visual Studio .NET 7.1" name="GENERATOR">
    <meta content="C#" name="CODE_LANGUAGE">
  <meta content="http://schemas.microsoft.com/Mobile/Page" name="vs_targetSchema">
</head>
<body>
  <mobile:Form ID="Form1" Runat="server">
    <mobile:Label ID="Label1" Runat="server">Change the value:</mobile:Label>
    <ApressMC:MCTextBox ID="MCTextBox1" runat="server"
    Text="Hi There!" MaxLength="15"
      Numeric="False" Password="False" Size="10"
      OnTextChanged="MCTextBox1_TextChanged">
     </ApressMC:MCTextBox>
    <mobile:Command ID="Command1" Runat="server">Command</mobile:Command>
    <mobile:Label ID="ChangeLabel" Runat="server">Message</mobile:Label>
  </mobile:Form>
</body>
```

Listing 10-17. *The MCTextBoxDemo.aspx File*

```
using System;

namespace ControlsBook2Mobile.Ch10
{
  public partial class MCTextBox : System.Web.UI.MobileControls.MobilePage
  {
    protected System.Web.UI.MobileControls.TextBox TextBox1;

    protected void Page_Load(object sender, System.EventArgs e)
    {
      ChangeLabel.Text = DateTime.Now.ToLongTimeString() + ": MCTextBox No change.";
    }

    #region Web Form Designer generated code
    override protected void OnInit(EventArgs e)
    {
      //
      // CODEGEN: This call is required by the ASP.NET Web Form Designer.
      //
      InitializeComponent();
      base.OnInit(e);
    }
```

```
    /// <summary>
    //      /// Required method for Designer support - do not modify
    /// the contents of this method with the code editor.
    /// </summary>
    private void InitializeComponent()
    {

    }
    #endregion

    protected void MCTextBox1_TextChanged(object sender, System.EventArgs e)
    {
      ChangeLabel.Text = DateTime.Now.ToLongTimeString() +
      ": MCTextbox Changed! " + MCTextBox1.Text;
    }
  }
}
```

The sample consists of MCTextBox, a Command button, and a Label to display a message. When the form first appears, the message label displays “No change”. Change the value in the MCTextBox control, and click the Command button.

When the mobile form reloads after the postback process, the message label displays an updated time and a message stating that the value changed. This shows that the server-side event process is correctly implemented.

The MCTextBox control will render correctly using both Pocket Internet Explorer and a WML emulator, demonstrating the extensibility of the ASP.NET Framework mobile server control architecture. This concludes our discussion of mobile control development.

Summary

In this chapter, we provided a quick overview of the web part infrastructure. Next, we created the WebPartPageController server control to provide a UI to the end user for manipulating the web part infrastructure. After that, we created two basic server controls and migrated them to web parts as a way to demonstrate the tasks that are typically required. We then walked through enabling web part connections between the web parts.

The next section began a discussion of adaptive control programming by customizing the HTML output of a server control without actually inheriting from the control. We walked through creating a simple control adapter to demonstrate how it works. The best examples of this are the DHTML control adapters available from Microsoft for download.

For device-specific programming, we covered the extensibility hooks for mobile server controls, which are the StyleSheet control, templates, device-specific UI choices, user controls, custom controls, and device adapters. ASP.NET provides three default StyleSheet Style attributes in the StyleReference property: error, subcommand, and title.

Mobile control technology includes user controls, composite controls, and custom-developed controls inherited from MobileControl. Creating custom mobile server controls is very similar to creating traditional mobile controls. The two major differences are ViewState management and the rendering process. Mobile server controls that inherit from MobileControl do not render themselves but instead rely on device adapters to handle their rendering. Device adapters render mobile controls on specific mobile devices, providing support for HTML, WML, cHTML, and XHTML. MobileCapabilties inherits from HttpBrowserCapabilities and aids in detecting the closest match of what device is currently browsing a web application.

CHAPTER 11

Design-Time Support

Design-time support refers to working with server controls within the Visual Studio development environment. Dragging controls onto the web page Component Designer surface from the Toolbox tool window, editing server control properties in the Properties tool window, and right-clicking a control to bring up a context menu are all examples of design-time support.

All these capabilities and more are made available to server control developers by the .NET Framework. In this chapter, we explore the design-time capabilities and techniques available in the .NET Framework for inclusion in custom-developed server control development efforts.

Professional Quality

Support for visual controls in rapid application development (RAD) environments on the Windows platform have existed since the early days of Visual Basic. As opposed to just working with a class in code, controls enhance the development environment experience and speed up development time. The qualities associated with a professional control include the following:

- Ease of installation
- High level of documentation
- Sample code that demonstrates control functionality
- Design-time support

In the remainder of this book, we aim to provide you with the requisite knowledge to assist you in developing professional quality controls. In this chapter we cover design-time support. We cover localization, help file integration, and deployment in the following chapters. In the next section, we take a look at the design-time architecture provided by the .NET Framework.

Design-Time Architecture

The .NET Framework provides design-time customizations for both Windows controls and web controls. The customizations available in each environment differ mostly as a result of rendering technology: ASP.NET server controls generate HTML; Windows Forms controls render using GDI+; and Windows Presentation Foundation controls render in DirectX 3D. This chapter focuses on design-time capabilities for web controls, but many of the concepts discussed here apply to the Windows Forms or Windows Presentation Foundation environment as well.

It is interesting to note that design-time support is built into the .NET Framework, not directly into Visual Studio. In the past, design-time support was built into editing tools or implemented on a component-by-component basis, such as ActiveX property pages. This is not the case with the .NET Framework.

For example, if you open a web form in Visual Studio, drag a `DataGrid` or `GridView` onto the Component Designer surface, and select the Control Tasks arrow in the upper-right corner of the control, a list of tasks, such as AutoFormat, is displayed. Now, perform the same steps in Visual Web Developer Express Edition (available at `http://www.asp.net`). Open a web form, place a `DataGrid` or `GridView` on the Component Designer surface, click the Control Tasks arrow in the upper-right corner of the control, and the same design-time UI is displayed. The UI is part of the control, not the development environment.

The .NET Framework provides rich design-time support, and Visual Studio 2008 provides rich extensibility points for tools as well as component vendors built on top of the .NET Framework. There are two primary facilities available for design-time programming:

- Design-time environment services
- Component-specific customizations

We next provide an overview of design-time environment services, and then we move on to cover component customization. As we implement component customization samples, we touch on the design-time environment services necessary to integrate into a design-time environment such as Visual Studio.

Environment Services Overview

The .NET Framework design-time environment services extend the capabilities and level of integration with a designer tool such as Visual Studio. To obtain a service, the `Component` class implements `IServiceProvider`, which has a method named `GetService` that can be used to obtain a reference to a service interface implemented by the design-time environment.

For example, a server control can use the `GetService` method in a UI type editor to obtain a reference to `IWindowsFormsEditorService`. Next, the control can call the `ShowDialog` method on the reference to have the design-time environment create a Windows Forms–based UI for editing a particular property. This is just one example of what is available in design-time environment services. Table 11-1 provides an overview of available design-time environment services.

Table 11-1. *Design-Time Environment Interfaces*

Interface	Description
`IComponentChangeService`	Permits a designer to receive notifications when components are changed, added, or removed from the design-time environment.
`IDesignerEventService`	Permits a designer to receive notifications when designers are added or removed, and notifications when the selected component changes.
`IDesignerFilter`	Permits a designer to add to the set of properties displayed in the property browser and filter the properties.

Table 11-1. *Design-Time Environment Interfaces*

Interface	Description
`IDesignerHost`	Used to add and retrieve services available in the design-time environment and handle events related to designer state. It provides support for detecting that a designer is loading and helps manage component and designer transactions.
`IDesignerOptionService`	Permits a designer to get and set property values displayed in the Windows Forms Designer property grid displayed when Tools ➤ Options is selected.
`IDictionaryService`	Provides a key-based collection for user-defined data for designers.
`IEventBindingService`	Permits a designer to expose events at design time for the selected component in a property browser.
`IExtenderListService`	Makes the currently active extender providers available to a designer.
`IExtenderProviderService`	Permits a designer to add or remove extender providers at design time.
`IHelpService`	Permits a designer to create and remove help service contexts and attributes, and display help topics by keyword and URL.
`IInheritanceService`	Permits a designer to search for components of derived classes and identify any inheritance attributes for each.
`IMenuCommandService`	Permits a designer to search for, add, remove, and invoke menu commands at design time.
`IReferenceService`	Permits a designer to obtain a reference to an object by name and type, and obtain a reference to the desired object's parent.
`IResourceService`	Permits a designer to obtain a culture-specific resource reader or writer.
`IRootDesigner`	Permits a designer to replace the root designer view with a custom designer view display.
`ISelectionService`	Permits a designer to get a set of references to currently selected components, select components(s), and determine what components are currently selected.
`IServiceContainer`	Permits a component or designer to add or remove services for use by other components or designers.
`ITypeDescriptorFilterService`	Permits a component or designer to filter attributes, events, and properties exposed by a component.
`ITypeResolutionService`	Permits a designer to add an assembly reference to a project, obtain a type or assembly by name, and obtain the assembly's path.
`IWindowsFormsEditorService`	Permits a UI designer to create a Windows Form UI for editing a property at design time.

As Table 11-1 shows, the .NET Framework includes quite a few interfaces to permit a high level of integration between the framework, the components, and the design-time environment.

We now move our discussion to the primary method to implement design-time capabilities: customizing component behavior.

Customizing Component Behavior

The .NET Framework provides the necessary interfaces and services to enable a rich design-time experience when working with controls. As we mentioned previously, the design-time architecture is shared between Windows Forms, Windows Presentation Foundation, and ASP.NET.

Windows Forms controls inherit from `System.ComponentModel.Component`, and we know that ASP.NET controls inherit from `System.Web.UI.Control`. Both classes implement the `IComponent` interface, which is in the `System.ComponentModel` namespace. The `System.ComponentModel.Design` namespace is where the majority of design-time classes exist.

Examine the design-time capabilities of the built-in `GridView` server control and you quickly see how extensive the support is. Customizations available at design time fall into the following categories:

- Designers
- Type converters
- UI type editors

The common root base class for both the Windows Forms and web forms custom designers is `System.ComponentModel.Design.ComponentDesigner`. Custom designers manage the UI and behavior of a component at design time. Customizations include changing the component's appearance, initialization, and interaction on the Component Designer surface. The `DesignerAttribute` associates a designer with a type.

A custom designer can modify what properties display in the property browser and provide methods that can be linked to component events or fired through the developer/user clicking a menu command. Designers are only used by controls at design time.

The base class for type converters is `System.ComponentModel.TypeConverter`. Type converters are generally implemented for control properties that are not readily converted to the `string` type. Type converters are also implemented for types that include subproperties, such as the expand/collapse UI for the `Font` property. `TypeConverterAttribute` associates a type converter with a type or type member. `TypeConverters` can be used by controls both at design time and runtime.

The root base class for UI type editors for Windows Forms, Windows Presentation Foundation, and web forms is `System.Drawing.Design.UITypeEditor`. A UI type editor can provide a custom user interface for editing property values. It displays a custom representation of a property at design time. UI type editors are type specific. An example is the `ForeColor` property of type `Color` that displays the various colors available, which makes it much easier to select a particular color than with a hex value or name. `EditorAttribute` associates a UI type editor with a type or type member. A UI type editor can be used by controls both at design time and runtime.

For a web form's design-time support, ASP.NET-specific base class implementations exist in the `System.Web.UI.Design` namespace. For example, the base class for ASP.NET server control custom designers is `System.Web.UI.Design.HtmlControlDesigner`, which inherits from `System.ComponentModel.Design.ComponentDesigner` (discussed previously).

HtmlControlDesigner provides basic designer functionality for server controls. The class that developers extend when building custom designer classes for ASP.NET server controls is System.Web.UI.Design.ControlDesigner.

Though Windows Forms, Windows Presentation, and web forms share a common architecture for design-time support, the recommendation here is to look to the rendering technology-specific design-time support namespaces first to ease development effort.

Attributes

As we mentioned previously, control customizations are applied using attributes. We provided an overview of attributes at the end of Chapter 3. Table 3-2 in Chapter 3 details basic design-time attributes such as DefaultProperty, DefaultValue, DescriptionAttribute, and so on. In the examples that follow, we apply several of these basic attributes as well as more advanced attributes related to this chapter's discussion. For more information on attributes, please refer to Chapter 3 or the .NET Framework documentation.

The TitledThumbnail Control

To demonstrate design-time behavior, we created a simple composite server control named TitledThumbnail. As you might have guessed, TitledThumbnail displays a thumbnail image with a title underneath. It has several custom properties including a complex property to help demonstrate design-time techniques. Figure 11-1 shows the control in a browser window.

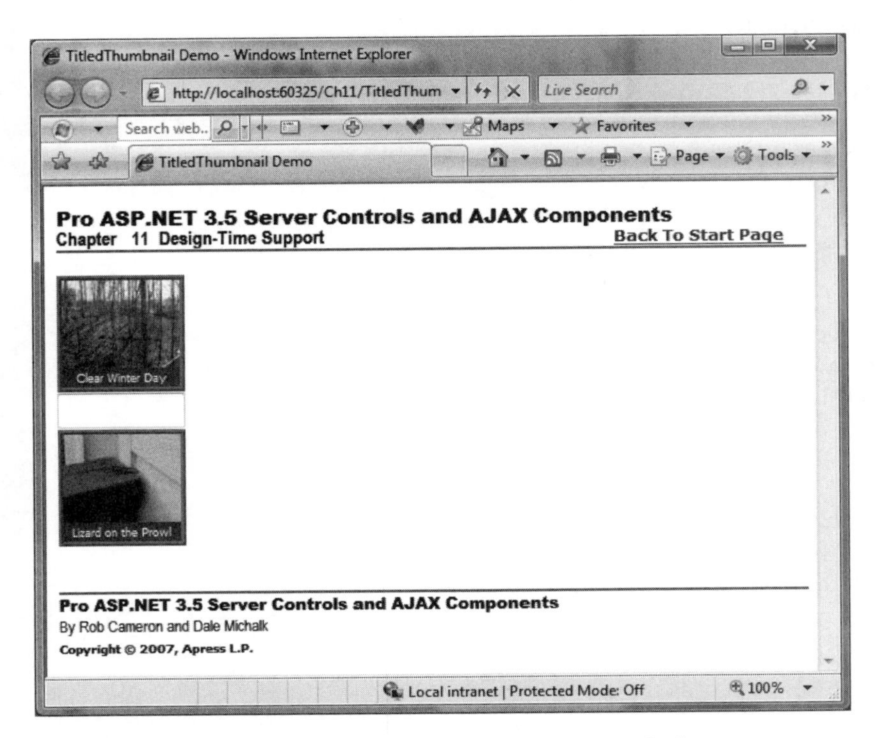

Figure 11-1. *The TitledThumbnail demonstration page in the browser*

There are two instances of the control displaying an image with a caption. We want to jump straight to our design-time discussion, and `TitledThumbnail` is so straightforward that we don't provide a discussion of how this control is constructed so we can go straight to the code. Listing 11-1 contains the source for the `TitledThumbnail` control.

Listing 11-1. *The TitledThumbnail Control*

```
using System;
using System.ComponentModel;
using System.Web.UI;
using System.Web.UI.HtmlControls;
using System.Web.UI.WebControls;
using ControlsBook2Lib.Ch11.Design;

namespace ControlsBook2Lib.Ch11
{
  public enum TitleAlignment { center, justify, left, right };

  [ToolboxData("<{0}:TitledThumbnail runat=server></{0}:TitledThumbnail>"),
  EditorAttribute(typeof(TitledThumbnailComponentEditor), typeof(ComponentEditor)),
  Designer(typeof(TitledThumbnailDesigner)),
  DefaultProperty("ImageUrl")]
  public class TitledThumbnail : WebControl
  {
    private Image imgThumbnail;
    private Label lblTitle;
    private ImageMetaData metaData;

    public TitledThumbnail()
      : base(HtmlTextWriterTag.Div)
    {

    }

    [DescriptionAttribute("Text to be shown as the image caption."),
    CategoryAttribute("Appearance")]
    public string Title
    {
      get
      {
        EnsureChildControls();
        object title = ViewState["title"];
        return (title == null) ? "" : (string)title;
      }
      set
      {
```

```
      EnsureChildControls();
      lblTitle.Text = value;
      ViewState["title"] = value;
    }
  }

  [DescriptionAttribute("The Url of the image to be shown."),
  CategoryAttribute("Appearance")]
  public string ImageUrl
  {
    get
    {
      EnsureChildControls();
      object imageUrl = ViewState["imageUrl"];
      return (imageUrl == null) ? "" : (string)imageUrl;
    }
    set
    {
      EnsureChildControls();
      imgThumbnail.ImageUrl = value;
      ViewState["imageUrl"] = value;
    }
  }

  [DescriptionAttribute("Set the alignment for the Image and Title."),
  CategoryAttribute("Layout"), DefaultValue("center")]
  public TitleAlignment Align
  {
    get
    {
      EnsureChildControls();
      object align = ViewState["align"];
      return (align == null) ? TitleAlignment.left : (TitleAlignment)align;
    }
    set
    {
      EnsureChildControls();
      this.Attributes.Add("align", Enum.GetName(typeof(TitleAlignment), value));
      ViewState["align"] = value;
    }
  }

  [DesignerSerializationVisibility(DesignerSerializationVisibility.Content),
  NotifyParentProperty(true), CategoryAttribute("MetaData"),
  DescriptionAttribute(
     "Meta data that stores information
     about the displayed photo image.")]
```

```
public ImageMetaData ImageInfo
{
  get
  {
    EnsureChildControls();
    if (metaData == null)
    {
      metaData = new ImageMetaData();
    }
    return metaData;
  }
}

public override ControlCollection Controls
{
  get
  {
    EnsureChildControls();
    return base.Controls;
  }
}

protected override void CreateChildControls()
{
  Controls.Clear();

  HtmlGenericControl divImageContainer = new HtmlGenericControl("div");
  divImageContainer.ID = "imageDiv";
  imgThumbnail = new Image();
  divImageContainer.Controls.Add(imgThumbnail);
  this.Controls.Add(divImageContainer);
  HtmlGenericControl divSpacer = new HtmlGenericControl("div");
  divSpacer.ID = "divSpacer";
  divSpacer.Attributes.Add("style", "margin:3px;");
  this.Controls.Add(divSpacer);
  lblTitle = new Label();
  lblTitle.ID = "imageTitle";
  lblTitle.ForeColor = System.Drawing.Color.White;
  this.Controls.Add(lblTitle);
}

protected override void AddAttributesToRender(HtmlTextWriter writer)
{
  writer.AddAttribute(HtmlTextWriterAttribute.Align, "center");
```

```
            writer.AddStyleAttribute(HtmlTextWriterStyle.BackgroundColor, "#2666A5");
            writer.AddStyleAttribute(HtmlTextWriterStyle.Width, "94px");
            writer.AddStyleAttribute(HtmlTextWriterStyle.Height, "88px");
            writer.AddStyleAttribute(HtmlTextWriterStyle.BorderColor, "silver");
            writer.AddStyleAttribute(HtmlTextWriterStyle.BorderStyle, "ridge");
            writer.AddStyleAttribute(HtmlTextWriterStyle.BorderWidth, "4px");
            writer.AddStyleAttribute(HtmlTextWriterStyle.FontSize, "XX-Small");
            writer.AddStyleAttribute(HtmlTextWriterStyle.FontFamily, "Tahoma");

            base.AddAttributesToRender(writer);
        }
    }
}
```

Listings 11-2 and 11-3 contain the source for the TitledThumbnail server control demonstration page and code-behind file.

Listing 11-2. *The TitledThumbnail Demonstration .aspx File*

```
<%@ Page Language="C#"
MasterPageFile="~/MasterPage/ControlsBook2MasterPage.Master"
    AutoEventWireup="true" CodeBehind="TitledThumbnail.aspx.cs"
    Inherits="ControlsBook2Web.Ch11.TitledThumbnail"
    Title="TitledThumbnail Demo" %>

<%@ Register TagPrefix="apress" Namespace="ControlsBook2Lib.Ch11"
  Assembly="ControlsBook2Lib" %>
<%@ Register Assembly="ControlsBook2Lib" Namespace="ControlsBook2Lib.Ch03"
   TagPrefix="cc1" %>
<asp:Content ID="Content1" ContentPlaceHolderID="HeadSection" runat="server">
</asp:Content>
<asp:Content ID="Content2" ContentPlaceHolderID="ChapterNumAndTitle" runat="server">
    <asp:Label ID="ChapterNumberLabel" runat="server"
    Width="14px">11</asp:Label>  <asp:Label
        ID="ChapterTitleLabel" runat="server" Width="360px">
        Design-Time Support</asp:Label>
</asp:Content>
<asp:Content ID="Content3" ContentPlaceHolderID="PrimaryContent" runat="server">
    <br />
    <apress:TitledThumbnail ID="TitledThumbnail1" Title="Clear Winter Day"
    runat="server"     ImageInfo-PhotographerFullName=
    "Robert Cameron" ImageInfo-ImageLongDescription=
    "Winter outdoor scene in February"
     ImageInfo-ImageDate="2007-09-01" ImageUrl="imgs/Outdoors.jpg"
     ImageInfo-ImageLocation="31N,123W">
    </apress:TitledThumbnail>
    <br />
```

```
    <apress:TitledThumbnail ID="Titledthumbnail2"
      Title="Lizard on the Prowl"
       runat="server"
      ImageInfo-PhotographerFullName="Rob Cameron"
      ImageInfo-ImageLongDescription=
      "A lizard on the side of a wooden deck."
      ImageInfo-ImageDate="2007-08-08" ImageUrl=
     "imgs/Lizard.jpg" ImageInfo-ImageLocation="32S,123E">
    </apress:TitledThumbnail>
    <br />
    <br />
</asp:Content>
```

Listing 11-3. *The TitledThumbnail Demonstration Page Code-Behind File*

```
using System;

namespace ControlsBook2Web.Ch11
{
  public partial class TitledThumbnail : System.Web.UI.Page
  {
    protected void Page_Load(object sender, EventArgs e)
    {

    }
  }
}
```

The `TitledThumbnail` control implements properties such as `ImageMetaData` and `Location` that do not configure the control; rather, they store data about the thumbnail image. Though this may or may not be a useful design, the properties help us demonstrate design-time customizations, which is this chapter's focus.

The TitledThumbnail Control at Design Time

Figure 11-2 displays an annotated screen shot of the `TitledThumbnail` control at design time. Item 1 in Figure 11-2 highlights a couple of properties displayed in the Properties window. We discuss customizations for the Properties window in the next section.

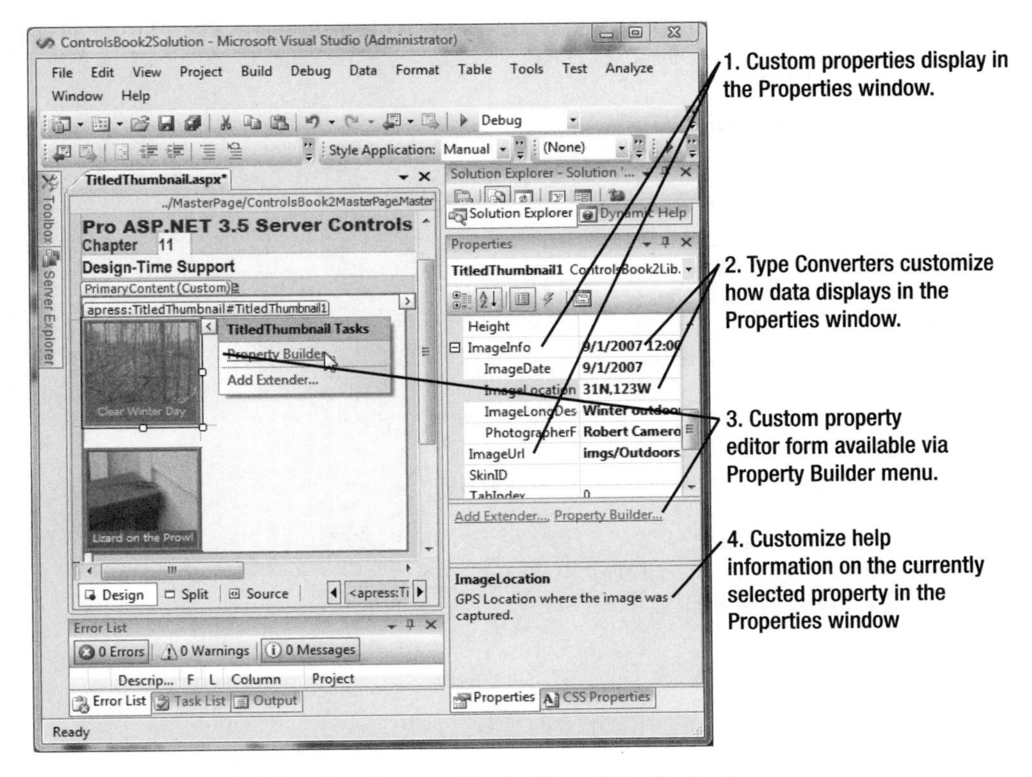

Figure 11-2. *The TitledThumbnail control in the Visual Studio Designer*

The Properties Window

Without any work by the developer, a control that inherits from `System.Web.UI.Control` displays simple properties in the property browser. Simple properties include `Boolean`, `string`, `integer`, `decimal`, and so on. Although not a simple type, `enumeration` types also display automatically, as does a drop-down list in the property browser.

Some easy customizations include applying the basic design-time attributes listed in Chapter 3. Here is an example from the `TitledThumbnail` control:

```
[DescriptionAttribute("Set the alignment for the Image and Title."),
    CategoryAttribute("Layout"),DefaultValue("center")]
```

The `DescriptionAttribute` displays the passed-in string at the bottom of the property browser, as pointed out by item 4 in Figure 11-2. The `CategoryAttribute` places the property in the passed-in category in the Properties window. Example property browser categories are `Layout`, `Behavior`, and so on. The last attribute, `DefaultValue`, sets the default value for the property. For an enumeration property, set the `DefaultValue` property to a string value representing the enumeration value, not the actual strongly typed enumeration value.

Attributes are generally named with the word “Attribute” appended at the end. However, the word “Attribute” is optional when applying the attribute. In the previous example, the text `DescriptionAttribute("..")` could be replaced with `Description("")`. Likewise, the actual class name of the `DefaultValue` attribute in the .NET Framework is `DefaultValueAttribute`.

The ImageInfo property on the TitledThumbnail control is of type ImageMetaData. Listing 11-4 contains the source for the ImageMetaData class.

Listing 11-4. *The ImageMetaData Class*

```
using System;
using System.ComponentModel;
using System.Drawing.Design;
using System.Globalization;
using System.Security.Permissions;
using System.Web;
using ControlsBook2Lib.Ch11.Design;

namespace ControlsBook2Lib.Ch11
{
  [TypeConverter(typeof(ImageMetaDataConverter)),
  AspNetHostingPermission(
  SecurityAction.LinkDemand,
  Level = AspNetHostingPermissionLevel.Minimal)]
   public class ImageMetaData
   {
      public ImageMetaData()
      {

      }

      public ImageMetaData(DateTime PhotoDate, Location Loc,
      string ImageDescription, string FullName)
      {
        PhotographerFullName = FullName;
        ImageDate = PhotoDate;
        ImageLongDescription = ImageDescription;
        ImageLocation = Loc;
      }

      [NotifyParentProperty(true),
      DescriptionAttribute("Name of the photographer who captured the image.")]
      public string PhotographerFullName {get; set;}

      [NotifyParentProperty(true),
      DescriptionAttribute("Date the image was captured.")]
      public DateTime ImageDate {get; set;}

      [NotifyParentProperty(true),
      DescriptionAttribute("Extended description of the image."),
      EditorAttribute(typeof(ControlsBook2Lib.Ch11.Design.SimpleTextEditor),
      typeof(UITypeEditor))]
```

```
      public string ImageLongDescription {get; set;}

      [NotifyParentProperty(true),
DescriptionAttribute("GPS Location where the image was captured.")]
      public Location ImageLocation {get; set;}

      [Browsable(false)]
      public bool IsEmpty
      {
         get
         {
            return ((ImageLongDescription == null) &&
                    (PhotographerFullName == null) &&
                    (ImageDate == null));
         }
      }

      public override string ToString()
      {
         return ToString(CultureInfo.CurrentCulture);
      }

      public string ToString(CultureInfo Culture)
      {
        return string.Format(CultureInfo.CurrentCulture, "[{0}: Date={1},
        LongDescription={2}, PhotographerName={3}]", new object[]
        { base.GetType().Name,
        this.ImageDate.ToShortDateString(),
        this.ImageLongDescription,
        this.PhotographerFullName });
      }
   }
}
```

ImageMetaData is a class containing simple types and a complex type named Location. Listing 11-5 contains the source for the Location class.

Listing 11-5. *The Location Class*

```
using System;
using System.ComponentModel;
using System.Globalization;
using ControlsBook2Lib.Ch11.Design;

namespace ControlsBook2Lib.Ch11
{
  [Serializable,TypeConverter(typeof(LocationConverter))]
   public class Location
```

```
{
   public Location()
   {
      Latitude = 0;
      Longitude = 0;
   }

   public Location(double Lat, double Long)
   {
      Latitude = Lat;
      Longitude = Long;
   }

   public double Latitude {get; set;}

   public double Longitude { get; set; }

   public bool IsEmpty
   {
      get
      {
         return (Latitude == 0 && Longitude == 0);
      }
   }

   //override ToString so that it displays the values of
   //its members as opposed to its fully qualified type.
   public override string ToString()
   {
      return ToString(CultureInfo.CurrentCulture);
   }

   public string ToString(CultureInfo Culture)
   {
     string Lat;
     string Long;
     TypeConverter DoubleConverter =
          TypeDescriptor.GetConverter(typeof(double));

     //Add N/S for latitude, E/W for longitude
     if (Math.Round(this.Latitude) >= 0)
     {
       Lat =
          DoubleConverter.ConvertToString(null,
          Culture, this.Latitude) + "N";
     }
```

```
        else
        {
          Lat =
             DoubleConverter.ConvertToString(null,
             Culture, Math.Abs(this.Latitude)) + "S";
        }

        if (Math.Round(this.Longitude) >= 0)
        {
          Long =
             DoubleConverter.ConvertToString(null,
             Culture, this.Longitude) + "W";
        }
        else
        {
          Long = DoubleConverter.ConvertToString(null,
             Culture, Math.Abs(this.Longitude)) + "E";
        }

        // Display lat and long as concantenated string with
        // a comma as the separator based on the current culture
        return String.Join(Culture.TextInfo.ListSeparator,
           new string[] { Lat, Long });
      }

      public override bool Equals(object obj)
      {
         Location Loc = (Location) obj;

         if (Loc != null)
         {
            return (Latitude == Loc.Latitude &&
               Longitude == Loc.Longitude);
         }
         return false;
      }

      public override int GetHashCode()
      {
         //XOR the latitude and logitude coordinates
         return Latitude.GetHashCode() ^ Longitude.GetHashCode();
      }
   }
}
```

The Location class stores a latitude and longitude as a decimal. To help display these properties in the property browser, we implemented the ImageInfoConverter and LocationConverter type converters. Type converters are the subject of the next section.

Type Converters

Type converter attributes are applied to type class definitions to assist with converting the type to other data types and vice versa. Generally, this conversion is to/from the `string` type. Type converters can also alter how a type appears in the property browser at design time.

■Note Never access a type converter directly. Instead, access the appropriate converter by using `TypeDescriptor`.

A custom type converter derives from `System.ComponentModel.TypeConverter` regardless of whether it is for a property of a Windows Forms or web forms control. The type converter for the `Location` class type has a type converter named `LocationConverter` that inherits from this class. The purpose of this type converter is to alter how the `Location` type displays in the property browser.

The LocationConverter Class

The `Location` class stores a latitude and longitude. An instance of this type is part of the `ImageMetaData` type. The `ImageMetaData` type uses the `Location` instance to store the location where the photo displayed by the `TitledThumbnail` control was taken. Latitude and longitude values are generally displayed using degrees/minutes/seconds notation or as a decimal with N/S, E/W appended to the decimal value.

Take a look again at Figure 11-2. Item 2 highlights the display for `ImageInfo` and `ImageLocation`. `ImageLocation` is of type `Location`. Notice the value displayed: 34S,150E. These values are easily understood to represent a latitude and longitude. If you look at the `Location` type, the underlying latitude and longitude values are of type `double` with a negative latitude representing south and a negative longitude representing east. The `LocationConverter` type converter makes this possible and is shown in Listing 11-6.

Listing 11-6. *The LocationConverter Source*

```
using System;
using System.ComponentModel;
using System.ComponentModel.Design.Serialization;
using System.Globalization;
using System.Reflection;

namespace ControlsBook2Lib.Ch11.Design
{
  public class LocationConverter : TypeConverter
  {
    public override object ConvertFrom(ITypeDescriptorContext
       context, CultureInfo culture, object value)
    {
```

```
    if (value.GetType() == typeof(string))
    {
      string str = (string)value;

      string[] propValues =
         str.Split(',');

      if (2 != propValues.Length)
      {
        throw new ArgumentException("Invalid Location.
        It must be in decimal form with N or S for latitude and E
       or W for longitude.  Example: 25.4N,123.3W.", "value");
      }

      //Peel off N/S for latitude and E/W for longitude
      string Lat = propValues[0];
      if ("N" == Lat.Substring(Lat.Length - 1))
      {
        string[] latParts = Lat.Split("N".ToCharArray());
        Lat = latParts[0];
      }
      if ("S" == Lat.Substring(Lat.Length - 1))
      {
        string[] latParts = Lat.Split("S".ToCharArray());
        Lat = "-" + latParts[0];
      }

      string Long = propValues[1];
      if ("W" == Long.Substring(Long.Length - 1))
      {
        string[] longParts = Long.Split("W".ToCharArray());
        Long = longParts[0];
      }
      if ("E" == Long.Substring(Long.Length - 1))
      {
        string[] longParts = Long.Split("E".ToCharArray());
        Long = "-" + longParts[0];
      }

      return new Location(Convert.ToDouble(Lat),
         Convert.ToDouble(Long));
    }
    else
      return base.ConvertFrom(context, culture, value);
  }
```

```
public override object ConvertTo(ITypeDescriptorContext context,
CultureInfo culture, object value, Type destinationType)
{
  if (destinationType == typeof(string))
  {
    Location Loc = (Location)value;
    string Lat;
    string Long;

    //Add N/S for latitude, E/W for longitude
    if (Math.Round(Loc.Latitude) >= 0)
    {
      Lat =
         (double)Loc.Latitude + "N";
    }
    else
    {
      Lat =
         (double)Math.Abs(Loc.Latitude) + "S";
    }

    if (Math.Round(Loc.Longitude) >= 0)
    {
      Long =
         (double)Loc.Longitude + "W";
    }
    else
    {
      Long = (double)Math.Abs(Loc.Longitude) + "E";
    }

    // Display lat and long as concantenated string with
    // a comma as the separator
    return Lat + "," + Long;
  }

  if (destinationType == typeof(InstanceDescriptor))
  {
    MemberInfo memberInfo = null;
    object[] memberParameters = null;

    Location Loc = (Location)value;
    Type doubleType = typeof(double);
    memberInfo = typeof(Location).GetConstructor(new Type[] { doubleType,
   doubleType });
```

```
        memberParameters =
          new object[] { Loc.Latitude, Loc.Longitude };
        return new InstanceDescriptor(memberInfo, memberParameters);
      }
      return base.ConvertTo(context, culture, value, destinationType);
    }

    public override bool CanConvertTo(ITypeDescriptorContext
       context, Type destinationType)
    {
      if ((typeof(string) == destinationType) ||
         (typeof(InstanceDescriptor) == destinationType))
      {
        return true;
      }
      else
        return base.CanConvertTo(context, destinationType);
    }

    public override bool CanConvertFrom(ITypeDescriptorContext
       context, Type sourceType)
    {
      if (sourceType == typeof(string))
      {
        return true;
      }
      else
        return base.CanConvertFrom(context, sourceType);
    }
  }
}
```

When the page parser encounters a type that has a type converter associated with it via the following syntax, it uses the type converter's methods to assist with parsing the property to/from a string value:

```
[TypeConverter(typeof(LocationConverter))]
   public class Location
   {
...
```

The .NET Framework also uses TypeConverters to stream types to/from ViewState during the page life cycle. TypeConverters provide methods to check whether a type conversion is supported as well as a method to make the conversion. The Location type converter implements four methods:

- CanConvertFrom(..)
- CanConvertTo(..)

- `ConvertFrom(..)`
- `ConvertTo(..)`

`CanConvertFrom` has logic that checks what type is passed in and returns true if the type is a type, such as string, that can be converted into the class type. `CanConvertTo` has generally the same logic, returning true if the target type is a type that the class type can be converted to.

`ConvertFrom` for the `LocationConverter` class has logic to ensure that the N/S, E/W values are appropriately handled; same for `ConvertTo`. This type converter provides nice functionality, altering how the type renders in the property browser so that it is more readable or in a format that makes more sense. Note that if the user decides to enter a latitude and longitude using this format, 34,–135 (34N,134E), the type converter logic is written in such a way to permit it.

We now move on to a discussion of the `ImageMetaData` class and its type converter.

The ImageMetaDataConverter Class

The `ImageMetaData` class is the type of the `ImageInfo` member on the `TitledThumbnail` control. The `ImageMetaData` class is a complex type that contains subproperties when viewed in the property browser, as shown in Figure 11-2. It contains the following properties:

- `ImageDate`
- `ImageLocation`
- `ImageLongDescription`
- `PhotographerFullName`

As we mentioned previously, unlike the other scalar types, `ImageLocation` is also a complex type of type `Location`. `LocationConverter` customizes how properties of type `Location` display in the Properties window.

Notice that the `ImageMetaData` class has a type converter associated with it:

```
[TypeConverter(typeof(ImageMetaDataConverter))]
  public class ImageMetaData
  {
```

This type converter inherits from `System.ComponentModel.ExpandableObjectConverter`, which provides functionality to display types with properties as subproperties similar to how the `Font` type displays in the Properties tool window. This type converter can also be used to alter what data shows for the value of the `ImageInfo` property listed in the property browser.

In Figure 11-2, you see that the data shown in the property field consists of `ImageInfo`'s subproperties, separated by a comma. This behavior is also similar to what the `Font` property displays for its value in the property browser. Listing 11-7 lists the source for the `ImageMetaDataConverter` class.

Listing 11-7. *The ImageMetaDataConverter Class*

```
using System;
using System.ComponentModel;
using System.ComponentModel.Design.Serialization;
```

```
using System.Globalization;
using System.Reflection;

namespace ControlsBook2Lib.Ch11.Design
{
  public class ImageMetaDataConverter : ExpandableObjectConverter
  {
    public override object ConvertFrom(ITypeDescriptorContext context, CultureInfo
   culture, object value)
    {
      if (null == value)
      {
        return new ImageMetaData();
      }

      if (value is string)
      {
        string str = (string)value;
        if ("" == str)
        {
          return new ImageMetaData();
        }

        string[] propValues = str.Split(',');

        if (4 != propValues.Length)
        {
          throw new ArgumentException("Invalid ImageMetaData", "value");
        }

        return new ImageMetaData(Convert.ToDateTime(propValues[0]),
           (Location)TypeDescriptor.GetConverter(typeof(Location)).
           ConvertFromString(propValues[1]),
           (string)propValues[2],
           (string)propValues[3]);
      }
      else
        return base.ConvertFrom(context, culture, value);
    }

    public override bool CanConvertFrom(ITypeDescriptorContext context,
     Type sourceType)
    {
      if (typeof(string) == sourceType)
      {
        return true;
      }
```

```
      else
        return base.CanConvertFrom(context, sourceType);
    }

    public override object ConvertTo(ITypeDescriptorContext context, CultureInfo
    culture, object value, Type targetType)
    {
      if ((targetType == typeof(string)) && (value is ImageMetaData))
      {
        ImageMetaData imageMetaData = (ImageMetaData)value;
        if (imageMetaData.IsEmpty)
        {
          return String.Empty;
        }
        return String.Join(culture.TextInfo.ListSeparator,
           new string[] {
                              imageMetaData.ImageDate.ToString(),
                              imageMetaData.ImageLocation.ToString(),
                              imageMetaData.ImageLongDescription,
                              imageMetaData.PhotographerFullName});
      }

      if ((targetType == typeof(InstanceDescriptor)) && (value is ImageMetaData))
      {
        ImageMetaData metaData = (ImageMetaData)value;
        ConstructorInfo cInfo = typeof(ImageMetaData).GetConstructor(new Type[] {
        typeof(DateTime), typeof(Location), typeof(string), typeof(string) });
        if (cInfo != null)
        {
          object[] obj = new object[] { metaData.ImageDate, metaData.ImageLocation,
         metaData.ImageLongDescription, metaData.PhotographerFullName };
          return new InstanceDescriptor(cInfo, obj);
        }
      }
      return base.ConvertTo(context, culture, value, targetType);
    }

    public override bool CanConvertTo(ITypeDescriptorContext context,
   Type destinationType)
    {
      if ((destinationType == typeof(InstanceDescriptor)) ||
     (destinationType == typeof(string)))
        return true;
      else
        return base.CanConvertTo(context, destinationType);
    }
  }
}
```

Without this type converter, the value displayed for `ImageInfo` would be what you would expect if you called the `ToString()` method, which is the fully qualified type name:

```
ControlsBookLib.Ch12.ImageMetaData
```

This is not a very useful value to display, which is why it is recommended that you build a type converter that inherits from `System.ComponentModel.ExpandableObjectConverter` to provide expand/collapse functionality in the property browser for complex types such as properties with subproperties. This also provides a more useful value for the complex type in the property browser.

UI Type Editors

UI type editors provide a pop-up UI for editing properties listed in the Properties window. An example is the Color Picker dialog box that displays when you click the button that appears when you click or tab into the `bgColor` property of the `Document` object in the Visual Studio property browser. This type editor provides a better UI than entering a hexadecimal color value by instead displaying the actual colors.

A UI type editor can have either a Windows Forms or a drop-down configuration UI for setting a property of a specific type. An example of the drop-down UI is the editor that displays when you click the button for the `BackColor` property of a `Label` control.

With this short discussion of UI type editors out of the way, we now implement a UI type editor for the `ImageInfo.ImageLongDescription` property of the `TitledThumbnail` control.

The SimpleTextEditor Editor

The `SimpleTextEditor` UI type editor provides a large editing area for a property of type `string`. Figure 11-3 shows the Windows Form UI.

Figure 11-3. *The SimpleTextEditor Windows Form UI*

The Windows Form class is named SimpleTextEditorDialog. It has a single property named TextValue. Otherwise, the rest of the code is generated by Visual Studio. Listing 11-8 shows the class listing.

Listing 11-8. *The SimpleTextEditorDialog Class*

```
using System.Windows.Forms;

namespace ControlsBook2Lib.Ch11.Design
{
  public partial class SimpleTextEditorDialog : Form
  {
    public SimpleTextEditorDialog()
    {
      InitializeComponent();
    }

    public string TextValue
    {
      get
      {
        return textString.Text;
      }
      set
      {
        textString.Text = value;
      }
    }
  }
}
```

Now that we have our UI built, we move on to create the UI type editor class. The SimpleTextEditor class inherits from UITypeEditor, the base class for type editors. The SimpleTextEditor includes two method overrides, EditValue and GetEditStyle. Listing 11-9 presents the source for SimpleTextEditor.

Listing 11-9. *The SimpleTextEditor Source*

```
using System;
using System.ComponentModel;
using System.Drawing.Design;
using System.Windows.Forms;
using System.Windows.Forms.Design;

namespace ControlsBook2Lib.Ch11.Design
{
```

```
    public class SimpleTextEditor : UITypeEditor
    {
        public override UITypeEditorEditStyle GetEditStyle(
            ITypeDescriptorContext context)
        {
            if (null != context)
            {
                return UITypeEditorEditStyle.Modal;
            }
            return base.GetEditStyle(context);
        }

        public override object EditValue(ITypeDescriptorContext context,
            IServiceProvider serviceProvider, object value)
        {
            if ((null  != context) && (null  != serviceProvider))
            {
                IWindowsFormsEditorService editorService =
                    (IWindowsFormsEditorService)serviceProvider.GetService(
                    typeof(IWindowsFormsEditorService));

                if (null != editorService)
                {
                    SimpleTextEditorDialog formEditor = new SimpleTextEditorDialog();
                    formEditor.TextValue = (string)value;

                    DialogResult DlgResult = editorService.ShowDialog(formEditor);
                    if (DialogResult.OK == DlgResult)
                    {
                        value = formEditor.TextValue;
                    }
                }
            }
            return value;
        }
    }
}
```

GetEditStyle takes ITypeDescriptorContext and returns UITypeEditorEditStyle. ITypeDescriptorContext implements IServiceProvider and is used for type conversion. In our case, though, we simply check to see whether or not it is null. If it is not null, then we know that it is design time, and we return a UITypeEditorEditStyle constant. The UITypeEditorEditStyle enumeration has three possible values:

- DropDown
- Modal
- None

The default value in the base class implementation is to return None. Returning None indicates that the editor does not have a GUI interface. In our case, we return Modal to indicate that the type editor's style is a modal form dialog box.

The EditStyle method does the bulk of the work in our UI type editor example. It creates the SimpleTextEditorDialog UI and returns the value back to the callee—in this case, Visual Studio. Earlier in this chapter, we discussed how Visual Studio provides design-time environment services.

The EditStyle method takes as parameters ITypeDescriptorContext, IServiceProvider, and an object that represents the current value of the property. We use the context parameter to determine that we are in a design-time environment. We next ensure serviceProvider is valid. If it is, we call GetService on serviceProvider to obtain a reference to an object that implements IWindowsFormsEditorService.

To implement a UI type editor that has a UITypeEditorEditStyle of DropDown as in the BackColor property of a Label control, call the DropDownControl method of IWindowsFormsEditorService. We call ShowDialog on editorService to display the SimpleTextEditorDialog UI. This simple form class has a property named TextValue to set and get the property value.

The Collection Editor

A collection editor provides you with the ability to add values to or remove values from an item's collection, as in the DropDownList or ListBox controls. The base class for collection editors is CollectionEditor in the System.ComponentModel.Design namespace.

As an example, ListItemsCollectionEditor implements a descendent class of CollectionEditor to provide the UI editor for the ListItemCollection type used in ListControl, the base class for both the DropDownList and ListBox controls.

Implementing a collection editor involves creating a custom collection type appropriate for your control. In the previous edition of this book, we implemented a custom collection class named MenuItemDataCollection and created a custom collection editor class as well. With the introduction of generic types in .NET Framework 2.0 and later, we no longer need to create a custom collection for MenuItemData; instead, we can rely on the built-in designer support.

For the built-in collection editor to provide the proper rendering and property access, we must apply a built-in type converter to the MenuItemData class like this:

```
[TypeConverter(typeof(ExpandableObjectConverter))]
public class MenuItemData
{
...
```

The built-in ExpandableObjectConverter type converter suffices for MenuItemData, because this class consists of simple property types. If this class had more complex properties, as was the case with the ImageMetaData class and its ImageLocation property of type Location, we would need to implement a custom ExpandableObjectConverter type converter. Figure 11-4 displays the built-in collection editor in action.

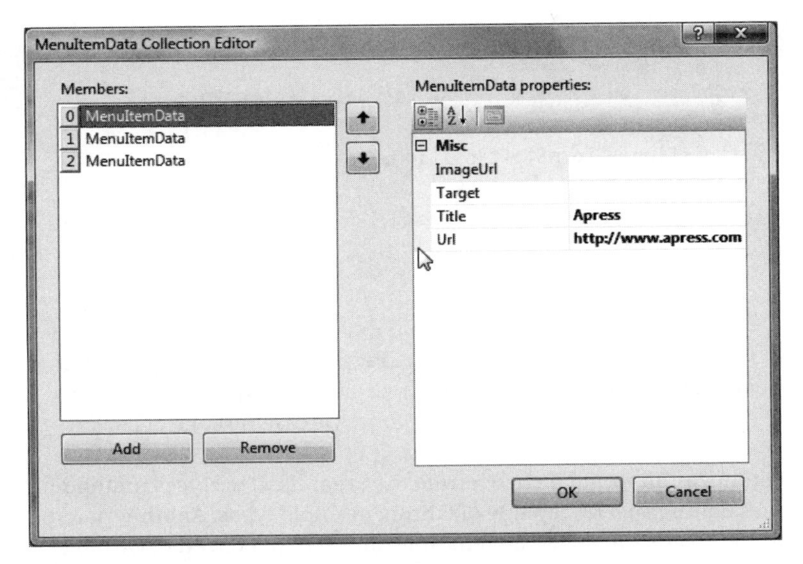

Figure 11-4. *The built-in collection editor Windows Form UI*

The built-in collection editor provides the exact same functionality as our custom collection editor from the previous edition of this book, so no further action is required. For reference purposes, Listing 11-10 presents the code for `MenuItemDataCollectionEditor`.

Listing 11-10. *The MenuItemDataCollectionEditor Source*

```
using System;
using System.ComponentModel;
using System.ComponentModel.Design;
using System.Design;
using System.Windows.Forms;
using System.Windows.Forms.Design;
using ControlsBook2Lib.Ch06;

namespace ControlsBook2Lib.Ch11.Design
{
   public class MenuItemDataCollectionEditor : CollectionEditor
   {
      public MenuItemDataCollectionEditor(Type type) : base(type)
      {
      }

      protected override
System.ComponentModel.Design.CollectionEditor.CollectionForm
```

```
CreateCollectionForm()
      {
         CollectionEditor.CollectionForm frm = base.CreateCollectionForm ();
         ((Form)frm).Width = 750;
         ((Form)frm).StartPosition = FormStartPosition.CenterParent;

         return frm;
      }
   }
}
```

The CollectionEditor class listing for MenuItemDataCollectionEditor is fairly short; it performs the one task of customizing how the collection editor displays, as noted previously. To modify the Width and StartPosition for the collection editing form, we cast the CollectionForm back to Form and perform the desired modifications.

Another potential customization would be to override the CreateNewItemTypes method in the event that the collection editor must be capable of editing multiple types. Another potential customization is to provide a custom collection editor form. With that covered, we next move on to another form of editor: the component editor.

Component Editors

A component editor is a modal dialog box that displays a property page similar to an ActiveX control's property page. Probably the most familiar component editor in ASP.NET is the DataGrid's component editor. It provides a convenient interface to quickly configure a DataGrid's numerous properties. You may have noticed this attribute on the previous TitledThumbnail server control:

```
EditorAttribute(typeof(TitledThumbnailComponentEditor),typeof(ComponentEditor))
```

This attribute is what associates the ComponentEditor with a server control. Building a component editor is different from what we have done so far, because component editors are considered part of .NET Windows Forms based on its namespace. The namespace for the base class ComponentEditor is System.Windows.Forms.Design.

Component editors consist of a ComponentEditor-based class and a ComponentEditorDlg Windows Form. The custom ComponentEditor class instantiates the component editor dialog box, initiates a DesignerTransaction, and either commits or rolls back any changes depending on whether the user clicks OK or Cancel on the component editor dialog box.

The Component Editor Dialog Box

Building the component editor dialog box is a matter of deciding what server control functionality to expose for configuration and laying out Windows Forms controls on the Windows Form that represents the editing dialog box on the Component Designer surface.

Because the component editor dialog box is a Windows Form, all the controls in .NET Windows Forms, such as the TabControl or TreeView, are available to provide a rich editing environment. For TitledThumbnailComponentEditorDlg, we expose the TitledThumbnail server control's main properties for editing on a simple form, as shown in Figure 11-5.

To create TitledThumbnailComponentEditorDlg, we start by adding a Windows Form to the project and setting the form's AcceptButton to buttonOK and CancelButton to ButtonCancel. Next, we edit its constructor to take a reference to a TitledThumbnail server control object. We need this reference to the TitledThumbnail server control in order to set its properties if the user clicks the OK button. Listing 11-11 shows the TitledThumbnailComponentEditorDlg class file.

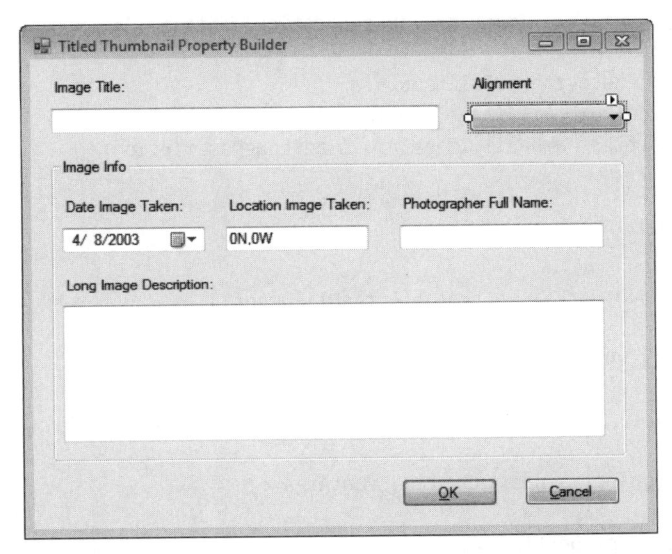

Figure 11-5. *The TitledThumbnail component editor dialog box*

Listing 11-11. *The TitledThumbnailComponentEditorDlg Class File*

```
using System;
using System.ComponentModel;
using System.Windows.Forms;

namespace ControlsBook2Lib.Ch11.Design
{
  public partial class TitledThumbnailComponentEditorDlg : Form
  {
    private TitledThumbnail titledThumbnail;

    public TitledThumbnailComponentEditorDlg()
    {
      InitializeComponent();
    }

    public TitledThumbnailComponentEditorDlg(TitledThumbnail component)
    {
      InitializeComponent();
```

```
    titledThumbnail = component;

    PopulateAlignment();

    cboAlignment.Text = Enum.GetName(typeof(TitleAlignment),
    titledThumbnail.Align);
    textImageTitle.Text = titledThumbnail.Title;
    textLocation.Text = titledThumbnail.ImageInfo.ImageLocation.ToString();
    textPhotographerFullName.Text =
     titledThumbnail.ImageInfo.PhotographerFullName;
    dtpImageTaken.Value = titledThumbnail.ImageInfo.ImageDate;
    textLongImageDesc.Text = titledThumbnail.ImageInfo.ImageLongDescription;
  }

  private void PopulateAlignment()
  {
    foreach (object Align in Enum.GetValues(typeof(TitleAlignment)))
    {
      cboAlignment.Items.Add(Align);
    }
  }

  private void buttonOK_Click(object sender, System.EventArgs e)
  {
    PropertyDescriptorCollection properties =
       TypeDescriptor.GetProperties(titledThumbnail);

    PropertyDescriptor Title = properties["Title"];
    if (Title != null)
    {
      try
      {
        Title.SetValue(titledThumbnail, textImageTitle.Text);
      }
      catch (Exception err)
      {
        MessageBox.Show(this,
           "Problem setting title property: Source:" +
           err.Source + " Message: " + err.Message, "Error",
           MessageBoxButtons.OK, MessageBoxIcon.Error);
      }
    }

    PropertyDescriptor alignment = properties["Align"];
    if (alignment != null)
    {
      try
```

```
  {
    alignment.SetValue(titledThumbnail, Enum.Parse(typeof(TitleAlignment),
    cboAlignment.Text));
  }
  catch (Exception err)
  {
    MessageBox.Show(this, "Problem setting align property: Source:" +
       err.Source + " Message: " + err.Message, "Error",
       MessageBoxButtons.OK, MessageBoxIcon.Error);
  }
}

PropertyDescriptorCollection imageInfoProps =
   TypeDescriptor.GetProperties(titledThumbnail.ImageInfo);

PropertyDescriptor imageDescription = imageInfoProps["ImageLongDescription"];
if (imageDescription != null)
{
  try
  {
    imageDescription.SetValue(titledThumbnail.ImageInfo,
    textLongImageDesc.Text);
  }
  catch (Exception err)
  {
    MessageBox.Show(this,
       "Problem setting image Long Description property: Source:" +
       err.Source + " Message: " + err.Message, "Error",
       MessageBoxButtons.OK, MessageBoxIcon.Error);
  }
}

PropertyDescriptor imageDate = imageInfoProps["ImageDate"];
if (imageDate != null)
{
  try
  {
    imageDate.SetValue(titledThumbnail.ImageInfo, dtpImageTaken.Value);
  }
  catch (Exception err)
  {
    MessageBox.Show(this,
       "Problem setting image date property: Source:" +
       err.Source + " Message: "
       + err.Message, "Error",
       MessageBoxButtons.OK, MessageBoxIcon.Error);
  }
}
```

```
        PropertyDescriptor photographerFullName =
        imageInfoProps["PhotographerFullName"];
        if (photographerFullName != null)
        {
          try
          {
            photographerFullName.SetValue(titledThumbnail.ImageInfo,
            textPhotographerFullName.Text);
          }
          catch (Exception err)
          {
            MessageBox.Show(this,
               "Problem setting photographer's full name property: Source:" +
               err.Source + " Message: " + err.Message, "Error",
               MessageBoxButtons.OK, MessageBoxIcon.Error);
          }
        }

        PropertyDescriptor imageLocation = imageInfoProps["ImageLocation"];
        if (imageLocation != null)
        {
          try
          {
            imageLocation.SetValue(titledThumbnail.ImageInfo,
            imageLocation.Converter.ConvertFrom(
            null, Application.CurrentCulture, textLocation.Text));
          }
          catch (Exception err)
          {
            MessageBox.Show(this,
               "Problem setting image location property: Source:" +
               err.Source + " Message: " + err.Message, "Error",
               MessageBoxButtons.OK, MessageBoxIcon.Error);
          }
        }
      }
    }
  }
```

The first step in the code is to initialize the form's controls with the TitledThumbnail's current values. The string properties ImageTitle, ImageLongDescription, ImageDate, and PhotographerFullName are simple string assignments. Initializing the Location TextBox takes advantage of the functionality provided by the LocationConverter type converter by calling the ToString() method on the Location object to get the customized display of the latitude and longitude. To initialize the Alignment ComboBox with values, we iterate over the custom enumeration TitleAlignment with this code:

```
private void PopulateAlignment()
{
   foreach (object Align in Enum.GetValues(typeof(TitleAlignment)))
   {
      cboAlignment.Items.Add(Align);
   }
}
```

This code sets the current value for Alignment:

```
cboAlignment.Text = Enum.GetName(typeof(TitleAlignment),titledThumbnail.Align);
```

The bulk of the other code in the TitledThumbnailComponentEditorDlg class is the OK button click method. This method starts by gaining a reference to the TitledThumbnail server control object's property collection. Next, for each property we obtain a PropertyDescriptor with code like this:

```
PropertyDescriptor Title = properties["Title"];
```

This code accesses the properties collection to obtain each property. The properties' ImageTitle and TitleAlignment are set by accessing the properties collection as follows:

```
alignment.SetValue(titledThumbnail,Enum.Parse(typeof(TitleAlignment),
cboAlignment.Text));
```

The TitledThumbnail server control contains a complex property of type ImageMetaData. To set these properties, another property collection is obtained for ImageInfo in this code:

```
PropertyDescriptorCollection imageInfoProps =
            TypeDescriptor.GetProperties(titledThumbnail.ImageInfo);
```

ImageLongDescription, ImageDate, and PhotographerFullName are straightforward assignments. For ImageLocation, we simply call ToString() on ImageLocation, which leverages the custom type converter LocationConverter under the covers. That is all the relevant code in the TitledThumbnailComponentEditorDlg class. In the next section, we cover the component editor class that manages the editing dialog box.

The Component Editor Class

The TitledThumbnailComponentEditor class inherits from WindowsFormsComponentEditor and is fairly short. This class overrides a single method named EditComponent, which is the only required override. Listing 11-12 contains the class file for TitledThumbnailComponentEditor.

Listing 11-12. *The TitledThumbnailComponentEditor Class File*

```
using System;
using System.ComponentModel;
using System.ComponentModel.Design;
using System.Windows.Forms;
using System.Windows.Forms.Design;
```

```
namespace ControlsBook2Lib.Ch11.Design
{
   public class TitledThumbnailComponentEditor : WindowsFormsComponentEditor
   {
      public override bool EditComponent(ITypeDescriptorContext context,
      object component, IWin32Window parent)
      {
         if ( !(component is TitledThumbnail) )
         {
            throw new ArgumentException("Must be a TitledThumbnail component",
            "component");
         }

         IServiceProvider serviceProviderSite =  ((TitledThumbnail)component).Site;
         IComponentChangeService changeSrvc = null;

         DesignerTransaction trans = null;
         bool changed = false;

         try
         {
            if (null != serviceProviderSite)
            {
               IDesignerHost designerHost = (IDesignerHost)serviceProviderSite.
               GetService(typeof(IDesignerHost));
               trans = designerHost.CreateTransaction("Property Builder");

               changeSrvc = (IComponentChangeService)serviceProviderSite.
               GetService(typeof(IComponentChangeService));
               if (null  != changeSrvc)
               {
                  try
                  {
                     changeSrvc.OnComponentChanging(
                    (TitledThumbnail)component, null);
                  }
                  catch (CheckoutException err)
                  {
                     if (err == CheckoutException.Canceled)
                        return false;
                     throw err;
                  }
               }
            }
```

```
            try
            {
               TitledThumbnailComponentEditorDlg propertyBuilderForm =
                           new TitledThumbnailComponentEditorDlg(
                           (TitledThumbnail)component);
               if (propertyBuilderForm.ShowDialog(parent) == DialogResult.OK)
               {
                  changed = true;
               }
            }
            finally
            {
               if (changed && (null != changeSrvc))
               {
                  changeSrvc.OnComponentChanged( (TitledThumbnail)component,
                  null, null, null);
               }
            }
         }
         finally
         {
            if (trans != null)
            {
               if (changed)
               {
                  trans.Commit();
               }
               else
               {
                  trans.Cancel();
               }
            }
         }
         return changed;
      }
   }
}
```

EditComponent starts off by ensuring that the component editor it is associated with is a TitledThumbnail server control. Next, EditComponent obtains a reference to the TitledThumbnail component's Site property. Every control has a Site property that is associated with the hosting designer environment, in this case, Visual Studio.

Site is of type ISite, which is an interface that derives from the IServiceProvider interface. IServiceProvider has a GetService method that permits the server control to gain access to design-time services, as described in Table 11-1. In our code, we get two services, one of type IDesignerHost and the other of type IComponentChangeService.

IDesignerHost is used to add and retrieve services available in the design-time environment and handle events related to designer state. IDesignerHost provides support for detecting a designer is loading and managing component and designer transactions. We use IDesignerHost to wrap component editing into a transaction of type DesignerTransaction.

IComponentChangeService permits a designer to receive notifications when components are changed, added, or removed from the design-time environment. We use IComponentChangeService to notify the hosting environment—in this case, Visual Studio—that the component is being edited. Note that this code will cause Visual Studio to want to check out the .aspx page for editing if the .aspx page is under source control:

```
changeSrvc.OnComponentChanging( (TitledThumbnail)component, null);
```

Once EditComponent initiates the DesignerTransaction and notifies Visual Studio that the page is about to be edited, it displays the TitledThumbnailComponentEditorDlg Windows Form. If the user clicks OK to set any changes, this code notifies Visual Studio that the component has changed:

```
changeSrvc.OnComponentChanged( (TitledThumbnail)component, null, null, null);
```

The next step is to either commit or cancel the DesignerTransaction, depending on whether or not the user clicked OK or Cancel on the component editor dialog box. That's it for the TitledThumbnailComponentEditor class.

When the TitledThumbnail server control is selected in the Visual Studio Designer, a Property Builder hyperlink appears at the bottom of the Properties window. Also, if you right-click the TitledThumbnail server control, you will see a context menu item titled with the same text. A custom designer provides this functionality and is the topic of the next section.

Custom Designers

The Designer classes in .NET customize how components in Windows Forms and server controls in ASP.NET appear and behave at design time. You can implement custom designers to perform custom initialization, access design-time services such as template editing, add menu items to context menus, or to adjust the attributes, events, and properties available in a server control.

■ **Note** You can use type converters and UI type editors both at design time and at runtime. You can use designers only at design time.

To associate a custom designer with a control, you apply the DesignerAttribute attribute. This is the code to apply the TitledThumbnailDesigner custom designer to the TitledThumbnail component:

```
Designer(typeof(TitledThumbnailDesigner))
```

All custom designers implement the IDesigner interface and provide customized methods and properties appropriate for the type of designer. IDesigner is a fairly simple interface, as you can see from Table 11-2.

Table 11-2. *IDesigner Interface*

Member	Description
`Component`	Property that holds a reference to the component associated with the designer class
`DoDefaultAction`	Method that executes the default action for the designer class
`Initialize`	Method that initializes the designer instance with its associated component
`Verbs`	Property that references a collection of design-time verbs provided by a designer class

`System.ComponentModel.Design.ComponentDesigner` is the base class for all designers, and it implements the `IDesign` interface. Both Windows Forms and server controls can have designers; however, because of the difference in rendering technologies and architecture, separate base designer classes that inherit from `ComponentDesigner` are required.

`System.Web.UI.Design.ControlDesigner` is the base class for ASP.NET server control designers and is associated with `System.Web.UI.Control`. To implement a custom designer for a server control, you must inherit from `ControlDesigner`. Table 11-3 describes the virtual members that you must implement when you create a custom designer class.

Table 11-3. *Required Overrides for a Custom Designer*

Method	Description
`GetDesignTimeHtml`	This method returns a string that contains the HTML to render the control it is associated with at design time.
`GetEmptyDesignTimeHtml`	This method returns a string that contains the HTML to render when a control has not been configured to render itself. Often, this text contains instructions on how to work with the control.
`GetErrorDesignTimeHtml`	This method returns a string that contains the HTML to render if the design-time parser encounters an error when parsing a control's tag
`.Initialize`	This method is invoked when the designer is initialized and applied to its associated component. This is the place to ensure that the designer has been associated with the correct control type.

The default behavior in `ControlDesigner` for `GetEmptyDesignTimeHtml` is to return the control type and its ID so that controls of the same type can be differentiated. You can customize this text by calling the helper method `CreatePlaceHolderDesignTimeHtml`. You can also use this method to customize the error message returned in `GetErrorDesignTimeHtml`. Otherwise, `ControlDesigner` returns an empty string for the error message.

For `GetDesignTimeHtml`, `ControlDesigner` calls the associated control's `RenderControl` method. For a composite control, this can cause a control to not render any design-time HTML if the control's child control collection, `Controls`, has not been created. We discuss a simple designer that addresses this issue in the next section.

The Control Designer and Designer Verbs

The TitledThumbnail component is a composite control that has a custom control designer associated with it via the DesignerAttribute attribute named TitledThumbnailDesigner. This control designer inherits from ControlDesigner, but with a couple of method overrides to further customize its functionality.

The first override is Initialize, in which we ensure that TitledThumbnailDesigner is associated with a TitledThumbnail component:

```
public override void Initialize(IComponent comp)
{
   if (!(comp is TitledThumbnail))
   {
      throw new
      ArgumentException("Must be a TitledThumbnail component.", "component");
   }
   base.Initialize(comp);
}
```

The next override is GetDesignTimeHtml, in which we customize behavior to display a message that the developer/user should set the ImageUrl property as a helpful tip:

```
public override string GetDesignTimeHtml()
{
   ControlCollection cntrls = ((Control)Component).Controls;
   if (((TitledThumbnail)Component).ImageUrl == "")
   {
      return CreatePlaceHolderDesignTimeHtml(
     "Set ImageUrl to URL of desired thumbnail image.");
   }
   else
   {
      return base.GetDesignTimeHtml();
   }
}
```

When the ImageUrl property is empty for the TitledThumbnail control, it displays the broken link image at design time, as shown in Figure 11-6.

With the override of GetDesignTimeHtml, the design-time view changes to Figure 11-7.

Instead of the broken image display, the developer/user now has a helpful hint as a guide to what the next step is to configure the control.

The final override in TitledThumbnailDesigner is the Verbs property of type DesignerVerbCollection. The Verbs collection is specified in the IDesigner interface as described in Table 11-2. Each designer verb represents a command usually presented to the developer/user by right-clicking the component. Visual Studio also displays designer verbs at the bottom of the Properties window as pointed to by item 4 in Figure 11-2.

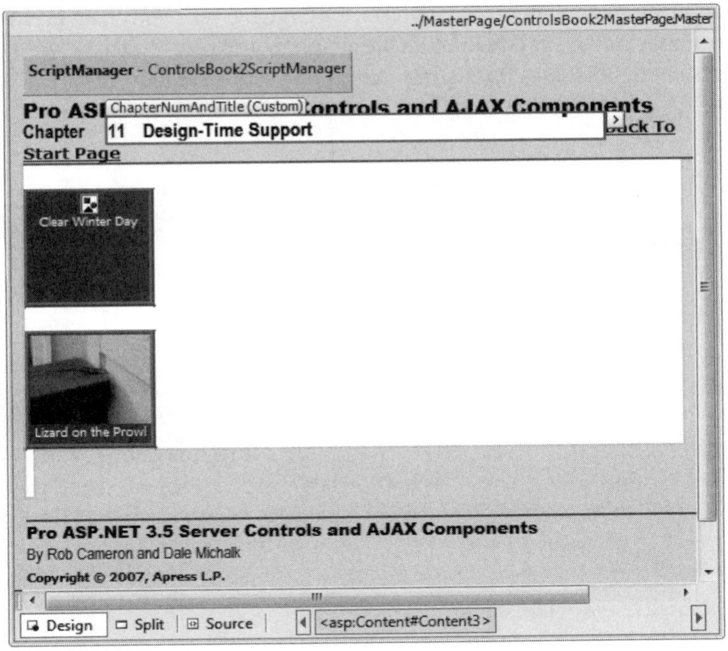

Figure 11-6. *TitledThumbnail at design time without the GetDesignTimeHtml override*

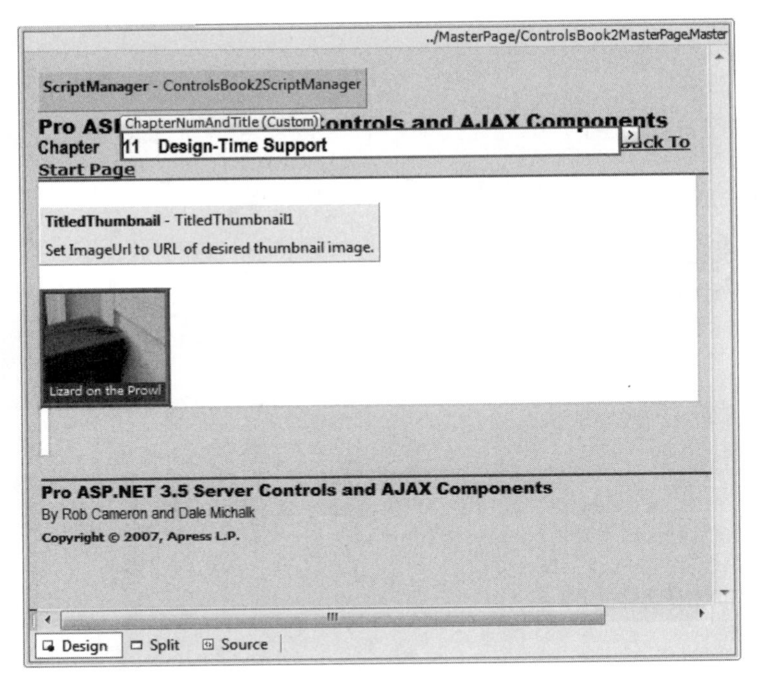

Figure 11-7. *TitledThumbnail at design time with the GetDesignTimeHtml override*

When the developer/user selects a menu item that represents a DesignerVerb object, an event handler associated with the designer verb is fired to execute the action. For TitledThumbnail, we want a menu item that when selected displays its custom component editor as described previously. To implement the desired menu item, we build an event handler to create the component editor UI:

```
private void OnPropertyBuilder(object sender, EventArgs e)
{
   TitledThumbnailComponentEditor TitledThumbnailPropsEditor = new
   TitledThumbnailComponentEditor();
   TitledThumbnailPropsEditor.EditComponent(Component);
}
```

The event handler creates a TitledThumbnailComponentEditor and calls its EditComponent method.

Listing 11-13 provides the source code for TitledThumbnailDesigner. In the listing, you find the override of the Verbs collection where a new DesgnerVerbCollection is created and the Property Builder menu item is added to the collection and associated with the OnPropertyBuilder event handler.

Listing 11-13. *The TitledThumbnailDesigner Class File*

```
using System;
using System.ComponentModel;
using System.ComponentModel.Design;
using System.Web.UI;
using System.Web.UI.Design;

namespace ControlsBook2Lib.Ch11.Design
{
   public class TitledThumbnailDesigner : ControlDesigner
   {
      private DesignerVerbCollection designTimeVerbs;
      public override DesignerVerbCollection Verbs
      {
         get
         {
            if ( null == designTimeVerbs)
            {
               designTimeVerbs = new DesignerVerbCollection();
               designTimeVerbs.Add(new DesignerVerb("Property Builder...",
               new EventHandler(this.OnPropertyBuilder)));
            }
            return designTimeVerbs;
         }
      }
```

```
      private void OnPropertyBuilder(object sender, EventArgs e)
      {
         TitledThumbnailComponentEditor TitledThumbnailPropsEditor =
         new TitledThumbnailComponentEditor();
         TitledThumbnailPropsEditor.EditComponent(Component);
      }

      public override void Initialize(IComponent comp)
      {
         if (!(comp is TitledThumbnail))
         {
            throw new ArgumentException("Must be a TitledThumbnail component.",
            "component");
         }
         base.Initialize(comp);
      }

      public override string GetDesignTimeHtml()
      {
         ControlCollection cntrls = ((Control)Component).Controls;
         if (((TitledThumbnail)Component).ImageUrl == "")
         {
            return CreatePlaceHolderDesignTimeHtml(
          "Set ImageUrl to URL of desired thumbnail image.");
         }
         else
         {
            return base.GetDesignTimeHtml();
         }
      }

      protected override string GetEmptyDesignTimeHtml()
      {
        return CreatePlaceHolderDesignTimeHtml(Component.GetType() + " control.");
      }
   }
}
```

In Chapters 6 and 7, we discussed templates and data binding respectively. In those chapters, we took advantage of a couple of designers to support our templated control, TemplateMenu, and our data-bound control, Repeater. In the next sections, we discuss these designer classes and how they support templates and data binding.

The Templated Control Designer

Earlier in this chapter, we covered the various services that a design-time environment such as Visual Studio can implement via interfaces to enhance the developer experience and reduce development time. One of these services is template editing by implementing the `ITemplateEditingService` service. We take advantage of this service to build a templated control designer.

The templated control `TemplateMenu` supports `Header`, `Separator`, and `Footer` templates. Although these templates can be manually edited by clicking the HTML tab in the Visual Studio Designer, it is also possible to provide a drag-and-drop UI editing interface for template editing, and that is what the `TemplateMenuDesigner` implements for the `TemplateMenu` control. Figure 11-8 shows the editing interface for `TemplateMenu`.

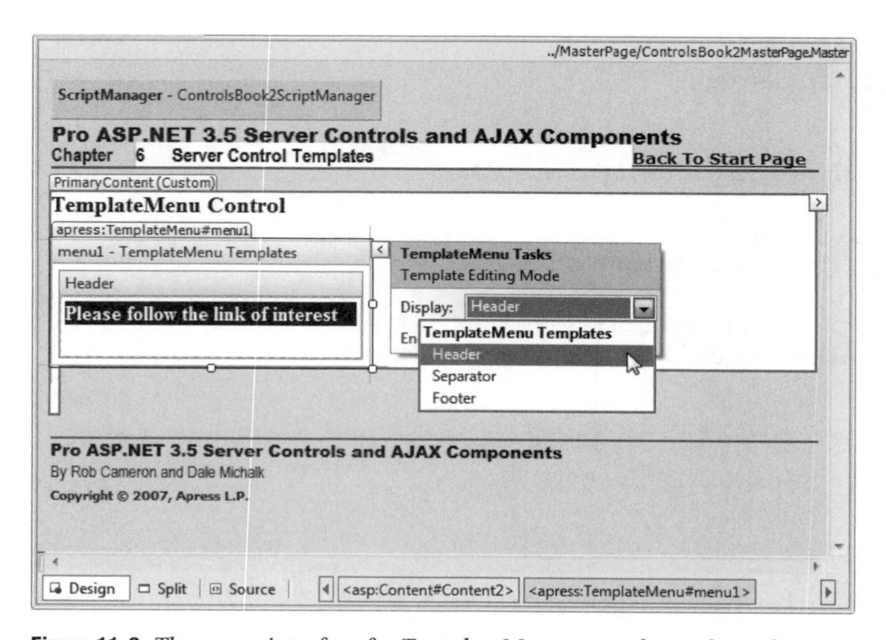

Figure 11-8. *The menu interface for TemplateMenu control template editing*

Figure 11-9 shows the editing UI for the `Separator` template after the developer/user clicks the action arrow at the upper right-hand corner of the control and selects Edit Templates on the `TemplateMenu` control.

The template editing interface allows the developer/user to drag and drop server controls from the Visual Studio Toolbox into the template editing area. The developer/user can also configure the template UI by editing properties such as style in the Properties window.

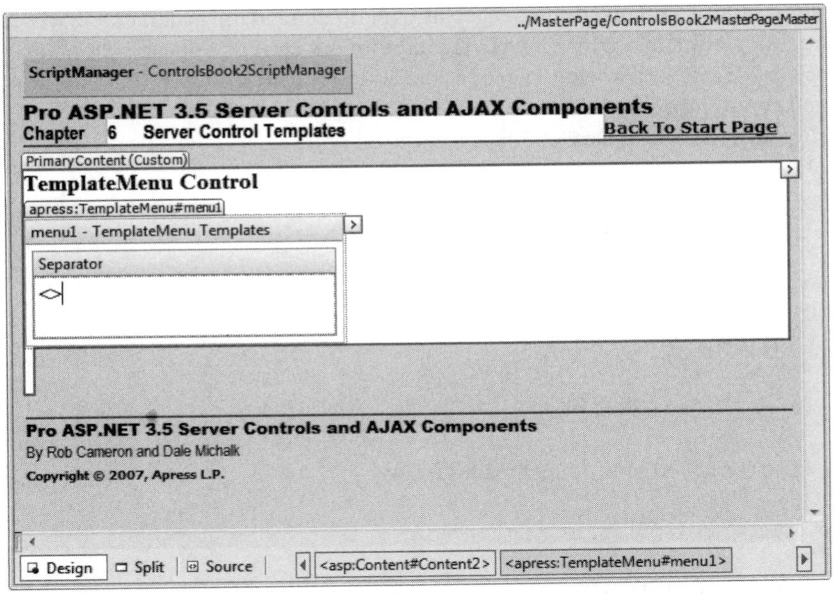

Figure 11-9. *Template editing UI for the TemplateMenu control Separator template*

The base class for `TemplateMenuDesigner` is `TemplatedControlDesigner`. `TemplatedControlDesigner` subclasses `ControlDesigner`, adding the key methods and properties listed in Table 11-4.

Table 11-4. *Key TemplateControl Designer Methods and Properties*

Member	Description
`CreateTemplateEditingFrame`	Creates a frame for template editing according to the specified designer verb selected, as demonstrated in Figure 11-9
`GetCachedTemplateEditingVerbs`	Obtains a reference to the cached verbs of type `TemplateEditingVerb` for template editing
`GetTemplateContent`	Returns the current template's content from the control's child tags in the `.aspx` page
`SetTemplateContent`	Creates a new template instance and sets the template's content to the desired content

As with previous designer classes, we override the `Initialize` method to ensure that the `TemplateMenuDesigner` class is associated with a `TemplateMenu` server control via the `Designer` attribute.

Because template editing is initiated through clicking a menu item on the action menu, we override `TemplateGroups` to return a `TemplateGroupCollection` for our control. For each template, we create a new `TemplateDefinition`, provide it a name, and add it to the `TemplateGroupCollection` object that is returned at the end of method.

Listing 11-14 provides the full source for `TemplateMenuDesigner`.

Listing 11-14. *The TemplateMenuDesigner Source*

```
using System;
using System.ComponentModel;
using System.Web.UI.Design;
using ControlsBook2Lib.Ch06;

namespace ControlsBook2Lib.Ch11.Design
{
  public class TemplateMenuDesigner : ControlDesigner
  {
    TemplateGroupCollection templateGroupCol = null;

    public override void Initialize(IComponent component)
    {
      base.Initialize(component);
      if (!(component is TemplateMenu))
      {
        throw new ArgumentException(
       "Component must be a TemplateMenu control for this custom designer."
          , "component");
      }
      else
      {
        SetViewFlags(ViewFlags.TemplateEditing, true);
      }
    }

    public override TemplateGroupCollection TemplateGroups
    {
      get
      {
        if (templateGroupCol == null)
        {
          // Get the base collection
          templateGroupCol = base.TemplateGroups;

          TemplateGroup templateGroup;
          TemplateDefinition templateDef;
          TemplateMenu ctl;
```

```
      //Get reference to the component as TemplateMenu
      ctl = (TemplateMenu)Component;

      //Create Template Group
      templateGroup = new TemplateGroup("TemplateMenu Templates");

      //Header
      templateDef = new TemplateDefinition(this, "Header",
          ctl, "HeaderTemplate", false);
      templateGroup.AddTemplateDefinition(templateDef);

      //Separator
      templateDef = new TemplateDefinition(this, "Separator",
           ctl, "SeparatorTemplate", false);
      templateGroup.AddTemplateDefinition(templateDef);

      //Footer
      templateDef = new TemplateDefinition(this, "Footer",
          ctl, "FooterTemplate", false);
      templateGroup.AddTemplateDefinition(templateDef);

      // Add the TemplateGroup to the TemplateGroupCollection
      templateGroupCol.Add(templateGroup);
    }

    return templateGroupCol;
  }
}

public override string GetDesignTimeHtml()
{
  //Return configuraiton instructions if no templates are set.
  if ((null == ((TemplateMenu)Component).HeaderTemplate) &&
     (null == ((TemplateMenu)Component).SeparatorTemplate) &&
     (null == ((TemplateMenu)Component).FooterTemplate))
  {
    return CreatePlaceHolderDesignTimeHtml(
    "Click here and use the task menu to edit  TemplateMenu Header,
    Footer, and Seperator template properties. " +
     "<br>A default template is used at run-time if the separator Template is
    not specified at design-time." +
     "<br>The Header and Footer templates are optional.");
  }
```

```
      //return configured html
      string designTimeHtml = String.Empty;
      try
      {
        ((TemplateMenu)Component).DataBind();
        designTimeHtml = base.GetDesignTimeHtml();
      }
      catch (Exception e)
      {
        designTimeHtml = GetErrorDesignTimeHtml(e);
      }
      return designTimeHtml;
    }

    protected override string GetErrorDesignTimeHtml(Exception e)
    {

      return CreatePlaceHolderDesignTimeHtml(
   "There was an error rendering the TemplateMenu control." +
          "<br>Exception: " + e.Source + "  Message: " + e.Message);
    }

    public override bool AllowResize
    {
      get
      {
        bool templateExists = null != ((TemplateMenu)Component).HeaderTemplate ||
                              null != ((TemplateMenu)Component).SeparatorTemplate ||
                              null != ((TemplateMenu)Component).FooterTemplate;
        return templateExists || InTemplateMode;
      }
    }
  }
}
```

The Data-Bound Control Designer

So far, we have built custom control designers to assist server controls with rendering at design time, to customize the context menu, to launch a custom property editor, and to demonstrate visual template editing for controls that support templates. Our next example includes some of those features, but the main focus is on interacting with other controls on the design surface to connect with design-time data sources.

In general, custom data-bound control designer classes inherit from `DataBoundControlDesigner`, which is what our `Repeater` control's designer `RepeaterDesigner` inherits. Not all data-bound controls inherit from `DataBoundControlDesigner`; they may instead inherit from `ControlDesigner` to gain additional control with added responsibilities. Data-bound controls that inherit from `ControlDesigner` directly may implement the `IDataSourceProvider` interface if a `DataMember` or `DataField` property is supported on the targeted server control for which the control designer needs to provide support. In our case, we found that the `DataBoundControlDesigner` base class proved more than adequate and reduced the amount of code required to provide design-time support. We strongly recommend looking first at the customized designer bases classes available in the .NET Framework 2.0 or later when adding design-time support in your own server controls.

The IDataSourceProvider Interface

`IDataSourceProvider` is an interface for control designers to use to provide access to a data source at design time when the server control requires design-time support for `DataMember` or `DataField`. The base designer class `DataBoundControlDesigner` implements this interface for you in inheriting from that base class. Table 11-5 lists the members of `IDataSourceProvider` and provides a short description of each.

Table 11-5. *IDataSourceProvider Members*

Member	Description
`GetResolvedSelectedDataSource`	Obtains a reference to the selected member or data table for the selected `DataSource` identified in `GetSelectedDataSource`.
`GetSelectedDataSource`	Obtains a reference to the selected data source. This method is called when a `DataSource` is selected in the design-time environment for the control.

`GetSelectedDataSource` provides access to design-time data sources such as a `DataSet` component through design-time services. `GetResolvedSelectedDataSource` is the place where component developers implementing a custom data-bound control designer class can provide support for objects that implement `IListSource` (i.e., `DataSet`), which can contain multiple objects that implement `IEnumerable` (i.e., `DataTable`), mapping the selected `IEnumerable` object to the `DataMember` property for the server control. See Chapter 6 for more information on data binding.

The RepeaterDesigner Class

The `Repeater` server control in Chapter 7 works just fine at runtime and is able to data bind with all the expected data containers, including `DataSet`. However, without the `RepeaterDesigner` associated with it via the `DesignerAttribute`, the `Repeater` control is not able to data bind to a design-time data source such as a `DataSet`.

Before we discuss `RepeaterDesigner`, we should mention that there are a couple of things you must set on the `Repeater` class itself to make sure the design-time functionality works correctly. The first item is to override the `DesignerSerializationVisibility` attribute for the `DataSource` property on the `Repeater` control and change it to `DesignerSerializationVisibility.Hidden`. This causes the `DataSource` property to persist on the `.aspx` page like this:

```
<apress:repeater ... " DataSource="<%# dataSetEmp %>" ...>
```

The other item is to ensure that this event is fired in the PerformSelect method override in the Repeater class:

```
OnDataBinding(System.EventArgs.Empty);
```

If this event is not fired in the Repeater class's PerformSelect method, the Repeater server control will not data bind to the design-time data source at runtime. An exception is not thrown. The Repeater simply renders blank, as if a DataSource was not set. With these items out of the way, we can now move on to our discussion of the RepeaterDesigner custom designer class.

The RepeaterDesigner class enables our Repeater to "see" DataSet objects at design time and bind to any available DataSet objects, displaying the data at runtime. The RepeaterDesigner also provides a design-time UI for the Repeater. Listing 11-15 provides the source for RepeaterDesigner.

Listing 11-15. *The RepeaterDesigner Class File*

```
using System;
using System.ComponentModel;
using System.Web.UI.Design;
using System.Web.UI.Design.WebControls;
using ControlsBook2Lib.Ch07;

namespace ControlsBook2Lib.Ch11.Design
{
  class RepeaterDesigner : DataBoundControlDesigner
  {
    TemplateGroupCollection templateGroupCol = null;

    public override void Initialize(IComponent component)
    {
      base.Initialize(component);
      if (!(component is ControlsBook2Lib.Ch07.Repeater))
      {
        throw new ArgumentException(
            "Component must be a ControlsBook2Lib.Ch06.
             Repeater control for this custom designer."
           , "component");
      }
      else
      {
        SetViewFlags(ViewFlags.TemplateEditing, true);
      }
    }

    public override System.Web.UI.Design.TemplateGroupCollection TemplateGroups
    {
      get
      {
```

```
    if (templateGroupCol == null)
    {
      // Get the base collection
      templateGroupCol = base.TemplateGroups;

      TemplateGroup templateGroup;
      TemplateDefinition templateDef;
      Repeater ctl;

      //Get reference to the component as Repeater
      ctl = (Repeater)Component;

      //Create Template Group
      templateGroup = new TemplateGroup("Repeater Templates");

      //Header
      templateDef = new TemplateDefinition(this, "Header",
          ctl, "HeaderTemplate", false);
      templateGroup.AddTemplateDefinition(templateDef);

      //Separator
      templateDef = new TemplateDefinition(this, "Separator",
          ctl, "SeparatorTemplate", false);
      templateGroup.AddTemplateDefinition(templateDef);

      ////Item
      //templateDef = new TemplateDefinition(this, "Item",
      //    ctl, "ItemTemplate", false);
      //templateGroup.AddTemplateDefinition(templateDef);

      ////Alternating Item
      //templateDef = new TemplateDefinition(this, "Alternating Item",
      //    ctl, "AlternatingItemTemplate", false);
      //templateGroup.AddTemplateDefinition(templateDef);

      //Footer
      templateDef = new TemplateDefinition(this, "Footer",
          ctl, "FooterTemplate", false);
      templateGroup.AddTemplateDefinition(templateDef);

      // Add the TemplateGroup to the TemplateGroupCollection
      templateGroupCol.Add(templateGroup);
    }
    return templateGroupCol;
  }
}
```

```
    public override string GetDesignTimeHtml()
    {
      //Return configuraiton instructions if no templates are set.
      if ((null == ((Repeater)Component).HeaderTemplate) &&
         (null == ((Repeater)Component).SeparatorTemplate) &&
         (null == ((Repeater)Component).ItemTemplate) &&
         (null == ((Repeater)Component).AlternatingItemTemplate) &&
         (null == ((Repeater)Component).FooterTemplate))
      {
        return CreatePlaceHolderDesignTimeHtml("Click here and use
            the task menu to edit Repeater Header, Footer, and
            Seperator template properties. " +
         "<br>A default template is used at run-time if the separator Template is
                  not specified at design-time." +
         "<br>The Header and Footer templates are optional.");
      }

      //return configured html
      string designTimeHtml = String.Empty;
      try
      {
        ((Repeater)Component).DataBind();
        designTimeHtml = base.GetDesignTimeHtml();
      }
      catch (Exception e)
      {
        designTimeHtml = GetErrorDesignTimeHtml(e);
      }
      return designTimeHtml;
    }

    public override bool AllowResize
    {
      get
      {
        bool templateExists =
             null !=((Repeater)Component).HeaderTemplate ||
             null != ((Repeater)Component).SeparatorTemplate ||
              null != ((Repeater)Component).FooterTemplate;
        return templateExists || InTemplateMode;
      }
    }
  }
}
```

Since RepeaterDesigner inherits from DataBoundControlDesigner, a lot of functionality such as managing the DataSource and DataMember properties, is handled automatically. We do not have to worry about manually populating these properties at design time so that they list any design-time data sources that are available on the web form.

The DesignTimeData Class

The .NET Framework's built-in `DesignTimeData` class provides helper methods for control developers implementing data-bound control designers. It is used to create design-time sample and dummy data. In the previous edition of this book, which targeted .NET Framework 1.1, we had to custom implement creating design-time sample and dummy data ourselves. In .NET Framework 2.0 or later, the `DataBoundControlDesigner` base class takes care of this automatically, but it is important to understand where the design-time data comes from in case you must create your own custom `ControlDesigner`.

Miscellaneous Design-Time Items

In this section, we tie up a couple of loose ends with respect to design-time support and development.

The Toolbox Icon

It is possible to provide a custom bitmap for the Toolbox icon for a custom server control. Simply add a 16×16 pixel bitmap to the custom server control's project and give it the same name as the component. The next step is to set its Build Action to Embedded Resource by right-clicking the image and expanding Advanced. Under Advanced, change the value for Build Action to Embedded Resource.

Next, apply the `ToolboxBitmapAttribute` attribute to the control's class. First, add a reference to `System.Drawing`, which is the namespace where this attribute exists. The name of the resource is the name of the bitmap file. For a control named `MyControl` and a bitmap named `MyControl.bmp`, the attribute looks like this:

```
[ToolboxBitmap(typeof(MyControl), "MyControl.bmp")]
```

The constructor we use here takes the type for the `MyControl` server control and looks for an embedded resource named `MyControl.bmp`. When the control is added to the Visual Studio Toolbox, it will display the custom bitmap instead of the default cog bitmap.

Debugging Design-Time Development

It is not possible to fully debug design-time code with a single instance of Visual Studio. With a single instance of Visual Studio, it is only possible to perform basic testing for design-time code. For example, to see if a custom designer renders the correct design-time HTML, you can create a custom designer class, apply the `Designer` attribute to the server control, recompile, and then flip to the test page hosting the desired server control to get a thumbs-up/thumbs-down judgment.

To fully debug design-time code with breakpoints, stepping through code, and so on, you must start up a second instance of Visual Studio and open the same project in the second instance of Visual Studio. Next, open the design-time code—for example, `RepeaterDesigner`—and set the desired breakpoints in one instance of Visual Studio. In the instance of Visual Studio with

RepeaterDesigner opened, select the Debug ➤ Processes menu item to display the Processes dialog box. Listed there is the other instance of devenv.exe, the filename for Visual Studio.

Then, you can either double-click devenv.exe or select devenv.exe and click Attach to display the Attach to Process dialog box. In this box, you just check Common Language Runtime. You should generally do this unless you have a need to select the other debugging program types. This speeds things up a bit. Next, click OK and then Close. You should now see the debug toolbar open with the Break All and Stop Debugging buttons enabled.

Now, you are ready to flip to the other instance of Visual Studio that is currently running under the debugger. In this example, if you bring up the Chapter 7 DataBoundRepeater.aspx sample test page and manipulate one of the Repeater controls at design-time, you hit the breakpoint that you set in the other instance of Visual Studio, and you can step through code.

■ **Tip** To quickly figure out which instance of Visual Studio is debugging and which instance is being debugged in the Windows taskbar, click the program group to display both instances of Visual Studio. The instance that has [run] in its caption is the instance that is debugging. The instance that has [design] in its caption is the instance being debugged.

Note that if you attempt to rebuild the project while running multiple instances of Visual Studio, you will get the following error message in the Output window in Visual Studio:

```
Cannot copy assembly 'ControlsBookLib' to file
'c:\ControlsBook\bin\ControlsBookLib.dll'.  The process cannot access the file
because it is being used by another process.
```

To make changes and rebuild the project, close the project in one of the instances of Visual Studio, make the desired changes, and then reopen the project in the second instance to begin debugging again.

Summary

Controls, as opposed to just working with a class in code, exist for the purpose of enhancing the development environment experience and speeding up development time. The .NET Framework provides design-time customizations for both Windows controls and web controls. The customizations available in each environment differ mostly as a result of rendering technology, with web controls generating HTML and Windows controls rendering using GDI+. Design-time customizations for controls are applied to a server control class through attributes primarily from the System.ComponentModel and System.Web.UI.Design namespaces.

The .NET Framework design-time environment services extend the capabilities and level of integration with a designer such as Visual Studio. To obtain a service, the Component class implements IServiceProvider, which has a method named GetService that can be used to obtain a reference.

Custom designers manage the UI and behavior of a component at design time. Customizations include changing the component's appearance, initialization, and interaction on the Component Designer surface.

Type converters are generally implemented for control properties that are not readily converted to the `string` type. Type converters are also implemented for types that include subproperties such as the expand/collapse UI for the `Font` property.

A UI type editor can provide a custom user interface for editing property values. It displays a custom representation of a property at design time. UI type editors are type specific.

Type converters and UI type editors can be used both at design time and at runtime, whereas designers can be used only at design time.

CHAPTER 12

Building a Complex Control

At this point in the book, we have covered all the major concepts in developing server controls. In this chapter and the next, we bring these concepts together and develop a powerful custom server control from the ground up to illustrate the techniques put forth in this book. This server control programmatically interacts with the Live Search web APIs to provide a nice package that can be dropped into an ASP.NET application to provide search functionality. We hope that it provides a useful example and framework for building your own custom server controls and serves as a useful addition to your server control toolkit.

We break into two chapters our discussion of our complex control to keep things manageable, as there is a lot of functionality to cover. In this chapter, we focus on the following aspects of our complex control:

- Understanding the Live Search web API
- Working with web services in server controls
- Using the global assembly cache (GAC) and strong-named assemblies
- Using configuration files
- Integrating the custom web service proxy class
- Designing the Live Search control architecture

In the next section, we dive into a discussion of the Live Search API and web service.

The Problem Domain

The Live Search web site provides access to search engine services that let users search its store of several billion URLs. To open this store to programmatic searches, Live Search provides a web service API to search the information store from code. Our task in this and the next chapter is to demonstrate how to build a suite of server controls that make it easy to consume the search feature of Live Search and make it simple to incorporate into an ASP.NET web application. Here's a summary list of the requirements for our control project:

- Completely handle all web services communications with the Live Search web service.
- Provide the ability to either use the Live Search web service or redirect queries to the Live Search web site directly.

- Display a text box and button to gather search input from the end user.
- Display both the status information and the list of search results from the search query.
- Provide the Live Search look and feel out of the box while supporting complete UI customization.
- Provide the ability localize the look and feel.
- Handle paging through the search results.
- Provide the ability to reconfigure the control without recompiling the control.
- Provide the ability to license access to the control.

The Live Search Web Service

Our first step when working with the Live Search web service is to understand what parameters we need to provide it and the data stream it returns. Live Search helps in this effort by providing a downloadable API from `http://dev.live.com` that provides documentation and sample code for invoking the Live Search service. Figure 12-1 shows the getting started page for the Live Search web service.

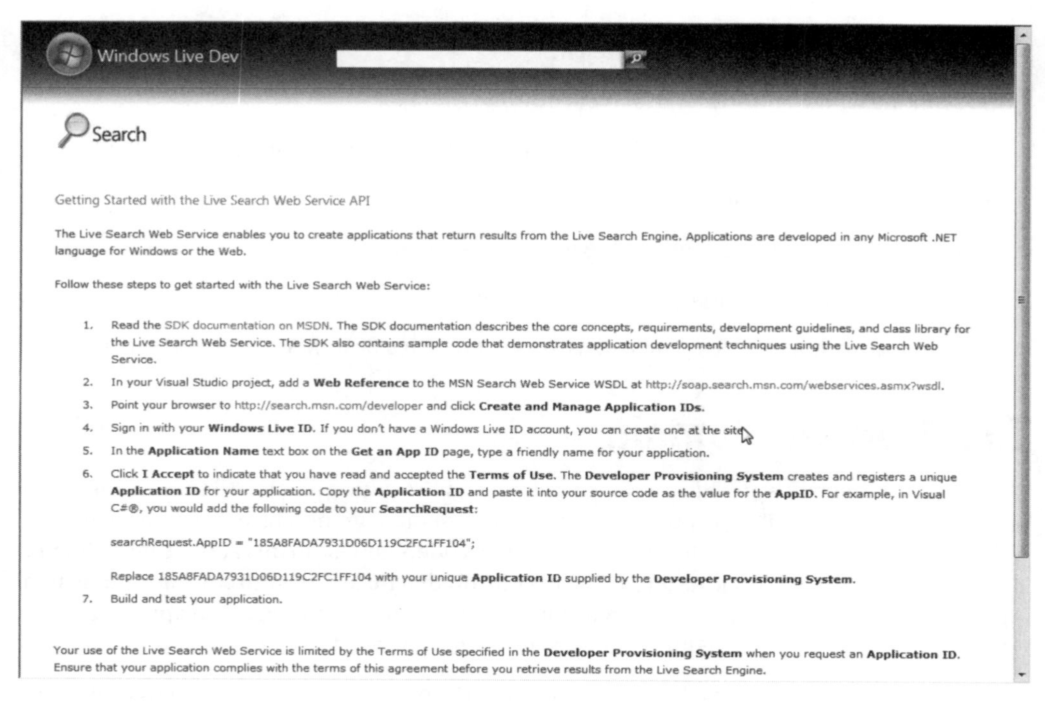

Figure 12-1. *The Live Search web service's getting started page*

In Figure 12-1, you can see that three steps are involved in using the Live Search service:

1. Add a web reference to the MSN Search Web Service WSDL.
2. Create a Live Search Application ID to gain access to the Live Search web API service.
3. Write code to access the Live Search Web API service.

It is a good idea to read the SDK documentation on MSDN as well as download the samples at `http://dev.live.com`. The second item, getting an application ID through Live Search's Create and Manage Application IDs, is a mandatory step, because the Live Search web APIs service requires authentication. The final step, programmatically accessing the Live Search web APIs service, is what the example code and discussion in this and the next chapter cover.

Web Services Description Language and .NET Web Service Proxies

Web services are described in full detail through Web Services Description Language (WSDL) files. WSDL files provide information on what XML is sent over the wire to communicate with the web service, and they also determine the protocol bindings and addressing information for the web service. The WSDL is available at this link:

```
http://soap.search.msn.com/webservices.asmx?wsdl
```

Because this is a book about building custom server controls, we do not examine the gory details of the XML contents of the WSDL file. Plenty of .NET web services books are available that cover that topic in depth. Instead, we show you how you can turn the WSDL file into a .NET class that handles the grunge work of working with XML and invoking the Live Search web service over the network.

One approach is to use the built-in Add Web Reference feature that comes with Visual Studio. This feature provides an automated way of generating the proxy code and is the tool most developers are familiar with. All developers have to do is click through a set of menus to browse to the WSDL file, and the proxy code is created behind the scenes.

In Visual Studio 2008 and .NET Framework 3.5, a new built-in feature called Add Service Reference generates a class proxy based on Windows Communication Foundation (WCF), which was first available in .NET Framework 3.0.

Windows Communication Foundation unifies Microsoft's various distributing technologies, such as remoting, ASMX Web Services, COM+, MSMQ, and WSE, into a single programming model. The programming model is focused on contract-first development, with .NET attributes available to decorate `Interface` and `class` to customize functionality. The actual protocol, such as remoting versus web services, can be applied via the `System.ServiceModel` configuration section in an application configuration file or in code.

While our preference is to use configuration files as much as possible for WCF development, we cannot count on the availability of a configuration file, nor do we want to burden the developer user with manually adding the configuration XML in an application configuration file to support making web service calls via WCF in the `Search` custom server control. Therefore, we programmatically create the necessary binding and channel to communicate with the Live Search service.

Instead of using the Add Service Reference functionality in Visual Studio 2008, we take a different route for our server control, because we want more predictability in the generated code, and we want to make changes to it without worrying about the changes being overridden by an automated process. For WCF, we use the command-line utility named `svcutil.exe` from a Visual Studio 2008 command prompt to generate a proxy class for the Live Search web service that is similar in its code-generation capabilities to the Add Web Reference tool in Visual Studio.

Make sure you use the command prompt that comes with Visual Studio or make sure the binary `wsdl.exe` file is in your path before you try the following command on the Live Search `SearchSearch.wsdl` description file:

```
svcutil.exe http://soap.search.msn.com/webservices.asmx?wsdl
/out:LiveSearchSearchService.cs /config:test.config
```

`Svcutil.exe` takes the provided WSDL and produces a proxy class file named Live Search `SearchSearchService.cs` in the same directory where the tool was run. Live Service `SearchSearch.cs` encapsulates the web service into a programmatically easy-to-use package. Notice that we also configure it to output a configuration file, so that we can take a quick look at the required configuration to help us write the programmatic code to achieve the same results.

At a later point in time, we will copy the code from the generated proxy class to our web control library project to add the necessary web service support for the server controls. If you peer inside the code file, you can see the various classes that communicate with the web service. You can also see the main web service method, `MSNSearchPortType.Search`, which we will invoke to perform searches with the Live Search web service. The code for `doLiveSearchSearch` is as follows:

```
EndpointAddress liveSearchAddress =
         new EndpointAddress(LiveSearchWebServiceUrl);
      BasicHttpBinding binding = new BasicHttpBinding();
      ChannelFactory<MSNSearchPortType> channelFactory =
        new ChannelFactory<MSNSearchPortType>(binding, liveSearchAddress);

      MSNSearchPortType searchService = channelFactory.CreateChannel();
      SearchRequest searchRequest = new SearchRequest();

      //Set mark query word.  Allows developer to highlight as desired
      searchRequest.Flags = SearchFlags.DisableHostCollapsing |
      SearchFlags.MarkQueryWords;
      searchRequest.Query = query;
      if (sourceRequests != null)
        searchRequest.Requests = sourceRequests;

      searchRequest.AppID = LiveSearchLicenseKey;
      searchRequest.CultureInfo = "en-US";

      SearchResponse searchResponse = searchService.Search(searchRequest);

      return searchResponse;
```

The internal implementation is not as important as understanding the types that are passed into the web service. The Search method takes a SearchRequest object as its sole parameter, which is configured with the search query string on its Query property. The SearchRequest object has a Requests property that takes an ArrayList of one or more SourceRequest objects. Each SourceRequest represents a search query, so it is possible to perform multiple searches in a single web service method call on MSNSearchPortType.Search. Configuring the SourceRequest object is the first step in performing a search request. Table 12-1 provides an explanation of the properties that can be configured on a SourceRequest object.

Table 12-1. *Properties Available for the SourceRequest Object*

Parameter	Type	Description
Count	Integer	Specifies the number of results to return
Offset	Integer	Specifies the offset from the starting point of the search that should be returned
Source	Enum	Object representing one or more sources listed in the SourceType enumeration
SearchTagFilters	string[]	Restricts the list of search tags returned by a query without otherwise affecting the results of the search
FileType	String	Specifies the type of files (.doc, .pdf, etc.) returned for a search
SortBy	Enum	Specifies the sort order of results returned from a PhoneBook SourceType search
ResultFields	Enum	Specifies the results fields returned in the result set based on the ResultFieldMask enumeration

Once one or more SourceRequest objects are configured, the array of SourceRequest objects is assigned to the SearchRequest.Request property. The other important properties on the SearchRequest class are CultureInfo, Query, and AppID. The CultureInfo property determines the Language and locale information for the search request and is a required parameter. The Query property represents the search criteria used by the Live Search service to look for matches and their URLs. The AppID parameter is the application ID that authenticates requests and allows access to the web service. You obtain an application ID by requesting one from Live Search at http://dev.live.com. Other parameters of interest that are part of our custom server control include the Flags property that accepts the enumeration type of SearchFlags to mark query terms with a nonprintable character, disable spell checking for special words, and disable host collapsing for multiple results for the same domain. The default Flags value is SearchFlags.None. Once the SearchRequest object is configured, it is passed in as the sole parameter to the MSNSearchPortType.Search method. Figure 12-2 shows this concept graphically. For a given search represented by the SearchRequest.Query property, each call to the web service requests a number of entries identified by Count, starting at the position in the result set identified by the SourceRequest.Offset parameter. We use these parameters to calculate a sliding window that pages through the search results with the page size equaling SourceRequest.Count, or less if it is the last page. So, based on the SourceRequest.Offset and SourceRequest.Count, we can calculate the start index and end index for the sliding window of search results displayed by the server control.

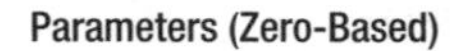

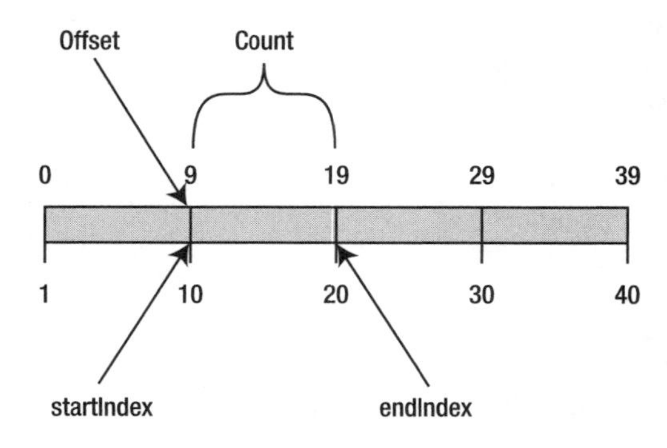

Figure 12-2. *The Live Search service paging results*

The result set returned from the doMSNSearchPortType.Search method is of type SearchResponse. The SearchResponse class contains a single property Responses, which is an array of one or more SourceResponse objects. The number of returned SourceResponse objects corresponds to the number of SourceRequest queries passed in as part of calling the MSNSearchPortType.Search method. All of the interesting information is contained in the SourceResponse class, which is described in Table 12-2.

Table 12-2. *The SourceResponse Class*

Parameter	Type	Description
Offset	integer	The actual zero-based offset returned for the search query
Results	LiveSearchService.Result	Array of returned results for the search query
Source	Enum	Represents the information source based on the SourceType enumeration
Total	integer	Estimate of the total number of results returned for the search query

While there isn't a start index or end index, these values can easily be calculated using the SourceResponse.Offset and SourceResponse.Total.

The actual results are in the Results ArrayList of Result items. The Result class holds the pertinent information for each URL match that was made against a search query. Table 12-3 lists the Result class's fields.

As you can see after reviewing Table 12-3, many types of searches are available via Live Search, such as a location, phonebook, or news search. For this example, we focus on returning a single web search result based on a query, but the example server controls could be extended to allow additional search customization. Please refer to the MSDN Live Search documentation for more information.

Table 12-3. *Live Search Web Service Result Object's Fields*

Field	Type	Description
Address	Address	Has a value of type Address if performing a PhoneBook SourceType search
CachedURL	string	Returns the URL to the cached version of the page
DateTime	DateTime	Returns a DateTime object containing the date and time the page was last indexed by the search engine
Description	string	Returns the description text for the search result
URL	string	Returns the URL for the search result
Location	Location	Returns the Location object associated with a PhoneBook or QueryLocation search
Phone	string	Returns the phone number as part of a PhoneBook search
Source	string	Returns the Source of a news or Encarta article search
Title	string	Returns the title for the search query
URL	string	Absolute path to the URL that matches the query

We don't dive into a discussion of the automatically generated service proxy, because it isn't pertinent to server control development. Likewise, we don't show the listing in this chapter, because it is all automatically generated code. Please see the code download for this book to peruse the LiveSearchService.cs automatically generated service proxy class file.

For additional information on WCF and calling web services, the MSDN documentation at http://msdn.microsoft.com provides many great resources including the documentation, articles, walkthroughs, and virtual labs. In the next section, we begin our discussion of building the custom server controls around the Live Search service.

Creating the Control Library Project

The first step in creating a control library is to ensure we have a well-organized namespace to identify and partition our controls from the rest of the control universe. A common paradigm for selecting such a namespace is to put business entities or organizations first, followed by a product or project title, followed by significant divisions within the actual product. For the Live Search web service control, we will use a namespace of ControlsBook2Lib.CH12.LiveSearchControls to follow the pattern used throughout this book. We give the Visual Studio project the same name (ControlsBook2Lib.CH12.LiveSearchControls), and we give the control assembly the output name of ControlsBook2Lib.CH12.LiveSearchControls.dll. Keeping the namespace and the assembly name in sync like this is not a requirement, but it is a good design guideline to follow because it is mimicked by system DLLs, such as System.Web.dll, that are part of the .NET Framework.

Strong-Named Assemblies and Versioning Attributes

After we decide on a namespace for our control project, the next step is to decide what sort of versioning policy we want to apply to it. We have two main options:

- Manually version code by releasing weak-named assemblies with documentation and hope consumers use the correct version.
- Take advantage of the built-in versioning in .NET available to strong-named assemblies, which ensures that the correct version of code is being used and provides a flexible policy for upgrade scenarios.

Although the process of taking a standard or weak-named assembly and converting it to a strong-named assembly isn't instant, it is pretty simple to do. Right-click the project in Solution Explorer, and select Properties. Click the Signing tab, and check the "Sign the assembly" box. In the "Choose a strong name key file" drop-down, select New to create a strong name key file in the project directory and update the project to ensure the generated assembly is signed.

To set the assembly version, open the project's properties, and click the Assembly Information button on the Application tab to fill in the assembly version, file version, title, and company information.

The final piece of information needed for making a strong-named assembly is the culture. The recommended culture setting for a primary assembly is the invariant culture, or a culture name with a blank string. This is achieved by leaving the default value of Neutral Language to (None) on the Assembly Information dialog. We discuss in depth how this setting impacts localization in the next chapter in the "Globalization and Localization" section.

At this point, we have specified full versioning information: name, public key, version, and culture. Clients that use our control will have metadata references using this strong name, and any changes to something (e.g., the version number) will cause a break in compatibility. Because of this, care should be taken when introducing bug fixes or new versions of a control library that supersede old versions. For more information on how to manage breaking changes, please see the .NET Framework SDK documentation.

Bin Directory or Global Assembly Cache Deployment

Once we have compiled the control library with a strong name, we can install it in either the bin directory of a web site or in the GAC, which is the .NET Framework–versioned code store. The GAC provides for ease of installation and reuse if several web applications need the same control library on a machine.

Regardless of the location of deployment for a strong-named assembly, we recommend that you provide strong-named controls for ease of versioned updates and the side-by-side deployment capabilities they provide in .NET. Both have the potential to significantly improve the reliability of web applications and ease the maintenance burden on the web administrator.

The strong-named assembly has built-in tamper-proof features, as we alluded to earlier. During the build process for the assembly, the compiler performs a hash on the contents of the assembly to create a digital signature. The public key information is also stored inside the assembly, so it can be verified by the runtime when it loads the assembly or when it is installed in the GAC. Any file tampering will cause an assembly load failure.

GAC installation provides a performance advantage over putting a strong-named assembly in the bin directory of the ASP.NET web application, because the verification process happens only once when the strong-named assembly is installed. If a strong-named assembly is loaded from an application's bin directory, the verification takes place each time on assembly load into an application.

Additional Assembly Attributes

As mentioned previously, additional information on the control library, such as the title, description, company, and so on, can be configured by going to project properties and clicking the Assembly Information button on the Application tab. To help out the Toolbox support of a web control, we recommend adding the `TagPrefixAttribute` at the assembly level. Here we use the `ControlsBook2Lib.LiveSearchControls` namespace and default to `ApressLive` as the prefix to put in front of our tags when they are used in an `.aspx` page:

```
// configure the tag/namespace to be used in the toolbox
[assembly: TagPrefix("ControlsBook2Lib.LiveSearchControls ","ApressLive") ]
```

Another useful attribute to have in your `AssemblyInfo.cs` file is the `CLSCompliantAttribute` class set to `true`. This ensures that all Common Language Specification (CLS)–compliant languages can work seamlessly with your code. This attribute causes the compiler to generate a warning if a public non-CLS-compliant member is present. Think of it as a safety net that keeps you from doing things that would make your control incompatible with its consumers. The final list of attributes in the `AssemblyInfo.cs` file is shown in Listing 12-1.

Listing 12-1. *The AssemblyInfo.cs Class File*

```
using System;
using System.Reflection;
using System.Runtime.CompilerServices;
using System.Web.UI;
using System.Runtime.InteropServices;

// General Information about an assembly is controlled through the following
// set of attributes. Change these attribute values to modify the information
// associated with an assembly.
[assembly: AssemblyTitle("ControlsBook2Lib.CH12.LiveSearchControls")]
[assembly: AssemblyDescription("Live Search Sample ASP.NET Controls")]
[assembly: AssemblyConfiguration("")]
[assembly: AssemblyCompany("Apress")]
[assembly: AssemblyProduct("ControlsBook2Lib.CH12.LiveSearchControls")]
[assembly: AssemblyCopyright("Copyright © Apress 2007")]
[assembly: AssemblyTrademark("")]
[assembly: AssemblyCulture("")]

// Setting ComVisible to false makes the types in this assembly not visible
// to COM components.  If you need to access a type in this assembly from
// COM, set the ComVisible attribute to true on that type.
[assembly: ComVisible(false)]
```

```
// The following GUID is for the ID of the typelib if this project is exposed to COM
[assembly: Guid("71bf600a-6b3d-458d-8645-bece292bdb03")]

// Version information for an assembly consists of the following four values:
//
//      Major Version
//      Minor Version
//      Build Number
//      Revision
//
[assembly: AssemblyVersion("1.0.0.0")]
[assembly: AssemblyFileVersion("1.0.0.0")]


// configure the tag/namespace to be used in the toolbox
[assembly: TagPrefix("ControlsBook2Lib.LiveSearchControls", "ApressLive")]

// ensure Common Language Specification (CLS) compliance
[assembly: CLSCompliant(true)]
```

Now that we have covered strong-named assemblies and how we implemented them in Live Search, in the next section we discuss how to store and retrieve configuration information using `.config` files.

Configuring the Search Settings

The Live Search search controls need a flexible way to retrieve configuration information that allows them to interact appropriately with the online web service. The following data is required:

- License key to authenticate with the Live Search web service
- URL of the Live Search search web service
- URL of a proxy server in situations in which the code is running behind a firewall

One approach to this sort of problem is hard-coding the configuration setting as string constants inside a control. Although simple in execution, this approach requires unnecessary recompilation steps that could hurt versioning and deployment maintenance of the web applications using the controls. A better approach is to use the XML configuration file mechanisms available to ASP.NET web applications.

Crafting the Configuration Section XML

Because we have several strings we want to use to configure our search controls, we decided to use a custom configuration section. This means we will have our own block of XML that is integrated as part of `web.config`. The following XML snippet is what we want to add to `web.config`:

```
<LiveSearchControls>
  <License
     LiveSearchLicenseKey="XXXXXXXXXXXXXXXXXXXXXXXXXXXXXXXXXXXXXXXX" />
  <Url
     LiveSearchWebServiceUrl="http://soap.search.msn.com:80/webservices.asmx" />
</liveSearchControls>
```

You can use whatever particular format suits your fancy as long as it is well-formed XML. Our custom configuration XML has the two configuration values that we need: LiveSearchLicenseKey and LiveSearchWebServiceUrl. You will need to obtain a valid Live Search license key from http://dev.live.com/livesearch/ and replace the string of Xs in the preceding code with your license key for the Live Search server controls to work properly.

Registering the Configuration Section

Now that we have defined the XML format for our configuration data and the requisite class to provide an object-oriented representation of the XML data, we need a way to tell ASP.NET what we are up to. Our next task is to register a configuration section handler so that ASP.NET can process our custom XML configuration settings when servicing client requests.

The configuration section handler is brought into the picture via an XML section that is added to the top of the web.config file underneath the root-level configuration XML element. configSections is a content-wrapping element that signifies we want to add additional content to the existing configuration sections, as shown here:

```
<sectionGroup name="system.web">
  <section name="liveSearchControls"
   type="ControlsBook2Lib.CH12.LiveSearchControls.LiveSearchConfigSectionHandler,
   ControlsBook2Lib.CH12.LiveSearchControls,
   Version=1.0.0.0, Culture=neutral, PublicKeyToken=9d0e1a77378e3a88" />
</sectionGroup>
```

An interesting read is searching for configSections in the machine.config file that comes with the .NET Framework installation. You can see all of the configuration sections (such as for session state, authorization, and so on) familiar to web developers in this section of the machine.config file.

sectionGroup is used to group configuration section entries to prevent naming conflicts. If you choose an existing sectionGroup name that is already used, the new, custom configSections entry is nested under that configuration element. In our case, we choose to put the Live Search web service data under the system.web elements in the web.config file. We could also have chosen a unique name to be a root-level sectionGroup just as easily.

The final XML element in the preceding snippet, and the one that declares a binding to the code that handles the configuration parsing, is named section. Notice that we give section a name, liveSearchControls, that corresponds to our top-level configuration section XML element. We also have to give it a fully qualified path to the class that implements the configuration section handler functionality, including the means to resolve the assembly containing the code.

Because we strongly named our control library project via the settings in the previously reviewed AssemblyInfo.cs file, we need to produce the name, version, culture, and public key token of the assembly. The easiest way to view this information is to use the shell extension GUI that is installed on a Windows machine along with the rest of the .NET Framework. Browse to the `C:\windows\assembly` folder. This folder has a special shell extension GUI that allows you to enumerate assemblies installed in the GAC, as shown in Figure 12-3.

Locate the assembly, right-click it, and select Properties. This action generates a pop-up dialog box with all the full versioning information of the assembly, as shown in Figure 12-4.

Assembly Name	Version	Cul...	Public Key Token	Processor Architecture
System.Data.OracleClient	2.0.0.0		b77a5c561934e089	x86
System.Data.OracleClient	2.0.0.0		b77a5c561934e089	AMD64
System.Data.SqlServerCe	9.0.242.0		89845dcd8080cc91	MSIL
System.Data.SqlServerCe	3.5.0.0		89845dcd8080cc91	MSIL
System.Data.SqlXml	2.0.0.0		b77a5c561934e089	MSIL
System.Deployment	2.0.0.0		b03f5f7f11d50a3a	MSIL
System.Design	1.0.500...		b03f5f7f11d50a3a	
System.Design	2.0.0.0		b03f5f7f11d50a3a	MSIL
System.DirectoryServices	1.0.500...		b03f5f7f11d50a3a	
System.DirectoryServices	2.0.0.0		b03f5f7f11d50a3a	MSIL
System.DirectoryServices.AccountManage...	3.5.0.0		b77a5c561934e089	MSIL
System.DirectoryServices.Protocols	2.0.0.0		b03f5f7f11d50a3a	MSIL
System.Drawing	1.0.500...		b03f5f7f11d50a3a	
System.Drawing	2.0.0.0		b03f5f7f11d50a3a	MSIL
System.Drawing.Design	1.0.500...		b03f5f7f11d50a3a	
System.Drawing.Design	2.0.0.0		b03f5f7f11d50a3a	MSIL
System.EnterpriseServices	1.0.500...		b03f5f7f11d50a3a	
System.EnterpriseServices	2.0.0.0		b03f5f7f11d50a3a	x86
System.EnterpriseServices	2.0.0.0		b03f5f7f11d50a3a	AMD64
System.IdentityModel	3.0.0.0		b77a5c561934e089	MSIL
System.IdentityModel.Selectors	3.0.0.0		b77a5c561934e089	MSIL

Figure 12-3. *Finding your assembly in the Windows Explorer assembly viewer*

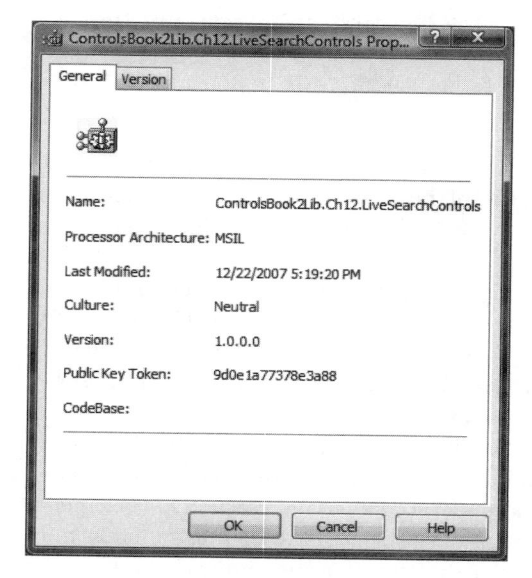

Figure 12-4. *The Properties dialog box from an assembly discovered by the assembly viewer*

Building a Configuration Section Handler Class

Now that the configuration section handler is identified, ASP.NET will query the class that represents the new configuration section anytime a request is made for it. To satisfy this request, we need to build a configuration section handler class based on the `ConfigurationSection` class.

The `ConfigurationSection` class provides a representation of a custom section type in a configuration file. The `LiveSearchConfigSectionHandler` class implements the `liveSearchControls` XML configuration section. The `liveSearchControls` configuration section contains two subsections titled `license` and `url`. Both of these subsections are represented by custom class implementations of the `ConfigurationElement` base class.

Implementing the `ConfigurationSection` and `ConfigurationElement` classes is a matter of providing properties that represent the attributes available on the configuration section or subsection. Listing 12-2 presents the full listing for `LiveSearchConfigSectionHandler` and the `LicenseConfigElement` and `urlConfigElement` classes.

Listing 12-2. *The Live SearchConfigSectionHandler.cs Class File*

```
using System;
using System.Configuration;

namespace ControlsBook2Lib.CH12.LiveSearchControls
{
  /// <summary>
  /// Retrieves instance of LiveSearchConfigSection fully
  /// populated from web.config
  /// </summary>
  public class LiveSearchConfigSectionHandler : ConfigurationSection
  {
    [ConfigurationProperty("License")]
    public LicenseConfigElement License
    {
      get
      { return (LicenseConfigElement)this["License"]; }
      set
      { this["License"] = value; }
    }

    [ConfigurationProperty("Url")]
    public UrlConfigElement Url
    {
      get
      { return (UrlConfigElement)this["Url"]; }
      set
      { this["Url"] = value; }
    }
  }
```

```
    public class LicenseConfigElement : ConfigurationElement
    {
      public LicenseConfigElement()
      {
      }

      public LicenseConfigElement(String licenseKey)
      {
        LiveSearchLicenseKey = licenseKey;
      }

      [ConfigurationProperty("LiveSearchLicenseKey", DefaultValue =
       "Your App Key Goes Here", IsRequired = true)]
      public String LiveSearchLicenseKey
      {
        get
        { return (String)this["LiveSearchLicenseKey"]; }
        set
        { this["LiveSearchLicenseKey"] = value; }
      }
    }

    public class UrlConfigElement : ConfigurationElement
    {
      public UrlConfigElement()
      {
      }

      public UrlConfigElement(String webServiceUrl)
      {
        LiveSearchWebServiceUrl = webServiceUrl;
      }

      [ConfigurationProperty("LiveSearchWebServiceUrl", DefaultValue =
  "http://soap.search.msn.com:80/webservices.asmx", IsRequired = true)]
      public String LiveSearchWebServiceUrl
      {
        get
        { return (String)this["LiveSearchWebServiceUrl"]; }
        set
        { this["LiveSearchWebServiceUrl"] = value; }
      }
    }
  }
```

Wrapping the Web Service Proxy in a Utility Method

To make it easier to work with the web service proxy, we wrap the creation and invocation process inside a utility class that abstracts all the details of communicating with the Live Search web service, as shown in Listing 12-3. This class also hides the work necessary to grab configuration information from the custom configuration section we created earlier in this chapter.

Listing 12-3. *The SearchUtility.cs Class File*

```
using System;
using System.Configuration;
using System.ServiceModel;
using System.Threading;
using System.Web;
using LiveSearchService;

namespace ControlsBook2Lib.CH12.LiveSearchControls
{
  /// <summary>
  /// Utility class for abstracting Live Search web service proxy work
  /// </summary>
  public sealed class SearchUtility
  {
    private const string ConfigSectionName = "controlsBook2Lib/liveSearchControls";
    /// <summary>
    ///   Static method for searching Live Search that wraps web service
          proxy code for easy invocation.
    /// </summary>
    /// <param name="query">Query to Live Search search web service</param>
    /// <param name="sourceRequests">Collection of search settings</param>
    /// <returns></returns>
    public static LiveSearchService.SearchResponse SearchLiveSearchService(
    string query, SourceRequest[] sourceRequests)
    {
      string LiveSearchLicenseKey = "";
      string LiveSearchWebServiceUrl = "";

      // get <liveSearchControl> config section from web.config
      // for search settings
      LiveSearchConfigSectionHandler config =
            (LiveSearchConfigSectionHandler)ConfigurationManager.GetSection(
            ConfigSectionName);

      if (config != null)
      {
        LiveSearchLicenseKey = config.License.LiveSearchLicenseKey;
        LiveSearchWebServiceUrl = config.Url.LiveSearchWebServiceUrl;
      }
```

```
        // if control is instantiated at runtime config section should be present
        else if (HttpContext.Current != null)
        {
          throw new Exception(
             "ControlsBook2Lib.LiveSearchControls.SearchUtility
              cannot find <LiveSearchControl> configuration section.");
        }

        EndpointAddress liveSearchAddress =
           new EndpointAddress(LiveSearchWebServiceUrl);
        BasicHttpBinding binding = new BasicHttpBinding();
        ChannelFactory<MSNSearchPortType> channelFactory =
          new ChannelFactory<MSNSearchPortType>(binding, liveSearchAddress);

        MSNSearchPortType searchService = channelFactory.CreateChannel();
        SearchRequest searchRequest = new SearchRequest();
        //Required parameters on SearchRequest
        searchRequest.Query = query;
        searchRequest.AppID = LiveSearchLicenseKey;
        searchRequest.CultureInfo = Thread.CurrentThread.CurrentUICulture.Name;
        //Optional parameters for SearchRequest
        if (sourceRequests != null)
          searchRequest.Requests = sourceRequests;
        //Set mark query word.  Non-printable character added to highlight query terms
        //Set DisableHostCollapsing to return all results
        searchRequest.Flags = SearchFlags.DisableHostCollapsing
       | SearchFlags.MarkQueryWords;

        //Conduct Search
        SearchResponse searchResponse = searchService.Search(searchRequest);

        return searchResponse;
      }
    }
}
```

The SearchUtility class provides a parameter list to its single static SearchLiveSearchService method that accepts the search query string entered by the user and an array of SourceRequest objects. This allows the custom server controls to customize what type of search is performed by setting properties on the SourceRequest objects. Consult Tables 12-1 through 12-4 for details on what settings are available. Now that we have covered how to work with the Live Search web service and the configuration architecture, we can focus on the custom server controls.

Designing the Control Architecture

At this point, you have an understanding of how to access the Live Search web service, and you have some code to invoke it to return a set of search results. In the next phase of this chapter, you will learn how to display and interact with results from the Live Search web service.

The result set returned by the Live Search web service does not have the tabular structure that traditional data-bound controls such as the Repeater control or the DataGrid control expect. The top-level Live SearchResponse class contains an array of SourceResponse objects that represents multiple search requests. A SourceResponse object contains the overall status information about the search result, which would more likely be used as a header format. The SourceResponse.Results property contains an array of Result instances with the URL data for display in a repeating item format. The control we need to build has to work with the data on these two separate levels to display it appropriately. We achieve this by having templates that bind to different portions of the data source. We discussed how to create templates in Chapter 6.

Another major consideration is how to abstract communications with Live Search so that a developer can quickly add search capabilities to his or her application. To provide this ease of use, we encapsulate the Live Search web service searching inside of our control's code base. We provide a public data-binding method to load up the control UI from the result set, but the means to do it are abstracted away from the developer. All a developer needs to do is customize the UI and let the control do the heavy lifting of communicating with Live Search and paging the result set.

The first major architectural decision is to factor out the responsibilities of the control library. Instead of one supercontrol, we factor the functionality into three major controls: Search, Result, and Pager. We also have the ResultItem class, which contains the output templates as a utility control in support of the Result server control. The diagram in Figure 12-5 shows the breakdown of responsibilities.

The Search control has the primary responsibility of gathering input from the user and setting up the Result control with the first page of results in a new search. We want to separate Search from Result to allow flexible placement of the Search control's text boxes. The text boxes can be deployed in separate locations on a web form so as not to constrain the web application developer from a UI perspective.

The Result control handles the display of search results returned by the Live Search web service. On the first query to Live Search, the Search control will set up the Result control's DataSource property with an instance of SearchResponse and call its DataBind method to have it bind its templates to the result set. This mimics the behavior of data-bound controls discussed in Chapter 7.

The Pager control is the third main control in our control library and is embedded as a child control of the Result control. If paging is enabled, the Result control passes the Pager control the result set so that it calculates the starting index offsets based on page size and renders page links.

Figure 12-6 shows the action that occurs with the Search, Result, and Pager controls on an initial search. The end result is a rendered page with embedded links that lets the page post back to itself to change the view of the search results.

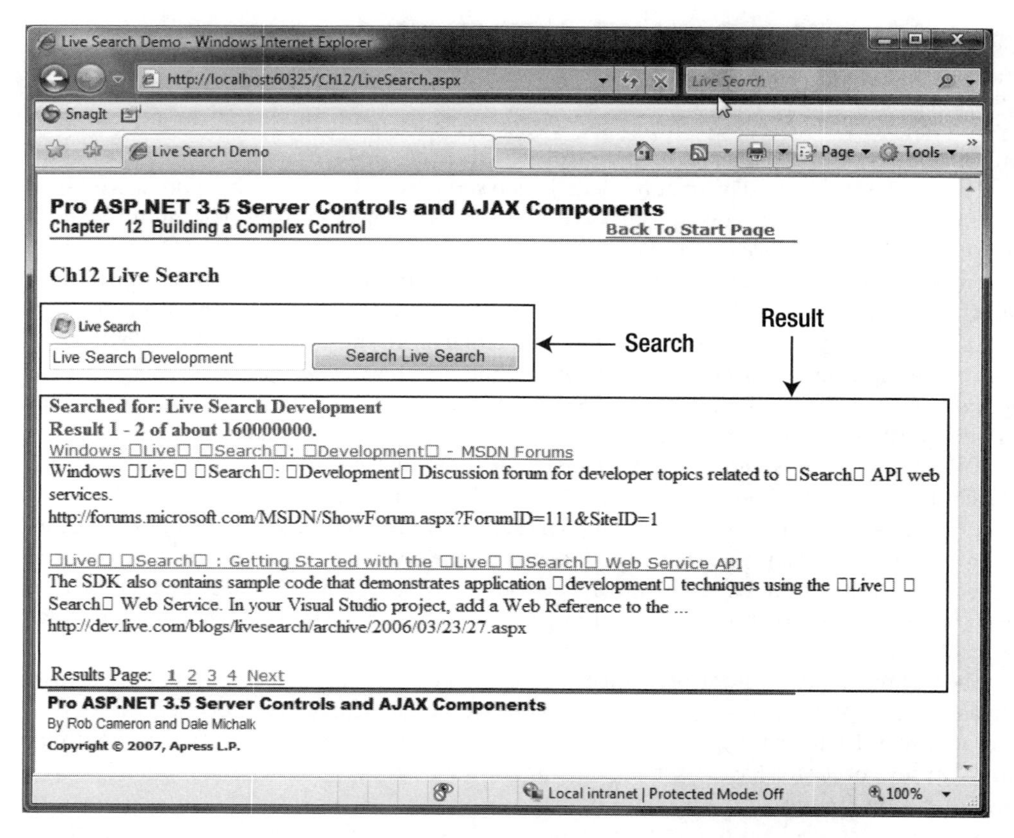

Figure 12-5. *The architecture of the Live Search controls*

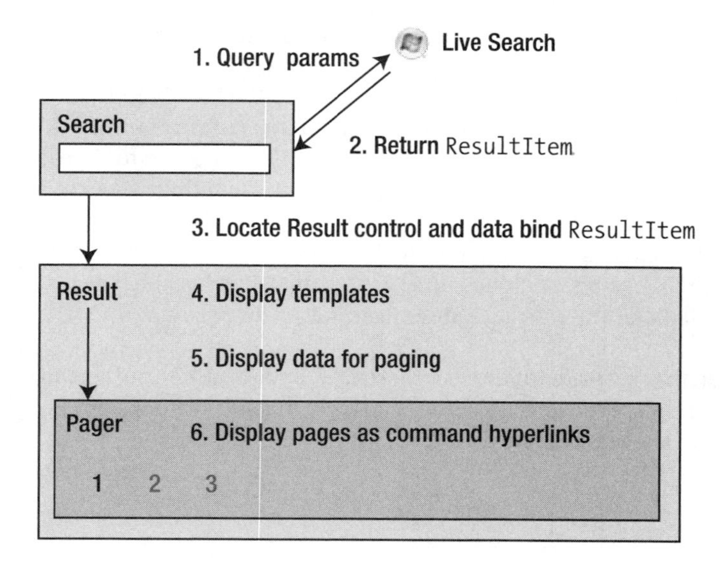

Figure 12-6. *Controls in action on an initial search*

Interacting with the paging features of the Result control is the next bit of functionality we discuss. When the links rendered by the Pager control are clicked, the control generates a server-side event. This event is mapped to the Result control, which then handles the process of going back to the Live Search web service and getting the desired page in the original result set. It sets its own DataSource property and calls DataBind on itself. This, in turn, starts the original binding process to render the new result set. Figure 12-7 shows the process graphically when the paging functionality of our control is exercised.

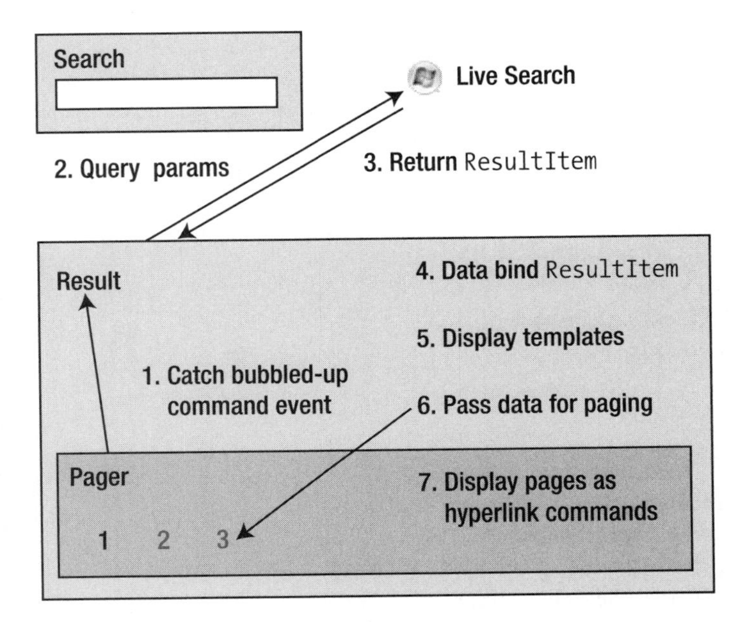

Figure 12-7. *Controls in action after the paging link is clicked*

Now that we have covered the overall design, we can move on to a more detailed analysis of the source code in each control, starting in the next section with the Search server control.

The Search Control

The Search control takes the input from the user to perform the search query. To accomplish this, we derive the control from the CompositeControl class. The Query property exposes the query string used to search the Live Search web service and is automatically set by the TextBox control, which is the primary input control for the Search control. The Search control does not expose a starting index property, as it assumes it will be on a one-based scale when it executes the query. RedirectToLiveSearch is a special property that provides the Search control the capability to ignore the Live Search web service and redirect the web form to the Live Search web site as if the user had typed in a query at the Live Search site directly.

The actual UI for the Search control is built in the composite control fashion of adding child controls from within the following CreateChildControls method. The first control added to the collection is a HyperLink to provide a clickable link back to Live Search as well. Note that the image is the official image made available by the Live Search service. The searchTextbox control is a TextBox control that grabs the input from the user. The searchButton control is a Button control that handles posting the page contents from the client back to the web server. Several LiteralControl instances are also added to the Controls collection to fill in the HTML spacing between the controls and provide breaks.

```
protected override void CreateChildControls()
{
  liveSearchLinkImage = new HyperLink();
  liveSearchLinkImage.ImageUrl = LiveSearchLogoImageUrl;
  liveSearchLinkImage.NavigateUrl = LiveSearchWebPageUrl;
  this.Controls.Add(liveSearchLinkImage);

  LiteralControl br = new LiteralControl("<br>");
  this.Controls.Add(br);

  searchTextBox = new TextBox();
  searchTextBox.Width = SearchTextBoxWidth;
  //searchTextBox.TextChanged += new
  //   EventHandler(SearchTextBoxTextChanged);
  this.Controls.Add(searchTextBox);

  br = new LiteralControl(" ");
  this.Controls.Add(br);

  // search button Text is localized
  ResourceManager rm = ResourceFactory.Manager;
  searchButton = new Button();
  searchButton.Text = rm.GetString("Search.searchButton.Text");
  searchButton.Click += new EventHandler(SearchButtonClick);
  this.Controls.Add(searchButton);

  br = new LiteralControl("<br>");
  this.Controls.Add(br);
}
```

Events are wired up in CreateChildControls as well. The Click event of searchButton and the TextChanged event of searchTextBox are the events of interest. These are routed to the SearchButtonClick and SearchTextBoxTextChanged private methods, respectively. All these events handlers really accomplish is passing the search query text over to the HandleSearch method, which does the majority of the work inside the Search control.

Handling the Search

The top of Search.HandleSearch has code that checks an internal Boolean variable named searchHandled to make sure that if both events fire on the same postback, we don't get duplicate searches occurring on the same query value unnecessarily, as shown here:

```
// check to see if search was handled on this postback
// (this prevents TextChanged and ButtonClicked from
// requesting the same query twice on the Live Search web service)
if (searchHandled == true)
  return;

// check for redirect of query processing to Live Search web site
if (RedirectToLiveSearch == true)
{
  this.Page.Response.Redirect(
     LiveSearchWebSearchUrl + "?q=" +
     HttpContext.Current.Server.UrlEncode(Query), true);
}
```

In `HandleSearch`, there is code that looks at the `RedirectToLiveSearch` property to decide whether to send the query back to the Live Search web site with `Response.Redirect`. The `Query` property is put on the URL string using the `q` variable on the HTTP GET string to accomplish this.

If we choose not to redirect the query to Live Search, we use the `SearchUtility` class to receive a `SearchResponse` from the web service proxy code it wraps. The `ResultControl` property of the `Search` control is used to do a dynamic lookup of the correct `Result` control via the `Page` `FindControl` method. Since `FindControl` is not recursive, we look for the `Result` control on the `Page` as well as at the same nesting level, which is the approach taken by the .Net Framework data-bound control's `DataSourceID` property.

We also use this control reference to infer the correct value for the `PageSize` along with the `Query` property value.

```
if (resControl == null)
  resControl = (Result)this.NamingContainer.FindControl(ResultControl);
if (resControl == null)
  throw new Exception("Either a Result control is not set on the " +
     "Search Control or the Result control is not located on the " +
     "Page or at the same nesting level as the Search control.");
  SourceRequest[] sourceRequests = new SourceRequest[1];
  sourceRequests[0] = new SourceRequest();
  sourceRequests[0].Count = resControl.PageSize;
```

After getting the result data from the web service, we raise an event to any interested parties. The type of this event is named `LiveSearchSearched`. This allows someone to use the `Search` control as a data generator and build his or her own custom UI from the result sets. We follow the design pattern for invoking this event through a protected method with `On` as the prefix to the search name, `OnLiveSearchSearched`, as shown here:

```
OnLiveSearchSearched(new
LiveSearchSearchedEventArgs(searchResponse));
```

The `LiveSearchSearchedEventArgs` class wraps the results of a Live Search web service query. We use that event argument's definition to create a `LiveSearchSearched` event handler. If you go back to the `Search` control source code, you can see the code that exposes the `LiveSearchSearched` event with this event definition. We use the generic `EventHandler<T>` class to help reduce memory footprint.

After the event is raised so that subscribers receive the Live Search web service search results, we continue processing in the `Search.HandleSearch` method to bind data to the `Result` control:

```
resControl.DataSource = searchResponse;
resControl.DataBind();
```

We set its `DataSource` property and call `DataBind` to have it fill its template structure with HTML that reflects the data of our web service query. The final step in the `HandleSearch` method sets the `searchHandled` Boolean variable to ensure the control does not fire two Live Search searches if both the `TextBox` `TextChanged` and the `Button` `Click` events fire on the same postback.

Listing 12-4 shows the source code for the `Search` control.

Listing 12-4. *The Search.cs Class File*

```
using System;
using System.ComponentModel;
using System.Resources;
using System.Web;
using System.Web.UI;
using System.Web.UI.WebControls;
using LiveSearchService;

namespace ControlsBook2Lib.CH12.LiveSearchControls
{
  /// <summary>
  /// earch control displays input textbox and button to
  ///capture input and start search process.
  /// </summary>
  [ParseChildren(true),
  ToolboxData("<{0}:Search runat=server></{0}:Search>"),
#if LICENSED
 RsaLicenseData(
     "55489e7a-bff5-4b3c-8f21-c43fad861dfa",

     "<RSAKeyValue><Modulus>mWpgckAepJAp4aUOAvEcGg3TdO+OVXws9Lji
SCLpy7aQKD5V7uj49Exh1RtcB6TcuXxmOR6dw75VmKwyoGbvYT6btOIw
QgqbLhci5LjWmWUPEdBRiYsOLDOh2POXs9xTvp4IDTKXYoP8GPDRKz
klJuuxCbbUcooESQoYHp9ppbE=</Modulus><Exponent>AQAB</Exponent>
</RSAKeyValue>"
     ),
  LicenseProvider(typeof(RsaLicenseProvider)),
#endif
 DefaultEvent("LiveSearchSearched"),Designer(typeof(SearchDesigner))]
  public class Search : CompositeControl
  {
    private const string LiveSearchWebPageUrl = "http://www.live.com";
```

```
    private const string LiveSearchWebSearchUrl =
      "http://search.live.com/results.aspx";
    private const string LiveSearch25PtLogoImageUrl =
      "http://go.microsoft.com/fwlink/?LinkId=89151";
    private const string LiveSearchLogoImageUrl =
      "http://go.microsoft.com/fwlink/?LinkId=89151";
    private const int SearchTextBoxWidth = 200;
    private const bool DefaultFilteringValue = false;
    private const bool DefaultRedirectToLiveSearchValue = false;
    private bool searchHandled;

    private HyperLink liveSearchLinkImage;
    private TextBox searchTextBox;
    private Button searchButton;

#if LICENSED
    private License license;
#endif


    /// <summary>
    /// Default constructor for Search control
    /// </summary>
    public Search()
    {

#if LICENSED

      // initiate license validation
      license =
        LicenseManager.Validate(typeof(Search), this);

#endif
    }

#if LICENSED

    private bool _disposed;
    /// <summary>
    /// Override Dispose to clean up resources.
    /// </summary>
    public sealed override void Dispose()
    {
      //Dispose of any unmanaged resources
      Dispose(true);
      GC.SuppressFinalize(this);
    }
```

```
    /// <summary>
    /// You must override Dispose for controls derived from the License class
    /// </summary>
    protected virtual void Dispose(bool disposing)
    {
      if (!_disposed)
      {
        if (disposing)
        {
          //Dispose of additional unmanaged resources here
          if (license != null)
            license.Dispose();
          base.Dispose();
        }
        license = null;
        _disposed = true;
      }
    }

#endif

    /// <summary>
    /// LiveSearchControls Result control to bind search results to for display
    /// </summary>
    [DescriptionAttribute("Result control to bind search results to for display."),
    CategoryAttribute("Search")]
    virtual public string ResultControl
    {
      get
      {
        object control = ViewState["ResultControl"];
        if (control == null)
          return "";
        else
          return (string)control;
      }
      set
      {
        ViewState["ResultControl"] = value;
      }
    }

    /// <summary>
    /// Search query string
    /// </summary>
    [DescriptionAttribute("Search query string."),
    CategoryAttribute("Search")]
```

```
virtual public string Query
{
  get
  {
    EnsureChildControls();
    return searchTextBox.Text;
  }
  set
  {
    EnsureChildControls();
    searchTextBox.Text = value;
  }
}

/// <summary>
/// Redirect search query to Live Search site web pages.
/// </summary>
[DescriptionAttribute("Redirect search query to Live Search site web pages."),
CategoryAttribute("Search")]
virtual public bool RedirectToLiveSearch
{
  get
  {
    object redirect = ViewState["RedirectToLiveSearch"];
    if (redirect == null)
      return DefaultRedirectToLiveSearchValue;
    else
      return (bool)redirect;
  }
  set
  {
    ViewState["RedirectToLiveSearch"] = value;
  }
}

/// <summary>
/// Click event handler for search button
/// </summary>
/// <param name="s">Search button</param>
/// <param name="e">Event arguments</param>
protected void SearchButtonClick(object source, EventArgs e)
{
  HandleSearch();
}
```

```
private void HandleSearch()
{
  // check to see if search was handled on this postback
  // (this prevents TextChanged and ButtonClicked from
  // requesting the same query twice on the Live Search web service)
  if (searchHandled == true)
    return;

  // check for redirect of query processing to Live Search web site
  if (RedirectToLiveSearch == true)
  {
    this.Page.Response.Redirect(
       LiveSearchWebSearchUrl + "?q=" +
       HttpContext.Current.Server.UrlEncode(Query), true);
  }

  if (ResultControl.Length != 0)
  {
    // lookup the Result control we are linked to
    // and get the PageSize property value
    Result resControl = (Result)Page.FindControl(ResultControl);
    if (resControl == null)
      resControl = (Result)this.NamingContainer.FindControl(ResultControl);
    if (resControl == null)
      throw new ArgumentException("Either a Result control is not set on the " +
          "Search Control or the Result control is not located on the " +
          "Page or at the same nesting level as the Search control.");
    SourceRequest[] sourceRequests = new SourceRequest[1];
    sourceRequests[0] = new SourceRequest();
    sourceRequests[0].Count = resControl.PageSize;
     //Specifies the number of results to return from offset
    sourceRequests[0].Source = SourceType.Web;
    //new search, always reset
    sourceRequests[0].Offset = 0; //start index for returned results
    sourceRequests[0].ResultFields = ResultFieldMask.All |
    ResultFieldMask.DateTime;

    // get search results from Live Search WCF service proxy
    SearchResponse searchResponse =
       SearchUtility.SearchLiveSearchService(
       Query, sourceRequests);

    // raise search results for any interested parties as well
    OnLiveSearchSearched(new LiveSearchSearchedEventArgs(searchResponse));
```

```
      // databind search results with the Result control
      // we are linked with
      resControl.Query = Query;
      resControl.PageNumber = 0;

      resControl.DataSource = searchResponse;
      resControl.DataBind();
    }
    // set bool that tells us the search has been handled on this
    // postback
    searchHandled = true;
  }


  public event EventHandler<LiveSearchSearchedEventArgs>
  LiveSearchSearched
/// <summary>
  ///   Protected method for invoking LiveSearchSearched event
  ///   from within Result control
  /// </summary>
  /// <param name="lse">Event arguments including search results</param>
  protected virtual void OnLiveSearchSearched(LiveSearchSearchedEventArgs e)
  {
    EventHandler<LiveSearchSearchedEventArgs> evnt = LiveSearchSearched;
    if (evnt != null)
      evnt(this, e);
  }

  /// <summary>
  /// Called by framework for composite controls to create control hierarchy
  /// </summary>
  protected override void CreateChildControls()
  {
    liveSearchLinkImage = new HyperLink();
    liveSearchLinkImage.ImageUrl = LiveSearchLogoImageUrl;
    liveSearchLinkImage.NavigateUrl = LiveSearchWebPageUrl;
    this.Controls.Add(liveSearchLinkImage);

    LiteralControl br = new LiteralControl("<br>");
    this.Controls.Add(br);

    searchTextBox = new TextBox();
    searchTextBox.Width = SearchTextBoxWidth;
    //searchTextBox.TextChanged += new
    //   EventHandler(SearchTextBoxTextChanged);
    this.Controls.Add(searchTextBox);
```

```
      br = new LiteralControl(" ");
      this.Controls.Add(br);

      // search button Text is localized
      ResourceManager rm = ResourceFactory.Manager;
      searchButton = new Button();
      searchButton.Text = rm.GetString("Search.searchButton.Text");
      searchButton.Click += new EventHandler(SearchButtonClick);
      this.Controls.Add(searchButton);

      br = new LiteralControl("<br>");
      this.Controls.Add(br);
    }

    /// <summary>
    /// Overridden to ensure Controls collection is created before external access
    /// </summary>
    public override ControlCollection Controls
    {
      get
      {
        EnsureChildControls();
        return base.Controls;
      }
    }
  }
}
```

Now that we have covered the search functionality, in the next section, we discuss how the returned results are processed in the Result control.

The Result Control

The Result control is the most complex control of the Live Search controls library. It is a templated, data-bound control that has the capability to page itself as well as access the web service to update the page range. The Result server control takes its cue from the Repeater control we developed in Chapter 7. It provides a robust set of templates: HeaderTemplate, StatusTemplate, ItemTemplate, AlternatingItemTemplate, SeparatorTemplate, and FooterTemplate. Each template also has a like-named Style object to modify the HTML that is rendered for style content: HeaderStyle, StatusStyle, ItemStyle, AlternatingItemStyle, SeparatorStyle, and FooterStyle. The embedded Pager control has its style properties exposed by a Result class property named PagerStyle.

Each template is pushed into an instance of the ResultItem control. This is the primary child control of Result, and it provides the means for achieving access to search results from a template data-binding expression. As we mentioned previously, Result offloads most of the paging work to a control class named Pager, which handles offset and range calculations. We stuff the Pager control inside a ResultItem, so that it can page content. Figure 12-8 shows the structural architecture of the Result control, including the portion handed off to the Pager control.

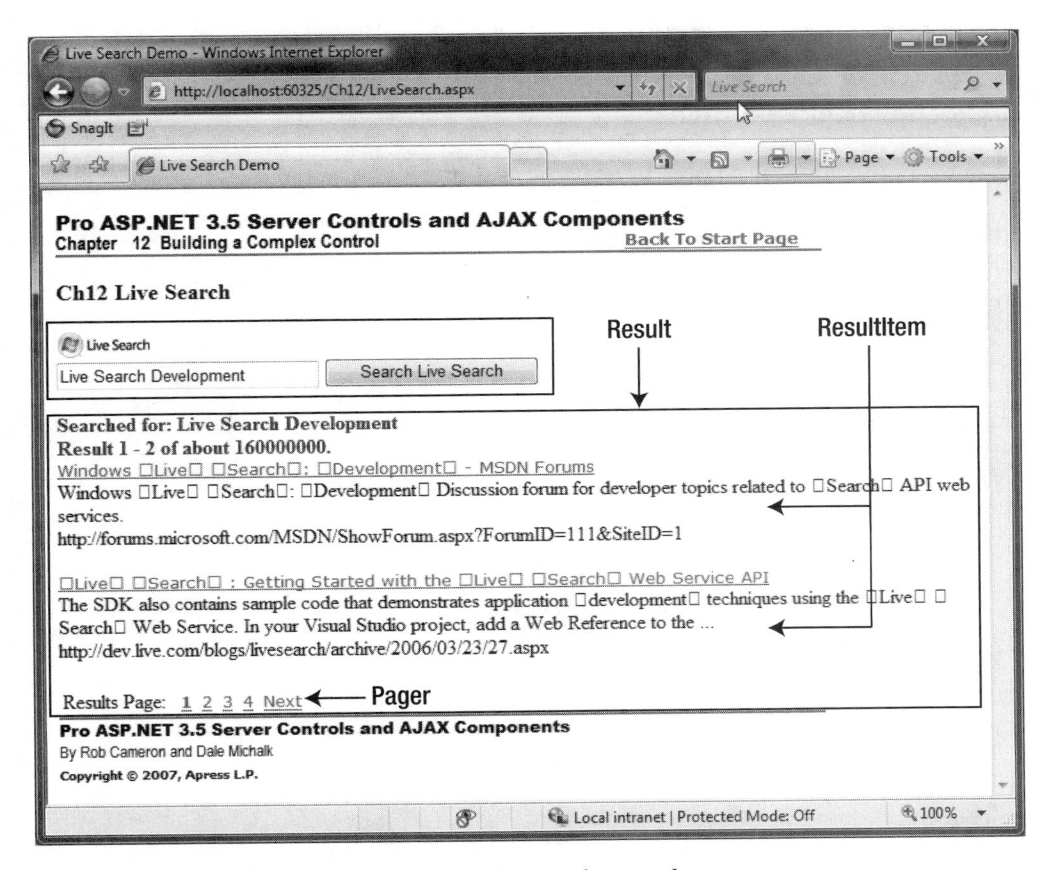

Figure 12-8. *The ResultItem structure inside the Result control*

Notice the square boxes around the search terms "Live", "Search", and "Development" in the returned search results in Figure 12-8. The square boxes are nonprintable characters, so that the developer can highlight search terms in the results if desired. In the next section, we discuss the details behind the ResultItem control class including how to fine-tune the search results such as adding the ability to highlight search terms.

The ResultItem Control

The ResultItem class takes on a structure that is common to containers used as data-bound templates. It has the well-known DataItem property, as well as ItemIndex and ItemType properties to store the index it occupies in the collection of ResultItem controls aggregated by its parent Result control. The ResultItemType enumeration matches up its usage with the templates and styles from the Result class as well.

Inside this file, we also have a ResultItemEventHandler signature of ResultItem events. These provide interested clients with the capability to receive the creation (ItemCreated) and data-binding events (ItemDataBound) events of the parent Result control class. Listing 12-5 presents the full text listing for the ResultItem control.

Listing 12-5. *The ResultItem.cs Class File*

```
using System;
using System.Web.UI.WebControls;

namespace ControlsBook2Lib.CH12.LiveSearchControls
{
  /// <summary>
  /// Enum which indicates what type of content/template/styles the
  /// ResultItem control represents
  /// </summary>
  public enum ResultItemType
  {
    /// <summary>
    /// Represents top of control output
    /// </summary>
    Header = 0,

    /// <summary>
    /// Represents status section below header
    /// </summary>
    Status,

    /// <summary>
    /// Represents search result item output
    /// </summary>
    Item,

    /// <summary>
    /// Represents search result alternating item output
    /// </summary>
    AlternatingItem,

    /// <summary>
    /// Represents separation between search result item or alternating item output
    /// </summary>
    Separator,

    /// <summary>
    /// Represents paging area below search result items
    /// </summary>
    Pager,
```

```
    /// <summary>
    /// Represents bottom of control output below paging area
    /// </summary>
    Footer
  }

  /// <summary>
  /// Primary child control of Result that contains all of the various templates
  /// when instantiated.
  /// </summary>
  public class ResultItem : CompositeControl
  {
    private object dataItem;
    private ResultItemType itemType;
    private int itemIndex;

    /// <summary>
    /// Default constructor of ResultItem control
    /// </summary>
    /// <param name="index">
    /// Index of control in collection of ResultItem controls under Result</param>
    /// <param name="type">
    /// Type of template the ResultItem control represents</param>
    /// <param name="dataItem">Data from search query</param>
    public ResultItem(int index, ResultItemType type, object dataItem)
    {
      this.itemType = type;
      this.dataItem = dataItem;
      this.itemIndex = index;
    }

    /// <summary>
    /// Data from search query
    /// </summary>
    public object DataItem
    {
      get
      {
        return dataItem;
      }
      set
      {
        dataItem = value;
      }
    }
```

```
    /// <summary>
    /// Index of control in collection of ResultItem controls under Result
    /// </summary>
    public int ItemIndex
    {
      get
      {
        return itemIndex;
      }
    }

    /// <summary>
    /// Type of template the ResultItem control represents
    /// </summary>
    public ResultItemType ItemType
    {
      get
      {
        return itemType;
      }
    }

  }

  /// <summary>
  /// Specialized EventArgs which contains a ResultItem instance
  /// </summary>
  public class ResultItemEventArgs : EventArgs
  {
    private ResultItem item;

    /// <summary>
    /// Default constructor for ResultItemEventArgs
    /// </summary>
    /// <param name="item">ResultItem control instance</param>
    public ResultItemEventArgs(ResultItem item)
    {
      this.item = item;
    }

    /// <summary>
    /// ResultItem control instance
    /// </summary>
    public ResultItem Item
    {
```

```
      get
      {
        return item;
      }
    }
  }
}
```

One thing to highlight regarding the Result control is how it binds different levels of data from the LiveSearchResult data source to the ResultItem based on its associated control template in use. The data-binding expressions reach into a different data objects when they reference the Container.DataItem property depending on which ResultItem is referenced. The StatusTemplate is bound to the top-level LiveSearchSearchResult class through the DataItem property. The ItemTemplate and AlternatingItemTemplate are alternately bound to each ResultElement class that makes up the search results. HeaderTemplate, FooterTemplate, and SeparatorTemplate are not bound to any data source and have a null DataItem value.

Building the Result Control

To provide a pleasing UI experience out of the box and let the control render something when it is blank or when it is data bound, we have three primary modes that the Result control operates in: blank, data binding, and postback. The blank mode is used for displaying a UI even when the user fails to link the control to a data source. Data-binding mode is used when a data source is provided and the user explicitly calls the DataBind method of the control. Postback is the mode the control takes on when it is sent back to the server from a postback event and the control hydrates its structure from ViewState.

The Blank Scenario

The default action of the Result control if you put it on a web form and leave it alone is triggered by code in its override of the following RenderContents method. If a Boolean named searchConducted is not set, it fires off a call to Result control's CreateBlankControlHierarchy method:

```
protected override void RenderContents(HtmlTextWriter writer)
{
   // if no search, create a hierarchy with header and
   // footer templates only
   if (!searchConducted)
   {
      CreateBlankControlHierarchy();
   }

   // prep all template styles
   PrepareControlHierarchy();

   // render all child controls
   base.RenderContents(writer);
}
```

After the call to the CreateBlankControlHierarchy method, the control next calls PrepareControlHierarchy to ensure all styles are applied to any user-provided templates. Last, the control calls the base class method of RenderContents to do its work of iterating through the child controls and rendering them.

If you look at CreateBlankControlHierarchy, you see that it looks for the HeaderTemplate and FooterTemplate templates and creates a ResultItem control to wrap them using the CreateResultItem helper method. We examine CreateResultItem in just a bit, but here is CreateBlankControlHierarchy:

```
private void CreateBlankControlHierarchy()
{
   if (HeaderTemplate != null)
   {
      ResultItem headerItem = CreateResultItem(-1, ResultItemType.Header, false,
                                                 null);
      items.Add(headerItem);
   }

   if (FooterTemplate != null)
   {
      ResultItem footer = CreateResultItem(-1, ResultItemType.Footer,
                                             false, null);
      items.Add(footer);
   }
}
```

It adds the ResultItem control to an internal ArrayList collection. This is a publicly reachable collection that is exposed via a top-level Items property on Result, as shown in the following code. Notice that we didn't add the ResultItem controls to the Controls collection of Result in CreateBlankControlHierarchy. This is handled by CreateResultItem, along with other things such as data binding and raising item-related events.

```
private Collection<ResultItem> items = new Collection<ResultItem>();
public Collection<ResultItem> Items
{
  get
  {
    return items ;
  }
}
```

The items collection takes advantage of the List generic type removing the need to create a custom strongly typed collection.

The DataBind Scenario

The next mode of creating child controls inside the Result control class focuses on what happens when the Search control executes a search, sets the DataSource property of the Result control, and invokes its DataBind method, as shown in the following code. The first task accomplished is clearing out child controls that might have been put into the collection manually and any information that might have been persisted to ViewState. We also set the all-important searchConducted Boolean value to true, so the control knows it is not in a blank control situation.

```
public override void DataBind()
{
   base.OnDataBinding(System.EventArgs.Empty);

   Controls.Clear();
   ClearChildViewState();
   TrackViewState();

   searchConducted = true;
   CreateControlHierarchy(true);
   ChildControlsCreated = true;
}
```

CreateControlHierarchy is used by DataBind to load up the control content and execute DataBind methods on each individual template. The Boolean value passed by DataBind is set to true to indicate to CreateControlHierarchy that we are in a data binding scenario. We examine the details of CreateControlHierarchy later in this chapter after we have covered our third mode, which deals with a rendered Result control rehydrating at the beginning of postback.

The Postback Scenario

The Result control's CreateChildControls method, shown in the following snippet, is called when a server control needs to build its control structure. This could happen as part of the blank control-building scenario or as part of postback from a client round-trip.

```
override protected void CreateChildControls()
{
  if (searchConducted == false &&
     ViewState["ResultItemCount"] != null)
  {
    CreateControlHierarchy(false);
  } }
```

The CreateChildControls method checks the searchConducted Boolean value to determine whether it has been called as part of the data-binding scenario. If the page has been manually data bound, we do not need to create the control hierarchy. We also check to see whether there is content in the ViewState variable ResultItemCount. If this is present, the page is coming back via postback, and we can call CreateControlHierarchy to have it repopulate the control structure based on ResultItemControl and have child controls retrieve their former values from ViewState. If the ViewState ResultItemCount variable is not present, we are in a blank control scenario, and we let the code we have in RenderContents handle the blank mode situation.

Creating a Control Hierarchy for Data Binding or Postback

Most of the heavy lifting to build the composite structure of the Result control occurs in the following CreateControlHierarchy for the data-binding and postback scenarios. This code is typical of your run-of-the-mill data-bound control:

```
private void CreateControlHierarchy(bool dataBind)
{
  Controls.Clear();
  SearchResponse result = null;

  // Result items
  items = new Collection<ResultItem>();

  int count = 0;

  if (dataBind == true)
  {
    if (DataSource == null)
      return;
    result = DataSource;

    // set ViewState values for read-only props
    ViewState["TotalResultsCount"] =
result.Responses[0].Total;
    ViewState["Offset"] = result.Responses[0].Offset;
    ViewState["Source"] = result.Responses[0].Source;

    count = result.Responses[0].Results.Length;
    ViewState["ResultItemCount"] = count;
  }
  else
  {
    object temp = ViewState["ResultItemCount"];
    if (temp != null)
      count = (int)temp;
  }

  if (HeaderTemplate != null)
  {
    ResultItem headerItem = CreateResultItem(-1,
ResultItemType.Header, false, null);
    items.Add(headerItem);
  }

  ResultItem statusItem = CreateResultItem(-1, ResultItemType.Status,
dataBind, result);
  items.Add(statusItem);

  // loop through and create ResultItem controls for each of the
  // result elements from the Live Search web service result
  ResultItemType itemType = ResultItemType.Item;
  for (int i = 0; i < count; i++)
```

```
{
  if (separatorTemplate != null)
  {
    ResultItem separator =
    CreateResultItem(-1, ResultItemType.Separator, false, null);
    items.Add(separator);
  }

  LiveSearchService.Result searchResultItem = null;
  if (dataBind == true)
  {
    searchResultItem = result.Responses[0].Results[i];
  }

  ResultItem item = CreateResultItem(i,
    itemType, dataBind, searchResultItem);
  items.Add(item);

  // swap between item and alternatingitem types
  if (itemType == ResultItemType.Item)
    itemType = ResultItemType.AlternatingItem;
  else
    itemType = ResultItemType.Item;
 }

 // display pager if allowed by user and if results
 // are greater than a page in length
 if (DisplayPager == true && TotalResultsCount > PageSize)
 {
   ResultItem pager = CreatePagerResultItem();
   items.Add(pager);
 }

 if (FooterTemplate != null)
 {
   ResultItem footer = CreateResultItem(-1, ResultItemType.Footer,
false, null);
   items.Add(footer);
 }
}
```

If we are in data-binding mode based on the passed-in Boolean parameter, the Result control examines the LiveSearchService.SearchResponse instance linked to the DataSource property of itself. DataSource is strongly typed in the implementation of Result to prevent someone from accidentally assigning a DataSet or other type of collection to it.

```
/// <summary>
/// Data source which takes a SearchResponse to build display.
/// </summary>
[DesignerSerializationVisibility(DesignerSerializationVisibility.Hidden),
      DefaultValue(null),
      Bindable(true),
      Browsable(false)]
public LiveSearchService.SearchResponse DataSource
{
  get
  {
    return dataSource;
  }
  set
  {
    dataSource = value;
  }
}
```

The CreateControlHierarchy code, when data binding, pulls key parameters from the data source like the number of results, the offset, and the source result set. The count variable is set to the size of the Results array returned to ensure accurate looping in the template creation process. If we are not in a data-binding scenario, yet we are creating the control hierarchy, we read ResultItemCount from the ViewState collection to set the count variable. Having a count is all we need, because we go through a loop that creates the correct number of ResultItem controls for each of the search results, and the controls then are able to pull their previous information from ViewState.

When the code loops through the result set items, it creates the required template for each item and data binds by calling the CreateResultItem method. As the result items are processed, the HeaderTemplate, FooterTemplate, and SeparatorTemplates templates are checked for null values, whereas the StatusTemplate and ResultItemTemplate templates are not. The reason for this difference is that ResultControl has two prewired template classes as default templates for the StatusTemplate and ItemTemplate if they are not specified by the user. You can see this by examining the CreateResultItem method, which is responsible for creating the ResultItem control instances that house the final template content.

Once we have looped through each ResultElement of the search query data set, we turn to creating the paging structure. Here we call a different method to create the ResultItem instance that houses the paging structure by calling the CreatePagerItem method. We also set up the ViewState to remember the count of elements added so we can rehydrate them from ViewState during postback.

Creating ResultItem Controls

CreateControlHierarchy offloads most of the work to the CreateResultItem method, as shown in the following code. The CreateResultItem method is the true workhorse of the Result class. It creates the major structures, adds them to the Controls collection, and manages events and data binding.

```
private ResultItem CreateResultItem(int index, ResultItemType itemType,
                                    bool dataBind, object dataItem)
{
   ITemplate selectedTemplate;

   switch (itemType)
   {
      case ResultItemType.Header :
         selectedTemplate = HeaderTemplate;
         break;
      case ResultItemType.Status :
         if (StatusTemplate == null)
         {
            // if no StatusTemplate, pick up the default
            // template ResultStatusTemplate
            selectedTemplate = new ResultStatusTemplate();
         }
         else
            selectedTemplate = StatusTemplate;
         break;
      case ResultItemType.Item :
         if (ItemTemplate == null)
         {
            // if no ItemTemplate, pick up the default
            // template ResultItemTemplate
            selectedTemplate = new ResultItemTemplate();
         }
         else
            selectedTemplate = ItemTemplate;
         break;
      case ResultItemType.AlternatingItem :
         selectedTemplate = AlternatingItemTemplate;
         if (selectedTemplate == null)
         {
            // if no AlternatingItemTemplate, switch to Item type
            // and pick up ItemTemplate
            itemType = ResultItemType.Item;
            selectedTemplate = ItemTemplate;
            if (selectedTemplate == null)
            {
               // if that doesn't work, pick up the default
               // template ResultItemTemplate
               selectedTemplate = new ResultItemTemplate();
            }
         }
         break;
```

```
        case ResultItemType.Separator :
           selectedTemplate = SeparatorTemplate;
           break;
        case ResultItemType.Footer :
           selectedTemplate = FooterTemplate;
           break;
        default:
           selectedTemplate = null;
           break;
     }

     ResultItem item = new ResultItem(index, itemType, dataItem);

     if (selectedTemplate != null)
     {
        selectedTemplate.InstantiateIn(item);
     }

     OnItemCreated(new ResultItemEventArgs(item));
     Controls.Add(item);

     if (dataBind)
     {
        item.DataBind();
        OnItemDataBound(new ResultItemEventArgs(item));
     }
     return item;
  }
```

The first task for CreateResultItem is to determine what type of ResultItem it is creating using a switch statement. The end result of the process is grabbing the correct template from the Result control's template properties and assigning it to the selectedTemplate method variable. For the Status and Item types, it also handles the case of a blank template by instantiating the built-in default ResultStatusTemplate and ResultItemTemplate classes. If the AlternatingItemTemplate property is blank, the Item type ResultItemTemplate default template is used.

After template selection, a brand-new ResultItem control is created and is passed its index in the parent Result control's Item collection, as well as its type and a potentially valid data source. After the ResultItem is minted, it receives the template control content via the Instantiate method of the ITemplate interface.

The final step is to fire the required events. Once the control is created, we raise an ItemCreated event and add the control to the Controls collection. The final step is to call DataBind on the ResultItem if we are in a data-binding scenario, which then raises an ItemDataBound event.

Creating the Child Pager Control

The Pager control is added to the Controls collection of the parent Result control in CreatePagerResultItem. This special-purpose creation method creates a new ResultItem control and adds a configured Pager control to it as follows:

```
private ResultItem CreatePagerResultItem()
{
  ResultItem item = new ResultItem(-1, ResultItemType.Pager, null);

  Pager pager = new Pager();
  pager.PageSize = PageSize;
  pager.PagerBarRange = PagerBarRange;
  pager.PagerLinkStyle = PagerLinkStyle;
  pager.TotalResultsCount = TotalResultsCount;
  pager.PageNumber = PageNumber;

  item.Controls.Add(pager);

  Controls.Add(item);

  return item;
}
```

Pager is configured based on information from the web service query and information that is exposed by the parent Result control. The PageSize property is the number of entries listed per page that are returned from the Live Search search results. PagerBarRange is the number of pages to display in numeric form at the bottom of the page to go along with the Previous and Next buttons, if applicable. PagerLinkStyle is of type ResultPagerLinkStyle declared as follows. It determines whether text links are displayed or text with DHTML is displayed.

```
public enum ResultPagerLinkStyle
{
   Text = 0,
   TextWithDHTML
}
```

We don't implement TextWithDHTML functionality for the Result control, but the ASP.NET AJAX functionality in HighlightedHyperLink could be leveraged to add DHTML functionality to the Pager's page numbers by inheriting from LinkButton and performing the same steps used with the HighlightedHyperLink to add DHTML functionality.

Notice that we don't have to explicitly pass LiveSearchService.SearchResponse to Pager in the CreatePagerResultItem method. It has code inside of it to deal with calculating and displaying the correct page ranges based on the TotalResultsCount, PageNumber, and PageSize property values.

Managing Paging

The Pager control that is part of the child control structure of a paging Result control will raise the correct command events when a page link is clicked to change the page of results displayed. The command event raised by the Pager control is intercepted by the parent Result control via the use of the OnBubbleEvent method override:

```
protected override bool OnBubbleEvent(object source, EventArgs args)
{
   // Handle events raised by children by overriding OnBubbleEvent.
   // (main purpose is to detect paging events)
   bool handled = false;
   CommandEventArgs cea = args as CommandEventArgs;

   // handle Page event by extracting new start index
   // and calling HandleSearch method, which does the
   // work of rebinding this control to the results
   // from the web service
   if (cea.CommandName == "Page")
   {
      StartIndex = Convert.ToInt32(cea.CommandArgument);
      HandleSearch();

   }

   return handled;
}
```

The `OnBubbleEvent` implementation in `Result` grabs the index of the new page to display with the `Result` control and then calls `HandleSearch`, which actually talks to Live Search. `HandleSearch` is similar to the method of the same name in the `Search` control, except that it doesn't have to look up a `Result` control; it simply sets the `DataSource` and calls `DataBind` on itself.

Styling the Result Control

After all of the child controls are created, either by `CreateBlankControlHierarchy` or `CreateControlHierarchy`, the styles exposed by the `Result` control are applied. This is handled in the `RenderContents` override discussed earlier. At the end of `RenderContents`, the code invokes `PrepareControlHierarchy` to make this happen. It loops through all the `ResultItem` controls and applies the appropriate `Style` object if the style was set on the `Result` control, as shown here:

```
protected void PrepareControlHierarchy()
{
   // apply all the appropriate style attributes
   // to the items in the result output
   foreach (ResultItem item in this.Items)
   {
      if (item.ItemType == ResultItemType.Header)
      {
         if (HeaderStyle != null)
            item.ApplyStyle(HeaderStyle);
      }
      else if (item.ItemType == ResultItemType.Status)
      {
```

```
         if (StatusStyle != null)
            item.ApplyStyle(StatusStyle);
      }
      else if (item.ItemType == ResultItemType.Item)
      {
         if (ItemStyle != null)
            item.ApplyStyle(ItemStyle);

      }
      else if (item.ItemType == ResultItemType.AlternatingItem)
      {
         if (AlternatingItemStyle != null)
            item.ApplyStyle(AlternatingItemStyle);
         else if (ItemStyle != null)
            item.ApplyStyle(ItemStyle);
      }
      else if (item.ItemType == ResultItemType.Separator)
      {
         if (SeparatorStyle != null)
            item.ApplyStyle(SeparatorStyle);
      }
      else if (item.ItemType == ResultItemType.Pager)
      {
         if (PagerStyle != null)
         {
            Pager pager = (Pager) item.Controls[0];
            pager.ApplyStyle(PagerStyle);
         }
      }
      else if (item.ItemType == ResultItemType.Footer)
      {
         if (FooterStyle != null)
            item.ApplyStyle(FooterStyle);
      }
   }
}
```

Because we know there is only one instance of the `Pager` server control stored as a `ResultItem`, we apply `PagerStyle` directly to this instance, as shown in the preceding code. Listing 12-6 shows the full source for the `Result` control.

Listing 12-6. *The Result.cs Class File*

```
using System;
using System.Collections.ObjectModel;
using System.ComponentModel;
using System.Web.UI;
using System.Web.UI.WebControls;
```

```
using ControlsBook2Lib.CH12.LiveSearchControls.Design;
using LiveSearchService;

namespace ControlsBook2Lib.CH12.LiveSearchControls
{
  /// <summary>
  /// Determines search results pager style
  /// </summary>
  public enum ResultPagerLinkStyle
  {
    /// <summary>
    /// Render pager with text hyperlinks for search result navigation
    /// </summary>
    Text = 0,

    /// <summary>
    /// Render pager DHTML for page link buttons in pager.
    /// Not implemented but a place holder for extension
    /// </summary>
    TextWithDHTML
  }

  /// <summary>
  /// Result control displays the formatted results from a query of the
  /// Live Search search web service.
  /// </summary>
  [ParseChildren(true),
  ToolboxData("<{0}:result runat=server></{0}:result>"),
  Designer(typeof(ResultDesigner)),
#if LICENSED
   RsaLicenseData(
      "55489e7a-bff5-4b3c-8f21-c43fad861dfa",

"<RSAKeyValue><Modulus>mWpgckAepJAp4aUOAvEcGg3TdO+OVXws9LjiSCLpy7aQKD5V7uj
49Exh1RtcB6TcuXxmOR6dw75VmKwyoGbvYT6btOIwQgqbLhci5LjWmWUPEdBRiYsOLDOh2POX
s9xTvp4IDTKXYoP8GPDRKzklJuuxCbbUcooESQoYHp9ppbE=</Modulus><Exponent>AQAB
</Exponent></RSAKeyValue>"
      ),
   LicenseProvider(typeof(RsaLicenseProvider)),
#endif
 DefaultEvent("LiveSearchSearched")
  ]
  public class Result : CompositeControl
  {
    // constants
    private const int defaultPageSize = 10;
    private const int defaultPagerBarRange = 4;
```

```
    private const int defaultPageNumber = 1;

    // style property fields
    private Style headerStyle;
    private Style statusStyle;
    private Style itemStyle;
    private Style alternatingItemStyle;
    private Style separatorStyle;
    private Style pagerStyle;
    private Style footerStyle;
    private ResultPagerLinkStyle pagerLinkStyle =
    ResultPagerLinkStyle.TextWithDHTML;

    // Template property fields
    private ITemplate headerTemplate;
    private ITemplate statusTemplate;
    private ITemplate itemTemplate;
    private ITemplate alternatingItemTemplate;
    private ITemplate separatorTemplate;
    private ITemplate footerTemplate;

    private bool searchConducted;
    private SearchResponse dataSource;
    private Collection<ResultItem> items = new Collection<ResultItem>();

#if LICENSED
      private License license;
#endif

    /// <summary>
    /// Default constructor for Result control
    /// </summary>
    public Result()
    {
#if LICENSED
          // initiate license validation
          license =
             LicenseManager.Validate(typeof(Search), this);
#endif
    }

    /// <summary>
    ///   Override bases Result control on div HTML tag
    /// </summary>
    protected override HtmlTextWriterTag TagKey
    {
```

```
        get
        {
          return HtmlTextWriterTag.Div;
        }
      }
      #region Dispose pattern

#if LICENSED
       private bool _disposed;
      /// <summary>
      /// Override Dispose to clean up resources.
      /// </summary>
      public sealed override void Dispose()
      {
        //Dispose of any unmanaged resources
        Dispose(true);
        GC.SuppressFinalize(this);
      }

      /// <summary>
      /// You must override Dispose for controls derived from the License clsas
      /// </summary>
      protected virtual void Dispose(bool disposing)
      {
        if (!_disposed)
        {
          if (disposing)
          {
            //Dispose of additional unmanaged resources here
            if (license != null)
              license.Dispose();
            base.Dispose();
          }
          license = null;
          _disposed = true;
        }
      }
#endif
      #endregion

      #region Search properties
      /// <summary>
      /// Number of search results returned with query and displayed on page.
      /// </summary>
      [Description(
     "Number of search results returned with query and displayed on page."),
       Category("Search"), DefaultValue(defaultPageSize)]
```

```
virtual public int PageSize
{
  get
  {
    object size = ViewState["PageSize"];
    if (size == null)
      return defaultPageSize;
    else
      return (int)size;
  }
  set
  {
    ViewState["PageSize"] = value;
  }
}

/// <summary>
/// Ending item index of search list results.
/// </summary>
[Browsable(true), DefaultValue(defaultPageNumber)]
virtual public int PageNumber
{
  get
  {
    object pageNumber = ViewState["PageNumber"];
    if (pageNumber == null)
      return defaultPageNumber;
    else
      return (int)pageNumber;
  }
  set
  {
    if (value < 1)
      value = 1;
    ViewState["PageNumber"] = value;
  }
}

/// <summary>
/// Estimated total results count from query.
/// </summary>
[Browsable(false)]
virtual public int TotalResultsCount
{
  get
  {
    object count = ViewState["TotalResultsCount"];
```

```
        if (count == null)
          return 0;
        else
          return (int)count;
      }

    }

    /// <summary>
    /// Search query string.
    /// </summary>
    [Browsable(false)]
    virtual public string Query
    {
      get
      {
        object query = ViewState["Query"];
        if (query == null)
          return string.Empty;
        else
          return (string)query;
      }
      set
      {
        ViewState["Query"] = value;
      }
    }

    #endregion

    #region Appearance properties

    /// <summary>
    /// Display paging links at bottom of search results.
    /// </summary>
    [Description("Display paging links at bottom of search results."),
    Category("Appearance")]
    virtual public bool DisplayPager
    {
      get
      {
        object pager = ViewState["DisplayPager"];
        if (pager == null)
          return true;
        else
          return (bool)pager;
      }
```

```
    set
    {
      ViewState["DisplayPager"] = value;
    }
  }

  /// <summary>
  /// Style of Pager control link display.
  /// </summary>
  [Description("Style of Pager control link display."),
  Category("Appearance")]
  public ResultPagerLinkStyle PagerLinkStyle
  {
    get
    {
      return pagerLinkStyle;
    }
    set
    {
      pagerLinkStyle = value;
    }
  }

  /// <summary>
  /// Number of pages displayed in pager bar.
  /// </summary>
  [Description("Number of pages displayed in pager bar."),
  Category("Appearance"), DefaultValue(4)]
  virtual public int PagerBarRange
  {
    get
    {
      object range = ViewState["PagerBarRange"];
      if (range == null)
        return defaultPagerBarRange;
      else
        return (int)range;
    }
    set
    {
      ViewState["PagerBarRange"] = value;
    }
  }
  #endregion
```

```
    #region Miscellaneous properties
    /// <summary>
    /// Data source which takes a SearchResponse to build display.
    /// </summary>
    [DesignerSerializationVisibility(DesignerSerializationVisibility.Hidden),
          DefaultValue(null),
          Bindable(true),
          Browsable(false)]
    public LiveSearchService.SearchResponse DataSource
    {
      get
      {
        return dataSource;
      }
      set
      {
        dataSource = value;
      }
    }

    /// <summary>
    /// Collection of child ResultItem controls
    /// </summary>
    [Browsable(false)]
    public Collection<ResultItem> Items
    {
      get
      {
        return items;
      }
    }
    #endregion

    #region Style properties
    /// <summary>
    /// The style to be applied to header template.
    /// </summary>
    [Category("Style"),
    Description("The style to be applied to header template."),

DesignerSerializationVisibility(DesignerSerializationVisibility.Content),
    NotifyParentProperty(true),
    PersistenceMode(PersistenceMode.InnerProperty),
    ]
    public virtual Style HeaderStyle
    {
```

```
      get
      {
        if (headerStyle == null)
        {
          headerStyle = new Style();
          if (IsTrackingViewState)
            ((IStateManager)footerStyle).TrackViewState();
        }
        return headerStyle;
      }
    }

    /// <summary>
    /// The style to be applied to status template.
    /// </summary>
    [Category("Style"),
    Description("The style to be applied to status template."),

DesignerSerializationVisibility(DesignerSerializationVisibility.Content),
    NotifyParentProperty(true),
    PersistenceMode(PersistenceMode.InnerProperty),
    ]
    public virtual Style StatusStyle
    {
      get
      {
        if (statusStyle == null)
        {
          statusStyle = new Style();
          statusStyle.ForeColor = System.Drawing.Color.Blue;
          statusStyle.Font.Bold = true;
          if (IsTrackingViewState)
            ((IStateManager)statusStyle).TrackViewState();
        }
        return statusStyle;
      }
    }

    /// <summary>
    /// The style to be applied to item template.
    /// </summary>
    [Category("Style"),
    Description("The style to be applied to item template."),

DesignerSerializationVisibility(DesignerSerializationVisibility.Content),
    NotifyParentProperty(true),
    PersistenceMode(PersistenceMode.InnerProperty),
    ]
```

```
    public virtual Style ItemStyle
    {
      get
      {
        if (itemStyle == null)
        {
          itemStyle = new Style();
          if (IsTrackingViewState)
            ((IStateManager)itemStyle).TrackViewState();
        }
        return itemStyle;
      }
    }

    /// <summary>
    /// The style to be applied to alternate item template.
    /// </summary>
    [Category("Style"),
Description("The style to be applied to alternate item template."),

DesignerSerializationVisibility(DesignerSerializationVisibility.Content),
NotifyParentProperty(true),
PersistenceMode(PersistenceMode.InnerProperty),
]
    public virtual Style AlternatingItemStyle
    {
      get
      {
        if (alternatingItemStyle == null)
        {
          alternatingItemStyle = new Style();
          if (IsTrackingViewState)
            ((IStateManager)alternatingItemStyle).TrackViewState();
        }
        return alternatingItemStyle;
      }
    }

    /// <summary>
    /// The style to be applied to the separator template
    /// </summary>
    [Category("Style"),
    Description("The style to be applied to the separator template."),

DesignerSerializationVisibility(DesignerSerializationVisibility.Content),
    NotifyParentProperty(true),
    PersistenceMode(PersistenceMode.InnerProperty),
    ]
```

```
    public virtual Style SeparatorStyle
    {
      get
      {
        if (separatorStyle == null)
        {
          separatorStyle = new Style();
          if (IsTrackingViewState)
            ((IStateManager)separatorStyle).TrackViewState();
        }
        return separatorStyle;
      }
    }

    /// <summary>
    /// The style to be applied to the pager template.
    /// </summary>
    [Category("Style"),
    Description("The style to be applied to the pager."),

DesignerSerializationVisibility(DesignerSerializationVisibility.Content),
    NotifyParentProperty(true),
    PersistenceMode(PersistenceMode.InnerProperty),
    ]
    public virtual Style PagerStyle
    {
      get
      {
        if (pagerStyle == null)
        {
          pagerStyle = new Style();
          if (IsTrackingViewState)
            ((IStateManager)pagerStyle).TrackViewState();
        }
        return pagerStyle;
      }
    }

    /// <summary>
    /// The style to be applied to the footer template.
    /// </summary>
    [Category("Style"),
    Description("The style to be applied to the footer template."),

DesignerSerializationVisibility(DesignerSerializationVisibility.Content),
    NotifyParentProperty(true),
    PersistenceMode(PersistenceMode.InnerProperty),
    ]
```

```
    public virtual Style FooterStyle
    {
      get
      {
        if (footerStyle == null)
        {
          footerStyle = new Style();
          if (IsTrackingViewState)
            ((IStateManager)footerStyle).TrackViewState();
        }
        return footerStyle;
      }
    }
    #endregion

    #region Style and ViewState management
    /// <summary>
    /// Manual override of ViewState save method to put in custom
    /// styles for control templates
    /// </summary>
    /// <returns>Object array to persist to ViewState</returns>
    override protected object SaveViewState()
    {
      object baseState = base.SaveViewState();
      object headerStyleState = (headerStyle != null) ?
((IStateManager)HeaderStyle).SaveViewState() : null;
      object statusStyleState = (statusStyle != null) ?
((IStateManager)StatusStyle).SaveViewState() : null;
      object itemStyleState = (itemStyle != null) ?
((IStateManager)ItemStyle).SaveViewState() : null;
      object alternatingItemStyleState = (alternatingItemStyle != null) ?
((IStateManager)AlternatingItemStyle).SaveViewState() : null;
      object separatorStyleState = (separatorStyle != null) ?
((IStateManager)SeparatorStyle).SaveViewState() : null;
      object pagerStyleState = (pagerStyle != null) ?
((IStateManager)PagerStyle).SaveViewState() : null;
      object footerStyleState = (itemStyle != null) ?
((IStateManager)FooterStyle).SaveViewState() : null;

      object[] state = new object[8];
      state[0] = baseState;
      state[1] = headerStyleState;
      state[2] = statusStyleState;
      state[3] = itemStyleState;
      state[4] = alternatingItemStyleState;
      state[5] = separatorStyleState;
```

```
    state[6] = pagerStyleState;
    state[7] = footerStyleState;

    return state;
  }

  /// <summary>
  /// Manual override of ViewState load method to retrieve custom styles
  /// for control templates
  /// </summary>
  /// <param name="savedState">Object array retrieved from ViewState</param>
  override protected void LoadViewState(object savedState)
  {
    if (savedState != null)
    {
      object[] state = (object[])savedState;

      if (state[0] != null)
        base.LoadViewState(state[0]);
      if (state[1] != null)
        ((IStateManager)HeaderStyle).LoadViewState(state[1]);
      if (state[2] != null)
        ((IStateManager)StatusStyle).LoadViewState(state[2]);
      if (state[3] != null)
        ((IStateManager)ItemStyle).LoadViewState(state[3]);
      if (state[4] != null)

        ((IStateManager)AlternatingItemStyle).LoadViewState(state[4]);
      if (state[5] != null)
        ((IStateManager)SeparatorStyle).LoadViewState(state[5]);
      if (state[6] != null)
        ((IStateManager)PagerStyle).LoadViewState(state[6]);
      if (state[7] != null)
        ((IStateManager)FooterStyle).LoadViewState(state[7]);
    }
  }

  /// <summary>
  /// Build child control structure
  /// </summary>
  protected void PrepareControlHierarchy()
  {
    // apply all the appropriate style attributes
    // to the items in the result output
    foreach (ResultItem item in this.Items)
    {
```

```
        if (item.ItemType == ResultItemType.Header)
        {
          if (HeaderStyle != null)
            item.ApplyStyle(HeaderStyle);
        }
        else if (item.ItemType == ResultItemType.Status)
        {
          if (StatusStyle != null)
            item.ApplyStyle(StatusStyle);
        }
        else if (item.ItemType == ResultItemType.Item)
        {
          if (ItemStyle != null)
            item.ApplyStyle(ItemStyle);

        }
        else if (item.ItemType == ResultItemType.AlternatingItem)
        {
          if (AlternatingItemStyle != null)
            item.ApplyStyle(AlternatingItemStyle);
          else if (ItemStyle != null)
            item.ApplyStyle(ItemStyle);
        }
        else if (item.ItemType == ResultItemType.Separator)
        {
          if (SeparatorStyle != null)
            item.ApplyStyle(SeparatorStyle);
        }
        else if (item.ItemType == ResultItemType.Pager)
        {
          if (PagerStyle != null)
          {
            Pager pager = (Pager)item.Controls[0];
            pager.ApplyStyle(PagerStyle);
          }
        }
        else if (item.ItemType == ResultItemType.Footer)
        {
          if (FooterStyle != null)
            item.ApplyStyle(FooterStyle);
        }
      }
    }
    #endregion
```

```
#region Template properties
/// <summary>
/// The content to be shown at header of control.
/// </summary>
[Browsable(false),
DefaultValue(null),
Description("The content to be shown at header of control."),
PersistenceMode(PersistenceMode.InnerProperty),
TemplateContainer(typeof(ResultItem))
]
public ITemplate HeaderTemplate
{
  get
  {
    return headerTemplate;
  }
  set
  {
    headerTemplate = value;
  }
}

/// <summary>
/// The content to be shown in status area below header template.
/// </summary>
[Browsable(false),
DefaultValue(null),
Description("The content to be shown in status area below header template."),
PersistenceMode(PersistenceMode.InnerProperty),
TemplateContainer(typeof(ResultItem))
]
public ITemplate StatusTemplate
{
  get
  {
    return statusTemplate;
  }
  set
  {
    statusTemplate = value;
  }
}
```

```
/// <summary>
/// The content to be shown with each item of the search result set.
/// </summary>
[Browsable(false),
DefaultValue(null),
Description("The content to be shown with each item of the search result set."),
PersistenceMode(PersistenceMode.InnerProperty),
TemplateContainer(typeof(ResultItem))
]
public ITemplate ItemTemplate
{
  get
  {
    return itemTemplate;
  }
  set
  {
    itemTemplate = value;
  }
}

/// <summary>
/// The content to be shown with alternating items in the search result set.
/// </summary>
[Browsable(false),
DefaultValue(null),
Description(
"The content to be shown with alternating items in the search result set."),
PersistenceMode(PersistenceMode.InnerProperty),
TemplateContainer(typeof(ResultItem))
]
public ITemplate AlternatingItemTemplate
{
  get
  {
    return alternatingItemTemplate;
  }
  set
  {
    alternatingItemTemplate = value;
  }
}
```

```
/// <summary>
/// The content to be put between each item in the search result set.
/// </summary>
[Browsable(false),
DefaultValue(null),
Description(
"The content to be put between each item in the search result set."),
PersistenceMode(PersistenceMode.InnerProperty),
TemplateContainer(typeof(ResultItem))
]
public ITemplate SeparatorTemplate
{
  get
  {
    return separatorTemplate;
  }
  set
  {
    separatorTemplate = value;
  }
}

/// <summary>
/// The content to be shown below search results at bottom of control.
/// </summary>
[Browsable(false),
DefaultValue(null),
Description(
"The content to be shown below search results at bottom of control."),
PersistenceMode(PersistenceMode.InnerProperty),
TemplateContainer(typeof(ResultItem))
]
public ITemplate FooterTemplate
{
  get
  {
    return footerTemplate;
  }
  set
  {
    footerTemplate = value;
  }
}
#endregion
```

```
#region Events and Event Handling
public event EventHandler<LiveSearchSearchedEventArgs> LiveSearchSearched;
/// <summary>
/// Protected method for invoking LiveSearchSearched
/// event from within Result control
/// </summary>
/// <param name="e">Event arguments including search results</param>
protected virtual void OnLiveSearchSearched(LiveSearchSearchedEventArgs e)
{
  EventHandler<LiveSearchSearchedEventArgs> evnt = LiveSearchSearched;
  if (evnt != null)
    evnt(this, e);
}

public event EventHandler<ResultItemEventArgs> ItemCreated;
/// <summary>
///   Protected method for invoking ItemCreated event from within Result control
/// </summary>
/// <param name="e">Event arguments</param>
protected virtual void OnItemCreated(ResultItemEventArgs e)
{
  EventHandler<ResultItemEventArgs> evnt = ItemCreated;
  if (evnt != null)
    evnt(this, e);
}

public event EventHandler<ResultItemEventArgs> ItemDataBound;
/// <summary>
///   Protected method for invoking ItemDataBound event
/// from within Result control
/// </summary>
/// <param name="e">Event arguments</param>
protected virtual void OnItemDataBound(ResultItemEventArgs e)
{
  EventHandler<ResultItemEventArgs> evnt = ItemDataBound;
  if (evnt != null)
    evnt(this, e);
}

/// <summary>
/// Handles bubbled up events from child controls to catch paging events
/// from Pager control
/// </summary>
/// <param name="sender">Control which is source of event</param>
/// <param name="e">Event arguments</param>
/// <returns></returns>
```

```
protected override bool OnBubbleEvent(object source, EventArgs args)
{
  // Handle events raised by children by overriding OnBubbleEvent.
  // (main purpose is to detect paging events)
  bool handled = false;
  CommandEventArgs cea = args as CommandEventArgs;

  // handle Page event by extracting new start index
  // and calling HandleSearch method which does the
  // work of re-binding this control to the results
  // from the web service
  if (cea.CommandName == "Page")
  {
    PageNumber = Convert.ToInt32(cea.CommandArgument);
    HandleSearch();
  }
  return handled;
}

private void HandleSearch()
{
  SourceRequest[] sourceRequests = new SourceRequest[1];
  sourceRequests[0] = new SourceRequest();
  sourceRequests[0].Source = SourceType.Web;
  sourceRequests[0].Count = PageSize;
 //Specifies the number of results to return from offset
  sourceRequests[0].Offset = PageSize * (PageNumber - 1);
//start index for returned results
  //For paging, specify new offset to get next results.
  //so for count of 5, to get 6-10 specify offset of 5 for page 2
  sourceRequests[0].ResultFields = ResultFieldMask.All |
   ResultFieldMask.DateTime;

  SearchResponse searchResults =
     SearchUtility.SearchLiveSearchService(
     Query, sourceRequests);

  OnLiveSearchSearched(new LiveSearchSearchedEventArgs(searchResults));

  this.DataSource = searchResults;
  this.DataBind();
}
#endregion

#region Control Creation/Rendering
private ResultItem CreateResultItem(int index, ResultItemType
itemType, bool dataBind, object dataItem)
```

```
{
  ITemplate selectedTemplate;

  switch (itemType)
  {
    case ResultItemType.Header:
      selectedTemplate = HeaderTemplate;
      break;
    case ResultItemType.Status:
      if (StatusTemplate == null)
      {
        // if no StatusTemplate, pick up the default
        // template ResultStatusTemplate
        selectedTemplate = new ResultStatusTemplate();
      }
      else
        selectedTemplate = StatusTemplate;
      break;
    case ResultItemType.Item:
      if (ItemTemplate == null)
      {
        // if no ItemTemplate, pick up the default
        // template ResultItemTemplate
        selectedTemplate = new ResultItemTemplate();
      }
      else
        selectedTemplate = ItemTemplate;
      break;
    case ResultItemType.AlternatingItem:
      selectedTemplate = AlternatingItemTemplate;
      if (selectedTemplate == null)
      {
        // if no AlternatingItemTemplate, switch to Item type
        // and pick up ItemTemplate
        itemType = ResultItemType.Item;
        selectedTemplate = ItemTemplate;
        if (selectedTemplate == null)
        {
          // if that doesn't work, pick up the default
          // template ResultItemTemplate
          selectedTemplate = new ResultItemTemplate();
        }
      }
      break;
    case ResultItemType.Separator:
      selectedTemplate = SeparatorTemplate;
      break;
```

```
      case ResultItemType.Footer:
        selectedTemplate = FooterTemplate;
        break;
      default:
        selectedTemplate = null;
        break;
    }

    ResultItem item = new ResultItem(index, itemType, dataItem);

    if (selectedTemplate != null)
    {
      selectedTemplate.InstantiateIn(item);
    }

    OnItemCreated(new ResultItemEventArgs(item));
    Controls.Add(item);

    if (dataBind)
    {
      item.DataBind();
      OnItemDataBound(new ResultItemEventArgs(item));
    }
    return item;
  }

  private ResultItem CreatePagerResultItem()
  {
    ResultItem item = new ResultItem(-1, ResultItemType.Pager, null);

    Pager pager = new Pager();
    pager.PageSize = PageSize;
    pager.PagerBarRange = PagerBarRange;
    pager.PagerLinkStyle = PagerLinkStyle;
    pager.TotalResultsCount = TotalResultsCount;
    pager.PageNumber = PageNumber;

    item.Controls.Add(pager);

    Controls.Add(item);

    return item;
  }
```

```
    private void CreateControlHierarchy(bool dataBind)
    {
      Controls.Clear();
      SearchResponse result = null;

      // Result items
      items = new Collection<ResultItem>();

      int count = 0;

      if (dataBind == true)
      {
        if (DataSource == null)
          return;
        result = DataSource;

        // set ViewState values for read-only props
        ViewState["TotalResultsCount"] =
result.Responses[0].Total;
        ViewState["Offset"] = result.Responses[0].Offset;
        ViewState["Source"] = result.Responses[0].Source;

        count = result.Responses[0].Results.Length;
        ViewState["ResultItemCount"] = count;
      }
      else
      {
        object temp = ViewState["ResultItemCount"];
        if (temp != null)
          count = (int)temp;
      }

      if (HeaderTemplate != null)
      {
        ResultItem headerItem = CreateResultItem(-1,
ResultItemType.Header, false, null);
        items.Add(headerItem);
      }

      ResultItem statusItem = CreateResultItem(-1, ResultItemType.Status,
dataBind, result);
      items.Add(statusItem);

      // loop through and create ResultItem controls for each of the
      // result elements from the Live Search web service result
      ResultItemType itemType = ResultItemType.Item;
      for (int i = 0; i < count; i++)
```

```
    {
      if (separatorTemplate != null)
      {
        ResultItem separator =
        CreateResultItem(-1, ResultItemType.Separator, false, null);
        items.Add(separator);
      }

      LiveSearchService.Result searchResultItem = null;
      if (dataBind == true)
      {
        searchResultItem = result.Responses[0].Results[i];
      }

      ResultItem item = CreateResultItem(i,
        itemType, dataBind, searchResultItem);
      items.Add(item);

      // swap between item and alternatingitem types
      if (itemType == ResultItemType.Item)
        itemType = ResultItemType.AlternatingItem;
      else
        itemType = ResultItemType.Item;
    }

    // display pager if allowed by user and if results
    // are greater than a page in length
    if (DisplayPager == true && TotalResultsCount > PageSize)
    {
      ResultItem pager = CreatePagerResultItem();
      items.Add(pager);
    }

    if (FooterTemplate != null)
    {
      ResultItem footer = CreateResultItem(-1, ResultItemType.Footer,
false, null);
      items.Add(footer);
    }
  }

  private void CreateBlankControlHierarchy()
  {
    if (HeaderTemplate != null)
    {
      ResultItem headerItem = CreateResultItem(-1,
```

```
ResultItemType.Header, false, null);
          items.Add(headerItem);
        }

        if (FooterTemplate != null)
        {
          ResultItem footer = CreateResultItem(-1, ResultItemType.Footer,
false, null);
          items.Add(footer);
        }
      }

      /// <summary>
      /// Called by framework for composite controls to create control hierarchy
      /// </summary>
      override protected void CreateChildControls()
      {
        if (searchConducted == false &&
           ViewState["ResultItemCount"] != null)
        {
          CreateControlHierarchy(false);
        }
      }

      /// <summary>
      /// Binds search control results to control contents
      /// </summary>
      public override void DataBind()
      {
        base.OnDataBinding(System.EventArgs.Empty);

        Controls.Clear();
        ClearChildViewState();
        TrackViewState();

        searchConducted = true;
        CreateControlHierarchy(true);
        ChildControlsCreated = true;
      }

      /// <summary>
      /// Overridden to ensure Controls collection is created before external access
      /// </summary>
      public override ControlCollection Controls
      {
```

```
    get
    {
      EnsureChildControls();
      return base.Controls;
    }
  }

  /// <summary>
  /// Override of base method of server controls that does
  /// rendering of HTML content
  /// between the outer div tags
  /// </summary>
  /// <param name="writer">Stream class for HTML output</param>
  protected override void RenderContents(HtmlTextWriter writer)
  {
    // if no search, create a hierarchy with header and
    // footer templates only
    if (!searchConducted)
    {
      CreateBlankControlHierarchy();
    }

    // prep all template styles
    PrepareControlHierarchy();

    // render all child controls
    base.RenderContents(writer);
  }
  #endregion
 }
}
```

Now that we have covered the Search and Result server controls, in the next section we discuss the Pager control.

The Pager Control

The Pager control wraps the cumbersome logic of calculating page ranges in the pager bar and determining whether or not to display a Previous or Next button. It takes the properties we discussed earlier—PageSize, PagerBarRange, TotalResultsCount, and PageNumber—and builds a composite child control structure to render the paging functionality. The interesting work it does is centered on its CreateControlHierarchy implementation.

The actual scaffolding for the Pager control is an HTML table that has a row for text links. You can break it down into the following sections: Results Page label, Previous link, page links, and Next link. Figure 12-9 shows the pager at the beginning of the search results without a Previous link displayed.

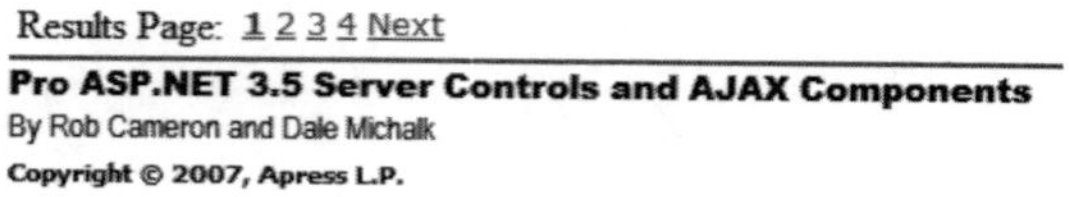

Results Page: 1 2 3 4 Next

Pro ASP.NET 3.5 Server Controls and AJAX Components
By Rob Cameron and Dale Michalk
Copyright © 2007, Apress L.P.

Figure 12-9. *A Pager control without a Previous link*

Figure 12-10 shows the situation in which there are pages before and after the current page.

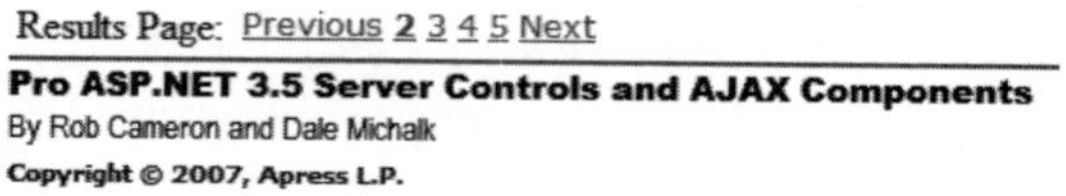

Results Page: Previous 2 3 4 5 Next

Pro ASP.NET 3.5 Server Controls and AJAX Components
By Rob Cameron and Dale Michalk
Copyright © 2007, Apress L.P.

Figure 12-10. *A Pager control with Previous and Next links*

In the scenario in which there are no subsequent pages in the page range, as shown in Figure 12-11, the Next link is omitted.

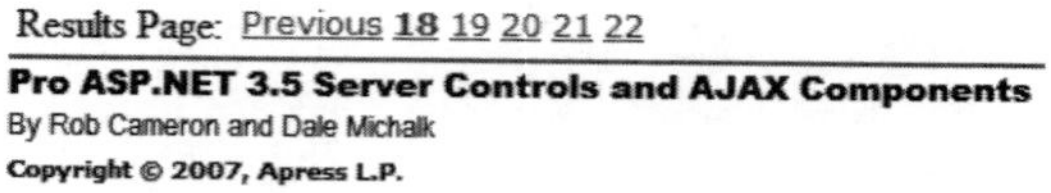

Results Page: Previous 18 19 20 21 22

Pro ASP.NET 3.5 Server Controls and AJAX Components
By Rob Cameron and Dale Michalk
Copyright © 2007, Apress L.P.

Figure 12-11. *A Pager control without a Next link*

Creating the Pager Results

The Pager control, like the Result and Search controls, is built using a composite control architecture. Because of this, it overrides the CreateControlHierarchy method to build up its HTML table structure:

```
private void CreateControlHierarchy()
{
   table = new Table();

   TableRow textRow = new TableRow();
   textRow.VerticalAlign = VerticalAlign.Top;

   // insert localized "Page Results:" text
   CreatePagerResults(textRow, PagerLinkStyle);
```

The first part of this method adds the Results section:

```
private void CreatePagerResults(TableRow textRow,
ResultPagerLinkStyle style)
{
   TableCell cell;

   cell = new TableCell();
```

```
    ResourceManager rm = ResourceFactory.Manager;

    cell.Text = rm.GetString("Pager.resultsPageCell.Text");
    cell.Wrap = false;
    cell.HorizontalAlign = HorizontalAlign.Center;
    textRow.Cells.Add(cell);
}
```

Creating the Pager's Previous Button

The next piece of code calculates the total number of pages based on the EndIndex and PageSize values. The current page is also determined by looking at the StartIndex of the current web service search and dividing it by PageSize:

```
// calculate the total number of pages based on the
// page size and the TotalResultsCount from the
// search service query
int numPages = (int) System.Math.Ceiling(
   (double) TotalResultsCount / PageSize);
```

The PageNumber value on Pager is provided by the Result control, so no calculation is required. The end page is calculated through some simple math calculations, as shown here:

```
int endPage = 0;
int calculatedEndPage = (int)System.Math.Floor((double)
  TotalResultsCount / PageSize);
if ((calculatedEndPage - PageNumber) > PagerBarRange)
  endPage = PageNumber + PagerBarRange - 1;
else
  endPage = calculatedEndPage;
```

The following CreatePagerPreviousButton method has code to create the Previous link. We use LinkButton for the text link as well.

```
private void CreatePagerPreviousButton(TableRow textRow,
   ResultPagerLinkStyle style, int prevIndex)
{

   TableCell cell;

   ResourceManager rm = ResourceFactory.Manager;

   cell = new TableCell();
   LinkButton prevButton = new LinkButton();
   prevButton.ID = "PrevButton";
   prevButton.Text = rm.GetString("Pager.prevButton.Text");
   prevButton.CommandName = "Page";
   prevButton.CommandArgument = prevIndex.ToString();
   cell.HorizontalAlign = HorizontalAlign.Right;
```

```
    cell.Controls.Add(prevButton);

    textRow.Cells.Add(cell);
  }
```

Crucial to the functioning of the parent Result control are the LinkButton objects that are configured to raise a specific command event named Page. The CommandArgument argument to the event is set to the numeric index of the page and is received by the Result control in its OnBubbleEvent override.

Creating the Pager's Bar Pages

The next section of code in CreateControlHierarchy deals with the page numbers that are directly displayed in the Results bar by the Pager control. The PagerBarRange property controls the size of this bar. Inside the code, we loop through each page, creating its content by invoking CreatePagerPageButton:

```
// loop through each page and spit out the page link
for (int pageNum = startPage; pageNum <= endPage; pageNum++)
{

   // insert Page number text
   CreatePagerPageButton(textRow, PagerLinkStyle,
   pageNum,  (currentPage == pageNum));
}
```

The code in the following CreatePagerPageButton creates the link for each page of results:

```
private void CreatePagerPageButton(TableRow textRow,
   ResultPagerLinkStyle style, int pageNum, bool currentPage)
{
  TableCell cell;
  LiteralControl lit;

  cell = new TableCell();
  cell.HorizontalAlign = HorizontalAlign.Center;

  // add extra separation between page numbers
  // if text only paging is used
  if (style == ResultPagerLinkStyle.Text)
  {
    lit = new LiteralControl();
    lit.Text = " ";
    cell.Controls.Add(lit);
  }
  //For TextWithDHTML functionality, you can create a
  //HighlightedLinkButton class similar to the
  //HighlightedHyperlink created in chapter 9
  //and render that instead of the basic LinkButton
```

```
  //based on the configured ResultPagerLinkStyle
  LinkButton pageButton = new LinkButton();
  pageButton.ID = "page" + pageNum.ToString() + "Button";
  pageButton.Text = pageNum.ToString();
  pageButton.CommandName = "Page";
  pageButton.CommandArgument = pageNum.ToString();
  pageButton.CausesValidation = true;
  if (currentPage == true)
    pageButton.ControlStyle.Font.Bold = true;

  cell.Controls.Add(pageButton);
  textRow.Cells.Add(cell);
}
```

Creating the Pager's Next Button

After we are done creating the page number links, we have code that is similar to the Previous button code. However, this code creates the Next button with a call to CreatePagerNextButton:

```
// insert a next link if less than max number of pages
if (calculatedEndPage > endPage)
{
  // insert Next text
  CreatePagerNextButton(textRow, PagerLinkStyle, PageNumber + 1);
}
```

The code for CreatePagerNextButton is as follows:

```
private void CreatePagerNextButton(TableRow textRow,
   ResultPagerLinkStyle style, int nextIndex)
{
  TableCell cell = new TableCell();
  LiteralControl lit;

  cell = new TableCell();

  // add extra separation between page numbers
  // if text only paging is used
  if (style == ResultPagerLinkStyle.Text)
  {
    lit = new LiteralControl();
    lit.Text = " ";
    cell.Controls.Add(lit);
  }

  ResourceManager rm = ResourceFactory.Manager;
```

```
    LinkButton nextButton = new LinkButton();
    nextButton.ID = "nextButton";
    nextButton.Text = rm.GetString("Pager.nextButton.Text");
    nextButton.CommandName = "Page";
    nextButton.CommandArgument = nextIndex.ToString();
    cell.HorizontalAlign = HorizontalAlign.Center;
    cell.Controls.Add(nextButton);

    textRow.Cells.Add(cell);
}
```

Ensuring Pager's Style Rendering

The Pager server control overrides the RenderContents methods for two primary reasons. First, it ensures that all child controls are correctly created in a design-time situation. It does that by having code that calls EnsureChildControls in the rendering override. Second, it ensures that the PagerStyle property maintained by the Result control and specifically passed by the code in its PrepareControlHierarchy implementation is rendered correctly as part of the internal structure of the Pager control.

```
protected override void RenderContents(HtmlTextWriter writer)
{
   EnsureChildControls();

   PrepareControlHierarchy();

   base.RenderContents (writer);
}
```

It uses a PrepareControlHierarchy implementation to grab the Table control, which is the major child structure, and applies its ControlStyle property to it if it has been set:

```
protected void PrepareControlHierarchy()
{
   // apply the Pager style attributes to the
   // table if they were specified by Result control
   if (this.ControlStyleCreated)
      table.ApplyStyle(this.ControlStyle);
}
```

At this point, we have a fully functional Pager control. Listing 12-7 presents the complete class file.

Listing 12-7. *The Pager.cs Class File*

```
using System.Resources;
using System.Web.UI;
using System.Web.UI.WebControls;
```

```
namespace ControlsBook2Lib.CH12.LiveSearchControls
{
  /// <summary>
  /// Pager control implements the paging functionality aggregated
  /// by the Result control
  /// </summary>
  internal class Pager : CompositeControl
  {
    private Table table;
    private ResultPagerLinkStyle pagerLinkStyle;
    private int pagerBarRange;
    private int pageSize;
    private int totalResultsCount;
    private int pageNumber;

    /// <summary>
    /// Pager is based on span tag
    /// </summary>
    protected override HtmlTextWriterTag TagKey
    {
      get
      {
        return HtmlTextWriterTag.Span;
      }
    }

    /// <summary>
    /// Number of search results returned with query and displayed on page.
    /// </summary>
    public int PageSize
    {
      get
      {
        return pageSize;
      }
      set
      {
        pageSize = value;
      }
    }

    /// <summary>
    /// Number of pages displayed in pager bar.
    /// </summary>
    public int PagerBarRange
    {
```

```
    get
    {
      return pagerBarRange;
    }
    set
    {
      pagerBarRange = value;
    }
  }

  /// <summary>
  /// Style of Pager control link display.
  /// </summary>
  public ResultPagerLinkStyle PagerLinkStyle
  {
    get
    {
      return pagerLinkStyle;
    }
    set
    {
      pagerLinkStyle = value;
    }
  }

  ///<summary>
  /// Current Page of search results.
  ///</summary>
  public int PageNumber
  {
    get
    {
      return pageNumber;
    }
    set
    {
      pageNumber = value;
    }
  }

  /// <summary>
  /// Estimated total results count from query.
  /// </summary>
  public int TotalResultsCount
  {
```

```
  get
  {
    return totalResultsCount;
  }
  set
  {
    totalResultsCount = value;
  }
}

private void CreatePagerResults(TableRow textRow,
   ResultPagerLinkStyle style)
{
  TableCell cell;

  cell = new TableCell();

  ResourceManager rm = ResourceFactory.Manager;

  cell.Text = rm.GetString("Pager.resultsPageCell.Text");
  cell.Wrap = false;
  cell.HorizontalAlign = HorizontalAlign.Center;
  textRow.Cells.Add(cell);
}

private void CreatePagerPreviousButton(TableRow textRow,
   ResultPagerLinkStyle style, int prevIndex)
{

  TableCell cell;

  ResourceManager rm = ResourceFactory.Manager;

  cell = new TableCell();
  LinkButton prevButton = new LinkButton();
  prevButton.ID = "PrevButton";
  prevButton.Text = rm.GetString("Pager.prevButton.Text");
  prevButton.CommandName = "Page";
  prevButton.CommandArgument = prevIndex.ToString();
  cell.HorizontalAlign = HorizontalAlign.Right;
  cell.Controls.Add(prevButton);

  textRow.Cells.Add(cell);
}
```

```
private void CreatePagerPageButton(TableRow textRow,
   ResultPagerLinkStyle style, int pageNum, bool currentPage)
{
  TableCell cell;
  LiteralControl lit;

  cell = new TableCell();
  cell.HorizontalAlign = HorizontalAlign.Center;

  // add extra separation between page numbers
  // if text only paging is used
  if (style == ResultPagerLinkStyle.Text)
  {
    lit = new LiteralControl();
    lit.Text = " ";
    cell.Controls.Add(lit);
  }
  //For TextWithDHTML functionality, you can create a
  //HighlightedLinkButton class similar to the
  //HighlightedHyperlink created in chapter 9
  //and render that instead of the basic LinkButton
  //based on the configured ResultPagerLinkStyle
  LinkButton pageButton = new LinkButton();
  pageButton.ID = "page" + pageNum.ToString() + "Button";
  pageButton.Text = pageNum.ToString();
  pageButton.CommandName = "Page";
  pageButton.CommandArgument = pageNum.ToString();
  pageButton.CausesValidation = true;
  if (currentPage == true)
    pageButton.ControlStyle.Font.Bold = true;

  cell.Controls.Add(pageButton);
  textRow.Cells.Add(cell);
}

private void CreatePagerNextButton(TableRow textRow,
   ResultPagerLinkStyle style, int nextIndex)
{
  TableCell cell = new TableCell();
  LiteralControl lit;

  cell = new TableCell();

  // add extra separation between page numbers
  // if text only paging is used
```

```
    if (style == ResultPagerLinkStyle.Text)
    {
      lit = new LiteralControl();
      lit.Text = " ";
      cell.Controls.Add(lit);
    }

    ResourceManager rm = ResourceFactory.Manager;

    LinkButton nextButton = new LinkButton();
    nextButton.ID = "nextButton";
    nextButton.Text = rm.GetString("Pager.nextButton.Text");
    nextButton.CommandName = "Page";
    nextButton.CommandArgument = nextIndex.ToString();
    cell.HorizontalAlign = HorizontalAlign.Center;
    cell.Controls.Add(nextButton);

    textRow.Cells.Add(cell);
  }

  private void CreateControlHierarchy()
  {
    table = new Table();

    TableRow textRow = new TableRow();
    textRow.VerticalAlign = VerticalAlign.Top;

    // insert localized "Page Results:" text
    CreatePagerResults(textRow, PagerLinkStyle);

    // if the page number greater than 1 you can put in a previous page
    // link
    if (PageNumber > 1)
    {
      // insert Previous text
      CreatePagerPreviousButton(textRow, PagerLinkStyle, PageNumber - 1);
    }

    int endPage = 0;
    int calculatedEndPage =
      (int)System.Math.Floor((double)TotalResultsCount / PageSize);
    if ((calculatedEndPage - PageNumber) > PagerBarRange)
      endPage = PageNumber + PagerBarRange - 1;
    else
      endPage = calculatedEndPage;
```

```
    // loop through each page and spit out the page link
    for (int pageNum = PageNumber; pageNum <= endPage; pageNum++)
    {

      // insert Page number text
      CreatePagerPageButton(textRow, PagerLinkStyle,
         pageNum,(PageNumber == pageNum));
    }

    // insert a next link if less than max number of pages
    if (calculatedEndPage > endPage)
    {
      // calculate the next index to link to
      int nextIndex = PageNumber + PagerBarRange;
      // insert Next text
      CreatePagerNextButton(textRow, PagerLinkStyle, PageNumber + 1);
    }

    // always display text links
    table.Rows.Add(textRow);

    Controls.Add(table);
  }

  /// <summary>
  /// Called by framework for composite controls to create control heirarchy
  /// </summary>
  override protected void CreateChildControls()
  {
    Controls.Clear();
    CreateControlHierarchy();
  }

  /// <summary>
  /// Overridden to ensure Controls collection is created before external access
  /// </summary>
  public override ControlCollection Controls
  {
    get
    {
      EnsureChildControls();
      return base.Controls;
    }
  }
```

```
    protected void PrepareControlHierarchy()
    {
      // apply the Pager style attributes to the
      // table if they were specified by Result control
      if (this.ControlStyleCreated)
        table.ApplyStyle(this.ControlStyle);
    }

    /// <summary>
    /// Overridden to ensure styles are properly applied
    /// </summary>
    protected override void RenderContents(HtmlTextWriter writer)
    {
      EnsureChildControls();

      PrepareControlHierarchy();

      base.RenderContents(writer);
    }
  }
}
```

This completes the first part of our discussion of the Live Search server control. In the next chapter, we dive deeper into the implementation details and test the functionality of the control.

Summary

In this chapter, we focused on putting together a full-featured control based on the Live Search web service. We covered the web service API and the design decisions that went into the control, and we provided detailed discussion of the individual controls. The discussion included information on building a control library in a strong-named assembly to allow it to deploy into the global assembly cache (GAC) for easy machine-level deployment and to provide built-in tamper-resistant facilities. We also demonstrated how to use the `web.config` configuration file system for our own purposes by developing a custom configuration section for our control library.

We rounded out this chapter with a detailed discussion of the individual controls that make up the Live Search control library. We also set the stage for the next chapter by implementing configuration management for licensing and deployment. In the next chapter, we finish our discussion of the Live Search control by covering design-time functionality, template support, globalization, localization, and tools to assist with quality and deployment.

CHAPTER 13

Packaging and Deployment

This chapter is second in our two-part discussion of the Live Search control. In the previous chapter, we covered the design of each control, configuration management, and of course, the Live Search API and the design decisions that went into the control to interact with the Live Search API. In this chapter, we start off with a discussion of design-time support in the Live Search control and then jump into the packaging and deployment using our Live Search control as an example. We focus on the following topics for packaging and deploying server controls:

- Design-time support (data binding and templates)
- Testing the Live Search controls
- Licensing
- Implementing globalization and localization
- Using Visual Studio Code Analysis for Managed Code to check design decisions and coding conventions
- Using XML comments in code to generate documentation

Designer Support

Oftentimes, what separates a good control from a great control is the design-time experience for users of a server control, or any component for that matter. We covered design-time support in detail in Chapter 11. In this section, we extend the discussion and cover the design-time support built into the Live Search web control library to provide a pleasant UI when working with the controls at design time.

Designers and Dummy Data Source

The designer support for the Live Search web control library centers on support for the two primary controls that are visible and reachable in the design-time environment. Both `Result` and `Search` have a designer built specifically for them. `SearchDesigner` is the simpler of the two. As shown in Listing 13-1, it is a typical composite control designer that implements the bare minimum to get it rendered correctly.

Listing 13-1. *The SearchDesigner.cs Class File*

```
using System;
using System.ComponentModel;
using System.Web.UI;
using System.Web.UI.Design.WebControls;

namespace ControlsBook2Lib.CH12.LiveSearchControls.Design
{
  /// <summary>
  /// Designer for LiveSearch Lib Search control
  /// </summary>
  public class SearchDesigner : CompositeControlDesigner
  {
    /// <summary>
    /// Initialize the resources of the designer
    /// </summary>
    /// <param name="component">Component which the designer is linked to</param>
    public override void Initialize(IComponent component)
    {
      if (!(component is Control) && !(component is INamingContainer))
      {
        throw new ArgumentException(
           "This control is not a composite control.", "component");
      }
      base.Initialize(component);
    }

    /// <summary>
    /// HTML rendered when control has an "empty" configuration
    /// </summary>
    /// <returns>HTML string</returns>
    protected override string GetEmptyDesignTimeHtml()
    {
      return CreatePlaceHolderDesignTimeHtml(
         Component.GetType() + " control.");
    }

    /// <summary>
    /// HTML rendered when control has an "error" in its configuration
    /// </summary>
    /// <returns>HTML string</returns>
    protected override string GetErrorDesignTimeHtml(Exception e)
    {
```

```
            return CreatePlaceHolderDesignTimeHtml(
               "There was an error rendering the" +
               this.Component.GetType() + " control." +
               "<br>Exception: " + e.Source + " Message: " + e.Message);
         }
      }
   }
```

ResultDesigner is more complex. Because it handles the large number of templates that the Result control exposes, it provides visual template editing support for the following templates: HeaderTemplate, StatusTemplate, ItemTemplate, AlternatingItemTemplate, SeparatorTemplate, and FooterTemplate. Figure 13-1 shows the template menu options.

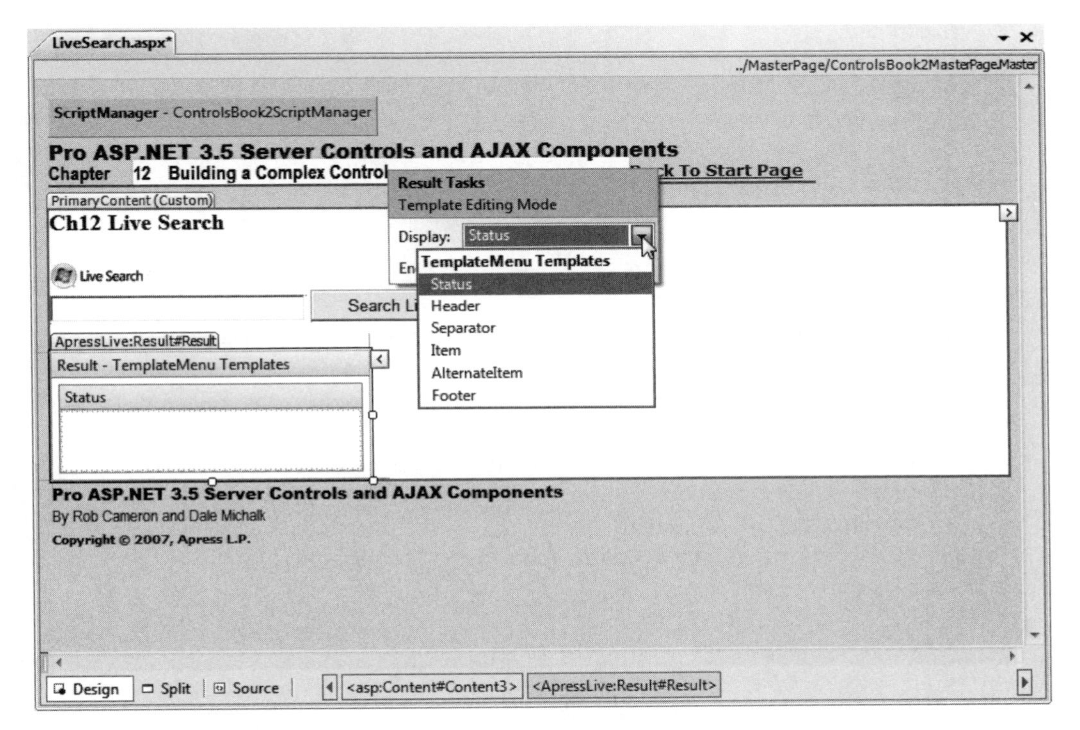

Figure 13-1. *The ResultDesigner template editing user interface*

The GetDesignTimeHtml method also uses a dummy data source instead of actually invoking the Live Search web service in the designer. ResultDummyDataSource has a method named GetLiveSearchSearchResults that takes as a parameter the page size so that it will create that many elements in the result set. ResultDesigner queries the Result control for its PageSize property value before invoking GetLiveSearchResults to make the design-time display more reflective of the execution display.

The full code for `ResultDesigner` is shown in Listing 13-2, and the code for `ResultDummyDataSource` is in Listing 13-3.

Listing 13-2. *The ResultDesigner.cs Class File*

```
using System;
using System.ComponentModel;
using System.ComponentModel.Design;
using System.Web.UI;
using System.Web.UI.Design;

namespace ControlsBook2Lib.CH12.LiveSearchControls.Design
{
  /// <summary>
  /// Designer class for the Result server control
  /// </summary>
  public class ResultDesigner : ControlDesigner
  {
    TemplateGroupCollection templateGroupCol;

    /// <summary>
    /// Initialize the resources of the designer
    /// </summary>
    /// <param name="component">Component which the designer is linked to</param>
    public override void Initialize(IComponent component)
    {
      base.Initialize(component);
      if (!(component is Result) && !(component is INamingContainer))
      {
        throw new ArgumentException(
           "This control is not a Result control.", "component");
      }
      else
        SetViewFlags(ViewFlags.TemplateEditing, true);
    }

    /// <summary>
    /// Pointer to template editing menu items
    /// </summary>
    public override TemplateGroupCollection TemplateGroups
    {
      get
      {
        if (templateGroupCol == null)
        {
          // Get the base collection
          templateGroupCol = base.TemplateGroups;
```

```
      TemplateGroup templateGroup;
      TemplateDefinition templateDef;
      Result ctl;

      //Get reference to the component as Result
      ctl = (Result)Component;

      //Create Template Group
      templateGroup = new TemplateGroup("TemplateMenu Templates");

      //Status
      templateDef = new TemplateDefinition(this, "Status",
          ctl, "StatusTemplate", false);
      templateGroup.AddTemplateDefinition(templateDef);

      //Header
      templateDef = new TemplateDefinition(this, "Header",
          ctl, "HeaderTemplate", false);
      templateGroup.AddTemplateDefinition(templateDef);

      //Separator
      templateDef = new TemplateDefinition(this, "Separator",
           ctl, "SeparatorTemplate", false);
      templateGroup.AddTemplateDefinition(templateDef);

      //Item
      templateDef = new TemplateDefinition(this, "Item",
          ctl, "ItemTemplate", false);
      templateGroup.AddTemplateDefinition(templateDef);

      //Alternate Item
      templateDef = new TemplateDefinition(this, "AlternateItem",
          ctl, "AlternateItemTemplate", false);
      templateGroup.AddTemplateDefinition(templateDef);

      //Footer
      templateDef = new TemplateDefinition(this, "Footer",
          ctl, "FooterTemplate", false);
      templateGroup.AddTemplateDefinition(templateDef);

      // Add the TemplateGroup to the TemplateGroupCollection
      templateGroupCol.Add(templateGroup);
    }

    return templateGroupCol;
  }
}
```

```
/// <summary>
/// Determines if designer allows control to be resized in editor
/// </summary>
public override bool AllowResize
{
  get
  {
    bool templateExists =
                    null != ((Result)Component).HeaderTemplate ||
                    null != ((Result)Component).StatusTemplate ||
                    null != ((Result)Component).AlternatingItemTemplate ||
                    null != ((Result)Component).ItemTemplate ||
                    null != ((Result)Component).SeparatorTemplate ||
                    null != ((Result)Component).FooterTemplate;

    return templateExists || InTemplateMode;
  }
}

/// <summary>
/// Provides HTML for the visual designer to display
/// </summary>
/// <returns>HTML string based on rendering the
/// control with a dummy data source</returns>
public override string GetDesignTimeHtml()
{
  Result control = (Result)Component;
  string designTimeHTML = null;

  // bind Result control to dummy data source
  // that has the appropriate page size
  control.DataSource =
     ResultDummyDataSource.GetLiveSearchResults(control.PageSize);
  control.DataBind();

  // let base class designer call Render() on
  // data-bound control to get HTML
  designTimeHTML = base.GetDesignTimeHtml();

  return designTimeHTML;
}

/// <summary>
/// HTML rendered when control has an "error" in its configuration
/// </summary>
/// <returns>HTML string</returns>
```

```
protected override string GetErrorDesignTimeHtml(Exception e)
{

  return CreatePlaceHolderDesignTimeHtml(
 "There was an error rendering the TemplateMenu control." +
     "<br>Exception: " + e.Source + "  Message: " + e.Message);
}


/// <summary>
/// Checks to see if any templates have their content set to a non-empty value
/// </summary>
protected bool TemplatesExist
{
  get
  {
    return (
       ((Result)Component).HeaderTemplate != null ||
       ((Result)Component).StatusTemplate != null ||
       ((Result)Component).ItemTemplate != null ||
       ((Result)Component).AlternatingItemTemplate != null ||
       ((Result)Component).SeparatorTemplate != null ||
       ((Result)Component).FooterTemplate != null
    );
  }
}

/// <summary>
/// Called when the component has been changed
/// </summary>
/// <param name="sender">Sender of the event</param>
/// <param name="e">Event data including member that was changed.</param>
public override void OnComponentChanged(
   object sender, ComponentChangedEventArgs ce)
{
  if (ce.Member != null)
  {
    string memberName = ce.Member.Name;
    if (memberName.Equals("HeaderStyle") ||
       memberName.Equals("StatusStyle") ||
       memberName.Equals("ItemStyle") ||
       memberName.Equals("AlternatingItemStyle") ||
       memberName.Equals("SeparatorStyle") ||
       memberName.Equals("PagerStyle") ||
       memberName.Equals("FooterStyle"))
```

```
          {
            OnStylesChanged();
          }
        }

        base.OnComponentChanged(sender, ce);
      }

      /// <summary>
      /// Override of method that is invoked when control styles change
      /// </summary>
      protected void OnStylesChanged()
      {
        //OnTemplateEditingVerbsChanged();
      }

      /// <summary>
      /// HTML rendered when control has an "empty" configuration
      /// </summary>
      /// <returns>HTML string</returns>
      protected override string GetEmptyDesignTimeHtml()
      {
        string text;

        if (!TemplatesExist)
        {
          text = "Click the arrow, select edit Template,
                      then choose a template to modify.";
        }
        else
        {
          text = "Switch to HTML view to edit the control's templates.";
        }
        return CreatePlaceHolderDesignTimeHtml(text);
      }
  }
}
```

Listing 13-3. *The ResultDummyDataSource.cs Class File*

```
namespace ControlsBook2Lib.CH12.LiveSearchControls
{
  /// <summary>
  /// Provides a fictional Data source to show control rendering of
  /// templates while control is in design-time mode
  /// </summary>
```

```
public sealed class ResultDummyDataSource
{
  private const int TotalResultsCount = 100;

  private ResultDummyDataSource()
  {
  }
  /// <summary>
  /// Returns a LiveSearchService.SearchResponse data set that is valid
  /// according to web service guidelines
  /// </summary>
  /// <param name="pageSize">
      page size of the LiveSearchService.SearchResponse set</param>
  /// <returns>LiveSearchService.SearchResponse instance
      with Service.resultElement
  /// entries present according to page size</returns>
  public static LiveSearchService.SearchResponse
  GetLiveSearchResults(int pageSize)
  {
    LiveSearchService.SearchResponse result = new
    LiveSearchService.SearchResponse();
    LiveSearchService.SourceResponse[] sr = new
    LiveSearchService.SourceResponse[TotalResultsCount];
    result.Responses = sr;
    sr.SetValue(new LiveSearchService.SourceResponse(), 0);
    result.Responses[0].Total = TotalResultsCount;
    result.Responses[0].Source = LiveSearchService.SourceType.Web;
    result.Responses[0].Offset = 0;
    // fill up 10 result elements
    result.Responses[0].Results = new LiveSearchService.Result[pageSize];
    for (int i = 0; i < pageSize; i++)
    {
      result.Responses[0].Results[i] = GetResult(i);
    }

    return result;
  }

  /// <summary>
  /// Returns a valid LiveSearchService.Result instance
  /// </summary>
  /// <param name="index">Index to help create title and url</param>
  /// <returns>Fully populated LiveSearchService.Result instance</returns>
  public static LiveSearchService.Result GetResult(int index)
  {
```

```
            LiveSearchService.Result result = new LiveSearchService.Result();
            result.Title = "Result Control " + (index + 1);
            result.Url = "http://apress.com/resultcontrol" + (index + 1);
            result.Summary = "Summary";
            result.Description = "Description";
            result.CacheUrl = "http://apress.com/cached" + (index + 1);
            return result;
        }
    }
}
```

In the next section, we discuss the default template support provided in the Result control.

Template Support in the Result Control

The Result control is able to display a decent stock Live Search look and feel even when dropped directly from the Toolbox. This is achieved through the use of two templates, ResultStatusTemplate and ResultItemTemplate, which are added to the control if the template structure is not set in the .aspx page containing the control. To provide implementation of the default templates, the template classes must implement the ITemplate interface and its InstantiateIn method. The signature for this method is as follows:

```
public void InstantiateIn(Control container)
{}
```

The template is given the container in which to instantiate its controls. In ResultStatusTemplate, we use InstantiateIn to add a Label control and a LiteralControl, which represents an HTML break:

```
public void InstantiateIn(Control container)
{
   Label header = new Label();
   header.DataBinding +=new EventHandler(BindResultHeader);
   container.Controls.Add(header);
   LiteralControl lit = new LiteralControl();
   lit.Text = "<br>";
   container.Controls.Add(lit);
}
```

We also map the DataBinding event exposed by the Label control to BindResultHeader. This allows us to later insert the correct information into our Label control when a data source is attached to the StatusTemplate of the Result control in its data-binding process. BindResultHeader uses a help method named GetResultControl, which is able to cast from the Label control upward to get at the Result control. We then use the GetResult helper method to grab the search result data from in the form of the LiveSearchResult class. The rest of the method is a process of building up a string that depicts the range of the search results, the number of total results, and the time it took for the query to happen. Listing 13-4 shows the full source code for ResultStatusTemplate.

Listing 13-4. *The ResultStatusTemplate.cs Class File*

```
using System;
using System.Resources;
using System.Text;
using System.Web.UI;
using System.Web.UI.WebControls;

namespace ControlsBook2Lib.CH12.LiveSearchControls
{
  /// <summary>
  ///  Default StatusTemplate implementation used by a
  ///  Stock Live Result control without a StatusTemplate
  /// </summary>
  public class ResultStatusTemplate : ITemplate
  {
    /// <summary>
    /// Method puts template controls into container control
    /// </summary>
    /// <param name="container">Outside control container to template items</param>
    public void InstantiateIn(Control container)
    {
      Label header = new Label();
      header.DataBinding += new EventHandler(BindResultHeader);
      container.Controls.Add(header);
      LiteralControl lit = new LiteralControl();
      lit.Text = "<br>";
      container.Controls.Add(lit);
    }

    private Result GetResultControl(Control container)
    {
      ResultItem itemControl = (ResultItem)container.Parent;
      Result resultControl = (Result)itemControl.Parent;
      return resultControl;
    }

    private void BindResultHeader(object source, EventArgs e)
    {
      Label header = (Label)source;
      Result resultControl = GetResultControl(header);

      StringBuilder section = new StringBuilder();

      // get ResouceManager for localized format strings
      ResourceManager rm = ResourceFactory.Manager;
```

```
        // Searched for: <searchQuery>
        section.Append(
        String.Format(
           rm.GetString("ResultStatusTemplate.SearchFor"),
           resultControl.Query));
        section.Append("<br>");

        // Result <StartIndex+1> - <EndIndex+1> of about
        // <TotalResultsCount> records
        // (accounting for zero based index)
        section.Append(
        String.Format(
           rm.GetString("ResultStatusTemplate.ResultAbout"),
        ((resultControl.PageNumber - 1) * (resultControl.PageSize)) + 1,
        resultControl.PageNumber * (resultControl.PageSize),
        resultControl.TotalResultsCount));
        section.Append("  ");

        header.Text = section.ToString();
      }
    }
}
```

ResultItemTemplate provides the default display for each item from the search results. The control content added inside the container includes a hyperlink displaying the title field Live Search Result and providing a hyperlink to the value of its URL field. It also adds a label to display the snippet field and a label to display the URL field. It uses three separate data-binding routines to accomplish the data loading: BindLink, BindSnippet, and BindUrl. Listing 13-5 presents the full source code.

Listing 13-5. *The ResultItemTemplate.cs Class File*

```
using System;
using System.Web.UI;
using System.Web.UI.WebControls;

namespace ControlsBook2Lib.CH12.LiveSearchControls
{
  /// <summary>
  ///  Default ResultItemTemplate implementation used by a
  ///  Stock LiveSearch Lib Result control without a ItemTemplate
  /// </summary>
  public class ResultItemTemplate : ITemplate
  {
    /// <summary>
    /// Method puts template controls into container control
    /// </summary>
    /// <param name="container">Outside control container to template items</param>
```

```
    public void InstantiateIn(Control container)
    {
      HyperLink link = new HyperLink();
      link.DataBinding += new EventHandler(BindLink);
      container.Controls.Add(link);
      container.Controls.Add(new LiteralControl("<br>"));

      Label snippet = new Label();
      snippet.DataBinding += new EventHandler(BindSnippet);
      container.Controls.Add(snippet);
      container.Controls.Add(new LiteralControl("<br>"));

      Label url = new Label();
      url.DataBinding += new EventHandler(BindUrl);
      container.Controls.Add(url);
      container.Controls.Add(new LiteralControl("<br>"));
      container.Controls.Add(new LiteralControl("<br>"));
    }

    private LiveSearchService.Result GetResultElement(Control container)
    {
      ResultItem item = (ResultItem)container;
      return (LiveSearchService.Result)item.DataItem;
    }

    private void BindLink(object source, EventArgs e)
    {
      HyperLink link = (HyperLink)source;
      LiveSearchService.Result elem = GetResultElement(link.NamingContainer);
      link.Text = elem.Title;
      link.NavigateUrl = elem.Url;
    }

    private void BindSnippet(object source, EventArgs e)
    {
      Label snippet = (Label)source;
      LiveSearchService.Result elem = GetResultElement(snippet.NamingContainer);
      snippet.Text = elem.Description;
    }

    private void BindUrl(object source, EventArgs e)
    {
      Label url = (Label)source;
      LiveSearchService.Result elem = GetResultElement(url.NamingContainer);
      url.Text = elem.Url;
    }
  }
}
```

Toolbox Image Icons

After the controls are built, we can ensure a nice experience in the Toolbox used by Visual Studio web forms when in design mode by adding Toolbox image icons. This task is accomplished by putting a 16×16 bitmap file with the same name as the control and settings its Build Action property in the Visual Studio Properties window to Embedded Resource. Once this is complete and the DLL representing the control library is built, you can add the controls in the DLL into the Toolbox via the Visual Studio Tools menu's Customize Toolbox dialog box, as shown in Figure 13-2.

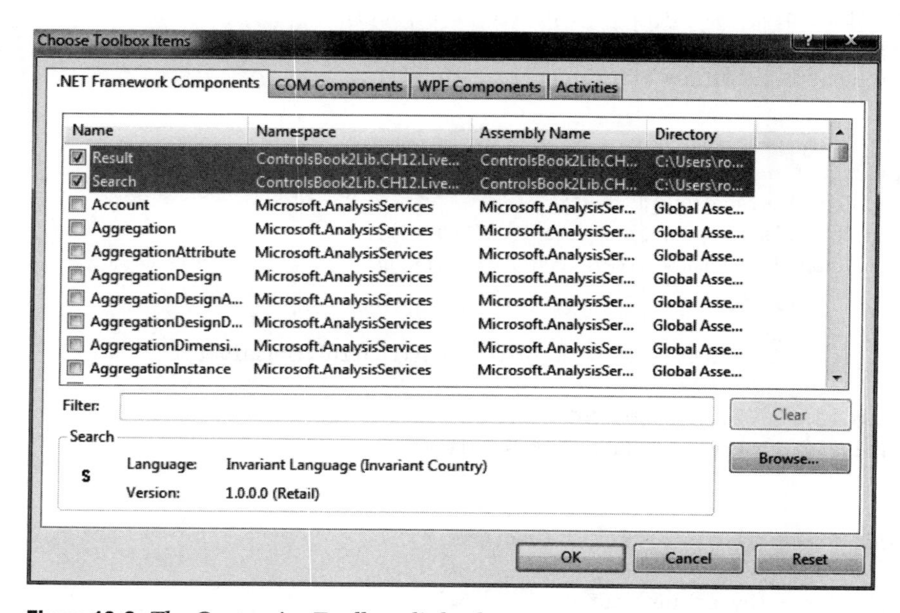

Figure 13-2. *The Customize Toolbox dialog box*

The end result of adding the new controls is a Toolbox tab like the one shown in Figure 13-3.

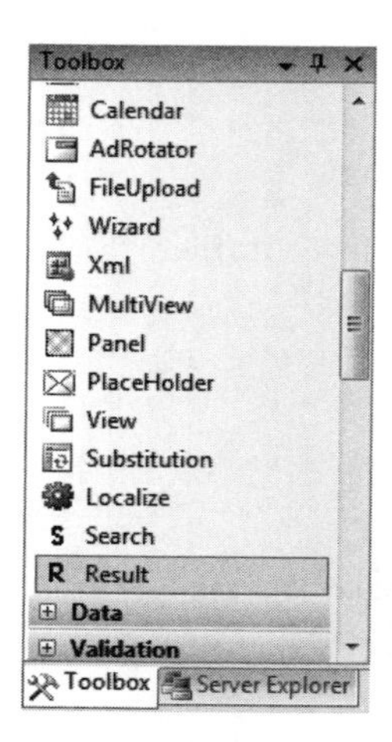

Figure 13-3. *Toolbox icons for the Live Search controls library*

In the next section, we put all the Live Search controls to work in a couple of demonstration web forms.

Testing the Live Search Controls

The default look and feel of the Live Search controls displays if you drag and drop the controls onto a web form. Both the `Search` and `Result` controls require little configuration effort to provide a pleasing display in the Visual Studio Control Designer, as shown in Figure 13-4.

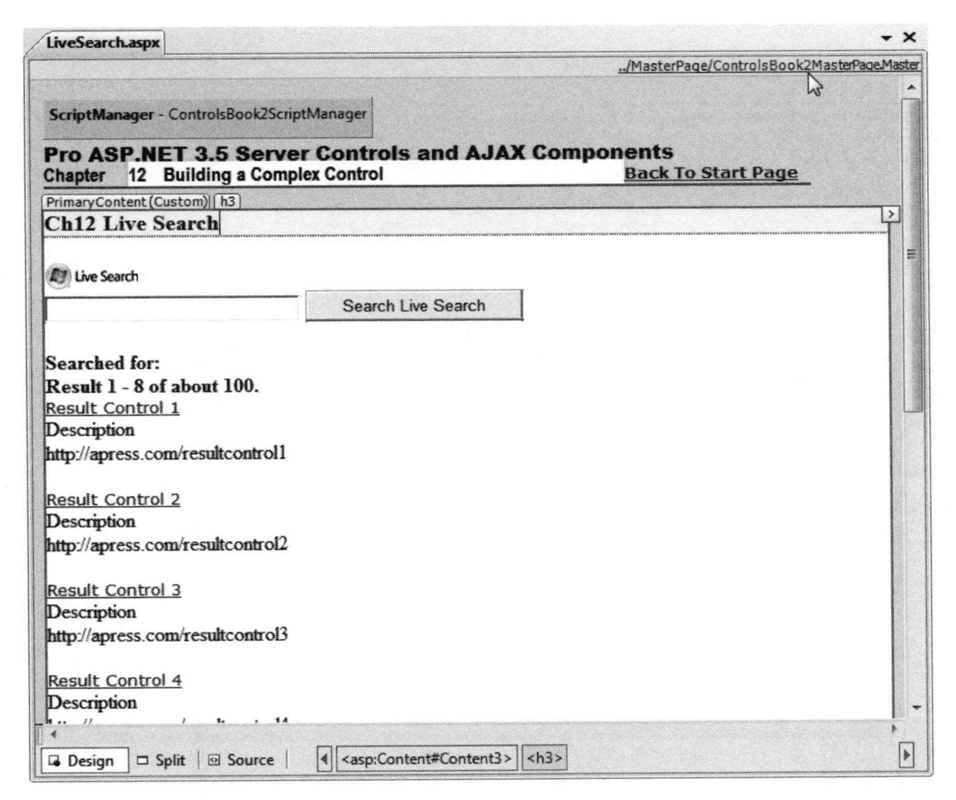

Figure 13-4. *The stock Search and Result controls in the Visual Studio Control Designer*

The Default Look and Feel

The same default look and feel shown at design time is generated in the browser. Figure 13-5 shows the initial page with just the `Search` control rendering its output. Type in a search query, and you can see the results in Figure 13-6.

■ **Tip** Remember to replace the settings in the `web.config` file of the web application project that relate to the Live Search Application ID as well as add the license file in order to get the samples shown in Figures 13-5 and 13-6 working.

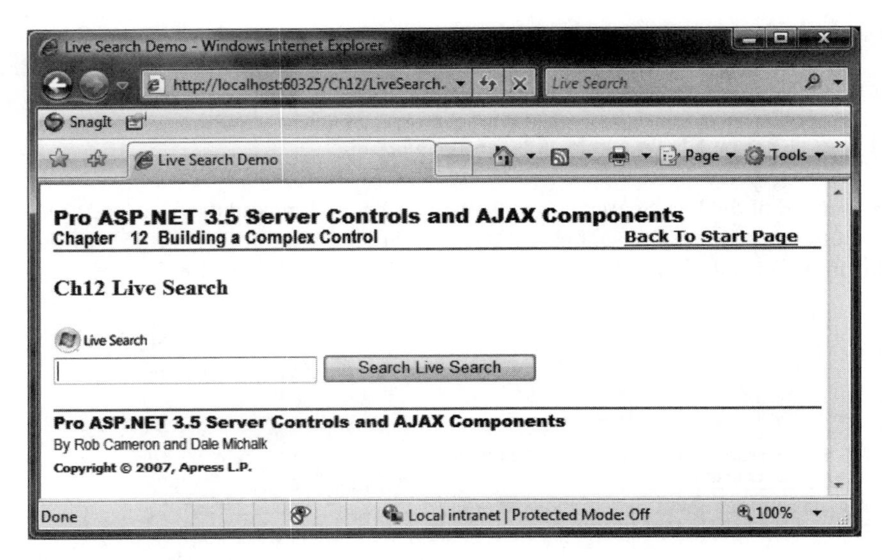

Figure 13-5. *A blank Live Search search page*

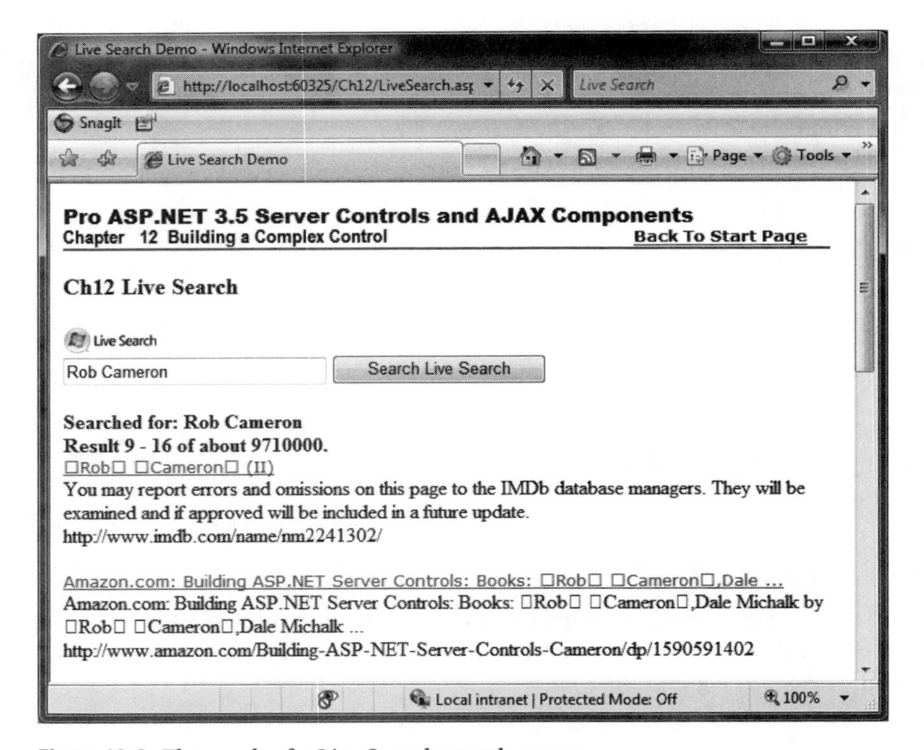

Figure 13-6. *The result of a Live Search search query*

Listings 13-6 and 13-7 contain the web form and the code-behind file, respectively.

Listing 13-6. *The LiveSearchSearch.aspx Page File*

```
<%@ Page Language="C#"
MasterPageFile="~/MasterPage/ControlsBook2MasterPage.Master"
  AutoEventWireup="true" CodeBehind="LiveSearch.aspx.cs"
  Inherits="ControlsBook2Web.Ch12.LiveSearch"
  Title="Live Search Demo" %>

<%@ Register TagPrefix="ApressLive"
Namespace="ControlsBook2Lib.CH12.LiveSearchControls"
  Assembly="ControlsBook2Lib.CH12.LiveSearchControls" %>
<asp:Content ID="Content1" ContentPlaceHolderID="HeadSection" runat="server">
</asp:Content>
<asp:Content ID="Content2" ContentPlaceHolderID="ChapterNumAndTitle" runat="server">
  <asp:Label ID="ChapterNumberLabel" runat="server"
   Width="14px">12</asp:Label>  <asp:Label
    ID="ChapterTitleLabel" runat="server" Width="360px">
    Building a Complex Control</asp:Label>
</asp:Content>
<asp:Content ID="Content3" ContentPlaceHolderID="PrimaryContent" runat="server">
  <h3>
    Ch12 Live Search</h3>
  <ApressLive:Search ID="search" runat="server" RedirectToLiveSearch="false"
    Width="426px"
    ResultControl="Result"></ApressLive:Search>
  <br />
  <br />
  <ApressLive:Result ID="Result" runat="server" PagerStyle="TextWithDHTML"
    PagerBarRange="4"
    PageSize="8" PageNumber="1" PagerLinkStyle="Text">
    <HeaderStyle Font-Bold="True" ForeColor="Blue" BorderColor="Blue"></HeaderStyle>
    <StatusStyle Font-Bold="True" ForeColor="Blue"></StatusStyle>
  </ApressLive:Result>
</asp:Content>
```

Listing 13-7. *The LiveSearchSearch.cs Code-Behind Class File*

```
using System;

namespace ControlsBook2Web.Ch12
{
  public partial class LiveSearch : System.Web.UI.Page
  {
    protected void Page_Load(object sender, EventArgs e)
    {

    }
  }
}
```

Customizing the Live Search Controls' Appearance

The Live Search controls we produced provide extensive support for customization through styles, templates, and data-binding overrides. The next web form demonstration takes advantage of all three features. The `CustomLiveSearch` web form implements its own version of `ItemTemplate`, `AlternatingItemTemplate`, and `StatusTemplate` to show a numbered list of the search results on the left side and a different color for each alternating row.

The work of keeping the item index is performed in the code-behind class file that links up to events exposed by the `Search` and `Result` controls. It resets the `resultIndex` variable when either `Search` or `Result` raises the `LiveSearchSearched` event. Then, on each `ItemCreated` event raised by the `Result` control, it increments its counter and inserts the number at the head of the `ResultItem` content for each row as part of the user interface. Figure 13-7 shows the result.

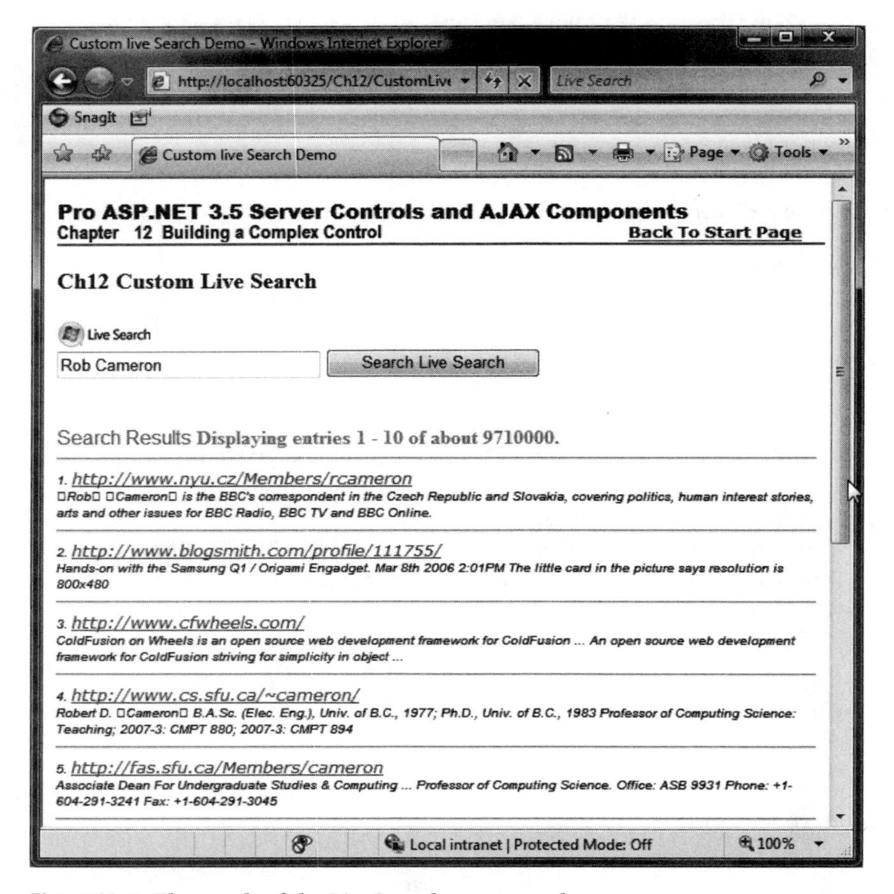

Figure 13-7. *The result of the LiveSearch.aspx search query*

Listings 13-8 and 13-9 show the web form and the code-behind file, respectively.

Listing 13-8. *The CustomLiveSearch.aspx Page File*

```
<%@ Page Language="C#" MasterPageFile="~/MasterPage/ControlsBook2MasterPage.Master"
  AutoEventWireup="true" CodeBehind="CustomLiveSearch.aspx.cs"
Inherits="ControlsBook2Web.Ch12.CustomLiveSearch"
  Title="Custom live Search Demo" %>

<%@ Register TagPrefix="ApressLive"
Namespace="ControlsBook2Lib.CH12.LiveSearchControls"
  Assembly="ControlsBook2Lib.CH12.LiveSearchControls" %>
<asp:Content ID="Content1" ContentPlaceHolderID="HeadSection" runat="server">
</asp:Content>
<asp:Content ID="Content2" ContentPlaceHolderID="ChapterNumAndTitle" runat="server">
  <asp:Label ID="ChapterNumberLabel" runat="server"
    Width="14px">12</asp:Label>  <asp:Label
    ID="ChapterTitleLabel" runat="server" Width="360px">
    Building a Complex Control</asp:Label>
</asp:Content>
<asp:Content ID="Content3" ContentPlaceHolderID="PrimaryContent" runat="server">
  <h3>
    Ch12 Custom Live Search</h3>
  <ApressLive:Search ID="search" runat="server" ResultControl="Result"
    RedirectToLiveSearch="false"
    OnLiveSearchSearched="search_LiveSearchSearched"
    onlivesearchsearchedeventhandler="search_LiveSearchSearched">
  </ApressLive:Search>
  <br />
  <br />
  <ApressLive:Result ID="Result" runat="server" DisplayPager="true"
  OnItemCreated="Result_ItemCreated"
    OnLiveSearchSearched="Result_LiveSearchSearched"
   onlivesearchsearchedeventhandler="Result_LiveSearchSearched"
    onresultitemeventhandler="Result_ItemCreated" PagerLinkStyle="Text">
    <ItemTemplate>
      <a href="<%# ((LiveSearchService.Result)Container.DataItem).Url  %>">
        <%# ((LiveSearchService.Result)Container.DataItem).Url%>
      </a>
      <br />
      <%# ((LiveSearchService.Result)Container.DataItem).Description%>
      <br />
    </ItemTemplate>
    <ItemStyle Font-Size="X-Small" Font-Names="Arial" Font-Italic="True">
    </ItemStyle>
    <FooterStyle Font-Italic="True" Font-Names="Arial" Font-Size="X-Small">
    </FooterStyle>
    <PagerStyle Font-Bold="True" ForeColor="Red"></PagerStyle>
    <AlternatingItemStyle Font-Italic="True" Font-Names="Arial"
      Font-Size="X-Small" />
```

```
      <HeaderTemplate>
        Search Results
      </HeaderTemplate>
      <StatusStyle Font-Bold="True" ForeColor="#CC9900"></StatusStyle>
      <HeaderStyle Font-Names="Arial" ForeColor="#339933" />
      <AlternatingItemTemplate>
        <a href=" <%# ((LiveSearchService.Result)Container.DataItem).Url  %>">
          <%#((LiveSearchService.Result)Container.DataItem).Url %>
        </a>
        <br />
        <%# ((LiveSearchService.Result)Container.DataItem).Description%>
        <br />
      </AlternatingItemTemplate>
      <StatusTemplate>
        Displaying entries
        <%# ((Result.PageNumber - 1) * (Result.PageSize)) + 1%>
        -
        <%# Result.PageNumber * (Result.PageSize)%>
        of about
        <%# Result.TotalResultsCount%>.<br />
      </StatusTemplate>
      <SeparatorTemplate>
        <hr />
      </SeparatorTemplate>
    </ApressLive:Result>
</asp:Content>
```

Listing 13-9. *The CustomLiveSearch.cs Code-Behind Class File*

```
using System;
using System.Web.UI;
using ControlsBook2Lib.CH12.LiveSearchControls;

namespace ControlsBook2Web.Ch12
{
  public partial class CustomLiveSearch : System.Web.UI.Page
  {
    private int resultIndex;

    protected void Page_Load(object sender, EventArgs e)
    {
    }
```

```
    protected void search_LiveSearchSearched(object sender,
      LiveSearchSearchedEventArgs lse)
    {
      resultIndex = lse.Result.Responses[0].Offset;
    }

    protected void Result_LiveSearchSearched(object sender,
      LiveSearchSearchedEventArgs lse)
    {
      resultIndex = lse.Result.Responses[0].Offset;
    }

    protected void Result_ItemCreated(object sender, ResultItemEventArgs e)
    {
      ResultItem item = e.Item;
      if (item.ItemType == ResultItemType.Item ||
          item.ItemType == ResultItemType.AlternatingItem)
      {
        item.Controls.AddAt(0, new LiteralControl
        ((((Result.PageNumber - 1) * Result.PageSize) +
             item.ItemIndex + 1).ToString() + "."));
        resultIndex++;
      }
    }
  }
}
```

Now that we have demonstrated the fully functioning search and result server controls, in the next section, we discuss how to add licensing support to a custom server control.

Licensing Support

We ignored two key aspects of the source code for the Search and Result controls to streamline our discussion: globalization and licensing. We start the process by drilling down into licensing. The licensing system that we provide for the Live Search control is based on the licensing framework that is already in place for .NET.

Several core classes provide the architecture and base foundation for adding licensing to components in the .NET Framework environment, as shown in Figure 13-8.

The primary class is the abstract LicenseProvider class, which ensures that a particular component has the necessary licensing information. To do its job, the LicenseProvider class relies on another abstract base class, the License class, to physically represent the licensing information. LicenseProvider has a key abstract method called GetLicense that validates and returns a License instance if it passes inspection. To link LicenseProvider to a component that needs license validation, the LicenseProviderAttribute attribute is provided to attach at the class level of the component. Once this is done, code is also manually added to the constructor to kick off the license validation process through the Validate method of the LicenseManager class.

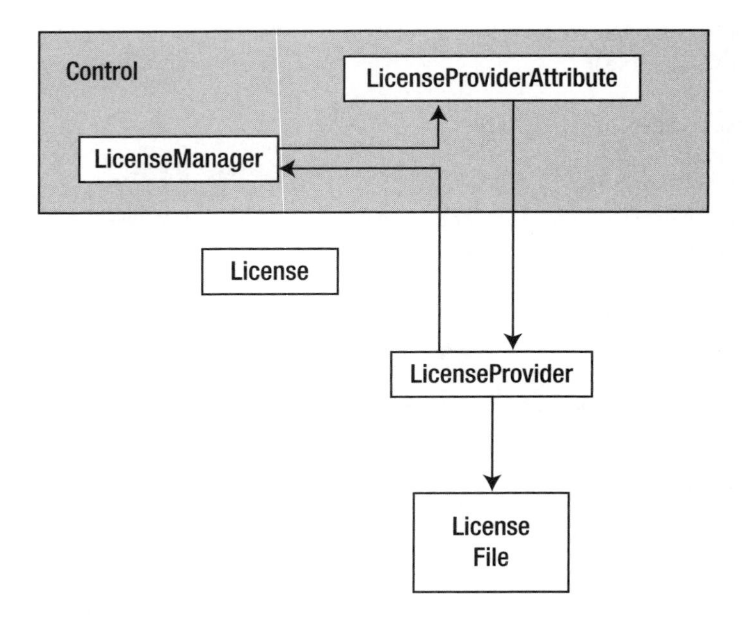

Figure 13-8. *The .NET licensing architecture*

The .NET Framework provides a trivial implementation of the abstract `LicenseProvider` class named `LicFileLicenseProvider` that provides a minimal licensing enforcement check. The only check it performs is for the presence of a `.lic` file with a text string in it, but it serves as a good starting point. We improve on this simple scheme in the following sections by writing a custom implementation of `LicenseProvider` and other related licensing classes using more advanced cryptographic techniques.

The RsaLicense License

The `License` class from the `System.ComponentModel` namespace represents the information used to direct the behavior of the license validation system and control feature enablement. For our licensing system, we rely on the following information stored in our custom license class:

- `System.Type` value of the control to which the license applies
- Globally unique identifier (GUID) for the particular build of the control for licensing purposes
- Expiration date for the license
- Full key string from the license file

The resulting class is simple because it is primarily a structure for information transport. Listing 13-10 shows the full code for our `RsaLicense` class.

Listing 13-10. *The RsaLicense.cs Class File*

```
using System;
using System.ComponentModel;

namespace ControlsBook2Lib.CH12.LiveSearchControls
{
  /// <summary>
  ///  License class for server controls using RSA crypto
  /// </summary>
  public class RsaLicense : License
  {
    private Type type;
    private string licenseKey;
    private string guid;
    private DateTime expireDate;
    private bool _disposed;

    /// <summary>
    ///   Constructor for RsaLicense control license class
    /// </summary>
    /// <param name="type">Type of server control to license</param>
    /// <param name="key">Full key value of license</param>
    /// <param name="guid">Guid for server control type build</param>
    /// <param name="expireDate">Date license expires</param>
    public RsaLicense(Type type, string key, string guid, DateTime expireDate)
    {
      licenseKey = key;
      this.type = type;
      this.guid = guid;
      this.expireDate = expireDate;
    }

    /// <summary>
    /// Full key value of license stored in license file
    /// </summary>
    public override string LicenseKey
    {
      get
      {
        return licenseKey;
      }
    }

    /// <summary>
    /// Server control type the license is bound to
    /// </summary>
```

```
public Type AssociatedServerControlType
{
  get
  {
    return type;
  }
}

/// <summary>
/// Guid representing specific build of server control type
/// </summary>
public string Guid
{
  get
  {
    return guid;
  }
}

/// <summary>
/// Expiration date of license
/// </summary>
public DateTime ExpireDate
{
  get
  {
    return expireDate;
  }
}

/// <summary>
/// You must override Dispose for controls derived from the License clsas
/// </summary>
public sealed override void Dispose()
{
  //Dispose of any unmanaged resourcee
  Dispose(true);
  GC.SuppressFinalize(this);
}

protected virtual void Dispose(bool disposing)
{
  if (!_disposed)
  {
    if (disposing)
    {
      //Dispose of additional unmanaged resources here
```

```
            //if (_resource != null)
            //_resource.Dispose();
          }

          // Indicate that the instance has been disposed.
          // Set additional unmanaged resources to null here
          //_resource = null;
          _disposed = true;
        }
      }
    }
}
```

License Cryptography

Now that we have reviewed the .NET representation of the licensing information, we next focus on the cryptographic techniques used by our system to authorize use of our control. We present a cursory review of public key cryptography and how it is used to secure the license file information in a tamper-proof manner. For a more detailed look at cryptography features in the .NET Framework SDK and for more information on this topic in general, please consult a text on cryptography.

Public key cryptography is a popular technique in the world of cryptography that helps with the traditional problem of exchanging private keys used for encryption and decryption. Instead of using a single private key that is shared by both parties—which is subject to interception or loss because it must be distributed to both parties—you use two keys that have different capabilities. Generally speaking, you can use one key to encrypt and the other key to read without knowing the private key. Figure 13-9 illustrates the differences between public and private key cryptography.

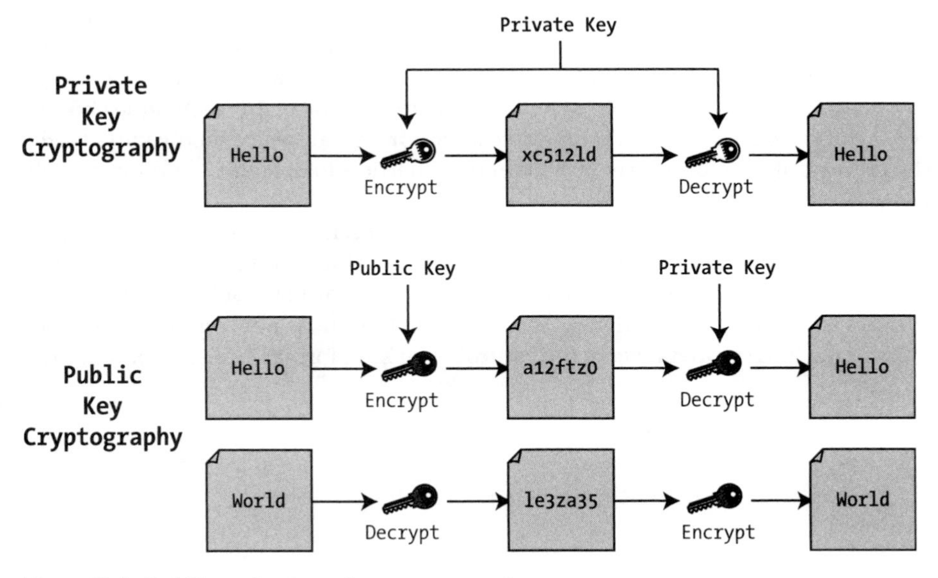

Figure 13-9. *Public and private key cryptography*

The asymmetric nature of the keys in public key cryptography provides us with the ability to distribute one side of the keys without compromising the other, meaning that the public key cannot be readily used to figure out the private key.

The general usage of public key cryptography falls into two patterns, encryption and digital signature, as shown in Figure 13-10. In encryption, someone is able to send an encrypted message using the public key that only the private key holder can read. A digital signature comes into play when the holder of the private key encrypts something to prove possession of that key to anyone holding the public key. This is traditionally the signature of a hash value to make that process as computationally friendly as possible. This public key technology is the basis of the technology we discussed earlier that is used by the .NET Framework to sign assemblies to prevent tampering.

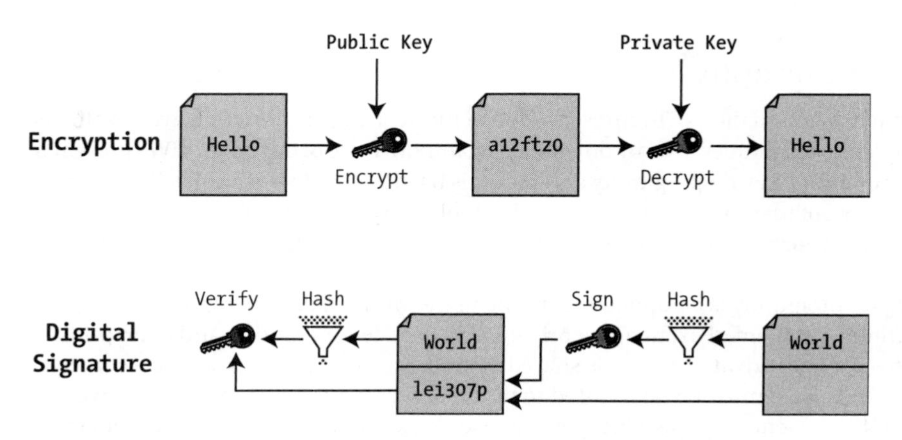

Figure 13-10. *Public key cryptography usage patterns*

We could have chosen a private key system for use with our control system. We moved away from this for two reasons. First, we want to demonstrate how to use public key cryptography in building control license schemes, and second, we want to solve the problem of how to embed the key in the code without giving away the secrets to the operation. This is not to say our approach is infallible or that private key techniques are any worse. Any technique chosen can be broken with patience through a brute-force attack or similar means on the part of the attacker. The purpose of encryption is to provide enough barriers to deter the effort for enough time to make attack less likely.

The starting point with building the licensing system is to generate a public and private key pair. An organization building a control library can use a tool such as the one we provide in the sample code project to generate all the necessary data. The control provider then keeps the generated private key in a secure location, so it is safe from loss and is not compromised. The public key is inserted into the metadata of the control in an XML format for use as part of the license validation process. We also take the extra step of inserting a GUID metadata value into the control to give us a way to version licenses without having to continually regenerate public/private key pairs.

The second process is the generation of the license file. It has the following format:

```
guid#expiration date#signature
```

The GUID matches up to the specific GUID that was embedded in the control library metadata. The expiration date puts an upper bound on how long the control can be used before the license is invalid. The signature of this licensing information is what makes the license file valid and tamper-proof through public key cryptography.

To create the signature for the license file string, we run a byte code value that represents the license data for the GUID and expiration data through the SHA-1 algorithm to generate a hash value. This algorithm has a reasonable guarantee of a unique output for its input to prevent someone from tampering to get the correct output value. For each change in the input, such as a single character, the output bytes will vary wildly.

After the hash is calculated, it is signed with the RSA algorithm using the private key of the control provider to protect the licensing values against tampering by including this digital signature. The process of verifying integrity when the control is deployed also unlocks the control functionality.

The process of validating the license file occurs in reverse order of the process for creating the digital signature. The first action the control licensing code takes is to locate and read the license file from a well-known location. In our case, we chose to put the license file into a directory of the web application for easy deployment. Once the licensing code locates the file, the control licensing code takes the clear text portion of the license string to parse its value. If the GUID in the license file equals the GUID in the metadata for the control and the expiration date has not been met, the process continues with verification of the digital signature. To do the verification, the licensing code calculates a hash of the clear text license key. After the hash is completed, the licensing code reaches into the metadata of the control to find the public key used to unlock the signature present in the license file. The public key is able to decrypt the signature and check to make sure that the decrypted hash and the separately computed hash are identical. If the two are equal, we make the assumption that the information the license file contains is valid and the control is allowed to continue its normal execution process.

Generating the License

To make this process easy on the control developer, we include source code for a rudimentary sample Windows Forms–based license generator that does the grunge work of creating the license file and handling the cryptography. It also makes it easy to reverify previously generated license data. Figure 13-11 shows what the application looks like.

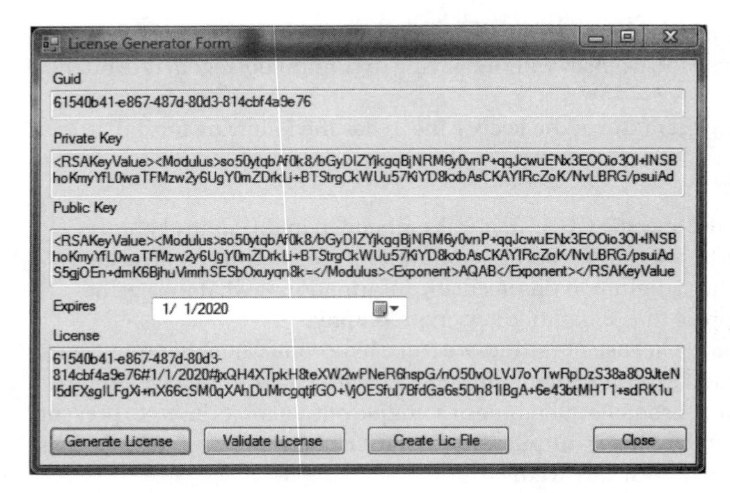

Figure 13-11. *The License Generator application*

The application is fairly simple to use. Click the Generate License button to populate the text box fields on the form with a new private/public key pair, a GUID, and a digital signature based on the expiration date. Make sure to copy and paste the public and private keys to a safe location for storage and use with the control building process. Click the Create Lic File button once this initialization step has occurred to enable you to save the licensing data in the correct `.lic` file format. Listing 13-11 shows the important code from the application.

Listing 13-11. *The License Generator Application Code*

```
private string GetLicenseText()
{
   return GUID.Text + "#" + Expires.Value.ToShortDateString() + "#";
}

private void btnGenLicense_Click(object sender, System.EventArgs e)
{
   GUID.Text = Guid.NewGuid().ToString();
   byte[] clear = ASCIIEncoding.ASCII.GetBytes(GetLicenseText());
   SHA1Managed provSHA1 = new SHA1Managed();
   byte[] hash = provSHA1.ComputeHash(clear);


   RSACryptoServiceProvider provRSA = new RSACryptoServiceProvider();
   PublicKey.Text = provRSA.ToXmlString(false);
   PrivateKey.Text = provRSA.ToXmlString(true);

   byte[] signature = provRSA.SignHash(hash, CryptoConfig.MapNameToOID("SHA1"));

   License.Text = GetLicenseText() +
   Convert.ToBase64String(signature,0,signature.Length);
}
```

The first thing the License Generator application does is create a new GUID. It then calls `GetLicenseText` to get the clear text license string with the expiration date. Next, it passes this as an array of bytes to `SHA1Managed`, the .NET-managed implementation of the SHA-1 hash algorithm, to create byte array for the hash with its `ComputeHash` method.

The byte array hash is passed to `RSACryptoServiceProvider`, which is initialized shortly afterward in the code. Notice how we use its `ToXmlString` methods to easily grab the newly generated public and private keys that are created when `RSACryptoServiceProvider` is initialized in a convenient-to-handle format.

The `SignHash` method on `RSACryptoServiceProvider` creates the digital signature needed to ensure integrity and validate the license information. The resulting final license text is put back together to include GUID, expiration date, and signature at the very end. The default license file that is included with the source code for the book contains the following data after all is said and done with the License Generator application (you can download the source code from the Source Code/Download area of the Apress web site, `http://www.apress.com`):


```
55489e7a-bff5-4b3c-8f21-c43fad861dfa#12/12/2017#R9COUxTZ4rU41A36WFjlM
x5ZjS9rwv4x6mTcNU3HOocCkHqw/7ZWrIyhVChyZfBYmtYWGjgvJ2gipIWzEobmyqvc2z
Tff2i8cRgOKuxaeTl8rKffRPLcAOOV3SiXuOF93MCBWcoxwLU3kPHRcQEz9NBnB5jWYqo
lK9FKQ7dvIFE=
```


The RsaLicenseDataAttribute Custom Attribute

After the license data is generated, we bind some of the information to the control itself to ensure linkage between the signature in the license file and the control. The important pieces of information are the GUID and the public key. Instead of putting them in hidden fields inside the control, we chose to store them in metadata that is easily accessible, because the public information in them does not compromise the integrity of the license system. `RsaLicenseDataAttribute` is a custom attribute that is built specifically for this purpose.

■ **Note** You can override the control implementation and replace the custom `License` attribute with a new value. One way to handle this situation is to make the `Search` and `Result` classes sealed. This requires some additional code reworking to remove the virtual/protected modifiers from several of the methods. We do not do this work here; rather, we leave it open for extension and further customization.

Listing 13-12 presents the full code for the custom attribute.

Listing 13-12. *The RsaLicenseDataAttribute Class File*

```
using System;

namespace ControlsBook2Lib.CH12.LiveSearchControls
{
  /// <summary>
  /// Custom attribute for annotating licensing data on LiveSearch Lib controls
  /// </summary>
```

```
  [AttributeUsage(AttributeTargets.Class, Inherited = false,
      AllowMultiple = false)]
  public sealed class RsaLicenseDataAttribute : Attribute
  {
    private string guid;
    private string publicKey;

    /// <summary>
    /// Constructor for RsaLicenseDataAttribute
    /// </summary>
    /// <param name="guid"></param>
    /// <param name="publicKey"></param>
    public RsaLicenseDataAttribute(string guid, string publicKey)
    {
      this.guid = guid;
      this.publicKey = publicKey;
    }

    /// <summary>
    /// Guid representing specific build of server control type
    /// </summary>
    public string Guid
    {
      get
      {
        return guid;
      }
    }

    /// <summary>
    /// Public key representing specific build of server control type
    /// </summary>
    public string PublicKey
    {
      get
      {
        return publicKey;
      }
    }
  }
}
```

Next, we discuss how to apply licensing to the Search and Result custom server controls.

Adding Licensing to the Search and Result Controls

The RsaLicenseDataAttribute attribute is applied with the appropriate values to both the Search and Result controls to provide the means of accessing the GUID and public key for validation.

We add `LicenseProviderAttribute` to link in our custom license provider, `RsaLicenseProvider`, which we cover in a moment. We use the following code:

```
#if LICENSED
 RsaLicenseData(
     "55489e7a-bff5-4b3c-8f21-c43fad861dfa",

     "<RSAKeyValue><Modulus>mWpgckAepJAp4aUOAvEcGg3TdO+OVXws9LjiSCLpy7aQKD5V7uj
49Exh1RtcB6TcuXxmOR6dw75VmKwyoGbvYT6btOIwQgqbLhci5LjWmWUPEdBRiYsOLDOh2POX
s9xTvp4IDTKXYoP8GPDRKzklJuuxCbbUcooESQoYHp9ppbE=</Modulus><Exponent>AQAB</
Exponent></RSAKeyValue>"),
  LicenseProvider(typeof(RsaLicenseProvider)),
#endif
```

The `LICENSED` keyword is a conditional compilation constant available in the C# language that allows the project to quickly and easily be compiled with or without licensing if needed. The default setting for `LICENSED` is defined in the Visual Studio project that comes with this book's source code.

You can change this setting by going to the LiveSearchControls project in the Visual Studio Solution Explorer, right-clicking, and selecting the Properties menu item to bring up the project Properties dialog box. On the Build tab, look for the "Conditional compilation symbols" constants section. Figure 13-12 shows what the dialog box for this build setting looks like. Remove LICENSED from the list, and the code between `#if` and `#endif` will be ignored in the compile process.

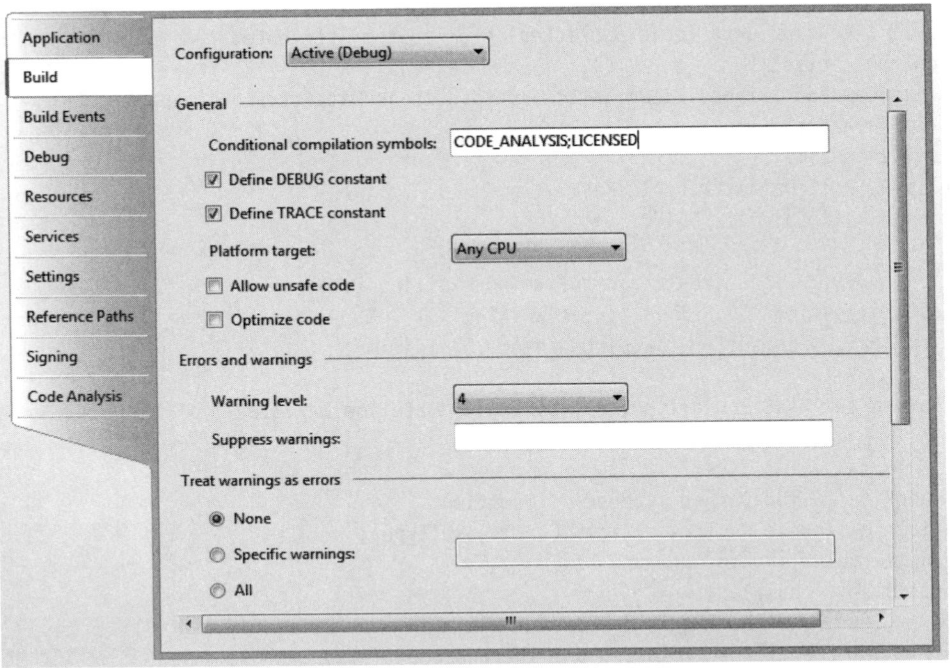

Figure 13-12. *Conditional compilation constant for licensing*

The RsaLicenseProvider Class

The heart of the validation process exists inside the RsaLicenseProvider class. It inherits from the base LicenseProvider class to implement the GetLicense method, which validates licensing data and then returns a valid license if successful in that process. The signature for GetLicense is as follows:

```
public override License GetLicense(LicenseContext context, Type type, object
                                   instance, bool allowExceptions)
{
```

The first parameter is an instance of LicenseContext that informs the LicenseProvider implementation what the current environment is. We use it to determine whether the server control is executing within a design-time environment. The Type parameter and the Object parameter provide access to the control type and instance that is validated. AllowExceptions is a Boolean that indicates whether LicenseProvider should throw a LicenseException to indicate that the control was unable to obtain a valid license. In our code, this is ignored, and instead of raising an exception, the code returns a null value. The full implementation for GetLicense is as follows:

```
public override License GetLicense(LicenseContext context, Type type, object
instance, bool allowExceptions)
{
   string attrGuid = "";
   string publicKey = "";

   // pull licensing data (guid/publickey) from custom attributes
   // on the control
   RsaLicenseDataAttribute licDataAttr = GetRsaLicenseDataAttribute(type);
   if (licDataAttr == null)
      return null;
   publicKey = licDataAttr.PublicKey;
   attrGuid = licDataAttr.Guid;

   // if in Design mode create and return nonexpiring license
   // so design-time ASP.NET is always working
   if (context.UsageMode == LicenseUsageMode.Designtime)
   {
      return new RsaLicense(type, "", attrGuid, DateTime.MaxValue);
   }

   // check cache for cached license information
   RsaLicense license =  licenseCache.GetLicense(type);
   string keyValue = "";
   if (license == null)
   {
      // check the license folder under the web root for a
      // license file and parse key data from it
      keyValue = LoadLicenseData(type);
```

```
      // validate the new license data key value
      DateTime expireDate = new DateTime();
      if (IsKeyValid(keyValue, publicKey, attrGuid, type, ref expireDate))
      {
         license = new RsaLicense(type, keyValue, attrGuid, expireDate);
         licenseCache.AddLicense(type, license);
      }

   }
   return license;
}
```

The first bit of code in GetLicense is responsible for grabbing the information from the custom attributes. This is handled by the GetRsaLicenseDataAttribute helper method:

```
private RsaLicenseDataAttribute GetRsaLicenseDataAttribute(System.Type type)
{
   RsaLicenseDataAttribute licDataAttr;
   object[] attrs = type.GetCustomAttributes(false);
   foreach (object attr in attrs)
   {
      licDataAttr = attr as RsaLicenseDataAttribute;
      if (licDataAttr != null)
         return licDataAttr;
   }
   return null;
}
```

Once GetLicense retrieves the licensing information, it obtains the public key and GUID value from the metadata and stores them in instance variables. Afterward, GetLicense checks to see if the control itself is running in design-time mode and, if so, it creates a valid license to permit the class to work in the designer.

After verifying that the server control is running in the design-time environment, GetLicense checks whether the license is in a custom cache class that holds licenses based on the type of the executing control. The cache class is named RsaLicenseCache and is based on a Hashtable collection with strongly typed methods. This is a static field of RsaLicenseProvider to save on the resource-intensive task of going to disk to examine and parse license information for each control instance. If the license is in the cache, GetLicense returns immediately to save on processing time. If not, GetLicense executes the validation process by examining the data in the license file. LoadLicenseData is the method responsible for looking up the control information:

```
protected string LoadLicenseData(Type type)
{
   // format of license files in web app folder structure
   // web root\
   // license\
   // Apress.LiveSearchControls.lic

   string keyValue = "";
```

```
    string assemblyName = type.Assembly.GetName().Name;
    string relativePath = "~\\license\\" + assemblyName + ".lic";
    string licFilePath = HttpContext.Current.Server.MapPath(relativePath);

    if (File.Exists(licFilePath))
    {
       // grab the first line that contains license data
       FileStream file = new FileStream(licFilePath,
          FileMode.Open, FileAccess.Read, FileShare.ReadWrite);
       StreamReader rdr = new StreamReader(file);
       keyValue = rdr.ReadLine();
       rdr.Close();
       file.Close();
    }

    return keyValue;
}
```

The location at which LoadLicenseData looks for the licensing information is a directory named "license" off of the web application directory. It looks for a file with the same name as the assembly but with a .lic extension. For our control library, this would be ControlsBook2Lib.CH12.LiveSearchControls.lic.

After the code returns from GetLicense, we have the license string ready for verification. The following IsKeyValid method takes care of this. If IsKeyValid returns true, GetLicense adds the license to the cache and returns a valid instance to signify the process was successful. The IsKeyValid method uses the String.Split method to separate the license string by the hash mark character (#) and checks compliance by validating against the date timestamp and the GUID returned from the control metadata:

```
protected bool IsKeyValid(string keyValue, string publicKey, string attrGuid,
System.Type type, ref DateTime expireDate)
{
   if (keyValue.Length == 0)
      return false;

   char[] separators = { '#' };
   string[] values = keyValue.Split(separators);
   string signature = values[2];
   string licGuid = values[0];
   string expires = values[1];

   // Convert the expiration date using the neutral
   // culture of the assembly(en-US)
   expireDate = Convert.ToDateTime(expires,
      DateTimeFormatInfo.InvariantInfo);
```

```
    // do a date comparison for expiration and make
    // sure we are matching control with right license data
    return (licGuid == attrGuid &&
       expireDate > DateTime.Now &&
       VerifyHash(publicKey, licGuid, expires, signature));
}
```

The IsKeyValid method then calls the VerifyHash method to perform the cryptographic work that verifies the digital signature:

```
private bool VerifyHash(string publicKey, string guid, string expires,
                        string signature)
{
   // recompute the hash value
   byte[] clear = ASCIIEncoding.ASCII.GetBytes(guid + "#" + expires + "#");
   SHA1Managed provSHA1 = new SHA1Managed();
   byte[] hash = provSHA1.ComputeHash(clear);

   // reload the RSA provider based on the public key only
   CspParameters paramsCsp = new CspParameters();
   paramsCsp.Flags = CspProviderFlags.UseMachineKeyStore;
   RSACryptoServiceProvider provRSA = new RSACryptoServiceProvider(paramsCsp);
   provRSA.FromXmlString(publicKey);

   // verify the signature on the hash
   byte[] sigBytes= Convert.FromBase64String(signature);
   bool result = provRSA.VerifyHash(hash, CryptoConfig.MapNameToOID("SHA1"),
      sigBytes);

   return result;
}
```

The SHA1Managed implementation of the SHA-1 hashing algorithm is used to create a computed hash value on the contents of the license file. Once this is complete, an instance of RSACryptoServiceProvider is initialized using the public key from the control metadata. The VerifyHash and RSACryptoServiceProvider methods next verify that the signature in the license file is valid according to the separately computed hash. The result of this check is returned from RSACryptoServiceProvider.VerifyHash to IsKeyValid, which, in turn, notifies the parent GetLicense of success or failure.

At this point, we have completed our discussion of license validation. Listings 13-13 and 13-14 contain the code for RsaLicenseCache and RsaLicenseProvider.

Listing 13-13. *The RsaLicenseCache.cs Class File*

```
using System;
using System.Collections;

namespace ControlsBook2Lib.CH12.LiveSearchControls
{
```

```
  /// <summary>
  ///   Custom cache collection built on Hashtable for storing RsaLicense instances
  /// </summary>
  internal class RsaLicenseCache
  {
    private Hashtable hash = new Hashtable();

    public void AddLicense(Type type, RsaLicense license)
    {
      hash.Add(type, license);
    }

    public RsaLicense GetLicense(Type type)
    {
      RsaLicense license = null;
      if (hash.ContainsKey(type))
        license = (RsaLicense)hash[type];
      return license;
    }

    public void RemoveLicense(Type type)
    {
      hash.Remove(type);
    }
  }
}
```

Listing 13-14. *The RsaLicenseProvider.cs Class File*

```
using System;
using System.ComponentModel;
using System.Globalization;
using System.IO;
using System.Security.Cryptography;
using System.Text;
using System.Web;

namespace ControlsBook2Lib.CH12.LiveSearchControls
{
  /// <summary>
  /// Custom license provider for LiveSearch Lib which use RSA crypto
  /// </summary>
  public class RsaLicenseProvider : LicenseProvider
  {
    static RsaLicenseCache licenseCache = new RsaLicenseCache();

    /// <summary>
    /// Called by LicenseManager to retrieve a license
```

```
/// </summary>
/// <param name="context">Context of request (design/runtime)</param>
/// <param name="type">Control type needing license</param>
/// <param name="instance">Control instance needing license</param>
/// <param name="allowExceptions">true if a LicenseException should be thrown
 when the component cannot be granted a license; otherwise, false.</param>
/// <returns></returns>
public override License GetLicense(LicenseContext context, Type type,
object instance, bool allowExceptions)
{
  string attrGuid = "";
  string publicKey = "";

  // pull licensing data (guid/publickey) from custom attributes
  // on the control
  RsaLicenseDataAttribute licDataAttr = GetRsaLicenseDataAttribute(type);
  if (licDataAttr == null)
    return null;
  publicKey = licDataAttr.PublicKey;
  attrGuid = licDataAttr.Guid;

  // if in Design mode create and return non-expiring license
  // so design time ASP.NET is always working
  if (context.UsageMode == LicenseUsageMode.Designtime)
  {
    return new RsaLicense(type, "", attrGuid, DateTime.MaxValue);
  }

  // check cache for cached license information
  RsaLicense license = licenseCache.GetLicense(type);
  string keyValue = "";
  if (license == null)
  {
    // check the license folder under the web root for a
    // license file and parse key data from it
    keyValue = LoadLicenseData(type);

    // validate the new license data key value
    DateTime expireDate = new DateTime();
    if (IsKeyValid(keyValue, publicKey, attrGuid, expireDate))
    {
      license = new RsaLicense(type, keyValue, attrGuid, expireDate);
      licenseCache.AddLicense(type, license);
    }
  }
  return license;
}
```

```
/// <summary>
/// Method to look up custom licensing attribute on server control
/// </summary>
/// <param name="type">Control type for custom attribute lookup</param>
/// <returns></returns>
private RsaLicenseDataAttribute GetRsaLicenseDataAttribute(System.Type type)
{
  RsaLicenseDataAttribute licDataAttr;
  object[] attrs = type.GetCustomAttributes(false);
  foreach (object attr in attrs)
  {
    licDataAttr = attr as RsaLicenseDataAttribute;
    if (licDataAttr != null)
      return licDataAttr;
  }
  return null;
}

/// <summary>
/// Methods retireves license key from license file
/// </summary>
/// <param name="type">Control type to retrieve license data for </param>
/// <returns></returns>
protected string LoadLicenseData(Type type)
{
  // format of license files in web app folder structure
  // web root\
  // license\
  // ControlsBook2Lib.LiveSearchControls.lic

  string keyValue = "";
  string assemblyName = type.Assembly.GetName().Name;
  string relativePath = "~\\license\\" + assemblyName + ".lic";
  string licFilePath = HttpContext.Current.Server.MapPath(relativePath);

  if (File.Exists(licFilePath))
  {
    // grab the first line which contains license data
    FileStream file = new FileStream(licFilePath,
       FileMode.Open, FileAccess.Read, FileShare.ReadWrite);
    StreamReader rdr = new StreamReader(file);
    keyValue = rdr.ReadLine();
    rdr.Close();
    file.Close();
  }
```

```
    return keyValue;
  }

  /// <summary>
  /// Method verifies the validaty of license key information
  /// </summary>
  /// <param name="keyValue">License key value</param>
  /// <param name="publicKey">Public key of version-specific control build</param>
  /// <param name="attrGuid">Guid of version-specific control build</param>
  /// <param name="type">Type of control being licensed</param>
  /// <param name="expireDate">Date license expires</param>
  /// <returns></returns>
  protected bool IsKeyValid(string keyValue, string publicKey, string guid,
DateTime expireDate)
  {
    if (keyValue.Length == 0)
      return false;

    char[] separators = { '#' };
    string[] values = keyValue.Split(separators);
    string signature = values[2];
    string licGuid = values[0];
    string expires = values[1];

    // Conver the expiration date using the neutral
    // culture of the assembly(en-US)
    expireDate = Convert.ToDateTime(expires,
       DateTimeFormatInfo.InvariantInfo);

    // do a date comparison for expiration and make
    // sure we are matching control with right license data
    return (licGuid == guid &&
       expireDate > DateTime.Now &&
       VerifyHash(publicKey, licGuid, expires, signature));
  }

  /// <summary>
  /// Helper method to verify hash value in license key using RSA
  /// public key crypto
  /// </summary>
  /// <param name="publicKey">Public key of version-specific control build</param>
  /// <param name="guid">Guid of version-specific control build</param>
  /// <param name="expires">Date of expiration for license</param>
  /// <param name="signature">Signature value in license key used for verification
      </param>
  /// <returns></returns>
```

```
    private bool VerifyHash(string publicKey, string guid, string expires,
    string signature)
    {
      // recompute the hash value
      byte[] clear = ASCIIEncoding.ASCII.GetBytes(guid + "#" + expires + "#");
      SHA1Managed provSHA1 = new SHA1Managed();
      byte[] hash = provSHA1.ComputeHash(clear);

      // reload the RSA provider based on the public key only
      CspParameters paramsCsp = new CspParameters();
      paramsCsp.Flags = CspProviderFlags.UseMachineKeyStore;
      RSACryptoServiceProvider provRSA = new RSACryptoServiceProvider(paramsCsp);
      provRSA.FromXmlString(publicKey);

      // verify the signature on the hash
      byte[] sigBytes = Convert.FromBase64String(signature);
      bool result = provRSA.VerifyHash(hash, CryptoConfig.MapNameToOID("SHA1"),
         sigBytes);

      return result;
    }
  }
}
```

Globalization and Localization

In this section of the chapter, we discuss issues surrounding developing server controls that work nicely in an ASP.NET application that is localized to cultures other than those using U.S. English. A key feature of a server control library is the capability to support modification techniques that make it easy to deploy to the appropriate culture. Two key definitions crystallize what needs to be done: globalization and localization. Globalization is the process of designing an application so that it can be easily modified or updated to support different cultures. Localization is the actual work it takes to modify the application for a specific culture. An application designed with globalization in mind makes the localization process very easy.

The CultureInfo Class

The international support in .NET focuses on the `CultureInfo` class in the `System.Globalization` namespace. The `CultureInfo` class stores information required by the rest of the .NET Framework to correctly process string, numeric, and date formats, as well as load resources based on current culture settings. To create an instance of the `CultureInfo` class, developers typically invoke its constructor by passing in a culture string. The format of the string is a two-part structure based on the RFC 1766 format that contains a language and a country/region in a primary two-digit format. The language is specified in lowercase letters, and the country/region is specified in uppercase letters. An example for Spanish as spoken in Mexico follows:

```
CultureInfo culture = new CultureInfo("es-MX");
```

In order for code that is currently executing to use the settings of an instance of CultureInfo, that CultureInfo instance must be assigned to the currently executing thread. The easiest way to do this is to use the static helper method CurrentThread of the Thread class in the System.Threading namespace:

```
Thread.CurrentThread.CurrentCulture = culture;
Thread.CurrentThread.CurrentUICulture = culture;
```

The demonstration code shows that the Thread class has both a CurrentCulture and a CurrentUICulture property that can be assigned by an instance of CultureInfo. The instance assigned to the CurrentCulture affects the formatting and comparisons of string, numeric, and date formats. The CurrentUICulture property setting affects resources such as strings and images that are loaded from assemblies. Setting both to the same value for a thread ensures that consistent culture settings are applied.

The ResourceManager Class

A key consideration when designing ASP.NET controls that support localization is to ensure that static control layouts accommodate for potential size changes due to language differences. You should avoid hard-coding any textual values; instead, you should rely on a resource-based approach. This approach supports localization with the side benefit of not requiring a full recompile of a control library just to modify language support.

With that in mind, we switch to looking at a snippet of the Search control, which loads the string for the Text property using the ResourceManager class:

```
// search button Text is localized
ResourceManager rm = ResourceFactory.Manager;
searchButton = new Button();
searchButton.Text = rm.GetString("Search.searchButton.Text");
searchButton.Click += new EventHandler(SearchButtonClick);
this.Controls.Add(searchButton);
```

The ResourceManager class exists in the System.Resources namespace and is responsible for locating the correct resources requested based on the CurrentUICulture setting on the thread that is executing. The preceding code indicates that the ResourceManager instance should retrieve a string value that is identified by the name "Search.searchButton.Text". Once it is located, the string value is assigned to the Text property.

The ResourceManager instance created in the preceding code snippet is retrieved by a utility class named ResourceFactory in the Live Search control library code. Listing 13-15 shows the full listing for this utility class.

Listing 13-15. *The ResourceFactory.cs Class File*

```
using System.Reflection;
using System.Resources;

namespace ControlsBook2Lib.CH12.LiveSearchControls
{
```

```
  /// <summary>
  /// Allows for efficient access to a single ResourceManager instance
  /// using a singleton type of factory pattern
  /// </summary>
  internal class ResourceFactory
  {
    private ResourceFactory()
    {
    }

    internal const string ResourceName =
    "ControlsBook2Lib.CH12.LiveSearchControls.LocalStrings";
    static ResourceManager rm;

    /// <summary>
    /// Retrieves static instance of ResourceManager class
    /// </summary>
    public static ResourceManager Manager
    {
      get
      {
        if (rm == null)
        {
          // Load the LocalStrings resource bound to the
          // main assembly or one of the language specific
          // satellite assemblies
          rm = new ResourceManager(ResourceName,
          Assembly.GetExecutingAssembly(), null);
        }
        return rm;
      }
    }
  }
}
```

ResourceFactory exists to provide easy, efficient access to an instance of the ResourceManager class. It does this through a static factory method approach so that each time we go for a localized resource we don't have to pay the price of initializing an instance of ResourceManager. The code also specifies the desired resource name for the ResourceManager instance:

```
internal const string ResourceName = "
ControlsBook2Lib.CH12.LiveSearchControls.LocalStrings";
```

The namespace of the control assembly is the prefix to the LocalStrings resource name. To create this resource, we add a resource file named LocalStrings.resx to the control project. LocalStrings.resx has an XML structure with a schema definition at the top and a data section at the bottom for holding pertinent text strings needed to localize the controls' textual output. Listing 13-16 shows the complete LocalStrings.resx file.

Listing 13-16. *The LocalStrings.resx Resource File*

```
<?xml version="1.0" encoding="utf-8" ?>
<root>
   <xsd:schema id="root" xmlns="" xmlns:xsd="http://www.w3.org/2001/XMLSchema"
    xmlns:msdata="urn:schemas-microsoft-com:xml-msdata">
      <xsd:element name="root" msdata:IsDataSet="true">
         <xsd:complexType>
            <xsd:choice maxOccurs="unbounded">
               <xsd:element name="data">
                  <xsd:complexType>
                     <xsd:sequence>
                        <xsd:element name="value" type="xsd:string" minOccurs="0"
                         msdata:Ordinal="1" />
                        <xsd:element name="comment" type="xsd:string"
                         minOccurs="0" msdata:Ordinal="2" />
                     </xsd:sequence>
                     <xsd:attribute name="name" type="xsd:string" />
                     <xsd:attribute name="type" type="xsd:string" />
                     <xsd:attribute name="mimetype" type="xsd:string" />
                  </xsd:complexType>
               </xsd:element>
               <xsd:element name="resheader">
                  <xsd:complexType>
                     <xsd:sequence>
                        <xsd:element name="value" type="xsd:string" minOccurs="0"
                        msdata:Ordinal="1" />
                     </xsd:sequence>
                     <xsd:attribute name="name" type="xsd:string" use="required" />
                  </xsd:complexType>
               </xsd:element>
            </xsd:choice>
         </xsd:complexType>
      </xsd:element>
   </xsd:schema>
   <resheader name="ResMimeType">
      <value>text/microsoft-resx</value>
   </resheader>
   <resheader name="Version">
      <value>1.0.0.0</value>
   </resheader>
   <resheader name="Reader">
      <value>System.Resources.ResXResourceReader, System.Windows.Forms,
 Version=1.0.5000.0, Culture=neutral, PublicKeyToken=b77a5c561934e089</value>
   </resheader>
   <resheader name="Writer">
      <value>System.Resources.ResXResourceWriter, System.Windows.Forms,
 Version=1.0.5000.0, Culture=neutral, PublicKeyToken=b77a5c561934e089</value>
```

```
    </resheader>
    <data name="Search.searchButton.Text">
      <value>Search Live Search</value>
    </data>
    <data name="ResultStatusTemplate.SearchFor">
      <value>Searched for: {0}</value>
    </data>
    <data name="ResultStatusTemplate.ResultAbout">
      <value>Result {0} - {1} of about {2}.</value>
    </data>
    <data name="ResultStatusTemplate.QueryTook">
      <value>Query took about {0} seconds.</value>
    </data>
    <data name="Pager.nextButton.Text">
      <value>Next</value>
    </data>
    <data name="Pager.prevButton.Text">
      <value>Previous</value>
    </data>
    <data name="Pager.resultsPageCell.Text">
      <value>Results Page:&amp;nbsp;</value>
    </data>
</root>
```

The controls that store values inside `LocalStrings` include the `Search` control and its button's `Text` property, and the `Pager` control and its Next/Previous buttons and `Results` text. The `ResultStatusTemplate` template also uses `LocalStrings` to build its content for search results.

Culture Types and Localizing Resource Files

The `LocalStrings.resx` resource file is an embedded resource for the primary culture of the assembly. To make this happen as part of the Visual Studio assembly build process, the Properties window for the `LocalStrings.resx` file has its Build Action property set to Embedded Resource. Figure 13-13 shows the compilation process and how it converts the `.resx` file to a binary resource file before it embeds it in the assembly.

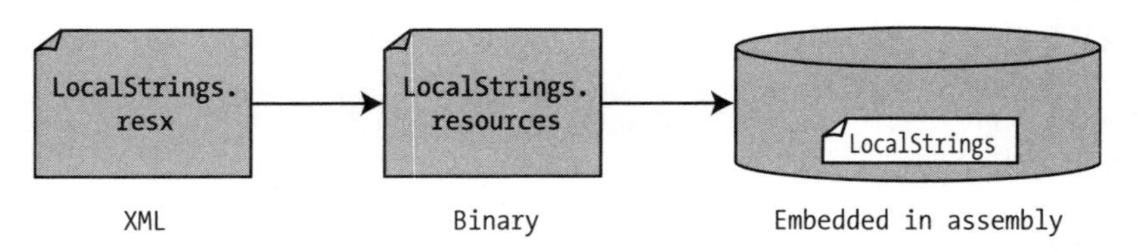

Figure 13-13. *Compiling a resource file and embedding it in an assembly*

The default culture for the `LocalStrings` resource is determined by the value of the `AssemblyCulture` assembly-level attribute:

```
[assembly: AssemblyCulture("")]
```

The blank value specified in the control library code indicates the use of the invariant culture. The invariant culture is the fallback culture that is used to resolve a lookup by ResourceManager if no other culture is specified or a culture cannot be matched using available resources.

Because we want to provide more than just an English version of output for our controls, we have to provide additional resource files that are localized for the cultures we want to support. We do this by creating a resource file with the same resource name as LocalStrings but with a language and/or culture/region as part of the filename right before the filename extension. To add support for Spanish spoken in Mexico, we would use the following filename:

```
LocalStrings.en-MX.resx
```

When we specify the full culture with both the language and the country/region, the culture we are targeting is called a specific culture. We can also specify just the language to create a neutral culture, such as the following for neutral German support:

```
LocalStrings.de.resx
```

Once you have added the desired resource files to the project, you need to copy the XML data section from the invariant culture resource file to ensure that the identifiers are the same. Once you have the structure for the resource files in place, unless you have language specialists on your staff, you will probably need the services of a translation agency. There are several commercial vendors who will accept a .resx resource file and return a localized version for the desired culture.

The data section for the Spanish as spoken in Mexico, es-MX, file translates to the following content:

```
<data name="Search.searchButton.Text">
   <value>Búsqueda Live Search</value>
</data>
<data name="ResultStatusTemplate.SearchFor">
   <value>Buscado para: {0}</value>
</data>
<data name="ResultStatusTemplate.ResultAbout">
   <value>Resultado {0} - {1} de alrededor {2}.</value>
</data>
<data name="ResultStatusTemplate.QueryTook">
   <value>Pregunta tomó sobre {0} segundos. </value>
</data>
<data name="Pager.nextButton.Text">
   <value>Después</value>
</data>
<data name="Pager.prevButton.Text">
   <value>Anterior</value>
</data>
<data name="Pager.resultsPageCell.Text">
   <value>Página De los Resultados:&amp;nbsp;</value>
</data>
```

```
The data section for the neutral German file looks like this:
   <data name="Search.searchButton.Text">
            <value>Suche Live Search</value>
   </data>
   <data name="ResultStatusTemplate.SearchFor">
      <value>Gesucht nach: {0}</value>
   </data>
   <data name="ResultStatusTemplate.ResultAbout">
      <value>Resultat {0} - {1} von ungefähr {2}.</value>
   </data>
   <data name="ResultStatusTemplate.QueryTook">
      <value>Frage nahm über {0} Sekunden.</value>
   </data>
   <data name="Pager.nextButton.Text">
      <value>Zunächst</value>
   </data>
   <data name="Pager.prevButton.Text">
      <value>Vorhergehend</value>
   </data>
   <data name="Pager.resultsPageCell.Text">
      <value>Resultat Seite:&amp;nbsp;</value>
   </data>
```

Now that we have our resource files in place, we next explore how to incorporate the localized resource files into a server control.

Satellite Assemblies and Resource Fallback

The localized resource files we add to the control project are not compiled by Visual Studio as resources to be embedded in the primary assembly. Instead, they become part of what is called a satellite assembly, which contains just the localized resources as part of its content. It does this in an organized fashion using a specific file folder structure so the `ResourceManager` class can find it. For the two preceding files, `LocalStrings.en-MX.resx` and `LocalStrings.de.resx` are located in the folder structure shown in Figure 13-14.

The `ResourceManager` resource resolution process first attempts to take an exact match if it is provided with a specific culture. An example of this type of specific culture string is "es-MX". In this case, there is a matching satellite assembly, so `ResourceManager` will pull the localized text from it.

The globalization support has a fallback mechanism in the event that an exact match cannot be found, as shown in Figure 13-15. If the fallback process cannot find an exact match, it continues until it either finds a suitable neutral culture match or winds up with the invariant culture in the main assembly. For example, if we specify a culture string of "fr-FR" for French spoken in France, we would end up with the English string from the main assembly, because we do not have a satellite assembly for the French language.

```
ControlsBook2Lib.CH12.LiveSearchControls
  bin
    debug
      ControlsBook2Lib.CH12.LiveSearchControls.dll
      de
      ControlsBook2Lib.CH12.LiveSearchControls.resources.dll
      es-MX
      ControlsBook2Lib.CH12.LiveSearchControls.resources.dll
```

Figure 13-14. *The satellite assembly folder structure*

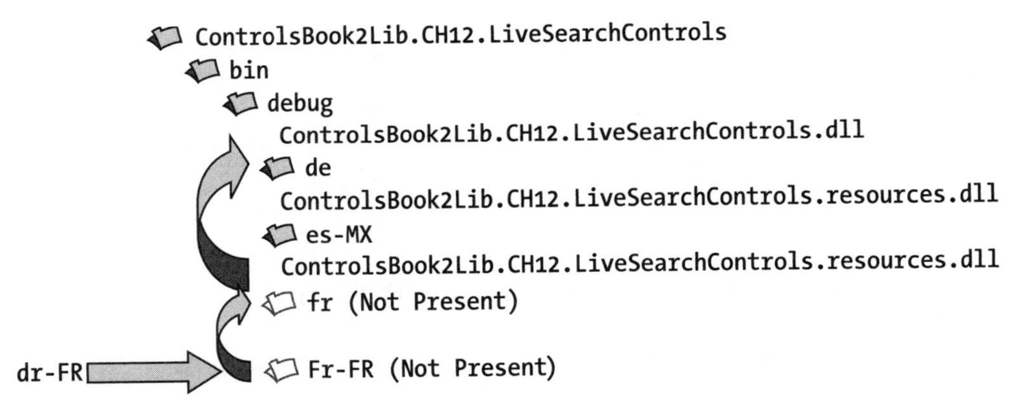

Figure 13-15. *The resource fallback process in action, part one*

If we specify a culture string of "de-AU" for German spoken in Austria, the ResourceManager would miss on the specific culture but pick up the German neutral culture (de) satellite assembly, as shown in Figure 13-16.

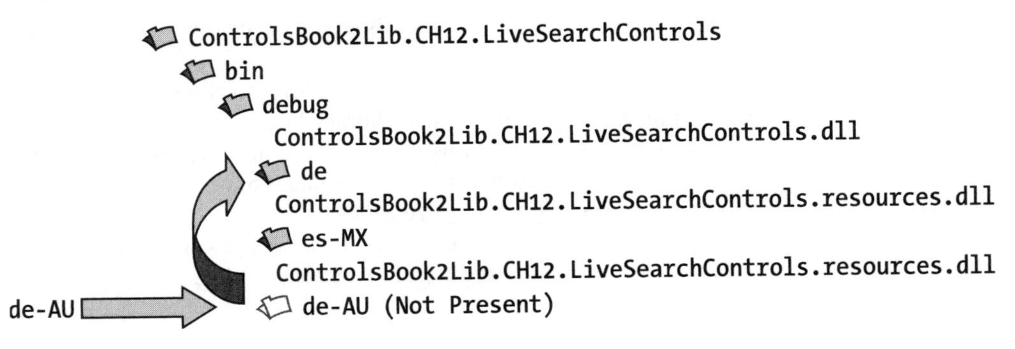

Figure 13-16. *The resource fallback process in action, part two*

Setting Thread Culture in the Global.asax File

To test the localization features, you must configure ASP.NET to identify the desired culture specified by the browser. This is best done in a centralized manner by overriding the `Application_BeginRequest` event in the `global.asax` file, as shown here:

```
protected void Application_BeginRequest(Object sender, EventArgs e)
{
   // find the preferred culture from the browser
   string culture = HttpContext.Current.Request.UserLanguages[0];

   CultureInfo info = null;

   // check for a neutral culture of length 2 (i.e., de or es)
   if (culture.Length == 2)
      // use CultureInfo to convert from neutral to specific culture
      // so we can assign to both CurrentCulture and CurrentUI Culture
      info = CultureInfo.CreateSpecificCulture(culture);
   else
      info = new CultureInfo(culture);

   // set it for both formatting/comparisons (CurrentCulture)
   // and resource lookup (CurrentUICulture)
   Thread.CurrentThread.CurrentCulture = info;
   Thread.CurrentThread.CurrentUICulture = info;
}
```

The first thing the code does is look at the HTTP client request variables for culture information that are available via the `Request` object's `UserLanguages` array. The array is populated from the web browser's `HTTP_ACCEPT_LANGUAGE HTTP` request header, and it has culture values that match those in RFC 1766, which is what the `CultureInfo` class expects. As a simplification to the process, we take the first language in the array. More robust code could be written to check if the site supported the first language and, if not, to walk along the array until a supported language was found.

The language header is manually controllable in Internet Explorer to allow you to easily test the localized resources built into the Live Search controls library. You control this by selecting Tools ➤ Internet Options to open the Internet Options dialog box. At the very bottom of the Internet Options dialog box is a Languages button. Click the Languages button to open another dialog box that presents the language settings (see Figure 13-17).

The Language Preference box gives you the option of adding languages and prioritizing the accepted languages in order. Now you can test different language settings.

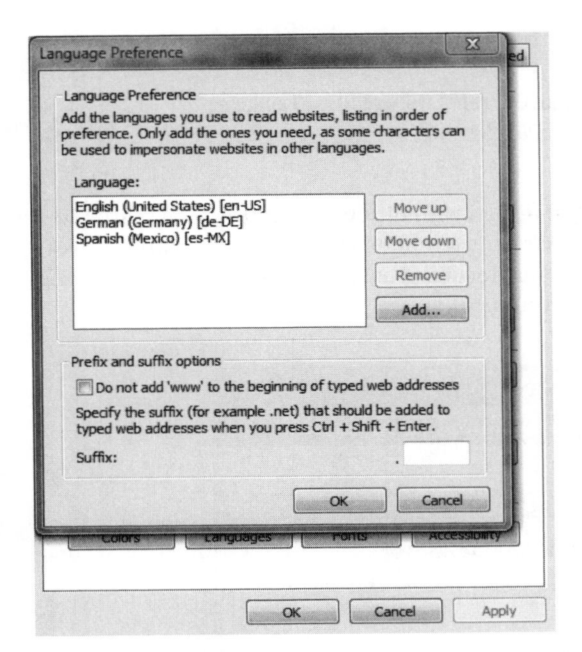

Figure 13-17. *Changing language settings in Internet Explorer*

Once the culture setting is retrieved from the browser, the `Application.BeginRequest` event handler checks to see if a specific culture with the language identifier is present. The `CurrentUICulture` class property works with a neutral culture, and the `CurrentCulture` property requires a specific culture to function correctly to do its formatting job, so we must account for the differences. We use the static helper method on the `CultureInfo` class named `CreateSpecificCulture` to do the conversion to a default specific culture from a neutral culture that might be passed in from the browser. The end result is a culture such as "de" getting transformed to "de-DE." Lastly, we assign the culture to the currently executing thread for the web application page to set up localized page rendering, which also sets the culture for the custom server control.

Viewing a Localized Web Form

`LocalizedLiveSearch.aspx` is a slightly modified web form from our previous Live Search search web form that has additional controls on it to show the current culture settings that the browser is providing to the web server. It has code in it to check the `Thread` for the `CurrentCulture` and display it in a `Label` control along with the current time to show the formatting differences:

```
private void Page_Load(object sender, System.EventArgs e)
{
  CultureLabel.Text = Thread.CurrentThread.CurrentCulture.DisplayName;
  DateTimeLabel.Text = DateTime.Now.ToLongDateString();
}
```

Figures 13-18, 13-19, and 13-20 show the results with different cultures for a search of "football". Notice how the button text and the status template change among cultures. Not only is the UI localized the actual search results are localized as well. We achieve this by setting the culture for the search to the current thread culture.

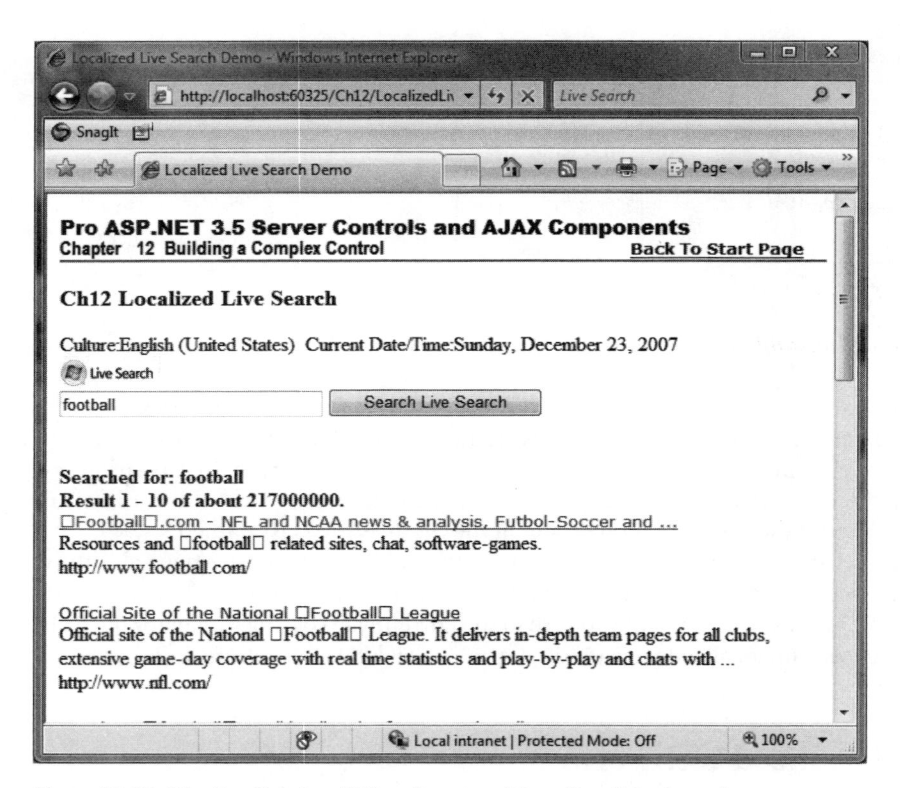

Figure 13-18. *The English (en-US) culture and LocalizedLiveSearch.aspx*

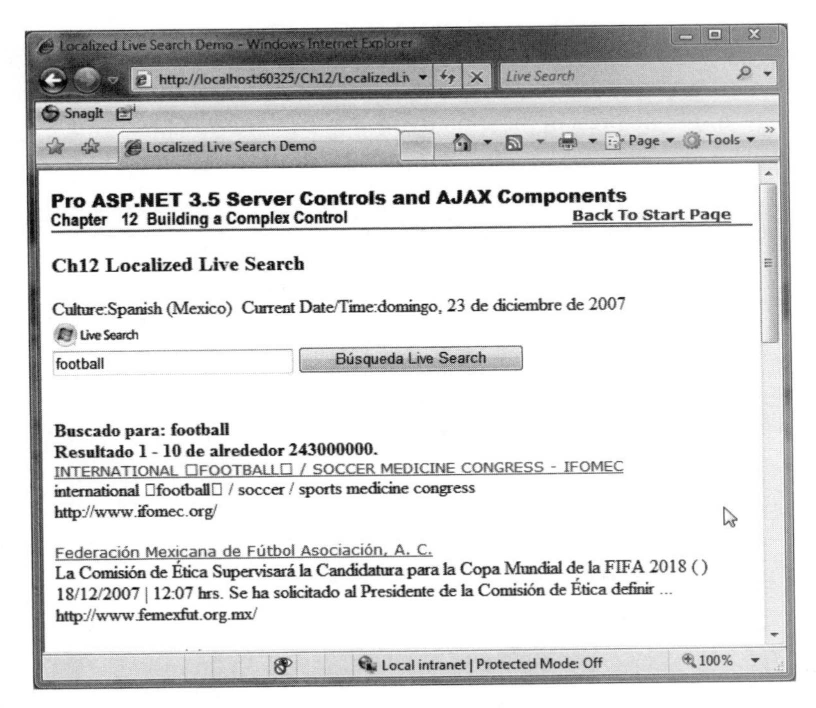

Figure 13-19. *The Spanish (es-MX) culture and LocalizedLiveSearch.aspx*

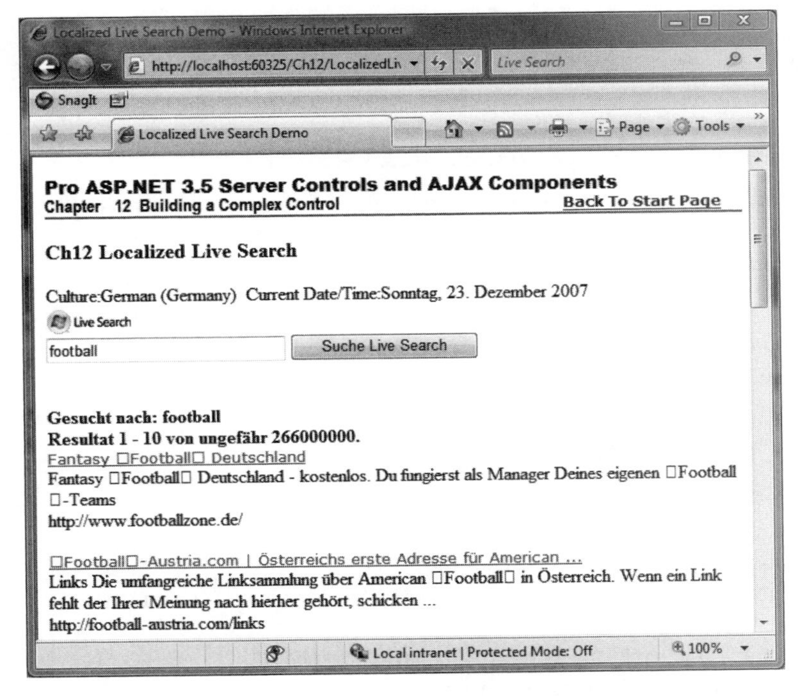

Figure 13-20. *The German (de) culture and LocalizedLiveSearch.aspx*

In Figure 13-21, notice that we fall back to the English invariant culture when a French culture setting is applied.

Notice that, even though the server control UI is not localized, the search results are in Figure 13-21. Listings 13-17 and 13-18 present the source code for the Localized Live Search web form.

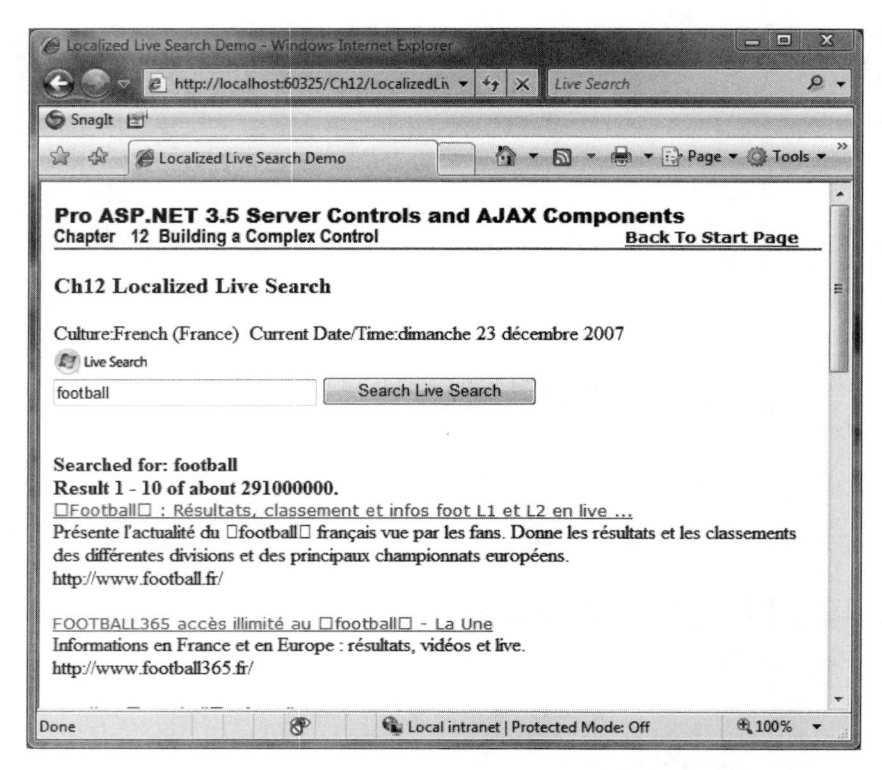

Figure 13-21. *The LocalizedLiveSearch.aspx reverted back to English for a nonimplemented culture.*

Listing 13-17. *The LocalizedLiveSearch.aspx Page File*

```
<%@ Page Language="C#"
MasterPageFile="~/MasterPage/ControlsBook2MasterPage.Master"
  AutoEventWireup="true" CodeBehind="LocalizedLiveSearch.aspx.cs"
  Inherits="ControlsBook2Web.Ch12.LocalizedLiveSearch"
  Title="Localized Live Search Demo" %>

<%@ Register TagPrefix="ApressLive"
 Namespace="ControlsBook2Lib.CH12.LiveSearchControls"
  Assembly="ControlsBook2Lib.CH12.LiveSearchControls" %>
<asp:Content ID="Content1" ContentPlaceHolderID="HeadSection" runat="server">
</asp:Content>
<asp:Content ID="Content2" ContentPlaceHolderID="ChapterNumAndTitle" runat="server">
  <asp:Label ID="ChapterNumberLabel" runat="server"
```

```
   Width="14px">12</asp:Label>  <asp:Label
    ID="ChapterTitleLabel" runat="server" Width="360px">
    Building a Complex Control</asp:Label>
</asp:Content>
<asp:Content ID="Content3" ContentPlaceHolderID="PrimaryContent" runat="server">
  <h3>
    Ch12 Localized Live Search</h3>
  Culture:<asp:Label ID="CultureLabel" runat="server"></asp:Label> 
   Current Date/Time:<asp:Label
    ID="DateTimeLabel" runat="server"></asp:Label>
  <br />
  <ApressLive:Search ID="search" runat="server" ResultControl="Result"
    RedirectToLiveSearch="false">
  </ApressLive:Search>
  <br />
  <br />
  <ApressLive:Result ID="Result" runat="server" PagerStyle="TextWithDHTML"
    PagerLinkStyle="Text">
    <StatusStyle Font-Bold="True" ForeColor="Blue"></StatusStyle>
  </ApressLive:Result>
</asp:Content>
```

Listing 13-18. *The LocalizedLiveSearch.cs Code-Behind Class File*

```
using System;
using System.Threading;

namespace ControlsBook2Web.Ch12
{
  public partial class LocalizedLiveSearch : System.Web.UI.Page
  {
    protected void Page_Load(object sender, EventArgs e)
    {
      CultureLabel.Text = Thread.CurrentThread.CurrentCulture.DisplayName;
      DateTimeLabel.Text = DateTime.Now.ToLongDateString();
    }
  }
}
```

This completes our discussion of globalization and localization. In the next sections, we discuss a few tools that can help you write robust, .NET Framework–friendly custom server controls.

Code Analysis for Managed Code

Code Analysis for Managed Code is the follow-on tool integrated with Visual Studio that supersedes FxCop. FxCop was developed by the .NET Framework team at Microsoft to help ensure compliance with name and coding conventions. It consists of a robust desktop application with a rules engine to check for common violations and errors. Code Analysis for Managed Code in Visual Studio 2008 is a superset of FxCop functionality, but the original FxCop is still available at `http://ww.gotdotnet.com/team/fxcop`.

You can configure Code Analysis for Managed Code to adjust the level of reporting it provides or the guidance it offers. It is a great automated form of code review, and you can adapt it by adding new rules to the system. Code Analysis is disabled by default. To enable it for a project, right-click the project; select Properties; click the Code Analysis tab; and check the setting Enable Code Analysis on Build. By default, all rules are enabled. While you can uncheck rules up front, we recommend building the application with all rules enabled and then reviewing each code analysis warning to decide whether or not to suppress it. Figure 13-22 displays the Code Analysis settings area.

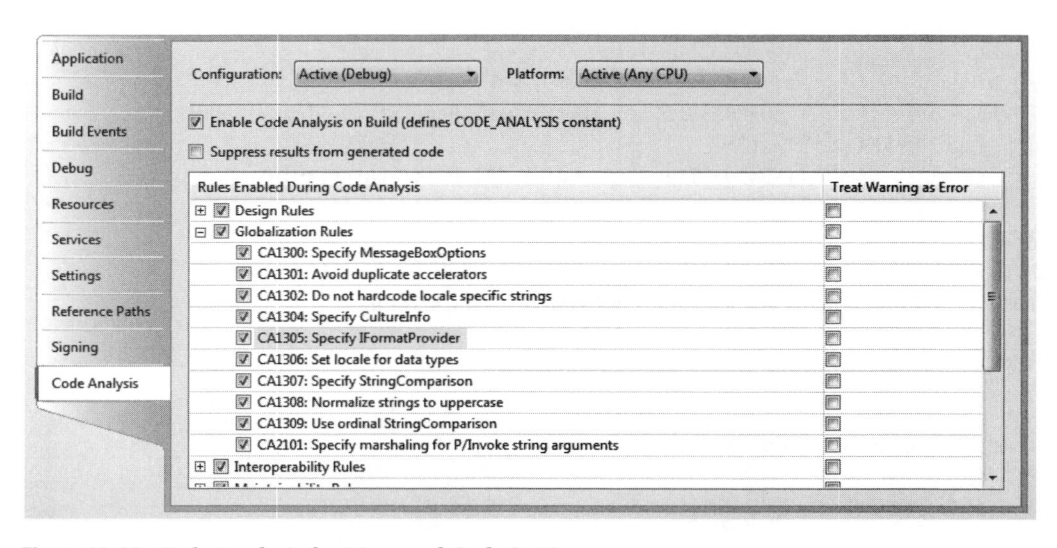

Figure 13-22. *Code Analysis for Managed Code Settings*

The best way to proceed is to enable Code Analysis up front when starting a new project, so that you can address the warnings as you code. Otherwise, if you enable it for a large project after the fact, you may see hundreds of new warnings and become discouraged. Even in this case, the user interface is very straightforward to allow you to suppress rules and quickly work through the warnings. We believe you will find it to be well worth your effort.

After enabling code analysis, the warnings appear in the Error List tool window when the project is built. You can also run code analysis by right-clicking the project and selecting Run Code Analysis in the context menu. You can force the messages to appear as errors if desired. To suppress a rule after determining that it doesn't apply or can be safely ignored, simply right-click the warning, and click Suppress Message(s). We recommend centrally locating suppressed warnings in one file, rather than throughout your project code, by choosing In Project Suppression File. Selecting this option results in the addition of a code file named `GlobalSuppressions.cs` to the project. Figure 13-23 shows the Error List UI.

If you look at the `GlobalSuppressions.cs` file in the `ControlsBook2Lib.CH12.LiveSearchControls` project, you will find several suppressed warnings. Some of them relate to retrieving numbers and calling `ToString`. In some cases, a retrieved number or a `DateTime` should be rendered in a localized way. In our case, none of the numbers would be different for the supported cultures (primarily, they are single-digit page numbers), so this rule can be suppressed.

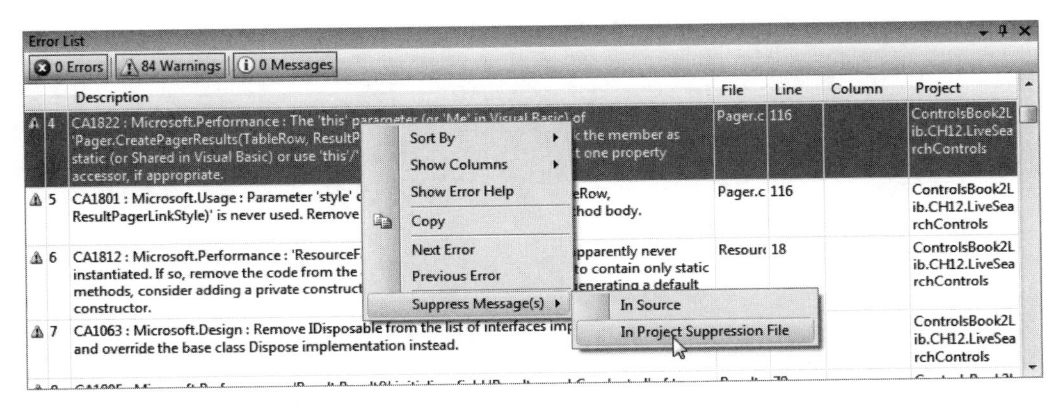

Figure 13-23. *Suppressing Code Analysis messages after review*

Another example is a rule that detected the string "url" in the property `UrlConfigElement`. It suggests adding support to take a parameter of type `System.Uri` as well as `string`. However, this support is not needed in our case, because the primary input is the `web.config` text file. These are just a couple examples of the type of checks that occur and why you may suppress some warnings in your own application.

While static code analysis is not a silver bullet for bug-free code, it can be helpful with finding unused local variables, obsolete methods, and so on, as well as informing the developer of coding issues not previously known. Think of it as another tool in the toolbox that allows you to approach your code from a different perspective. Odds are pretty good that you will find useful tidbits that are well worth the time spent analyzing code.

Documentation

The downloadable code for this book has additional content for the source code listed in this chapter, because it contains XML comments that were pared to shorten the chapter text. We took advantage of the XML comment system built into the C# language and Visual Studio to generate documentation for us once we were finished coding.

This functionality is configured by going into the Visual Studio project properties for the Live Search controls library. Go to Configuration Properties; select the Build section; and look for the XML Documentation File setting. We decided to generate an XML file with all the comments named `ControlsBook2Lib.CH12.LiveSearchControls.XML`, as shown in Figure 13-24. Now, when the project is built, Visual Studio will parse the XML comments out of the code and insert it into our XML file.

Raw XML is not the best documentation form, but many tools are available to generate nice documentation from the XML file, such as the Visual Studio Power Toys, NDocs, or plain old XSLT. Here is a link to Visual Studio Power Toys:

http://msdn2.microsoft.com/en-us/vstudio/aa718340.aspx

The key step is to keep up with the XML comments as you code. The MSDN documentation has information on what tags are available to make the comments as useful as possible.

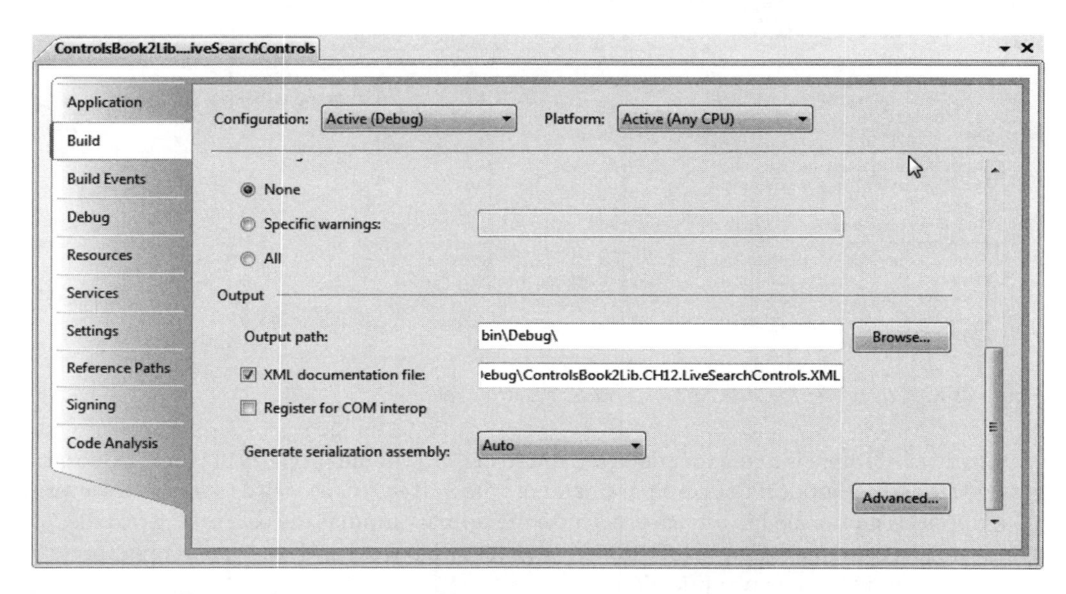

Figure 13-24. *The XML documentation file settings*

Summary

In this chapter, we started off with a discussion of design-time support to include data binding and template support. After testing out the Live Search control, we next covered how to implement licensing as part of server control deployment. We also covered the globalization/localization features available when building custom server controls and provided an example of how to add these features to the Live Search control. Finally, we discussed the use of the XML comment system in ASP.NET to generate documentation based on source code comments.

Index

B

E

I

J

L

M

N

T

W

X

Z